Principles of Behavior Analysis

Lyle Grant

Athabasca University

Annabel Evans

Concordia College

HarperCollins*CollegePublishers*

To Bob, Onerva, Lois, and Lee

To Daniel and Lucas

Sponsoring Editor: Catherine Woods
Project Coordination, Text and Cover Design: Proof Positive/Farrowlyne Associates, Inc.
Production Manager: Kewal Sharma
Compositor: Proof Positive/Farrowlyne Associates, Inc.
Printer and Binder: R. R. Donnelley & Sons Company
Cover Printer: R. R. Donnelley & Sons Company

Principles of Behavior Analysis, First Edition

Library of Congress Cataloging-in-Publication Data

Grant, Lyle.
    Principles of behavior analysis / Lyle Grant, Annabel Evans.—1st ed.
        p.   cm.
    Includes bibliographical references and index.
    ISBN 0–06–500366–7
    1. Behavior modification. 2. Behavior modification—Case studies. 3. Reinforcement (Psychology). 4. Reinforcement (Psychology)—Case studies. I. Evans, Annabel. II. Title.
BF637.B4G736 1994
150.19'43—dc20   93–36624
                                                                                              CIP

98 99 9 8 7 6 5

Table of Contents

chapter 13 Pavlovian Conditioning   376

chapter 14 Stimulus and Response Classes: Conceptual Behavior Generalized Response Classes and Equivalence Classes   426

Conceptual Exercise Analyses

Preface

The content of the present textbook represents a combination of several themes within behavior analysis. First, behavior analysis is a strongly empirical field that is based on the experimental analysis of behavior. Behavior analysts are people who are guided by their data. We have conceived our role as being a conduit between experimenters and students. To this end, we have largely avoided fictional descriptions of the behavior of imaginary people in favor of simply describing the experiments that behavior analysts have conducted.

Second, behavior analysis has well-established roots in the field of conceptual-discrimination training and programmed instruction. We have tried to capitalize on this strength of behavior analysis through our extensive use of conceptual exercises. In this respect, we have used behavior analysis principles to teach behavior analysis, following the fine example originally provided by Miller and Weaver (1976). We have empirically validated the instructional effectiveness of our exercises in two field tests. These field tests have indicated that students using the present text can successfully learn the concepts and principles of behavior analysis, as the ability to recognize novel examples of those concepts and principles illustrates. Instructors who wish to use them may obtain our empirically validated test items from the publisher.

Third, we have tried to emphasize the "analysis" part of behavior analysis. In recent years, behavior analysis work with people has sometimes been chided for being too practical and insufficiently concerned with underlying principles. In this text, we have tried to highlight experiments that attempt to answer the "whys" of human behavior as well as representing those that illustrate practical behavior changes. Although the present text does not include extensive discussions of theoretical issues, in places we have touched upon aspects of these issues in order to illustrate that the discipline has a theoretical orientation.

Fourth, behavior analysis is a discipline that emphasizes that enduring value of rewarding experiences in altering behavior. To this end, we have tried to write a book that students will enjoy. Our field tests have indicated that our use of real-life examples, our use of many concrete examples, and our focus on human behavior are features of this text that students like. Our experience is that in an introductory behavior analysis course, many students are unfortunately deterred by animal research. As such, in this book we have included experiments with people almost exclusively. Of course, behavior analysis is a discipline that has its origins in animal behavior research, and this type of research continues to be of immense importance to the discipline. However, it is our experience that the more abstract experimental questions posed and answered through animal research are best appreciated by those students whose work in behavior analysis continues beyond the introductory course. Students should nonetheless be aware that behavior analysis has an additional level of richness, provided by animal research, that is not represented here.

A few caveats are necessary. First, we have made extensive use of case studies to illustrate behavioral procedures. The experimental design of these case studies is such that it does not allow firm conclusions to be drawn about the effectiveness of procedures. However, in instances where we have used a case study for illustrative purposes, other sound experimental data are available showing the general effectiveness of the procedures described. We have also made use of correlational evidence at certain points where experimental data were not available, and have presented this as suggestive rather than definitive evidence.

Second, although this text consists mainly of true stories, in some cases we have altered aspects of the stories. Especially in the conceptual exercises, we have given the subjects names to make the material more readable. In other cases in the conceptual exercises, we have made omissions and minor alterations in aspects of the studies for illustrative purposes. However, we feel we have described the research in a way that allows for brevity and teaching effectiveness without sacrificing the main purposes and results of the studies. In a few cases in which we have made substantial alterations of experiments, we have suggested that interested readers compare (cf.) our rendition to the original source.

Instructors and students who use this text may occasionally disagree with the interpretations we have given to items in the exercises and on quizzes. One feature of the concept-teaching approach we are using is that the extensive use of concrete examples sometimes leads naturally to controversies about the nature of the concepts. The examples and nonexamples lay the subject matter open for close inspection and criticism. In contrast, more traditional abstract (i.e., based on definitions rather than extensive sets of examples and nonexamples) presentations of instructional content often hide these natural controversies under the ambiguities of verbal abstractions. Grant and Spencer (1983) have emphasized that one of the benefits of the extensive use of concrete examples and nonexamples in teaching is that it allows subject matter experts to refine their conceptual schemes. This process of refinement of concepts and principles is an important feature of scientific progress (Skinner, 1957, Chapter 18). This refinement is made possible, in part, by lively student inquiry and associated controversies. We look forward to learning from students and faculty about these areas of controversy so as to allow us to improve our treatment of the concepts and principles of behavior analysis.

Finally, we wish to thank several individuals for providing, at one time or another, helpful perspectives regarding the concepts, principles, and instructional format represented in this text. These people include Ansley Bacon, Wesley Becker, Steve Bono, Will Ellis, Allan Hayduk, Don Hake, Brandon Hall, Linda Hayes, Dan Hursh, Ed Huth, Harvey Jacobs, Jack Keenan, Mari-Carmen Luciano, Rogers McAvoy, Richard Malott, Jack Michael, Don Prue, Hayne Reese, Bob Spencer, Julie

Vargas, Tom Werner, Mike Wesolowski, Don Whaley, and Richard T. Walls. Special thanks are due to Gloria Gasparotto for her very helpful review of the text and for testing it with her students. Thanks are due to Lynn Miller for her work in copyediting of the text. Other reviewers who provided helpful comments include Eric Cooley, Western Oregon College; Gary McClure, Georgia Southern University; Jay Moore, University of Wisconsin, Milwaukee; David Mostofsky, Boston University; Robyn Rogers, Southwest Texas State University; Janet St. Lawrence, Jackson State University; and Matthew Westra, Longview Community College. Any errors or faults in this book occurred despite the efforts of these individuals. We would also like to thank our editor, Catherine Woods, for her patience and guidance.

Lyle Grant
Athabasca, Alberta

In order to grasp the truth it is necessary, once in a lifetime, to discard all the concepts that one has received and to reconstruct from the very beginning and from their very foundations all systems of knowledge.

—René Descartes

chapter 1

Behavior and Behavior Analysis

We are what we do. During the course of our lifetimes, we constantly engage in some type of behavior. It is our behavior that defines what kind of people we are, whether we are productive or wasteful, kind or cruel, and wise or foolish. It is our behavior that causes others to laugh or cry, to praise us or blame us, and to love us or hate us. It is our behavior that importantly determines whether we are successful or unsuccessful and whether we are happy or sad. Ultimately, our behavior—how we act toward each other and toward the physical environment—will determine the fate of our species and of our planet.

Almost everybody will admit that behavior is important, but for various reasons people are generally ineffective in managing and changing behavior. One of the great paradoxes of modern life is that our knowledge in the physical sciences and engineering has advanced at a rapid rate, but our knowledge of behavior and the forces that cause it have not kept pace (Skinner, 1953, 1971). As a result, in daily life we constantly find huge differences between our abilities to manage technology and ourselves. We can fly across oceans in a few hours, but we live in a world where terrorist bombings destroy airplanes. We can use agricultural technologies to grow enough for everyone to eat, but we cannot organize the behaviors necessary to teach people how to use the technologies and distribute the food. We can build factories and machines that offer us a huge range of goods, services, and conveniences, but we cannot manage to induce ourselves to cease destroying the environment. We can create weapons of war and destruction that are more effective all the time, but we have created a world where people want to kill each other rather than protect each other. Our information technologies have reached new heights with the help of computer science, but efforts to teach people basic reading and writing skills fail. Advancements in communications provide us access to the messages of political candidates, but failures in our abilities to impart wisdom and reason have left us with campaigns that appeal to prejudices and simple emotions. In a world in which there is so much to share with others, many people are desperately lonely because their social behaviors are inadequate. In each case, the advancements of the physical sciences and technology are matched by ineptness in our ability to teach ourselves to behave well and successfully.

The discipline of behavior analysis represents an organized and systematic approach to understanding behavioral processes and solving behavior problems through behavior change. It seeks, in part, to develop an applied science that can enable us to manage and change our actions.

In this chapter, we will first take a closer look at behavior and then examine the characteristics of behavior analysis, a discipline devoted to the study of behavior and how to change it. Finally, we will consider the problem of selecting behaviors for change and examine several methods that have been developed for identifying important worthwhile behavior.

Describing Behavior

Behavior consists of specific categories of actions people perform, what people do. In order to change behavior, we must define the categories carefully and specifically so there is minimal doubt about whether or not a behavior has occurred. For example, "said hello," "smiled," "remained in her seat for five minutes," and "ran a mile in five minutes" are all descriptions of specific categories of behavior that people engage in. "Was friendly," "studied hard," and "ran fast" are less specific descriptions that are less useful if our goal is to change behavior.

Behaviors have certain physical or *topographical* features. These features are often movements through space. For example, the topography of a dancer or an athlete's behavior consists of the specific form that movement takes. Dance instructors and athletic coaches pay close attention to the topography of behavior and increasingly use videotape and computer graphics to plot behavior topographies with precision.

Behaviors also have other important properties. Specifically, behaviors may be measured in terms of *frequency, duration, latency,* and *percentage correct.* Behavior frequency or *rate* is the number of times a behavior occurs per unit time. For example, when we say a typist works at 60 words per minute or a poet writes at 5 words per minute, we are considering behavior in terms of its frequency. In general, frequency is an important aspect of behavior because we so often identify proficiency and skill with high frequency performances. For example, a child who can solve a certain type of math story problems at a rate of 10 problems per hour is less proficient than a child who can solve the same problems at a rate of 20 problems per hour. Speaking a foreign language at a high rate is likewise a measure of fluency in the language and how well the language has been learned. Educators who have concentrated on improving the rates of student academic performances have had considerable success in improving student learning (Johnson & Layng, 1991; Lindsley, 1992). Generally, once a student is able to perform an academic task correctly, additional improvement at the task can be achieved through *fluency building,* by teaching the student to engage in the task at a higher rate. For example, through fluency building, students learn to read, solve math problems, or generate metaphors at higher response rates.

Another measure of behavior is its duration, how long an episode of behavior lasts from beginning to end. The length of time students spend in and out of their seats, reading, drawing, or swimming are all examples of using duration to measure behavior. Duration of behavior is the basis of payment of employees who work by the hour. Although behavior duration is a useful measure of behavior, it is sometimes flawed because it does not tell us much about the quality of performance. For example, a frequency measure tells us that a runner is running at a rate of one mile every 7 minutes, while a duration measure tells us only that the runner ran for 7 minutes.

Latency of behavior is the time that elapses between occurrence of a stimulus and the onset of a response to that stimulus. A sprinter's reaction time to the starter's pistol is an example. The latency of the response would be the time elapsing between the firing of the pistol and the onset of running. Latency is sometimes used as a measure of learning. For example, we tend to say that a child who rapidly responds to solving a multiplication problem has learned to solve that problem better than problems that require a considerable delay in response time. Similarly, the debater who swiftly responds to an opponent's challenges is thought to be better prepared than one who is able to think of an appropriate response only after the debate is over.

You are certainly aware of the use of percentage correct as a measure of behavior, because it is the most common measure by which students are graded. Percentage correct is useful in situations in which people are given multiple opportunities to respond, as typifies most school examinations. Percentage correct is obtained by dividing the total correct responses by the total opportunities to respond, and multiplying this ratio by 100.

In general, the behavior analyst uses the word *behavior* in a broader way than is the case in ordinary language. Specifically, the behavior analyst considers "private" activities such as thinking specific thoughts, dreaming, and hearing a melody "to yourself" to be behaviors. Behavior analysts sometimes refer to behaviors such as thinking as covert behaviors. The behavior analyst also classifies sensory activities such as seeing and hearing as forms of behavior.

Although behavior analysts often directly observe behavior, they also examine *tangible products* of behavior for measurement purposes. A tangible product of behavior is some physical thing that behavior produces. For example, a student's essay exam is clearly not behavior, but a tangible product that the student's writing behavior generates. In analyzing such an essay, the behavior analyst can count words, grammatical constructions, instances of original metaphors, and so forth, and thereby apply precise and thorough measurement procedures to describe what the student has done. Although measuring tangible products of behavior is often convenient, there is always an advantage to observing behavior directly. For example, in teaching handwriting it is important to attend to the specific topography of the student's hand and finger movements rather than merely to evaluate the written products of handwriting.

Behavior and Labels

In everyday language we often talk about people's actions without reference to specific behaviors. For example, *nice, happy, vile, wicked, satisfied, arrogant, confident, shy, greedy,* and *loving* are but a few of the terms that people use to refer to human actions. When we use such terms, we are not speaking of specific behaviors but instead of a number of different behaviors that have something in common. For example, the person who acts *wickedly* engages in many behaviors that violate codes of ethics and that bring harm to others who have done nothing to warrant it. Likewise, a person who is *shy* engages in many different behaviors involved in avoiding or being uncomfortable in social situations.

Summary labels or *summary terms* refer to a set of different behaviors that have something in common. Summary labels differ from behavior because, while behaviors refer to specific behavioral categories, summary labels refer to a number of different behavior categories that are related in some fashion. Behavior analysts generally feel that summary labels have major disadvantages, although there is a key advantage: A summary label can quickly provide information about the categories of behavior a person is likely to engage in. If we are told someone is shrewd in business dealings, for example, we may then proceed with caution when doing business with this person. Similarly, if we have it on good authority that someone is likable, we can often benefit from his or her acquaintance.

There are four major disadvantages of summary labels. First, because they provide only broad information about behavior categories, they can sometimes mislead. We don't know whether a boy labeled *wicked* has merely been into the cookie jar without permission or whether he physically abuses others. Unscrupulous people use the ambiguities of summary labels to their advantage. Some candidates for political office often apply negative summary labels to their opponents in order to sway voter support. For example, suppose a candidate for political office accuses an opponent of being "unpatriotic." "Unpatriotic" can mean almost anything from not singing the national anthem loudly enough to selling secret information to foreign agents. Because of their multiple meanings, summary labels are often the source of a good deal of misinformation.

A second disadvantage of summary labels is that they do not permit a quantitative treatment of behaviors. Because of the labels' ambiguity, it is impossible to get agreement on what is nice or nasty, foolish or wise, and thoughtless or thoughtful. This characteristic makes it impossible to measure the summary labels using frequency, duration, latency, and percentage correct measures in any straightforward way.

A third disadvantage of summary labels is that they can change or maintain our reactions to the labeled individual when this is counterproductive (Bromfield, Bromfield, & Weiss, 1988; Bromfield, Weisz, & Messer, 1986; Link, Cullen, Frank, & Wozniak, 1987). For example, a child might initially be labeled *unintelligent* because she was ill and absent from school during the time some key concepts were presented. Suppose the student is then able to overcome the problems created by her absence from school. Even if this happens, the label *unintelligent* might still stick. School personnel can continue to respond to the child as unintelligent, and to expect and demand little from the student beyond minimum standards of performance.

Bromfield, Bromfield, and Weiss (1988) investigated the influence of the label *sexually abused*. Junior high and high school teachers read a brief story about a 6-year-old girl who was having difficulty in putting together a 10-piece jigsaw puzzle. One group of teachers was told that the girl was being treated for sexual abuse, but another group was not given this label. The teachers given the label *sexually abused* were less likely to encourage the girl to persist at solving the puzzle and predicted a less successful future for the girl than the teachers who were not given the label. Bromfield, Weisz, and Messer (1986) found similar effects with the label *mentally retarded*. Children watched a videotape in which a girl was trying to solve a puzzle. When told the girl was mentally retarded, the children were less likely to urge her to persist at trying to solve the puzzle than when she was not labeled.

In general, once an individual has been labeled, we continue to respond to that person in terms of the label. In addition, labeled individuals tend to be affected by the way other people respond to them so that their behavior comes to match the label. A *labeling effect*, also known as a self-fulfilling prophecy, occurs when a summary label is applied to an individual and causes other people to respond to that individual in terms of the label. This effect may in turn result in the labeled individual's behavior becoming more and more appropriate to the label. Surprisingly, many labeling effects appear to be mainly self-induced. Many people give themselves negative labels and spend much of their lives feeling inadequate and ashamed of themselves, all because they have stereotyped themselves using negative labels. Self-help books written by those knowledgeable in behavior analysis (e.g., Kassorla, 1984) are of great use because they encourage people to ease up on their negative self-labeling.

A fourth disadvantage of summary labels is that they may lead to the conclusion that the label is a "thing" inside the labeled individual that causes him or her to act in a way appropriate to the label. When this occurs, the summary label has come to function as an *explanatory fiction* (Skinner, 1953). For example, suppose a student who has difficulty with math is described as having "math anxiety." If we then ask why the student has difficulty with math, and are given the answer that the cause of the student's problem is math anxiety, that label is used both as a summary label for describing the problem and as a cause of the problem. At this point the label math anxiety has become an explanatory fiction, an inner explanation of behavior derived from observations of behavior.

When used as explanatory fictions, terms like math anxiety are harmful because they put the problem inside the person where it cannot be solved. In particular, explanatory fictions often deflect attention from environmental causes of the problem that can be solved. For example, it is possible to solve the problem of a student who responds fearfully to math by having the student practice math while remaining calm in a nonthreatening context. Explanatory fictions often hinder the search for solutions to behavior problems; because false causes of behavior are supposed to more or less permanently reside within the person, they suggest that behavior problems cannot be solved. Math anxiety is only one example of an explanatory fiction. Others are jealousy, hatred, love, shame, personality, intelligence, a poor memory, and so forth. These summary terms are not necessarily harmful in themselves, but only when they are used as causes of behavior.

Comparing Behavior Definitions and Summary Labels

As we have seen, behavioral definitions and summary labels are both means of describing what people do. Summary labels have one advantage over behavior definitions. They can quickly provide us with a description of the general categories of behavior someone can be expected to engage in. This convenience comes at a price, however. Compared to behavior definitions, summary labels are ambiguous and confusing, cannot be subjected to a quantitative analysis, are liable to perpetuate stereotyped behavior patterns associated with labeling effects, and can be misinterpreted as explanatory fictions.

In contrast to summary labels, specific behavior definitions require effort to formulate them and put them into use. For example, a single summary label (e.g., "bad boy") might have to be translated into a large number of behavior definitions (e.g., hits other children, fails to clean his room, and so on). However, the effort put into constructing behavior definitions usually has several payoffs. Once constructed, behavior definitions provide a clear statement of the problem to be solved. Once behaviors are defined they can then be measured and quantitatively analyzed using frequency, duration, latency, and percentage correct data, so that even a small change in behavior will not go unnoticed. Even if a behavior is difficult to change, our quantitative analysis will permit us to say precisely how *resistant to change* the behavior is—how difficult the behavior is to change.

Because behavior descriptions are specific, they are unlikely to cause the labeling effects that summary labels often do. In addition, behavior descriptions are unlikely to be mistaken for causes of behavior, as are summary labels when they are transformed into explanatory fictions. Finally, once we have defined a *target behavior*, a behavior selected for change, the problem lends itself to treatment because behavior analysts have developed a large number of treatment procedures aimed at changing specific and measurable behaviors.

Behavior Analysis

Behavior analysis is the study of behavior and the variables that influence behavior. Behavior analysis began as a discipline with the work of Dr. B. F. Skinner during the 1930s, as represented in his work *The Behavior of Organisms* (Skinner, 1938). Skinner's work was in the *experimental analysis of behavior*, a part of behavior analysis that is concerned with the study of the principles that describe animal and human behavior. Researchers who work in the experimental analysis of behavior are often concerned with abstract principles that often do not have immediate or direct application to solving human problems. In another part of behavior analysis, called *applied behavior analysis*, behavioral principles are used to solve human problems. For example, a study in applied behavior analysis might be concerned with how to encourage people to recycle waste products, engage in safe-sex practices, or teach children how to read or to solve special types of math problems. Many behavior analysts work in both experimental and applied fields, sometimes studying behavior principles in the abstract, and at other times applying the principles to solve specific behavior problems. In the present text, we have included a mix of the experimental analysis of behavior and applied behavior analysis to illustrate how both fields contribute to our understanding of behavior. We have also included studies outside the field of behavior analysis when this research bears upon some issue or aspect of behavior analysis.

Although behavior analysts engage in diverse activities, seven general features are common to most work in behavior analysis. These include (a) a focus on behavior; (b) a scientific approach to the study of behavior, (c) a pragmatic approach to changing behavior, (d) clear definitions of procedures and principles, (e) an emphasis on the environmental causes of behavior, (f) avoiding the use of certain types of hypothetical inner causes of behavior, and (g) an optimistic, idealistic, and sometimes utopian outlook on the possibilities for improving the human condition through behavior analysis.

First, behavior analysts consider behavior to be the focus of their work (Baer, Wolf, & Risley, 1968, 1987; Skinner, 1953). As we have already seen, the focus on behavior provides us with several important advantages over the use of summary labels, including an emphasis on precisely defining and quantifying behavior using frequency, duration, response latency, and percentage correct measures. In addition, because it is essential that observations of behavior be reliable, behavior analysts typically have several observers record instances of behavior to ensure that they agree that behaviors have indeed occurred.

Often people misunderstand the behavior-analytic focus on behavior as denying that people have thoughts and feelings, for example. However, as we have suggested, the behavior analyst's general definition of behavior is broad even though individual instances of behavior must be precisely defined and measured for purposes of study. As such, behavior analysts consider thoughts and feelings as forms of behavior to be studied in much the same way as other types of behavior. For example, in this book, thoughts in the form of self-rules are treated in Chapter 11, and the emotional behaviors called feelings are treated in Chapter 13.

Second, behavior analysts apply scientific methods to the study of behavior. The main method behavior analysts use is the experimental method, in which some measure of behavior, a dependent variable is shown to be influenced by some cause or independent variable. Behavior analysts constantly search for new methods to change behavior, and these methods must pass experimental tests that demonstrate a cause-effect relationship between the method of change and the change itself. Behavior analysts have devised a set of special experimental techniques called *single-subject research designs*. For example, in the present text, many of the graphs show how the behavior of one or a few people is influenced by a behavior-change procedure. Part of the reason for this emphasis on individuals is that behavior analysts like to demonstrate clearly that their procedures can produce important changes in one individual's behavior rather than generally influence the behavior of a group of people as a whole. [See Sidman (1960) and Johnston and Pennypacker (1981) for detailed treatments of single-subject research designs and other features of behavior analysis research methods.]

Third, behavior analysts, especially applied behavior analysts, take a pragmatic approach to behavior and behavior change (Baer et al., 1968, 1987). The pragmatic nature of behavior analysis is seen in several forms. One of these is technical terms and concepts that behavior analysts use. They tend to invent and retain concepts, principles, and terms that enable them to change behavior more effectively and discard those that do not produce practical benefits (Day, 1980; Skinner, 1957, Chapter 18; 1969). Because behavior analysis operates on the basis of this kind of practical effectiveness, the concepts and principles of the discipline are always evolving toward ones that produce greater effectiveness.

The pragmatic approach of behavior analysts is also seen in an emphasis on being inventive, in doing what is necessary to change behavior even when this means setting cherished principles aside for the moment. In changing behavior, the behavior analyst focuses attention mainly on the behavior of the subjects. This focus on behavior can often lead the behavior analyst to intuitions and discoveries that would not be possible by thinking only in terms of established principles (Skinner, 1956). The success of behavior change methods is evaluated on pragmatic grounds. For example, it is not enough merely to show a quantitative change in behavior. It is also important for other people to agree that a change in behavior has been of practical importance. This consensus ensures that an important behavior has been changed, that the amount of change is significant, and that the change is a lasting one (Baer et al., 1968, 1987).

Over the years, the pragmatic aspect of behavior analysis has attracted many students to the discipline. Many idealistic students who begin studying psychology in order to help other people find that they end up studying things that are of little practical benefit to anyone. Such students are often attracted to behavior analysis because its methods can produce behavior changes that benefit many people.

Fourth, behavior analysts use principles and procedures that can be precisely defined and described (Baer et al., 1968) so that other people can use the procedure. This feature of behavior analysis is one aspect of its scientific character, because a key feature of science is careful description of activities that allow other scientists to engage in the same activity to see if they get the same results. In general, behavior analysts have a reputation for careful use and description of even small details of their activities, and normally it is attention to precise details of behavior-change procedures that determines their effectiveness or failure.

Fifth, behavior analysts tend to use behavior-change procedures that rely on altering environmental stimuli. In this respect, behavior analysts tend to be strong environmentalists. Indeed, virtually all the principles covered in later chapters of this book consist of specific ways to change environmental stimuli in order to change behavior.

The behavior analyst's emphasis on the environment is sometimes misunderstood. They do not claim that environmental stimuli are the only causes of behavior, but see genetic and biological factors as important determinants of behavior (Reese, 1986; Skinner, 1969). For example, some behavior analysts study how genetic and biological variables work together with environmental stimuli to change behavior. In some cases this work includes how behavior changes can override genetic and biological deficits. For example, schizophrenia is a psychological disorder suspected to be due to genetic and biological abnormalities. However, Liberman and his associates (Liberman, 1992) have had impressive success in treating schizophrenic patients by establishing a learning environment for teaching them job-seeking skills, family-living skills, independent-living skills, and symptom-management skills. According to Liberman, his colleagues are sometimes puzzled by how teaching the patients skills can be so successful with a biologically based disorder. These successes are less puzzling if both the environment and biological factors are seen as important causes of behavior.

Sixth, in keeping with their emphasis on behavior and on the environment, behavior analysts reject explanations of behavior based on hypothetical processes going on inside the person, such as explanatory fictions, as we discussed earlier.

Generally, behavior analysts attempt to trace the causes of behavior to the environment and avoid the explanation of behavior in terms of desires, urges, needs, wants, disordered minds, madness, anxieties, fears, and the like. Part of the reason for this is practical: When the environmental causes of a problem are discovered, the environment can be altered so as to cause the behavior to change. For example, sometimes the problems of children who have difficulty in learning are attributed to a short attention span. Frequently, behavior analysts have found that children said to have short attention spans shift their attending behavior from a difficult task, such as studying, to an easy task, such as playing a video game. Essentially, the short attention span is a form of behavior that is rewarded by escape from a difficult task, rather than being a thing inside the child. Treatment often consists of changing the child's environment to maintain the child's attending behaviors with respect to difficult tasks.

Behavior analysts are often interested in the role of inner events in causing behavior. However, when behavior analysts speak of inner events, they are talking about private stimuli and responses that other people cannot see. When behavior analysts refer to inner events, they are not referring to inner processes that are essentially different from the stimuli and responses we can see in the external world. For example, in Chapter 10 we will examine research that indicates that when someone imagines another person performing a behavior correctly, such as giving a speech, this serves to improve the speech-giving skills of the person who is imagining the act. We can say that imagining, a private activity, causes an improvement in observable behavior. However, imagining is considered a type of private or covert behavior and the stimuli this activity generates are private stimuli. Behavior analysts consider these private behaviors and private stimuli to have similar roles and properties as observable behaviors and observable stimuli.

Seventh, behavior analysts generally have an optimistic, idealistic, and sometimes utopian outlook on the possibility of improving human well-being through the use of behavioral principles. After some initial experiences in applying behavioral principles successfully, most behavior analysts believe that behavior problems can be solved to a much greater extent than is commonly supposed. Behavior analysts who work with severely handicapped individuals recognize that these people can learn far more than most people expect. Behavior analysts who practice in schools are struck with how teaching practices could be greatly improved to enable students to make the best of themselves.

Behavior analysts generally believe that people punish one another too frequently, and that society could be greatly improved if people used rewards and kindnesses to influence others. Behavior analysts also recognize that virtually all social, economic, and political institutions could be reorganized using behavioral principles to alleviate many needless forms of human suffering and allow people to achieve their full potential. These expansive attitudes are a natural outcome of seeing that behavioral principles can be effective in many facets of life.

The behavior analyst's interest in improving the human condition is seen in its most comprehensive form in an interest in the development of utopian communities. B. F. Skinner outlined one such behavioral utopia in his novel *Walden Two* (Skinner, 1948). In this novel, Skinner described how using behavioral principles in the design of an entire society promised a better life for the average person. Some behavior analysts, following the example of *Walden Two*, have organized communal societies. As several observers have noted, Skinner's version of a utopian society is only one person's vision of what a society might be like (Morris, 1992). Many behavior analysts feel that the importance of *Walden Two* is conceptual in that it combines the timeless appeal of building a better world with a set of practical and effective behavioral principles to achieve such a goal. At present, however, most behavior analysts have concentrated on improving their personal and professional environments through behavior principles rather than opting for large-scale utopian experimentation. Nonetheless, most behavior analysts can see that their practices, if applied more widely in society, could significantly improve human welfare.

Selecting Target Behaviors

When facing a behavioral problem, one of the first things behavior analysts must do is to identify what is to be changed. As we have emphasized, it is important for the behaviors to be clearly defined in measurable terms. The behavior analyst will often identify both undesirable behaviors to be eliminated or reduced, and desirable behaviors. The desirable behaviors will include (a) behaviors to be maintained and increased and (b) behaviors to be learned.

The problem of selecting appropriate target behaviors, behaviors to be changed, confronts far more people than behavior analysts. Businesspeople must decide what they are going to pay their employees to do. Legislators must decide what behaviors they wish to encourage and discourage through laws. Physicians must decide what medical procedures are the treatments of choice. In democracies, citizens identify target behaviors by voting for leaders who engage in those responses.

Parents make many of the most important decisions about target behaviors when they are confronted with a perplexing range of questions about what behaviors they should encourage and discourage in their children. Should children be taught pre-reading skills at a very early age or might this be a waste of time or harmful to the child? At what point does the parent distinguish between spirited play to be encouraged and aggression to be discouraged? Should the child be prohibited from engaging in possibly damaging exploratory behaviors or will doing so curtail the child's enthusiastic and curious behaviors that will be important later in life? Should the child who is reluctant to play a musical instrument or learn a foreign language be compelled to do so because it is in her best interest, or will harmful consequences result from this practice? Should children be taught to be honest even when it means losing out on something important or be taught to lie and cheat when necessary?

Educators face a similar array of questions. Should children be taught to read phonetic units or individual words? What should be the proper mix of science and arts courses in a curriculum? Should students who are poor at learning some subjects be encouraged to forgo those and study subjects at which they excel? Should parent training and sex education courses be required of students? Should moral and patriotic values be taught as a part of the curriculum? If so, which ones?

As you can surmise, questions of selecting target behaviors are difficult and often controversial. Because we are what we do, questions of selecting appropriate behaviors strike to the heart of the matter of what sort of people we are and wish to become. We cannot avoid these questions. For instance, parents who claim not to explicitly encourage or discourage their children's behaviors cannot in practice avoid doing so; by default, they teach by the example of their own behavior [see Chapter 10].

Because decisions about target behaviors involve value judgments and philosophical considerations (Nelson & Hayes, 1979), we cannot make recommendations about specific target behaviors to be encouraged. Instead, we will generally consider practical issues about the relationship between behavior and outcomes and identifying worthwhile target behaviors. Following this, we will consider several methods that behavior analysts have developed for identifying worthwhile target behaviors.

Practical Considerations: Behavior and Outcomes

The value of what we do is not in our behavior but in what our behavior accomplishes, in what worthy achievements and desirable goals our behavior produces. Gilbert (1978) distinguishes between behavior and accomplishments. Accomplishments are worthy outcomes of behavior. Behavior in itself is important only insofar as it results in accomplishments. For example, the behavior invested in studying and learning calculus may or may not result in any accomplishments. If the student never again uses calculus, little is accomplished. But if the student goes on to be a physicist or an engineer, the use of calculus will of course be essential for producing accomplishments. Table 1.1 provides contrasts between behavior and accomplishments in several different fields.

Table 1.1	*Behavior and Accomplishments*
Behavior	**Associated Accomplishments**
Handling building materials	Building a house
Planting/tending a garden	Harvesting a crop
Exercising	Improving cardiovascular system
Talking	Winning a debate
Listening to a lecture	Applying a useful fact
Handling a carburetor	Rebuilding a working carburetor
Reading Shakespeare	Successfully applying insights
Taking photos	Viewing and enjoying good photos
Going to an art museum	Greater appreciation of visual experience
Manipulating shoelaces	Tying shoelaces

It is often difficult for behavior analysts to identify behaviors that are worth engaging in and that really do produce accomplishments and worthwhile outcomes. There is always a risk that the target behaviors will not be related or will be only partially related to accomplishments (Hawkins, 1975; Kazdin, 1985; Mash, 1985). One problem is selecting target behaviors that are easy to define and measure rather than those that produce accomplishments.

Two examples illustrating the distinction between behavior and accomplishments come from behavior analysis research. Early work showed that if grade school students were rewarded for paying attention to their tasks and for not disrupting the class, they would pay attention more and disrupt less. This result seemed worthwhile. However, further research (Ayllon & Roberts, 1974; Ferritor, Buckholdt,

Hamblin, & Smith, 1972; Harris, 1986a; Hay, Hay, & Nelson, 1977; Kirby & Shields, 1972, Marholin & Steinman, 1977; Winnett & Roach, 1973) showed that increasing the students' levels of paying attention and decreasing disruptions often had little or no effect on academic performances such as accuracy in solving math problems. Only when academic performances were selected as targets of behavior change did these behaviors show improvement. Further, when academic performance levels were targeted and increased, the students paid attention more and disrupted less even though these behaviors were not the direct focus of the behavior change procedures.

Another example of the distinction between behavior and accomplishments comes from the field of geriatric care. Initial research showed that serving refreshments to elderly patients increased their level of interaction with others, a seemingly worthwhile outcome in nursing homes, where patients often have difficulty enjoying conversation. However, Carstensen and Erickson (1986) found that these interactions consisted of ineffective statements (e.g., "Angels coming then") that everyone ignored and that accomplished nothing. Serving refreshments actually *decreased* the patients' rate of stating facts and opinions, behaviors more representative of interesting conversation. Measuring the patient's interactions was relatively easy and convenient, but the interactions were not worthwhile behaviors to be targeted. The experimenters suggested that in future work, the quality of interactions should be assessed.

Another problem is a tendency to focus upon only a single target behavior when accomplishment in an area involves multiple target responses (Kazdin, 1985). For example, consider the goals of a university education. It is desirable for a university graduate to have a general knowledge of human history and Western civilization, to be able to write essays, to speak effectively in debates and dialogues, to interpret current affairs in the light of historical parallels and contexts, to know how to use a library and find additional sources of information, to pursue independent study, and to have expertise in the student's area of specialization. In addition, certain institutions have the goal of developing well-rounded students who have social skills, athletic interests and accomplishments, leadership abilities, and the like. Focusing on any one of these target behaviors to the exclusion of others would not result in the education of fully accomplished students.

Identifying Worthwhile Target Behaviors

Many of our beliefs about the relationship between behaviors and accomplishments are not based on research. For example, in the recent past, rote memorization of long passages of text, physical punishment, and the study of ancient Greek and Latin were firmly considered to be essential to producing worthy educational outcomes. In child rearing, it was generally accepted that children were to be seen and not heard. Today, education and parenting seldom emphasizes these kinds of target behaviors. Often, we base our knowledge of appropriate target behaviors largely on tradition and speculation rather than on proven facts.

Behavior analysts have been especially concerned with establishing a firm basis for deciding what behaviors are desirable and undesirable. As behavior analysts have come to recognize that behavior is important only insofar as it is tied to accomplishments, they have developed methods to attempt to make connections between behaviors and worthy outcomes. We will consider three basic methods, the experimental criterion validation method, the social comparison method, and the subjective evaluation method.

Experimental Criterion Validation Methods

To use the experimental criterion validation method, the researcher conducts an experiment in which the effect of engaging in a behavior is assessed using some widely accepted criterion of accomplishment. For example, good grades in school, high performance on standardized achievement tests, economic prosperity, excellent physical health, low infant mortality, long life expectancy, low nonrenewable resource use, and maximized recycling of waste products are all generally accepted as desirable standards of accomplishment. Behaviors that produce these outcomes can therefore be considered to be worthy.

Richards (1975) used the experimental criterion validation method to examine study behavior. Ninth-grade students in inner-city Chicago used a technique called self-monitoring in which every day the students recorded and graphed the number of pages they read and the number of hours they studied. A cause-effect relationship between studying and improvement in the students' grades was established by comparing the students who used self monitoring with a control group of students who did not use the technique. The students who used self monitoring received better grades than the control group. This is an example of the experimental criterion validation method because Richards experimentally demonstrated a cause-effect relationship between self monitoring and improved grades and because good grades are generally accepted standards of accomplishment for students.

Criterion validation is an excellent method for relating behavior to worthwhile outcomes and thereby providing a means of selecting useful target behaviors. However, an important disadvantage of this method is that criterion validation methods can be used only when there are clear and well accepted criteria defining desirable outcomes. For example, people's tastes in food, art, music, humor, appropriate social behavior, and so forth are not based on clear criteria but on subjective judgments. As such, worthy behaviors that produce desirable outcomes in these fields cannot be identified using criterion validation methods because these methods depend on the use of well accepted criteria.

Social Comparison Methods

Social comparison methods of identifying target behaviors consist of several techniques, each of which involves some comparison between "successful" and "unsuccessful" performers at a given task or enterprise. There are two main types of social comparison methods used: for data collection and for intervention purposes.

The Data Collection Phase.   In the data collection phase of the social comparison method, data comparing behaviors of two or more groups of successful and unsuccessful performers are merely collected. By comparing the successful and unsuccessful performers, it is possible to identify how they differ in terms of successful and unsuccessful behaviors. For example, Biglan et al. (1985) made use of the collection phase of the social comparison method. In comparing average married couples with married couples in which the wife was depressed, they found that the depressed women and their husbands confided in each other less than the normal married couples. This finding suggests that the behavior of confiding in one's spouse is important in contributing to happiness and preventing depression.

The data collection phase of social comparison methods is used in other disciplines. For example, medical research demonstrating the dangers of smoking, excessive dietary fat consumption, obesity, excessive alcohol use, exposure to cancer-causing toxic wastes, failures to take medication, and so forth, has shown that these behaviors result in harmful outcomes and are therefore worth changing. A group of people with a medical disorder is compared to a similar group of people without the disorder. The two groups are then examined to determine how their behavioral practices differ. In this way, investigators can collect statistical evidence regarding behaviors that appear to prevent and cause the disorder.

The Intervention Phase.   In the intervention phase of the social comparison method (Kazdin, 1982a; Kendall & Grove, 1988), two or more groups of people are compared. A "successful" group made up of average people might be compared to an "unsuccessful" group of people with behavior problems or deficiencies. Alternatively, a successful group of accomplished performers might be compared to a less successful group of ordinary performers or people of lesser accomplishments (Van Houten, 1979). The behaviors of the successful performers are used as standards of accomplishment to be achieved by the unsuccessful performers, who are trained in the target behaviors. For example, if they had used the intervention phase in the Biglan et al. (1985) study cited above, they might have taught the troubled couples to confide in each other more often.

Considerations in Using Social Comparison Methods.   Social comparison methods are useful in identifying potentially important target behaviors. However, merely because successful and unsuccessful people differ in the occurrence of a particular behavior does not necessarily prove that the behavior is at the heart of the problem. For example, suppose that happily married people have more children than unhappily married people. One possible conclusion from such a finding would be that the way to improve the quality of marriages is to have more children, based on the theory that children promote a happy home. A problem with this conclusion is that many children might be *the effects* of a happy marriage in that happily married people decide to have more children because they are happy. The behaviors that are actually *the* *causes* of happy marriages may remain to be identified. In general, when social comparison methods are used there is a risk of misidentifying some variable as a cause of a behavioral problem.

Subjective Evaluation Methods

Subjective evaluation methods use a group of people to evaluate the quality or competence of an individual's performance. These evaluators are sometimes experts in the performance evaluated (e.g., teachers evaluating students), are sometimes the people in a position directly to benefit or suffer from the performance (e.g., parents evaluating children), and are sometimes peers of the individuals evaluated (e.g., students evaluating other students). As with the social comparison methods, the subjective evaluation method can be used at both data collection and intervention phases.

The Data Collection Phase.   In the data collection phase of the subjective evaluation method, the evaluators merely rate the usefulness, competence, or worthiness of different behaviors and no effort is made to modify the behavior. This practice provides data about the comparative value of different behaviors. For example, suppose a group of accomplished educators rate the value of reading different books for junior high and high school students who intend to pursue university studies. Experts' ratings of books suitable for these purposes is an example of the data collection phase applied to reading behaviors (e.g., Carlsen, 1971). Similarly, film, music, and book reviews are examples of the data collection phase of the subjective evaluation method in that expert reviewers specify whether behavior invested in encountering these forms of art would be worthwhile.

The Intervention Phase.   In the intervention phase of the subjective evaluation method, the evaluators rate the usefulness, competence, or worthiness of a performance usually both before and after a behavior change takes place (Kazdin, 1977a, 1982a; Wolf, 1978). After-ratings that are better than the before-ratings are evidence that the behavior change has been a worthwhile accomplishment. For example, Minkin et al. (1976) trained social skills among court-referred pre-delinquent and delinquent girls from a residential group home. They specified two target behaviors, questioning and providing positive feedback, and successfully taught the target behaviors to the girls. Adult judges rated the quality of the girls' social skills before and after training. Their subjective evaluation indicated that training improved the girls' social skills.

Considerations in Using Subjective Evaluation Methods.   Subjective evaluation ratings are useful for determining if the target behaviors actually represent problems to be solved or produce accomplishments worth attaining. However, one disadvantage of subjective evaluation ratings is that they are only the judges' verbal reports, and it is sometimes not clear how these reports are related to other accomplishments (Wolf, 1978; Nelson & Hayes, 1979). For example, in training social skills, the most important outcomes concern how the trainees make use of those skills in making friends, getting on well with people, and enhancing the quality of social interactions. If judges' ratings do not reflect these worthy outcomes of social skills training, the subjective evaluations will be misleading.

Another potential problem with subjective evaluation methods is that they represent prevailing standards of judgment regarding a target behavior and this may bias the evaluators against target behaviors that have yet to gain popular acceptance. For example, especially in music, literature, and the visual arts, many innovative and original activities were rejected when they were first introduced, only to gain popular acceptance years later. If judges' ratings merely reflect existing standards without allowing for spontaneity and change in what behaviors we consider desirable, we may freeze standards and stultify innovation and change.

Summary

The central concern of the behavior analyst is behavior, or what people do. For the behavior analyst, behavior consists of specific activities people engage in, activities that have defined forms called topographies. An important feature of behavior is that it is measurable by frequency, duration, latency, or percentage correct. Each of these measures has an important role in the definition of behavior problems and in teaching of new behaviors. Precise behavior measurement allows behavior analysts to be specific about the severity of behavior problems and to be continually aware of progress in solving those problems. In general, behavior analysts use the word *behavior* in a much broader sense than it is used in ordinary language. For behavior analysts, behavior encompasses thoughts, inner imaginings, and sensory responses such as seeing and hearing. Although behavior analysts make considerable use of direct observations of behavior, they also observe tangible products of behavior, such things as a child's drawing or a student's essay.

In day-to-day life, many human activities are described in terms of summary labels rather than in terms of specific behaviors. Labels such as *shy, wicked,* or *happy* do not specify easily definable characteristics of behavior. Rather, they are global references to large categories of behaviors. Summary labels have an important advantage over specific behavioral descriptions because labels can quickly inform us of important general information about the kinds of behavior we can expect of other people. However, there are important disadvantages in using summary labels to describe behavior. First, they are ambiguous about the specific behaviors the labeled person is likely to engage in, which can lead to misconceptions about the labeled person. Second, summary labels do not permit a direct measurable and quantitative treatment of the labeled person's activities. Third, labels can continue to influence our expectations and interactions with the labeled person, even in the light of specific behavioral evidence contrary to the label. When we respond to a labeled person in terms of the label, we say a labeling effect has occurred. Fourth, summary labels describing behavior are sometimes misinterpreted as causes of behavior. In other words, the label is used not only to describe the behavior but also to explain the behavior. When this occurs, the label has become an explanatory fiction.

In comparison with summary labels, specific behavioral descriptions have much to recommend them, at least for the purposes of the behavior analyst. Specific behavioral descriptions are unambiguous and therefore cannot mislead us. Specifically defined behaviors can be assessed using measures of frequency, duration, latency, and percentage correct, permitting quantitative treatment of our subject matter. Because behavior descriptions are specific, they are neither likely to lead to labeling effects nor to be the basis for explanatory fictions.

Behavior analysis has two main branches, the experimental analysis of behavior, which is concerned with the formulation of behavior principles, and applied behavior analysis, which applies behavior principles to solve human problems. The seven characteristics common to work in behavior analysis are (a) a focus on behavior; (b) a scientific approach to the study of behavior, (c) a pragmatic approach to changing behavior, (d) clear definitions of procedures and principles, (e) an emphasis on the environmental causes of behavior, (f) avoiding the use of certain types of hypothetical inner causes of behavior, and (g) an optimistic, idealistic, and sometimes utopian outlook on the possibilities for improving the human condition through behavior analysis.

Behavior analysts have an important role to play in the selection of target behaviors to be modified. It is insufficient merely to define a problem in terms of a specific behavior. Certain philosophical issues involving value judgments arise. Any behavior-change enterprise has important implications for defining what kind of people we aspire to be and the kind of world in which we wish to live.

Behavior analysts must also be concerned with identifying target behaviors that produce worthwhile accomplishments. Merely changing behavior is no guarantee that any useful outcome has been achieved. Behaviors that are easy and convenient to modify sometimes are unrelated to accomplishments. Often, changing a single behavior will not lead to the accomplishment of anything important because many behavior problems require multiple behavior changes.

Over the years, behavior analysts have devised and made use of several methods for identifying target behaviors that produce worthwhile accomplishments. These methods include the experimental criterion validation method, the social comparison method, and the subjective evaluation method. When using criterion validation methods, an experiment is conducted to demonstrate a cause-effect relationship between a behavior change and an outcome that is generally recognized as worthwhile. In the social comparison method, a group of adequately functioning people is compared to a group of people with a behavior problem. Differences between the two groups are examined in an attempt to identify those behavioral variables at the root of the problem. Once the important differences have been identified, behavior modification techniques are used to make the problem group more like the adequately functioning individuals. With the subjective evaluation method, expert evaluators judge the adequacy of people's behavior. These judgments are often made before and after a set of behaviors has been modified. If the post-change evaluations are better than the prechange evaluations, we may assume the modified behaviors were worth changing. Behavior modifiers take into account the strengths and weaknesses of all three methods when planning their programs.

| **Conceptual Exercise**   *Describing Behavior* |

In each of the following items, several words and phrases are highlighted and identified by letters. For each identified word or phrase, specify whether it is a description of (a) behavior, (b) a summary label, (c) a labeling effect, or (d) an explanatory fiction. If more than one word or phrase is involved, answer separately for each instance. Confirm your decisions by consulting the analyses in the back of the book. Use the following definitions and provide a rationale for your answer:

Behavior: A specific action an organism engages in that has a topography and can be described in terms of frequency, duration, or latency.

Summary label: A label applied to a person because she has been observed to have a number of different behaviors that have something in common.

Labeling effect: A label is applied to an individual and the label causes people to respond to that individual in terms of the label.

Explanatory fiction: The use of a summary label as a cause for one of the behaviors it labels.

Note: A labeling effect is different from an explanatory fiction. In a labeling effect, people respond to a labeled person differently than if that person had not been labeled. In an explanatory fiction, a summary label is used as a cause or reason for someone's behavior. With a labeling effect, there is no direct suggestion that the label is a cause for behavior. With an explanatory fiction, the label is explicitly cited as a cause for behavior.

1. Erin was incredibly (a) **creative** and all her friends admired her for it. As a student teacher, Erin (b) **constructed attractive mobiles** with multiplication table problems on them to encourage students in her class to learn.

2. Ms. Adams was a sixth-grade teacher who gave her class a personality test at the beginning of the year. The test was designed to identify (a) **introverts,** people who are quiet and unsociable, and (b) **extroverts,** people who are outgoing and sociable. The test did this by sampling the students' behavior with respect to various questions about how outgoing and sociable they were. On the basis of the scores on the test, Ms. Adams identified one fourth of the students as extroverts and one fourth as introverts and (c) **these labels caused her to begin responding differently toward the two groups.** As a result, when she readministered the personality test at the end of the year (d) **the extroverts had become more extroverted than before and the introverts had become more introverted than before.**

3. Because Arnie worked hard in all his classes and received good grades, many people came to regard him as extremely (a) **intelligent.** When asked to explain why Arnie got good grades, Mr. Jacobs, the school principal, cited Arnie's (b) **intelligence** as the cause of his good grades.

4. Wilbur was at a picnic at the city park. He hadn't brought any food along himself. In a nearby bower of trees, some people were cooking steaks on their grill. Wilbur (a) **smelled steaks cooking** and followed the smell into the trees, where he began talking

to the people, hoping they would invite him to eat with them. They didn't and Wilbur continued his walk through the park. He again (b) **smelled steaks cooking** and followed the smell into the trees, where he found that he had been mistaken because there was no one at all in the area.

5. Carol (a) **missed her boyfriend** Todd after he graduated from their high school and went to a university several hundred miles away. She had (b) **deep longings** for Todd that remained stronger than ever. She would often (c) **stare at his picture** and (d) **recall scenes from their past**, especially their day hikes in the mountains. She would do this even when she was supposed to be listening to lectures in school.

6. Because she engaged in many activities involving sports, recreation, and the arts, Betty was known as having a lot of (a) **enthusiasm.** One day Ross was asked to explain why Betty had volunteered to be captain of the volleyball team at the plant. He said, "Of course the reason she volunteered is that Betty has so much (b) **enthusiasm.**"

7. Selden was having a terrible vacation. He was (a) **being chased by two bears** who had just eaten a stack of pancakes that he was eager to eat himself. He (b) **ran as fast as he could to a nearby lake** and (c) **dove into the cold water**. That night Selden had a nightmare in which the day's events were replayed. In the nightmare he was (d) **being chased by the two bears** that had eaten his pancakes. He (e) **ran as fast as he could to a nearby lake** and (f) **dove into the cold water**. He (g) **swam backstroke** to see if the bears would follow him.

8. Because Duane avoided and postponed many of his tasks at work, several of his coworkers, his superiors, and Duane himself came to describe him as (a) **lazy**. Duane had been passed over for a promotion several times. When asked to explain why he had not kept his customer files up to date, Duane said it was because he was (b) **lazy.**

9. Ansley was walking along the beach (a) **looking for sea shells**. She (b) **saw a sea shell** and after she drew closer to it she saw that it was pretty. Later, she (c) **saw an object she thought was a sea shell** but after she drew closer to it she saw that it was a candy bar wrapper.

10. Within the last year, Diane had been arrested for both shoplifting and writing bad checks, had been divorced, had gone bankrupt and had lost her job. She usually ignored direct questions put to her and when she did answer, her answers often made no sense. As a result of these incidents, Wayne, one of Diane's friends, said that she had a (a) **disordered personality**. Later, when Wayne was asked to explain why Diane screamed at him when he told her that she should see a psychologist, he cited Diane's (b) **disordered personality** as the cause.

11. During the winter symphony season Sandra was at an auditorium (a) **listening to Ravel's Piano Concerto in G Major**. Because it was one of her favorite pieces of impressionist music, she swooned with rapture. During the following summer, Sandra was out sailing in the sound. The rhythm of the waves lapping against the boat and the sound of the wind blowing against the sails reminded her of a musical

passage from Maurice Ravel's Piano Concerto in G Major. She (b) **listened to the concerto as she recalled it**.

12. Dominick was a second-grader who had become known as (a) **mildly retarded** because he did poorly in school. The reason he did so poorly was because he needed glasses to see the blackboard. After he got glasses, he could see the blackboard clearly. However, (b) **he continued to do poorly in school because the teachers continued to respond to him as though he were retarded**.

13. Stephen was in a psychology experiment in which subjects' reactions to tactile stimuli were being tested. He was blindfolded and told that an ice cube would be applied to the back of his neck. Just after that he (a) **felt an ice cube against the back of his neck**. When asked what he felt he told the experimenter that he felt the ice cube. He then learned that he had been correct and an ice cube had been used. Later another stimulus was applied and he (b) **felt an ice cube against the back of his neck**. When asked what he felt he told the experimenter that he felt an ice cube. He then learned that he had been mistaken and a piece of plastic had been used.

14. Ruth was having difficulties in keeping her class orderly. Therefore, she began using a procedure in which any time students (a) **spoke without first raising their hands** and being called on, they would have to stay after school for half an hour. With another class Ruth tried a different technique. She began using a procedure in which, for (b) **every hour that elapsed without anyone speaking without first raising his/her hand**, five minutes of story reading would be added at the end of the day.

15. Because she ordered the new recruits to do a good deal of extra work, Sergeant Reynolds was said by some of the recruits to have an (a) **authoritarian personality**. One day Sergeant Reynolds ordered the recruits to march five miles more than the other instructors did. Alex, a recruit, said the reason Sergeant Reynolds made them march so far was that she had an (b) **authoritarian personality.**

16. On a test in his art history class, Tom was the only student to correctly (a) **identify the role of the late thirteenth- and early fourteenth-century Italian painter Giotto** on the development of high Renaissance painting in the fifteenth century. Tom was considered extremely (b) **intelligent.**

17. Senator Morley had described his campaign opponent, Alan Howard, as a (a) **wimp** because Howard opposed the death penalty and military intervention in foreign countries. When Howard announced that he was also in favor of a commission to investigate charges of brutality by the state police, Senator Morley said the reason for Howard's position on this issue was that he had a (b) **wimpy personality.**

18. Brandon was coming out of the movie theater into the bright light of day. As he did, (a) **the pupils of his eyes constricted,** which allowed less of the bright light to go through his pupils and reach the retina, the light-sensitive part of the eye. At that time he also (b) **lifted his hand to shield his eyes from the light.** This also allowed less of the bright light to reach his retina.

19. Margaret smoked cigarettes, normally about a pack a day. Sometimes people who

smoke are said to have a (a) **tobacco habit**. When Pat was asked to explain why Margaret smoked cigarettes, he cited her (b) **tobacco habit** as the cause of her smoking.

20. Josie was concerned about her young son Jason because he hadn't been feeling well, having contracted a bad case of the flu. By evening he was feeling a little better, although he was (a) **sneezing once every few minutes**. A few months later, Josie was concerned because Jason had been (b) **sneezing once every few minutes,** but otherwise he seemed well. Upon further investigation, Josie learned that Jason had been sneezing in order to get attention, not because he was ill.

21. Mr. Marco was a teacher at Cody High School. One student had heard from a friend that Mr. Marco was a (a) **cold person** and this student informed the other students in his class that Mr. Marco was cold. As a result of this, the students in the class (b) **interacted with Mr. Marco very little in class, didn't like him, and said he wasn't a good teacher.**

22. Allison was quite good at multiplication. She was presented with the problem 34 X 40 = ? in her textbook and she (a) **quickly calculated the answer** ("1360") to herself without using paper and pencil. A classmate, Beth, was also presented with the problem 34 X 40 = ? in her textbook and she (b) **quickly calculated the answer** by using paper and pencil.

23. After George's mother died, he went through a difficult period. One day at school he jumped out of a classroom window and didn't come back to school for a week. On another occasion, he tore the pages out of a library book. As a result of these two incidents, the school nurse told the teachers that George was (a) **mentally ill** and word of this got out to the students as well. Consequently, the teachers and students (b) **initiated interactions with George much less often and behaved as if he were dangerous.** This in turn caused George (c) **to behave in a more bizarre fashion than he had before.**

24. On a dark and stormy evening, Basil sat in his favorite chair (a) **silently reading a ghost story to himself**. On another dark and stormy evening, Basil sat in his favorite chair (b) **reading a ghost story aloud to those gathered around him.**

25. During the past week Ben had forgotten his wallet at home before going to work, had not recalled an appointment with his boss, and had failed to remember his wife's birthday. As a result of these incidents Ben concluded that he had (a) **a poor memory.** When he then neglected to remember to pay his phone bill, he felt that the reason for this was his (b) **poor memory.**

26. Because Janet frequently thought about Bob, wrote affectionate prose to him daily, and often called him to talk, Janet described herself as having (a) **love** for Bob. Janet knitted Bob a sweater for his birthday and when Bob was asked to explain why Janet did this he said the reason was Janet's (b) **love** for him.

Conceptual Exercise   *Selecting Target Behaviors*

Each of the following items represents a method of selecting target behaviors, the criterion validation method, the social comparison method, or the subjective evaluation method. For each item, specify which method is represented and explain your decision. If the item is an example of the social comparison method or the subjective evaluation method, also specify whether the data collection phase was used alone or with the intervention phase. Confirm your decisions by consulting the analyses in the back of the book.

Experimental criterion validation method: An experiment is conducted in which the effect of engaging in a behavior is assessed (e.g., one group of people performs the behavior while another group does not). The effects that the behavior produces must be generally accepted as worthy outcomes (e.g., good grades in school or reductions in infant mortality).

Social comparison methods: Successful and unsuccessful performers at a given task or enterprise are compared to see what behaviors they engage in or fail to engage in. In this way, we can infer what behaviors produce success and failure. During the data collection phase of the social comparison method, the behaviors of successful and unsuccessful performers are merely compared. During the intervention phase of the social comparison method, the group of unsuccessful performers is taught to engage in the behaviors performed by the successful performers.

Subjective evaluation methods: A group of evaluators, often experts in an area, judges the quality or competence of an individual's performance. In the data collection phase of this method, the evaluators simply judge the value of a performance (e.g., a film critic evaluates the quality of the performances of actors and actresses). In the intervention phase of this method, the evaluators rate the worthiness of a performance usually both before and after a behavior change takes place. After-ratings that are better than the before-ratings are evidence that the behavior change has been a worthwhile accomplishment.

1. Professor Perkins was conducting a study of poets. He gave both good and poor poets a test in which their task was to provide words and phrases that satisfied certain conditions. For example, the poets were told to list the characteristics of an apple (e.g., red, has a stem, tart, and so on). In general, he found that the good poets had greater verbal fluency than the ordinary poets in that they were able to list more words and phrases per given unit of time than the ordinary poets.

2. A group of art students was shown a variety of objects and asked to draw a still life drawing that included these objects. On the basis of the quality and originality of the drawings, the students were categorized as "good" or "ordinary" artists. The students were also questioned about their techniques in drawing. In general, it was found that the good artists spent more time than the ordinary artists arranging and rearranging the still life objects in an attempt to "find" an interesting artistic problem to solve. The good and ordinary artists did not differ in their technical artistic skills.

3. Several third-grade children were trained in fire safety skills involving responding to emergency fire situations. A group of professional firefighters evaluated the chil-

dren's training by, for example, judging the likelihood that the children would die or be burned severely because of their skill levels. The firefighters judged that the children were much less likely to die or be burned severely in a fire emergency after the training than before.

4. Three underachieving fifth-grade students were given training in certain self-control procedures designed to improve their performance in arithmetic drills. The students' arithmetic performances improved as a result of the training. After the training was complete, their teachers rated the training on a 5-point scale as helpful and easy to use. They said they would use it again with other underachieving students.

5. A research project was designed to teach problem-solving skills to a group of delinquent teenagers committed to a state mental hospital after being diagnosed as having conduct disorders. Target behaviors were to apply problem-solving techniques to avoid potentially troublesome social situations (e.g., what to do when you want to watch a television show and someone else is watching a different show). Target behaviors were identifying the problem, defining the goal, generating alternative solutions, comparing the consequences of the alternatives, and selecting the best alternative. A group of normal teenagers was used as a comparison group. At first, target behaviors of the conduct-disordered teenagers were far lower than those of the normal teenagers. However, after the conduct-disordered teenagers were trained in problem solving, they surpassed the levels of target behaviors that the normal adolescents had achieved.

6. Speeding, defined as driving a vehicle in excess of posted speed limits, was selected as a target behavior in experiments in Canada and Israel. It was found that feedback signs effectively reduced speeding behavior, and the reduction in speeding caused a substantial reduction in injury accidents, a well-accepted standard of desirability in traffic safety.

7. Twelve children who were at least 20% overweight participated in a behavioral program designed to change their eating habits. Their parents were trained in the use of behavior analysis principles to modify the eating behaviors of the children. The experiment showed that the training caused the children to lose weight. Weight reduction among overweight people is a well-accepted accomplishment in the fields of health and fitness.

8. Several videotapes were prepared showing different situations in which a "victim" responded to aggressive criticism. The videos showed the victim responding nonassertively, aggressively, or in one of two assertive styles. A group of 16 female undergraduates, whose dormitory co-residents judged them to be particularly effective at handling criticism, watched the tapes and rated how effective the victim's responses to aggressive criticism were on a 1 to 7 scale. The researchers found that the women rated the two assertive styles to be more effective than either nonassertive responding or aggressive responding.

9. Eighteen elementary and junior high schools participated in a program designed to reduce school vandalism, a generally recognized problem in modern society. School personnel were trained to reduce disruptive behavior and vandalism through posi-

tive techniques, including praising students for desirable behavior. These methods caused a 78.5% reduction in vandalism compared to schools that were not in the program.

10. In research concerned with behaviors contributing to marital satisfaction, 10 happy couples were compared to 10 unhappy couples. Researchers found that the happiest couples rewarded one another for being in each other's presence, while the unhappiest couples punished one another for being in each other's presence. Moderately happy couples defined "pleasant" in terms of those desirable behaviors their spouse engaged in. Moderately unhappy couples defined "pleasant" in terms of those undesirable behaviors their spouse did not engage in.

11. Six retarded adults participated in a social-skills training program in which several target behaviors, including appropriate gesturing, posture, speech loudness, intonation, and eye contact, were selected. Before training, a group of judges rated the overall interpersonal effectiveness of the trainees at an average of 1.72 on a 5-point scale. After training, this value increased to 4.36.

12. A research project compared two groups of married people. In one group the wives were depressed and in the other, they were not. It was found that in the group with depressed wives, the frequency of positive social contacts with people other than the husband was lower than in the group of nondepressed wives.

13. An experiment was conducted to learn if a package of behavioral techniques would lead to increased energy conservation. The package included a 20-minute television program made available on cable television to 575 homes in Virginia. The television program demonstrated energy-saving behaviors, including selective use of air conditioning, closing blinds and windows, and insulating water heaters. The investigators found that the package of techniques substantially reduced the residents' electricity use, a well-recognized standard of desirability in the field of energy conservation.

14. In a study designed to determine the elements of conversational skill, observers rated 15 videotapes of two people conversing. In addition, the people in the conversations also rated their partners' conversational skills. The observers rated the use of questions, proximity, and voice volume as important aspects of good conversation, while the participants themselves rated facial expressiveness, topic variety, and voice clarity as important aspects.

15. Five senior citizens living in nursing homes had a problem with incontinence, generally recognized as a serious problem among older people. In order to manage the problem, staff at the nursing homes checked the patients once per hour for signs of wetness, prompted the patients to use the toilet, praised the patients for dryness, and reprimanded the patients who had wet themselves. These procedures caused a reduction in incontinence from about 30% before use of the procedures to 15% afterwards.

16. Three low-income women who spoke to groups about community issues enrolled in a public-speaking training program. They were successfully taught target behaviors

including eye contact, use of gestures, and a variety of other public-speaking behaviors. Audiences of between 6 and 42 people rated the performances of the three women from 1 (very poor) to 7 (very good). These ratings were higher after training than before.

17. Students who were studying introductory psychology participated in an experiment. They read some material in a text using the SQ3R study method, which consists of surveying the chapter, constructing questions about the material, reciting answers to the questions, and reviewing the material. It was found that use of the SQ3R method enabled the students to do better on quizzes assessing academic achievement.

18. A training program was used to teach five retarded women to color coordinate their clothes. Observers stationed in a shopping mall recorded the color combinations female shoppers wore. The color combinations of 600 regular female shoppers were compared to those of the retarded women. Initially, the retarded women did not select the popular color combinations that the other women wore. The most popular color combinations the shoppers wore were used as standards of good taste to train the five retarded women. The women were successfully trained to dress in the popular color combinations.

19. Steve was a 7-year-old boy in a special class for students with behavior problems. He would often steal from other students and from the school. A program was used to reduce Steven's stealing behavior. All of Steve's belongings were marked, and he was periodically rewarded if he possessed only his marked belongings. If he possessed the unmarked belongings of others, he was verbally reprimanded. Experimental evidence indicated that this method reduced Steve's thefts substantially.

20. Twelve mentally retarded adults were in a program to train appropriate mealtime behaviors. A training procedure greatly reduced the number of eating errors the trainees made. Also, observers watched general customers at a restaurant and recorded their frequency of eating errors. It was found that before training, the eating errors of the trainees were higher than those of the general restaurant customers. After training, however, the trainees exhibited fewer eating errors than the restaurant customers.

21. Fourth-, fifth-, and sixth-grade students were taught to write stories that contained a variety of adjectives, action verbs, and sentence beginnings. The teaching procedures were successful in increasing the frequency of these target behaviors. In addition, two experts in language skills ranked compositions the students wrote before training and after training. Compositions written after training were ranked as more creative than those written before training.

22. Several people, suffering from a disorder called *caffeinism* (i.e., excessive caffeine consumption), enrolled in a program designed to help them solve their problem. (This disorder, considered a health risk, can cause nervousness, restlessness, and headaches.) The project supervisors conducted an experiment and found that a gradual reduction in caffeine intake was effective in allowing the people to function without excessive caffeine.

23. In research concerned with the problem of post-traumatic stress disorder (PTSD) among Vietnam combat veterans, two groups of veterans were examined, one with many PTSD problems and another with few such problems. It was found that the veterans with many problems had a) less social support and b) more combat exposure than those with few problems.

24. At a prison, a group of men who had been convicted of rape was compared to a group of men who had been convicted of nonsexual crimes. Both groups listened to audiotapes depicting sex scenes in which a female took an active or passive role in sexual acts or was portrayed as being raped. The rapists responded sexually to all the scenes, but the nonrapists responded sexually only to those scenes in which the women did not give anti-approach cues.

25. In a study concerned with interpersonal attraction, children were shown videos of two boys playing together. In the videos, one boy made a suggestion to the other in either a cooperative or an uncooperative manner. The second boy either agreed with the first boy's suggestion or did not. The refusals were accompanied either with a statement giving an explanation for the refusal or a neutral remark. The children viewers rated cooperative behavior and agreeableness to suggestions higher than uncooperative responding or refusals of suggestions. Also, when a suggestion was refused, it was rated higher when accompanied by an explanation than by a neutral statement.

chapter 2

Positive Reinforcement

Mr. and Mrs. Orr were a prosperous older couple who had been looking forward to the extra leisure time they would have together during their retirement years. Unfortunately, at the age of 67, Mr. Orr suffered a stroke. One effect of the stroke that was particularly distressing to Mrs. Orr was her husband's inability to converse in the way he formerly had.

Loss of conversational skills is especially cruel for the elderly. Although we cannot be expected to enjoy as many physically strenuous activities as we approach old age, partial compensation for that loss are conversation and reminiscences of one's youth, friendships, adventures, and successes. Through conversation it is possible for the elderly to remain mentally alert and able. In addition, the loss of the ability to speak, impedes people's access to a variety of services, including medical care. In the past, such a disability has often been considered as an untreatable brain abnormality. Many older people who have lost speech skills have lived out lonely lives in institutions, their thoughts and feelings held captive within themselves by their disability.

Three months after his stroke, Mr. Orr was discharged from the hospital and referred to the Elderly Support Project, which specialized in the treatment of geron-tological disorders, problems of the elderly. Mr. and Mrs. Orr were fortunate to be referred to three behavior analysts, Glenn Green, Nathan Linsk, and Elsie Pinkston, who had experience in treating problems similar to Mr. Orr's.

The team began by assessing the Orr's home environment. They decided that treatment would take place right there, with Mrs. Orr acting as the therapist. The first step in this program, as in most applications of behavior analysis, was for Mrs. Orr to define precisely Mr. Orr's conversational difficulties. After consulting with the team, Mrs. Orr identified two specific behaviors that were at the crux of the prob-lem. The first of these target behaviors was Mr. Orr's correct responses to questions, determined by the content, duration, and timing of his answers. For example, if Mr. Orr said nothing in response to a question or said something irrelevant to the ques-tion, this was considered an incorrect response. The second target behavior was Mr. Orr's spontaneous verbalizations, which included appropriate utterances when he was not directly questioned or otherwise prompted. If Mr. Orr said something inap-propriate, such as "It's hot outside" in midwinter, this was not counted as an appro-priate spontaneous verbalization.

The team of behavior analysts then trained Mrs. Orr to use a positive reinforce-ment procedure. This procedure consisted of training Mrs. Orr to reward Mr. Orr with a touch, praise, and a smile whenever Mr. Orr answered questions appropriately or spontaneously spoke out.

During one hour of each day, the team instructed Mrs. Orr to ask her husband at least five questions, some "yes-no" questions and some requiring a longer answer. If Mr. Orr answered the questions appropriately within one minute, Mrs. Orr would touch him, praise him, and smile proudly at him. Mrs. Orr's touches were directed to the left side of her husband's body because that side had not been damaged by the stroke.

Under the direction of the team, Mrs. Orr received extensive practice in using positive reinforcement to help her husband. The team emphasized that Mrs. Orr had to touch, praise, and smile immediately after Mr. Orr engaged in a target behavior and that she had to be scrupulously consistent in her use of the technique, making sure that Mr. Orr's desirable behaviors were always rewarded.

At first, Mr. Orr's "question-answering" and spontaneous verbalizations were merely recorded during a baseline or pretreatment period. During this time, Mr. Orr answered questions correctly 67% of the time and spontaneously spoke less than once per hour. After Mrs. Orr was taught to use the reinforcement procedure, a problem developed. Not fully understanding the reinforcement procedure, Mrs. Orr sometimes failed to touch, praise, and smile at her husband when he per-formed the target behaviors. With additional training, however, Mrs. Orr learned how to use the technique properly. Mr. Orr's correctness of question-answering increased to 84% and his spontaneous verbalizations more than doubled to 2.5 per hour. Mrs. Orr was very encouraged with the significant change in her husband's conversational ability.*

*Based on Green, Linsk, and Pinkston (1986).

Influencing Behavior With Rewards

Although behavior analysis consists of many principles and procedures, the basic idea that *rewards influence behavior* is the single most powerful and important fact about behavior you can ever learn. By learning a few basic principles about how rewards change behavior, you will have knowledge that can help you change not only the behavior of others, but also your own behavior.

That rewards influence behavior may seem like common sense. However, this notion is far more complex and poorly understood than you might think. For example, it is not generally appreciated that small rewards can have a big impact on behavior. As the example of the Orrs illustrates, even a few touches, smiles, and words of praise can be the keys to recovering the companionship between a wife and husband that seemed lost. At times, however, trying to use rewards to influence behavior can be wrong, and using fewer or less obvious rewards can be right. Aside from a knowledge of behavior principles, using rewards effectively requires perseverance, consistency, and patience. All sorts of complexities, nuances, mysteries, and paradoxes must be considered, many of which do not arise from common sense.

One of these complexities involves the use of the term *reward*. Reward is an everyday word and, as a result, there are some disadvantages to using it in a scientific discipline like behavior analysis. For example, the term reward usually involves giving material things to people for doing good work. Indeed, what first comes to mind when you hear the term reward? Many people think of money offered to encourage people to turn in lost pets or escaped convicts, or trophies given to winners of sporting events. When we think of rewards, we tend not to think of more subtle things such as praise, smiles, hearing someone address you warmly by name, the experience of reading a good book, or learning something new. These kinds of things neither ordinarily come to mind when we think of rewards nor are they normally given to induce people to do things.

A second problem is that common use of the term reward implies something that is clearly pleasurable and the notion of *pleasure* is far too narrow for our purposes. Pleasure is a subjective term and what is pleasurable for me may not be so for you. It is desirable, therefore, to find a term for reward that doesn't necessarily connote pleasure. Rather, we need a word to stand for *anything for which people will work to obtain.*

Describing Positive Reinforcement

The solution behavior analysts have adopted is to replace the term reward with a more precise term, *positive reinforcer*. Using a positive reinforcer to change behavior is called *positive reinforcement*, a process that behavior analysts describe in the following way:

- a response-dependent consequence is presented;
- the response occurs more often;
- the response occurs more often because of the response-consequence relationship, not for some other reason (Catania, 1984; Higgins & Morris, 1985).

If these criteria are all met, we call the consequence a positive reinforcer. Let us consider each of the three criteria of this definition.

A response-dependent consequence is one that follows only the response in question. That is, when the response occurs, the consequence occurs, and whenever the response fails to occur, the consequence also fails to occur. When such a relationship exists, the consequence is said to be dependent on (or contingent on) the response (Lattal & Poling, 1981). For example, Mrs. Orr's praise, smiles, and touches were response-dependent consequences for Mr. Orr's appropriate answers to questions and for his spontaneous speech because when these target behaviors occurred, the consequences occurred, and when these target behaviors failed to occur, the consequences also did not occur. By *consequence,* we mean a stimulus change that follows the response. Positive reinforcement will always involve a change from no stimulus (e.g., no praise, smiles, or touches) to the presence of a stimulus (e.g., praise, smiles, and touches). Technically, it is this stimulus change that is the reinforcer.

Imagine what might have happened if Mrs. Orr praised, touched, and smiled at Mr. Orr whether the target behaviors occurred or not. Mr. Orr might have concluded that his wife would shower him with attention no matter what he did. Had this happened, the consequences would be said to be response-independent. In other words, there would be no relationship between the occurrence of particular responses and consequences.

The second defining feature of positive reinforcement is that the behavior occurs more often. There must be an increase in some measure of the behavior in order to say that positive reinforcement has taken place. In Mr. Orr's case, both his answers to questions and his spontaneous speech occurred more often than they had before, using frequency of responses and percentage of questions answered correctly. If a duration measure had been used in the study, the amount of time Mr. Orr spent speaking would have been used. Which measure a behavior analyst chooses depends on both the nature of the problem and the situation.

The requirement that the behavior occurs more often makes the definition of reinforcement *functional:* What is and is not a reinforcer depends on the function or effect the procedure has on someone's behavior. Nobody can say for sure if a given consequence will act as a reinforcer until the consequence can be shown to make a behavior occur more often. In addition, if a given consequence fails to make behavior occur more often, this does not mean that reinforcement has failed to work. Instead, it means that we have not yet identified a true reinforcer. In the example of the Orrs, Mrs. Orr's smiles and touches could be said to be reinforcers only after they had been shown to increase the frequency of Mr. Orr's responses. Had the smiles and touches failed to increase Mr. Orr's responding, this would not be a violation of the principle of reinforcement but rather an indication that the smiles and touches were not functioning as reinforcers.

The third defining feature of positive reinforcement is that increases in some measure of behavior must be shown to be due to response-dependent consequences, not to some other influence. It is important that the behavior increases in rate as a result of the positive reinforcer, not for some other reason. Let us imagine a scuffle between two children. We want to know whether one child's name-calling is a positive reinforcer for another child's hitting. After one child hits the other, the second child calls the first child a name. This occurs several times, making name-calling a response-dependent consequence for hitting, and satisfying the first requirement for positive reinforcement.

Further, suppose that the target behavior, hitting, occurs more often than it did before name-calling was dependent on it. This condition would satisfy the second requirement for positive reinforcement, that the response occurs more often. In order to satisfy the third requirement, that the increase in behavior rate is due to the response-consequence relationship and not to some other influence, it would be necessary to do some experimentation. For example, we might find that when a certain child is called a name, she hits, even though name-calling had occurred before hitting, and is therefore not dependent on hitting. In such a case, we would have to conclude that the response-consequence relationship between the hits and the name-calling was not why name-calling increased hitting, but instead the increase in hitting was due to some other reason. Specifically, name-calling would have been a prompt for hitting, not a positive reinforcer. Indeed, in ordinary life, most of the time name-calling does not act as a positive reinforcer for hitting, but as a prompt for hitting. As you can see, proving that something is unquestionably a positive reinforcer requires experimentation.

The term positive reinforcement avoids the two problems associated with the term reward. First, positive reinforcers can include typical rewards like food, money, or presents, but they can also include praise, smiles, subtle expressions of affection, or the opportunity to listen to music, and so forth. Second, positive reinforcers can be any response-dependent consequences that increase some measure of behavior, not necessarily consequences we would typically consider pleasurable. Making use of the concept of positive reinforcement makes it unnecessary to decide what is pleasurable and what is not. Further, making use of the concept of positive reinforcement does not entail adopting a hedonistic view of human nature, that people are motivated only by pursuit of pleasures (cf., Keller & Schoenfeld, 1950, p. 278).

Several conventions should be observed when discussing positive reinforcement and positive reinforcers. Positive reinforcement refers to the process of response-dependent stimulus presentation that causes some measure of the response to increase. Positive reinforcer (and also positive reinforcement) refers to the *stimulus* whose response-dependent presentation increases some measure of behavior. As discussed earlier, a key feature of reinforcement is the response-dependent stimulus change, the change from no reinforcer to a reinforcer. If you wish to refer precisely to this stimulus change, you can speak of the reinforcing stimulus change.

We speak of reinforcement of a response, not of a person, because it is the response that is strengthened, not the person. If you wish to speak of the effect of reinforcement on behavior without being specific about which measure of behavior is altered, you may speak of the strengthening of the response or an increase in the level, probability, or likelihood of the response. Finally, if you wish to speak of positive reinforcement without having proven that some measure of behavior is actually increased, you may speak of use of a positive reinforcement procedure, response-dependent presentation of a suspected reinforcer.

Describing Positive Reinforcers

A positive reinforcer is an event that is dependent on a behavior and causes that behavior to increase in strength. Positive reinforcers can be described in a variety of ways, but it is customary to distinguish between various types of positive reinforcers. These include unconditioned and conditioned reinforcers, token and back-up reinforcers, social and nonsocial reinforcers, activity reinforcers, intrinsic and extrinsic reinforcers, and natural and contrived reinforcers.

Unconditioned and Conditioned Reinforcers

An *unconditioned reinforcer,* also called a *primary reinforcer,* is one whose reinforcing properties are not learned. Because air, food, water, and an agreeable temperature are all examples of stimuli whose reinforcing properties are unlearned, they may serve as unconditioned reinforcers. These act as reinforcers without learning through association with other reinforcers.

In contrast, *conditioned reinforcers,* also called *secondary reinforcers,* acquire their reinforcing effectiveness through a learning process in which they are associated with other reinforcers. Verbal praise, money, subway tokens, good grades in school, and fashionable clothes are all examples. These do not act as reinforcers unless they are associated with other reinforcers. For example, infants are not particularly reinforced by money except for its use as a play object, and we are unaffected even by lavish praise if given in a foreign language.

Although the distinction between unconditioned and conditioned reinforcers is well-accepted, in practice it is sometimes difficult to determine which reinforcers are learned and unlearned. For example, it is not known whether the sight of attractive people of the opposite sex is an unconditioned or conditioned reinforcer for most people. It is known that standards of physical attractiveness are similar across racial and ethnic groups. This suggests, along with intuitive, introspective reports (Skinner, 1980; Stendhal, 1926), that physical attractiveness is at least a partially unlearned reinforcer. Similarly, it is difficult to determine whether our appreciation of music and language patterns (e.g., rhyming) are learned or unlearned behaviors. Fortunately, it is not necessary to determine whether a reinforcer is unconditioned or conditioned to make effective use of it for the purpose of changing behavior.

The clearest examples of conditioned reinforcers are seen when things quickly acquire or lose their status as reinforcers. People will work hard to acquire fashionable clothes when they are in style, but will not be caught dead wearing them once they are passé. A trendy phrase or greeting will be a reinforcer for a while, but will be met with derision when it goes out of style.

Table 2.1   *List of Reinforcers Available for Tokens*

Reinforcer	Number of Tokens Required Daily
I. Privacy	
Selection of bedroom	0–30
Personal chair	1
Room divider	1
Choice of bedspread	1
Coat rack	1
Personal cabinet	2
Placebo	1–2
II. Leave from the ward	
20-min walk on hospital grounds	2
30-min grounds pass	10
Trip to town	100
III. Social interaction with staff	
Private audience with chaplain, nurse	5 min free
Private audience with ward staff, physician	5 min free
Private audience with ward psychologist	20
Private audience with social worker	100
IV. Devotional opportunities	
Extra religious services on ward	1
Extra religious services off ward	10
V. Recreational opportunities	
Movie on ward	1
Listen to live band	1
Exclusive use of radio	1
Choice of television program	3
VI. Commissary items	
Consumables (candy, milk, cigarettes, coffee)	1–5
Toiletry items	1–10
Clothing and accessories	12–400
Reading and writing materials	2–5
Miscellaneous items	1–50

Token and Back-up Reinforcers

One reinforcement system that behavior analysts pioneered is called a *token economy,* wherein tokens, often poker chips or other small pieces of plastic, are awarded to program participants for engaging in specified desired behaviors (Ayllon & Azrin, 1968; Kazdin, 1977b). Participants may exchange these tokens for *back-up rein-forcers,* things such as food, privileges, trips, or toys. Ted Ayllon and Nate Azrin (Ayllon & Azrin, 1965) established one of the first token economies for 45 psychotic female patients in a mental hospital. The patients could earn tokens for work on jobs including helping in the kitchen, clerking at the ward commissary, performing secretarial duties, assisting with laundry, doing janitorial work, and assuming self-care. They could exchange the tokens for a variety of reinforcers, as Table 2.1 shows.

Ayllon and Azrin found that when the tokens were given on a job-dependent basis, the patients reliably performed their duties. However, when the tokens were distributed on a job-independent basis (i.e., whether or not the jobs were done), the tasks were not performed.

Token economies have also been used extensively in elementary school classrooms where a teacher might give tokens for correct answers in reading, spelling, handwriting, arithmetic, and language arts assignments. The students would then redeem their tokens for free time, extra recreation periods, the opportunity to listen to stories or to watch a film, and so forth.

Two important benefits are associated with token economy systems: First, tokens can be easily distributed and collected with minimum interference to ongoing activities. Second, because participants can exchange tokens for a wide variety of back-up reinforcers, it is likely that the tokens will always act as reinforcers.

Token reinforcers are one example of *generalized reinforcers.* A generalized reinforcer is more-or-less effective all the time, while a *nongeneralized reinforcer* is effective only when we have been deprived of the reinforcer. For example, money is a generalized reinforcer because it is always effective, while food is not a generalized reinforcer because it is effective as a reinforcer only when we have gone without food for a period of time. Generalized reinforcers like money are powerful reinforcers because they can be traded for many different reinforcers. For example, money can be exchanged for food, water, a warm place to stay, or social contact with other people.

Social and Nonsocial Reinforcers

Social reinforcers involve the actions of other people. For example, response-dependent praise, smiles, kisses, and applause are all social reinforcers because these consequences consist of things people do that typically strengthen behaviors they are dependent on. In contrast, *nonsocial reinforcement* consists of consequences that do not involve the behavior of other people. Picking fruit from a tree, receiving a drink from a vending machine, and reaching your destination on a walk are all examples of nonsocial reinforcement.

Social reinforcers are highly effective for most people and are important deter-minants of our everyday interactions with others (Snyder & Patterson, 1986). Social reinforcers are thought to be powerful because they are associated with many differ-ent kinds of reinforcers. From the time we are born, we receive so many reinforcers from other people that signs of friendliness and kindness from others become estab-lished as powerful reinforcers.

The considerable power of social reinforcement was illustrated by an experi-ment in which a social reinforcer was pitted against a nonsocial reinforcer. Gallimore, Tharp, and Kemp (1969) had fourth-grade children engage in a button-pushing task in which flashes of a light on a display panel followed correct responses and incorrect responses were followed by face-to-face contact with the experimenter, who said, "You're wrong." Many children who were socially deprived were more likely to respond incorrectly and receive the negative face-to-face attention than children who were not socially deprived. This result strongly suggests that many children deprived of social reinforcement will seek it out in whatever form it becomes available, even when it consists of reprimands and other seemingly unpleasant forms of social con-tact (Madsen, Becker, Thomas, Koser, & Plager, 1968). Many forms of poor con-duct by both children and adults are suspected to be due to the fact that misbehav-ior, because it is difficult to ignore, often results in attention from others, a powerful social reinforcer. In contrast, attention for desirable behaviors is often earned only after considerable effort and hard work, and sometimes not even then.

Activity Reinforcers

Another important kind of reinforcer is an *activity reinforcer*, the opportunity to engage in a favored behavior or activity. According to the Premack principle, named for psychologist David Premack (1959), who introduced this concept, the opportu-nity to engage in a frequently performed behavior may be used as a reinforcer for an infrequently-performed behavior.

For example, in one of the first applications of the Premack principle, Homme, deBaca, Devine, Steinhorst, and Rickert (1963) worked with nursery school children who paid little attention to what they were told, and spent most of their time run-ning about the room screaming and pushing chairs about. In order to get the chil-dren to sit quietly and look at a blackboard, the opportunity to run around the room and scream was made dependent on sitting quietly and looking at the blackboard. The children were soon reliably engaging in the desirable behaviors so much so that anyone who saw them sitting quietly would have assumed they were doing so out of fear of punishment, rather than looking forward to the opportunity to run and scream.

Activities that serve as reinforcers are sometimes surprising. Taffel and O'Leary (1976), for example, worked with two fourth-grade math classes. After the children had worked on a set of problems for 30 minutes, their answers were scored. If a student met a criterion based on improvement over his or her previous performance, the child was given the opportunity to do more math problems. Comparisons with children in a control group indicated that the opportunity to do more math problems acted as a reinforcer that increased the initial problems the students completed and the time spent working on the initial problems. Of course, during the time the students were doing the extra problems, they were also learning more. This study shows that activities that seem dull and commonplace to students should not be overlooked as possible reinforcers.

Another example of the effectiveness of unusual activity reinforcers was described by Charlop, Kurtz, and Casey (1990) in their work with autistic children. Identifying effective reinforcers for autistic children can be a difficult problem. Often they do not respond to stimuli, such as toys or praise, typically used with other children. Activities that many autistic children prefer are stereotypical, perseverative behaviors such as self-stimulation. Charlop and her colleagues (1990) compared the reinforcing effectiveness of these preferred activities with more conventional stimuli, such as food as reinforcers for various academic task behaviors. In general, task performance was highest when the opportunity to engage in aberrant behavior depended upon correct performance. Edible reinforcers were the least effective in promoting correct task performance. This study demonstrates the need for creativity on the part of the behavior analyst designing behavioral intervention programs.

Activity reinforcers are particularly useful when appropriate reinforcers for someone's behavior are not apparent. In these situations, behavior analysts can simply observe the individual's behavior to see what activities occur often, and then attempt to use these activities as reinforcers. An example of activity reinforcers in a token economy was seen in Ayllon and Azrin's (1965) study in which, for example, the opportunity to watch films and television and to listen to live music was made dependent on payment of tokens.

Extrinsic and Intrinsic Reinforcers

Extrinsic reinforcers are consequences external to ourselves, such as money, applause, and verbal praise from others. These extrinsic consequences do not automatically occur as a result of engaging in a behavior. In contrast, *intrinsic reinforcers*, also called *automatic reinforcers* (Vaughan & Michael, 1982), are consequences that result automatically from engaging in the behavior. Solving a crossword puzzle, viewing attractive paintings, listening to beautiful music, and reading a good novel are all possible intrinsic reinforcers because the consequences of these behaviors occur automatically. The behavior involved in solving a crossword puzzle is intrinsically or automatically reinforced by completion of the puzzle. The behavior of looking at the painting is reinforced by the intrinsic appreciation of color, texture, and content. Reading is reinforced by identifying the theme of a novel, relating symbols to themes and to characters, seeing the plot thicken, and finding out how the story ends.

Natural and Contrived Reinforcers

Natural reinforcers are recurring consequences that are typically dependent on the behavior of skilled or mature individuals. *Contrived reinforcers*, in contrast, are non-recurring consequences not typically dependent on the behavior of competent performers. Contrived reinforcers are consequences that are added specifically in order to increase the level of weak behavior on the part of those in training to be competent performers. For example, suppose a student who has learned Russian well at school travels to Russia, asks for directions from natives, and receives them. Receiving directions is a natural reinforcer because they are recurring consequences that are typically dependent on, in this case, the behavior of skilled speakers of Russian. In contrast, suppose a student studying Russian at school asks for directions in Russian as a part of an oral quiz, and receives a good grade on the quiz for asking correctly. The good grade is a contrived reinforcer because (a) a good grade is a nonrecurring consequence not typically dependent on asking questions in a foreign language and (b) the grade is a consequence that has been added to increase the language proficiency of those learning to speak Russian competently. Note that natural reinforcers are recurring reinforcers because they continue to be received in the natural environment as long as the behavior is executed properly; contrived reinforcers are nonrecurring reinforcers, because they are received only while the individual is in training and are not available outside the training situation or after a training period.

Many behavior analysis procedures make extensive use of contrived reinforcers because behavior analysts so often are concerned with strengthening weak or nonexistent behavior. One primary purpose of behavior analysis is to develop procedures that train people to become competent performers. However, once a behavior has been increased to an adequate level, it is essential to replace the contrived reinforcers with natural reinforcers. Although good grades encourage students to learn a language, the eventual goal of foreign language instruction is to allow the natural reinforcers to take over, those reinforcers that consist of successfully communicating with foreign language speakers.

Note that the distinction between intrinsic and extrinsic reinforcers is different from the distinction between natural and contrived reinforcers. First, all intrinsic reinforcers are also natural reinforcers, but not all natural reinforcers are intrinsic reinforcers. Because intrinsic reinforcers occur automatically as a result of engaging in a behavior, all intrinsic reinforcers are natural reinforcers also because they are recurring consequences that are typically dependent on the behavior of competent performers in the natural environment. For example, an artist's sketch can be both an intrinsic reinforcer for drawing because it is an automatic result of drawing, and a natural reinforcer because sketches are recurring consequences that skilled artists typically receive in the natural environment.

Second, not all natural reinforcers are intrinsic reinforcers. For example, if you ask for directions in Russia, the directions are not automatically forthcoming; the Russian being asked might not know the answer or might be too busy to respond at all. Similarly, applause is a natural reinforcer for the skilled work of those in most of the performing arts and in sports, but applause is far from an automatic consequence of even excellent performances.

A Positive Approach to Changing Behavior in the Real World

A working premise of behavior analysis is that the world as we know it is flawed because people's desirable behaviors are not positively reinforced (Skinner, 1953, 1971). Instead of making use of positive reinforcement techniques, our entire society is set up to induce people to behave well through threats, punishment, and coercion (Sidman, 1989).

Students learn because they fear the consequences of not learning, rather than because of the positive reinforcers associated with knowledge and skills. Employees work because they will be fired, rather than because they obtain positive reinforcement from the goods they produce and services they provide. People obey laws because of the punishment for disobeying, rather than because the social harmony associated with an organized lawful society acts as a positive reinforcer. People are threatened by minority groups and try to oppress them, rather than seeking the positive reinforcement that results from friendship. Nations compete with one another militarily out of mutual fear of aggression, rather than obtaining the positive reinforcement that accrues through cooperation.

Almost all applications of behavior analysis are concerned with replacing aversive (i.e., punitive or coercive) forms of suppression of undesirable behavior with positive reinforcement techniques in which people are given reasons to act desirably.

Making Positive Reinforcement Effective

By definition, a positive reinforcer must be a consequence that increases some measure of behavior. Yet, not all reinforcers are equal. The effectiveness of positive reinforcers varies and behavior analysts have acquired considerable, but by no means complete, knowledge, about the reasons for this variation. Nine factors that influence the effectiveness of positive reinforcement are:

- deprivation and satiation;
- instructions;
- reinforcer amount;
- predictive conditioned reinforcers;
- reinforcer variety;
- response energy;
- reinforcer contrast effects;
- extraneous reinforcers; and
- reinforcement delay.

Deprivation and Satiation

A state of deprivation is said to exist when a person has not had contact with a particular reinforcer for a period of time and that reinforcer has become effective. A state of satiation exists when the person has had contact with a particular reinforcer recently and that reinforcer is no longer effective, at least temporarily. Depriving someone of a reinforcer is called an establishing operation because it establishes the effectiveness of that reinforcer.

The principle of deprivation states that the longer a person has been deprived of a reinforcer, the more effective that reinforcer will be. The specific length of deprivation will depend on the reinforcer being used. For example, sleep is effective as a reinforcer after a day of deprivation, food and water reinforcers become effective after several hours of deprivation, and air is highly effective as a reinforcer after only a few seconds of deprivation. Through personal experience it is clear to us that deprivation indeed establishes the unconditioned reinforcing effectiveness of food, water, air, and sleep.

However, the principle of deprivation also applies to conditioned social reinforcers such as attention and praise (Eisenberger, 1970, Gewirtz and Baer, 1958a, 1958b). For example, Kozma (1969) conducted an experiment in which third-grade children were initially put in an isolation room for 3, 6, 12, or 18 minutes. A control group of children was not isolated. All the children were then shown two cards, one with a picture of a dog and one with a picture of a cat. The experimenter had each child select the picture he or she preferred. The experimenter then told the child that they would play a game in which the child would guess if the next card drawn from a deck of 50 cards would be a dog or a cat. If the child had initially said that he or she preferred the cat picture, a deck containing 35 dog pictures and 15 cat pictures was used. Alternatively, if the child had initially said he or she preferred the dog picture, the deck contained 35 cat pictures and 15 dog pictures.

As you can surmise, the child's guesses would be correct much more often if she learned to "guess against" her initial preference for dogs or cats. During the game, correct guesses were followed by the experimenter saying "Good," "Right," or "Fine." In effect, the experimenter was testing the power of these social reinforcers to induce the children to guess correctly. Figure 2.1 shows the results of the experiment.

The results indicated that the children who were isolated guessed correctly more often than those who were not, showing that the social reinforcers delivered by the experimenter were more effective for the isolated children. In addition, the results generally suggested that the longer the length of the isolation, the greater the effectiveness of the social reinforcers, though there was little difference between the 12- and 18-minute isolation conditions.

We see the principle of deprivation and satiation of conditioned reinforcers in everyday life. After a few hours traveling alone, many people find that the social reinforcers associated with conversation with strangers are more effective than usual. The longer people have been deprived of favored things and activities, including reading, seeing a film, listening to music, watching a sports event, or the opportunity to wear

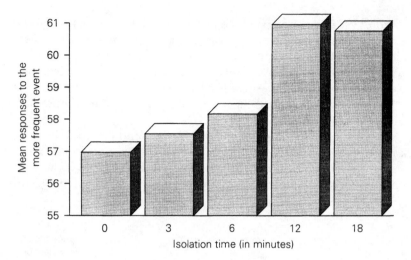

Figure 2.1 *The Relation Between the Duration of Social Reinforcer Deprivation and the Effectiveness of Social Reinforcement*

In Kozma's (1969) experiment, the longer that children were isolated prior to social reinforcement, the more effective the social reinforcers were in increasing the frequency of the reinforced responses. Figure adapted from Kozma (1969).

a preferred item of clothing, the more effective these reinforcers become. Absence, within limits, makes the heart grow fonder.

Depriving a person of a reinforcer has two effects. It will:

• increase the effectiveness of the reinforcer; and

• induce behavior that had previously been successful in producing the reinforcer.

We have considered the first effect and given examples of it. The second effect is also of interest. We know that when we are hungry, for example, we often find ourselves thinking of and searching for food. Wispe and Drambarean (1953) studied the effect of deprivation on inducing food-related responses by depriving subjects of food for either 0, 10, or 24 hours. The subjects looked into a device that flashed words on a screen for less than a quarter of a second. It was found that food-deprived subjects were able to recognize food words (e.g., *dine, waffle, nibble, cake*) presented at briefer durations than nondeprived subjects were. The deprived and nondeprived subjects did not differ in recognition of nonfood words. In this study, food deprivation had the effect of strengthening food-word recognition responses.

Instructions

The effects of reinforcement occur more quickly if the person whose behavior is being reinforced is told that a reinforcer is dependent on a specific behavior. Ayllon and Azrin (1964) demonstrated the influence of instructions on reinforcer effective-ness among female patients in a mental hospital. At meal times, patients would go through a food line with trays. They would receive food but often neglected to pick up eating utensils and would eat with their hands. For 20 meals, Ayllon and Azrin gave patients who picked up utensils a choice of candy, a cigarette, or extra coffee or milk. As the second panel of Figure 2.2 illustrates, this procedure had little if any effect on the target behavior.

For the next 10 meals, an attendant in the food line told the patients, "Please pick up your knife, fork, and spoon and you will have a choice of extra milk, coffee, cigarettes, or candy." As the last panel of the figure shows, the addition of the instructions induced an immediate and large increase in the target behavior.

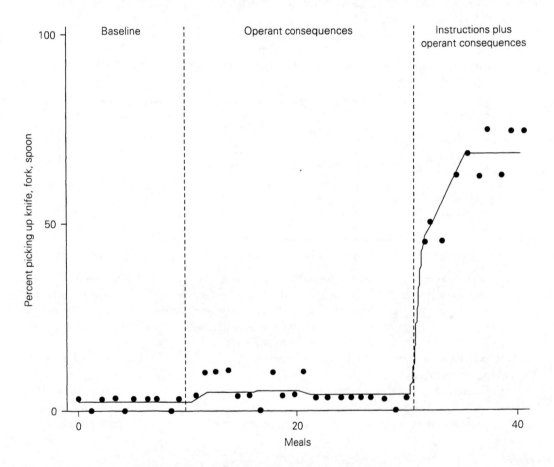

Figure 2.2   *The Effect of Instructions on the Effectiveness of Reinforcement*

Adapted from Ayllon and Azrin (1964). In their study, reinforcers without instructions increased the frequency of the patients' picking up eating utensils only a small amount. After instructions specifying the relationship between the response and the reinforcers were added, the patients' frequency of picking up their utensils increased substantially.

Amount of the Reinforcer

In general, the greater the amount of a reinforcer, the more effective it will be. This relationship has been most consistently shown by research in which people are given the opportunity to engage in two or more different behaviors and the amount of the reinforcer for those behaviors is varied (Cuvo, 1974; Hom, 1967; King & Logue, 1990; Logue, Pena-Correal, Rodriguez, & Kabela, 1986; Wolf, Giles, & Hall, 1968).

For example, Wolf et al. (1968) set up a token economy in a remedial classroom in which points were earned and could be exchanged for such things as candy, food, novelties, clothing, and opportunities to go to sports events and movies. Students could choose from a wide range of materials to use in the classroom. In one experiment, the researchers wanted to see if they could influence the students' choice of activities by varying the number of points awarded for an activity. One boy known as KT was given either 52 points or 90 points for completing each unit of a story reading assignment. Completing a unit meant that the student was able to answer a set of

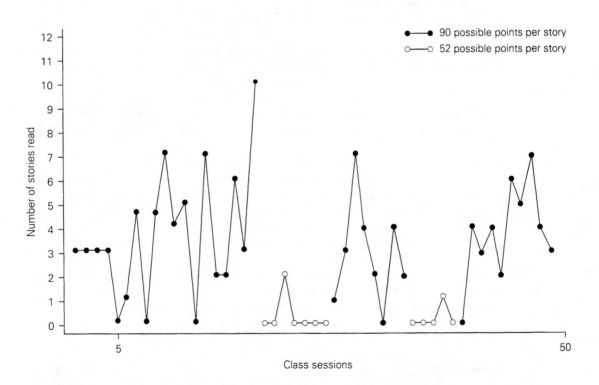

Figure 2.3   *The Effect of Amount of the Reinforcer on Reinforcer Effectiveness*

When a relatively large amount of the point reinforcers was dependent on doing the story assignments, KT did many more assignments than when a lesser amount of points was dependent on doing the assignments. Figure adapted from Wolf, Giles, and Hall (1968).

questions about the content and vocabulary of the stories. As Figure 2.3 shows, KT seldom read stories worth only 52 points, but he read a great many stories when he could earn 90 points. Even though KT could choose to do many other things, when enough points were provided for reading, he chose to do so.

Although greater amounts of reinforcement will influence our choice of activities, behavior analysts often use only the minimum amount of the reinforcer necessary to maintain the individual's participation in the activity. One reason for this is that when they use greater amounts of reinforcement, satiation sets in more quickly and the reinforcer loses its effectiveness. As we have seen, even conditioned reinforcers such as attention are subject to the process of satiation. Because most behaviors worth learning are learned only after a good deal of training, it is important to extend the life of reinforcers by dispensing them in relatively small amounts.

Predictive Conditioned Reinforcers

Conditioned reinforcers gain their value through association with other reinforcers. If a conditioned reinforcer is to be effective, it must sometimes signal or predict that other reinforcers are on the way.

Lauten and Birnbrauer (1974) demonstrated the principle of predictive conditioned reinforcers in an experiment in which retarded children engaged in a button-pushing task. Correct responses by children in one group were followed by the experimenter saying "Right" and then delivering candy. In another group, "Right" and candy were presented independently of one another so that "Right" did not reliably predict candy delivery. On some trials, candy would follow "Right," on some trials, candy would not follow "Right," and on some trials, candy delivery would not be preceded by "Right." On trials that tested the children's learning, the group in which "Right" reliably predicted candy did better than the group in which "Right" and candy delivery were unrelated. This study and others (Cairns, 1967, 1970; Cairns & Paris, 1971; Lovaas et al., 1966; Steinman, 1968; Warren & Cairns, 1972) have clearly shown that the effectiveness of social and other conditioned reinforcers depends on whether they reliably predict the delivery of additional reinforcers.

The principle of predictive conditioned reinforcement often applies in everyday experience. For example, consider a boss who is forthcoming with verbal praise for your work, but gives raises and promotions to others. Or consider a girl or boyfriend who insists on her/his love for you, but who otherwise has little time for you. The principle of predictive conditioned reinforcement specifies that the boss's praise and a friend's declarations of love will ring hollow over time and eventually lose their reinforcing effectiveness, because they do not reliably predict other reinforcers.

Reinforcer Variety

The principle of reinforcer variety states that the more varied and diverse the reinforcers, the more effective they will be. Egel (1981) studied the effects of reinforcer variety with autistic boys. The boys were given different tasks to perform including

(a) identifying the odd picture from a set of three pictures, two of which were the same; (b) identifying a picture that showed a specific type of action when presented with two pictures (e.g., "Which picture shows a boy running?"); and (c) identifying *more* and *less* when shown different amounts of things. Edible treats reinforced correct responses on these tasks. Part of the time, a single type of edible reinforcer was used, such as grapes, potato chips, or small candies, while at other times, Egel used all three types of edible reinforcers.

Egel found that when three different kinds of reinforcers were used, the boys worked hard on the tasks, responding correctly often, until the end of the experimental sessions. However, when only a single type of reinforcer was used, the boys began the session by responding correctly, but seemed to lose interest in the tasks. By the end of these sessions, the boys were seldom responding.

The principle of reinforcer variety can be considered a special case of the principle of satiation/deprivation. When different types of reinforcers are used, the individual may become satiated on some of them but not on others, leaving some effective reinforcers still available to improve or maintain desirable behavior. Note that the principle of reinforcer variety is part of the reason for the effectiveness of token reinforcers, the effectiveness of which are maintained by a wide variety of back-up reinforcers in a properly designed token economy.

Response Energy

The principle of response energy is that the greater the energy or effort a response requires, the less effective reinforcement will be. Schroeder (1972) studied the effects of response energy on the effectiveness of reinforcement in a sheltered workshop, a workplace where the employees are mentally handicapped. In one experiment, an employee was given the job of unscrewing nuts from studs. The nuts had been tightened with a torque wrench so that during some sessions, the nuts on the studs required a force of 1 inch/pounds to unfasten them, while during other sessions the required force was set at 2 inch/pounds or 4 inch/pounds. During one part of the experiment, as the employee worked, a visible counter registered points, with one point earned for every five nuts that were unfastened. At the end of the sessions, the employees could exchange the points for tokens, which could in turn be exchanged for items at the workshop store or turned into cash to spend during weekend outings. As Figure 2.4 indicates, there was an inverse relationship between the amount of energy required to unfasten the bolts and the amount of work accomplished. That is, the more energy that was required, the less work was accomplished.

The principle of response energy is always present in day-to-day life. For example, the invention of machines to perform labor-intensive activities serves to decrease required response energy and increase the strength of the response and the amount of work accomplished. Similarly, good managers are sensitive to the physical arrangement of offices in the workplace. If two departments or two employees are not communicating properly, one possible solution to the problem is to move their offices closer together in order to decrease the energy required to communicate and

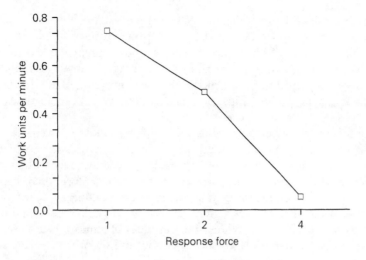

Figure 2.4   *The Influence of Response Energy on the Effectiveness of Reinforcement*

When nuts could be tightened with a lesser amount of force, 1 inch per lb, reinforced nut-tightening occurred frequently. As nuts required greater amounts of force, 2 inch per lb or 4 inch per lb, the amount of responding was progressively reduced. Figure adapted from Schroeder (1972).

thereby to increase the level of communication. Teachers use the reverse procedure when they physically separate the desks of disruptive students in the classroom in order to decrease disruption.

Reinforcer Contrast Effects

The principle of reinforcer contrast specifies that the effectiveness of a reinforcer will depend on the person's prior history of reinforcement. There are two possibilities.

First, if a person has been reinforced with a relatively high quantity or quality of a reinforcer in the past and then the quantity or quality of the reinforcer is reduced, the reduced quality or quantity of the reinforcer will be less effective than if the person had not first experienced the higher quantity or quality of reinforcement. This penomenon is called a *negative contrast effect*.

Second, if a person has been reinforced with a relatively low quantity or quality of a reinforcer and is then switched to a higher quantity or quality reinforcer, the larger amount of the reinforcer will be more effective than if the person had not first had the low quantity or quality reinforcer. This occurrence is called a *positive contrast effect*. Both positive and negative contrast effects are sometimes referred to as *Crespi effects*, after Crespi (1942), who studied them in animals.

Kobre and Lipsitt (1972) studied negative contrast effects in 25 newborn human infants ranging in age from 45 to 105 hours old. An artificial nipple apparatus permitted the infants' behavior to be measured and recorded as number of sucking responses per minute. Three groups of infants were studied, each over a period of 20 minutes. One group of infants received a solution of water and 15% sugar during the entire 20 minutes. A second group received plain water during the 20 minutes. A third group received the sugar water during the first five minutes, plain water during the second five minutes, sugar water during the third five minutes, and plain water during the final five minutes. This experiment was designed to examine contrasting effects by examining the performance of the group who was switched from a higher quality reinforcer, the sugar water, to a lower quality reinforcer, the plain water. Figure 2.5 illustrates the results of the experiment.

As you can see, Group 3 responded at relatively low rates during the second and fourth 5-minute blocks, when they sucked plain water after having previously sucked sugar water. In comparison, the rate of responding of Group 2, who received water throughout the entire 20 minutes, was more-or-less constant during the experiment. The decline in rate of responding of Group 3 compared to Group 2 during the second and fourth 5-minute periods illustrates that the reinforcing effectiveness of the plain water was substantially reduced because it was preceded by the

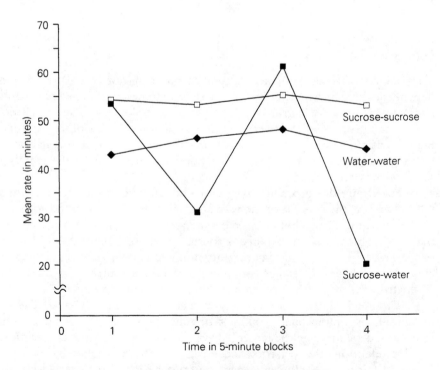

Figure 2.5   *The Influence of Contrast on the Effectiveness of Reinforcers*

When switched from a high-quality sugar water reinforcer to a lower-quality water reinforcer, the water reinforcer was less effective than what it was for infants who had not previously experienced the sugar water reinforcer. Figure adapted from Kobre and Lipsitt (1972).

sugar water. This is a negative contrast effect because reduction in the quality of the reinforcer, from sugar water to plain water, diminished the effectiveness of the plain water reinforcer compared to what it would otherwise have been. In other words, for Kobre and Lipsitt's infants, the sugar water was a tough act to follow.

Kobre and Lipsitt also found a hint of a positive contrast effect. As Figure 2.5 indicates, during the third 5-minute time period, when switched from plain water to sugar water, the infants sucked at a slightly higher rate than the infants who received sugar water during the entire experiment. This suggested a positive contrast effect in which the effectiveness of a higher quality reinforcer is increased because it is switched to from a lower quality reinforcer. However, this effect was too small and unreliable to illustrate a clear positive contrast effect.

Positive and negative contrast effects are apparent in everyday experience. Live entertainers know that it is difficult to reinforce the behavior of an audience when the previous performers have been received enthusiastically. This condition would be a negative contrast effect. You may have benefited from a form of a positive contrast effect that occurs when students' essays are graded. Essay markers will give higher grades to "average" essays if a few relatively poor essays have immediately preceded them.

Extraneous Reinforcers

The amount of time we spend engaged in one behavior is due to the reinforcers dependent on that behavior and also to the extraneous reinforcers dependent on alternative behaviors (Herrnstein, 1970). For example, Ayllon and Michael (1959) convinced nursing staff at a mental institution to reinforce a woman's normal, sensible conversation by paying attention when she engaged in such behavior, and not when she engaged in "psychotic talk" about her illegitimate child and about men she thought were chasing her.

For a time this procedure seemed to be effective in producing more sensible talk. However, the content of the woman's talk then took a turn for the worse. She began engaging in psychotic talk more frequently. Ayllon and Michael discovered that the problem was an extraneous source of reinforcement: A social worker was conversing with the woman, paying attention to and thereby reinforcing the psychotic talk. This circumstance, of course, provided a source of reinforcement that competed with the staff's reinforcement for sensible conversation.

This incident demonstrates that if you are attempting to increase a response by using positive reinforcement, you must be concerned with (a) making sure that reinforcers are dependent on the target behavior and (b) making sure that reinforcers are not dependent on other behaviors incompatible with the target behavior.

In addition to reinforcers dependent on behavior incompatible with the target behavior, another factor that will diminish the effectiveness of reinforcement is **response-independent reinforcement** (McDowell, 1988). Response-independent reinforcement is presenting reinforcement whether or not the target response has occurred. For example, Brigham, Finfrock, Breunig, and Bushell (1972) were teaching handwriting to kindergarten children. During one phase of the experiment, tokens exchangeable for the opportunity to engage in various play activities were dependent on the quality of the children's handwriting. During another phase of the experiment, all the tokens were given to the children at the beginning of their handwriting lesson on a response-independent basis, without regard to the quality of their handwriting. The results of the experiment indicated that the response-independent reinforcement produced poorer performance than response-dependent reinforcement. Whenever the children were switched from response-dependent reinforcement to response-independent reinforcement, their percentage of correct handwriting responses decreased; whenever the children were switched from response-independent to response-dependent reinforcement, their handwriting improved.

Reinforcement Delay

Research with humans has often shown that *immediate reinforcers* are more effective than *delayed reinforcers* (King & Logue, 1990; Logue et al., 1986; Ramey & Ourth, 1971; Terrell & Ware, 1963; Ware & Terrell, 1961). For example, Ramey and Ourth reinforced infant vocalizations by lightly touching the infant's stomach, smiling, and saying, "That's a good baby." They did this either immediately following infant vocalizations or 3 or 6 seconds after an infant vocalization. As Figure 2.6 illustrates, only the immediate reinforcers were effective in strengthening vocalizations (cf., Millar & Watson, 1979).

As you can see, only when the reinforcers were presented immediately after the vocalizations were the reinforcers effective in increasing the frequency of the vocalizations. During baseline (B) and extinction (E1 and E2) periods, vocalizations were measured but not reinforced.

Although immediate reinforcers are sometimes more effective than delayed reinforcers, for three reasons it is misleading to conclude that immediate reinforcement should always be used in behavior change programs. First, much research has shown that delayed reinforcement is not always less effective than immediate reinforcement (e.g., Goldstein and Siegel, 1971, 1972; Renner, 1964). A conclusion drawn from this research is that delayed reinforcement decreases reinforcer effectiveness only when methods are not used to specify the response-reinforcer relationship and bridge the delay between the response and the reinforcer (Brackbill & Kappy, 1962; Fowler & Baer, 1981; Terrell, 1965). These methods can include using instructions to specify the response-reinforcer relationship or providing other stimuli that bridge or mediate the delay between response and reinforcer (e.g., Erikson & Joyce, 1990; Goldstein & Siegel, 1972).

For example, suppose a child is promised a weekend outing if she does her homework every weekday evening. Suppose further that the outing is delayed. If the child is given instructions about the homework-outing dependency, either by her parents or by herself in the form of self-reminders, delayed reinforcement may be effective. This instruction to do homework to get to the zoo is an example of the use of a *verbal mediator* to bridge the delay between response and reinforcement.

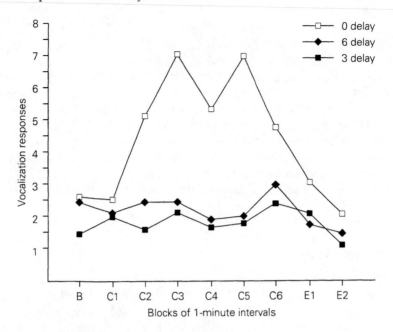

Figure 2.6   *The Relation Between Reinforcement Delay and Reinforcer Effectiveness*

During the treatment phase of Ramey and Ourth's (1971) study (periods C1 through C6), infant vocalizations were reinforced immediately or after a delay of 3 or 6 seconds. Only when reinforcement was immediate was it effective in increasing the frequency of vocalizations. Figure adapted from Ramey and Ourth (1971).

Similarly, the use of tokens in token economies mediates the delay between a response and a reinforcer (Brigham & Sherman, 1973).

Second, immediate reinforcement is often not available in the natural environment. In human affairs, the natural reinforcers that maintain behavior that we admire are often delayed, and for this reason it is desirable for our behavior to be maintained by delayed rewards rather than immediate rewards (Taffel, O'Leary, & Armel, 1974). For example, the natural reinforcer of having an attractive body is a delayed reinforcer for dieting. The natural reinforcer of getting a good job is a delayed reinforcer for engaging in educational activities. The natural reinforcer of having many friends is a delayed reinforcer for the consistent use of social skills. The natural reinforcer of having bright children is a delayed reinforcer for years of working with them on educational activities.

Another line of research has suggested that it is desirable to teach people to learn to avoid immediate reinforcers in favor of larger delayed reinforcers (Mischel, 1984, 1986). Mischel (1984) found that preschool children who had the ability to delay their reinforcers had, when they reached adolescence, more social competence, better thinking and coping skills, and better school achievement than their counterparts who were unable to delay their reinforcers. Similarly, the notion of self-control has been identified with the ability to choose a larger delayed reward rather than a smaller immediate reward, while the concept of impulsiveness has been identified with choosing a smaller immediate reward rather than a larger delayed reward (Rachlin, 1974; King & Logue, 1987).

A third reason that delayed reinforcers may be more desirable than immediate reinforcers is that behavior reinforced by delayed rewards is more durable over time than behavior maintained by immediate rewards (Dunlap, Koegel, Johnson, & O'Neill, 1987; Fowler & Baer, 1981; Schwarz & Hawkins, 1970; Stokes & Baer, 1977). This effect will be considered more extensively in Chapter 9.

In summary, immediate reinforcement is generally more effective than delayed reinforcement because the effectiveness of delayed reinforcement depends on the ability to comprehend instructions, to learn that a delayed response-reinforcer dependency exists, and to bridge delays with mediators. For this reason, it is best to use immediate reinforcement when a response is just being acquired, if the task is difficult, or if the person being reinforced cannot comprehend instructions or bridge delays between responses and reinforcers (cf., Fowler & Baer, 1981). On the other hand, once a response has been acquired, it is often desirable to maintain it by delayed reinforcers, especially when those reinforcers are naturally delayed. These considerations suggest that behavior analysts be concerned with methods and techniques that increase the relative effectiveness of delayed reinforcers (e.g., Skinner, 1948; Walls & Smith, 1970), rather than always relying on immediate reinforcers.

Summary

The notion that rewards influence human behavior is one of the most important, yet unappreciated, ideas in psychology. Within behavior analysis, this idea has been refined into the principle of positive reinforcement. We say that positive reinforcement has taken place when:

• a consequence is dependent on a response;

• the response occurs more often or is otherwise strengthened; and

• the increase in the strength of the response is due to the response-consequence relationship, not because of some other factor.

We have considered several different types of reinforcers: unconditioned and conditioned reinforcers, token and back-up reinforcers, social and nonsocial reinforcers, activity reinforcers, extrinsic and intrinsic reinforcers, and natural and contrived reinforcers. A knowledge of these types of reinforcers and their advantages and disadvantages is important in applying behavior analysis principles.

We also have considered the general position of behavior analysis concerning the degree to which positive reinforcement is used to influence behavior relative to punishment and coercive forms of behavior influence. Essentially, behavior analysts feel that many of the problems of humankind are due to the failure to use positive reinforcement and the overuse of punishment and coercion.

Many factors are important in making positive reinforcement effective, including satiation and deprivation, instructions, amount of the reinforcer, predictive conditioned reinforcers, variety of reinforcers, required response energy, reinforcer contrast effects, extraneous reinforcers, and reinforcement delay. Each of these factors determines whether a particular application of positive reinforcement will be effective. Successful use of positive reinforcement therefore requires not only a knowledge of the basic principles, but a sophisticated knowledge of characteristic effects of the conditions that contribute to the effectiveness of positive reinforcement.

Conceptual Exercise   *Positive Reinforcement*

For each of the following items, decide if the item is an example of positive reinforcement of the highlighted target behavior and justify your decision with a brief explanation. Confirm your decisions by consulting the analyses provided in the back of the book.

1. In early Greece, citizens were expected to attend the daily *ecclesia* or General Assembly where various issues were discussed and voted on. Attendance at these sessions was a problem. In order to increase **attendance,** each citizen was given a clay tablet at the beginning of the session. These tablets could be exchanged at the end of the session for money. This method was very successful in improving attendance.

2. In a junior high home economics classroom, the students were working on sewing projects, but often the level of disruptive noise in the classroom rose so high that it impaired the students' work on their projects. In order to solve this problem, an apparatus was constructed that measured the overall noise level in the room. If the noise stayed below a level that the teacher had determined was disruptive to the students' work, radio music would come on. As a result of this procedure, the noise level in the classroom stayed **below a disruptive level** more often than it had before.

3. Three 4-year-old girls were participating in research designed to study creative behavior. The children were given building blocks and invited to play with them. The teacher began using a procedure in which she expressed delight and enthusiasm when the child **constructed a shape or form she had not constructed before** (i.e., a novel form). As a result of this procedure, the children constructed novel forms more often than they had before.

4. It is very important for cystic fibrosis patients to keep their lungs clear. Chest physiotherapy (CPT) is used to help clear mucous out of the lungs. Carol Ann had been diagnosed as having cystic fibrosis when she was just an infant. Her mother took her to the Mississippi Medical Center when Carol Ann was 12, because she would refuse to **do her CPT**. Behavior analysts at the medical center taught Carol Ann's mother to use treats, privileges, and activities dependent on Carol Ann doing her CPT. Carol

Ann and her mother signed a contract specifying what Carol Ann was expected to do and what the consequences would be. Carol Ann soon began doing her CPT regularly, both Carol Ann and her mother reported that they rarely argued anymore, and Carol Ann was proud of herself and her control over her treatment. Carol Ann was seen several weeks later and continued to do her CPT on schedule.

5. Debbie wasn't doing well in her sixth grade math class. Her teacher told her parents that Debbie handed in fewer that 50% of her homework assignments. Consequently, her parents told Debbie that for any day on which she did not hand in her homework, she would be sent to bed right after dinner. As a result of this procedure, Debbie **handed in her assignments** 95% of the time.

6. One day Dave was **teasing Marsha about her weight**. This angered Marsha so she slapped Dave in the face. As a result, Dave began teasing Marsha about her weight more often than he had before.

7. Dr. Arnold was working with Greg, a physically disabled four-year-old boy who had few movements and no speech because he had been in an automobile accident. At first Greg would **smile** only about twice a day, but as a result of Dr. Arnold talking to him, Greg's smiling increased to about once a minute.

8. Mark had just bought a new car. One feature it had was a computer with a voice that told Mark to **buckle his seat belt** when Mark started the car. As a result of the computer voice, Mark buckles his seat belt much more often than he did before.

9. At a Mexican factory, the workers were often late for work. A new procedure was put into effect in which, for each time a worker arrived on time for work, he would receive a bonus of 10 pesos. Before the procedure was used, 85% of the workers **arrived on time** for work. As a result of the bonus procedure, 97% of the workers arrived on time for work.

10. The residents in a complex of 166 apartments in Baltimore participated in an electrical conservation study. During any month when the amount of electricity the residents used was less than the amount of electricity the electric company predicted on the basis of the outside temperatures, the cost savings of the difference in these values was rebated to the residents in the form of a check. This procedure resulted in a decrease in electricity use of 6.2%. The target behaviors here are those **behaviors that conserve electricity**.

11. Florida households were selected to participate in a trash recycling program wherein residents were encouraged to separate newspaper and aluminum products for collection. It was found that a brochure that informed residents about the program increased the number of people who **separated their trash** for recycling.

12. Several kindergarten children participated in a project to teach them drawing skills. The children were given a lesson that taught them to draw a few types of simple shapes and these responses were defined as **correct responses** if the children performed them appropriately. After every fourth or fifth correct response, the teacher gave the child a token that could later be exchanged for trinkets and edible treats. It

was found that giving the children tokens for correct responses resulted in more correct responses than when tokens were given to the children whether or not they responded correctly.

13. In a program designed to teach junior high school students social skills, a researcher was interested in encouraging the students to **ask follow-up questions** during discussions. Whenever Zeke, one of the students, asked a follow-up question, the researcher would praise him and comment upon what an interesting question Zeke had asked. Although Zeke, who seldom received praise, was overjoyed with this attention and felt a sense of accomplishment, his rate of asking questions did not change.

14. Norm was an 8-year-old boy who had been removed from a regular school classroom and put in a special education class because he would follow the teacher's instructions only after long delays. A procedure was set up to encourage him to **follow instructions rapidly**. This procedure consisted of giving Norm tokens when he complied with the teacher's instructions within a given time limit. Norm could use the tokens to buy toys or play periods. This procedure caused Norm to follow the teacher's instructions rapidly much more often than he had before.

15. Three 3-year-old children attended nursery school. It was noticed that the children's favorite activities were running around the room and screaming, while sitting quietly and looking at the blackboard seldom occurred. A procedure was used in which, when the children were observed to be sitting quietly and paying attention to the blackboard, they were told, "Run and scream." They immediately did so. As a result of this technique, the children **sat quietly and paid attention** to the blackboard much more often than they had before.

16. In a large department store, 33 retail sales employees participated in an experiment. The salespeople's behavior was classified into functional responses (conversing with customers, showing merchandise, ringing up sales) and dysfunctional responses (socializing with co-workers, idle standing or sitting, and being absent from assigned tasks without reason). The salespeople were observed and for each week they engaged in the **functional responses** 90% of the time or more, they would receive four hours off with pay. In addition, for each day a salesperson met the 90% standard, her name would be entered into a pool. The winner of the pool would receive two airplane tickets to Hawaii or the cash equivalent. As a result, the salespeople engaged in functional responses more often than they had before, and more often than other employees who were not participating in the experiment.

17. Twenty-seven children in a first grade and second grade classroom were participating in a project to improve their dental hygiene. Tooth brushing was measured by the amount of plaque on their teeth. Students whose plaque level was below a selected criterion had their photographs displayed on a bulletin board at the front of their classroom. As a result of this procedure, the students' level of **tooth brushing,** as measured by plaque reduction, increased.

18. In a residential treatment program for emotionally and behaviorally disturbed youths, a case manager log book was used to record information about when case

managers **visited their clients**. In order to better coordinate services and planning for the youths, case managers were required to sign the book and list the date and the name of the client they were visiting. Each week on the average, case managers visited 40% to 45% of the youths in the program. It was decided to send response-dependent thank-you letters to case managers each time they visited a client. These letters thanked the case manager for his or her visit, stressed the importance of the visits, and indicated that the supervisor was sent a copy. As a result of these thank-you letters, the average percentage of youths visited each week increased to 74% to 81%.

19. Martha was a 5-year-old girl who attended preschool. She seldom **played with the other children**. Workers at the preschool began praising and admiring Martha frequently throughout the day and, as a result, Martha's rate of cooperative play with the other children increased.

20. Dee was a 3-year-old girl enrolled in nursery school. She crawled, crouched, or sat 93% of the time at school and was **on her feet** only 7% of the time. The teachers used a procedure in which whenever Dee was off-feet, she was made to stand in a corner of the room for 5 minutes with her back to the room. This procedure resulted in Dee's engaging in on-feet behavior almost all the time, like the other children at the school.

21. In an elementary school classroom, research was conducted to study the effects of teacher behavior on student behavior. During one phase of the study, the teacher began disapproving of the students' **disruptive behaviors** when they occurred, resulting in increased disruptive behaviors.

22. Students in Professor Ohno's class were given a weekly quiz. Over the years, Professor Ohno had given a lecture in which he gave the students two rules for success in his class: study hard and pay careful attention to your work. Ohno would sometimes give the lecture before the students had done any work and would sometimes give it after they had taken several quizzes. No matter when he gave the lecture, it would always improve the student's **percentage correct quiz responding**.

23. When Lewis' classmates misbehaved by **speaking out without being called on,** the teacher made them stay after school and perform special chores including washing the blackboards. This procedure caused Lewis's classmates to speak out more often than they would have had they not been made to stay after school and wash the blackboards.

24. Six children ranging in age from 7 to 10 years old participated in an experiment to reduce nighttime fear behavior. Each of the children was reported by his or her parent as having severe fear of the dark as evidenced by unwillingness to go to bed, unwillingness to sleep alone, inability to sleep through the night and so forth. The parents monitored the behavior of their children throughout the procedure. Part of the treatment involved training the children and parents in relaxation techniques and cognitive self-instruction strategies with tokens presented to the children for appropriate nighttime behaviors, such as going to bed within a reasonable time, going to bed without complaining, or sleeping through the night. The tokens could be traded

in for the opportunity to attend a party. Parents were instructed to practice the exercises nightly. This procedure was successful in increasing **appropriate nighttime behaviors** in five of the six children.

Conceptual Exercise   *Describing Reinforcers*

Describe the reinforcer involved in each of the following situations using the following terms:

- an unconditioned or a conditioned reinforcer;
- a token reinforcer;
- a social reinforcer;
- an activity reinforcer;
- an extrinsic reinforcer or an intrinsic reinforcer; reinforcer; and
- a natural reinforcer or a contrived reinforcer.

Indicate all the above terms that apply to each reinforcer.

1. A child 's good behavior on outings is reinforced by a candy bar.

2. Attending the ballet is reinforced by an excellent performance.

3. Completing homework is reinforced by the opportunity to play ice hockey.

4. Paying a dollar to someone in the "kissing booth" at the fair is reinforced by the opportunity to hug and kiss that person.

5. Being kind and considerate to someone is reinforced by the opportunity to hug and kiss.

6. Writing a musical score is reinforced by the opportunity to hear the work played.

7. Dishwashing is reinforced by points that can be traded in for a night out at the movies.

8. Driving a car is reinforced by reaching a destination.

9. Smiling at an attractive classmate is reinforced by being invited to go for coffee.

10. Engaging in educational activities is reinforced by being awarded a university degree.

11. Inventive activities are reinforced by the creation of a new type of easy-to-use measuring cup.

12. A physically disabled child's putting weight on his legs is reinforced by spoonfuls of frozen yogurt.

13. Politely asking a librarian for help is reinforced by obtaining a desired library book.

14. A child's cleaning of his room is reinforced by a weekly allowance.

15. A child's cleaning of his room is reinforced by a clean room.

16. A student's reading of a novel is reinforced by a good grade on a quiz about the novel.

17. A student's reading of a novel is reinforced by the exciting content of the novel.

Conceptual Exercise *Making Positive Reinforcement Effective*

In this chapter we examined the following factors that influence the effectiveness of positive reinforcement:

- deprivation/satiation;
- instructions;
- amount of the reinforcer;
- predictive conditioned reinforcers;
- reinforcer variety;
- response energy;
- reinforcer contrast effects (positive contrast and negative contrast);
- extraneous reinforcers; and
- reinforcement delay.

Each of the following items could be altered in some way to make positive reinforcement more effective. Specify what should be altered and explain why.

1. Mr. Kersey taught a first-grade class. He had read about the use of positive reinforcement and decided to use this principle in his classroom. Whenever one of his students correctly answered one of the questions he posed correctly, Mr. Kersey marked it on a piece of paper. At the end of the day, students who had three or more marks beside their names would make the honor roll for that day, and their names would be posted on the bulletin board during the next school day. Mr. Kersey did not tell the students what method he used to determine which students made the daily honor roll, because he didn't want them to answer questions correctly simply for the sake of making the honor roll. The students did not know if they had made the honor roll until the next morning when they saw the posted names. To Mr. Kersey's dismay, the system didn't seem to work very well. How and why should this situation be altered?

2. Mr. Durer worked as a graphic artist at an automobile company. He worked on the same floor as the offices of the company's sales staff, so he often consulted with them about his work. One day Mr. Durer was relocated two floors below the offices of the company sales staff. As a result, he consulted with the sales staff much less

than he had before, even though the sales staff were the ones who decided if his work would be used and who often provided Mr. Durer with reinforcing praise for his work. How and why should this situation be altered?

3. Adele and Fred were a suave and sophisticated dance duo who opened a vaudeville show consisting of various kinds of entertainment. Adele and Fred were so good that they received standing ovations night after night. Because Adele and Fred were so much better than the other acts, the audience's reaction to the following acts was much less enthusiastic than if Adele and Fred had not preceded them. Many of the other acts were pretty good. How and why should this situation be altered?

4. June's parents, Bob and Eileen, were concerned, because June was so shy that she would not speak to anyone to whom she was introduced. They decided to use a positive reinforcement technique to induce June to speak to people she met. Bob and Eileen instructed her that she would receive attention from her parents only if she talked on the appropriate occasions, at which time they would immediately give her sufficient attention to reinforce her speech. Before June was to meet someone, Bob and Eileen would go out of their way to pay attention to June to ensure that she was in a good mood. They coupled their attention with other reinforcers June would receive, and provided her with a variety of different types of attention reinforcers. Bob and Eileen's initial response requirement was merely for June to say, "Hi." How and why should this be altered?

5. Bob was a teacher in a nursery school. Every day he read the students a story and, as he progressed through the story, he would pose questions to the students to ensure they were listening to and comprehending the story. Students who answered a sufficient number of questions correctly would be allowed to play in a special play area that was supplied with two jigsaw puzzles. The students were instructed about the relationship between answering the questions and playing with the puzzles. The questions were not unduly difficult and did not require long answers. No important extraneous reinforcers interfered with the program. How and why should this be altered?

6. Jim's well-heeled parents offered him and his friend Tamara $5 to wash the family car throughout the summer. Jim and Tamara were also being paid by Tamara's parents to keep their car clean, but Tamara's parents were paying them $10 for each cleaning. To Jim's parents' surprise, Jim and Tamara spent much more time over at her house washing the family car than they did at Jim's house. As a result, Jim's parents' car was dirty for much of the summer. How and why should this be altered?

7. Lionel's parents had become concerned about his use of grammatically incorrect language. They used a positive reinforcement procedure in which they would attend to Lionel when he spoke correctly. Lionel's parents did not satiate him with their attention, they reinforced grammatically correct language immediately, they provided sufficient and varied forms of attention to strengthen grammatical language, they made sure their attention predicted other reinforcers, they instructed Lionel that their attention was dependent on his using appropriate language, and they required only modest amounts of correct speech from Lionel for reinforcement. Away from home,

Lionel's peers paid extra attention to him when he used grammatically incorrect language. How and why should this be altered?

8. Mr. Neville worked in a prison. He set up a system in which the prison inmates could earn points for a variety of desirable behaviors including treating other prisoners and prison staff courteously, doing their assigned daily work assignments, and keeping their cells clean. Inmates would receive points immediately upon completion of the desirable behavior. More difficult or less pleasant jobs would earn more points than easy tasks, and the inmates received menus specifying the relationship between behaviors and points. The points that each inmate earned were posted daily on a large bulletin board. Problems with extraneous reinforcers were minimized. How and why should this plan be altered?

9. Mr. Bothwell taught English in high school. Every semester he assigned three books for students to read: A boring book of literary criticism, a moderately interesting play, and a fascinating novel. He scheduled the fascinating novel to be read first in the semester, then the boring criticism, then the play. He found that because of the order in which he scheduled the readings, the students all read the novel very thoroughly, but many students merely skimmed the play and the book of criticism or gave up reading them altogether. How and why should this sequence be altered?

Conceptual Exercise   *Usage of Terms*

For each of the following items, decide if the italicized term in the sentence is used correctly or not. Explain your reasons. Use the following hints:

- positive reinforcement is presenting a response-dependent stimulus or event that strengthens the response.

- a positive reinforcer (or a positive reinforcement) is a stimulus, the response-dependent presentation of which strengthens the response.

- to positively reinforce is to present a response-dependent stimulus or event that causes the response to be strengthened.

- to say something is reinforcing is to say that it is able to strengthen responses when it is dependent on those responses.

- a positive reinforcement procedure is the response-dependent presentation of a suspected reinforcer.

1. *Positive reinforcement* was used to improve Barb's attendance at work.

2. The *positive reinforcements* for Barb's attendance at work were comments of praise from her co-workers and boss.

3. In a project designed to teach Randall how to speak, bites of cereal were used as *positive reinforcers* for any kind of vocalizations he made.

4. Cereal was used to *positively reinforce* Randall's vocalizations.

5. Alex was *reinforced* with pieces of Belgian chocolates.

6. The *positive reinforcement* procedure was used to encourage Ivan's quiet play behavior.

7. The research showed that the cartoons were *positively reinforcing* stimuli for the children's correct identifications of colors being taught to them.

8. I find you highly *reinforcing,* darling.

chapter 3

Decreasing Responding:
Extinction, DRO, and DRI

Clarence, 33, had been classified as both retarded and psychotic. He lived at the Winnebago State Hospital, where many staff members had concluded there was no hope to change his bizarre behaviors.

When given a chance, Clarence would pound his head hard into the nearest available object, be it a chair, a table corner, or the floor. He would run up and down the length of a room, whacking his head against walls. When he wasn't hurting himself, he would attack other patients and staff, especially women, seemingly at random. Because of his dangerous outbursts, he had been kept carefully bound in a restraint chair for seven years.

If his arms and hands were not kept securely bound in the restraint chair, Clarence would rip out his own fingernails, leaving bloody stubs of flesh. He would also break his fingers, push pins or paper clips deeply into his flesh, and burn his arms and hands with cigarettes. In addition, he would twist pieces of cigarette-package cellophane into sharp points and stab himself. In order to prevent these horrific behaviors, Clarence had to wear mittens on his immobilized hands. Besides being tied up in a restraint chair all day, Clarence was also strapped into his bed at night.

Dr. Robert Lane and Dr. Richard Domrath were two psychologists who were familiar with behavior analysis techniques. Upon learning of Clarence's case, they immediately realized that many people would be much better off if Clarence could somehow be trained not to hurt himself and others. As it was, the staff spent much time binding Clarence in and out of restraints and the other patients were noticeably upset because Clarence was always strapped down. On humanitarian grounds, it would be much better if Clarence could be released from his bonds to live a life of more freedom.

Accordingly, Dr. Lane and Dr. Domrath considered the use of positive reinforcement. They noted that Clarence craved coffee, so much so that he would eat food he had left untouched on his plate if promised an extra cup of coffee after his meal. The two clinicians decided to try a differential reinforcement of zero responding method (DRO), in which positive reinforcement is dependent on not engaging in a behavior for a specified length of time. For Clarence, DRO would consist of being given coffee when he did not harm himself.

Before Clarence's DRO procedure was put into effect, word about the treatment circulated among hospital staff. One group of aides felt so confident the treatment was doomed to fail that they saw it as an opportunity to make some easy money at the expense of the two naive psychologists. This group of aides pooled their money and offered the therapists a $50 bet that Clarence's treatment wouldn't work. However, Dr. Lane and Dr. Domrath were wise enough reinforcement theorists not to accept the bet. They knew that the full cooperation of the aides was important if the treatment were to succeed. By accepting the $50 bet, the therapists would be reinforcing the aides to the tune of $50 for whatever they did, even unconsciously, to cause the treatment to fail.

At first, Clarence was unbound and his mittens were removed for only 15 brief seconds. If he didn't pull his fingernails—his favorite form of self-injury—he could drink a small cup of coffee, eight tablespoons' worth. The doctors conducted daily sessions using this method three times a day, each session continuing until Clarence had consumed a small thermos of coffee.

At the outset, Clarence often couldn't wait 15 seconds and began to injure himself. His mittens were immediately replaced and he got no more coffee for that session. However, Clarence made it through an increasing number of the 15-second intervals and got his coffee. He was so successful that it was possible for the aides administering the procedure to go out of sight during the 15-second intervals. During these occasions, Clarence could be seen eyeing both his hands and the coffee.

After three weeks, Clarence had learned to sit completely alone during the time intervals. At this point, the length of the intervals was varied so that sometimes Clarence could have coffee after less than or more than 15 seconds. Over weeks, the interval lengths were gradually and carefully increased to 15 minutes, then to an hour. With continued application of the procedures, Clarence was able to sit unrestrained in the day room for several hours. Further into treatment, Clarence was able to shed his day and night restraints completely. He spent his typical day watching television with the other patients, or leafing through a magazine.*

A Constructional Approach to Behavior Change

Behavior analysis is most successful when it takes a constructional approach to behavior change by defining what behaviors are desirable and to be encouraged, rather than a pathological approach that focuses on eliminating unwanted behaviors (Goldiamond, 1974). When people learn to engage in new desirable behaviors, they are acquiring new ways of successfully interacting with their physical and social environments, and they thereby become established as successful individuals. For example, our idea of social competence is based mainly on the socially effective behaviors we have. If competent behavior in any area of human performance is defined by what was not done, inanimate objects would qualify as models of excellence. Despite the apparent attractiveness of a constructional approach to solving problems, much of psychology, medicine, and other social institutions make use of the pathological approach. The focus is too often on problems rather than on successes.

The usefulness of the constructional approach is illustrated in the work of Liberman and his coworkers (e.g., Eckman et al., 1992; Liberman, 1992; Liberman, Corrigan, & Schade, 1989; Wallace et al., 1992; Wirshing, Eckman, Liberman, & Marder, 1989), who have worked with chronic mental patients diagnosed as schizophrenic. People diagnosed with this label often have many bizarre behaviors and some theorists, therefore, define the problem as reducing the strange behaviors. Liberman has instead adopted a skill-building approach to solve the problem. The focus of treatment has been on teaching the patients social skills, coping skills, skills relevant to community adaptation, job-seeking skills, family-living skills, and symptom-management skills. The approach has been highly successful. For example, in one study in which job-seeking and holding was taught, 65 percent of the patients were able to seek and retain a job. Because the focus of treatment is on skill building, the former patients are able to use the skills to function in the real world. In contrast, if the focus of treatment had been on reducing undesirable behaviors, most of the patients would probably have fewer undesirable behaviors, but would be living out their lives in institutions.

The importance of a constructional approach to behavior problems was also illustrated in the Williams (1979) study touched upon in Chapter 1. Williams found that with happily married couples, spouses defined what was "pleasant" about their partner by the desirable behaviors the partner engaged in. In contrast, with the unhappy couples, spouses defined what was "pleasant" about their partner in terms of the undesirable behaviors their partner did not perform. Essentially, the happy couples took a constructional approach by defining real behaviors that composed the basis for the relationship. In contrast, the unhappy couples did not identify desirable

*Based on Lane and Domrath (1970)

behaviors their partner performed that could form the basis for improving the relationship. Extending this finding, it is reasonable to suppose that happy behavior analysts are the ones on the lookout for good behaviors to teach and maintain, while unhappy behavior analysts are the ones out on search and destroy missions to eliminate bad behaviors. A maxim among behavior analysts who work with children is, "Catch 'em being good": Reinforce the children's behavior when you find them behaving well (Madsen, Becker, & Thomas, 1968). The phrase catches our attention because it is such a contrast to normal punitive disciplinary procedures in which children are caught only when they behave badly.

The road to happiness, however, is not the easiest to travel. As seen in Chapter 1, defining what is desirable requires imagination, research, and philosophical contemplation. It is inappropriate merely to eliminate behaviors unmindfully that are irritable, inconvenient, or threatening to those in authority.

These considerations aside, behavior analysts do come across behavior problems that require that an undesirable behavior be eliminated before serious attempts can be made to build successful behaviors. Such behaviors include self-destructive activities, aggressive behaviors that harm other people, and behaviors that prevent the individual from learning adaptive behaviors. In this chapter, we will focus on three useful methods designed to reduce or eliminate undesirable behavior.

Extinction

Extinction is withholding a reinforcer for a previously reinforced response that causes a decline in the level of that response. For example, suppose a student in a classroom waves her arms in wild, exaggerated motions because doing so has caused the teacher to call on her. The teacher would be using extinction if he or she withheld reinforcement for wild arm waving by not calling on that student, thus causing a reduction in the level of arm waving.

Recall that reinforcement will always involve a response-dependent stimulus change. In the above example, wild arm waving produced a change from no opportunity to speak out to being called on to speak. When the teacher began using extinction, the wild arm waving produced no stimulus change at all. One important cue that extinction is being used is that the response declines because it no longer produces a stimulus change. In other words, when the response occurs, nothing happens.

A response is said to be *on extinction* if it no longer produces a reinforcing stimulus change. We can use these terms even if the response has not been eliminated or reduced. However, to say that a response is extinguished is to say that it no longer occurs as a result of nonreinforcement. We extinguish behavior, not people.

While reinforcement strengthens responding, extinction weakens it. However, not all response-weakening effects are due to extinction. In particular, extinction is different from forgetting and punishment. The response-weakening effect of extinction is due to nonreinforcement, while the response-weakening effect of forgetting is due to the passage of time during which the response does not occur. Punishment differs from extinction because with extinction no stimulus change is dependent on the response, while with punishment, a stimulus change is dependent on the response. To tell the difference between examples of punishment and extinction, ask yourself what happens following the response that is being weakened. If nothing happens following the response, it is apt to be an example of extinction, while if some change in the environment follows the response, it is apt to be an example of punishment.

Two Initial Effects of Extinction

While the effect that defines extinction is a decrease in the level of the response, extinction sometimes also produces some other effects. One of these is an extinction burst, an initial temporary increase in the level and intensity of the response (Skinner, 1938). For example, Williams (1959) used extinction with a young child who screamed and howled if his parents neglected to sit with him as he fell asleep each night. When the parents attempted to leave the room, the child would scream, and one of the child's parents would return to the child, thereby reinforcing the child's screams. Using extinction, the parent no longer returned when the child screamed. Extinction was eventually effective in eliminating the screaming, but on the first night, the child screamed for 45 minutes, quite an ordeal for both the parents and the child.

Because extinction sometimes results in a temporary increase in the level of a problem behavior, you should be prepared for the possibility that the behavior problem will get worse before it gets better. Although it often requires considerable patience to endure, the extinction burst will subside in time if the procedure is properly used.

Another effect of extinction is an increase in frequency of emotional behaviors in the form of aggression or annoyance. This effect, called extinction-induced aggression, has been documented in both animals (Azrin, Hutchinson, & Hake, 1966) and humans (Kelly & Hake, 1970; Nation & Cooney, 1982). Kelly and Hake conducted an experiment using teenage boys as subjects. When the boys pulled a knob 200 times, they would receive a nickel. At the same time, an unpleasant tone would sound once per minute. The tone could be prevented or turned off in one of two ways: by pushing a button with 1.5 pounds of force or by punching a cushion with 20 pounds of force, the latter considered to be an aggressive response. Kelly and Hake found that when knob-pulls were put on extinction, the frequency of aggressive cushion-punches increased. Figure 3.1 shows data from the experiment.

The increase in punches occurred despite the fact that they required far more effort than the button-pushes, which turned off the tones just as effectively. Normally, when two responses that produce the same consequence differ in the amount of energy they require, the response requiring less energy will occur more often. This suggests that the increase in punches during extinction was an example of extinction-induced aggression.

Experience in everyday life parallels the situation in these studies showing the relationship between extinction, and aggression or annoyance. Most people become at least mildly annoyed when someone else completely ignores what they say, when

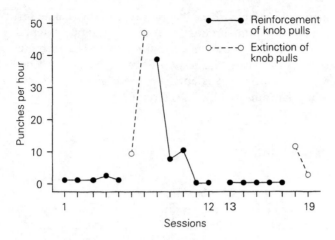

Figure 3.1   *The Influence of Extinction on Aggression*

When a teenage boy's knob pulls were reinforced with nickels, virtually no aggressive punching occurred. However, when knob pulling was put on extinction, aggressive punching increased dramatically. Adapted from Kelly and Hake (1970).

vending machines fail to operate, when "easy-to-assemble" merchandise fails to work after proper assembly, when phone calls fail to go through or be returned, when a car fails to start, when letters go unanswered, and so forth.

Despite the fact that extinction can induce aggression and annoyance, it is inappropriate to conclude that extinction is an undesirable behavior-change procedure. Indeed, whenever positive reinforcement is used, we selectively reinforce certain responses and fail to reinforce (i.e., extinguish) other responses, so extinction is usually a silent partner of positive reinforcement. Anything worth doing carries with it both the possibility of success and positive reinforcement on the one hand, and failure and extinction on the other. Moreover, the reinforcers involved in our successes are made all the more effective by previous failures to succeed, according to the principle of positive contrast discussed in Chapter 2.

The best means of eliminating or at least coping with extinction-induced aggression and milder forms of extinction-induced annoyance is to provide positive reinforcers for desirable alternative behaviors, a procedure that should always be used in conjunction with extinction. In addition, many of the negative emotional reactions people have to extinction occur when extinction is inconsistently or capriciously used. As a behavior change procedure, extinction should be used together with instructions that specify what behaviors will meet the criteria for reinforcement and extinction.

Types of Extinction

Some notable varieties of extinction include social extinction, nonsocial extinction, and sensory extinction.

Social extinction occurs when a social reinforcer is no longer dependent on a previously reinforced response and that response is weakened. Social extinction usually takes the form of simply ignoring a response. For instance, in the example of extinction of hand waving mentioned earlier, the teacher weakened hand waving by ignoring it. Because social reinforcement is so important in human behavior, examples of social extinction are numerous; when asked to give an example of extinction, students usually give an example of ignoring misbehavior.

One problem with the popularity of social extinction as a behavior-change procedure is that beginning students often fail to recognize examples of nonsocial extinction as extinction. Nonsocial extinction occurs when the physical or nonsocial environment is changed so that a reinforcer is no longer dependent on a response. For example, suppose you move the location of a light switch in your bathroom. At night you are apt to reach for the old location for a period of time before this response undergoes extinction. Likewise, if you normally wear a wristwatch and then go without it, you will find yourself looking to your wrist for the time until this response is extinguished.

Another type of extinction is called sensory extinction (Rincover, 1978a; Rincover, Cook, Peoples, & Packard, 1979). Sensory extinction is a form of nonsocial extinction in which the sensory stimulus changes that reinforce a response are removed and the response becomes less apt to occur. Researchers developed sensory extinction procedures through work with autistic children who engage in repetitive self-stimulatory behaviors that interfere with their ability to learn new activities or play normally. One theory of self-stimulatory behavior is that this behavior is excessively reinforced by the sensory consequences that result when engaging in the response. If procedures are used to stop self-stimulation, normal appropriate play behaviors will naturally replace it (Koegel, Firestone, Kramme, & Dunlap, 1974; Epstein, Doke, Sajwaj, Sorrell, & Rimmer, 1974).

Rincover et al. (1979) applied sensory extinction procedures to solve the problems of several autistic children. One child named Reggie engaged in twirling plates and similar objects on a hard surface. The investigators noticed that when spinning plates, Reggie would lean over and listen intently to the sound, suggesting that the sound of the plate was the reinforcer for plate spinning. Sensory extinction was used by carpeting the table Reggie used, eliminating the auditory stimulus change dependent on plate spinning. Reggie ceased spinning plates and this behavior was replaced with play with musical toys.

Another child, Karen, would toss pieces of feather, lint, and string into the air, making arm movements in an apparent attempt to keep these items airborne. In this case, sensory extinction consisted of turning off the electric lights when Karen engaged in self-stimulation, therein eliminating the visual sensory consequences. Karen could no longer see the items floating through the air with the lights out, although the room remained sufficiently well-lit by daylight for most other activities, and her self-stimulatory behavior ceased. It was eventually replaced by blowing bubbles.

Sensory extinction has also been used to modify self-destructive behavior. Unfortunately, many mentally handicapped people engage in self-destructive behavior such as head banging. One theory of the cause of this behavior is that the sensory stimulation the head-banging response produces acts as a reinforcer. Dorsey, Iwata, Reid, and Davis (1982) found some support for this theory by outfitting Ron, a 16-year-old mentally retarded boy, with a football helmet and foam-padded gloves that would withhold the stimulation of head banging and hand biting. Through skillful implementation of this sensory extinction procedure and other procedures, Dorsey et al. (1982) were able to remove Ron's helmet and gloves without resumption of the self-destructive behaviors.

Sensory extinction also appears to occur in normal day-to-day situations. For example, you will cease writing when your pen runs out of ink because the sensory consequences that have formerly been dependent on writing movements are now no longer forthcoming. Gibson and Yonas (cited in Winner, 1982) found that children who had formerly engaged in scribbling with a marking pen ceased scribbling movements when given one that left no traces on paper. Impairment of vision and hearing that occurs in old age also functions to withhold sensory consequences and extinguishes behavior that those consequences previously maintained. Skinner and Vaughan (1983) offer excellent practical advice about how to cope with the sensory extinction that occurs in old age.

Making Extinction Effective

Several conditions are important in making extinction procedures effective. These include the extent of previous reinforcement of the response, the reinforcement of alternative behaviors, the availability of extraneous reinforcers for the target behavior, instructions, the context and consistency of extinction, and the effectiveness of the withdrawn reinforcer.

Extent of Previous Reinforcement.   In general, the more often a response has been reinforced, the more resistant to extinction it will be. It may be hard to teach an old dog new tricks, but it is also hard to extinguish an old dog's old tricks, ones which have been repeatedly reinforced. Siegel and Foshee (1953) demonstrated the basic relationship between the number of previous reinforcers and resistance to extinction using children ranging in age from about 3 to 6 years. Pieces of candy were dispensed down a chute when the children pressed a lever. Four groups of 20 children participated in this experiment; one group received 2 reinforcers, one received 4 reinforcers, one received 8 reinforcers, and one received 16 reinforcers. After the children had received the planned number of reinforcers, lever-pressing was put on extinction and the number of responses the children made was measured for a 3-minute period. Figure 3.2 shows the results of this experiment.

As indicated, there was a direct relationship between the number of reinforcers and resistance to extinction: The more reinforcers the children had previously received, the more responses the children made during extinction.

Siegel and Foshee (1953) demonstrated the effect of the number of reinforcers on resistance to extinction in an experiment that lasted only short periods of time (Thompson, Heistad, & Palermo, 1963). Siegel and Foshee's study took about 15

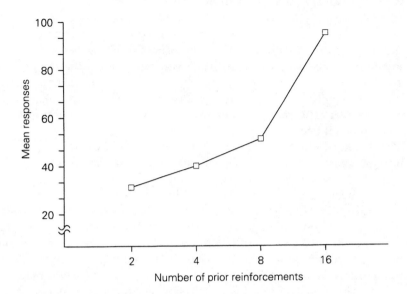

Figure 3.2   *The Influence of the Extent of Previous Reinforcement on Resistance to Extinction*

The greater the number of times children's lever-presses had been reinforced with candy, the more resistant to extinction lever-pressing became. Adapted from Siegel and Foshee (1953).

minutes per child. The rapidity with which this effect can be demonstrated attests to the powerful influence the number of previous reinforcers has on resistance to extinction, and gives us some insight into the reason for persistence of problem behaviors. We are sometimes puzzled about why people fail to quit smoking or cease consuming high-fat foods even after these people have had serious medical disorders that their own behavior causes. These phenomena are made less mysterious when we take into account the powerful effect of years of repeated reinforcement of behavior.

Reinforcement of Alternative Behaviors.   Whenever possible, extinction should be combined with positive reinforcement for some desirable alternative behavior. When response-reduction procedures such as extinction are used, the level of the target behavior is reduced, but the level of behaviors other than the target behavior may increase (Sajwaj, Twardosz, & Burke, 1972). There is no guarantee that the other behaviors that show an increase in level will be desirable behaviors (Ullmann & Krasner, 1975) unless desirable alternative behaviors are specifically reinforced.

When extinction is used without combination with reinforcement for an alternative behavior, a phenomenon known as symptom substitution may occur (Ullmann & Krasner, 1975). For example, suppose a child whines frequently, successfully getting the parents' attentions. They then use extinction to decrease the child's whining, and the frequency of whining indeed declines. However, the child continues to receive minimal parental attention, and begins complaining of headaches, which in fact do not exist. Complaints of headaches secure the reinforcing attention of the parents once again. As you can surmise, the real problem here is a lack of parental attention for desirable child behavior. This phenomenon is sometimes called symptom substitution, because new behavior problems continue to appear as long as the real problem—the lack of parental attention for desirable behavior—has not been addressed.

Symptom substitution is a concept that was once used by opponents of behavior analysis. It is the idea that if you solve one behavior problem by changing a behavior, another behavior problem will soon appear because the root of the problem has not been solved. Behavior analysts have largely discredited the basic idea of symptom substitution because they have shown their procedures to be effective both in long-term maintenance of behavior change and in producing consumer satisfaction with those changes (Kazdin, 1982b). Research has shown that when one behavior problem is solved, others do not materialize as a result. However, one exception to this premise may occur when extinction is not combined with positive reinforcement for an alternative response. The behavior on extinction may be eliminated, but another problem behavior may appear.

Availability of Extraneous Reinforcers.   In an extinction procedure, a suspected reinforcer for a response is withheld. Extinction procedures will not be effective if the reinforcer we suspect is maintaining the behavior is not the only reinforcer for the behavior. For example, Madsen, Becker, and Thomas (1968) used an extinction procedure in a classroom in which the teacher ignored disruptive student behavior. Although the reinforcer, teacher attention, was withdrawn for the disruptive responses, disruptive responses increased rather than decreased, suggesting that some unknown reinforcer other than teacher attention was responsible for the disruptive behavior.

Parents and teachers have come to realize that the cause of child misbehavior is often not adult attention, but the attention from peers. Carlson, Arnold, Becker, and Madsen (1968) dealt with this problem in the course of working with an 8-year-old girl. At school, Diane threw tantrums in which she swore, screamed, ran about the room wildly, threw chairs, and so on. Previously, the tantrums had received considerable attention from the teacher, the school secretaries, the school principal, a social worker, Diane's mother, and, of course, Diane's classmates. In order to solve the problem, extinction was combined with positive reinforcement for desirable behavior. As a part of the extinction procedure, Diane's classmates were told that anyone who did not turn around to watch her throw a tantrum would receive a piece of candy. Diane's classmates ignored her tantrums, and over the course of 6 weeks, her tantrums became less frequent and were eliminated.

Often, the behavior analyst, the teacher, or the parent will not have control of sources of extraneous reinforcement for the behavior that is put on extinction. In such cases, extinction cannot be expected to be used successfully. For example, parents do not have control over the reinforcers involved in the sexual behavior of their teenage children. Similarly, using extinction by ignoring theft cannot be expected to

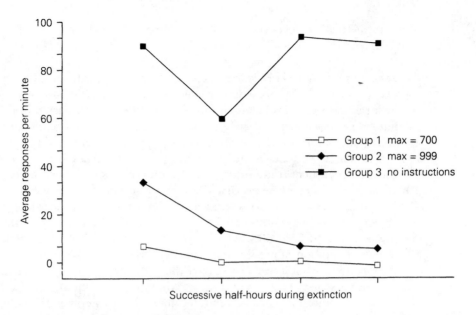

Figure 3.3   *The Influence of Instructions on the Effectiveness of Extinction*

Group 1, correctly instructed that extinction was in effect, responded very little during extinction. In contrast, Group 2, given false instructions about extinction, and Group 3, given no instructions, responded a good deal even though their behavior was on extinction. Drawn from Weiner's (1970) data.

be successful. In these cases, behavior analysts must rely on procedures other than extinction.

Instructions.   Extinction will be more effective if combined with instructions that specify that a response will go unreinforced. For example, Weiner (1970) had subjects engage in a lever-pressing task in which every 10th response was reinforced with a penny. The maximum any subject could earn was 700 pennies. One group was correctly informed that the maximum they could earn was 700 pennies, a second group was misinformed that they could earn a maximum of 999 pennies, and a third group was told nothing about a maximum. After the subjects had earned 700 pennies, the lever-presses of all three groups were put on extinction for 2 hours.

As indicated in Figure 3.3, subjects in the group that was told the correct maximum earnings responded very little during extinction. For these people, the extinction procedure, combined with instructions that specified that extinction was in effect, virtually eliminated all responding as soon as the extinction period began. In contrast, subjects in the group that was not given instructions about maximum earnings continued to respond during extinction. Subjects in the group that was told false maximum earnings responded at an intermediate level. For these subjects, instructions that there was a maximum to be earned, although inaccurately high, served to reduce the level of responding compared to that of subjects not told of a maximum earnings value.

The Context and Consistency of Extinction.   Like reinforcement, extinction is affected by its context, particularly by preceding events. In general, extinction will occur more rapidly if the response has been reinforced each time it has occurred in the past (i.e., continuous reinforcement) than if some responses have been reinforced and some have not (i.e., intermittent reinforcement) (Neisworth, Hunt, Gallop, & Maddle, 1985; Schmid, 1986). Lewis and Duncan (1956) investigated this type of contrast effect in an experiment using undergraduate university students as subjects. The students operated a slot machine that dispensed a nickel for each winning lever-pull. The slot machines were fixed so that it was predetermined how often the students would win. One group won on all 8 trials (100% reinforcement), while the 6 remaining groups received 75%, 50%, 37.5%, 25%, 12.5%, and 0% reinforcement. After the first 8 trials, operation of the slot machine for all the groups was put on extinction.

As Figure 3.4 indicates, the greater the percentage reinforcement the students received, the less they responded during extinction before quitting. In other words, the greater the intermittency of reinforcement, the greater was the subjects' resistance to extinction. This relationship is sometimes referred to as the partial reinforcement effect. In a clinical application of this principle, Neisworth et al. (1985) found that extinction of a retarded man's self-stimulatory hand-flapping responses was more effective after each response occurrence had been reinforced.

When using extinction, the behavior analyst must be rigidly consistent in ensuring that the target behavior goes unreinforced. Even occasional reinforcement makes the behavior resistant to extinction, but it is often difficult to use extinction consistently. Because many undesired behaviors are hard to ignore, they are strengthened and maintained. Intermittent schedules make behavior more resistant to extinction.

We saw an example of the danger of inconsistent extinction in the Williams (1959) study in which parents sat with their howling child at bedtime until he fell asleep. Advised by a behavior analyst, the parents were initially successful in extinguishing the bedtime crying and howling, as Figure 3.5 illustrates.

However, one night when an aunt put the child to bed, he began screaming and howling as he had before, causing the aunt to rush to the child and sit with him as he fell asleep. This single instance of reinforcement made it necessary to put the child's bedtime tantrums on extinction once again. As Figure 3.5 illustrates, the second use of extinction was successful, but it required a substantial amount of time for the behavior to be reextinguished.

Effectiveness of the Withdrawn Reinforcer.   In general, the greater the effectiveness of the reinforcer that has previously maintained the response to be extinguished, the more difficult it will be to extinguish the response (i.e., the greater the resistance to extinction). As such, conditions that we discussed that contribute to the effectiveness of a positive reinforcer will contribute to the resistance to extinction when the positive reinforcer for the response is withheld. Conversely, anything that can be done to

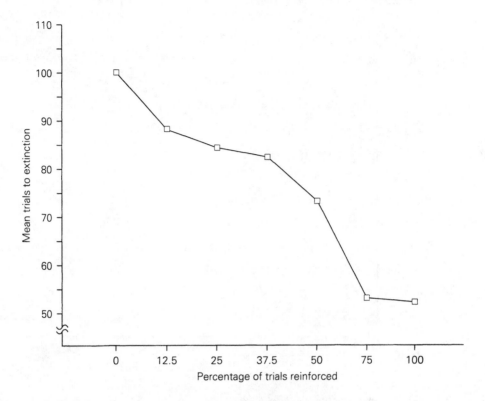

Figure 3.4   *The Effect of the Context of Extinction on Resistance to Extinction*

The greater the intermittency of money reinforcement of slot-machine lever pulls, the more the subjects responded when lever-pulling was put on extinction. Figure adapted from Lewis and Duncan (1956).

minimize the effectiveness of a reinforcer will make behavior that that reinforcer maintains less resistant to extinction (easier to extinguish). Therefore, contributors to making extinction more effective include:

• the absence of instructions that a response will be reinforced;

• a decreased amount of a reinforcer;

• use of unpredictive conditioned reinforcers; and

• using little variety in reinforcers.

Lewis and Duncan (1957) conducted an experiment that showed the relationship between the amount of a reinforcer and the effectiveness of extinction on behavior that the reinforcer previously maintained. Undergraduate university students pulled the lever of the slot-machine apparatus described earlier. Different groups of students had their lever-pulls on the slot machine reinforced by 1¢, 10¢,

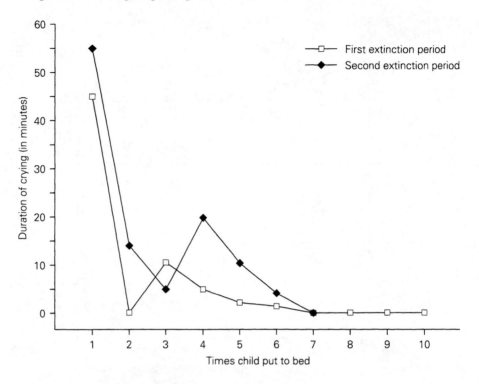

Figure 3.5   *The Effect of Inconsistent Extinction*

During the first period of extinction, a child's bedtime crying had been eliminated. However, after the child's aunt reinforced bedtime crying, it was necessary to put the behavior on extinction a second time, which required an additional 7 days. Figure adapted from Williams (1959).

25¢, or 50¢. As indicated in Figure 3.6, the greater the amount of the reinforcer that was used to establish and maintain plays on the slot machine, the greater was the response's resistance to extinction.

Unfortunately, weakening the effectiveness of a reinforcer in order to make behavior maintained by that reinforcer easier to extinguish is rarely a feasible way of increasing the effectiveness of extinction. For example, suppose parental social reinforcement maintains a child's tantrums. When the child throws a tantrum, the parents pay a good deal of attention to the child. Reducing the effectiveness of parental attention would clearly be a highly undesirable option, because it would also reduce the effectiveness of parental attention as a reinforcer for the child's desirable behaviors.

Situations in which it is possible to increase the effectiveness of extinction by decreasing the effectiveness of the withdrawn reinforcer are those in which the reinforcer itself is undesirable. For example, suppose parents wish to eliminate a child's

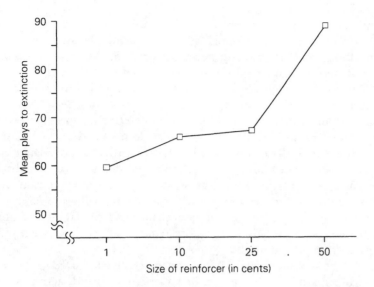

Figure 3.6   *The Influence of Amount of the Reinforcer on Resistance to Extinction*

The more money that subjects had received for slot-machine lever-pulls, the more the subjects responded when lever-pulls were put on extinction. Adapted from Lewis and Duncan (1957).

previously reinforced requests for nonnutritious snacks such as candy and potato chips. In principle, extinction of the child's requests would be easier if, before using extinction, the parents reduced the amount of the snacks they provided. It is speculative whether the advantage gained of less resistance to extinction would be worth the trouble of using the gradual-reduction procedure.

DRO and DRI

Two other procedures designed to reduce or eliminate behavior are differential reinforcement of zero responding, or DRO, and differential reinforcement of incompatible behavior, or DRI. In a DRO procedure, also known as omission training, the level of a behavior is reduced due to a stimulus change dependent on the absence of the behavior for a given period of time. The story of Clarence at the beginning of this chapter is an example.

The parents of a family with six children used another example of a DRO procedure. For every year that passed without one of the children smoking, that child would be awarded $25; if the child reached the age of 21 without smoking, she or he would receive a $250 bonus. This example is a DRO procedure because presentation of the money was dependent on the absence of smoking for given periods of time, and because it prevented smoking from occurring. There was no actual reduction in smoking, because smoking never occurred. However, it is a reinforcement procedure because it maintained the zero rate of smoking throughout the children's adolescence, a time when social pressures encourage young people to become addicted to tobacco.

Some evidence indicates that DRO is more effective in eliminating behavior than extinction (Homer & Peterson, 1980). Johnson, McGlynn, and Topping (1973) found that DRO eliminated behavior more rapidly than extinction. Following reinforcement training, one group of university students had their presses on a telegraph key put on extinction, while another group of students, a DRO group, was reinforced for every 5 seconds that elapsed without a lever-press occurring. The reinforcers used were points exchangeable for credit in fulfilling their course requirements. The DRO procedure reduced responding much more rapidly than the extinction procedure did.

In differential reinforcement of incompatible behavior (DRI), a behavior that is physically incompatible with a target behavior is reinforced, acting to reduce the level of the target behavior. In Chapter 1, an example of DRI was cited in which the rate of off-task and disruptive behavior was reduced by reinforcing academic responding, such as accuracy in solving math problems. Desirable academic performances were incompatible with undesirable off-task and disruptive behaviors, so by reinforcing the desirable academic behaviors, the levels of incompatible undesirable behaviors were reduced. DRI should be familiar to you at this point because, in most respects, DRI is simply a standard positive reinforcement procedure. The only difference is that DRI is defined by the reduction in the level of the behavior incompatible with the reinforced behavior, while standard positive reinforcement is defined by an increase in the level of the reinforced behavior.

DRI is a highly desirable procedure because it represents a constructional approach to behavior change. In DRI, an undesirable response is weakened at the same time that a desirable alternative response is strengthened. As such, when DRI is used, the behavior analyst is compelled to identify useful forms of behavior rather than simply identifying problem responses. Use of the DRI procedure redirects the focus of behavioral problems from eliminating bad behaviors to encouraging desirable behaviors. For example, suppose parents are concerned that too often their children are playing video games and watching television. Alternative desirable activities the parents might identify include a regular program of family outings to plays, museums, and libraries, or arranging to teach the children skills in music, dance, art, or creative writing. Conceiving of desirable behaviors and arranging for them to occur are essential features of the DRI method that require creativity, inventiveness, time, and energy.

DRO and DRI are similar in that both procedures are defined in terms of the reduction of the level of the target behaviors. However, in DRO, reinforcement is dependent on a period of time passing during which the target behavior does not occur, while in DRI, reinforcement is dependent on the occurrence of a specific behavior or behaviors that are incompatible with the target behavior.

An important advantage of DRO and DRI procedures is that students, parents, staff, and children have consistently rated them as more acceptable procedures than other methods of eliminating behavior such as extinction, punishment, and medication (Kazdin, 1980a, 1980b, 1981; Singh & Katz, 1985; Singh, Watson, & Winton, 1987). When behavior change procedures are favorably evaluated, those procedures are more likely to be sought out and used by people who stand to benefit from them (Kazdin, 1980a). For these reasons, DRO and DRI are generally the preferred methods of first resort when the goal is to eliminate an undesirable behavior. Even if DRO and DRI procedures do not work by themselves, other response reduction procedures can be combined with DRO and DRI methods to change behavior in an acceptable manner.

One reason why people favor DRO and DRI procedures is because they have few adverse side effects (Homer & Peterson, 1980), a factor that causes people to respond unfavorably to behavior-change procedures (Kazdin, 1981). In their review, Harris and Ersner-Hershfield (1978) reported mainly desirable side effects of DRO, but in some cases, increases in the level of undesirable behaviors accompanied the decrease in the level of the target behavior. As we have seen, even apparently harmless procedures like extinction are capable of producing the undesirable side effects of annoyance and aggression, but generally, these types of effects have seldom been reported with DRO or DRI procedures. An exception was an experiment in which Cowdery, Iwata, and Pace (1990) found that a child sometimes cried when scheduled DRO reinforcers were not delivered, due to occurrence of the self-destructive target behaviors.

Making DRO and DRI Effective

Because DRO and DRI both involve the delivery of reinforcers, the parameters influencing their effectiveness include those that affect positive reinforcement: Deprivation and satiation, instructions, reinforcer amount, predictive conditioned reinforcers, reinforcer variety, response energy, reinforcer contrast effects, extraneous reinforcers, and reinforcement delay. Each of these conditions may be assumed to influence the effectiveness of DRO and DRI in the same way they influence standard positive reinforcement. For example, Corte, Wolf, and Locke (1971) used a DRO procedure to reduce the self-destructive slapping of a profoundly retarded adolescent who lived at a state institution. Using spoonfuls of malted milk as a reinforcer, the experimenters held sessions at 3:00 P.M. daily. On days when the subject had not had lunch, the DRO procedure reduced the self-destructive responses to zero, but on days when the subject had eaten lunch, about 20 responses occurred per day. As such, this study showed that satiation and deprivation operations affect DRO procedures in essentially the same way that they affect standard positive reinforcement procedures.

In addition to the basic parameters that make positive reinforcement effective, a parameter important in making DRO and DRI effective is the nature of the reinforced behavior. Two additional parameters in making DRO effective include (a) whole-interval and momentary DRO procedures, and (b) graduated interval sizes.

Nature of the Reinforced Behavior.   When using DRO procedures, reinforcement is dependent only on the absence of a target behavior. Therefore, behavior other than the target behavior replaces the target response. One problem may arise if the behavior replacing the target behavior in DRO is either clearly worse than the target behavior or is not a desirable behavior. To take an extreme case, if you are using DRO to eliminate a child's aggression toward others and the child begins engaging in self-destructive behavior, it would certainly be inappropriate to reinforce self-destruction, even if no aggression toward others had occurred.

One solution to this problem with DRO is to provide opportunities for the occurrence of desirable, or at least neutral, behaviors. For example, Zeiler and Fite (1975) used DRO to decrease the rate of a key pressing a target key. Simply by providing alternative keys, they found that DRO was more effective in reducing the rate of pressing the target key. This method was effective even though no consequences were dependent on pressing the alternative keys. This strategy might improve the effectiveness of DRO for a child's aggressive behaviors. By providing an opportunity for other behaviors such as playing with toys and games, watching television, or reading, DRO might work more effectively.

Another solution to this problem with DRO is to use DRI. Users of DRI can be assured that the incompatible behavior strengthened is not worse than the target behavior, because they have specifically selected it for reinforcement. Therefore, DRI is recommended in cases in which the person whose behavior is being modified is engaging in many different undesirable behaviors most of the time.

When using DRI, it is important to select a target response as incompatible as possible with the target behavior. For example, Young and Wincze (1974) worked with a woman who engaged in two self-destructive behaviors, fist-to-head hits, and hitting her head against the back handle of her wheelchair. Merely reinforcing eye contact with the experimenter did not reduce the rate of self-destructive behaviors, because eye contact and self-destruction could occur at the same time. The experimenters also tried reinforcing the woman's response of sitting erect with her hands on the arms of her wheelchair. This procedure was effective in reducing the level of the woman's fist-to-head hits, but it increased the frequency of the woman's hitting her head against the handle of her wheelchair. This example illustrates that some behaviors are more incompatible than others, and when using DRI, it is desirable to select behaviors that are as physically incompatible as possible with the target behavior.

Whole Interval and Momentary DRO.   In DRO, reinforcement is dependent on a time interval elapsing without the target behavior occurring. Repp, Barton, and Brulle (1983) were interested in the specific role of this time interval. Working with mildly retarded 7-year-olds, they identified several disruptive classroom behaviors as target responses to be eliminated, including being off-task, being out-of-seat, and interrupting the teacher. One method they used was called whole-interval DRO. In whole-interval DRO, the students received candy or cereal if they had not engaged in any disruptive target behaviors during an entire 5-minute interval. As such, this use of whole-interval DRO represents the standard use of DRO because reinforcement was dependent on a period of time elapsing without the target behavior occurring. The whole-interval DRO method was compared with momentary DRO, in which the students received candy or cereal at the end of each 5-minute interval when the target responses were not occurring precisely when the interval ended. As such, in whole-interval DRO, the students had to refrain from engaging in disruptive responses for the entire 5 minutes; in momentary DRO, all they had to do was not engage in the target behaviors at the moment the 5-minute interval ended.

The results of the Repp et al. (1983) study showed that whole-interval DRO more effectively reduced the rate of the disruptive target behaviors than momentary DRO. In later work, Barton, Brulle, and Repp (1986) showed that the momentary DRO procedure could be effective with target behaviors that the whole-interval DRO method had previously modified. Although the momentary procedure is less effective than the whole-interval method, the momentary procedure is less time-consuming and easier to use because you have only to observe whether the behavior is occurring at the moment the interval ends. When using the whole-interval method, it is necessary to observe during the entire interval.

Graduated Interval Size. Several studies (Cross, Dickson, & Sisemore, 1978; Repp & Slack, 1977; Topping, Larmi, & Johnson, 1972) demonstrated the value of beginning DRO training with a relatively small time interval and gradually increasing the size of the interval. For example, Cross et al. (1978) engaged retarded teenagers in a lever-pressing task. At first, poker chips exchangeable for money were dependent on lever presses, and all the subjects learned to press the lever. Then two DRO procedures were compared. Subjects in a constant-DRO group received poker chips dependent on 8 seconds elapsing without a lever press. In contrast, subjects in a gradual-DRO group first received poker chips for 2 seconds elapsing without a press, then 4 seconds, then 6 seconds, and finally 8 seconds. Results indicated that the level of the gradual-DRO group's responding declined more than that of the constant-DRO group. These data indicate that when using DRO, the time interval for reinforcement should first be set at a relatively small value at which reinforcement can be achieved, and be increased gradually.

DRO: Some Advanced Considerations

DRO procedures have always had a curious place within behavior analysis. Some observers feel that DRO is a punishment procedure, because occurrence of a response in DRO postpones delivery of the reinforcer. We have classified DRO as a reinforcement procedure, however, because the reinforcing consequence in DRO is immediately dependent on the absence of the target response. When the target behavior occurs under DRO, nothing happens (i.e., no stimulus change occurs). It is only when the response has been absent for a specified period of time that the reinforcing stimulus change occurs.

Uncertainty about DRO procedures arises because of the notion of "other behavior" or "not-responding." Perhaps living as we do in a material world, most people are more comfortable with behaviors that can be seen and counted than with ambiguous other behaviors or, worse, not-responding. However, as Lewis Carroll— a logician familiar with the pairwise nature of assertion and negation—was often fond of pointing out in *Alice's Adventures in Wonderland,* whenever we define an event like a response, we automatically single it out from everything else, creating a measurable and material response unit. In the same stroke, we define what that response is not, immaterial not-responding. As such, the paradox of defining one behavior—what a behavior is—is that another behavioral phenomenon is automatically defined: what that behavior is not, or not-responding.

This paradox of defining things is important because so many behavior-analysis procedures consist of providing differential consequences. In standard positive reinforcement, reinforcing consequences are made dependent on a selected response and are withheld for the absence of that response (for not-responding). In DRO these conditions are reversed: Reinforcing consequences are made dependent on not-responding and are withheld when the response occurs. Essentially, in using behavioral procedures, the behavior analyst must be concerned with what is going on both after a response occurs and after it fails to occur, with responses and with nonresponding. Recently, this concern with what happens both to responses and nonresponding has been highlighted by work in which the effects of using a behavior analysis procedure with one behavior are assessed on that behavior and other behaviors (Epling & Pierce, 1983; Kazdin, 1982b; McDowell, 1982, 1988).

Other observers accept that DRO is a reinforcement procedure, but are uncertain about precisely what is learned through DRO (Woods, 1983). One view of DRO is the specific-behavior-replacement theory. According to this view, when we use DRO, some measure of the target behavior declines because specific behaviors occurring immediately before delivery of the reinforcer are strengthened. For example, suppose the absence of a child's tantrums is reinforced every 20 minutes. At the end of the first three 20-minute periods, just before reinforcer delivery, the child might be reading, working with a coloring book, or doing jumping jacks. According to the specific-behavior-replacement theory, tantruming is reduced because reading, coloring, and playing replace it. Reading, coloring, and playing would be said to be accidentally reinforced, because reinforcement would not be specifically dependent on these specific behaviors. These behaviors were reinforced because they happened to be occurring immediately before the reinforcer was delivered. They would be said to be accidentally reinforced behaviors, because the reinforcer that strengthened the behaviors was not dependent on those behaviors (i.e., the reinforcer was response-independent).

According to an alternative theory, a response property, the absence of the target behavior, is reinforced when we use DRO. This response-property theory of DRO holds that DRO reinforcers strengthen not merely the specific responses occurring at the moment of reinforcer delivery, but all behavior that shares the response property, the absence of the target behavior. This theory designates that decline in the target behavior is due to its replacement with the entire class of behavior that shares the reinforced response property, rather than specific accidentally reinforced behaviors. For example, in the case of the child's tantruming, the response-property theory of DRO would predict that tantruming would decline due to replacement by the entire class of behaviors that possess the property of the absence of tantruming, not by a few specific behaviors that occur just before the moment of reinforcer delivery. The response-property theory of DRO has received some support from research in the reinforcement of creative responding, in which behavior showing the property of novelty, not having been previously performed, can be reinforced (Goetz & Baer, 1973; Pryor, Haag, & O'Reilly, 1969). The class of behaviors that the property of response novelty defines is reinforceable and, like the class of behavior defined by the absence of a response, is defined by what the behavior is not.

At present, there is no easy way to decide between the specific behavior replacement theory and response-property theory of DRO; perhaps both are correct. Early during the use of DRO procedures, there could be accidental reinforcement of specific other behaviors, while after extended exposure to DRO, a class of not-responding might be strengthened. Woods (1983) has called for experimentation to determine whether DRO reinforcers strengthen specific behaviors, or whether they strengthen a nonspecific class of responses that the absence of the target behavior defines.

Summary

Behavior analysis is at its best when it takes a constructional approach, by concentrating on building repertoires of behavior that people can use to function independently and successfully. However, sometimes behaviors exist that are self-destructive or that prevent the individual from acquiring desirable behavior. Under these conditions, it becomes necessary to consider response-reduction procedures, three of which are extinction, differential reinforcement of zero responding, and differential reinforcement of incompatible behavior.

Extinction, the withholding of reinforcement for a previously reinforced response, causes a reduction in the level of the response. In extinction, the response produces no stimulus change, and in this way extinction differs from punishment, wherein the response does produce a stimulus change. The response reduction due to extinction differs from forgetting, because in extinction the response occurs, goes unreinforced, and is weakened due to nonreinforcement. In forgetting, a period of time passes during which the response does not occur, and the response is weakened for this reason.

A temporary increase in the level of the response on extinction often accompanies extinction, and it may also cause aggressive behavior and annoyance on the part of the person whose behavior is being extinguished. Extinction of our behavior may involve withholding both nonsocial and social reinforcers. Sensory extinction can be used to reduce the level of undesirable behaviors maintained by sensory consequences.

Whenever possible, extinction should be accompanied by reinforcement of desirable alternative behaviors. Extinction should also be used consistently, combined with instructions, and the behavior analyst should make sure that no extraneous reinforcers are dependent on the response that is put on extinction.

Differential reinforcement of zero responding (DRO) and differential reinforcement of incompatible behaviors (DRI) are response-reduction procedures that people have rated as most acceptable, and are therefore the procedures of first resort when it is necessary to eliminate or reduce undesirable behavior. Very few harmful side effects of DRO and DRI procedures have been documented.

In order to ensure the effectiveness of DRO and DRI procedures, it is necessary to pay attention to all the parameters that make standard positive reinforcement effective. An important factor that must be considered when using both DRO and DRI is the nature of the reinforced behavior. When using DRO, it is important to (a) reinforce the absence of responding only when it is indeed absent for the entire duration of the specified interval, and (b) begin with short-duration intervals and gradually progress to intervals of longer duration.

Finally, we considered certain ambiguities of DRO procedures. Some observers classify DRO as a punishment procedure, while others view it as a reinforcement procedure, but are unsure of the nature of the reinforced behavior in DRO. Two theories of DRO are discussed, but at present neither theory has been proven correct.

Conceptual Exercise   *DRO, DRI, and Extinction*

For each of the following, decide if the item is an example of extinction, DRO, DRI, forgetting, or none of these. The target behavior is highlighted.

If you have difficulty deciding if an item is an example of extinction or forgetting, ask yourself whether or not an event that previously reinforced the response has been withdrawn and the response has decreased in strength as a result. If so, the loss of strength is due to nonreinforcement or extinction. If the response has lost strength because there has been a period of time during which there was no opportunity to respond, this is forgetting.

Remember that DRO is a procedure where the reinforcing consequence is dependent upon nonresponding. DRI involves the reinforcement of *a response which is incompatible with the target behavior*. With DRO, reinforcement is dependent on *the passage of an amount of time during which the response does not occur*. With DRI, reinforcement is dependent not on the passage of time, but on the occurrence of a specific incompatible response.

Note: In most of the studies of extinction, it was combined with some form of positive reinforcement for an alternative behavior. For purposes of clarity, several items in this exercise omit the description of the positive reinforcement that was combined with extinction. In practice, however, remember that extinction should be used with some form of positive reinforcement for a desirable alternative response.

1. Gail was a 22-year-old retarded woman. She had once lived at home, but she had to be sent to an institution because of **aggressive and destructive behavior toward herself, her parents, and household furniture.** In five years at the institution, Gail had continued being aggressive to staff and residents and had destroyed much furniture. She was thought to be a hopeless case. A procedure was used in which a female staff member at the institution posed as an unresponsive victim of Gail's attacks. When Gail attacked the "victim," the woman would absorb Gail's blows and casually ignore the attack as much as possible. As a result of this method, Gail's attacks against the victim, other people, herself, and the furniture decreased to near-zero levels.

2. Newborn infants, ranging in age from 51 to 96 hours, were subjects in an experiment. One group of these infants was given a baby bottle nipple whenever they **turned their head 10 degrees or more.** Then, nipple presentations no longer followed head turns, and this caused the frequency of head turns to decline.

3. Fay was a friendly and polite 5-year-old. She was normal in most respects, but for a year she had **scratched herself** so much that she often bled. Large scars and scabs had formed on much of her face and on one arm and leg. In order to try to solve this problem, Fay's mother began praising and approving her after every 20-to 30-minute period of time that passed without any scratching. In addition, Fay's mother gave her a gold star to paste in a booklet. For every three gold stars that Fay earned, she received a cookie, candy, or a glass of a drink she liked. Further, at noon and at supper time, her mother would count the stars and give Fay an inexpensive trinket. The period of time required for praise and stars was gradually lengthened until, at the end of 6 weeks, Fay's wounds were healed and her scratching had ceased.

4. Thomas had mastered his ABCs as a result of his parents' use of drill and praise. Then his parents took a 3-week trip to Europe, while Thomas stayed with his grandmother. She gave him lots of attention, but didn't drill him on the alphabet. When his parents returned, they found that Thomas was no longer **able to say the whole alphabet.**

5. Tim was a 4-year-old retarded boy who was a student in a remedial classroom. He would spend most of his time lying on the floor and **squirming** in odd positions. The teacher began a procedure in which Tim received toys, teacher praise, and tokens when he assumed a seated position. The tokens were exchangeable for candy and trinkets. As a result of this procedure, the duration of time Tim spent squirming on the floor decreased. The target behavior is Tim's squirming on the floor.

6. Lucy was a 17-year-old retarded girl who suffered from motor epilepsy and had about 15 **seizures** per day. Just before a seizure, her body would become rigid, she would clench her fist, raise her arms at a 90 degree angle from her body, grimace,

and snap her head back. In order to try to reduce the seizures, a procedure was implemented in which Lucy's arms were placed at her sides when she had raised them and she was then praised lavishly and given candy for keeping her arms lowered. This procedure resulted in a reduction of seizures to near-zero levels.

7. Laura was a 9-year-old girl who had several handicaps. Six months after admission to a school for the retarded, she began **vomiting in class** every day. This soiled her dress and she was sent to her dormitory residence hall after each incident. As a result of her vomiting, Laura was dropped from school for 2 months. However, after that time, a new teacher volunteered to work with Laura, and tried a new technique: Whenever Laura vomited, class continued normally, and she was not sent back to the dorm. This procedure remained in force even though Laura vomited as many as 21 times per day. As a result of the procedure, Laura's vomiting declined in frequency over time and by the end of 30 class days, Laura no longer vomited.

8. Anna, a patient in a mental hospital, engaged in much delusional talk about her trip to another planet in an alien spaceship and the unfriendly aliens she believed were trying to kidnap her. A program was established whereby staff responsible for Anna ignored her **psychotic talk**.

9. Linda was a retarded woman who had been living in an institution for many years. Linda had two self-destructive behaviors: pounding her head against a table and pinching herself. A procedure was implemented whereby Linda was praised and given tasty snacks for sitting up straight with her hands at her sides. As a result, Linda's head-to-table hitting decreased, but her level of **self-pinching** was unchanged.

10. Fred, 52, was a retarded man who often unzipped his pants and showed his penis to others. In order to reduce this behavior, staff at the institution where Fred lived began praising Fred and giving him a hug for every 10 minutes that passed without Fred's **exposing himself**. Eventually this procedure eliminated Fred's self-exposures.

11. When she was in the 5th grade, Julie had learned to **recite the capital cities of 100 of the world's most populous countries**. However, after a period of 2 years had elapsed without recalling the cities, Julie was able to recite only 75 capital cities when given the names of the 100 countries.

12. Elaine had frequently used the side door of her house, before she had it nailed shut to prevent burglary. She lived in a bad neighborhood, and because the side door could not be viewed from the street, it was an invitation to thieves. Despite this, she sometimes found herself **trying to use the door**, but her twists and tugs at the knob were to no avail. Eventually, this caused her to cease attempting to open the door.

13. Sidney was an 11-year-old boy. He lived in a residential treatment center for emotionally disturbed children, where he attended school. Several times each week he **threw a temper tantrum** in which he screamed and thrashed about on the floor, drawing a crowd of staff who watched him. One of the teachers arranged it so that

when Sidney threw a tantrum, he was not allowed to watch television or listen to the radio for the rest of that day. This procedure was continued for several weeks until Sidney's tantrums ceased completely.

14. Ruth, a 9-year-old retarded girl who had been diagnosed as being schizophrenic, would often engage in **self-destructive behaviors** including head banging and arm banging. A procedure was devised in which she was praised for engaging in "appropriate musical behaviors," which included hand clapping, rocking in time to the music, and singing the correct words at the right time. As a result of this method, Ruth's self-destructive behaviors declined to very low levels.

15. Henry was a kindergarten student. Although he was a good boy and a good student in many respects, he would often **pull clothes off other children**. When this happened, class was disrupted because all the students would laugh. The teacher began sending Henry to the school principal whenever he tried to take other students' clothes from them. After several days, this procedure eliminated the problem.

16. Three retarded people engaged in stereotypic **self-stimulatory responses** of the sort that interfered with efforts to teach them appropriate behavior. One, a 12-year-old female, would flap her lips with her fingers. Another, a 22-year-old female, would rock constantly. A third, a 23-year-old male, would wave his hands in front of his face. Staff at the institution first tried to say "No" when the self-stimulatory responses occurred, with little effect. A procedure was used in which the staff gave hugs and praise whenever the self-stimulatory activities had ceased for a few minutes. As a result of this procedure, the self-stimulatory responses were virtually eliminated in each of the three people.

17. After she took a photography course, Mavis had learned to **compose photographs very well**. However, after taking the course, Mavis took a full-time job that kept her so busy she was unable to take photographs. When she resumed photography, her pictures were not as well-composed as they had been formerly.

18. Bob, 14, was a retarded boy who lived at a state institution. Since the age of 5, he had often behaved aggressively, including hitting, scratching, kicking, and biting. He often bruised and drew blood from his victims. In the past, Bob had been **aggressive** in situations in which he was required to follow instructions or when other demands were made of him. Conversely, when he engaged in aggression, he was put in a situation in which no demands were made of him. In order to try to solve this problem, Bob was placed in a seat belt in a chair across from the experimenter and remained there for an hour no matter how much aggression he engaged in when demands were made of him. As a result of this procedure, within four sessions his aggression dropped to low levels. His low aggression was eventually maintained even when his seat belt was removed.

19. Henry was a 7-year-old boy who had been diagnosed as having asthma. He had frequent **asthma attacks,** consisting of wheezing and coughing, despite changes in his diet and use of various types of medication. It was noticed that Henry received medi-

cine and much sympathetic attention from his mother during asthma attacks that occurred at bedtime. In order to try to solve the problem, when Henry had bedtime asthma attacks, he was no longer given any attention and his medication was discontinued. This procedure caused the duration of Henry's asthma attacks to drop from over an hour per evening to about 5 minutes per evening.

20. Sam was a 3-year-old boy who had been hospitalized for lead poisoning for the second time. Lead poisoning, often due to chewing or eating flaking lead-based paints, can cause neurological disorders, mental retardation, and death. Sam was presented with a board to which a flour and water mixture that resembled flaking paint had been applied. Sam was also shown several inedible objects. The researcher wanted to reduce Sam's **pica behavior,** consisting of mouthing inedible objects, eating the simulated paint, mouthing his body parts, and touching paint chips. Sam was given raisins, cheese, and crackers for every 10 minutes that passed without any pica behavior. As a result of this method, Sam's pica behavior was reduced to zero. Sam's parents were taught to use this method, and a year later, the lead in Sam's blood was no longer at a dangerously high level.

21. Elvira had frequently used a basement sink in her house, but she had the water shut off because the pipes began leaking. Despite this, she sometimes found herself trying to **use the taps at the sink,** but her turns of the taps were to no avail.

22. Lee was a 3-year-old boy who was being treated for **toe walking,** a disorder in which a child walks on the balls of the feet without the heels touching the ground. In severe cases, this condition requires surgery, so a group of behavior analysts wanted to see if they could correct the problem using behavioral techniques. At first, Lee was outfitted with a pair of heavy boots that weighed down his feet and produced a partial reduction in toe walking. Two weeks later, they put into effect a procedure whereby they gave Lee candy, snacks, and tokens for every 15 seconds that passed without toe walking. He could trade in tokens for food and play materials. This procedure caused a further reduction in toe walking. Lee's mother continued using these methods at home, and toe walking was eliminated completely in a few weeks.

23. Shortly after her admission to a school for the retarded, Leslie began **vomiting** in class every day. This soiled her dress and she was sent to her dormitory residence hall after each incident. As a result of her vomiting, Leslie was dropped from school for 2 months. However, after that time, a new teacher volunteered to work with her and tried a new technique: Whenever Leslie vomited she was required to completely clean up the mess she had made. This procedure remained in force even though Leslie vomited as many as 21 times per day. As a result of the procedure, Leslie's vomiting declined in frequency over time and by the end of 30 class days she no longer vomited.

24. Sally was a 28-year-old woman who had Prader-Willi syndrome, a condition in which the person is mentally retarded, short, and very obese. She was 4 feet 8 inches tall and weighed 253 pounds. Like many people with this syndrome, She would often **steal food.** She was secretly observed in rooms where food was in view. Although she was told not to steal any of this food, she did so, sometimes as often

as twice a minute. A procedure was then used: Sally would receive praise and tokens for every 30 seconds that elapsed without any food theft. Tokens could be traded in for low calorie drinks and food as well as for magazines and cosmetics. This procedure caused a rapid decline in food stealing. Later this method was combined with other techniques, and helped Sally to lose 81 pounds.

25. Bob was a 19–year-old retarded man who would often **ruminate,** a behavior disorder in which previously swallowed and partially digested food is brought up, re-chewed and re-swallowed. This disorder can cause malnutrition and death. Trainers gave Bob small bits of a cookie and dabs of peanut butter for every 10 seconds that he did not ruminate, and this 10-second time criterion was gradually increased until, eventually, Bob's rumination decreased to nearly zero.

26. Harry was a 22-year-old mildly retarded man who had been diagnosed as an epileptic. He lived as an inpatient at a psychiatric unit of a university mental health center. Harry would engage in **seizure-like behaviors** seven times per day. During these apparent seizures, Harry would jerk his body about, make strange noises, masturbate, put his hand in his mouth, and hyperventilate. Harry often expressed a desire to get outside the facility and into the local community, so he was allowed to go for a half-hour walk any day when he had not had a seizure during the previous 24 hours. This procedure resulted in a reduction of Harry's seizure-like behaviors by over half, to about 3 per day.

27. Bill was a 4-year-old enrolled in preschool. He was popular with the other children. His language skills were very good and he was persuasive in his interactions with both teachers and classmates. However, Bill cried frequently, about 5 to 10 times per morning. Minor physical injuries, frustrations, and threats of any kind of physical attack would cause Bill to **scream and cry**. When this happened, class activities would cease for everyone until Bill had been comforted by the teacher for several minutes. Only then would he stop crying. In order to solve this problem, the teacher began completely ignoring Bill when he cried, except for a brief glance at him to make sure he was not in any danger. After 5 days, this procedure resulted in Bill's crying from zero to two times per day, and eventually the crying was eliminated.

28. In an experiment, two researchers set up a token economy in a 2nd-grade classroom. Tokens were exchangeable for a variety of games and materials including a ball, puzzles, dolls, and art supplies. The researchers gave students praise and tokens when they **raised their hands after completing reading workbook assignments**. This procedure caused a reduction in the students' frequency of correct answers to the reading lesson and on-task behaviors, including talking to the teacher, looking toward materials, and having one's pencil in position for writing.

29. Rae was a 24-year-old woman. She was of normal intelligence, but she had had a heart attack five years earlier that had caused some apparent neurological damage. She would often **open her mouth rapidly and forcefully,** resulting in her jaw sometimes becoming dislocated. Rae was treated by giving her a flash of a light and praise for every 5 seconds that passed with her mouth closed. This value was increased to 10 seconds and then 15 seconds. The procedure resulted in a substantial reduction in Rae's quick, forceful mouth openings.

30. In a 3rd-grade classroom, the teacher was troubled by the high level of **disruptive behaviors,** including making noise with objects, touching other students' materials, hitting, kicking, and talking without permission. One day the teacher set a kitchen timer for 5 minutes and let it run as long as no disruptive behavior occurred. When the timer bell rang, the teacher praised the students and told them they had all earned 1 minute of free time. This method continued and the number of minutes of free time the students earned was displayed to them on a flip-card stand. Free time was awarded by terminating class as much as 10 minutes early. As a result of this method, disruptive behavior was reduced by about two thirds in both math and language arts classes.

31. Rob was a six-year-old retarded and multiply handicapped child. For 18 months he had **bit himself on his forearm,** resulting in the development of large callouses. In order to correct this problem, Dr. Luiselli outfitted Rob with a pliable plastic tube on each of his arms. When he wore the tubes, Rob's bites to his arm no longer produced marks or wounds, and his frequency of arm bites decreased to low, manageable levels.

32. Hendrick was an 11-year-old boy. During current events period, his teacher would ask him to read a short newspaper article to the class. Hendrick would begin to read, but would then **laugh and giggle** without completing the article. At first the teacher was patient with Hendrick and would ask him what was so funny. One day the teacher began shouting angrily at Hendrick for laughing and giggling and this resulted in an immediate and permanent cessation of his laughing and giggling.

Conceptual Exercise   *Making Extinction, DRO, and DRI Effective*

In each of the following items, something should be altered to make the extinction, DRO, or DRI procedures more effective. Describe what should be altered and explain why in terms of the parameters that make extinction, DRO, and DRI effective. In some cases, it is possible that there is more than one problem with the example. If you feel this is so, identify all the possible problems and explain your reasoning. The analysis-answers to these items contain a single key problem with the example.

1. Tanya was working with Chester, a multiply handicapped child. One problem in teaching him was that Chester would begin waving his hands in front of his face, which would interfere with his training. In order to solve this problem, Tanya used a DRO procedure with Chester. Training sessions were held after Chester had eaten lunch, so that he wouldn't be cranky. Tanya used a variety of edible treats as reinforcers, and reinforced the absence of hand waving with an initial interval of 5 seconds and planned to increase the interval duration gradually as training progressed. How and why should this procedure be altered?

2. The Acme Insurance Company was interested in encouraging drivers to drive safely and stay out of accidents. In order to do this, they implemented a DRO procedure:

Any driver who went 10 years without an accident or a traffic ticket would be sent a rebate on their insurance. The average value of the rebate would be about $150. Clients of the company were informed of this policy through use of an attractive brochure. How and why should this procedure be altered?

3. Ophelia was concerned that her boyfriend, Hamlet, would talk of nothing else except his delusions about seeing his father's ghost. In order to try to solve this problem, she decided to use a DRO procedure. Whenever Hamlet went 10 minutes without talking about ghosts, she would stroke his forehead while he rested his head on her lap, something that seemed to soothe him. Ophelia gave Hamlet clear instructions that her attentions were dependent on his ceasing delusional talk about ghosts, and she planned to increase gradually the duration of the time interval required for reinforcement. Hamlet met the criterion for reinforcement when he went on enthusiastically talking about his plans to murder his uncle for 20 minutes, so Ophelia reinforced the absence of talk of ghosts. How and why should this procedure be altered?

4. Peter, a swim coach, was having a problem with Ken, one of his swimmers. Ken's problem was that during relay races, he would dive into the water too soon, before the teammate preceding him in the relay had touched the wall. This false start had resulted in the team being disqualified twice. In order to solve the problem, Peter decided to use a DRI procedure in which he would reinforce Ken's waiting to dive, a behavior incompatible with diving. Peter used instructions to specify the relationship between waiting to dive and receiving reinforcers. In practice, the first time Ken waited long enough to dive, Peter praised him with a half-hour speech of congratulation. How and why should this procedure be altered?

5. Rachel owned an advertising agency. She was having a problem with a new employee, Dave, who didn't dress well. Part of Dave's job was to interact with potential clients, but because Dave wore ties that were short, five inches wide, and in patterned material that would be more appropriate for a circus-clown suit, he was failing to establish credibility with clients. Rachel recognized the problem, but not wanting to hurt Dave's feelings, she did not tell him exactly what was wrong with his appearance. Instead, she decided to use a DRI procedure in which she would praise Dave and take him out to lunch on those rare days when he wore an attractive tie. How and why should this procedure be altered?

6. Sandy, a 3rd-grade teacher, was having difficulty with disruptive student behaviors during the time students were supposed to be reading. In order to address this problem, she decided to use a DRI procedure whereby she would give students stick-on stars as reinforcers for correct answers to reading quiz questions. Sandy used instructions to specify the relationship between correct responding and awarding of the stars. How and why should this procedure be altered?

7. Roger was a boy who would constantly shake his head from side to side, preventing his trainer from teaching him anything. In order to solve this problem, the trainer used a DRO procedure. For every 10 seconds that passed without Roger shaking his head, he would receive a spoonful of baked beans. The trainer planned to increase gradually the time interval required for reinforcement, and gave Roger clear instruc-

tions that he would receive food only when he did not shake his head. How and why should this procedure be altered?

8. Ted was a high school teacher. One problem he noticed among his students was that they would spend most of their time outside school drinking and taking drugs. To deal with this problem, Ted decided to use a DRI procedure. He assigned 40-page typewritten essays due every 2 weeks from each student. Ted felt that if the students were busy doing schoolwork, they would drink and do drugs less. He talked to local business owners and convinced them to provide him with a wide variety of gift certificates as reinforcers for those students who turned in their essays, with extra reinforcers available for students who did especially good ones. Ted gave the students clear instructions about the relationship between doing the essays and receiving the awards. How and why should this procedure be altered?

9. Ms. Hagey was using a DRO procedure with Jack, one of the boys in her classroom, who would constantly touch and push other students. In order to solve the problem, Ms. Hagey decided to use a DRO procedure. Once every 10 minutes, Ms. Hagey would check to see what Jack was doing. If he wasn't touching or pushing other students, Ms. Hagey would place a token on his desk that would be exchangeable for a variety of awards and privileges. Ms. Hagey planned to increase the size of the time interval required for reinforcement when Jack was meeting the 10-minute criterion. She clearly specified to Jack that receiving the tokens was dependent on not touching the other students. How and why should this procedure be altered?

10. Marvin and Sally worked together in an accounting firm. One problem Sally had with Marvin is that he would often make sexist comments that demeaned her abilities, and only rarely would he say anything complimentary about her skills. Among other things, Marvin often aired his views that women made poor accountants because they lacked mathematical aptitude. In order to try to solve this problem, Sally decided to use an extinction procedure in which she ignored Marvin's demeaning comments about her and other women accountants. She also made it clear to Marvin that she wouldn't listen to his comments about women's abilities. How and why should this procedure be altered?

11. Phil was a student teacher assigned to a 7th-grade classroom full of children who engaged in a variety of disruptive behaviors. One of the children, Lionel, was an expert at making and launching paper airplanes, which delighted the other children in the class, who would cheer on flights of long duration. Phil attempted to deal with this problem using extinction of airplane throwing, combined with positive reinforcement for Lionel's correct responding on his assignments. Phil made it clear to Lionel that he wouldn't receive any attention from him for throwing the airplanes. How and why should this procedure be altered?

12. After playing outside, Benny would often run home screaming and show his mother, Kathryn, a minor scratch or nick. Although Kathryn could see that the problem wasn't serious, she would often hug Benny to calm him down. One day Kathryn decided to use an extinction procedure to deal with the problem. When Benny came home screaming with a very minor injury, she ignored him while he screamed. During this time she made an extra effort to reinforce Benny's wholesome play outside that did not culminate in minor injuries and screaming. She also made sure no one else gave Benny attention for screaming after minor injuries. How and why should this procedure be altered?

chapter 4

Punishment

Baby Sandra came from a poor rural family. During the first months of her life, her family life was unstable. She was cared for by a variety of people, including her mother, her aunt, and even children who lived in the neighborhood. She had failed to gain weight as rapidly as she should have. It was strongly suspected she had been neglected.

When Sandra was 6 months old, her aunt took her to the University of Mississippi hospital. The doctors who examined her found her thin, malnourished, and dehydrated. Normal, healthy 6-month-old infants are responsive to their surroundings, smile or babble frequently, and grasp objects presented to them. Sandra did none of these things. She did cry, but only a little. She spent most of her time lying passively in her crib. Sandra's doctors believed her condition was so grave that she might even die.

Sandra's problem was rumination, bringing up previously swallowed food that is then spit out or reswallowed. After being fed with a liquid formula, Sandra would open her mouth, fold her tongue and elevate it, thrust her tongue forward and backward, and slowly bring up the formula, which dribbled out of her mouth. This process continued for 20 to 40 minutes, until Sandra had lost all the formula she had initially consumed. She appeared to feel no pain or discomfort while she was ruminating, a condition typical of ruminating infants. Studies of infantile rumination have shown that it is a serious problem. Between 10 and 20% of ruminating infants die from malnourishment, dehydration, or lowered resistance to disease.

Sandra was given an extensive set of medical tests to determine if there might be an organic or physical cause for her disorder, but none was found. Three behavior analysts, Thomas Sajwaj, Julian Libet, and Stewart Agras were brought in to work on the case. One option they first considered was to give Sandra electric shock to discourage this behavior when she engaged in rumination. Previous work had shown that shock could be used successfully to treat rumination. However, the behavior analysts did not want to use electric shock for three reasons. First, shock is painful and causes suffering, something Sandra already had had enough of during her young life. Second, the behavior analysts felt that if they used shock, the staff on the pediatrics ward where Sandra was being treated would view the treatment as inhumane and be less likely to cooperate with the procedure. A third consideration was that after Sandra was discharged from the hospital, her caretakers would need to continue the treatment if necessary. The behavior analysts felt that shock treatment was inappropriate considering the instability in Sandra's home life.

Instead, the behavior analyst team decided to use lemon juice to discourage her rumination behavior. Although the taste of lemon juice is unpleasant for infants, it is not painful. It is easy to administer and does not require the close supervision of highly-trained professionals. The regular ward staff could be easily trained to carry out the treatment. Before treatment began, the team carefully measured Sandra's rumination behavior using a technique known as interval recording. They divided time periods into 10-second intervals, and behavior observers noted each interval during which Sandra engaged in the target behavior: the tongue-thrusting movements characteristic of her rumination. They also observed Sandra for 20 minutes immediately after feeding, and she was weighed daily.

This period of time before treatment begins, when the behavior is merely observed and recorded, is called a baseline phase, which provides a record of the level of the behavior before any attempts are made to change it. During baseline, Sandra ruminated during 40% to 70% of the time intervals. Following the baseline phase, the treatment period began. Each time Sandra engaged in the tongue-thrusting movements characteristic of her rumination, lemon juice was squirted into her mouth and she was observed for the next 30 to 60 seconds. If she engaged in the tongue-thrusting movements again after the 30 to 60 second interval had passed, lemon juice was again administered.

As seen in Figure 4.1, during the first 16 feedings when the lemon-juice method was used, rumination was reduced substantially. It occurred in only 10% of the measured time intervals. For the next two feedings the therapy was discontinued and rumination increased to an average of 50% of the measured time intervals. These two feedings were called a reversal phase because the treatment method was withdrawn or reversed. Behavior analysts use reversal to determine if the withdrawal of

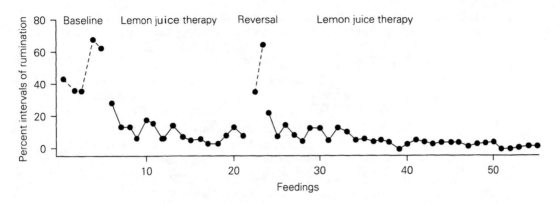

Figure 4.1   *The Effects of the Lemon-Juice Therapy Procedure on Baby Sandra's Eating Behavior*

The incidence of Sandra's ruminating declined during the first lemon-juice therapy phase, returned to baseline levels during reversal, and declined during the second treatment phase. Figure adapted from Sajwaj, Libet, and Agras (1974).

the treatment procedure causes the behavior to revert to its former level. If the behavior change is a result of something other than the treatment, then withdrawal of treatment would not affect its rate. Sandra's ruminating behavior did indeed revert to its former level, providing evidence that there was a cause-effect relationship between the lemon-juice treatment and the reduction in the level of rumination.

Following the brief reversal phase, the lemon-juice therapy was reinstituted and rumination decreased rapidly. After the 12th day of treatment, Sandra no longer brought up formula and the target behaviors, the tongue movements, were reduced to low levels. The behavior observers felt that the rumination behaviors they recorded after the 12th day consisted of nothing more than Sandra's normal lip and tongue movements. However, because rumination was defined in terms of these movements, the observers dutifully continued to record them as instances of rumination.

As the therapy continued, Sandra's physical health improved significantly and her behavior resembled that of a normal infant. During the 8 weeks between initiation of the treatment and Sandra's discharge from the hospital, her weight increased from 8 pounds to 12 pounds. She began smiling, babbling, playfully grasping objects, and paying attention to those around her. After Sandra's discharge from the hospital, she was placed in the care of foster parents, who were trained to use the lemon-juice therapy. After remaining with her foster parents for 5 months, she was returned to her natural parents. Although the behavior analysts feared that Sandra might once again be neglected, continuing follow-up visits to Sandra's home indicated that she remained healthy. At a 10-month follow-up visit, she was given tests of infant development and was found to be only slightly behind the norms for her age. At a 1-year follow-up Sandra's weight had increased to 24 pounds, still light for an infant girl of her age but within an acceptable range.*

*Based on Sajwaj, Libet, and Ágras (1974)

Punishment

Sometimes methods such as extinction, DRO, and DRI are not effective in reducing the level of an undesirable behavior. In Sandra's case, for example, extinction would have been difficult because aspects of the behavior itself likely reinforced her rumination behavior. DRO and DRI would have been difficult because her rumination behavior was at a high level after feeding, leaving little opportunity to reinforce non-rumination or incompatible behaviors. Under conditions like these, behavior analysts must turn to other methods for a solution to the problem. Punishment is a general name for many of these methods. Like DRO, punishment is a response-reduction method that does not build new behavior. It is therefore used within the context of larger programs designed to teach people to behave successfully.

Punishment is a procedure in which a response-dependent stimulus change functions to weaken behavior. In Baby Sandra's case, a stimulus change from no lemon juice to a squirt of lemon juice in her mouth was dependent on her rumination. The reversal phase of her treatment showed that response-dependent use of the lemon juice was indeed responsible for the reduction in Sandra's rumination. Therefore, we can say that Sandra's rumination behavior was punished and that the application of the lemon juice acted as a punisher. Actually, a better test for punishment would be to compare the amount of response reduction that occurred under conditions of response-dependent and response-independent consequences. In Sandra's case this would have meant applying lemon juice independently of rumination responses (i.e., whether or not rumination was occurring). If her ruminating behaviors decreased under these conditions, we could not say that punishment was responsible because punishment must entail response-dependent reductions in behavior. However, because this "better" test of punishment involves more discomfort for the person being treated, it is often omitted.

Punishment always involves the occurrence of a response-dependent stimulus change. In some cases, the stimulus change will involve the presentation of a stimulus; for example, lemon juice was presented to Baby Sandra. In other cases, the stimulus change will involve the removal of a stimulus. Suppose in a token economy we take away a person's tokens dependent on a specific misbehavior and we find that this dependency serves to reduce the level of the misbehavior. This example would also be an example of punishment.

The word *punisher* is often used to refer to a stimulus that, when presented dependent on a response, functions to weaken some measure of the response. For example, the lemon juice used with Baby Sandra was a punisher in this sense. However, technically, the important consequence in punishment is the stimulus change (e.g., the stimulus change from no lemon juice to lemon juice; or the change from a certain quantity of tokens possessed to a reduced quantity of tokens possessed). As such, the word *punisher* can also refer to the stimulus change involved in a punishment procedure. To refer specifically to this stimulus change in punishment procedures, one can talk about the punishing stimulus change.

 As with the definition of reinforcement, the definition of punishment is functional, because it is based on whether the consequence acts or functions to weaken behavior. As such, a punisher for the behavior of one person, like a scolding or a spanking, may not function as a punisher for the behavior of another person. Indeed, for some people, scoldings and spankings are positive reinforcers. As with reinforcement, we say that it is the response that is being punished, not the person.

When a punisher that previously followed a response is withdrawn and the response is strengthened, recovery is said to have occurred. During Baby Sandra's treatment, for example, there was an instance of recovery during the reversal phase when the lemon juice was not administered. Recovery of rumination occurred because the punisher was no longer dependent upon the response. Recovery is to punishment as extinction is to reinforcement. In extinction, discontinuing reinforcer delivery causes a decrease in some measure of the response; in recovery, discontinuing punisher delivery causes an increase in some measure of the response.

In many respects, it is unfortunate that behavior analysts adopted the use of the term *punishment,* because people react to it emotionally and associate the word with cruelty and vindictiveness. When you consider the range of things you call *punishment,* you are likely to think of at least a few instances of beating and torture, for example. These types of activities are not the kind of responsible procedures that behavior analysts use (Mulick, 1990).

Grant and Evans (1992) conducted an experiment in which introductory psychology students studied a lesson designed to teach the concept of punishment. For one group of students, the lesson was entitled "Punishment" and the word *punishment* was used frequently to describe the concept being taught. Two other groups of students studied the same lesson, except that all references to punishment were replaced either by *disinforcement* (Harzem & Miles, 1978) or *attenuation.*

When the procedures were labeled as *disinforcement* or *attenuation,* the students rated them as more acceptable, as having more appropriate uses, and as being more likable than when those same procedures were labeled as *punishment.* As you can see, some negative attitudes that people have about punishment are due to the connotations of the word itself. These connotations sometimes mislead even professional behavior analysts when they discuss this topic (Oldenquist, 1990). Therefore, as you read about the methods described in this chapter, try not to be influenced by any negative feelings you might have about the word *punishment.*

Types of Punishment

Behavior analysts have devised many variations on punishment procedures. The major forms of punishment behavior analysts use are physical punishments, reprimands, timeouts, response costs, and activity punishers.

Physical Punishment

Physical punishers, or unconditioned punishers, are stimuli that act as punishers without having been associated with other punishers. You may recall that uncondi-

tioned reinforcers are similar in that they act as reinforcers without having been associated with other reinforcers. Examples of physical punishers behavior analysts have
used to reduce undesirable behaviors include electric shock, lemon juice, Tabasco
sauce, the smell of ammonia, water-mist spray, loud noises, ice, and tickling. Special
care must be exercised when using physical punishers. For example, lemon juice can
have harmful effects on tooth enamel, and for this reason its use is no longer permitted in many places.

When you think of physical punishment, you may tend to think of painful
things that people do to one another. However, many physical punishers occur naturally in our environment (Azrin & Holz, 1966). Losing your balance is punished by
a skinned knee, careless handling of a hot drink is punished by a burn, gulping food
or water is punished by choking, running through underbrush is punished by scrapes
from thorns, going outside on a very hot or cold day is punished by extremes of
temperature, a child's rough play with a pet is punished by a scratch or a bite, and
inattentive use of tools is punished by injury. Even among infants, a downward view
from a high place acts as a punisher (Walk & Gibson, 1961). Although behavior
analysts seek to minimize the amount of punishment people must encounter, keep in
mind that because of the vulnerability of our bodies and the natural hazards of the
environment in which we live, physical punishment is a fact of life for all of us.

We will consider later in some detail several disadvantages of punishment.
However, one special disadvantage of using physical punishment as a behavior-
change technique is that it is consistently rated as less acceptable than other types of
punishment. For example, Witt and Robins (1985) found that teachers rated corpo-
ral punishment the least acceptable of several response-reduction procedures.
However, even the use of electric shock, considered to be the least acceptable of all
response-reduction methods (Kazdin, 1980a; Miltenberger, Lennox, & Erfanian,
1989; Tarnowski, Mulick, & Rasnake, 1990; Tarnowski, Rasnake, Mulick, & Kelly,
1989), can be viewed as an acceptable procedure if applied to very serious behavior
problems, such as self-destructive behavior, that other methods have failed to solve
(Spreat, Lipinski, Dickerson, Nass, & Dorsey, 1989).

Reprimands

All of us have had the experience of being reprimanded, of having our behavior punished by the words of others. A commonly used reprimand in behavioral treatment is
the simple word "No" made dependent on an undesirable behavior.

Rolider and Van Houten (1984) used reprimands to discourage the physically
abusive behaviors of a 4-year-old Israeli girl named Limor. Limor would hit, pinch,
push, and bear-hug Adi, her 9-month-old baby sister, a decided problem for Adi.
Ever since Adi's birth, Limor had appeared to be jealous of the attention her sister
was getting. Behavior analysts tried a DRO procedure first. For every 15 minutes
that passed without physical abuse of Adi, Limor received a hug, a kiss, and a trinket.
Unfortunately, as Figure 4.2 illustrates, this procedure did not reduce Limor's physically abusive behavior.

The next step in the project was to combine the DRO procedure with reprimands dependent on physical abuse. Every time Limor abused Adi, her mother took Limor by the shoulders, looked her straight in the eyes, told her to stop abusing Adi, that she was hurting Adi, and she was not to do this again. As Figure 4.2 illustrates, adding the reprimand to the DRO method eliminated Limor's abusive behaviors. Over time, Limor's parents ceased using the DRO procedure, but praised Limor when she played with Adi appropriately. They continued using reprimands when necessary, but Limor's physical abuse seldom occurred.

Reprimands have the advantage of being convenient to use and many types of reprimands are relatively acceptable. Under certain conditions, they can be more effective than other types of punishers that take much more time to use (Doleys, Wells, Hobbs, Roberts, & Cartelli, 1976). The ease by which reprimands can be issued can, of course, lead to overuse of them, as suggested by the principle of response energy discussed in Chapter 2.

A concern with the use of reprimands is that they make up a large class of punishers, the individual effects of which can differ a great deal. Reprimands can be very mild, but they can also include some of the cruelest things that people can do to one another. Within behavior analysis, reprimands used to modify behavior have included relatively benign and simple stimuli, not verbalizations that ridicule, embarrass, or belittle the person whose behavior is being punished.

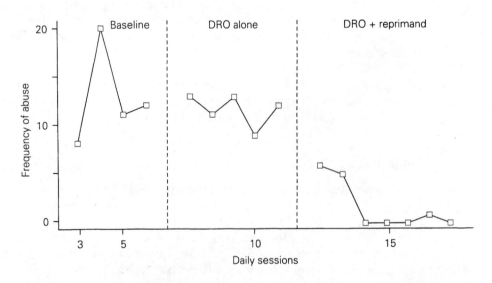

Figure 4.2   *The Effects of DRO Alone and DRO Combined with Reprimands*

The frequency of Limor's aggressive behavior was not reduced by the DRO procedure alone but was virtually eliminated when a reprimand was added. Figure adapted from Rolider and Van Houten (1984).

Timeout

Timeout is a punishment procedure that day-care workers and schoolteachers often use. In timeout, punishment consists of a temporary loss of opportunities for reinforcement. The two major types of this procedure are called exclusionary timeout and nonexclusionary timeout.

Zeilberger, Sampen, and Sloane (1968) used an exclusionary timeout procedure with a boy named Rorey, a 5-year-old who engaged in various forms of physical aggression including hitting, kicking, biting, screaming, and bossing other children. In addition, Rorey would seldom follow his mother's instructions. In order to solve these problems, the behavior analysts stripped one of the bedrooms in Rorey's house of all items that might interest him, and used it as a timeout room. Every time Rorey was aggressive or did not do as he was told, his mother put him in the timeout room for 2 minutes. If he threw a tantrum or cried during the timeout period, 2 more minutes of timeout were added after the tantrum or crying ceased. This procedure, combined with positive reinforcement for Rorey's good behaviors, increased Rorey's compliance with instructions from 30% to 78%, and almost completely eliminated his physical aggression. Rorey was even observed to refrain from retaliating when other children behaved in an aggressive fashion toward him. It seemed to Rorey's parents and several of the neighbors that he was a different boy. Even Rorey's screaming diminished, even though timeout was not dependent on this behavior.

The procedure used with Rorey was exclusionary timeout, sometimes also called isolation timeout, because it consisted of removing Rorey from the situations where his undesirable behaviors occurred. Less severe forms of exclusionary timeout can include chair timeouts, in which a child is made to sit in a chair facing a wall, but in the same room in which the misbehavior occurred.

Griffiths, Bigelow, and Liebson (1977) used nonexclusionary timeout procedures to suppress alcoholics' drinking. The procedures were used on a hospital ward for alcoholic men. During afternoons and evenings, the men could drink up to 17 alcoholic drinks per day, 1 every 40 minutes. During baseline conditions, no consequences were dependent on having a drink, and the men drank close to the maximum permitted. Later, however, a social timeout procedure was used: While drinking, the men were not permitted to socialize with anyone else, although they could engage in recreational activities such as playing pool, watching television, and reading magazines. An activity timeout procedure was also instituted: While drinking, the men were required to sit in a chair for 40-minute periods. During this time, they were not permitted to read, play games, or use any other recreational materials. Finally, investigators combined the social and activity timeout procedures to see what effect this would have on drinking. All three timeout procedures reduced drinking: The social timeout procedure reduced drinking to 71% of the level of baseline drinking, while the activity timeout procedure and the combined social and activity timeout procedure reduced drinking to 36% and 24% of the level of baseline drinking. These methods are called nonexclusionary timeout procedures because the men were permitted to remain on the ward while drinking; timeout curtailed their access to social and activity reinforcers, not to the environment in which drinking took place.

An important advantage of nonexclusionary timeout procedures is that they are likely to be acceptable to people because they do not involve physical isolation and they do not require a special timeout area (Foxx & Shapiro, 1978). However, often an additional back-up punisher must supplement nonexclusionary timeout methods if the individual misbehaves during timeout. For example, Griffiths et al. (1977) levied stiff token fines for men who broke the timeout rules. Similarly, Roberts (1988) showed that brief exclusionary timeouts, such as removal to a timeout room, could enforce timeouts in which a child was required to sit in a timeout chair. Kazdin (1980b) found that university students rated exclusionary timeout as more acceptable when it was used as a back-up punisher to enforce nonexclusionary time-outs than when used as alone.

Timeout can sometimes be ineffective. For example, Solnick, Rincover, and Peterson (1977) found that putting an autistic girl in timeout for throwing tantrums increased rather than decreased the rate of her tantrum behavior. The researchers discovered that while in timeout, the girl engaged in self-stimulation, a highly reinforcing behavior for many autistic children. Similarly, when the normal or "timein" environment places demands on the individual's performance, timeout can serve as a relaxation break and thereby reinforce misbehavior (Plummer, Baer, & LeBlanc, 1977). A child who finds schoolwork difficult and demanding may well prefer time-out because demands to perform are no longer present. In such a case, timeout serves as a reinforcer rather than a punisher.

Response Cost

Response cost is a punishment procedure in which previously earned or awarded reinforcers are removed dependent on a response, and are not necessarily returned. Common examples include token fines for breaking the rules of a token economy and money fines. For example, Miller (1972) used a response-cost procedure to reduce the problem drinking of a 44-year-old married man. The man signed a contract in which he agreed to pay his wife $20 if he consumed more than 3 drinks per day or consumed any alcohol when he was away from his wife. His wife was required to spend the money frivolously. In turn, the wife agreed to pay her husband $20 if she complained about his drinking or responded to it negatively in any way. At first, the man's drinking remained high, at about 7 or 8 drinks per day. However, after the first month, during which he was fined several times, his drinking diminished to fewer than 3 drinks per day. A 6-month follow-up indicated that his drinking remained under the agreed-upon limit. Both the husband and the wife reported that their relationship was much improved.

Response cost is a convenient means of reducing the rate of problem behavior. If the cost is sufficiently high, the response can often be quickly reduced. In addition, because response cost is a commonly used method of punishing violations of legal codes, most people are familiar with it and view it as an acceptable method of reducing behavior problems.

Response cost, sometimes confused with nonexclusionary timeout procedures, involves the more-or-less permanent withdrawal of reinforcers that the individual has previously earned. Nonexclusionary timeout, on the other hand, involves the temporary withdrawal of reinforcement opportunities for a specified period of time, the timeout interval. For example, if a teacher levies a point fine on a child for shouting out in class, this is a response cost procedure because it involves the permanent removal of a reinforcer that the child has previously received. In contrast, if a teacher declares that a child is ineligible for token reinforcement for 10 minutes dependent on that child's shouting out, this is a timeout procedure. Under conditions of timeout then, reinforcers or the opportunities for reinforcement are removed for a specified period of time.

Activity Punishers

In our discussion of the Premack principle in Chapter 2, you saw that preferred, highly probable activities can serve as reinforcers for less preferred, low-probability behaviors. The reverse is also true: A less preferred, low-probability activity may act as a punisher if it is made dependent on a high-probability response. For example, Fischer and Nehs (1978) used a simple activity punisher to reduce the swearing of an 11-year-old boy named Mark. At the dinner table, Mark swore 10.8 times during each 30-minute dinner period. His foster parents, upset with this behavior, had been unable to persuade him to stop swearing. The problem was solved by requiring Mark to engage in 10 minutes of window washing for each time he swore at dinner. This procedure eventually succeeded in virtually eliminating Mark's swearing.

Discussion follows of several types of activity punishers: Arbitrary activity punishers, restitutional overcorrection punishers, positive-practice punishers, and habit reversal punishers.

Arbitrary Activity Punishers. An arbitrary activity punisher is one that bears no logical relationship with the undesirable behavior. Punishing Mark's swearing with required window washing is an example, because window washing behavior is not related in any logical way to swearing behavior. Requiring Mark to write a 500-word essay on why swearing is undesirable, on the other hand, would not be arbitrary because the task has a logical relationship to swearing.

Overcorrection Activity Punishers. With overcorrection activity punishers, the punisher is engaging in an activity that is the opposite of the punished response. One form of overcorrection is called *restitutional overcorrection*, wherein the misbehaving individual is required to overcorrect or overrestore the environmental damage the misbehavior caused. For example, Foxx and Azrin (1972) used a restitutional overcorrection procedure with retarded and brain damaged patients who overturned tables or chairs. The patients were not only required to return the furniture to the correct position, but also to straighten the other furniture in the entire hospital ward. Similarly, when patients frightened or annoyed other people through disruptive behavior, the patients were required to apologize to all those who had been present and to assure everyone that the disruptive acts would not happen again. When patients became agitated and aggressive, they were required to lie down calmly for 15 minutes, a procedure known as quiet training. Finally, when a patient's aggression resulted in wounding a victim, the patient would be required to help clean, medicate, and dress the wound as well as to help fill out accident reports. In each of these cases of restitutional overcorrection, you can see that the activity required of the misbehaving individual produces results opposite to those produced by the punished behavior: Overturned furniture is opposite to upright furniture; frightened people are opposite to reassured people; a wound is opposite to its healing. Because the punished behavior and the overcorrective activity function to produce contrary results, we say that these consequences are functionally opposite.

In another type of overcorrection called *positive-practice overcorrection,* a misbehaving individual is required to practice an appropriate alternative to the punished response. For example, positive-practice overcorrection for a child who has a toileting accident is to require the child to engage repeatedly in proper toileting activities including walking to the toilet, pulling pants down, sitting on the toilet, pulling pants up, and so forth (Foxx & Bechtel, 1983). Azrin and Powers (1975) required students who spoke out in class without being called upon to practice repeatedly raising their hands and waiting for their teacher's permission to speak. In treating self-destructive behavior, Gibbs and Luyben (1985) required a retarded teenager to hold his hands stationary in different positions (e.g., down at the sides, over the head). These hand positions were appropriate response alternatives to the self-destructive response, hand-to-head hits.

Positive-practice overcorrection procedures appear to be useful in promoting the practiced behavior as well as diminishing the punished response. For example, Carey and Bucher (1981) studied a positive-practice overcorrection method in which retarded adults were required to practice 10 correct knife and fork eating movements, with no actual eating, dependent on messy eating. This procedure increased proper eating habits more than another procedure in which the subjects were required to practice a pegboard-puzzle task. In addition, the positive practice made up of correct knife and fork movements promoted correct eating habits more than a restitutional-overcorrection method in which subjects were required to clean themselves, the table, and the floor for 2 minutes, dependent on messy eating. This experiment shows that positive-practice overcorrection can teach desirable behavior at the same time the activity functions as an activity punisher.

Both restitutional and positive-practice overcorrection procedures require the person whose behavior is being punished to engage in an activity. If the misbehaving individual does not follow instructions to perform the activity, part of the overcorrection procedure then is to guide manually the person's body through the required response activity. If the individual then begins performing the activity without assistance, manual guidance is discontinued. Because of the use of manual guidance and careful supervision, overcorrection can require considerable effort to use.

Distinguishing between restitutional and positive-practice overcorrection procedures is not always simple, because the activity punisher will sometimes both overcorrect a harmed environment and be an activity that is an appropriate response alternative to the punished behavior. For example, Azrin and Wesolowski (1974) used an overcorrection procedure called *theft reversal* with retarded adults. The behavior analyst totally eliminated thievery by requiring the thief to return to the victim the stolen item, plus an identical item. This procedure can be considered restitutional overcorrection because the social environment was restored to a better-than-original state: The theft victim was better off materially. It can also be considered positive-practice overcorrection, because the behavior of giving valued items to others is an appropriate response alternative to stealing valued items from others.

In positive-practice overcorrection, subjects repeatedly perform an appropriate response alternative. You may wonder whether repeatedly performing a desirable response alternative is itself sufficient to diminish an undesirable response. Gibbs and Luyben (1985) tested this idea by comparing response-dependent positive practice with response-independent positive practice in attempting to reduce self-destructive behavior. They found that the overcorrection procedure was effective only when it was dependent on the response, indicating that the positive practice was indeed an activity punisher.

A key advantage of overcorrection procedures is that they tend to be viewed as more acceptable response reduction methods than some other forms of punishment. For example, Singh and Katz (1985) found that psychology students rated positive-practice overcorrection to be as acceptable as DRO, and that they rated both these methods as more acceptable than timeouts. Kazdin, French, and Sherick (1981) found similar results for parents and institutional staff. The fact that overcorrection procedures are seen as helping rather than penalizing the individual (Azrin & Powers, 1975; Foxx & Bechtel, 1983) may explain in part the acceptability ratings. Some evidence, however, indicates that the acceptability of overcorrection procedures depends on the specific features of the method. Overcorrection procedures in which the individual learns desirable response alternatives appear to be seen as more acceptable than less constructive procedures (Miltenberger et al., 1989).

Habit Reversal Punishers.   Another type of activity punisher is known as habit reversal (Azrin & Nunn, 1973). Habit reversal procedures have been used to reduce various nervous muscle and vocal tics including eye blinking, mouth twitching, head jerking, hair pulling, nail biting, barking, and throat clearing. In habit reversal, the individual is required to engage repeatedly in a competing response, one that is incompatible with the undesirable response. For example, habit reversal procedures have been used to treat Tourette syndrome, a disorder in which the person suffers from frequent muscular and vocal tics (Azrin & Peterson, 1988). In this study, a 42-year-old man had suffered from head jerks, barking, coughing, and throat clearing for 32 years. The treatment required the man to engage in neck muscle contraction, a response that is opposite to head jerking. In addition, he was to practice rhythmic deep breathing with his mouth closed, a response opposite to barking, coughing, and throat clearing. During the first month, the habit reversal procedure reduced muscular and vocal tics 74% in the clinic and 66% at the man's home. These reductions were maintained after 8 months.

Several recent findings have enhanced our understanding of the effectiveness of habit reversal. Miltenberger and Fuqua (1985) found that response-dependent practice of the competing response weakened the target behavior but response-independent practice did not. This finding suggests that habit reversal is effective because it serves as an activity punisher. Sharenow, Fuqua, and Miltenberger (1989) reported that practice of either a similar or a dissimilar response could punish nervous tics. A woman's mouth twitches were effectively punished by requiring her to tighten her right arm muscle and to clench her left fist for 3 minutes after a mouth twitch had occurred. Later, requiring the woman to clench her jaw for 3 minutes dependent on mouth twitches also continued to punish the response. These data suggest that the physical nature of the competing response is not a key feature of habit reversal techniques.

Advantages of Punishment

Research has shown that punishment does have some advantages in rapid elimination of the undesirable response and desirable changes in unpunished behaviors.

In many instances of punishment, the procedure is successful in rapidly reducing or completely eliminating an undesirable behavior. Several of the examples we have considered, including the case of Baby Sandra, have illustrated this feature of punishment. In contrast, DRO and DRI procedures often take weeks of careful use before they produce a substantial weakening of the undesired response. This rapid-elimination feature of punishment is particularly useful for behaviors such as self-destructive or extremely aggressive behaviors that are not tolerable even when they occur at a very low rate.

To be effective in rapidly reducing the rate of an undesirable response, punishment must be reasonably intense, which presents an ethical question. Suppose we have a response that causes harm to the person who engages in it or harm to others. Is it better to eliminate that response rapidly with a relatively intense punisher or is it more humane to use a weaker procedure and be content with gradual or incomplete response elimination? This question is a focus of continuing debate.

Another advantage to punishment is *desirable change in nontarget behavior.* Many studies have reported both increases in desirable behaviors and decreases in undesirable unpunished behaviors due to the use of various forms of punishment (Brantner & Doherty, 1983; Foxx & Bechtel, 1983; Johnston, 1972; Lichstein & Schreibman, 1976; Matson & Taras, 1989).

Several of the studies we have examined in this chapter illustrate beneficial by-products of punishment procedures. You may recall that Baby Sandra showed an increase in smiling, babbling, and playing with objects, even though none of these behaviors were target behaviors. In the example of Limor, the girl who abused her baby sister, her "jealous" imitation of the baby's movements and verbalizations decreased, even though these behaviors were not punished. Rorey, who was treated with response-dependent timeout for aggressive behavior, stopped yelling, even though yelling was not specifically punished. In the case of the man whose alcohol consumption was decreased through response cost, observers noted improvements in his and his wife's social behaviors. In Foxx and Azrin's (1972) study, two of the women treated through restitutional overcorrection procedures increased their appropriate social interactions, and one of them began paying more attention to her personal appearance. In their study of positive-practice overcorrection to reduce messy eating, Carey and Bucher found that the procedure encouraged the positively practiced behavior, the use of a knife and fork. Finally, Azrin and Peterson found that one of their Tourette syndrome subjects treated through habit reversal was able to cease taking a drug to control his condition. As you can see even from this small sample of studies, much evidence indicates that punishment procedures have desirable effects beyond simply reducing the targeted response.

Disadvantages of Punishment

Some research has reported undesirable side effects associated with the use of punishment. These side effects have included emotional behaviors, aggression, inappropriate response substitution, the imitation of the use of punishment, the self-perpetuating nature of punishment, the establishment of inappropriate conditioned punishers, and escape and avoidance. Another disadvantage of punishment is that people find these methods less acceptable than other behavior-change techniques. Planners of a behavioral program must carefully consider the disadvantages of punishment. Nonetheless, much research indicates that their are conditions in which the benefits of punishment procedures can outweigh the disadvantages (Foxx & Bechtel, 1983; Lichstein & Schreibman, 1976; Matson & Taras, 1989; Newsom, Favell, & Rincover, 1983).

Emotional Behaviors

Emotional side effects of punishment include crying, tantrums, and agitation. As with extinction, one typically sees these types of effects when punishment is initially used. For example, in the Zeilberger et al. (1968) study, Rorey threw tantrums during much of the 19 minutes he spent in the first timeout period, but after the first day, his tantrums were brief.

Aggressive Behaviors

Aggression can also be produced by punishment. Oliver, West, and Sloane (1974) had 10 inpatient alcoholic men work on a plunger-pulling task. Tokens exchangeable for money or cigarettes reinforced the task. During some sessions, the men received strong response-independent shocks, but during other sessions they did not. By flipping a switch, the men could themselves shock a man they were told was an observer. The observer, who sat with the men, was really an experimenter. During the shock sessions, the men shocked the observer at an average rate of 16 times per session, but during no-shock sessions, the men shocked the observer only 1.7 times per session. Shocks to the observer had no effect on the shocks the men received.

Undesired Response Substitution

A rare effect of punishment is elimination or reduction of the target behavior along with an increase in another undesirable behavior. Miltenberger, Fuqua, and McKinley (1985) found such an effect in their study of habit reversal. Treatment of a facial tic was successful in eliminating the tic, but a new problem behavior, teeth tapping and grinding, emerged. However, this new behavior was less frequent and much less annoying than the original problem. A suspected cause of inappropriate response substitution is a poorly planned behavior change program in which one behavior is punished without reinforcing an appropriate alternative response (Reese, Howard, & Reese, 1978, p. 73). As we have emphasized, punishment should be used only as one component of a larger program that teaches effective behaviors.

Undesired Response Imitation

A story is told of a household in which a parent while spanking her child says, "This will teach you to hit other children." It is wise to consider what lessons others learn from us when we use behavior-change techniques. When we use punishment, we are demonstrating the fact that punishment works, and this demonstration may result in inappropriate imitation of the act of punishment.

Gelfand et al. (1974) examined this effect in an experiment with first and second graders. The children played a game by dropping marbles into a box. Some of the drops were hits and made a green light flash and a high tone sound, while other drops were misses that made a red light flash and a low tone sound. Hits and misses had nothing to do with the children's accuracy, but were predetermined according to a schedule that was the same for all the children: 15 hits and 15 misses. The children were given 30 pennies to start. One group of children worked with an adult who fined the children one penny for each miss. In another group, an adult was present while the children played the game, but that adult did not reinforce or punish the children's responding. After working with the adult, each child then became a "teacher" child who worked with a "learner" child who had not been given any training. All the teacher children were told they could give points exchangeable for pennies for hits or subtract pennies dependent on misses. The results showed that the teacher children who had been previously fined by the adults, themselves fined the learner children for almost all misses. However, the teacher children not previously fined by the adult very seldom fined the learner children for misses. Essentially, the children imitated the procedure to which they themselves had been subjected.

The imitation of punishment is a difficult problem because much of the time when a punishment procedure is used, those who observe it learn that punishment can effectively put a stop to unwanted behavior. In contrast, most observers are less likely to see that other methods to treat the problem have failed, that the use of punishment is being combined with slower acting reinforcement as a part of a larger program, and that many precautions and considerations have been observed in deciding whether and how to use punishment.

The Self-perpetuating Nature of Punishment

Parental use of punishment as a behavior control technique is prevalent, perhaps because of the reinforcing effect on the behavior of the parent who administers punishment. Administering a punisher is often immediately followed by the cessation of the undesirable behavior, a result that is highly reinforcing. The use of punishment to accomplish this effect often requires little energy, as in a reprimand. In contrast, when techniques such as DRO, DRI, and extinction are used to reduce an undesirable response, a considerable amount of effort is required to establish the program, and when favorable results are achieved, they are often not immediate. For these reasons, many people fall into a trap of constantly using punishment to reduce undesirable behaviors. When used prudently, punishment has the advantage of producing rapid behavior change and seems particularly useful for behaviors that are dangerous to the individual engaging in them or to others in the social environment. When other behavior-change techniques have been tried and found wanting, punishment may be the treatment of choice.

Inappropriate Conditioned Punishers

When punishment is used, the punisher is associated with all the stimuli in the surrounding environment, possibly establishing these stimuli as conditioned punishers. These conditioned punishers can sometimes be undesirable. For example, when a person of a different nationality punishes someone's behavior, there is a chance that the nationality itself can become established as a conditioned punisher. This once happened to the eminent behavior analyst, B. F. Skinner. Although normally a very polite and courteous man, Dr. Skinner (1983, p. 270) made some self-described errors in his social behavior, and his British hosts punished these errors. For several months afterward, Dr. Skinner found that British accents, British films, and even references to the city of London were conditioned punishers. In this case, nothing about the Britishness of Dr. Skinner's hosts had anything to do with his misbehavior or with the delivery of the punishers. The mere fact that the punishment occurred in a British environment was sufficient to establish the British stimuli as punishers.

When punishment is used, there is a great risk that any stimuli in the environment in which punishment occurs will become conditioned punishers. One often sees these types of effects in day-to-day life. As Dr. Skinner's example suggests, many ethnic fears and prejudices appear to be due to punishing experiences. Similarly, for children punished in educational environments, books, teachers, and the learning process itself can become established as conditioned punishers.

Escape and Avoidance

Punishers act to weaken responses on which they are dependent. However, another common effect of punishers is to encourage behavior that allows either escape from or avoidance of the punishing consequence (Boren & Colman, 1970; Morris & Redd, 1975; Azrin & Powell, 1968; Redd, Morris, & Martin, 1975). Morris and Redd studied this aspect of punishment with three nursery school boys who were working on a color-sorting task. All the children worked with men who (a) praised on-task behaviors; (b) reprimanded off-task behaviors; (c) both praised on-task behavior and reprimanded off-task behavior; or (d) were present but ignored the child's behavior. Results of the study showed that when the children worked with men who used reprimands or with men who used a combination of reprimands and praise, the children got to work sooner, spent more time on-task, and sorted more colors than when the children worked with men who used only praise or with men who ignored them. However, when children selected the men they would most like to play with, the man who used only praise was most preferred as playmate. The man who ignored the child was the next most preferred, and the man who used both praise and reprimands was the third most preferred. The man who used only reprimands was by far the least preferred. These data show that even when punishment eliminates undesirable behaviors, the person who administers the punishers may be avoided.

Lack of Acceptance of Punishment

In general, punishment procedures are rated as less acceptable response-reduction techniques than DRO and DRI (Kazdin, 1980a, 1980b; Kazdin, French, & Sherick, 1981; Miltenberger et al., 1989; Singh & Katz, 1985; Singh, Watson, & Winton, 1987; Tarnowski et al., 1989; Tarnowski et al., 1990; Witt & Robbins, 1985).

Behavior analysts have studied some of the conditions that make procedures acceptable. Singh and Katz found that by teaching students about the nature and purpose of punishment procedures, the students were more likely to find punishment techniques acceptable. Tarnowski et al. (1989) found that behavioral procedures were more acceptable to staff at institutions that made use of those procedures compared to institutions that did not. Kazdin (1980b) found that another way to increase the acceptability of punishment is to have the individual whose behavior is being punished to sign a "contingency contract" in which the individual agrees to the procedure in advance. Therefore, familiarity with punishment procedures and advance agreement to their use serve to increase their acceptability.

Making Punishment Effective

Important parameters of punishment include the use of reinforcement of alternative behaviors, consistency of punishment, instructions, minimizing reinforcement of the punished response, the extent of previous unpunished responding, punisher variety, delay of punishment, the rapidity of punishment, punishment intensity, using predictive conditioned punishers, and punishment contrast effects.

Reinforcing a Desirable Alternative Behavior

When punishment must be used, it is desirable to combine the procedure with reinforcement of a desirable alternative response (Herman & Azrin, 1964; Holz, Azrin, & Ayllon, 1963; Perry & Parke, 1975). Punishment is a response elimination procedure that does not in and of itself teach new behavior. Appropriate use of punishment carries with it the responsibility to specify desirable behaviors that natural reinforcers will ultimately sustain.

Perry and Parke studied the influence of reinforcing an alternative response on the effectiveness of punishment using first, second, and third grade boys. Each boy was presented with two toys, an attractive one and an ordinary one. When boys in a punishment group chose to play with the attractive toy, a loud buzzer would sound and the experimenter would issue a reprimand. In a punishment plus reinforcement group, the buzzer and reprimand also punished choice of the attractive toy, but these boys were also prompted to play with the ordinary toy and praised when they did so. On later test trials, the experimenter left the room and the boys were observed to see if they would play with the prohibited toy. The boys in the group in which the alternative response, play with the ordinary toy, had been reinforced, chose to play with the prohibited toy less often than the boys in the group in which the alternative response had not been reinforced.

In much applied research, it is not difficult to determine which alternative responses should be reinforced. For example, Larson and Ayllon (1990) used parental attention to reinforce quiet, alert behaviors of babies troubled with infantile colic. Andrews (1989) treated a woman who had been brain damaged by a drug overdose in a suicide attempt. As a part of a timeout program to eliminate her screaming episodes, she was placed in a busy passageway where people could interact with her when she was behaving well.

Often, behavior analysts must be creative in finding an alternative response to reinforce. Lane, Wesolowski, and Burke (1989) worked with a brain-injured man named Stan who collected and hoarded garbage. Several response-reduction procedures had been tried but were found ineffective and had caused emotional side effects. The solution to the problem was to combine timeout with reinforcement of two alternative behaviors: collecting baseball cards and collecting and disposing of trash. Initially, Stan was taught to collect baseball cards. When cards had become reinforcers for his behavior, he was told to pick up and dispose of trash with a glove and apron to keep him clean. Trash pickup and disposal was reinforced with baseball cards. In this way, hoarding garbage was eliminated. At the same time Stan found a hobby he could enjoy. Later, the success of the program led to Stan being hired at a local campground where he picked up and properly disposed of trash littered there.

Consistency of Punishment

In general, the greater the proportion of responses made that are punished, the more effective punishment will be (Acker & O'Leary, 1988; Clark, Rowbury, Baer, & Baer, 1973; Kircher, Pear, & Martin, 1971; Pierce & Risley, 1974). Therefore, to make punishment most effective, each instance of the undesirable behavior should be punished. Clark et al. (1973) worked with an 8-year-old retarded girl named Bertha who was attending preschool. Bertha, who was older and larger than the other children in the preschool, engaged in several behaviors that disrupted school activities and were dangerous to other children. Target behaviors selected for change included choking, bear hugging, throwing other children to the floor and pouncing on them, and damaging schoolroom materials. Three different types of intermittent punishment were examined: (a) punishing an average of one out of every eight occurrences of the target behavior; (b) punishing an average of one out of every four occurrences of the target behavior; and (c) punishing an average of one out of every three occurrences of the target behavior. The results of the experiment are illustrated in Figure 4.3.

As you can see, the greater the percentage of responses punished, the more effective punishment was in reducing the level of the aggressive and disruptive behavior.

Why is consistency of punishment so important? Behavior analysis principles suggest that undesirable responses often occur because they are being reinforced in some way, even though we may not be aware of the specific nature of that reinforcer. Failure to punish an occurrence of the response should not, therefore, be seen as having no effect on behavior strength. It is more likely to be the case that each time the response goes unpunished, it is also being strengthened because it is reinforced in some way.

Problems with inconsistent punishment are commonplace in our natural environment. Children misbehave because they are inconsistently punished and so some instances of misbehavior are reinforced. Our system of law enforcement, from traffic ordinances to criminal statutes, is essentially a system that seeks to deter violations of

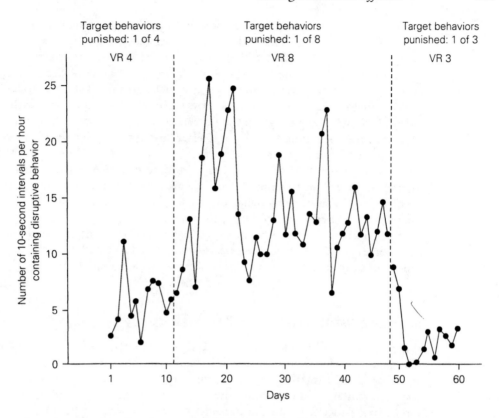

Figure 4.3   *The Influence of the Consistency of Punishment on the Effectiveness of Punishment*

The incidence of Bertha's disruptive behavior was much lower when the behavior was punished on an average of one of every three or four occurrences than an average of one of every eight. Figure adapted from Clark et al. (1973).

the law through intermittent punishment because it is not feasible to observe and punish each violation. Unfortunately this pragmatic constraint results in lowered effectiveness of the punishment procedure.

Instructions

Punishment procedures should be accompanied by instructions that clearly specify the undesired response and its consequences. Instructions that specify not to perform the undesired response (e.g., "I don't want you to do X") are more effective than instructions that only specify engaging in a desired alternative response (e.g., "I want you to do Y") (Redd, Amen, Meddock, & Winston, 1974).

   There is also evidence that instructions should specify why the punished response is undesirable. For example, Parke (1969) placed toys in view of first- and second-grade boys. One group of boys were told not to touch some of the toys: If they did, a loud buzzer would sound. A second group of boys, given the same instructions, were provided with a reason for the restriction: The toys would break or wear out such that they could no longer be used. The boys were trained and tested one at a time. During training, the loud buzzer punished the touching of the prohibited toys. During testing, the boys were left alone in a room with the toys in view. The boys who were given the instructions with a reason touched the forbidden toys less often, less quickly, and for a lesser amount of time than the boys given the instructions without the reason.

Aside from their effect in increasing the effectiveness of punishment, it is important to use instructions because they increase the acceptability of punishment procedures. When people's behavior is punished without their first being told about the response-punisher dependency, they are apt to view the procedure as unfair and the undesirable side-effects of the procedure worsen. In contrast, when the response-punisher dependency is clearly specified and agreed to by all concerned, punishment procedures are apt to be seen as more acceptable (Kazdin, 1980b).

Minimizing Reinforcement of the Punished Response

When using punishment, it is crucial to do everything possible either to eliminate or minimize the effectiveness of possible reinforcers for the punished response. There are two reasons for this. First, lessening reinforcers dependent on the punished response will assist in weakening the response through punishment. Second, if reinforcers are associated with the punisher or with delivery of the punisher, there is a danger that the punisher itself will become a signal for reinforcement.

Some research has explored the extent to which reinforcers can compete with and override the effects of punishers (McGovern, Ditzian, & Taylor, 1975; Thomson, 1983). For example, McGovern et al. (1975) used an experimental arrangement in which male university students were faced with a situation in which they could choose to accept an electric shock or let the shock be delivered to a woman. The woman posed as a subject, but was really assisting with the experiment. The woman told one group of men "Thank you" when they complied with her request to accept a shock. She did not tell another group of men "Thank you" if they complied with the request. From that point in the experiment, the men she told "Thank you" a single time went on accepting many shocks, while the men not told "Thank you" accepted far fewer shocks.

Making both reinforcers and punishers dependent on the same response is a dangerous mix. It is often difficult for parents and others who use punishment to avoid reinforcing the behavior targeted for punishment. For example, often a child who cries when his or her behavior is punished receives sympathy and attention, reinforcers that can strengthen the undesirable behavior and thereby teach the child that punishment is a signal for forthcoming reinforcing attention and sympathy. Couples who mix affection with rebuke for one another create the same paradox: They establish negative behaviors as cues for reinforcement. A much better practice is to administer punishment unemotionally, and to save expressions of affection for later instances of desirable behavior.

Minimizing reinforcement for the punished response is a special concern with social punishers such as reprimands. Because reprimands are a form of attention, there is a danger that the attention of the reprimand will act as a reinforcer at the same time the content of the reprimand acts as a punisher for the undesirable response (Gallimore, Tharp, & Kemp, 1969; Jones, Sloane, & Roberts, 1992; Madsen, Becker, Thomas, Koser, & Plager, 1968). Research has shown that it is best for reprimands to be kept brief (Abramowitz, O'Leary, & Futtersak, 1988; Pfiffner & O'Leary, 1989). Brief reprimands minimize the amount of reinforcing attention provided for the punished response.

Recall that in Chapter 2 we discussed several conditions that influence the effectiveness of reinforcement, including satiation, reinforcer amount, predictive conditioned reinforcers, reinforcer variety, response energy, and reinforcement delay. Each of these conditions can be used to decrease the effectiveness of reinforcement of the punished response and thereby increase the effectiveness of punishment. For example, suppose a responsible municipality wishes to reduce the number of handguns registered and uses a response-cost procedure by requiring a $1,000 fee for handgun registration. This punishment procedure could, in principle, be made even more effective by increasing the response energy needed by making applicants fill out a long form, thereby suppressing the number of frivolous and impetuous registrations.

Extent of Previous Unpunished Responding

The principle of previous unpunished responding is that the lesser the extent of previous unpunished responding, the greater the effectiveness of the punisher. Karsh and Williams (1964) studied this principle in an experiment using kindergarten children as subjects. The researchers taught the children to press a lever by making candy dependent on lever presses. Lever pressing of one group of children went unpunished for 1 day, followed by 2 days during which the candy reinforcers were also accompanied by 2 punishers, a loud noise, and the experimenter's reprimand. For a second group of children, candy reinforced lever pressing for 3 days, followed by 2 days during which the 2 punishers were also made dependent on lever pressing. A control group of children received 5 days of reinforced responding without punishment. Using response latency as a measure, Karsh and Williams showed that the punishers were effective in slowing down the responding of the children whose behavior was punished after only a single day of unpunished training. However, the punishers for the group who had 3 days of unpunished training were ineffective.

Punisher Variety

As with reinforcement, punishment is more effective if several different punishers are made dependent on the response. Charlop, Burgio, Iwata, and Ivancic (1988) demonstrated this aspect of punishment in work with three retarded children who were between 5 and 7 years old. The children engaged in several undesirable behaviors including aggression, self-stimulation, and self-destruction. During some of the other sessions, experimenters alternated three different punishers to punish the children's behaviors. The punishers included overcorrection, presentation of a loud noise, timeout, and the reprimand "No." During other experimental sessions, the children's behaviors were punished using only one of the punishers. For all three children, the alternating use of three different punishers was more effective in reducing the frequency of the undesirable responding than application of a single punisher.

In many instances, use of intense punishers is prohibited or discouraged, making it necessary to use only mild punishers. An important practical implication of the varied punishment procedure is that it can enhance the effectiveness of several mild punishers (Charlop et al., 1988). Although investigators do not fully understand the reason for the effectiveness of varied punishers over a single punisher, Charlop et al. (1988) considered several possible explanations. One possibility is habituation, a reduction in responding to a stimulus due to continued exposure to that stimulus. For example, Weinstein (1969) found that continued application of shock decreased its effectiveness as a punisher for the behavior of students working on math problems. Use of varied punishers may minimize this effect because each punisher is repeatedly presented much less than when a single punisher is used.

Delay of Punishment

Two major principles are concerned with delay of punishment. The principle of immediate punishment is that the shorter the delay between the completion of the response and the occurrence of the punisher, the more effective the punisher will be (Banks & Vogel-Sprott, 1965; Setterington & Walters, 1964; Vogel-Sprott, 1967; Walters, 1964). Vogel-Sprott demonstrated this principle in an experiment in which she instructed undergraduates to push four buttons in a display panel. Successful button-pushing patterns resulted in the immediate presentation of a sum of money. One group of students received an electric shock at the same time that they received the money, but for three other groups the shock was delayed for 10 seconds, 20 seconds, or 30 seconds following the correct response.

Results of the study, illustrated in Figure 4.4, showed that the immediately punished group emitted fewer correct responses on 20 test trials than the 3 delayed-punishment groups. Although immediate punishment is most effective and should be used whenever possible, delayed punishment, like delayed reinforcement, can be made effective if a verbal mediator bridges the delay. For example, Verna (1977) found that a 4-hour delay of response-cost punishment could be as effective as immediate punishment if the children were given specific verbal instruction about why their behavior was being punished.

One problem with punishment is that an appropriate person is not always available to present the punishing event immediately upon the occurrence of the undesir-

Figure 4.4   *The Influence of Immediacy of Punishment on the Effectiveness of Punishment*

The students emitted fewer button-pushing responses when punishment was immediate than when punishment was delayed. Figure adapted from Vogel-Sprott (1967).

able behavior. For example, student misbehavior is probably more appropriately punished by parents rather than by teachers, but parents are often not available to provide immediate consequences for undesirable classroom behaviors. Bailey, Wolf, and Phillips (1970) addressed this problem in a study in which teachers gave students a daily report card that indicated whether the student had worked hard at school and had obeyed school rules. When the students' report cards indicated they had not studied and disobeyed the rules, parents punished these behaviors by withdrawing privileges such as snacks, television, and outdoor play. Students could earn back these privileges only by doing extra chores. Even though punisher delivery was delayed several hours, the procedure was effective in virtually eliminating violations of school rules.

One situation when many parents have difficulty applying immediate punishment is in a public place, where accusing and annoyed glances from bystanders inhibit adherence to the principle of consistent punishment. Rolider and Van Houten (1985a) addressed this problem in work with a 10-year-old boy named Michael who had been labeled psychotic and who frequently threw public tantrums. Treatment consisted of audiotaping those tantrums. Later at home, Michael's mother and father played back the tape to Michael, who was then put into timeout by being put in a corner for 35 seconds during which he was not permitted to move. This method of playing the tape and using timeout was repeated 3 times. This procedure, called audiotape-mediated punishment, successfully eliminated Michael's public tantrums.

Van Houten and Rolider (1988) explored another method of delayed punishment called re-create-the-scene. Shawn, a 4-year-old boy, bit other children and stomped on their feet. When it was learned that Shawn had bitten another boy, behavior analysts enlisted that boy's help. They re-created the biting scene by having Shawn sit next to his victim as he had when the misbehavior originally occurred. Next, when Shawn's face came close to the boy's cheek, the boy cried, as he had been told to do. Experimenters then immediately and firmly restrained Shawn's head and guided it toward his victim's face with Shawn's lips pulled back to expose his teeth. Shawn was then reprimanded and given a corner timeout with no movement permitted. A similar method was used to discourage Shawn's foot stomping. These procedures eliminated both biting and foot stomping.

A second principle concerned with delayed punishment is the principle of early punishment: In general, the earlier an ongoing response is punished following its onset, the more effective the punisher will be. Often an undesirable response consists of a sequence of ongoing behavior. The earlier the punisher occurs within this response sequence, the more effective the punisher will be (Abramowitz & O'Leary, 1990; Aronfreed & Reber, 1965; Cheyne, 1971; Fonagy & Slade, 1982; Parke, 1969; Walters, Parke, & Cane, 1965). The principles of immediate and early punishment are similar, but not identical. The immediate punishment principle specifies that if the response has already ceased, the punisher should be delivered as soon as possible. The early punishment principle is that an ongoing response should be punished as soon as possible after it begins occurring. Some behaviors, such as out-of-seat behavior in the classroom, are clearly definable as undesirable when they begin occurring. For such responses, the early punishment principle applies. However, other behaviors, such as misspelling or incorrect arithmetic problem solving, are definable as undesirable only after they have ceased to occur. For these responses, the immediate punishment principle applies.

Cheyne (1971) studied the early punishment principle using first-grade boys as subjects. With an experimenter present in the room, several toys were placed on a table at which a boy was seated. In an early punishment group, when a boy reached for a forbidden toy, this response was punished by either a loud buzzer or the experimenter's reprimand of "No, that's wrong." In a late punishment group, experimenters permitted 6 seconds of play with the toy before delivering the punisher. Later, when the experimenter left the room, observers watched the boys through a one-way mirror. Boys in the late punishment group played with the forbidden toys sooner and longer than boys in the early punishment group, showing the increased effectiveness of delivering the punisher early in the behavioral sequence rather than later.

Abramowitz and O'Leary studied the principle of early punishment in a classroom setting. Reprimands were more effective in reducing student socializing if delivered as soon as the behavior occurred than if delivered only after 2 minutes of socializing. The researchers explained this effect in terms of the way early punishers prevent reinforcement of the undesirable behavior. Specifically, early punishers can suppress the response before there is an opportunity for the response to be strengthened through reinforcement. In contrast, when a response is punished late in a response sequence, after reinforcement has occurred, the weakening effects of the punisher must compete with the strengthening effects of the reinforcer.

Punishment Intensity

In general, the greater the magnitude or intensity of the punisher, the more effective it will be. Burchard and Barrera (1972) studied the effects of both timeout and response cost procedures on the behavior of 6 mildly retarded teenage boys who engaged in high levels of antisocial behavior. Target behaviors in the study included swearing, personal assaults, property damage, and stealing. The purpose of the study was to assess the effects on behavior of timeout duration and severity of response cost. On some days, the timeout period was 5 minutes while on others it was 30 minutes. Similarly, on some days, response cost was 5 tokens while on others it was 30 tokens. A visual signal posted in the unit dayroom informed the boys about the specific penalty in effect that day.

Figures 4.5a and 4.5b show that Burchard and Barrera found that the greater the amount of the punisher, the more effective the punisher was. The 30-token penalties were more effective than the 5-token penalty and the 30-minute timeout duration was more effective than the 5-minute timeout duration.

Like reinforcers, punishers consist of a change from one stimulus condition to another, from a prechange to a postchange stimulus condition. The change from the normal environment to the timeout environment is an example of such a change. Therefore, we can increase the intensity of a punisher by making the postchange conditions more aversive or by making the prechange conditions more reinforcing. For example, Solnick, Rincover, and Peterson (1977) initially found that a timeout

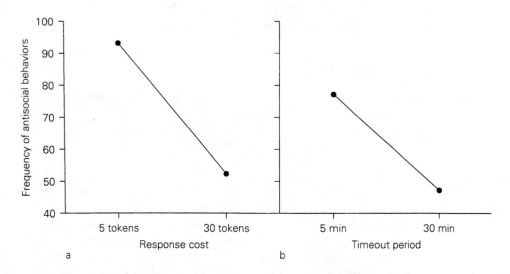

Figure 4.5　　*The Influence of Amount of the Punisher on the Effectiveness of the Punisher*

The boys' antisocial behavior was reduced much more when the response cost was 30 tokens than when it was 5 tokens. The 30-minute timeout reduced the boys' antisocial behavior much more than the 5-minute timeout. Figures adapted from Burchard and Barrera (1972).

procedure was ineffective in reducing the spitting and self-destructive behaviors of a retarded teenager. However, when the normal or "timein" environment was made more attractive through the addition of toys and music, the timeout procedure was effective in reducing the undesirable behaviors to low levels.

In everyday life, one sees examples of the ineffectiveness of punishment due to an unreinforcing normal environment. For a homeless person in harsh weather, going to jail for committing a minor crime can be a reinforcing rather than a punishing consequence. For a youth who has known only poverty and abuse at home, the "punishments" that society has to offer are often only marginally effective.

Other work addressing the issue of punishment-intensity effects has shown that punishers are summative in their effects: Making two different punishers dependent on a response is more effective than is either punisher used alone. For example, Van Houten, Nau, MacKenzie-Keating, Sameoto, and Colavecchia (1982) worked with two boys who engaged in a variety of disruptive classroom behaviors. When the teacher's verbal reprimands were made dependent upon the disruptive responding, these responses became less frequent. However, nonverbal reprimands, consisting of the teacher making eye contact with the boys and holding them by the arm while delivering the verbal reprimand, reduced the frequency of the disruptive behaviors more than verbal reprimands used alone.

Although punishers of greater intensity tend to be more effective than weaker punishers, it does not follow that punishers should always be intense. Intense punishers are apt to produce more undesirable side effects. Using intense punishers for relatively minor transgressions is apt to violate our sense of fairness and be considered unacceptable. For these reasons, punishers should only be used in intensities sufficient to eliminate the undesirable response.

Predictiveness of Conditioned Punishers

Like conditioned reinforcers, conditioned punishers gain their effectiveness through association with other punishers. In order to be effective, conditioned punishers must reliably predict that other punishers are on the way.

The principle of predictive conditioned punishers is applicable to reprimands, an important form of conditioned punishers that behavior analysts use. Dorsey, Iwata, Ong, and McSween (1980) worked with two retarded women, Cindy, 21, and Sally, 26, who bit their hands. The experimenters had used various procedures to solve this problem, but without success. At first, the word "No" was made dependent on hand-bites, but saying "No" failed to reduce the target behavior. Afterward, "No" was combined with a spray of water mist directed toward Cindy's and Sally's faces, establishing "No" as an effective punisher. Afterward, saying "No" alone was capable of punishing Cindy's and Sally's hand biting in situations other than the situation in which "No" was combined with water mist.

One often sees the principle of predictive conditioned punishers in day-to-day life. A parent's reprimands will work after they are backed up by physical punishment, response-cost, or timeout, but over time when they no longer predict other punishers, they lose their effectiveness. On the other hand, when it predicts other punishers to come, a gesture as slight as a raised eyebrow can be a very effective punisher.

Punishment Contrast Effects

As with reinforcers, a prior history of punishment influences the effectiveness of punishers. One documented kind of contrast effect is a negative contrast effect, which a sequence of conditions defines: A response is initially punished by a relatively intense punisher, the intensity of the punisher is reduced, and because of the reduction in punishment intensity, the weaker punisher is less effective than it would have been if the stronger punisher had not preceded it.

White, Nielsen, and Johnson (1972) reported a negative punishment contrast effect in a study of timeout duration. Twenty retarded children who lived in a state institution engaged in several disruptive behaviors including aggression, self-destruction, tantrums, and running away from their cottage. To solve the problem, the investigators placed the children in a timeout room when they engaged in the disruptive behaviors. Length of stay in the timeout room was 1 minute, 15 minutes, or 30 minutes. Three different orders of timeout duration were used. Group A received the 1-minute timeout first, the 15-minute timeout second, and the 30-minute timeout third. Group B received the timeouts in the sequence of 30 minutes, 1 minute, and 15 minutes. Group C received the timeouts in the order of 15 minutes, 30 minutes, and 1 minute. The results showed that the 1-minute timeout was most effective for Group A, which received it first, and least effective for Group C, which received it last, after a history of longer timeout periods. Figure 4.6 shows how effective the 1-minute timeouts were for Groups A, B, and C.

One must consider negative punishment contrast effects when selecting the initial intensity of the punisher. Consider what might happen if we choose a relatively weak punisher and find that it does not work. We are then confronted with a situation in which we must increase punisher intensity more than would have been necessary had we not used the weak punisher to begin with. On the other hand, consider what might happen if we choose an initial punisher that is too intense. Undesirable side effects may be increased and people might view the procedure as unfair and unacceptable. In addition, increasing pressure from government agencies and interest groups encourages initial use of relatively weak punishers before using more powerful ones.

All these considerations make selection of the initial intensity of a punisher a difficult problem. If the initial level is too weak, it is best to increase the intensity of punishment by a relatively large amount. For example, Barton, Brulle, and Repp (1987) found success in using timeout in which an initial timeout period of 1 minute was followed by a later duration of 3 minutes and a final duration of 7 minutes. Like other behavior-change techniques, punishment procedures must be chosen and practiced prudently.

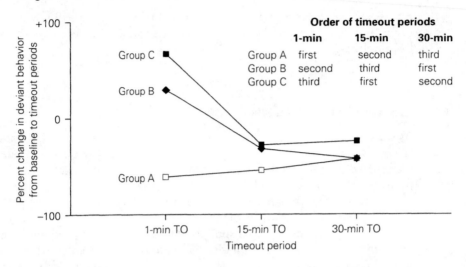

Figure 4.6   *The Influence of Contrast on the Effectiveness of Punishment*

The 1-minute timeout was most effective in reducing deviant, aggressive behaviors when it was used first (before longer timeouts) and least effective when it was used third (after longer timeouts). Figure adapted from White et al. (1972).

Punishment: Some Advanced Considerations

As we discussed in Chapter 3, there are two theories of the function of DRO, one that emphasizes the strengthening of behaviors other than the target behavior and one that emphasizes the weakening of the target behavior itself. Two parallel types of theories of punishment also exist. One of these, the escape-avoidance theory of punishment, proposes that punishment does not reduce behavior directly but strengthens responses that escape or avoid the punishing stimulus change (Dinsmore, 1977). According to the escape-avoidance theory of punishment, reinforcement and punishment are not opposite processes. Reinforcement is seen as a response-strengthening procedure but punishment is not a response-weakening procedure; instead, punishment strengthens behaviors other than those punished because engaging in those behaviors serves to avoid punishment. Remember Baby Sandra? An escape-avoidance punishment theorist would claim that the effect of the lemon-juice therapy was to increase normal food-intake behaviors because these behaviors permitted Sandra to avoid unpleasant lemon juice.

Most behavior analysts have adopted the response-weakening theory of punishment, which defines punishment as a response-weakening procedure opposite to that of reinforcement. They view increases in behaviors other than the punished responses as, at best, side effects of the main effect of punishment, the weakening of the punished response. In the case of Baby Sandra, these behavior analysts would say that the lemon-juice therapy was effective in directly suppressing rumination behavior.

Advocates of the response-weakening theory of punishment point out that it is more straightforward to define punishment in terms of a decline in an observed and measured response, especially when that response has been observed and counted, while supposedly strengthened other behaviors have not been counted or measured. Often the other behaviors consist of doing nothing in particular, as in the case of Baby Sandra when she digested her food without ruminating. However, escape-avoidance theorists would counter that whether a response is easily measured or countable should not be the route we use to define punishment.

If you are confused at this point, do not despair. For the time being, think of punishment in the way we have defined it, as a response-weakening procedure. However, in the future, two promising developments in behavior analysis offer some hope of clarifying and possibly integrating the two theories of punishment. One of these developments is the measurement and analysis of many different target behaviors in behavior analysis research (e.g., Becker, Turner, & Sajwaj, 1978). This method offers the hope of better understanding how behavioral procedures, including punishment procedures, affect different behaviors. A second development in behavior analysis has been the introduction of mathematical treatments of the way in which behavioral procedures alter different behaviors (McDowell, 1982, 1988).

Summary

It is sometimes necessary to reduce an undesirable response as a part of a behavior change program. Punishment is a name for a collection of methods that reduce responding. We say that punishment has occurred when:

- a consequence is dependent on a response;

- some measure of the response decreases or is otherwise weakened; and

- the weakening of the response is due to the response-consequence relationship, not to some other reason.

Because of its use in everyday language, the term *punishment* carries with it negative connotations for many people, an unfortunate situation for behavior analysts. Research has shown that the name *punishment* misleads people into responding unfavorably to punishment procedures. *Disinforcement* is a word behavior analysts invented to help distinguish their response-reduction methods from harsh and cruel practices that the term *punishment* suggests.

Punishment procedures reduce or eliminate behavior. Because they do not establish successful new response patterns, punishment procedures must be used within the context of a larger program designed to promote adaptive, useful new behavior.

Several different types of punishers have been shown to be effective in reducing or eliminating a variety of undesirable behaviors. Each has advantages and disadvantages that designers of behavior change programs must consider.

One advantage of punishment over other response-reduction procedures is that it can be used relatively quickly to reduce or completely eliminate responding. Another advantage is that punishment can produce beneficial changes in responses not directly punished. Many studies of punishment have shown that it can both increase desirable behaviors and decrease unpunished inappropriate behaviors.

Although negative side effects of punishment procedures have been reported, such effects are not inevitable and are often short-lived. A more important disadvantage of punishment is that the general public does not accept it as well as other response-reduction methods such as DRO and DRI. Behavior analysts have found that teaching people about punishment procedures can increase the acceptance of the procedures.

There are a variety of conditions that contribute to the effectiveness of punishment and each of these may contribute to the failure or the success of a punishment procedure.

Punishment is seen by most behavior analysts as a response-weakening procedure that parallels the view that reinforcement is a response-strengthening procedure.

Conceptual Exercise   *Punishment*

For each of the following items, decide if the illustration is an example of punishment and if so, whether it is an example of the use of physical punishment, reprimands, exclusionary timeout, nonexclusionary timeout, response cost, arbitrary activity punishers, restitutional overcorrection, positive-practice overcorrection, or habit reversal. In each item, the target behavior is highlighted.

Note: Applications of punishment are often combined with other procedures, sometimes including positive reinforcement of an alternative response. However, in many items, these other procedures have been omitted for purposes of clarity.

1. HR1 was a 60-year-old woman who had been troubled by a facial tic for 2 to 3 years. She would frequently **protrude her lips from her face**. In order to solve the problem, she was required to press her lips tightly together for 3 minutes dependent on each instance of the tic. As a result of using this method, HR1's tic was eliminated in a little over 2 weeks with no return of the problem at a 7-week follow-up check.

2. Peter was a retarded 4-year-old boy whose mother had taken him to a psychologist because Peter's behavior had gone out of her control. He kicked objects and people, took off his clothes, called people vile names, pushed his sister, threatened others, and hit and bit himself. A procedure was implemented to reduce Peter's **objectionable behaviors**: Every time he behaved objectionably he was sent to his room for a minimum of 5 minutes. This method resulted in a decline in Peter's objectionable behaviors to low, manageable levels.

3. Raymond was a 6-year-old who often misbehaved. He threw objects, hit people,

screamed as loudly as he could, and scratched himself. A procedure was implemented to reduce Ray's **misbehaviors**: Every morning his father announced to him a list of behaviors that he was not to perform. This method resulted in a decline in Ray's objectionable behaviors to low, manageable levels.

4. Psychiatric ward patients at the Brockton Veterans Administration Hospital were in a token economy program. They could earn up to 50 tokens per day for grooming, cleaning, using free time appropriately, and positive social behavior. However, the patients did **break some ward rules**, so a system of fines was set up in which errant patients would receive tickets that specified how many tokens they had lost (e.g., 3 tokens for spitting on the walls or floor, 5 tokens for stealing, 15 tokens for destroying property). The ticketing system worked very effectively. Baseline fines of 22.37 tokens per week per patient were reduced to 5.47 tokens per week by the eighth week of the program. Reductions in the fines, of course, indicated similar reductions in rule-breaking behaviors.

5. Elizabeth was a 14-year-old girl who, for two years, had **picked her face** with her hands, leaving patches of unattractive raw skin. In order to solve this problem, every time Elizabeth engaged in face-picking she was taken to the bathroom and required to clean the wounds on her face for 1 minute. This procedure produced an 86% reduction in face-picking.

6. Psychiatric patients in a token economy ward of a hospital could earn up to 50 tokens per day for grooming, cleaning, using free time appropriately, and positive social behavior. The patients did **break some ward rules**. In an effort to "show the patients who was boss," several times a week at randomly selected hours of the day all patients would be fined 10 tokens no matter what they had been doing. This method caused a reduction in rule-breaking.

7. In Cecil's kitchen an electrical problem had developed in the butter compartment, which was located in the door of his refrigerator. The electrical problem caused Cecil's radio, which he listened to constantly, to emit a very loud and unpleasant buzz. Cecil could stop the buzz by **giving the refrigerator door a sharp rap** about once an hour. One day Cecil's wife scolded him after he hit the door because she noticed the door was becoming dented. As a result, Cecil ceased giving the door sharp raps and put up with the buzz.

8. In Cecil's kitchen an electrical problem had developed in the butter compartment, which was located in the door of his refrigerator. The electrical problem caused Cecil's radio, which he listened to constantly, to emit a very loud and unpleasant buzz. Cecil could stop the buzz by **giving the refrigerator door a sharp rap** about once an hour. One day when Cecil rapped sharply on the door the buzzing did not stop. After this, Cecil no longer rapped on the door.

9. Donald was a 23-year-old college student. His problem was **jaw-popping,** moving his jaw from one side of his mouth and then quickly to the other, which threw his jawbone out of joint temporarily. Donald had to take medication to control the pain when this happened. The problem was treated by requiring Donald to engage in an

opposite competing response every time he engaged in jaw-popping or felt an urge to do so. The competing response was to close his mouth and bite until he felt tension in his jaw. He did this for 3 minutes. The procedure eliminated Donald's jaw-popping, allowing him to cease taking pain medication.

10. Ever since telephone lines had been installed in Prairieville, citizens had been able to **call directory assistance** without charge. Then the telephone company changed its policy and directory assistance calls were charged at 20¢ per call. The citizens were outraged about this change in policy.

11. Dave would always **wave at the elderly lady** sitting on her porch when he passed her on his way to work. She never waved back, but he continued to wave every day. Then one day she began returning his waves, causing Dave to wave less often after that.

12. Mike was a 7-year-old boy who had been diagnosed as autistic. He was socially unresponsive and almost constantly engaged in a self-stimulatory response, **clapping his hands,** preventing him from learning new skills. In order to reduce Mike's hand-clapping, whenever he began clapping he was required to practice appropriate alternative hand responses for 5 minutes. These alternatives included putting his hands above his head, in front of him, in his pockets, and behind his back. As a result of this procedure, Mike's hand-clapping was eliminated.

13. Reston was a 15-month-old boy. He was normal in most respects, but when confronted by threatening situations he would **hold his breath,** a disorder known as apnea. In order to solve this problem, nurses at the children's ward would hold a crushed vial of aromatic ammonia four inches away from Reston's nose when he held his breath. This method eliminated Reston's breath-holding after five days of treatment.

14. Four university students had volunteered to be subjects in an experiment. At the experimental site, they were each put into a room alone and told to talk about whatever they liked. If they had trouble thinking of a topic, they could draw a card with a topic word on it and talk about that topic. During baseline periods, there were no consequences for talking. During an experimental period, **speech disfluencies** including "er," "um," "uh," or sound repetitions produced a 1-point reduction in a number that was displayed to the subjects on a television screen. The number was initially set at 200, and the subjects were told that at the end of the session they would receive 1¢ for each point they had remaining. Data from the experiment indicated that the subjects' speech disfluencies were reduced substantially due to the point-loss arrangement.

15. Maybelline was a 5-year-old who **sucked her thumb**. On every hour, her mother would remind her not to suck her thumb. As a result of this method, Maybelline's thumb sucking declined to almost zero within a few days.

16. Peter was 10 years old, retarded, and legally blind. He was enrolled in a program for severely disturbed children. Two of Peter's problems were **nonverbal aggression,**

including hitting, kicking, choking, pulling, and pushing others, and **aggressive comments,** including threats to kill others and to step on their faces. A treatment used with Peter required him to stand up and sit down 10 times after each instance of nonverbal aggression and after each aggressive comment. This method produced a decline in nonverbal aggression from an average of over 60 responses per day to fewer than 5 per day, and a decline in aggressive comments from about 25 per day to fewer than 10.

17. Through a computer error, Glenda had been mistakenly billed for $3,000 on her credit card. She **wrote letters** to tell the bank to correct the problem, but she received no replies. This result caused Glenda to cease writing letters to the bank.

18. Eight retarded adults who lived at a state mental hospital engaged in a variety of **aggressive and disruptive behaviors** including screaming, self-injury, tantrums, threats, cursing, and crying. In order to try to solve these problems, when the people engaged in the target behaviors, they were put to bed and required to relax for at least 15 minutes. Relaxation was selected as the required activity because the outcome of relaxation was considered to be the opposite of the agitation that the target behaviors produced. The procedure produced a 95% decline in the aggressive and disruptive behaviors soon after it was implemented.

19. Mordred was a 20-year-old woman who was depressed. She would often **cry** for no apparent reason, would seldom talk, and when she did speak she talked about fear, personal injury, and death. She lived in a psychiatric hospital on a ward that used a token economy. One treatment used with Mordred was to fine her one token whenever she cried. As a result of this procedure, after 8 weeks, Mordred's *crying* declined from over 25 responses per day to fewer than 4 responses per day.

20. Dr. Ellis was working with Freddie, a man who was normal in many respects. However, whenever the subject of his mental life would come up, Freddie would **claim that the Greek playwright Aristophanes had somehow been trapped inside him.** In partial treatment for the problem, Dr. Ellis would pay attention to Freddie only after every 1 minute of conversation that did not include claims that Aristophanes was inside him. As a result of this method, Freddie's claims declined to zero.

21. Kate was an 11-year-old girl who attended junior high school. Her problem was that **she pulled out her hair,** a disorder called trichotillomania. Kate's behavior problem had left her partially bald. A procedure was used in which, every time Kate pulled her hair out or felt an urge to do so, she was required to clench her fist for 2 minutes. This procedure reduced the frequency of hair pulling, allowing her hair to grow back normally.

22. Reggie was a severely retarded 16-year-old who lived in an institution. Reggie and 15 other residents often engaged in inappropriate mealtime behaviors including **eating with their fingers and "pigging," eating spilled food.** A procedure was used in which every time Reggie emitted an inappropriate mealtime behavior, his food tray was removed from him for 15 seconds. This procedure was implemented in the winter and by spring it caused Reggie and the other residents to become much more refined diners, engaging in the inappropriate behaviors only 5% of the time, compared with 36% prior to treatment.

23. Celia was a retarded and hearing-impaired 5-year-old girl. A big problem with her was that she would **scratch other people.** In order to solve this problem, her teacher put Celia behind a freestanding room divider for several minutes where she could not see other children in the classroom. This procedure happened when Celia had scratched others twice after being warned the first time. The procedure caused Celia's scratching to decline from 0.15 scratches per minute to 0.05 scratches per minute, and eventually it almost completely eliminated scratching.

24. Brenda was a 7-year-old who had engaged in **nighttime head-banging** since she was 3 years old, leaving her with a bald patch on her head. Once her head-bang had been so forceful she had put a hole in a plaster wall next to her bed. To correct the problem, Brenda's parents woke up when she banged her head and required her to engage in an alternative appropriate response: Getting on her hands and knees as if she were going to bang her head, saying "Stop," and lying down on her bed and covering herself. She was required to do this 10 times for each instance of head-banging. This procedure almost eliminated Brenda's nighttime head-banging.

25. Chuck was a 9-year-old retarded boy who attended a special education class in a state institution. He often **engaged in disruptive behaviors including loud yelling, banging objects, and pinching others.** In order to solve this problem, Chuck and four other students wore a colored ribbon in bolo tie fashion around their necks as long as they were behaving well. When they behaved disruptively, the ribbon was removed for 3 minutes. During the 3 minutes, the offender could watch classroom activities but could not participate in them. The teacher ignored the offender, and objects near him were removed from reach. As a result of this method, the disruptive behavior of Chuck and the other students declined to very low levels.

26. Joey would continually **bang his head against his playpen.** After several days of this behavior, he seemed to be increasing the force with which he propelled his head against the playpen, and welts, bruises, and sores appeared on his head. Nonetheless, he continued to pound his head against the playpen, to the horror of his parents.

27. Barbara, 8, was a severely retarded girl enrolled in a day-care program. She would pick up all sorts of objects and put them in her mouth. For objects too heavy for her to lift, Barbara would put her lips and tongue on the object and **mouth** it in this fashion. To treat this problem, a procedure was used in which, for every time Barbara mouthed an object, she was required to brush her teeth and gums with mouthwash for 2 minutes. This method reduced mouthings from over 150 per hour to none.

28. Shelby was a retarded teenager who engaged in **body-rocking,** quick forward and backward movements of his upper body. This behavior was self-stimulatory and prevented him from being trained in more appropriate activities. To solve the problem, Shelby was required to play catch with a rubber ball with his teacher whenever he

engaged in body rocking. (It had been previously observed that Shelby disliked play-ing with the rubber ball.) As a result of this procedure, Shelby's body rocking was reduced by about 50%.

29. Eight female teenagers were in the custody of a county family and children services department. They lived in a cottage residence, where they were required to return by 9:45 P.M. on Sunday through Thursday. Curfew violations were a problem, so a sys-tem was set up in which residents who arrived late on any given evening would cause the next evening's curfew to be moved up for all the cottage residents. As a result of this method, the frequency of **late arrivals** declined substantially.

30. William was a 69-year-old man who lived in a psychiatric institution on a ward for psychotic patients. He engaged in several aggressive behaviors toward other patients and staff including both physical aggression and **verbal aggression.** Physical aggression included hitting, kicking, pushing, and throwing objects. Verbal aggression included cursing and screaming. In order to solve these problems, when-ever William engaged in an aggressive act he was immediately placed in an empty room for 10 minutes. This procedure resulted in substantial decline in both physical and verbal aggression, although neither set of behaviors was eliminated completely.

31. Martin was a patient in a mental hospital. He would occasionally become very aggressive, **striking and biting the other patients, nurses, and attendants.** In order to quell his aggression a physician administered a heavy dose of a tranquilizer every morning at 7:00 A.M., causing Martin to become quite placid, his aggression eliminated.

32. Velma was a 32-year-old profoundly retarded woman who was blind and deaf. A behavior problem she had was **bruxism,** a grinding of the teeth that can cause dam-age to the teeth, gums, and jaw. Before treatment, Velma engaged in bruxism during more than 60% of the time intervals measured. A treatment was used in which a piece of ice was applied to Velma's cheek or chin when she ground her teeth. This procedure reduced teeth grinding such that it occurred during only about 11% of the time intervals measured.

33. Pam, Nyree, Denise, and Leanne were four moderately retarded girls who were attending a special school and learning to read. When the girls made **oral reading errors,** defined as mispronunciations, omissions, and word substitutions, they were required to say the word they missed five times and then read the entire sentence in which the word occurred. This procedure caused oral reading errors to decline.

34. Vulcan was a 4-year-old boy who was fascinated by fire and would spend long hours playing with matches and lighting fires. At the request of his troubled parents, the local fire chief had given Vulcan a stern lecture on the dangers of **playing with fire,** but this did not influence Vulcan. In order to solve the problem, when Vulcan played with matches or set fires, he was required to spend 1 hour working, doing jobs like scrubbing the back porch, washing walls, and cleaning kitchen tiles with a tooth-brush. As a result of this method, Vulcan's play with fire was eliminated, as was his animated conversation when discussing fire-related topics.

Conceptual Exercise   *Making Punishment Effective*

In each of the following items a principle of punishment effectiveness has been violated. Identify what was done wrong and how the procedure could be improved.

1. Bruce was a 5-year-old boy who couldn't resist playing with one of his father's new and cherished possessions, a small glass unicorn that was displayed prominently in his father's study. His father was afraid that someday Bruce would break the unicorn, and so decided to use a punishment procedure with Bruce. Sometimes when Bruce touched the unicorn his father would immediately say, "No, Bruce," in a very threatening tone of voice. On other occasions, Bruce's dad would put him on timeout for 2 minutes. Bruce's father was careful to be consistent in his use of the punishers. How and why should this procedure be altered?

2. Gertrude was a 2-year-old who had recently begun throwing tantrums when she went grocery shopping with her mother. As soon as Gertrude began a tantrum, her mother would raise her voice, and say, "Stop that." When Gertrude stopped the tantrum and began to play with objects in the grocery cart, her mother was careful to hug her and praise her for being so good. When her mother was particularly tired, she sometimes neglected to follow her plan and would fail to reprimand Gertrude when she threw tantrums. Instead, her mother would quickly finish her shopping and take Gertrude home. How and why should this procedure be altered?

3. In the Loving Care Day-Care Center, there was a room where the children were not allowed to go because unsafe and dangerous items were stored there. When children approached the storeroom they were immediately reprimanded and removed to a play area where they were praised for alternative behavior, such as playing with the many toys. The day-care workers were careful to be very consistent in their reprimand behavior. The children were heard discussing the possibility that the storeroom contained especially wonderful toys. How and why should this situation be altered?

4. Julie was in third grade and came from a very large family. Because of the size of her family Julie didn't get very much attention at home. In her classroom she would often disrupt the class. When she did this, her teacher would take her aside and chastise her for her disruptive behavior. This lecture often lasted 5 minutes or more. Her teacher was careful always to chastise Julie when she disrupted the class and to praise Julie when she was behaving appropriately. Julie enjoyed attention very much. How and why should this method be altered?

5. John attended the first three grades in a very permissive school where disruptive behavior, fighting, and stealing were rarely punished. When John's parents moved to a different area of town, John attended a much stricter school with many more rules than he was used to. Children in this school who broke the rules were immediately sent to the principal, who would give serious reprimands, remove privileges, and administer other punishing stimuli. All the children were carefully told what

appropriate and inappropriate behaviors were and the teachers were careful to praise appropriate behavior. Although most of the children in John's new school were well behaved, it took a long time for John to adjust. How and why should this procedure be altered?

6. A forensic facility for young offenders had been using a token economy for some time. Offenders could earn tokens for a variety of appropriate behaviors and could exchange them for privileges. Staff punished misbehavior by withdrawing tokens. A new program was established in the facility where misbehavior was punished by withdrawal of exercise time. The staff were careful to be consistent in their punishment procedure; to explain the difference between misbehavior and appropriate behavior and to reinforce appropriate behavior when it occurred. The new program was not as successful as the token economy program. How and why should this procedure be altered?

7. Amanda was a 2-year-old who would often misbehave. Her mother would report this misbehavior to Amanda's father when he got home from work, at which time he would punish Amanda's behavior by sending her to her room for 5 minutes. Amanda's father was consistent in his punishment procedure and explained to Amanda why she was being punished, but Amanda seemed confused. She began to fear her father's return from work. How and why should this procedure be altered?

8. Jillian was a teenager who went out at least six times a week to movies and other recreational places. She was expected to be home by 10 on weeknights and 12 on weekends. If she was late, her parents would punish her by not allowing her to go out on the following Monday night. This punishment was consistent, and Jillian understood the relationship between her behavior and its consequences. Although Jillian's parents were careful to praise her when she came home on time, this procedure had little effect on Jillian's behavior. How and why should this procedure be altered?

9. Tommy was a difficult 2-year-old. He would hit his sister, break things, run away, and generally torment his parents. His parents consistently spoke loudly to Tommy when he misbehaved and explained that the consequences would be severe if Tommy continued to behave badly, but Tommy's parents rarely carried through with their threats. How and why should this procedure be altered?

10. In a strict school, the principal punished misbehavior by severely reprimanding the child. Joy had attended this school for some time and had misbehaved quite a bit. When Joy moved to a new school, she was amazed to find that misbehavior resulted in a mild "talking to" by the principal. The children understood the relationship between their misbehavior and its consequences and the principal consistently used the punishment procedure. Appropriate behavior was always reinforced. This procedure worked very well for most of the children, but Joy misbehaved more often than the others did. How and why should it be altered?

chapter 5

Escape and Avoidance

People can be so cruel and insensitive that sometimes it's easier to avoid them altogether. At least that's how it seemed to Vivian, a woman in her late 50s. Vivian was born with a cleft palate and although it had been repaired surgically, she was left with some facial disfigurement and a related speech impediment.

Vivian's difficulties with people had started when she was a young woman. Frequently while waiting for or riding on a bus, Vivian would be approached by people who would say, "What happened to you?" or "Did you get into some kind of accident?" She even had been told, "You look terrible." The cumulative effects of these incidents took a psychological toll on Vivian, and she was being treated for depression and social isolation as a day patient at a hospital. One particular problem, apparently caused by her earlier experiences, was a well-established fear of riding on a bus. Vivian reported that she had taken a bus only once during the previous 7 years, a fact that her husband confirmed.

Vivian's problem behavior came to the attention of Dr. Steve Hayes and Dr. David Barlow, two behavior analysts who had successfully treated phobias (irrational and maladaptive fears). Although Vivian's fear of bus riding apparently had a rational basis because it enabled her to avoid unpleasant confrontations, it was maladaptive because it prevented her from traveling and, therefore, limited her activity. Dr. Hayes and Dr. Barlow's previous experience had led them to believe that the key to Vivian's treatment was to teach her to respond assertively to people's questions and comments regarding her disfigurement. They wanted Vivian to learn to respond in a matter-of-fact way, "I have [or 'was born with'] . . . a cleft palate. This is why I look [or 'sound'] the way I do" (Hayes & Barlow, 1977, p. 743). The behavior analysts realized that it would not be easy for Vivian to learn this assertive response, the target behavior. She had a well established and long-standing pattern of avoiding social situations rather than confronting them assertively.

As a part of Vivian's treatment, the team initially prepared two types of "scenes" or scripts: "bus-incident" scenes and an "aversive" scene. The bus-incident scenes were hypothetical scenarios in which people asked Vivian questions about her disfigured face and her speech abnormalities or commented critically on her appearance. The aversive scene described Vivian's typical thoughts and feelings when she encountered the bus-incident scenes. Many of these thoughts were self-depreciating. For example, the aversive scene would include statements such as, "You think, 'Oh, I must look awful.' Your heart pounds and you can feel your face flush" (p. 743).

Vivian's therapy was a lot like a stage play, with Vivian rehearsing for the starring role and the behavior analysts serving as playwrights, stage directors, drama coaches, and behind-the-scenes producers. Part of the treatment used an avoidance procedure wherein one behavior analyst read a bus-incident scene to Vivian, after which she had 3 seconds to make the assertive response. If she failed to make that response, the aversive scene was described to her in a very realistic manner, and halted only when Vivian made the assertive response. An avoidance procedure is one where failure to engage in a behavior produces an (aversive) event. Because the aversive scene was dependent on Vivian's failure to make the assertive response, the doctors used an avoidance procedure. Avoidance procedures motivate behavior by making an aversive-stimulus change dependent on the nonoccurrence of the target behavior.

As another part of the treatment, the behavior analysts used an escape procedure. A bus-incident scene would be read to Vivian, followed immediately by the aversive scene. After 10 seconds of exposure to the aversive scene, an assertive response from Vivian would terminate the aversive scene. An escape procedure is one where the occurrence of the target behavior terminates or stops an aversive event. The therapy was designed to teach Vivian that, at least in the structured therapy situation, she could avoid or escape from the aversive scene by behaving in an assertive manner. The assertive response was difficult for Vivian, but because it permitted her to avoid or escape from the even more difficult aversive scene, the behavior analysts hoped that Vivian could be motivated to respond assertively. In turn, they hoped that this assertive behavior would be useful in Vivian's everyday life.

Vivian's therapy took place during two 2-hour sessions of scenes repeatedly presented to her using both the escape and avoidance procedures. At first, Vivian failed to emit the assertive response, causing her to be confronted with the aversive scene for longer than necessary. However, after the first few trials, Vivian promptly responded assertively, indicating that she had learned how to avoid and escape the aversive scene. Vivian's success in rehearsing her role in therapy was matched by success in real life. A month after the therapy sessions, she was riding the bus regularly, traveling to do volunteer work, making shopping trips, and going to church. The real test came when on two occasions people questioned Vivian about her facial disfigurement and she had no difficulty responding assertively. A 3-month follow-up found Vivian with a new full-time job to which she commuted daily by bus. Six months later, Vivian continued to be successful in her new, productive life.*

Escape Conditioning

At this point, we have discussed one way of motivating or increasing the level of a behavior, through positive reinforcement. Two other ways, as Vivian's example illustrates, are through escape and avoidance conditioning.

Escape conditioning strengthens behavior through the response-dependent removal of a stimulus. We say that escape conditioning has occurred when three conditions have been met:

- The stimulus or event is removed, dependent on a response,
- The response occurs more often or is otherwise strengthened, and
- The increase in response strength is due to the response-consequence relationship, not some other factor.

We can say that escape conditioning occurred with Vivian because the target response terminated the aversive scene and caused assertive responding to occur more often.

Escape responding is common in day-to-day life. Rolling up a car window is strengthened by removal of traffic noise or rain. Closing a dull book is strengthened by cessation of boring reading activity. Saying good-bye to a rude person is strengthened by the cessation of insults. Running out of a burning building is strengthened by removal of smoke and fire.

Escape conditioning is also called *negative reinforcement*. You will recall that in positive reinforcement, the presentation of a stimulus or event strengthens behavior. In negative reinforcement, behavior is strengthened by removal of a stimulus or event. We can say, for example, that Vivian's assertive responses were negatively reinforced by removal of the aversive scene.

Although people often confuse negative reinforcement with punishment, the two concepts are very different. Negative reinforcement is a response-strengthening procedure, but punishment is a response-weakening procedure. We use negative reinforcement for the same reason that we use positive reinforcement: to increase the level of a desirable behavior.

*Based on Hayes and Barlow (1977)

When escape conditioning is used as a behavior change technique, it is necessary to create a state of aversive stimulation that an escape response can terminate. In Vivian's example, reading the aversive scene to her created a state of aversive stimulation, or an establishing operation because it established removal of the aversive stimulation as a reinforcer. In Chapter 2, we indicated that reinforcer deprivation is an establishing operation for positive reinforcement because deprivation of the reinforcer makes the positive reinforcer effective. Creating a state of aversive stimulation serves the same purpose for negative reinforcers involved in escape conditioning: It makes them effective.

One should observe certain usages when discussing escape conditioning. The procedure of removing a stimulus dependent on a response that results in an increase in response strength is called either escape conditioning or negative reinforcement. The stimulus removed in escape conditioning is called a negative reinforcer.

An *aversive stimulus* is a stimulus that functions as a punisher when it is presented, or as a negative reinforcer when it is removed. It is sometimes convenient to talk about certain stimuli without being specific about their function. The term *aversive stimulus* (and also, aversive activity, or aversive event) permits us to do this. For example, consider a child who, put in timeout for disruptive behavior, decreases disruptions. This effect would make timeout a punisher for disruptions. Further suppose that we make escape from timeout dependent on quiet behavior, thus causing an increase in the amount of quiet behavior while the child is in timeout (e.g., Hobbs & Forehand, 1975). This stipulation would make timeout a negative reinforcer because removal of timeout would strengthen quiet behavior. By referring to timeout as an aversive event, we can refer both to the punishing and negatively reinforcing aspects of timeout. An example is in our penal system. Criminals are jailed for engaging in criminal behavior; criminal behavior is thereby punished. Through good behavior, prisoners can escape from confinement; good behavior is thereby negatively reinforced.

Another term is an *aversive stimulus change*. As we have seen, behavior analysts use the term *aversive stimulus* to refer to stimuli like electric shocks or timeouts, the presentation of which functions as a punisher and the removal of which functions as a negative reinforcer. When we talk about an aversive stimulus change, we refer specifically to response-dependent changes in the environment that function either as punishers or negative reinforcers. As such, aversive stimulus changes are not physical stimuli like shocks, timeouts, candy, or money; aversive stimulus changes refer specifically to the action of presenting and removing stimuli. Aversive stimulus changes include the presentation of punishers and the removal of reinforcers (i.e., response cost). When response-dependent aversive stimulus changes function to decrease some measure of behavior, they are *punishing stimulus changes*. When response-dependent aversive stimulus changes function to increase some measure of behavior, they are (*negatively*) *reinforcing stimulus changes*.

Escape responding, behavior strengthened by escape conditioning, can also be extinguished. When an escape response is extinguished, removal of a stimulus is no longer dependent on the response. For example, suppose the window crank on your car breaks such that it turns, but does not roll up the window. When it begins rain-ing, the escape response of turning the window crank would be extinguished because it would no longer stop the rain.

Avoidance Conditioning

Avoidance conditioning, like escape conditioning, has three defining features:

- A consequence is dependent on the *failure* to engage in a particular response within a specified period of time,
- The response occurs more often or is otherwise strengthened, and
- The increase in response strength is a result of the response-consequence relationship, not some other factor.

There are many instances of avoidance conditioning in everyday life. In such instances, an aversive stimulus change is dependent on the failure to perform a behavior within a given time limit. Failing to pay our bills within a specified period of time produces late charges or repossessions, and these dependencies strengthen bill paying. We say we avoid the late charges by paying the bills. Failing to paint your house within a given time interval results in weather damage, a dependency that strengthens house painting. We say that we avoid a damaged or ugly house through painting. Failing to water the house plants within a certain interval of time results in severely wilted or dead plants, a dependency that strengthens watering the plants. We say we avoid wilted plants by watering them. Failing to put on warm clothes before going outside in cold weather results in frozen body parts, a dependency that strengthens dressing appropriately. We say we avoid the pain produced by the cold by wearing warm clothes. The failure of world leaders to negotiate with one another during critical intervals of time may produce conflict and war, dependencies that we hope will strengthen negotiation behaviors. We say that leaders avoid the consequences of conflict and war through timely negotiation.

Avoidance conditioning is also viewed as strengthening a response because the response prevents or postpones the delivery of a punisher (e.g., Reese, Howard, & Reese, 1978) or an aversive stimulus. This is another way of saying that the failure of the response to occur produces the aversive stimulus change: When the response occurs, this prevents or postpones the aversive stimulus change; when the response fails to occur, this produces the aversive stimulus change. For example, in the case of Vivian, we could say that her assertive avoidance responses prevented the therapists from reading the aversive scenes to her or we could say that her failure to perform the assertive avoidance responses produced the aversive scenes. As you can see, we can look at avoidance conditioning in either of these two ways. In the conceptual exercise in this chapter, we have emphasized the definition of avoidance conditioning in terms of the aversive stimulus changes being dependent on a failure to respond. We have found that this definition expedites the correct identification of examples of avoidance.

Like escape conditioning, (avoidance conditioning is often considered a form of negative reinforcement. In negative reinforcement, behavior is strengthened by removal of a stimulus or event. We saw that with escape conditioning, negative reinforcement consists of the removal of an aversive stimulus that is present at the time the escape response is made. In avoidance conditioning, negative reinforcement is slightly different: It consists of preventing or postponing an aversive stimulus change. The aversive stimulus change is said to be removed in the sense that its future delivery is prevented or postponed.)

Avoidance conditioning and escape conditioning are similar because both procedures strengthen some measure of the target behavior. In this respect, both escape and avoidance differ from punishment, a procedure that weakens some measure of the target behavior. Always remember that escape and avoidance procedures increase the level of some measure of behavior, whereas punishment procedures decrease the level of some measure of behavior.

Escape and avoidance procedures are different. In escape conditioning, an aversive stimulus is present at the time the response is made, and this stimulus is removed dependent on the response. We see an example illustrating the difference between escape and avoidance conditioning in social interactions. Suppose you work at an office where you have an aversive colleague, Mr. X, who pulls you aside whenever he sees you, brags about his many talents and great deeds, points out that you ought to be more like him, mentions that it is interesting how good-looking people like him also tend to be great achievers, discloses that he is thinking of allowing a team of experts to examine his brain to find out why it works so well, and so on. An escape response would be one that terminates interactions with Mr. X. For example, citing an excuse to leave and saying good-bye would be an escape response strengthened by the termination of the aversive stimulus, the interaction with Mr. X.

In contrast, an avoidance response would not immediately terminate an ongoing aversive interaction with your colleague. For example, suppose you work at an office with Mr. X and that you arrive every morning at 9 A.M. for work. Suppose Mr. X has office hours every morning from 11 A.M. until noon, and that by closing your office door during the interval of time before Mr. X's arrival, an interaction with Mr. X will not occur. However, by failing to engage in the target door-closing behavior before 11 A.M., the aversive stimulus change from no Mr. X to a Mr. X interaction will occur at 11 A.M. In this case, the door-closing avoidance response is strengthened by the dependency between failing to close the door and the appearance of Mr. X. We say that closing the door avoids, prevents, or postpones interactions with Mr. X.

Like escape behavior, avoidance (behavior may be weakened through extinction.) When an avoidance response is extinguished, an aversive event is no longer dependent on the failure of the response to occur, causing weakening of the response. For example, suppose your electric bill-paying behavior is strengthened through avoidance: You pay your bills because failure to do so results in a fine or disconnection of your electricity. Further suppose that a computer malfunction provides you with free electricity whether you pay your bills or not. Under these conditions, behavior analysis would predict a weakening of bill-paying behavior due to extinction of avoidance responding.

One notable feature of avoidance behavior is that it can be difficult to extinguish (Higgins & Morris, 1984; Malloy & Levis, 1988; Miller, Kalin, Eckenroth, & Meyer, 1970; Miller, Kalin, & Meyer, 1970). For example, some people called compulsive checkers spend hours checking their home for some particular problem, such as leaving running water on. This behavior is maladaptive because so much time is spent checking that more important activities cannot be performed. In many cases, checking behavior was originally strengthened because failure to check produced some aversive consequence, such as a small flood. However, the avoidance response, checking, continues to occur despite, in some cases, years of no aversive consequences. Normally, we would expect the avoidance response to undergo extinction, but extinction fails to occur. We will consider some of the reasons for this later.

(Avoidance conditioning can be either signaled or unsignaled. In signaled avoidance conditioning, a warning signal precedes the onset of the aversive event. The signal indicates that avoidance responses will be negatively reinforced. In unsignaled avoidance conditioning, no warning signal is used. Most behavior-change programs use signaled avoidance. For example, in the case of Vivian, behavior analysts used signaled avoidance because reading the bus-incident scene alerted Vivian to the fact that in responding assertively she would avoid exposure to the aversive scene.

Escape and Avoidance Conditioning as Behavior Change Procedures

Escape and avoidance procedures often go hand in hand in behavior change programs. First, a behavior is established through escape conditioning and then continues to be strengthened through avoidance conditioning. For example, in Vivian's case, the assertive response was initially made as an escape response to the aversive scene. However, later she learned to engage in the assertive response as an avoidance response; it served to avoid the aversive scene, which she never encountered after a few initial exposures to it.

Positive reinforcement is generally the treatment of choice for promoting desirable behavior. Although escape and avoidance conditioning are effective behavior-change techniques, both make use of aversive stimuli and have the potential for undesirable side effects. However, under some conditions at least, people do not appear to favor positive reinforcement over avoidance as a means of strengthening behavior. For example, when Iwata and Bailey (1974) compared a token economy based on response cost to one based on positive reinforcement, students did not prefer one method to the other.

There are two major conditions when one considers escape and avoidance. First, sometimes positive reinforcement procedures will fail or not be completely successful in attempts to encourage and maintain desirable behaviors (Fichter, Wallace,

Liberman, & Davis, 1976; Foxx, 1984; Kazdin, 1973; Sullivan & O'Leary, 1990). When this happens, escape and avoidance procedures are options that may be useful.

For example, Warzak, Kewman, Stefans, and Johnson (1987) worked with a 10-year-old boy named Adam. Adam had been a normal healthy boy until he contracted a respiratory infection. Simultaneously, Adam claimed he had lost the ability to read; printed words blurred and seemed to move about on the page. Physicians could find no physical cause for this problem and, indeed, Adam was seen to play computer games with remarkable skill. Although consequences such as praise, game-playing, and visits from his family seemed to reinforce many of Adam's behaviors powerfully, they failed to reinforce reading.

The therapists required Adam to follow avoidance conditioning procedures, including two boring visual exercises of eye movements: one in which he had to look up, down, right, and left 10 times, and one in which he had to identify large shapes close to him. Initially, Adam's target behavior was to read one word aloud. If he failed that, he was required to engage in the boring eye exercises; if he did read, he was not required to do the eye exercises any more that day. This successful technique was was avoidance conditioning because (a) an aversive activity, the boring exercise, was dependent on failure to engage in reading, the target behavior, and (b) this dependency caused the target behavior to be strengthened.

Treatment progressed by requiring Adam to read more and more words. After several weeks, Adam was reading well and he was able to be discharged from the hospital and returned to his school. At a one-year follow-up, he had become an above-average student and reported no problems seeing. Adam's parents and the hospital staff found the treatment highly acceptable.

A second condition when one considers escape and avoidance procedures is when the desired behavior in the natural environment is partially motivated by escape and avoidance dependencies. For example, in the case of Vivian, assertive responding permitted escape from or avoidance of the aversive scene. You'll recall that the aversive scene described Vivian's typical thoughts when she was confronted, which often consisted of negative evaluations of herself. In the natural environment, competent people avoid this kind of negative self-talk through assertive behavior. The success of the therapy with Vivian may have been partially a result of her learning to avoid her own negative self-talk, a natural consequence of assertive responding.

One example is in establishing conversational skills. Heckel, Wiggins, and Salzberg (1962) conducted group therapy sessions with patients, and long silences in conversation had become a problem. For skilled conversationalists, long pauses in conversations are aversive, and part of learning to be a good conversationalist is learning how to avoid prolonged silences (Hansen, St. Lawrence, & Christoff, 1988). Heckel et al. (1962) taught their patients to avoid silences by sounding a loud noise if 10 seconds passed without conversation. If a patient then said something, the noise stopped. This method reduced pauses in the conversation, even when the escape-avoidance dependency was no longer used, suggesting that the silences had become conditioned aversive stimuli for the patients, as they are for skilled conversationalists.

Types of Aversive Stimuli Used in Escape and Avoidance Conditioning

The same types of aversive stimuli that have been used in punishment procedures have also been used in escape and avoidance procedures. Physical stimuli (i.e., unconditioned aversive stimuli), reprimands, timeout, response cost, aversive activities, and overcorrection have all been used in escape-avoidance conditioning. In addition, some research has been conducted using social aversive stimuli.

Physical Aversive Stimuli

White, Mathews, and Fawcett (1989) used physical or unconditioned aversive stimuli to deal with the problem of pressure sores among people who use wheelchairs. This problem is serious and sometimes fatal for people whose physical mobility is restricted by a handicap. Two 11-year-olds, Teri and Peter, were born with spina bifida, a spinal cord disorder that prevents normal mobility. The target behaviors in the study were wheelchair push-ups, in which Teri and Peter would raise themselves from their wheelchairs with their arms in an exercise known to prevent pressure sores. A loud alarm sounded for 6 seconds for every 30 minutes that passed without Teri or Peter spending at least 3 seconds doing push-ups. This method substantially increased their time doing push-ups. This method was an example of avoidance conditioning because the stimulus change, the presentation of the loud alarm, was dependent on the failure of the target behavior, the push-ups, to occur, and because this dependency increased the duration of the target behavior.

Reprimands

Doleys et al. (1976) used reprimands in an avoidance conditioning procedure with four mentally retarded children who were noncompliant: They failed to obey instructions. If a child failed to obey an instruction within 10 seconds from the time it was issued, the experimenter held the child by the shoulders, gave a verbal reprimand, and then glared at the child for 40 seconds. As a result, the children obeyed instructions much more frequently than they had before treatment. This method was an avoidance conditioning procedure because the consequences, the reprimands, were dependent on the failure of the target behavior to occur within the 10-second time interval.

Timeout

Timeout has been used in much the same way as reprimands in the avoidance conditioning of children's compliance with their parents' instructions (Doleys et al., 1976; Hobbs, Forehand, & Murray, 1978; Scarboro & Forehand, 1975). If the child fails to obey the parental instruction, the child is sent to an exclusionary timeout area or, in the case of nonexclusionary timeout, access to a reinforcer is denied for a specific length of time.

Schrader and Levine (1989) described the use of escape and avoidance conditioning using timeout with television audiences. A public broadcasting station in San Francisco, KQED, sometimes interrupts its normal programs with "pledge breaks," in which viewers are repeatedly told to send money to the station to cover operating costs. The pledge breaks can be considered a form of nonexclusionary timeout because they are a temporary withdrawal of reinforcement opportunities—the opportunities to enjoy the normal programs. Station KQED uses an avoidance contingency by making the pledge break timeouts dependent on the failure of a sufficient number of the viewers to call in and contribute a certain amount of money. According to Schrader and Levine, the avoidance contingency has successfully motivated the viewers to contribute money and thereby avoid interruptions in the normal programming.

Response Cost

Response cost procedures have also been used effectively in avoidance conditioning. For example, Little and Kelley (1989) worked with three families in which children failed to comply with their parents' instructions. Part of the procedure was to put the children—Lauren, 10, Jenny, 6, and Sam, 7—on point systems. The day was divided into several time intervals. At the beginning of an interval, the children were awarded points in the form of a row of smile faces printed on a sheet of paper. When the children failed to comply with their mothers' instructions after being given a warning, one of the smile faces would be crossed out. At the end of the time interval, the smile faces were exchanged for privileges including television watching, having a friend over, or playing a game with their mother or father. This method was an avoidance conditioning procedure because the response-cost penalty was dependent on the failure of compliant behavior to occur.

At first, if the children had lost only 50% of the faces, they were given privileges at the end of the interval. Later, as the procedure became more successful, the privileges were dependent on losing fewer faces. This method was successful in improving the children's compliance with the instructions. Aversive behaviors on the part of both children and mothers also declined, a desirable side effect of the procedure. All three mothers were satisfied with the success of the procedure, and rated response cost as more acceptable than spanking or timeout.

Avoidance conditioning through response cost is often used in behavioral contracts to promote desirable behaviors. For example, Nurnberger and Zimmerman (1970) worked with a 31-year-old university professor who was having problems writing his thesis, a long research paper required for many postgraduate degrees. The professor agreed to meet specific daily and weekly writing requirements. As a part of the agreement, he was required to select three organizations he thoroughly disapproved of and write checks to each one. He chose the Ku Klux Klan, the American Nazi Party, and the John Birch Society. He gave these checks to his therapist, whose job it was to mail these checks to the organizations if the professor failed to meet his writing requirements. This method motivated the professor to complete his thesis, an accomplishment that pleased his wife and had the added benefit of improving their marriage. This avoidance conditioning procedure included an aversive event—sending the checks to the organizations—that was dependent on the failure of writing behavior to occur.

Aversive Activities

Aversive activities have been extensively used in escape and avoidance conditioning. We have already considered two examples, in Vivian having to listen to an aversive scene and in Adam having to do boring eye exercises.

This approach has also been used to treat people with severe burns. Exercise is very painful for burn patients but it is extremely important because it promotes proper healing and prevents muscle weakening. Hegel, Ayllon, VanderPlate, and Spiro-Hawkins (1986) worked with three men: two had been injured at their jobs at a steel mill when molten steel had erupted, and the third had been burned in a fire at his home. Every day, staff measured the men's range of motion of their joints and set a goal for improvement. If the men failed to exercise on their own, as they had been encouraged to do, they also failed to meet their improvement goals and were required to participate in a painful physical therapy session in which their limbs were guided through a range of movements. However, if they did engage in self-exercise and met their goal, they were not required to undergo the physical therapy session. This was an avoidance conditioning procedure because the aversive activity requirement was dependent on the failure to exercise. Results of the procedure were encouraging. Each of the men gradually improved the range of motion of his affected joints to nearly normal levels. The success of the avoidance dependency also benefitted the hospital staff. Conventional physical rehabilitation for burn patients demands individual attention from a physical therapist. The avoidance procedure made it possible for the physical therapists to devote their time to more seriously incapacitated patients who were unable to exercise on their own. Although the procedure was an aversive one, the men were enthusiastic about the treatment program and never showed any stress or anxiety, despite the painfulness of the self-exercises.

Aversive activities have also been used as a part of overcorrection procedures to produce avoidance conditioning. When used in avoidance conditioning programs, restitutional overcorrection activities produce outcomes that are functionally opposite to an undesired behavior; positive-practice overcorrection activities used in avoidance conditioning consist of desirable alternatives to some undesired response.

Aversive Social Stimuli

The reactions of other people sometimes serve as aversive stimuli that can promote escape or avoidance behavior. Escape and avoidance conditioning procedures have been used to promote altruistic or helping behavior (Weiss, Boyer, Lombardo, & Stich, 1973; Weiss, Cecil, & Frank, 1973), assertive responding in conversation (Weiss, Lombardo, Warren, & Kelley, 1971; Weiss, Feinberg, Cramer, & Schoedel,

1976), escape behavior from aversive group situations (Seybert & Weiss, 1974), and advice-seeking about how to avoid threatening conditions (Cecil, Weiss, & Feinberg, 1978).

Weiss, Buchanan, Altstatt, and Lombardo (1971) had university students watch a "victim" perform a task in which the victim, apparently suffering pain from constant electric shock, was actually in league with the experimenter, and only pretended to be in pain. The students were told to evaluate the victim's performance on the task by turning dials and, when a light came on, to press a button to record the evaluations.

Button-presses stopped the victim's apparent suffering for 10 seconds but the students were not informed about this relationship. The button-presses were escape responses because they terminated the victim's suffering, the aversive stimulus.

Response latency, the time that passed from light onset to button-pressing, was measured. Students under these experimental conditions pressed the button more rapidly than students in a control group where no victim appeared to be suffering pain. This result showed that "altruistic reinforcement" strengthened the students' behavior in the form of the removal of the victim's suffering. Weiss, Buchanan, Altstatt, and Lombardo (1971) likened this kind of reinforcement for escape responding to other situations in which people help others who are in difficulty.

Escape and Avoidance Conditioning as the Basis for Undesirable Behaviors

We have seen how escape and avoidance conditioning can be used to strengthen desirable behavior. Behavior analysts are also interested in the role of escape and avoidance dependencies in promoting undesirable and self-defeating behaviors. It is important to know whether escape-avoidance dependencies or other factors cause inappropriate behavior, because only then can we devise solutions keyed to the specific problem (Repp, Felce, & Barton, 1988; Steege, Wacker, Berg, Cigrand, & Cooper, 1989).

Inappropriate Escape Behavior

Research has shown that a good deal of inappropriate behavior is due to escape conditioning. For example, suppose a primary school child is having difficulty learning the skills required to master long division. For such a child, the learning activity could function as an aversive activity, and misbehavior that brings the activity to a halt would be reinforced through escape from the activity. In general, removal of an effortful or otherwise difficult task can be a reinforcer (Carr & Durand, 1985; Iwata, Pace, Kalsher, Cowdery, & Cataldo, 1990; Miller, 1968a).

Steege et al. (1989) studied the self-injurious hair-pulling of a 4-year-old named Johnny, who was observed under various conditions. Behavior analysts noted that hair-pulling occurred only when Johnny was ordered to participate in an academic task, and they decided to treat the problem by reinforcing incompatible behavior and redirecting Johnny to the academic task dependent on his self-injury. This latter procedure served to extinguish escape behavior because the reinforcer for the response, removal of task demands, was withdrawn; self-injury no longer produced escape from the academic task.

If we know that escape motivates an undesirable behavior, we can be more successful at changing the behavior. For example, if Steege et al. (1989) had not known that Johnny's hair-pulling was reinforced by escape, they might have used a timeout procedure. If so, hair-pulling would have been even more effective in producing escape from the academic task (Durand & Carr, 1987). Plummer, Baer, and LeBlanc (1977) found just such an effect in their work with special preschool children. Timeout appeared to reinforce disruptive responses because a student's disruptive behavior and going to timeout stopped the teacher's demands. Disruptive responses were eliminated through extinction of escape responding: Disruptions no longer produced escape from the teacher's instructions.

Other behavior analysts have used a variety of imaginative techniques to solve the problem of misbehaviors motivated by escape from demands. These have included reducing task demands (Gaylord-Ross, Weeks, & Lipner, 1980; Weeks & Gaylord-Ross, 1981), making the task easier by increasing the child's familiarity with it (Mace, Browder, & Lin, 1987), making escape dependent on a desirable behavior (Steege et al., 1990), teaching proper requests for help with difficult tasks (Durand & Carr, 1987), teaching proper requests for rest periods (Durand & Kishi, 1987), and mixing in instructions to perform demanding tasks with instructions to perform easy tasks (Mace & Belfiore, 1990).

Undesirable behavior motivated by escape from demanding situations is common in everyday life. It seems easier sometimes to tell a lie and escape from a threatening line of questioning than to tell the truth and face the consequences. Many students escape school demands by daydreaming or gazing vaguely out the window. Escape behavior is seen by some as a broad social problem in life today. Certain television, movie, and other low-grade mass media reinforcers may encourage people to escape from the responsibility of solving personal and social problems. More broadly, some observers view dictatorial political systems as a form of reinforcing escape from the challenges, choices, and other demands that confront individuals living in a free society.

Inappropriate Avoidance Behavior

Avoidance conditioning is also thought to be responsible for a wide range of inappropriate behaviors. For example, Freud's early clinical work was with women suffering from hysterical paralysis that had no organic cause. Freud recognized that in many cases the disorder allowed the patient to avoid confronting some type of aversive stimulus or activity. We see these kinds of disorders even today. Hendrix, Thompson, and Rau (1978) worked with a 14-year-old girl whose clenched fist served to enable her to avoid school. Mizes (1985) studied a 13-year-old girl whose back pain and stiffness allowed her to avoid academic and athletic demands. You may remember Adam, whose report of a visual disorder was thought to be a means of avoiding school.

Some behavior analysts think avoidance conditioning is responsible for many psychological disorders. Ullmann and Krasner (1975), for example, suggest that many patients learn a set of "sick role" behaviors that enable them to be cared for and thereby avoid confronting the problems of normal day-to-day life. Boyd and Levis (1980) and Biglan et al. (1985) believe that some depressive behaviors are avoidance responses. Biglan et al. (1985) examined the way depressed women and their husbands treated each other. They found that depressive behaviors by the women (e.g., complaints about oneself, frowns, downcast eyes) resulted in less aggressive behavior by their husbands. It appeared that by acting depressed, the wives could avoid their spouses' aggressiveness. Although more research is needed to clarify this finding, it may be, as Ullmann and Krasner suggest, that subtle avoidance dependencies such as this cause many behavioral problems.

Making Escape and Avoidance Conditioning Effective

Several of the conditions that influence the effectiveness of punishment have similar influences on the effectiveness of escape and avoidance conditioning. These conditions include the consistency of the aversive consequence, instructions, response energy, using a variety of aversive consequences, delay of the aversive consequence, intensity of the aversive consequence, using predictive conditioned aversive stimuli, and contrast effects.

As Iwata (1987) has noted, avoidance conditioning has not been studied as much as other behavior change techniques. For this reason, less research is available concerning the factors that make avoidance effective. We will therefore discuss only the roles of instructions, consistency, delay, response energy, and intensity as examples of how principles of punishment effectiveness also apply to escape and avoidance. Further, we will examine four additional conditions that influence the effectiveness of escape and avoidance: The effectiveness of reinforcers for alternative behaviors, removing punishers for the escape or avoidance responses, the size of the time interval in avoidance, and the extent of previous response-independent aversive consequences.

Instructions

As we have seen with many other behavior change techniques, escape and avoidance conditioning are more effective when instructions are used to specify the relationship between the response (or nonresponse) and its consequences (Galizio, 1979; Higgins & Morris, 1984; Moffat & Miller, 1971).

Miller, Kalin, Eckenroth, and Meyer (1970) examined the effect of instructions on escape and avoidance on four groups of university students. The students sat in chairs with handgrips within reach. The experimenters placed an air nozzle behind the students' heads. If the students failed to press a button on the handgrip within 2 seconds of the start of an experimental trial, they would receive an annoying blast of air directed just behind the ear. A light signaled the beginning of each trial. Students in one group were told only that there was a way to control what happened to them. In a second group, they were told to grasp the handgrip. Students in a third group were told to grasp the handgrip and that they were allowed to press the button. In a fourth group, they were told that they would receive blasts of air that could be prevented if they pressed the button in the handgrip.

As Figure 5.1 shows, the more information the students were given about the avoidance dependency, the more effective the avoidance conditioning procedure was in strengthening avoidance responses.

Instructions that specify the avoidance dependency can sometimes be effective in increasing desirable behaviors in natural settings. For example, Rogers, Rogers, Bailey, Runkle, and Moore (1988) wanted drivers of vehicles owned by the state of Florida to buckle their seat belts. An avoidance dependency already existed: Drivers involved in accidents who had failed to buckle their seat belts received a 25% reduction in workers' compensation benefits. Rogers et al. (1988) put stickers on the windshields of the vehicles informing the state employees about this avoidance dependency, and had the employees sign forms indicating that they were aware of

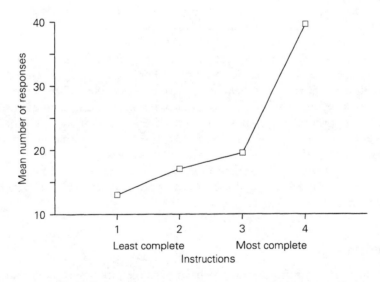

Figure 5.1   *The Relation Between Instructions and the Effectiveness of Avoidance*

The students made more responses when they were well informed about the relation between their behavior and consequences than when they were not well informed. Figure redrawn from the data of Miller et al. (1970).

the dependency. Before these stickers were used, only about 10% of the drivers buckled their seat belts; after they were used, about 50% buckled up.

Consistency of the Aversive Consequence

As we saw with punishment, escape and avoidance conditioning are more effective when the consequence occurs more, rather than less, frequently (O'Leary, 1974; Weiss, Boyer, Lombardo, & Stich, 1973; Weiss, Lombardo, Warren, & Kelley, 1971). O'Leary (1974) studied the role of the consistency of the aversive consequence on avoidance behavior with kindergarten children. The children listened to stories on audiotape. If they failed to press a lever five times within 10 seconds, a bell would sound. If they then failed to press a lever five times within the next 10 seconds, a 10-second story timeout (i.e., a story interruption) would sometimes occur. For one group of children, the story timeout occurred 100% of the time. For two other groups of children, the story timeouts occurred 60% and 20% of the time. One measure of the effectiveness of the different percentages of the aversive consequence is in the frequency of the children's responding during the second 10-second period.

As Figure 5.2 shows, when the story timeouts were dependent on failures to lever-press only 20% of the time, lever pressing was less frequent than when the

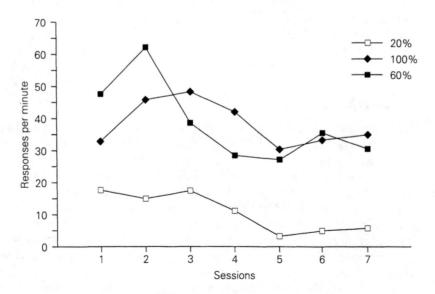

Figure 5.2   *The Influence of Consistency of Application of the Aversive Consequence on the Effectiveness of Avoidance*

The children's avoidance responses occurred much less often when the story timeouts occurred only 20% of the time compared to 60% or 100% of the time. Figure adapted from O'Leary (1974).

dependency between lever-presses and timeout was either at 60% or 100%. One often sees this consistency effect in day-to-day life. When a child is reprimanded only occasionally for failing to perform chores, performance is apt to be poorer than when the failure to perform is reprimanded consistently. In general, lack of consistency gives a mixed message that will always interfere with the effectiveness of behavior change procedures.

Aversive Consequence Delay

The shorter the delay between the response and its consequence, the more effective escape and avoidance conditioning will be. In an experiment similar to the altruistic reinforcement study described earlier, Weiss, Cecil, and Frank (1973) showed that delay of reinforcement influences the effectiveness of escape conditioning. Students watched a "victim" perform a task in which the victim appeared to be suffering pain from continuous electric shock. The students were told their job was to evaluate the victim's task performance by turning a dial. Following the evaluation, a light signaled the students to press a button to record their evaluations. Button presses stopped the victim's apparent suffering for 10 seconds. For one group of students, the button pushes relieved the victim's suffering immediately, while for two other groups there were delays of 1 or 2 seconds. The strength of the escape response was measured using response latency, the time that elapsed between onset of light and button-pressing. Response latency was briefest for the group of students whose button presses immediately stopped the victim's apparent suffering, and progressively longer for the 1-second and 2-second delay groups.

Response Energy

The principle of response energy is that the greater the energy required of the escape or avoidance response, the less effective the aversive consequences will be in strengthening the response (Miller, 1968a, 1968b).

Matthews and Shimoff (1974) studied the role of response energy in avoidance responding. Three female university students were taught to press a key that required 0.2 pounds of force to operate. Each trial was 10 seconds long. Key presses (or the failure to key press) produced no stimulus changes during the first 9 seconds. However, during the final 1 second of the trial, loss of 10 points on a response counter was dependent on the failure to press the key. This was an avoidance dependency because the stimulus change, point loss, was dependent on the failure to respond during the 1-second interval. The students who lost the fewest points could trade points for money. The principle of response energy was demonstrated by replacing the key with a high-effort response button that required 16 pounds of force to operate. For two of the three subjects, the use of the high-effort response button reduced the rate of avoidance responses, showing that increasing response energy reduced the effectiveness of the avoidance dependency.

Aversive Consequence Intensity

The greater the intensity or magnitude of the aversive stimulus, the more effective it will be in strengthening escape or avoidance responses. For example, Moffat (1972) studied avoidance conditioning in first-grade children through music timeouts, temporary interruptions of recorded music. Failure of the children to push a button produced the music timeouts. When the timeouts consisted of interruptions in the soundtrack from a children's movie, avoidance responses were more frequent than when the timeouts consisted of interruptions of classical music.

Weiss, Boyer, Lombardo, and Stich (1973) examined the effectiveness of escape conditioning using different intensities of an aversive stimulus. They used the procedure described earlier in which subjects perceive a victim as suffering from continuous shock. For a high-magnitude reinforcement group, the victim working on a task would appear to be in great pain and the subject's button-pushes appeared to eliminate the victim's pain for 10 seconds. For a medium-magnitude reinforcement group, the subject's button-pushes appeared to reduce but not eliminate the victim's pain. For a control group, button-pushes had no apparent effect on the victim's pain. The effectiveness of the escape conditioning was measured using response latency. The high-magnitude reinforcement group had the lowest response latencies, indicating the most effective conditioning, while the control group had the highest response latencies, indicating less effective conditioning. The medium-magnitude reinforcement group's latencies were at an intermediate level.

Reinforcers for Alternative Behaviors

The effectiveness of escape and avoidance conditioning will depend on reinforcers available for responses other than escape and avoidance. As such, when the escape or avoidance response is a desirable behavior, reinforcers for alternative responses should be removed or made as ineffective as possible. Conversely, if the escape or avoidance response is an undesirable behavior, reinforcers for alternative responses should be used and made effective.

The importance of reinforcing alternative behaviors has been shown in several cases where inappropriate escape behavior was weakened through reinforcement of an alternative response. For example, Plummer et al. (1977) worked with a retarded 5-year-old boy who escaped from teacher instructions by various misbehaviors including rocking, playing with his fingers, throwing food around, and spitting. These escape behaviors were weakened by making the reinforcers of teacher praise and favored bites of food dependent on following the teacher's instructions.

Removing Punishers for the Escape or Avoidance Response

Escape and avoidance conditioning procedures will be more successful if punishers dependent on the escape or avoidance responses are removed or minimized. For example, in the story of Vivian that began this chapter, the behavior analysts made sure that Vivian's assertive behavior was never punished, by teaching the escape and avoidance responses in a structured role-playing environment. Had they merely instructed Vivian to take a ride on a bus and try out her assertive behavior, these behaviors might have been punished by impolite people. By providing Vivian with an unpunished history of assertive responding, the therapists increased the likelihood that she would continue to be assertive in more realistic settings.

Time Interval Sizes in Avoidance

In avoidance conditioning, an aversive stimulus change is dependent on the failure of a response to occur during a given interval of time. Evidence shows that avoidance responses are best acquired when the length of the time interval is kept relatively short, at least during the initial stages of learning (Sidman, 1966). In one study illustrating this principle, medical and graduate students were subjects in an experiment in which they could avoid shocks to their legs by pressing a button (Ader & Seibetta, 1964). In general, the students acquired the response most rapidly when shocks were dependent on failing to respond every 5 seconds rather than every 10 or 15 seconds. Another variable that made avoidance conditioning more rapid was the length of time that a response postponed shocks. In general, the longer the shocks were postponed, the more rapidly the students acquired the avoidance response.

Previous Response-Independent Aversive Stimulation

Research has shown that a history of response-independent aversive stimulation will lessen the effectiveness of escape and avoidance conditioning. In other words, a person who in the past has received aversive stimulation independent of his or her behavior may in the future fail to learn to avoid or escape aversive stimulation even when it is possible to do so. This outcome is called *learned helplessness*. Hiroto and Seligman (1975) conducted an experiment in which one group of university students could press a button four times to escape a loud tone. Another group of students had to listen to the same loud tones, but their button presses had no effect on the tones. After this, both groups of students were tested on an shuttle-box avoidance task: The subjects were presented with an apparatus in which a sliding knob could be moved from one side of a box to the other. They could avoid loud noises by moving the knob to one side of the box on one trial, and then moving the knob to the opposite side of the box on the next trial. The shuttle-box avoidance conditioning procedure was more effective with the students for whom noise escape had been dependent on button presses than with the students for whom noise escape was independent of button pressing.

As the term *learned helplessness* suggests, people who receive response-independent aversive stimulation appear to learn to give up trying to solve the insoluble task. When they are then presented with soluble escape and avoidance tasks, their previous experience of being helpless serves to maintain nontrying behavior, and they have learned to be helpless. Generally, when people are given response-independent aversive stimulation, they cease seeking solutions to problems and become passive. A history of response-independent aversive events is suspected to cause many psychological disorders, including depression (Miller & Seligman, 1975). Learned helplessness is also suspected to be a factor in passive student behaviors that result in poor academic achievement, behavioral disorders of old age, and the problems of battered women (Peterson & Bossio, 1989). Aside from the learned helplessness effect itself, response-independent aversive stimulation is a very harmful procedure that worsens the undesirable side effects of aversive procedures (Oliver, West, & Sloane, 1974) without eliminating undesirable behaviors or promoting desirable responses.

Avoidance: Some Advanced Considerations

Traditionally, avoidance conditioning has been one of the more puzzling processes in behavior analysis. Even today, behavior analysts debate among themselves about what consequences strengthen avoidance responses, why avoidance responses are difficult to learn, and why they are difficult to extinguish. One of the puzzles of avoidance responses is that they are strengthened even though they do not produce an immediate consequence. In avoidance conditioning, failure to engage in a response during an interval of time produces an aversive stimulus change at the end of the interval. When an avoidance response occurs, the aversive stimulus change is prevented or postponed seconds, minutes, hours, or months into the future.

One proposed solution to the problem of lack of an immediate consequence in avoidance responding is called the two-factor theory of avoidance (Mowrer, 1947). According to this theory, an immediate consequence is indeed dependent on avoidance responses: Once the avoidance response is made, there is an immediate reduction in fear or anxiety. For example, suppose you have just watched a play at a theater in a large city. Because it is a pleasant evening for a walk, you begin doing so, but as you walk you feel a sense of apprehension. You think about violent crimes you have read about in the news and seen depicted in movies. You run into a cafe, call a cab, and experience an immediate reduction in your fears and thoughts of personal danger. According to two-factor theory, these fear- and thought-reductions strengthen avoidance behavior.

Two-factor theory gets its name because two processes are assumed to be involved in strengthening avoidance responding. First, there is a process whereby a stimulus or situation provokes fear. In our example, in large cities many people fear walking the streets at night because crimes and violence have been associated with such activities. Second, there is a process whereby the avoidance response reduces the fear: Calling the taxi reduced the fear.

The two-factor theory of avoidance is intuitively appealing for at least two reasons. One is that it suggests an immediate consequence, fear reduction, for the avoidance response. Another is that many behavior therapists find the theory helpful in explaining certain puzzling aspects of maladaptive avoidance behavior (Levis & Malloy, 1982). For example, earlier we briefly discussed people called compulsive checkers, who repeatedly check things to ensure that some harmful event has not happened. Such people get out of bed to check for natural gas odors, refuse to leave their home before checking to see that each door and window is locked, and so on. In extreme cases, the checkers spend most of their day doing nothing else but checking. Roper, Rachman, and Hodgson (1973) found that compulsive checkers rated themselves as less anxious after checking than when their checking was prevented. If fear reduction is what strengthens compulsive checking, then it is possible for avoidance behavior to be maintained in the absence of any external aversive consequence as long as fear (or at least discomfort) is reduced through compulsive checking. As such, if fear reduction is important in strengthening avoidance behavior, then we have a better explanation for the resistance to extinction of avoidance behavior.

Many behavior analysts do not like the two-factor theory of avoidance because it makes use of unobservable explanatory events: fear, anxiety, or discomfort. Some behavior analysts feel that many, if not most, instances of avoidance behavior can be explained through relationships between responses and external consequences without any need to refer to events like fear or anxiety reduction. These two perspectives on avoidance behavior represent a current controversy within behavior analysis that has yet to be fully resolved.

Summary

In this chapter we have considered two means of strengthening responding: Escape conditioning and avoidance conditioning. Escape conditioning is the response-dependent removal of a stimulus that strengthens a response. Escape conditioning is also sometimes called negative reinforcement. Avoidance conditioning is making a stimulus change dependent on the failure to respond and that causes the response to be strengthened. Avoidance conditioning is also considered as a form of negative reinforcement in the sense that the avoidance response serves to prevent or postpone the aversive stimulus change.

Both escape and avoidance conditioning make use of aversive stimuli. An aversive stimulus is a stimulus that generally functions either as a punisher to weaken behavior, or functions to strengthen behavior when used in escape or avoidance conditioning. Use of the term *aversive stimuli* allows behavior analysts to talk about stimuli that generally serve both types of response-weakening and response-strengthening functions.

✓ Both escape and avoidance responding may be subject to extinction. Extinction of escape responding occurs when the response is weakened because it no longer terminates the aversive stimulus. Extinction of avoidance responding occurs when an aversive stimulus no longer is dependent on the avoidance response. ✓

Both escape and avoidance conditioning procedures involve the use of aversive stimuli, so the side effects we saw associated with punishment are also of concern with these procedures. Escape and avoidance procedures should be considered under two conditions. First, if various types of positive reinforcement procedures have been unsuccessful in strengthening a desired response to an adequate level, escape and avoidance might be an effective accompaniment. Second, if behavior in the natural environment is maintained by escape and avoidance dependencies, then using escape and avoidance as behavior-change techniques may also be useful.

The subtypes of escape and avoidance conditioning procedures parallel the types of punishment procedures. Aversive physical stimuli, reprimands, timeout, response cost, and aversive activities have all been used to condition escape and avoidance responses. In addition, aversive social stimuli have been shown to promote escape behavior.

Escape and avoidance conditioning is also of interest to behavior analysts because a great deal of inappropriate behavior is strengthened by escape and avoidance dependencies. Daydreaming, ritualistic behaviors, self-destruction, and other forms of misbehavior have all been shown to be strengthened by escape from demanding activities. Various methods have been successfully used to solve the problem of escape-motivated misbehaviors. Much maladaptive behavior is also motivated by avoidance dependencies. Hysterical reactions and depressive behaviors are examples.

A variety of conditions have been shown to influence the effectiveness of escape and avoidance conditioning, including many of the same factors that influence the effectiveness of punishment. A knowledge of these factors is very important in both using escape and avoidance conditioning as behavior change procedures and in reducing the effectiveness of escape and avoidance dependencies that motivate undesirable behaviors.

The two-factor theory of avoidance conditioning holds that avoidance behavior is strengthened by the reduction of fear or anxiety that had been associated with the stimulus event or situation.

Section Summary

To this point we have discussed positive reinforcement, DRO and DRI, punishment, avoidance, and escape. You have learned all the basic behavior analysis relationships between responses and consequences that are important in changing behavior. Now we will focus on (a) variations in the way consequences can be dependent on behavior and (b) the effects of using stimulus cues to signal response-consequence relationships. Table 5.1 summarizes the basic response consequence relationships we have covered to this point.

As Cell 1 indicates, in both positive reinforcement and escape conditioning, responding is strengthened through a response-dependent stimulus change. In positive reinforcement, the stimulus change is one of stimulus presentation, while in escape conditioning, the stimulus change is one of stimulus removal.

As Cell 2 shows, punishment is a response-dependent stimulus change that weakens the response. We can distinguish between those forms of punishment in

Table 5.1   *Table of the Behavioral Elements*

	Effect of the Procedure	
	Strengthening of the target behavior	Weakening of the target behavior
Consequent stimulus change dependent on response	**CELL 1** Positive reinforcement Escape conditioning	**CELL 2** Punishment through stimulus presentation Punishment through response cost
Consequent stimulus change dependent on the absence of the response	**CELL 3** Avoidance	**CELL 4** Differential reinforcement of zero responding (DRO)

which a punisher is presented and those forms of punishment in which reinforcers are removed, as in response-cost and nonexclusionary time-out.

As Cell 3 shows, in avoidance conditioning a stimulus change is dependent on the failure of the response to occur, a procedure that strengthens the response. As Cell 4 illustrates, in DRO a stimulus change is dependent on the failure of a response to occur, a procedure that weakens the response.

Note that it is also possible to break down both avoidance conditioning and DRO in terms of stimulus presentations and removals. For example, the aversive event in some forms of avoidance is response cost, removal of already acquired reinforcers. The reinforcing event in some forms of DRO is removal of a stimulus dependent on the absence of a response. (See Tryon (1976) for a separate classification of the two forms of avoidance and the two forms of DRO.)

Woods (1974) and Tryon (1976, 1978) have pointed out that behavior analysis charts like Table 5.1 are comparable to the Periodic Table of the Elements in chemistry. The Periodic Table of the Elements shows the properties and relationships among the components of the material world. Likewise, Table 5.1, and Woods' and Tryon's expansions of it, depict the essential behavior-environment relationships in behavior analysis procedures and show how they are related. Tryon (1978) has illustrated how consulting such behavioral tables can clarify response-consequence dependencies for the behavior analyst when such dependencies become complex and potentially confusing.

Conceptual Exercise   *Escape and Avoidance*

For each of the following items, decide if the item is an example of escape, avoidance, both escape and avoidance, or neither escape nor avoidance. In each case the target behavior is highlighted. Justify your answer with a brief explanation. Check your answers as you go along with the analyses provided in the back of the book.

Note: Both escape and avoidance produce increases in the level of the target behavior and they are often used together in applications of behavior modification. When these procedures are used together, it is necessary to determine whether any increase in the level of the target behavior is due to avoidance or to escape. If the level of the target behavior increases only when the aversive stimulus is being applied, then the increase in behavior is due to escape conditioning. However, if the level of the target behavior increases at times other than when the aversive stimulus is actually being applied, then the increase in behavior is not due to escape conditioning but to avoidance conditioning. If the increase in the level of the target behavior occurs both when the aversive stimulus is being applied and when it is not, then the increase would be due to both escape and avoidance.

1. Kathy, 31, was a mildly retarded woman who had lived in an institution for 20 years. She resided on an exit ward where she was being prepared to leave the institution and live in the outside world. However, she often would not **attend classes** teaching grooming skills. To encourage her to attend classes, for every absence, Kathy was required to go to a small room equipped with grooming supplies. Once there, she was required to give a profoundly retarded woman from another ward a manicure, a hair combing, and an application of makeup. If Kathy refused to comply, she was manually guided through the activities. As a result of this method, Kathy's attendance at grooming class increased from about 20% to 100%.

2. Barbara, 21, was a mildly retarded woman who had lived in an institution for 20 years. She resided on an exit ward where she was being prepared to leave the institution and live in the outside world. However, she often would not **attend classes,** teaching grooming skills. In order to encourage her to attend classes, every time Barbara attended class, she was allowed to go to a small room equipped with grooming supplies. Once there, she was permitted to give a profoundly retarded woman from another ward a manicure, a hair combing, and an application of makeup. As a result of this method, Barbara's attendance at grooming class increased from about 20% to 100%.

3. Twenty-five employees at Anna State Hospital had volunteered for a study designed to improve their posture. The people wore a device around their necks. When they slouched, the device would sound a loud 500 hertz tone until they **assumed an upright posture.** Because of using this device, the employees assumed an upright posture quickly after the tone sounded, something they had rarely done before.

4. Twenty-five employees at Anna State Hospital had volunteered for a study designed to improve their posture. Whenever the employees **assumed an upright posture,** the experimenter would play beautiful Montovani music. As a result, the employees assumed and maintained an upright posture much more often than they had before.

5. Jerry's aunts and uncles would often send him presents, but Jerry would seldom **write thank-you letters.** In order to solve this problem, the Supreme Being sent a scary monster to visit his room at night whenever a week had elapsed without his writing a thank-you letter for a present. As a result of this method, Jerry's letter writing increased and now he always writes thank-you letters as soon as he receives a present.

6. Jerry's aunts and uncles would often send him presents but Jerry would seldom **write thank-you letters.** In order to solve this problem, Jerry's father told him that a scary monster would visit Jerry in his room at night whenever a week had elapsed without his writing a thank-you letter for a present. As a result of this method, Jerry now always writes thank-you letters as soon as he receives a present.

7. Mary was a 40-year-old mentally retarded woman who had been hospitalized for 22 years. She spent much of her day reclining on chairs rather than **going to occupational therapy sessions.** Therapists used a procedure in which every time she did not go to an occupational therapy session, prices were doubled for goods she could purchase with her token economy earnings. Before using this procedure, she did not go to occupational therapy at all. As a result of implementing the procedure, she began going to the occupational therapy sessions five times per week.

8. Mike, 8, was an autistic boy; Wilma, 8, and Doug, 6, were severely retarded children. One problem they had in common was a failure to **make eye contact with the therapist for at least 2 seconds within 5 seconds after receiving a "Look at me" instruction from the therapist.** In order to solve this problem, every time the child failed to respond to the "Look at me" prompt within 5 seconds, the therapist would give a "Head up," "Head straight," or "Head down" command and would manually guide the child's head in the appropriate direction within 1 second. Combined with reinforcement (praise and edibles) for eye contact, this procedure produced a 90% level of correct responding, a major improvement over the 55% level of correct eye contact responding that praise and edible reinforcement alone obtained.

9. After Cinder's father died, her stepmother took complete charge of the household. The stepmother would yell at Cinder much of the time. At first Cinder thought if she **did her homework and several chores around the house,** she wouldn't get yelled at. However, her stepmother still yelled at Cinder whether or not she did the homework and chores. As a result of the yelling, though, Cinder did her homework and the chores more often than she had before.

10. Joe, 21, diagnosed as a schizophrenic, lived in a psychiatric ward. Two of Joe's problems concerned his conversational skills: He failed to **speak loudly enough to be understood** and he failed **to speak in durations longer than 15 seconds.** In order to improve his conversational skills, a "nagging" procedure was used in which, when

Joe failed to speak loudly enough or long enough, the staff told him "Louder" or "Longer" as applicable, at 3 second intervals, until Joe complied with the request. Four times per day the ward staff would ask Joe to tell them something about a topic, including what he had read in the newspaper that day. Staff measured only **Joe's first responses** (i.e., before nagging) **to a topic.** This approach improved Joe's appropriate speech volume from 17% to 91% and improved his appropriate speech durations from 0% to 96%.

11. Gabby was a 27-year-old officer in the navy. He had no history of psychological problems but he **talked in his sleep.** He had begun to share his apartment with a friend who was disturbed by his frequent and often noisy sleep talking. In addition, the content of the sleep talk, though mostly nonsense, sometimes embarrassed Gabby. Drugs and hypnosis had failed to solve this problem, so Dr. LeBoeuf had Gabby put a device near his bed. Whenever Gabby talked in his sleep, a loud tone would sound through an earphone for 5 seconds, awakening him. This method eliminated sleep talk within about 3 weeks.

12. Martha never heated her house well at night because she was trying to reduce her heating bill. On some cold mornings, she would jump out of bed and her feet would "freeze" when they hit the cold tile. However, if she **put her slippers on** first, her feet would remain warm. As a result , Martha put her slippers on before touching her feet to the tile much more often than she had before.

13. Phoenecia was a 67-year-old woman who had had a stroke 6 months earlier. As a result, she was unable to **flex her left elbow.** In an attempt to solve this problem, researchers attached electrodes to Phoenecia's right forearm and administered an electric shock to her. Phoenecia could turn off the shock by flexing her left forearm 5 degrees. As a result of this method, when the shock came on, Phoenecia flexed her elbow much more often than she had before. After 19 sessions, Phoenecia could flex her elbow as much as 70 degrees.

14. Students living in a university dormitory would often not **lock their doors** before going to sleep. One researcher attempted to solve this problem by phoning all the students at 2:30 A.M. who had failed to lock their doors, and telling them to lock up. As a result of this procedure, door locking among the students increased from about 75% to 100%.

15. Keith was a four-year-old boy who had several behavior problems including **repetitive stereotyped acts,** such as lying on the floor for long periods while he stared at a pair of shoes, kissing and fondling a pair of shoes, and repeating "Shoes" as part of a strange ritual. Whenever Keith would engage in repetitive stereotyped acts, a therapist would hold one hand over Keith's eyes and the other hand behind his head for 30 seconds. This method rapidly reduced the repetitive acts, which were eventually eliminated.

16. Randy was living in a country where the electricity was very expensive. During the first month of his stay, he neglected to **turn off his hot water heater** every night. Consequently, Randy received a huge electricity bill at the end of the

month because the water was being heated when it wasn't needed. As a result of this, Randy turned off the hot water heater for the night most of the time.

17. During recreation period, Nancy would sometimes fail to **remain on the school playground**. In order to solve this problem, the teacher who supervised students on the playground told Nancy that if she wandered off the playground she would be harshly reprimanded. As a result of this warning, Nancy thereafter remained on the playground.

18. Allan was a 9-year-old boy who had been referred to Dr. Hansen by an urologist. Allan's problem was bed-wetting. Part of the treatment for the problem was use of a device that sounded a moderately loud tone when the child wet his bed. If Allan then failed to **get up and flip a switch that turned off the first tone,** a second much louder and more unpleasant tone would sound within 7 seconds. At first Allan failed to get up to turn off the first tone, but after a few experiences with the loud tone, he learned always to turn off the first tone whenever it sounded. Eventually, Allan also learned to stop wetting his bed.

19. The students at Discordia College were angry with the administration for not supporting various student rights. In order to change things, the students staged sit-ins in the president's office. The students ended their sit-ins only when the **president agreed to give students particular rights.** Sometimes the students had to sit for as long as 3 days, but the sit-in caused the president to give up and agree to give the students the rights they wanted. Before the sit-ins, the president had never given the students any rights.

20. Jeanette, 26, was a woman who had several behavior problems, including conversational skill deficits. Some difficulties were that she would pause too long between statements and before answering questions, make insufficient eye contact, and provide too much detail. In order to treat this problem, whenever Jeanette failed to **engage in an appropriate conversational skill,** a shrill tone would go on and stay on until Jeanette executed the skill being taught. As a result, whenever the tone came on, Jeanette would quickly perform the skill.

21. Six women staff members at Anna State Hospital had volunteered for a research project concerned with encouraging people to take prescribed medication at appropriate times. The women carried a device that would sound a tone when it was time to take a pill. **Turning a knob** on the device would end the tone and dispense a pill. As a result of this method, the women turned the knob every time the tone came on, but never when the tone was off.

22. Gaetan was taking a psychology course in which students had to pass a series of quizzes. Students earned 4 points for each quiz they passed. They could take quizzes at various times during the week and could take as many or as few as they wanted. However, if Gaetan and the other students in his group failed to **take quizzes often enough to meet a minimum rate of progress,** they would lose 25 points per day until they passed a quiz. This point loss dependency was found to improve the rate at which Gaetan and his fellow students progressed through the course.

23. Joan was a 12-year-old girl who had suffered from constipation for five years. She

also had encopresis, an accompaniment of constipation in which fluid from her stomach and small intestine seeps out at night, soiling her bedclothes. Three years of humanistic, self-awareness therapy had failed to help Joan. In order to solve this problem, a new procedure was put into effect. Upon awakening every morning, Joan was required to sit on the toilet for 20 minutes, or until she had a bowel movement. If she failed to **defecate,** at 1:00 P.M. she was required to sit on the toilet for 40 minutes, or until she had a bowel movement. If she failed to defecate at the 1:00 P.M. session, at 7:30 P.M. she was required to sit on the toilet for 90 minutes or until she had a bowel movement. Joan was not allowed to read or engage in any activity while on the toilet. As a result of this method, Joan began defecating in the toilet more often and soiled herself at night less. Within 14 months, she was defecating on a normal schedule.

Conceptual Exercise   *Making Escape and Avoidance Conditioning Effective*

In each of the following items, a principle of escape and avoidance conditioning effectiveness has been violated. Indicate what was done wrong and what should be done to make the procedure more effective.

1. In the Enlightened Day-Care Center, children were timed-out for engaging in undesirable behavior. If the children were quiet during the two-minute timeout, they could escape the timeout room. The workers were careful to be consistent with their use of the escape procedure, and minimized extraneous reinforcers and punishers. In addition, the children were told about the relationship between desirable quiet behavior and release from the timeout room. Usually, the children at the Enlightened Day-Care Center behaved well. At the Not-on-the-Ball Day-Care Center, a similar procedure was used. In this center, however, the children were not told about the consequences of quiet behavior in the timeout room.

2. Matilda frequently returned home from school without her galoshes. Her mother, a busy woman, sometimes reprimanded Matilda for forgetting her galoshes, but sometimes she didn't bother. The reprimand was quite severe and occurred as soon as Matilda got home. Matilda understood that she was supposed to return home with her galoshes.

3. When Jill came home from school, she was expected to do her homework before she was allowed to go out to play. Jill was aware of her parents' expectations. When Jill came home from school complaining of a sore tummy or with a headache, she was not required to do her homework. Jill began coming home with various physical complaints more and more often.

4. Biff was a rude child who had very poor manners. If he wanted a toy, he would just grab it from another child. His teachers decided to time Biff out whenever he was rude and grabbed toys. If he asked nicely for a toy, however, he would receive the toy and avoid timeout. The teachers noticed that when Biff asked some of the children nicely for a toy, they would yell at him and be mean to him. As a result, Biff's polite behavior was not increasing as quickly as they had hoped.

5. Students in first-year law school discovered that with one of their professors, they could avoid being called on to answer questions for the entire class period if they themselves made an unsolicited comment soon after class began. In another class, they discovered that an unsolicited comment only briefly postponed being called on. Students in the former class made many comments very quickly, but students in the latter class made fewer comments, and did so more slowly.

6. The students in Mr. Green's history class never seemed to do anything right. It seemed that Mr. Green would criticize them no matter what they were doing. Ms. Farrara was puzzled when some of these same students began her art class and made no attempt to avoid poor marks, even though she didn't demand a lot from them.

chapter 6

Shaping and Schedules of Reinforcement

Dicky had been a normal infant until, at about 9 months of age, cataracts developed in both of his eyes, causing clouding of the lens of the eyes and loss of visual acuity. Dicky began to have temper tantrums and difficulty sleeping. His visual problems worsened and during his second year, several eye operations were required. Eventually it became necessary to remove the lens in each of Dicky's eyes. Because his natural lenses were gone, it was crucial for Dicky to wear eyeglasses at all times, which became a serious problem in his family. For more than a year, Dicky's parents were unable to make him wear his glasses. Finally, Dicky was seen by several specialists, whose diagnoses of Dicky's condition included mental retardation, brain damage, and psychosis. One specialist thought that Dicky should be placed in an institution for the retarded. Dicky's refusal to wear his eyeglasses was just one of his many serious problems. Temper tantrums, including head banging, face slapping, face scratching, and hair pulling, often left him bleeding and bruised. This situation was so hard on Dicky's mother that she needed psychiatric help for depression and anxiety. Dicky himself was finally placed in a state psychiatric hospital for 3 months with a diagnosis of childhood schizophrenia. Dicky was only 3 years old.

During his stay in the psychiatric facility, Dicky's behavior began to improve somewhat, although he still refused to wear his glasses. An ophthalmologist who examined Dicky said that unless he began wearing his glasses, he would be permanently blind within 6 months. Dicky was referred to the Developmental Psychology Laboratory (DPL) at the University of Washington, where a team of behavior analysts took on the task of training Dicky to wear his eyeglasses.

The behavior analysts decided to use a method called *shaping* to get Dicky to wear his glasses. Shaping is a procedure in which a goal behavior is defined and responses that are increasingly like the goal behavior are reinforced. In order to expedite the use of immediate reinforcement, they initially established a conditioned reinforcer wherein they paired the noise of a toy clicker with delivery of candy and fruit. The clicker was easy to use and quickly accessible whenever Dicky made an appropriate response. Several pairs of glasses were placed in the room where training took place. If Dicky picked up a pair of glasses, this behavior was reinforced with the clicker. Although picking up the glasses is a very different behavior from the goal behavior of wearing the glasses, it was a first step. Next, reinforcement was made dependent on holding the glasses. When this behavior was established, reinforcement was made dependent on Dicky's carrying the glasses around. Once Dicky was carrying the glasses around, the behavior analysts reinforced movements that brought the glasses closer and closer to his eyes. At this point in the shaping process, a problem developed. Although Dicky was now wearing the glasses, at least in a technical sense, they were of no use to his vision because they were positioned improperly. The earpieces were usually upside down and the lenses were not in front of Dicky's eyes.

When anyone tried to touch Dicky's head to adjust the glasses, he became upset. Rather than trying to change Dicky's behavior at this point, the behavior analysts took a more practical approach and changed the glasses themselves. They added large adult earpieces and bars so that the glasses fit like a cap and did not easily slide off Dicky's head. Meanwhile, the shaping procedure had been used for several weeks with only slow progress. The behavior analysts realized that the fruit and candy reinforcers were not as effective as they should have been partly because Dicky was rarely deprived of food items. On a day when Dicky had not had much for breakfast or lunch, they used a different reinforcer, ice cream, and progress was rapid. Dicky was wearing the glasses properly within 30 minutes of the introduction of ice cream, and before long, Dicky was wearing his glasses throughout most meal sessions. Over time, activity reinforcers such as going for walks, taking car rides, and playing outdoors were made dependent on wearing the glasses. When Dicky was discharged from the hospital he was wearing his eyeglasses 12 hours per day.

Training Dicky to wear his eyeglasses was of primary concern to the behavior analysts because of the danger of vision loss, but there were other problems. Dicky's severe temper tantrums were treated with exclusionary timeouts and DRO procedures, as described by Wolf, Risley, and Mees (1964). After his discharge from the hospital, Dicky was enrolled at the DPL preschool where he was trained to speak and later to read. He was also taught more appropriate social behavior.

After 2 years at the preschool, Dicky enrolled in a public school special education class intended for mentally retarded students. After spending 2 years there and learning a great deal, he was placed in a special class for physically handicapped students, also for 2 years. He continued to be successful and was enrolled in a regular fourth-grade class. Dicky remained in a regular school and continued to perform adequately through the sixth grade. His teacher thought of him as a kind and considerate student who took pride in his work. He was well-liked by other students, and represented his homeroom class at student government meetings.*

To this point, you have studied the basic response-consequence relationships that behavior analysts use to change behavior: positive reinforcement, DRO, DRI, extinction, punishment, escape conditioning, and avoidance conditioning. In this chapter, we will examine two additional types of response-consequence relationships, shaping and schedules of reinforcement. Shaping is a procedure that can be used to teach new behaviors. Schedules of reinforcement can be used to ensure that behaviors we already possess continue to occur over time.

Shaping

Suppose you wish to strengthen a response using positive reinforcement. What if the goal response does not occur? In the case of Dicky, if the team of behavior analysts had sat around waiting for Dicky to put on his glasses so that they could reinforce this behavior, they may have had a long wait indeed. When the target behavior occurs infrequently or does not occur at all, we will have to "shape it up."

Shaping is a behavior change technique that promotes gradual improvement from some initial behavioral state to the desired goal state. In shaping, reinforcement is dependent on behaviors that are increasingly like some terminal or goal response.

With Dicky, the goal response was for him to wear his glasses all the time. At first, reinforcement was dependent on his picking up the eyeglasses. When this was achieved, reinforcement was made successively dependent on holding the glasses, carrying them around with him, moving them toward his face, putting the glasses on, putting them on properly, and then wearing them for longer and longer periods of time. Eventually, the goal response of wearing the glasses all the time was reached. This example illustrates shaping, because reinforcement was dependent on responses that were increasingly like the goal response.

Shaping shares certain features of the children's game of "hot and cold" (Morgan, 1974). An object is hidden, and the goal is for the player to find the object. Movements toward the object are reinforced by saying "hotter," and when the player moves away from the hidden object, she is told "colder." In general, the reinforcing consequence, "hotter," occurs only when the movement is closer to the object than previous movements. In this way, only those responses that are increasingly like the goal response are reinforced.

*Based on Wolf, Risley, and Mees (1964), and Nedelman and Sulzbacher (1972)

Certain usages apply to shaping. First, shaping is a special type of reinforcement procedure in which the goal response is reached by reinforcing behaviors that are increasingly like the goal response. It is incorrect to say that simple reinforcement techniques that do not require stepwise changes in the reinforced response are examples of shaping. Second, we say that responses that are increasingly like the goal response *successively approximate* the goal response. We call responses that are increasingly like the goal response *successive approximations* of the goal response. Third, in shaping we change the response requirement by reinforcing responses that are more and more like the goal response. Neither the stimulus for the response nor the reinforcer for the response change. Fourth, as with reinforcement, extinction, and punishment, we say that behavior is shaped, not people.

Types of Shaping

Behavior consists of many *dimensions* or *features,* ways in which behaviors are similar and different. For example, consider the features of your current behavior in reading this text. Your eyes are a certain distance from the page, you are sitting or lying down, or you have assumed another posture. Reading at a certain rate measurable in words per minute, you will read for a measurable duration of time before moving to another activity. A period of time elapsed (latency) between your opening the book and the onset of reading. As you can see, there are a large number of dimensions of your behavior.

When using shaping, we reinforce responses that are increasingly similar to a goal behavior. The specific ways in which the responses are similar to each other and to the goal behavior are called the shaping dimensions. Among the many dimensions along which behavior can be shaped, including temporal and intensive dimensions, are two basic shaping types: topographical dimensions and quantitative dimensions.

In shaping behavior along a topographical dimension, reinforcing response movements that are increasingly like the goal response shape a new response form or topography. Most of the shaping procedures used with Dicky are examples of *topographical shaping,* because it achieved a new response form (putting on the glasses) by reinforcing response forms that were more and more like the goal response. When topographical shaping is used, the shaping procedure consists of reinforcing different types of movements until, eventually, a new response is learned.

Another type of shaping is *quantitative shaping* in which reinforcement is dependent on either an increasing or decreasing quantity of some measure of behavior. Quantitative shaping is also referred to as using an *adjusting schedule of reinforcement.* In quantitative shaping, a new response topography is not learned. Instead, the person whose behavior is being shaped learns to engage in a previously learned response according to some measure of behavior that is progressively changed. For example, in shaping the rate of the response, reinforcement for the response is made dependent on either progressively higher response rates or progressively lower response rates.

For example, Epstein, Repp, and Cullinan (1978) used a shaping procedure to eliminate obscene language in a class of six behaviorally disordered children. At first, 20 bonus tokens were dependent on three or fewer instances of obscene language per day. After 12 days the rate of obscene language had diminished to an average of 1.4 responses per day. Next, the bonus tokens were dependent on two or fewer responses per day. After 5 days, the average rate of responding diminished to 0.47 responses per day. Then, the tokens were dependent on no more than a single response per day, further reducing responses to an average of 0.37 per day. Finally, a DRO procedure was used in which the tokens were dependent on a zero rate of obscene utterances per day, eliminating obscene verbal behavior during the last five days of the procedure. This example was a response rate-shaping procedure, because reinforcement was dependent on progressively lower response rates, until the goal of a zero rate of responding was achieved. Figure 6.1 present the data for one of the subjects. Clearly, the stepwise nature of the procedure gave the student an incentive and opportunity gradually to learn to reduce inappropriate utterances.

It is also possible to shape a higher rate of responding. For example, in a laboratory study, Scott, Peters, Gillespie, Blanchard, Edmunson, and Young (1973) shaped increases in a man's heart rate though the use of response-dependent television viewing. Television viewing was initially dependent on a heartbeat rate of 5 beats per minute over the man's normal baseline rate. When this increase in heart rate was achieved, television viewing was made dependent on an additional 5 beat

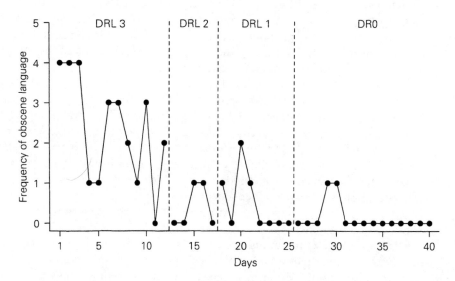

Figure 6.1   *The Effects of Shaping Response Frequency Downward*

The shaping procedure gradually reduced the child's obscene language to zero when the DRO procedure was in effect. The DRL (differential-reinforcement-of-low-rate-behavior) values refer to the maximum number of responses permitted in order to obtain reinforcement. Figure adapted from Epstein et al. (1978).

per minute increase in heart rate. This stepwise change in the criterion for reinforcement continued until the man achieved the goal response of a 20% increase in heart rate.

We can shape response latency in much the same way as we shape response rate. We can shape longer latencies by making reinforcement dependent on progressively longer delays between a stimulus and a response, or shorter latencies by making reinforcement dependent on shorter delays between a stimulus and a response. Dahlquist (1990) used a response-latency shaping procedure to eliminate vomiting in a 13-year-old boy. The boy, who had been hospitalized for his disorder, would vomit any liquid he consumed within 7 to 11 seconds after swallowing. Response-latency shaping was used by making points dependent on progressively longer latencies between swallowing and vomiting. For each second the boy exceeded a goal latency, he was awarded extra points exchangeable for the opportunity to play video games, watch television, and spend time with visitors. At first, points could be earned after latencies of only 12 seconds, but the required latencies were gradually increased to 18, 28, and 60 seconds. Combined with other procedures, this method eliminated the boy's vomiting within 15 days.

We can encourage a behavior by making reinforcement dependent on engaging in it for progressively longer periods of time, or discourage a behavior by making reinforcement dependent on engaging in it for progressively shorter periods of time. In this procedure, behavior duration is used as the shaping dimension. For example, Brown, Copeland, and Hall (1974) worked with an 11-year-old sixth-grade student named Fred, who was frequently absent from school. The behavior analysts suspected that the reason for his poor attendance was a punishing experience he had had with his fourth-grade teacher; he had been made to stand before the class wearing a dunce cap for failing to answer a question correctly.

Because of his problems, Fred had been transferred to a special school where behavior analysis methods were often used. There, the school principal set the goal of normal school attendance for Fred. Learning that Fred was a football fan, the principal set up a system whereby Fred could earn points exchangeable for tickets to see the Kansas City Chiefs, his favorite team. At first, points were dependent on Fred's being in the school library or hall for 3 hours in the morning or the afternoon. After 10 days of this method, during which Fred spent about 5 hours per day at school, points were made dependent on his spending at least 30 minutes in the classroom. As Fred spent more and more time in the classroom, the criterion for reinforcement was increased to 90 minutes, 2 hours, 3 hours, and finally 6 hours. Fred's data are presented in Figure 6.2. As you can see, Fred began attending school on a near-normal schedule and maintained this behavior in Grades 6 and 7.

In this example, duration of time was the shaping dimension; virtually any measure of behavior can serve as a shaping dimension.

In the forms of shaping we have considered, it is clear that responses are becoming more and more like some goal response. In topographical shaping, the responses become similar in form to the goal response, while in quantitative shaping, the responses become similar in some measure of amount, duration, or latency (quantitative dimensions). However, sometimes the shaping dimensions are less clear

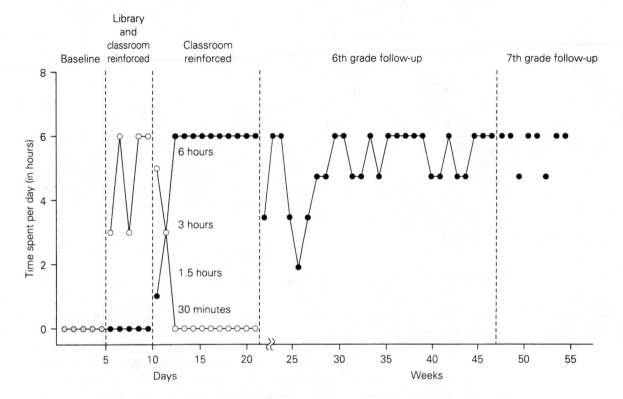

Figure 6.2   *The Effects of Shaping the Duration of a Response*

The duration of Fred's school-attending behavior was gradually shaped to the point where he was attending on an normal schedule, and this behavior persisted at follow-up. Figure adapted from Brown et al. (1974).

and less easily measured. For example, in shaping humor, we can differentially reinforce responses we identify as progressively funnier, but we would often be hardpressed to explain what makes one joke funnier than another, much less come up with some quantitative measure of hilariousness. We can similarly distinguish improvements in other important features of behavior including persuasiveness, politeness, clarity of expression, and so forth, but it is also often difficult to specify the dimensions that might be used as a shaping procedure. Shaping nonetheless takes place; we do not need to specify why one joke is funnier than another to laugh more at it.

Making Shaping Effective

Important factors in using shaping effectively are the selection of the goal response, the selection of the starting behavior, the selection of the shaping dimension, and the selection of stepwise criteria to be used in the shaping process.

The Goal Response

Before beginning the shaping process, define a specific goal response. It should represent a behavior that can produce accomplishments, as discussed in Chapter 1. This step helps to ensure that the goal behavior is clear and easily measurable. Many teachers fail because, although they recognize and reinforce improvements in student behavior, they do not have a clearly defined goal response. For example, one English professor we know recognizes and reinforces improvements in his student's writing, but has never explicitly defined good writing skills. As a result, the students lack an ultimate goal, and often their gains in writing improvement are incomplete.

The Starting Behavior

A common complaint among would-be behavior analysts goes, "I can't use shaping because there is nothing at all to reinforce." In such cases, usually the novice behavior analyst is unrealistic in requiring a starting behavior that is very close to the terminal response. In selecting the starting behavior, you must be content with a very distant approximation of the goal response. Look for a response that has something, however small, in common with the goal behavior and that occurs often enough to be reinforced. For example, Kirsch, Wolpin, and Knutson (1975) wished to shape public speaking behaviors in university students who feared public speaking. Although the students experienced much discomfort reading a prepared speech to others, they had much less trouble reading lists of unrelated words to an audience. Therefore, list reading was selected as the initial step in the shaping process. Behavior analysts must be creative in selecting a starting behavior and imaginative about how to shape this response in the direction of the goal response.

The Shaping Dimension

In selecting a shaping dimension, we are concerned with identifying a feature of behavior that will be changed to become more and more similar to the goal behavior. In shaping a response topography, our concern is with shaping behavior that is more physically like the goal behavior. In quantitative shaping, our concern is with shaping some measure of the behavior so that it eventually matches the goal, the desirable measure of the behavior to be achieved.

It is important that the shaping dimension matches the goal behavior. For example, if a manager's goal behavior is to increase employee productivity, in many cases, rather than to shape the length of time the employees sat at their desks, it would be more desirable to select dimensions that better indicate productivity.

Shaping Steps

Shaping steps should be large enough so that progress is rapid but small enough to be attainable. If too large a step is required, the behavior may be "lost" and the response must be reshaped by reverting to an earlier step.

With responses that are difficult to shape, it may be necessary to remain at an early step for a relatively long period of time. Koegel, O'Dell, and Dunlap (1988) compared two methods to teach autistic children to speak, a shaping method in which motor responses increasingly like speech were reinforced, and another method in which any verbal attempts to speak were always reinforced. With the attempts method, all that the children were required to do was to vocalize with normal loudness, orient themselves toward the trainer or the task materials, and give the appearance that the vocal response had something to do with the task.

The attempts method produced greater enthusiasm, interest, and happiness on the part of the children as well as more improved speech than the shaping method. These researchers believed that their results may have been due to the greater amount of reinforcement that occurred in the attempts method. In the shaping method, the children's behaviors were less frequently reinforced, because shaping demands ongoing progress toward the goal response (speech). Data from this study suggest remaining at one shaping step (e.g., attempting to speak) for a long period of time if requiring improvements reduces the reinforcers available to the person whose behavior is being shaped.

Other Variables

As a procedure, shaping formally involves only the use of reinforcement of responses. However, when shaping a response, it is important to do everything possible to induce the behavior, including giving verbal prompts (e.g., "Put your hand here"), gestures that indicate what the person should do next, time schedules for performing the response, and so forth. For example, consider what Wolf, Risley, and Mees did to help the shaping procedure along. They used several pairs of eyeglasses to make picking them up more likely. They had special glasses built in order to make it easy for Dicky to put them on his head. They switched reinforcers to make the procedure more effective. Once they got Dicky to put the glasses on, they put interesting objects in front of him in the hope of naturally reinforcing the response. When we use shaping, our job is not to adhere to the definition of shaping, but to use all our skills as behavior analysts to get the desired response to occur. Sometimes this means deviating from the shaping procedure as formally defined.

Schedules of Reinforcement

In everyday life, often your behavior is not reinforced each time it occurs. You knock on a door and no one is home. You place a phone call, and get a busy signal. You apply for a job, but fail to get it. You take a photograph and discover the lighting was poor. All of these are examples of *intermittent reinforcement,* cases in which behavior is reinforced only some of the time. Intermittent reinforcement contrasts with continuous reinforcement, reinforcement of a response each time it occurs.

A *schedule of reinforcement* is a system or plan that specifies which responses will be reinforced and which will go unreinforced. Discussion of important types of reinforcement schedules follows.

Fixed-Ratio Schedules

In a fixed-ratio schedule of reinforcement, reinforcement is dependent on the completion of a fixed number of responses. For example, Kirby and Shields (1972) worked with a 13-year-old seventh grader named Tom, who was not paying attention to his school work and was doing poorly on his arithmetic problems. The behavior analysts used a procedure in which they praised Tom for completing two problems. This method is called a fixed-ratio 2 (FR 2) schedule of reinforcement. Over time, reinforcement was made dependent on completion of an increasingly larger number of problems. Tom's problem completion was put on an FR 4 schedule of reinforcement, in which he was praised for completing four problems, then put on an FR 8 schedule, and finally an FR 16 schedule, in which reinforcing praise was dependent on Tom's completion of 16 problems. This procedure was highly successful. Tom's rate of correct problem solving increased from about 0.5 responses per minute to about 1.5 correct responses per minute, a threefold increase. In addition, Tom's percentage of attending behaviors increased from 50% to 100%. This gradual decrease in the number of responses being reinforced is called *thinning the reinforcement schedule.*

Laboratory work indicates that fixed-ratio schedules give rise to a special pattern of responding. Before reinforcement, response rate is high and uniform; the person on the FR schedule responds frequently. Immediately after reinforcement, however, a brief pause in responding takes place, after which responding again occurs at a high rate. The postreinforcement pause, long a subject of considerable interest to behavior analysts, has been compared to the impulse we feel to take a break after we have successfully completed a major project. Miller (1968a) reinforced vocal responses with escape from a high-force response requirement. He put vocal responses on different fixed-ratio schedules of reinforcement (FR 1, FR 5, FR 10, and FR 50) and examined the length of the postreinforcement pause in each schedule. The results from one of the subjects in this study are shown in Figure 6.3.

As shown, the greater the size of the fixed-ratio schedule, the longer was the pause after reinforcement. Miller's results suggest that when you complete a big job, you will schedule a longer vacation from work than when you complete a small one.

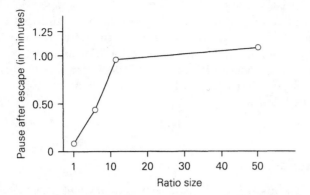

Figure 6.3   *The Relation Between the Size of a Fixed Ratio and the Length of the Postreinforcement Pause*

The length of the pause after reinforcement by escape from high force requirement increased with the size of the fixed ratio required. The FR 1 schedule produced the shortest postreinforcement pause and the FR 50 schedule produced the longest pause. Figure adapted from Miller (1968a).

Variable-Ratio Schedules

In a variable-ratio schedule, reinforcement is dependent on a number of responses that varies from reinforcement to reinforcement. For example, Saari and Latham (1982) used a variable-ratio schedule of reinforcement in a study of the work performance of 12 mountain-beaver trappers in Washington state. The mountain beaver is a rodent that eats newly planted trees, impairing the growth of new forests. For part of the time, the trappers were paid on a continuous reinforcement schedule in which each response was reinforced: Every rodent caught could be traded in for $1. At other times, the trappers were paid on a variable-ratio 4 (or VR 4) schedule of reinforcement. On this schedule, every time the trapper brought a rodent to his supervisor, the trapper would receive $4 dependent on correctly predicting the odd or even outcome of 2 rolls of a die. The chance of guessing correctly both times is 1 in 4. This was a VR 4 schedule of reinforcement because reinforcement was dependent on an *average* of every 4 responses. The number of responses varied from reinforcement to reinforcement. Sometimes the trappers would receive, for example, $4 two or three times in a row, while other times they would not receive any money even after making a long series of responses. However, on the average, every fourth response was reinforced, making it a VR 4 schedule.

Results of the study showed that both the continuous reinforcement schedule and the VR 4 schedule increased the trapper's productivity compared to the usual method of paying the trappers by the hour. In addition, the trappers were more productive on the VR 4 schedule than on the continuous schedule. The trappers rated the VR 4 schedule more favorably on a questionnaire than the continuous schedule.

Laboratory research has shown that variable-ratio schedules generate the highest rates of responding of all the reinforcement schedules. Unlike fixed-ratio schedules, VR schedules do not generate a postreinforcement pause. Much gambling behavior is reinforced according to variable-ratio schedules, and the great interest people have in various types of gambling has been attributed to the power of variable-ratio schedules to induce high rates of behavior. For example, consider a slot machine. Responses are seldom reinforced, but it is possible for responses to be reinforced twice in a row, causing people who have won a bit of money to continue playing even after they have won.

Fixed-Interval Schedules

In a fixed-interval schedule (FI), reinforcement is dependent on the first response after the passage of a fixed period of time since the last reinforcement. For example, Alexander and Apfel (1976) used a fixed-interval schedule in a classroom situation. Every 3 minutes a bell would sound and the teacher would look up at the class and observe which students were on-task. On-task students were given tokens that could later be exchanged for toys, candy, or free time. This was a fixed-interval schedule (FI 3') because reinforcement was dependent on passage of the fixed interval of time, 3 minutes, followed by the response, on-task behavior.

With fixed-interval schedules it doesn't matter what is going on during the interval; only postinterval responding is reinforced. The students in Alexander and Apfel's study could have been off-task during most of the time and still have earned tokens if they switched to on-task behavior as the end of the 3-minute interval approached. Laboratory experiments with animals have indicated that this pattern of switching from nonresponding to responding often occurs with fixed-interval schedules. Immediately after reinforcement, response rate is low but as the fixed interval of time passes, response rate increases to a maximum just before reinforcement. Because fixed-interval schedules promote desirable target behaviors only during a limited period of time, behavior analysts seldom use them in behavior change projects.

Fixed-interval schedules occur often in everyday life. Baking bread is an example. The response of removing bread from an oven is reinforced only after the passage of a fixed-interval of time. Responses occurring before the interval has passed will not be reinforced because the bread is not properly baked.

Many fixed-interval schedules of reinforcement also have limited-hold (LH) dependencies. In a limited-hold dependency (or limited-hold contingency), there is a limited period of time after passage of the fixed interval when the response can be reinforced. For example, in baking bread, there is a limited amount of time after the fixed interval has passed when taking the bread out of the oven can be reinforced. Responses occurring long after the interval has passed will not be reinforced because the bread will be overcooked or burned. In general, the effect of limited-hold dependencies is to reduce the length of pauses between responses and, in this way, to increase overall response rate. Because of the limited-hold dependency, the experienced baker checks the bread relatively frequently.

Variable-Interval Schedules

In a variable-interval schedule, reinforcement is dependent on the first response after the passage of a period of time that changes from reinforcement to reinforcement. For example, after using the FI 3' schedule for two days, Alexander and Apfel changed to a variable-interval 3-minute schedule (VI 3'). In this kind of schedule, the amount of time that passed before the experimenters looked about the room and gave tokens to on-task students varied. Sometimes only a few seconds passed between token deliveries, while at other times 5 or 6 minutes passed between reinforcement opportunities. On the average, on-task behavior was reinforced every 3 minutes.

The VI 3' schedule has a key advantage over the FI 3' schedule. With the FI 3' schedule, it would be possible for clever misbehaving children to consult their wristwatches and be on task only for a few seconds once every 3 minutes. However, with the VI 3' schedule, the children could not predict when the token reinforcement would become available, so the best strategy would be to be on-task all the time to get the most reinforcers in the shortest amount of time.

Variable-interval schedules generally result in a uniform rate of sustained responding. These types of schedules do not generate as high a rate of behavior as variable-ratio schedules because in a variable-interval schedule, very high response rates won't result in more reinforcers; the time period must pass. Variable-ratio schedules, on the other hand, generate very high rates of responding because more responses per unit time result in more reinforcement. However, one practical advantage of variable-interval schedules is that you do not need to count each instance of the target behavior, as is required when using variable-ratio schedules. For this reason, variable-interval schedules are often used in group teaching situations where teacher time is limited.

Fixed-Duration Schedules

In a fixed-duration schedule, reinforcement is dependent on engaging in a behavior for a fixed amount of time. For example, Semb and Semb (1975) used a fixed-duration schedule in a summer remedial-reading class for children in grades three through six. During one part of the study, reinforcement from the teacher was dependent on engaging in workbook assignment activity for a fixed duration of time. However, this schedule was less effective than a fixed-page schedule in which reinforcement was dependent on completing a fixed number of workbook pages. For this reason, Semb and Semb recommended that teachers should make reinforcement dependent on completion of a set amount of work rather than on the amount of time engaged in the activity.

Fixed-duration schedules are best used in teaching situations where the duration of the activity represents a measure of good performance. For example, in a swimming class, an instructor might make reinforcers dependent on treading water for a fixed duration of time. Fixed-duration schedules are also seen in certain forms of timeout. In activity-suppression timeout, for example, a misbehaving individual is required to sit still for a fixed amount of time before exiting timeout.

Perhaps the most familiar form of fixed-duration schedule is the hourly wage. Employees receive their pay after engaging in work behavior for a fixed duration of time, the scheduled work hours. In many work situations, however, additional avoidance dependencies are in effect. For example, for many employees, failure to produce some minimal levels of output results in being fired.

Some evidence indicates that the hourly wage system is a relatively poor means of maintaining behavior when compared to fixed- and variable-ratio schedules or other methods of making pay dependent on employee productivity (George & Hopkins, 1989; Pritchard, Hollenback, & DeLeo, 1980; Prichard, Leonard, Von Bergen, & Kirk, 1976). For example, George and Hopkins compared the fixed-duration hourly wage system for waitpersons to a performance-dependent pay in which the waitpersons received 7% of their total sales. Under the performance-dependent pay arrangement, the waitpersons sold more food per hour and earned more money. In this way, the performance-dependent pay system benefited both the waitpersons and their employers. [See George and Hopkins for a discussion of the relative merits of fixed-duration and performance-dependent pay systems.]

Variable-Duration Schedules

In a variable-duration schedule, reinforcement is dependent on engaging in a behavior for an amount of time that changes from reinforcement to reinforcement. As with fixed-duration schedules, little work has been done using variable-duration schedules to solve behavior problems. However, one example would be a parent who praises the quiet play of children in durations that vary from reinforcement to reinforcement. We see variable-duration schedules in everyday life. Waiting in line at the grocery store is reinforced on a variable-duration schedule because the time you must stand in line before receiving reinforcement varies from one time to the next, depending on the speed of the cashier and the number of customers preceding you.

Fixed- and variable-duration schedules are similar to but not the same as fixed- and variable-interval schedules. In duration schedules, reinforcement is dependent on engaging in the behavior for the entire amount of time specified. In interval schedules, reinforcement is dependent on merely one response that occurs after the interval has passed.

Differential-Reinforcement-of-Low-Rate-Behavior Schedules

In a differential-reinforcement-of-low-rate-behavior (DRL) schedule, reinforcement is dependent on a response rate that is below a specified response rate. Two types of DRL schedules are *spaced-responding DRL* and *interval DRL* (Deitz, 1977).

In spaced-responding DRL, reinforcement for a response is dependent on the passage of a minimum amount of time since the last response. For example, Lennox,

Miltenberger, and Donnelly (1987) used spaced-responding DRL with three retarded people who ate so quickly that they would choke on their food. A DRL 15" schedule was used in which the opportunity to have a bite of food was dependent on the passage of 15 seconds since the last attempt to have a bite of food. This method was effective in reducing the rate of eating when combined with a prompting technique that promoted waiting between bites.

Another type of DRL schedule is interval DRL. In interval DRL, reinforcers are given to an individual at the end of a time period dependent on the occurrence of fewer than a specified number of responses during that time period. If more than the specified number of responses occurs during a time period, the opportunity for reinforcement during that time period is lost and a new time period is set. For example, Deitz (1977) used interval DRL to reduce the talking out of a 6-year-old girl who attended the first grade in an Atlanta public school. A chocolate caramel was made dependent on every 5 minutes that passed during which the girl had talked-out fewer than two times. If she talked out more than once during a 5-minute interval, a timer was reset and the girl was required to talk out fewer than twice during the new 5-minute interval. This method reduced the frequency of talking out to a low level.

A special case of interval DRL is called *full-session DRL*. As in interval DRL, in full-session DRL, reinforcers are given to an individual at the end of a time period, dependent on the occurrence of fewer than a specified number of responses during that time period. However, in full-session DRL, reinforcement can be earned only during one interval. In interval DRL, if the person fails to meet the criterion for reinforcement, the interval is reset and there is another chance for reinforcement during the next interval. In full-session DRL, the interval length is set for the full period of time during which reinforcement is possible.

For example, Deitz and Repp (1973) used full-session DRL to reduce the talk-out behaviors of an 11-year-old retarded boy. Talk-out behaviors included verbalizations that were made without the teacher's permission. If three or fewer talk outs occurred during a 50-minute session, a rate of 0.06 or fewer per minute, the boy was given 5 minutes of free playtime at the end of the day. If more than three talk outs occurred during the 50-minute session, no free play was awarded that day. Figure 6.4 presents the data during baseline when no dependency was in effect and during the treatment phase where the DRL dependency was in effect.

This method reduced responding from an average of 0.11 responses per minute during baseline to an average of 0.02 responses per minute while the DRL dependency was in effect. Indeed, the boy's rate of talking out was below the DRL criterion throughout treatment and he received his reward of free time every day.

DRL dependencies are appropriate to use with behaviors that are acceptable as long as they occur at low, manageable rates. For example, eating is clearly a desirable behavior, but not when it occurs at too high a rate. Deitz and Repp's modification of talk-out behaviors is another example. If talk-out behaviors occurred without restriction, classrooms would be chaotic places where little learning could take place. However, permitting a low rate of talk-out behavior allows students greater freedom to communicate without unduly disrupting the learning environment.

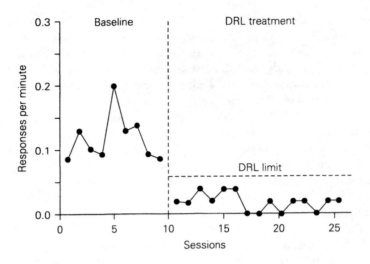

Figure 6.4   *The Effects of a DRL Schedule*

When the DRL dependency was in effect, the boy's rate of talking out decreased to well below the criterion requirement for reinforcement. Figure adapted from Dietz and Repp (1973).

As we saw in discussing shaping, DRL schedules can be used to shape progressively lower rates of responding. Epstein, Repp, and Cullinan (1978) shaped progressively lower rates of obscene language by using DRL schedules that required progressively lower rates of responding.

Natural DRL schedules are common in daily life. Taking a walk through an art museum or down a garden path are examples. Walking and observing at a sufficiently slow rate enables the viewer to have enough time to notice aspects of art or nature that are pleasing or visually interesting. In contrast, when we hurry through these activities, these reinforcers are not available.

Differential-Reinforcement-of-High-Rate-Behavior Schedules

In a differential-reinforcement-of-high-rate-behavior (DRH) schedule, reinforcement is dependent on a rate of responding that is above a specified response rate. DRH schedules are normally set up such that a minimum number of responses are required during a given unit of time. In one application of DRH schedules, Arnett and Ulrich (1975) assigned a 5-year-old girl several household tasks, including cleaning a bathroom sink, emptying a wastebasket, washing a television screen, emptying ashtrays, and setting the table. The girl performed her chores, but often did so very slowly. A DRH schedule was put into effect in which tokens exchangeable for candy were made dependent on performing the chores within a set time limit. The fastest previous task performance determined the time limit. Figure 6.5 presents the

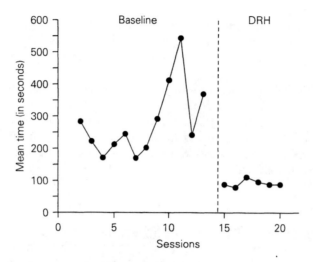

Figure 6.5   *The Effects of a DRH Schedule*

When reinforcement was dependent on doing her chores within a set time limit, the girl's performance rate improved considerably. Figure adapted from Arnett and Ulrich (1975).

mean results of this treatment for the five tasks assigned. As you can see, this method increased the rate at which the girl performed the chores.

DRH schedules are common in daily life. Any athletic competition in which winning is dependent on engaging in some activity faster than an opponent is a DRH schedule. People who work under the pressure of deadlines are on DRH schedules. Students who must cram before a final exam are also on DRH schedules in which the reinforcer of a good grade is dependent on rapid acquisition of course material.

Many routine activities like washing dishes and taking out the trash are influenced by natural DRH schedules. When you perform routine activities at a high rate, more time is available to engage in other more reinforcing activities.

Differential-Reinforcement-of-Paced-Responding Schedules

A differential-reinforcement-of-paced-responding (DRP) schedule is a combination of DRL and DRH schedules. In a DRP schedule, reinforcement is dependent on a response rate that is both below a specified maximum response rate and above a specified minimum response rate. Howie and Woods (1982) used a DRP schedule in work with men who had problems with stuttering. During one part of the treatment, token reinforcement was dependent on a rate of nonstuttering speech that was either 20 syllables per minute above or below a set criterion. The goal of this work was to increase the rate of the men's nonstuttering speech gradually. Setting a lower limit on speech rate helped give the men an incentive to increase their speech rate and become more fluent speakers. Setting an upper limit helped prevent the men from speaking too rapidly before they had reliably learned to do so without stuttering.

Many examples of DRP schedules occur in everyday life. For instance, music teachers often make reinforcement dependent on a rate of playing an instrument that is neither too slow nor too fast. Setting a lower limit for response rate ensures that the student will be challenged to play more fluently. Setting an upper limit for response rate ensures that the student will not play so rapidly that errors occur and poor playing techniques are acquired.

Characteristics and Advantages of Reinforcement Schedules

Students sometimes wonder why schedules of reinforcement are used as behavior change procedures. If positive reinforcement is so good, they ask, then isn't it best to reinforce each response rather than reinforcing only some responses? The answer to this question is yes . . . and no.

For a response that is just being learned, the answer is yes; each instance of newly acquired responses should be reinforced. In this way, weak, newly learned behavior can be quickly strengthened. However, once a response has been acquired, the answer is no; intermittent reinforcement is preferred for several reasons. Its advantages include economizing on reinforcers and behavioral observations, building persistent behavior, and improving correct responding on certain types of tasks.

Economizing on Time and Reinforcers

When we use intermittent reinforcement, we free ourselves from the job of observing and reinforcing each response. For example, in teaching situations, using continuous reinforcement often demands that a teacher observe one student at a time and be prepared to dispense a reinforcer when a response occurs. When reinforcement is intermittent, teachers can monitor the performance of larger numbers of students.

Intermittent reinforcement also has the advantage of conserving available reinforcers. In token economies or in the workplace, thinning the reinforcement schedule makes it possible to strengthen more behavior at less cost. In addition, when responding is intermittently reinforced, more responses can occur before satiation than when continuous reinforcement is used.

Building Persistent Behavior

Another advantage of intermittent reinforcement over continuous reinforcement is that behavior that has been intermittently reinforced is more resistant to extinction than behavior that has been continuously reinforced. We briefly examined this feature of intermittent reinforcement in Chapter 3 in our discussion of extinction. Extinction is less effective with behavior that has been intermittently reinforced rather than continuously.

The role of intermittent reinforcement in promoting resistance to extinction is important because in the natural environment there will be times when good behavior is at least temporarily on extinction. Less courteous participants in social situations often ignore good manners. A student's discovery of the correct solution to a math problem will sometimes be unnoticed by the teacher. A spouse's noble efforts to hold a good marriage together may be to no avail. A diplomat's attempts to convince bitter enemies to cease conflict frequently will be unsuccessful. Scientific work, more often than not, consists of a long series of dead ends and false starts.

The success of most worthwhile human activities requires that we persevere despite extended periods of nonreinforcement. Thomas Edison once said ". . . I have not failed. I've just found 10,000 ways that won't work." Through intermittent reinforcement we learn to be persistent.

The advantage of intermittent reinforcement in building persistent behavior has been documented in many studies. Kazdin and Polster (1973) dramatically illustrated this feature of intermittent reinforcement in work with two retarded men employed at a sheltered workshop. Both men had a social skills deficit: They would rarely talk with their co-workers. In order to solve this problem, tokens were made dependent on the men's social interactions, defined as one of the men saying something to a co-worker, who in turn said something in reply. Simple questions the men directed at co-workers, however, did not count. Further, the men were required to speak about some topic (e.g., the weather or sports) and make declarations about the subject.

Both men's rate of social interaction increased as a result of the continuous token reinforcement. For one of the men, an intermittent schedule was then introduced. During the first week of intermittent reinforcement, two-thirds of his interactions were reinforced. During the second week, the schedule was further thinned such that only one-third of the interactions were reinforced. In contrast, the other man's social interactions continued to be reinforced continuously with tokens. After this 2-week period, token reinforcement for both men was discontinued. As you can see in Figure 6.6, the results suggested that intermittent reinforcement was a much more desirable procedure. The man whose behavior was intermittently reinforced continued to interact with his co-workers frequently, while the man whose behavior was continuously reinforced reverted to his previous pattern of social isolation.

Improving Correct Responding

A third advantage of intermittent reinforcement over continuous reinforcement is improved performance in discrimination tasks. Koegel, Schreibman, Britten, and Laitinen (1979) worked with autistic children, training them to tell the difference between visual stimuli. During each training trial, the children were shown two picture cards. For example, on one card were pictures of a bird and a squirrel while on

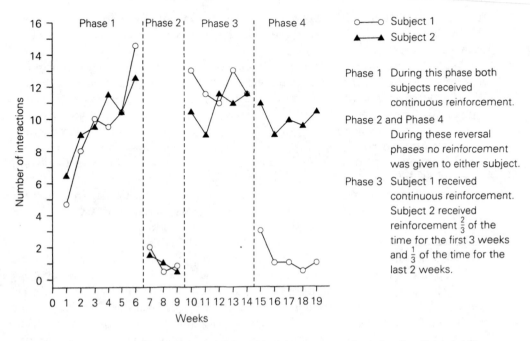

Figure 6.6   *The Influence of Intermittency of Reinforcement on Long-Lasting Behavior Changes*

Subject 2 continued to interact with his co-workers during extinction when he had been previously reinforced on an intermittent schedule. The interactions of Subject 1, however, dropped significantly during extinction. Subject 1 had been continuously reinforced for interactions. Figure adapted from Kazdin and Polster (1973).

the other card were pictures of a flower and a butterfly. The child's pointing to the picture of the bird-squirrel card was reinforced, while pointing to the flower-butter-fly card was put on extinction. For one group of children, pointing was continuously reinforced. For another group, pointing was reinforced on a variable-ratio 3 schedule of reinforcement. After this training, the children were shown cards with only one picture on them—for example a bird, a squirrel, a flower, or a butterfly. Correct responses to these one-picture cards were pointing to the pictures that had previous-ly been associated with reinforcement. In our example, pointing to the bird or the squirrel would be correct, while pointing to the flower or the butterfly would be incorrect.

Results of the study showed that the children given VR 3 training performed better on the one-picture tests than students given continuous reinforcement train-ing. These researchers suggest the VR 3 schedule may have caused the children to pay more attention to both figures on the training card than the continuous rein-forcement schedule. In particular, when the children's responses went unreinforced, they may have paid more careful attention to all the stimuli involved in the task.

Something similar may happen when, for example, you dial a phone number, get no answer, and you recheck the phone number to ensure that you have the correct number. Increased attending behavior induced by nonreinforcement may explain why intermittent reinforcement sometimes improves performance at tasks requiring people to make discriminations (e.g., Calicchia, 1973; Freed & Freed, 1977; Gross & Gutman, 1988; Stephens, Pear, Wray, & Jackson, 1975). However, this effect of intermittent reinforcement is not currently well understood.

The results of the Koegel et al. (1979) study illustrate another important feature of intermittent schedules, that they cause responding to become more diverse and variable than when every response is reinforced. In general, when your responding goes unreinforced, you are more likely to alter your ongoing behavior. These changes in your responding can, in turn, cause you to discover a more successful mode of responding. Response variability induced by nonreinforcement may explain why intermittent reinforcement sometimes improves performance in various types of tasks.

Eckerman and Vreeland (1973) examined this aspect of intermittent schedules of reinforcement in a study with university students. The students were told to put an "X" anywhere on a piece of paper, after which they received either a yellow card, indicating their placement of the "X" was correct, or a white card, indicating their placement of the "X" was incorrect. During different periods of the study, the "X" placement responses were (a) reinforced continuously; (b) reinforced on a VR 3 schedule; or (c) put on extinction. Results of the study indicated that the marks were placed at more diverse locations on the page during VR 3 periods than during continuous reinforcement.

Making Schedules of Reinforcement Effective

The effectiveness of reinforcement schedules is importantly determined by the same variables that influence the effectiveness of reinforcement. As such, schedules of reinforcement will be influenced by deprivation and satiation, instructions, reinforcer amount, predictive conditioned reinforcers, reinforcer variety, response energy, reinforcer contrast effects, extraneous reinforcers, and reinforcement delay.

One additional factor important in making reinforcement schedules effective is gradually thinning the reinforcement schedule, moving from continuous to progressively more intermittent reinforcement. There are two reasons for this gradual reduction in the frequency of reinforcement. First, if the intermittency of reinforcement is increased too rapidly, the response will go repeatedly unreinforced too many times and may undergo extinction. This phenomenon occurs with ratio schedules when the response requirement is increased too quickly and is called *ratio strain*. When ratio strain occurs, the response must be reinforced more often. Sometimes it is necessary to return to a continuous reinforcement schedule for awhile before making reinforcement intermittent again.

A second reason for gradually thinning the schedule was reported by Steeves, Martin, and Pear (1970), who found that aggression and undesirable emotional behavior can occur when intermittent reinforcement is introduced. Recall that one of the effects of extinction can be an increase in aggression. Moving to a more intermittent schedule of reinforcement is like extinction because both situations entail an increase in nonreinforced responses. It is desirable to decrease the frequency of reinforcement gradually in order to minimize possible aggressive and emotional effects of nonreinforcement.

Behavior analysts must give careful consideration to the effects of the reinforcement schedule when they plan their behavioral intervention programs. In general, it is often best to begin training with continuous reinforcement with the intention of gradually thinning the schedule, once the behavior has been well established.

Some Advanced Considerations

As you have seen, intermittent reinforcement causes more persistent responding during extinction than continuous reinforcement. Several theories have been developed to explain this intermittent reinforcement effect, including the discrimination hypothesis, of which there are several different versions. One of these is called the generalization-decrement hypothesis.

The generalization-decrement hypothesis asserts several things. First, when we are on a reinforcement schedule, reinforcement and nonreinforcement become established as cues for our behavior. Second, when we have learned to respond to a cue for a behavior, alterations in that cue will cause us to perform the behavior less often or less well than when the original cue is present. One example of this is in studying. Research has shown that when you study in the same room in which you take an examination, you will tend to do better on the exam than if you study in a different room (e.g., Abernethy, 1940; S. M. Smith, 1979). Essentially, the stimuli in the place where you study become established as cues for the academic responses you learn while studying. The third assertion of the generalization-decrement hypothesis is that if your behavior has been intermittently reinforced and then put on extinction, there is less alteration of the cues for the behavior than when your behavior has been continuously reinforced and then put on extinction. Nonreinforcement occurs in both intermittent reinforcement and in extinction, but it never occurs during continuous reinforcement. Because the change from continuous reinforcement to extinction represents a greater alteration of cues for responding than the change from intermittent reinforcement to extinction, there is less responding in extinction after continuous reinforcement than after intermittent reinforcement.

One problem with theories of the intermittent reinforcement effect, including this version of the discrimination hypothesis, is that they have been developed from the findings of animal research. In animal research, an extrinsic reinforcer such as food is used and it is normally the sole reinforcer for the behavior being studied. In contrast, in applied work with people, often the goal is not so much to maintain behavior during extinction but to shift the reinforcer for a response from an contrived reinforcer to a natural reinforcer. For example, in Kazdin and Polster's study, token reinforcement was used to strengthen social interactions. Eventually those interactions were maintained by their natural consequences, but this occurred only when the token reinforcement was made progressively more intermittent. At this time, the role of intermittent reinforcement in easing the transition from contrived to natural reinforcers is not as well understood as is the role of intermittent reinforcement in maintaining behavior during extinction.

Summary

In this chapter we examined two topics, shaping and schedules of reinforcement. Whereas shaping is used to establish new behaviors, schedules of reinforcement are used to ensure that previously established behaviors continue to occur.

Shaping is a method of gradual behavior change. In shaping, reinforcement is dependent on behaviors that are increasingly like some terminal or goal response. The responses that are increasingly like the goal response are said to successively approximate the goal response, and these responses are called successive approximations to the goal response.

In shaping, behavior becomes more like the goal response in certain respects called shaping dimensions. Two basic types of shaping dimensions are topographical dimensions and quantitative dimensions. When topographical shaping is used, the form of the response becomes more like the form of the goal response. In quantitative shaping, some quantitative measure of the behavior, such as response rate, becomes more and more like the measure of the goal behavior. Behavior analysts have made extensive use of both topographical and quantitative shaping procedures.

In making shaping effective, important considerations are the selection of the starting behavior, the selection of the shaping dimension, and the selection of the steps to be used in the shaping process. It is important that there is a clear specification of the behaviors at each stage of the shaping process and that the steps in the shaping procedure are the appropriate size. In addition, when using shaping the behavior analyst should be inventive in order to find creative ways of getting the goal behavior to occur, even if this means using methods other than shaping.

Schedules of reinforcement are generally concerned with the question of which responses will be reinforced and which will not. Essentially, a schedule of reinforcement is a plan or a system that specifies those responses that will be reinforced. In a fixed-ratio schedule of reinforcement, reinforcement is dependent on a fixed number of responses, while in a variable-ratio schedule, reinforcement is dependent on a variable number of responses. In fixed-interval schedules, reinforcement is dependent on the passage of a certain fixed period of time before a response will produce reinforcement. Variable-interval schedules follow this pattern, except that the time interval between reinforcements varies.

In duration schedules, reinforcement is dependent on engaging in the target behavior for a specified amount of time. In fixed-duration schedules, the behavior must be performed for a fixed amount of time. In variable-duration schedules, the time interval during which the behavior must be performed varies or changes from reinforcement to reinforcement.

In other types of schedules, reinforcement is dependent on the rate of the response. In a differential-reinforcement-of-low-rate (DRL) schedule, reinforcement is dependent on a rate of the response that is below a maximum standard. In contrast, in a differential-reinforcement-of-high-rate (DRH) schedule, reinforcement is dependent on a rate of response that is above a minimum standard. Finally, a differential-reinforcement-of-paced-responding schedule combines the requirements of the DRL and DRH schedules: Reinforcement is dependent on a response rate that is neither too high nor too low.

Reinforcement schedules are useful because they allow the behavior analyst to change behavior while economizing on reinforcers and behavioral observations. Reinforcement schedules also play an important role in building persistent behavior. In addition, reinforcement schedules can promote more correct responding on certain types of tasks.

Important considerations in making reinforcement schedules effective include the same variables that influence the effectiveness of reinforcement. In addition, intermittent reinforcement is more effective if the level of intermittency is introduced gradually.

Finally, we briefly considered one theory of reinforcement called the generalization-decrement hypothesis. This theory attempts to explain the effect of reinforcement schedules in making behavior more persistent.

Conceptual Exercise   *Shaping*

For each of the following items, decide if the item is an example of shaping and, if it is, identify the shaping dimension. Justify your decision with a brief explanation. Confirm your decisions by consulting the analyses provided in the back of the book.

1. A preschool girl named Ann always played by herself rather than with the other children. In order to get her to play with other children, the teacher initially paid attention to Ann when she was near other children, watching them play. When this behavior was established, the teacher reinforced the children's play when it occurred alongside the other children. Finally, the teacher reinforced the children with attention only when they were playing with the other children.

2. Retarded children who lived at a state hospital had to be taught to feed themselves. The goal was for the boys to learn a self-feeding cycle: to scoop food from their plates, take it to their mouths, and eat. When they succeeded, their trainer praised them. As a result, many of the children learned to eat properly.

3. Subject Two was a 61-year-old man who suffered from anxious behavior and an elevated heart rate. The goal of therapy was to reduce the man's heartbeat to more normal levels. To accomplish this, the man was allowed to view television only when his heart rate was 5 beats per minute less than what it was before. When this reduction

was achieved, the criterion for being able to view the television was decreased by another 5 beats per minute. This procedure continued until the man's heart rate was 71 beats per minute, within the normal range.

4. Patient A, 40, had lived in a mental hospital for 19 years. He had not spoken since shortly after he began living in the hospital. Three behavior analysts working with Patient A made saying something a treatment goal. At first, they reinforced Patient A's lip movements with a stick of gum. Then, gum was made dependent on a vocalization. After several weeks, Patient A was given gum when he said words that were increasingly like the word "gum." Eventually this method resulted in Patient A saying "gum," as well as answering questions about his name and age.

5. Felicity attended a school for behaviorally disordered students. She had difficulty paying attention, so for a week-long period she received 5 minutes of reinforcing free play for every 5 minutes she spent with her eyes oriented toward the teacher during lesson presentations. This method seemed to work well, and during the next week Felicity was awarded 10 minutes of free play for every 5 minutes of attention. During the following week, 15 minutes of free play was dependent on 5 minutes of paying attention to the teacher.

6. Three university students had problems with hoarse voice quality. One goal of their speech therapy was for them to be able to speak clearly in ordinary conversation. The problem was addressed by dividing up the components of clear speech into a series of steps, each of which was made up of responses that were increasing like clear speech. Praise from the speech therapist was dependent on the students' completing each step. As a result of the program, all the students learned to speak clearly.

7. Mike was a 14-year-old boy whose problem was adipsia, an abnormal avoidance of fluid consumption. When shown a glass of fluid he would turn his head away. He spit out fluid from his mouth. The goal of Mike's therapy was to get him to drink a normal, healthful amount of fluids. Treatment required Mike to consume milk from a 1/4 teaspoon measuring spoon. Throughout treatment, praise and applesauce were dependent on Mike's drinking. When he was reliably swallowing the 1/4 teaspoon drinks, he was required to swallow 1/2 teaspoon drinks. As Mike's drinking was successfully established with smaller amounts, he was progressively required to drink from 1 teaspoon, 1 tablespoon, 2 tablespoons, 1/4 cup, 1/2 cup, and 1-cup containers. In this way, the goal of normal fluid consumption was achieved.

8. Sandy's parents were training her to speak. At first, they gave Sandy bits of food when she correctly identified a pictured object. Later, the parents began pairing the food with verbal approval, and the procedure continued to work well. Finally, the parents reinforced Sandy's correct responses with verbal approval in the absence of food. This method continued to work well.

9. Gordon was a retarded 8-year-old whose problem was an inability to chew solid food. One goal of the treatment was to get Gordon to bite through a graham cracker. In order to establish food chewing, Gordon's family provided him with reinforcing praise and cottage cheese when he exerted pressure on a graham cracker. When he

did this, reinforcement was made dependent on increased amounts of pressure on the graham cracker. This procedure continued until Gordon crunched and bit through the graham cracker.

10. As part of a procedure to increase the cooperative play of socially withdrawn retarded children, a goal was set for two children to roll a ball to the experimenter. At first, candy was dependent on the children's releasing the ball. Then, candy was made dependent on rolling the ball longer and longer distances until eventually the children were able to roll the ball the full distance required.

11. Ben, 39, Frank, 63, and Will, 44, were all longtime residents at a state mental hospital. Their problem was that they mumbled at such a low volume that they could not be heard. The goal of treatment was to increase the volume of the men's speech. The volume of the men's speech was measured using an electronic device. Treatment consisted of making candy and praise dependent on a minimum speech volume level. As the men learned to speak more loudly, the speech volume criterion for reinforcement was progressively increased until the men were reliably speaking at normal levels. Ben and especially Frank increased their ability to communicate with others a great deal as a result of the training.

12. Martha was a 35-year-old woman whose problem was pollakiuria, urinating too often. She had accumulated over $10,000 in medical expenses trying to solve her problem. The goal of the treatment was to get Martha to urinate at a normal frequency. A schedule for urination was established that specified a maximum number of urinations per day. Adhering to the schedule was reinforced with things like cigarettes and the opportunity to go on shopping trips. Reinforcement of the response gradually became dependent on longer and longer intervals between urinations. Eventually this procedure resulted in Martha urinating four or five times per day, a normal frequency.

13. Jane was a hospitalized and bedridden 13-year-old girl who said she was unable to bend at the waist or move normally, although no medical cause could be found for her problem. The goal of treatment was to induce Jane to move normally. Reinforcement, in the form of the opportunity to watch television, visit with her parents, and use a telephone was made dependent on tensing her stomach muscles. When she did this, reinforcement was made dependent on raising her legs. As she became adept at this, reinforcement was made dependent on a series of additional behaviors, including walking down a long hallway, back-bending exercises, and sitting in a chair for 2 hours. Eventually this method enabled Jane to move reasonably normally, be discharged from the hospital, and resume her schooling.

14. Sue was a 6-year-old girl who had difficulty swallowing the pills that controlled her hyperactivity. A goal was set for Sue to be able to swallow big pills. As she learned to swallow very small candy pills, the reinforcer was the candy itself. Similarly, she learned to swallow medium pills. Finally, she learned to swallow large candy pills. As a result of this method, Sue began swallowing her medication without any problems.

15. Jerry had difficulty responding correctly to symbols, although he could respond to

colors. Early in training, he was shown his name spelled correctly in red letters and misspelled in white letters. His task was to point to the correct name. When he learned to do this, Jerry's misspelled name was shown to him in progressively increased red hues, beginning with light pink. This process continued until Jerry was correctly selecting his name when it and the misspelled names were both shown in the same red hues. Trainers used praise consistently to reinforce correct responses.

16. Ten female students at the University of Vermont had a fear of snakes. They volunteered for a study in which they would unlearn their fear of snakes. The goal response was defined as being able to move close to a caged snake. Reinforcement in the form of praise from the experimenter was dependent on the students' moving increasingly closer to a snake in a glass cage. This method enabled the students to approach the snake much closer than formerly.

17. Eleven children from 9 to 16 years old were being treated for extreme shyness. During one part of the treatment, the therapist made reinforcers dependent on progressively longer periods of eye contact between the therapist and the child. Different reinforcers were used with different children. Through this method, the therapist achieved the goal of establishing normal levels of eye contact with the children.

18. Doreen was a 24-year-old woman who would often eat massive quantities of food at night and then induce vomiting to prevent herself from gaining weight, a disorder called bulimia nervosa. The goal of treatment was for Doreen to completely cease her binges. In order to accomplish this, she gave all her jewelry to the therapist. During the first two weeks of treatment, return of her jewelry was dependent on two nights without binges. Over time, the number of days that had to pass without any binges was gradually increased until after several weeks, return of the jewelry was dependent on no binges at all during the week. This procedure resulted in Doreen ceasing her binges.

Conceptual Exercise   *Making Shaping Effective*

In each of the following items, something should be altered to make the shaping procedure more effective. Describe what should be altered and explain why.

1. At the University of Greater Knowledge, the goal of the educational process was to produce good citizens. The educational plan was to shape good citizenship gradually over students' 4-year attendance. A variety of incentives and rewards were available to reinforce improvement toward good citizenship. Unfortunately, although the faculty agreed that good citizenship was a worthwhile goal, they did agree on what specific behaviors were necessary in order to produce good citizens.

2. Mary was in a special class for children with speech disfluencies. Mary, a stutterer, could rarely complete a full sentence without stuttering. One of the goals of the special class was for each student to conduct a full 50-minute class session without speech disfluencies. The teacher planned to use a shaping procedure using points as

reinforcers that students could exchange for a wide variety of privileges. His plan was to begin by requiring each student to give a 10-minute speech to the class. If the student was able to do so with no speech disfluencies, the student would receive points. The teacher then planned to gradually increase the length of the speech until the students reached the 50-minute goal. Unfortunately, neither Mary nor any of the other students were able to succeed in the initial 10-minute speech requirement.

3. Roy was hired as lion tamer at a local circus. His job was to train lions to jump through burning hoops. He began by requiring the lion to walk through a hoop at ground level. After a few trials, he was successful and rewarded his lion with a lion treat. Next he required that the lion jump through a hoop 12 feet off the ground. He was disappointed to see that his lion would not even approach the hoop, let alone jump through it.

4. Harry was a competitive swimmer who had a problem with his backstroke. He would fling his arms out of the water at an incorrect angle. His coach decided to improve his backstroke with a shaping procedure. When Harry completed one lap of the pool under a particular time limit, this behavior was reinforced with a variety of swimmer needs such as goggles, caps etc. Gradually the coach decreased the time limit that Harry had to meet for reinforcement. Harry soon learned to swim the backstroke much more quickly than before although he still flung his arms out at the wrong angle.

5. Lulu had transferred to a new school where the class she was in was learning handwriting. The teacher used a shaping procedure where the students received praise and stars for correct handwriting responses. The teacher began by reinforcing small improvements in the students' responses, and patiently continued doing this with each student. Lulu had already learned a lot about handwriting at her previous school and was soon seen doodling and fooling around during handwriting exercises that she found much too easy.

6. Anna was a graduate student in psychology. As part of her training, her advisor required her to go to a workshop where she learned how to solder electrical connections. This skill was important in building apparatuses for use in psychological experiments. During the workshop, the training reinforced correct soldering responses in step-by-step fashion, making sure to reinforce improvements in the students' soldering. However, Anna already had considerable skills in soldering because she had built her own personal computer. She therefore dropped out of the workshop.

7. Jill took a very long time to get dressed in the morning, averaging 2 hours from the time she arose until she got dressed. Her mother wished to get Jill to dress more rapidly, and therefore decided to use a shaping procedure in which Jill received points that could be exchanged for privileges and money if she dressed progressively more rapidly. During the first day of the procedure, Jill's mother required that Jill dress within 1 hour, 55 minutes to obtain reinforcement. This duration was reduced 5 minutes on each of the next 2 days. The plan worked so well that on the fourth day, Jill's mother reduced the requirement to 15 minutes. However, Jill failed to meet the time requirement and both Jill and her mother were emotionally upset.

8. Jimmy was an autistic child who was learning to pay attention. Jimmy had trouble paying attention, and would gaze off in space in a self-stimulatory way. His teacher would say, "Jimmy, look at me," and if Jimmy did, the teacher gave him a small treat that he liked very much. The teacher planned to reinforce progressively longer durations of Jimmy's eye contact, but during the first few trials the teacher was a little late with the treat and Jimmy got the treat after he was no longer making eye contact. Jimmy did not progress as well as his teacher had hoped.

Conceptual Exercise   *Schedules of Reinforcement*

This conceptual exercise presents examples of reinforcement schedules. Your job is to identify the type of reinforcement schedule from among the following:

> Fixed ratio (FR)
> Variable ratio (VR)
> Fixed interval (FI)
> Fixed interval with limited hold (FI/LH)
> Variable interval (VI)
> Variable interval with limited hold (VI/LH)
> Fixed duration (FD)
> Variable duration (VD)
> Differential reinforcement of low rates (DRL)
> Differential reinforcement of high rates (DRH)
> Differential reinforcement of paced responding (DRP)

In analyzing examples of reinforcement schedules, you may find it useful to ask yourself the following series of questions:

Was reinforcement dependent on the target behavior occurring a specific or fixed number of times? If the answer to this question is yes, the reinforcement schedule is fixed-ratio.

Was reinforcement dependent on the target behavior occurring a number of times that varied from reinforcement to reinforcement? If yes, the schedule of reinforcement is variable-ratio.

Was reinforcement dependent on the target behavior occurring after the passage of a specific or fixed amount of time? If yes, the schedule of reinforcement is fixed-interval.

If the target behavior was reinforced according to a fixed-interval schedule, was reinforcement available for only a limited period of time? If yes, the schedule is fixed-interval with a limited hold.

Was reinforcement dependent on the target behavior occurring after the passage of an amount of time that varied from reinforcement to reinforcement? If yes, then the schedule of reinforcement is variable-interval.

If the target behavior was reinforced according to a variable-interval schedule, was the reinforcement for the response available only for a limited period of time? If yes, then the schedule is variable-interval with a limited hold.

Was reinforcement dependent on the target behavior occurring for a specific or fixed duration of time? If yes, then the schedule of reinforcement is fixed-duration.

Was reinforcement dependent on the target behavior occurring for a period of time that varied from reinforcement to reinforcement? If yes, then the schedule of reinforcement is variable-duration.

Was reinforcement dependent on a maximum rate of the target behavior? If yes, then the schedule is differential reinforcement of low rates.

Was reinforcement dependent on a minimum rate of the target behavior? If yes, then the schedule is differential reinforcement of high rates.

Was reinforcement dependent on both a minimum and a maximum rate of the target behavior? If yes, then the schedule is differential reinforcement of paced responding.

For each of the following items, identify the type of reinforcement schedule that is illustrated. Briefly explain the reason for your answer. Confirm your decisions by consulting the analyses provided in the back of the book.

1. Every day Sam's teacher induced him to do his math assignments by allowing him to go to gym period (a reinforcer for Sam's behavior) only after he had worked on the problems for 90 minutes. As a result, Sam worked on his math assignments for the required 90 minutes per day, and began to excel at math. The target behavior in this example was Sam's work on his math assignments.

2. Dr. Hake and Dr. Foxx were studying methods to get people to conserve gasoline by driving less. Using university student volunteers as subjects, first, they had the students measure the baseline number of miles they drove for about a month. Then, they arranged a dependency in which the drivers who drove 10% below their baseline rate of driving amount received $1 per week and $5 per month. The students could earn even more through additional reductions in their driving. As a result of these dependencies, the student's driving was reduced substantially. The money was a reinforcer for the students. The target behavior was the students' rate of driving per week and per month.

3. Loretta was blind and in order to earn a livelihood she made macrame plant hangers. The company she worked for paid her $2.50 for each batch of 10 plant hangers she made. The money was a reinforcer for her making the hangers, and she worked busily during the day fashioning the hangers. The target behavior was making one plant hanger.

4. Six drug addicts were in a program in which they took a drug called methadone. The drug prevents physiological withdrawal symptoms from heroin but without the "high" that heroin produces. Desirable target behaviors for the addicts included passing a drug-use test, arriving on time to the methadone clinic, arriving on time to work, and increasing body weight. Each time a target behavior occurred, the addict rolled a die. If some numbers came up on the die, the addict would receive credits that could be traded for home delivery of methadone, late privileges, tickets to events, special food, bus tokens, free lunches, and less frequent meetings with pro-

bation officers. However, if other numbers came up on the die, the addict would receive no credits. The program was successful with three of the six addicts.

5. Marvin's favorite food was a baked potato. He would often ask his parents to cook one for him in their microwave oven. It took seven minutes to cook. The microwave was on the kitchen counter and too high up for little Marvin to see inside. He would keep asking, ``Is the potato almost ready yet?'' during the time it was cooking. If there were fewer than 30 seconds left, his parents would answer his question, ``Yes,'' but if there were more time to go, they would say, ``No.'' A ``yes'' answer to his question was a reinforcer for Marvin's behavior. The target behavior in this case was Marvin's asking if the potato were ready.

6. Bob's television set was not working properly. The picture would roll repeatedly, much to Bob's frustration. However, Bob found that if he hit the top of the set, it would stop rolling and deliver a really good picture. The number of times he had to hit the set before it stopped rolling wasn't the same each time. Sometimes he would have to pound it only once, but other times he had to smack it four, five, six, seven, or even as many as eight times before it would operate correctly. The change from a rolling picture to a good picture was a reinforcer for Bob's behavior. The target behavior in this case was hitting the top of the television set once.

7. Harry was applying for several jobs that required skills in typing. Getting any of the jobs for which Harry was applying was dependent on a typing speed of at least 50 correct words per minute. Getting a job was a reinforcer for Harry's behavior. The target behavior was typing.

8. Lola had moved to a new town and enjoyed receiving letters from her friends and family back home. She would check her post office box to see if any letters had arrived for her. Some days she would receive a letter, but on other days she would not. Receiving a letter was a reinforcer for Lola's behavior. The target behavior in this example was checking the post office box.

9. Mike was a 12-year-old boy in a class for children with behavior disorders. In order to get Mike to work harder, points were made dependent on Mike's correctly solving at least 61 math problems during a 1-hour math period (61 responses per hour). Mike could earn even more points by solving more than 61 problems correctly per hour. The points, which could be traded for free time in a room full of interesting play materials, were reinforcers for Mike's behavior. The target behavior was Mike's correct rate of problem solving.

10. Homer worked in a sewer so after a hard day at work he liked to take a shower to wash up. Some days he would be especially dirty and would have to shower and scrub for about 30 minutes before he was clean. On other days he wasn't as dirty, and 5 to 10 minutes would suffice. Being clean after a day at work was a reinforcer for Homer's behavior. The target behavior was showering and scrubbing.

11. Sally had a 10-speed bicycle with tires that lost air pressure rapidly. When her tires had lost all their air, she would have to pump them up with a hand pump she owned. When the tire was completely flat, she had to operate the pump 100 times in

order to fill the tire to its recommended pressure. A filled tire was a reinforcer for Sally's behavior. The target behavior was pumping the pump once.

12. Stephen was the class clown and would entertain the class every morning by telling jokes. Mr. Huth, the teacher, found that Stephen was so good at telling jokes that the other students would laugh uproariously, fall out of their seats and sometimes have to leave the classroom because they were having difficulty catching their breath. As a result, Mr. Huth imposed a dependency on Stephen's behavior. If during the morning class session Stephen told fewer than three jokes, the class would be able to leave 15 minutes early at the end of the day. Consequently, the number of days on which Stephen told fewer than three jokes increased. The target behavior was Stephen's joke telling.

13. Sixteen third and fourth grade children were doing poorly in school and were attending an after-school remedial class. In order to get the children to be in their seats more often, a timer would ring every 20 minutes, on the average. Sometimes it would ring immediately after the previous ring, while sometimes it would ring as long as 40 minutes after the previous ring. Every student who was engaging in in-seat behavior when the timer rang would receive 5 points. Points could be traded for snack foods, candy, clothing, and the opportunity to go on field trips. The points were reinforcers for the children's behavior. This method increased the level of the target behavior, in-seat behavior.

14. Gwendolyn's great preoccupation in life was observing if the local groundhog would see his shadow on groundhog day. Observing whether the groundhog would see or not see his shadow on February 2 was a reinforcer for Gwendolyn's behavior. The target behavior was Gwen's observing the groundhog.

15. Janna was learning to read English with the help of her tutor, Kris. Twice a week they met and during part of their session Janna read practice exercises out loud. Kris reinforced Janna's reading with praise and nods when it occurred at a moderate rate, but not when it occurred at too high or low a rate. Janna made too many errors when she tried to read too fast, and when she read too slow she was not learning to read at an adequate rate. The target behavior was Janna's reading.

16. Edmund enjoyed viewing the rings of Saturn and other astronomical phenomena through his telescope during the evening hours. However, occasionally it was too cloudy to see anything. Sometimes he had to wait several evenings before viewing conditions were right; on other occasions he was able to get excellent and unobstructed views skyward night after night without interruption. A clear, unclouded sky was a reinforcer for Edmund's behavior. The target behavior in this example was looking at heavenly bodies through his telescope at night.

17. Fenwick received a large allowance from his mother at the beginning of every month. He sometimes tried to collect his allowance early, but without any success. The allowance was a reinforcer for Fenwick's behavior. The target behavior was trying to collect the allowance.

18. Patty got a big thrill out of viewing thunderstorms. They occurred only during the summer, however, and even then she had to wait several days or even weeks for a

thunderstorm. Viewing thunderstorms was a reinforcer for Patty's behavior. The target behavior was observing the sky to see if there was a thunderstorm.

19. Riders on a campus bus in University Park consisted of students, faculty, and local residents. Two researchers wanted to encourage more people to ride the bus in order to reduce automobile gas consumption, pollution, and traffic congestion. In order to accomplish this, they presented a token to an average of one out of every three people who boarded the bus. As such, any one person would receive a token every third time she boarded the bus, on the average. The tokens, which were reinforcers for the behavior of the bus riders, were pink credit-card sized items exchangeable for a variety of things including free bus rides, beer, ice cream, and hamburgers. This method caused more people to use the bus. The target behavior was boarding the bus.

20. The Cosmos Insurance Company had a policy by which an insurance premium was lowered for drivers who went a year having only one accident of less than $200 damage. A lowered insurance premium was a reinforcer for the driver's behavior. The target behavior was getting into an accident in which less than $200 damage was done, or avoiding accidents altogether.

21. Astin would take a bus ride every month to visit his family in a neighboring city. The trip would take an average of about 1 hour, but sometimes road construction, bad weather, frequent intermediate stops, and so forth would slow the bus, making it take almost 2 hours. Other times, good weather and few required stops would cut down traveling time to 40 minutes. Arriving in the neighboring city was a reinforcer for Astin's behavior. The target behavior in this case was riding on the bus.

22. Jethro loved to go fishing more than anything else, but because he lived on a farm there were plenty of chores that were more important than his fishing. After he sneaked away from the farm for a few days in a row, his parents hid his fishing gear and told him that he would get it back only after he had worked at least 6 hours a day. Thus, if he started work at 5:00 A.M. he could be finished an hour before noon and have the rest of the day to fish. Going fishing was a reinforcer for Jethro's behavior. The target behavior was working on the farm.

23. Leon, a long-distance runner, was working with Coach Nurmi. Leon's problem was that during the first kilometer of a 10-kilometer run, he would either run too fast or too slow. When he ran too fast, he would exhaust himself too soon and when he ran too slow, he let his competitors get too far ahead for him to catch up later in the race. In order to solve this problem, Coach Nurmi reinforced Leon's first kilometer of running with praise and jelly beans when it occurred at a moderate rate, but not when it occurred at too fast or too slow a rate. The target behavior is Leon's running of the first kilometer in a 10-kilometer race.

24. Harold liked to listen to the news on the radio every hour to keep posted on the latest developments. Because he lived in an isolated community, there was only one radio station, and it broadcast the news only once an hour for 5 minutes. Listening to the news was a reinforcer for Harold's behavior. The target behavior in this example was being in a location to be able to listen to the news.

25. Jane was a 16-year-old retarded resident at a state institution. One problem she had was spilling her food while eating. She was trained to eat without spilling. After she learned how to eat without spilling, a dependency was established whereby every seventh correct eating response was reinforced with a sip of chocolate milk and a token. Tokens could be traded for 1 minute of conversation with a staff member later in the day. Later, as Jane became better at eating, she received the reinforcers for every 10th response. The target behavior was a correct eating response, taking food from plate to mouth without spillage.

chapter 7

Stimulus Discrimination

For most of us, music is one of the great pleasures in life. Music, like art, enriches our lives, but not everyone shares the ability to appreciate the beauty of music. Some children grow up without being able to appreciate music fully because they have difficulty telling different pitches of sound apart.

During the early 1930s, Manuel Wolner, a graduate student at what is now called Wayne State University in Detroit, was studying the writings of prominent psychologists of the day. These learned scholars were claiming that pitch discrimination, telling the difference between musical tones, was an ability that some learners could not fully acquire no matter how much training they were given. Wolner and his graduate advisor, Dr. William H. Pyle, were not so sure. They decided to conduct a study to determine whether or not children with poor pitch discrimination could be trained to improve this ability.

Music teachers at three Detroit elementary schools were contacted and asked to identify the students who had the worst skills in pitch discrimination, students who might be classified as "tone-deaf." From among this woeful group of fifth, sixth, and seventh graders, Wolner and Pyle selected seven students, three boys and four girls, who were the worst of the lot in pitch discrimination.

In spite of taking several years of music classes, none of the students could sing. Some of them could not tell the difference between notes an entire octave apart, and none of them could tell the difference between notes that were 30 cycles per second apart. (At the midrange of the piano, being able only to tell the difference between pitches 20 cycles per second apart is considered poor.)

Over a course of 81 days, every morning for 5 days a week, the students received 20 minutes of pitch discrimination training. At first, middle C on the piano was sounded and the students were asked to sing the note as best they could. The students were told when they were right and wrong, and whether they needed to raise or lower the pitch of their voice. After a student had learned to sing middle C, Wolner and Pyle trained her to sing D. They then trained alternating between the two notes and increasingly more notes until students learned the entire octave.

Another part of the students' training was to discriminate between two tones of different pitches presented sequentially, and to tell whether the second tone was higher or lower than the first. The students were told when they were correct. If incorrect, they were required to try to sing the two notes. As the students improved on this task, the tones were presented to them using tuning forks, enabling the experimenter to present tones that were more similar in pitch to each other than could be presented on the piano.

Aside from these procedures, the trainers gave the students instruction in the quality of musical sound, taught them to concentrate and imagine pitches that had just been played for them, and generally taught other skills necessary for an understanding of music. When one type of drill procedure became too tiresome, the trainers would alter it in some way to provide the students with more variety.

At times, the results were discouraging, requiring much patience, but training continued. The students progressed at very different rates, and training was often individually tailored to problems the students were having. By the end of training, however, the results were indeed impressive. All the students had learned to tell the difference among a range of four octaves of notes. Four of the students were trained to tell the difference between notes that differed in pitch by only 0.5 cycles per second. (Being able to tell the difference between notes one cycle per second apart is considered above average.) Two other students learned to discriminate between tones differing by 3 cycles per second in frequency and another student learned to discriminate between tones that differed by 5 cycles per second.

The students also learned how to sing. One sang several songs flawlessly, another was able to vocalize songs and scales, but without words, two other students were able to sing intervals and scales, and the remaining three students were able to sing with errors, but sing, nonetheless.

Wolner and Pyle apparently did not follow the course of the students' lives after they were trained. We can perhaps safely speculate, however, that whatever happened to them after the study, their appreciation of the world of music was enhanced by stimulus discrimination training.*

*Based on Wolner and Pyle (1933)

Stimulus Discrimination Training and Stimulus Control

To this point we have been concerned with response-consequence relationships. We have seen how positive reinforcement, escape conditioning, avoidance conditioning, schedules of reinforcement and shaping procedures can strengthen behavior and how extinction, DRO, DRI, and punishment procedures can weaken it. Stimulus discrimination is concerned with strengthening a response under certain stimulus conditions and weakening that response under other stimulus conditions. The same behavior in response to two different stimuli can be totally appropriate in one case and totally inappropriate in the other. Sexual deviance, for example, may be seen as a stimulus control problem. Sexual response can come under the control of stimuli that most people view as inappropriate, whereas that same behavior may be viewed by society as quite appropriate under different stimulus conditions.

Stimulus discrimination training refers to a variety of procedures designed to teach the learner to respond selectively to different stimuli. To *respond selectively* means that different responses are trained to different stimuli. This selective responding is brought about by providing differential consequences for responding to different stimuli. The term *differential consequences* means that one type of consequence is dependent on correct responses while a different consequence is dependent on incorrect responses. For example, Wolner and Pyle used stimulus discrimination training in teaching the students to tell the difference between pitches.

The most basic type of stimulus discrimination training is to reinforce a response in the presence of one stimulus and extinguish the response in the absence of that stimulus. Rabin-Bickelman and Marholin (1978) used this type of stimulus-discrimination procedure with a retarded man. The man, seated at a table across from the experimenter, worked at placing blocks into containers. When a 40-watt light bulb on the table was lit, the experimenter reinforced the man's work on a VI 30-second schedule, using ice cream and positive comments. However, when the light was turned off, the man's work went unreinforced. As a result of this procedure, the man came to engage in the task much more frequently when the light was on than when it was off.

Several terms are used to describe aspects of stimulus discrimination training. The stimulus in the presence of which responses are strengthened is called a discriminative stimulus. For example, in the study of the man's work task, the light bulb on was a discriminative stimulus because in its presence, responding was strengthened. A discriminative stimulus is designated by either the symbols S+ (ess-plus or positive stimulus) or S^D (ess-dee). The stimulus in the presence of which a response is not reinforced or otherwise weakened is called either an S− (ess-minus or negative stimulus) or an S^Δ (ess-delta). In the light-on, light-off study, the S− was the light off because in its presence, responding was weakened through extinction.

A related concept is that of *stimulus control*. Stimulus control is said to exist when the presentation of a stimulus changes some measure of behavior. For example, in Rabin-Bickelman and Marholin's study, turning the light on increased the man's work behaviors. The lit bulb can therefore be said to have exerted stimulus control over work activities. The lit bulb exerted *excitatory stimulus control,* because presenting the light, the S+, strengthened the work behaviors.

A second type of stimulus control is called *inhibitory stimulus control,* which exists when the presentation of a stimulus (S–) causes a weakening of some measure of behavior. For example, when someone puts an index finger to his or her lips and makes a shushing noise, it often causes us to reduce the rate and loudness of our speech. This gesture can therefore be said to exert inhibitory stimulus control over loud speech.

Taylor and Rickard (1974) used an inhibitory stimulus at a summer camp for behaviorally disturbed children. At the dining hall, when a camp leader raised her hand with the index and middle fingers extended, being served the meal was dependent on the absence of loud behavior, a DRO procedure. As a result of this method, presenting the hand signal caused an immediate weakening of loud behavior among the campers.

A wide variety of events exert stimulus control over our everyday behavior. Looking at a clock in the morning serves as an S+ for arising and an S– for continued sleep. Hearing a weather report predicting rain serves as an S+ for wearing a raincoat and an S– for washing the car. Seeing a close friend you haven't seen for awhile serves as a S+ for a greeting and an S– for hurrying away. As you are reading this page, each written word is an S+ for your reading responses. As you can see, stimulus control is something that is affecting your behavior virtually all the time.

Stimulus control can sometimes cause amusing incidents when one stimulus has too much control. Such a situation occurred to a Washington, D.C., radio news broadcaster named Ed Myer ("Quotation on Stimulus Control," 1977). For many years, Ed's boss called him after his 8:30 A.M. morning news broadcast to give him his daily assignment as a news reporter. After receiving the call, Ed would drive off to do the assignment. The boss's phone call had been firmly established as an S+ for Ed's leaving work, getting into his car, and driving away. However, one morning Ed's boss phoned him before his 8:30 A.M. broadcast, not after, and the phone call still acted as an S+. Consequently, Ed drove off from the radio station. As he sat in his car in the morning traffic a few minutes later, Ed heard himself being introduced on the radio. Only then, as he sat unable to deliver his newscast, did he realize what had happened.

Stimulus-control processes are often at work in cases of Dr. Jekyll-Mr. Hyde changes in behavior. We note that the same person who appears decent and benevolent at church is unethical and shady in business dealings. The children who are well-behaved when their regular teacher is present behave poorly when a substitute teacher fills in. The friendly looking neighbor who keeps her lawn nicely trimmed and smiles a lot turns out to be a mass murderer. In each case, a desirable behavior occurs in one stimulus situation and an undesirable behavior occurs in another because of differences in the consequences dependent on the behaviors in the two situations. Unethical behavior in church, student misbehavior with a regular teacher, and violence in a public place all would be met with immediate aversive consequences, consequences not as likely to be forthcoming in the alternative stimulus conditions.

The basic pattern of stimulus discrimination training is illustrated by a situation in which a response is reinforced in the presence of the S+ and extinguished in the presence of an S–. However, stimulus discrimination training may also occur with other types of consequences as long as there are response-strengthening consequences dependent on the response in the presence of the S+ and response-weakening consequences dependent on the response in the presence of the S–. For example, it is possible to punish a response in the presence of an S–. It is also possible to use a DRO procedure to reduce a response in the presence of an S–.

Natural and contrived consequences often work together in stimulus discrimination training. For example, the natural consequences of children's loud boisterous behavior maintain it on the playground, but often response-reduction procedures such as punishment or DRO must be used to suppress these responses at school and in many home situations. In order to bring the behavior under stimulus control, a punishment or DRO procedure could be used to establish the school or home as an S– for loud, rough play. It would not be necessary to reinforce the response on the playground, because it is reinforced naturally there.

Discriminative stimuli are sometimes confused with reinforcers. However, a discriminative stimulus is present before a response occurs and it is often present while a response is occurring. In contrast, a reinforcer is a stimulus change that occurs after a response occurs. In everyday language, we speak of S+ and S– as signals or cues for a response, not as rewards for a response. In simple discrimination training, we could diagram the relationship in the following way.

A response that occurs in the presence of the S+ is reinforced whereas that same response in the presence of the S– is extinguished.

Students sometimes confuse stimulus discrimination with differential reinforcement. Differential reinforcement is a procedure where one response is reinforced and a different response is extinguished. The purpose of differential reinforcement is to increase the strength of a particular response and decrease the strength of different response. In stimulus discrimination, however, a response is reinforced in the presence of the S+ and that same response is not reinforced in the presence of the S–. The purpose of stimulus discrimination is to increase the strength of a particular response in the presence of one stimulus and to decrease the strength of that same response in the presence of another stimulus.

Types of Stimulus Discrimination Training and Stimulus Control

The many different types of stimulus discrimination and stimulus control procedures include simultaneous and successive stimulus discrimination, social discrimination, verbal discrimination, multiple-stimulus multiple-response discrimination, matching-to-sample discrimination, and multiple-cue discrimination.

Simultaneous and Successive Discrimination

In a *simultaneous discrimination*, both the S+ and the S– are presented at the same time. Learner responses to the S+ are reinforced, while responses to the S– are not. For example, Simmons (1964) taught 1-year-old infants to discriminate between red and blue, using a simultaneous discrimination method. The infants were seated in front of a display board with two panels. On each experimental trial, one of the panels was red and the other was blue. For one group of infants, chimes would sound if the infant touched the red panel, but nothing would happen if the infant touched the blue panel. For a second group of infants, the sound of chimes was dependent on touches to the blue panel, while touches to the red panel were put on extinction. The procedure served to establish the red light as an S+ and the blue light as an S– for panel-touching for the first group of infants and to establish the blue light as an S+ and the red light as an S– for a second group of infants. This example is a simultaneous discrimination procedure because the S+ and S– were presented to the infants at the same time.

In a *successive discrimination,* the S+ and the S– are each presented at different times. For example, Bijou (1961) taught a 4-year-old boy to respond to an amber light, and not to a blue light, using a successive discrimination procedure. When the S+ (the amber light) was on, the child's lever presses were reinforced with trinkets, small cookies, and candy on a VR 50 schedule of reinforcement. When the S– (the blue light) was on, lever presses were put on extinction. The S+ and S– were alternated in 2-minute periods. The boy learned to respond rapidly when the S+ was on, and to cease responding when the S– came on.

Simultaneous discrimination is often the best procedure to use when the discrimination between the S+ and the S– is difficult, especially during the early stages of discrimination training (Loess & Duncan, 1952), because simultaneous discrimination allows the learner to easily compare the two. For example, suppose we have been assigned the task of training soldiers to discriminate between friendly and enemy fighter planes. During early training, it would be useful to use a simultaneous discrimination procedure in which two similar planes are presented side by side, highlighting the differences between the two planes. However, the ultimate goal of the training procedure would be for the trainees to identify each type of plane when presented alone because this is how the planes would normally appear under natural conditions. Therefore, later in training, it would be desirable to use a successive discrimination procedure in which the planes were presented alone; then the learner's task would be to respond differently to them. As this example illustrates, the decision whether to use simultaneous or successive discrimination will depend on the ultimate goal of stimulus discrimination training.

Social Discrimination

Other people serve as discriminative stimuli for our behavior. For example, with some of your friends you are likely to tell jokes and stories, while with other peers you may merely get together and study. You act in a different way when you greet your instructors than when you greet small children. In general, people perform tasks better when they are being watched by others than when they are performing alone.

Redd and Birnbrauer (1969) studied the effects of people as discriminative stimuli. Severely retarded boys were visited by a woman for 5 minutes. She reinforced the boys' play behaviors with candy, ice cream, and drinks of Coke on a fixed-interval 45-second schedule with a 15-second limited hold. After this, a man visited the boys and gave out the reinforcers every 60 seconds, on a response-independent basis. As a result of this method, when the woman entered the room, the boys immediately began playing, showing that she had become established as an S+ for play behavior. However, when the man entered the room, the boys' behavior showed no change. When the man and the woman reversed roles the man became the S+ for play and the woman came to have no effect on the boys' behavior. When the man and the woman entered the playroom together, the boys began playing.

Redd and Birnbrauer compared their experiment to a family situation in which one parent reinforces appropriate child behavior while the other parent gives rewards to children in response-independent fashion. In such a situation, one parent can be expected to come to be an S+ for desirable behavior, while the children's behavior would be unpredictable in the presence of the other parent.

Azrin and Hayes (1984) studied another type of social discrimination, training men to tell when women are interested in them. Young men in their late teens and 20s viewed a series of videotapes showing men and women in conversation. The subjects were asked to rate the degree to which the women in the videotapes were interested in the men with whom they were conversing. After viewing each scene, the subjects were given the woman's rating of how much she was actually interested in the man with whom she had interacted. This training enabled the men to improve their ability to discriminate the women's interest levels, and this improvement was seen in ratings of women not used during discrimination training.

Verbal Discrimination

In verbal discrimination training, a verbal stimulus such as a word or a command becomes established as an S+ for a response. A familiar example is training children to comply with commands and instructions. Wahler (1969) worked with two elementary school boys named Billy and Sammy who seldom complied with their parents' requests. The boys' parents had brought each of them for psychological treatment, because their behavior had become unmanageable. Discrimination training consisted of (a) the parents giving attention and approval whenever the children complied with a request or command and (b) the boys being given a 5-minute time-out if they did not comply with their parents' requests. As a result of this training, the parents' requests were established as S+s for the boys behavior: the boys began complying with their parents requests quickly after they were made. Soon the boys and their parents began to enjoy one another's company much more than they had before.

Multiple-Stimulus Multiple-Response Discrimination

The simplest form of discrimination occurs when a response is reinforced in the presence of an S+ and not reinforced when it occurs in the presence of an S−. A more complex form of discrimination is a 2-stimulus 2-response discrimination. An example is meeting two people named Lisa and Laura and learning to call each by name. Lisa is an S+ for the verbal response "Lisa" and is an S− for the response "Laura." Laura is an S+ for "Laura" and at the same time an S− for "Lisa."

An even more complex type of discrimination is required when there are more than two stimuli and responses required. For example, learning the alphabet is an example of a multiple-stimulus, multiple-response discrimination. Each letter of the alphabet is an S+ for a response, the name of that letter. At the same time, each letter of the alphabet is an S− for all the other letter names except its own. Another example is learning the multiplication table. The problem 2 x 2 is an S+ for the answer "4" and an S− for any other answer. Each problem must be established as an S+ for the correct answer to that problem and an S− for other answers.

Another name for multiple-stimulus multiple-response is *conditional discrimination*. It is called conditional discrimination because the correct responses to be reinforced are conditional on the particular S+ that is present.

The many other examples of multiple-stimulus multiple-response learning include learning the names of colors, animals, trees, chemical elements, rocks and minerals, and the countries on a blank world map. As you can see, much of language learning, especially the learning of nouns, involves this type of discrimination.

Matching-to-Sample Discrimination

Matching-to-sample discrimination training is a procedure often used in research and teaching. In matching-to-sample, a stimulus called a sample stimulus is first presented. Then, two or more additional stimuli (comparison stimuli) are presented. One of the comparison stimuli is the same as the sample stimulus and the others are different. The correct response is to select the comparison stimulus that is the same as the sample stimulus (that matches the sample). For example, the sample stimulus might be the letter "p," while the two comparison stimuli might be the letters "q" and "p." The correct response in this matching-to-sample task would be to select the "p" comparison stimulus.

A variant of matching-to-sample is called oddity matching, also with a sample stimulus and comparison stimuli. The correct response in oddity matching, however, is to select the stimulus that is different from the sample stimulus. It would be the letter "q" in the task we have described. Another variant of matching-to-sample is called symbolic matching. In symbolic matching, a picture of an apple might be the sample stimulus and the comparison stimuli might be two spellings of apple: *aple* and *apple*. The learner's task would be to select the correct spelling of apple.

Multiple-Cue Discrimination Learning and Attending Behavior

We often pay attention to different aspects of stimuli. You may be listening to music you have heard many times before and hear, for the first time, notes played by an instrument you had not noticed before. On your way to work or school you might pay attention to a tree or house that had formerly escaped your attention. Have you ever noticed how frequently a word, whose meaning you have just learned, seems to pop up in your reading although you hadn't noticed this word in the past? All of these are examples of selective attention: Paying attention to certain stimuli and certain aspects of stimuli and ignoring other stimuli or aspects of stimuli.

Selective attention can sometimes be a problem in multiple-cue discrimination training, a type of stimulus discrimination training in which the S+ consists of more than one feature or cue. For example, Lovaas and Schreibman (1971) gave autistic and normal children discrimination training. The children's lever presses were reinforced with food treats in the presence of a red light accompanied by white noise. (White noise is sound that contains many different frequencies of sound. The roar of the ocean or the sound of a radio that is not tuned to a station are examples of white noise.) In the absence of the red light/white noise, the S– lever-presses were extinguished. This training was an example of multiple-cue discrimination learning because there were two stimulus cues in the presence of which the response was reinforced: the red light/white noise.

Over time, all the children learned to respond when the red light/white noise came on and learned to cease responding when it went off. However, Lovaas and Schreibman were especially interested in how the children would respond to the two stimuli, the red light and the white noise, when each was presented alone. Figure 7.1 presents the data for a typical normal subject and a typical autistic subject. As you can see, the normal child responded to both the red light and the white noise when each was presented alone. This indicated that for this child, the red light and the white noise had each become S+s for responding. However, with the autistic child, only the white noise became established as an S+.

This effect was similar for most of the children in the study. The normal children attended to both cues whereas the autistic children tended to selectively attend to only one of the two stimuli during training, causing it alone to become an S+. This effect, in which only one cue of a multiple-cue stimulus becomes established as an S+ during discrimination training, is called *stimulus overselectivity.*

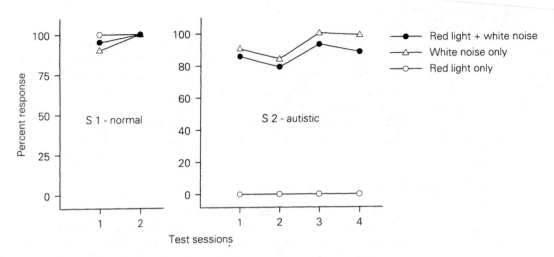

Figure 7.1   *The Effects of a Multiple-Cue Stimulus Discrimination Procedure on the Behavior of a Normal Child and an Autistic Child*

For the normal child, both the white noise and red light became S+s for responding, but for the autistic child, only the white noise was established as an S+. The autistic child's behavior is said to represent stimulus overselectivity. Figure adapted from Lovaas and Schreibman (1971).

Making Stimulus Discrimination Training Effective

The effectiveness of stimulus discrimination training will depend on the effectiveness of the response-strengthening and response-weakening procedures used. For example, if stimulus discrimination training makes use of positive reinforcement in the presence of one stimulus and extinction in the presence of the other stimulus, then the effectiveness of the training will depend on the effectiveness of the reinforcement and extinction procedures used. As such, the principles that make positive reinforcement and extinction effective will also help make stimulus discrimination effective. Otherwise, if the discrimination training is based on combinations of other response-consequence dependencies like avoidance, escape, DRO, DRI, or punishment, the effectiveness of the training will depend on the effectiveness of each of these procedures.

Several other conditions also influence the effectiveness of stimulus discrimination training, including instructions, active responding, pretraining procedures, the similarity of the stimuli, the relationship between the training and goal stimuli, the rate of stimulus presentation, the order of stimulus presentation, and stimulus-specific reinforcement. Two additional sets of methods for improving the effectiveness of stimulus discrimination training are prompting and fading procedures, discussed in Chapter 8.

Instructions

Stimulus discrimination training is often complicated. For learners who can under-stand language, instructions can be used to describe the task, describe the S+ and the S– and how they differ, indicate the consequences of correct and incorrect responses, and so forth. Instructions should normally be used during the initial presentation of the stimuli to be discriminated. Differences between the stimuli should be explained to the learners and highlighted.

Instructions can be useful in helping the learner attend to the discriminative stimulus. Ziegler (1987) used attending instructions in training beginning tennis students to discriminate a moving tennis ball. As part of the training method, the students were instructed to watch the ball from the first moment it was directed at them and to focus on the path of the ball. These procedures improved forehand and backhand returns by 45% over baseline performance.

Instructions are also useful in helping the learner understand the difference between correct and incorrect responses. Spence, Armstrong, and Conrad (1969) studied the influence of instructions about correct responses and consequences in discrimination learning. Grade school students were given a task in which they were presented with two words (e.g., apple, orange). One word was an S+ for choosing that word while the other word was an S– for choosing it. Correct responses were followed by "right," while incorrect responses were not followed by any conse-quence. One fully instructed group of students was told that correct responses would be followed by "right" and incorrect responses would not be followed by a consequence. A partially informed group of students was told only that "right" would follow correct responses. A noninstructed group was told only that they would find out when they gave correct responses as they engaged in the task. Some of the results of this experiment are presented in Figure 7.2.

As you can see, the fully instructed group of students learned the discrimina-tion best, followed by the partially instructed and noninstructed group.

A major problem for the two groups who were not fully instructed is that the students did not know whether to interpret the absence of a consequence for a response as an indication that the response was correct or incorrect. When using dis-crimination training, it is important to explain fully to learners what consequences will follow correct and incorrect responses.

Active Responding

The principle of active responding is that discrimination learning is improved when the learner responds to the stimuli being presented. Narayan, Heward, Gardner, Courson, and Omness (1990) examined this principle in a fourth-grade classroom. During 20-minute sessions, a teacher presented a lesson to students and, after each fact or concept had been presented, asked the students questions about what she had just presented. During part of the study, the students answered the questions in the standard way by raising their hands and being called on. During another part of the

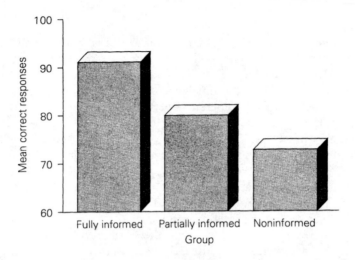

Figure 7.2   *The Influence of Instructions on the Effectiveness of a Stimulus Discrimination Procedure*

The students who were informed about the consequences of correct responding responded at the highest level. Students who were not informed about response consequences responded at the lowest level. Figure drawn from the data of Spence et al. (1969).

experiment, the students were provided with 9″ by 12″ white laminated boards on which to write answers to the teacher's questions.

By using the boards, each student actively responded to each of the teacher's questions. After the lessons, the students took quizzes in which they answered questions similar to those the teacher had posed during the lesson. When the students used the response boards, they did better on the quizzes than when they used the traditional hand-raising method. The quiz questions had been established as more effective S+s for correct responding because the students had actively responded to the training stimuli, the teacher's questions during the lesson.

The principle of active responding is often not properly applied in much instruction. For example, when viewing television programs, children certainly attend to the screen, but opportunities for active responding are normally lacking. Because of the absence of active responding, children often fail to learn to do anything when viewing television, even when the programs have educational value. Similarly, university lectures are often long monologues with no opportunities for the students to respond. In all types of instruction, applying the behavior analysis principle of active responding means breaking the task down into steps and pausing to allow the learners to respond to what they are learning (e.g., Keller, 1968; Skinner, 1968).

Pretraining Procedures

Pretraining procedures can improve stimulus discrimination training by causing the learner to attend to differences between the stimuli to be discriminated.

Hendrickson and Muehl (1962) used a pretraining procedure to train kindergarten children to discriminate between the letters "b" and "d." An experimental group of children was given two arrows that pointed left and right. The experimenter explained the way in which the "b" "points" to the right and "d" to the left.

The children were then required to select arrows that pointed in the same way as the "b"s or "d"s did, when presented with these letters. The children selected the arrows by moving one of two levers that moved in the directions of the selected arrow. If the children moved the correct lever, a bell would ring. This pretraining procedure, which induced to children to attend to the differences between "b" and "d," helped the children respond correctly on a later task in which they used "b" and "d" to name pictures.

Other pretraining procedures that have been shown to be helpful include practice in responding to discrimination problems. For example, Vance and Siegel (1971) had first-grade children look at pairs of pictures of cats that differed only slightly (e.g., a curved versus straight tail). Children who were required to look at the pictures and decide if they were the same or different learned the discrimination faster than children who were merely told to look carefully at the pictures. The group required to decide if the cats were the same or different appeared to do well because the pretraining task induced them to attend to differences between the stimuli.

In another experiment showing the value of practice on discrimination learning, Walk (1966) found that university students became better at judging differences among 5 varieties of wine, as a result of trials when students decided if two samples of tasted wines were the same or different. The students were 62% correct on a pretest, but 71% correct on a posttest after 20 training trials. This improvement in performance occurred even if no feedback was provided about whether the student's judgments were correct, showing that attending to stimulus differences can improve discrimination performance even in the absence of feedback.

Similarity of the Stimuli

The greater the similarity between the stimuli to be discriminated, the more difficult stimulus discrimination training will be. By difficulty, we mean that more errors will be made in training or that training will require more trials or time.

Spiker and Holton (1959) studied the effects of stimulus similarity with fourth-grade children in multiple-stimulus multiple-response discrimination training. The task required that the children respond to four lights that differed in intensity by pushing one of several buttons when a light of a particular intensity came on. When the intensity was similar, the children made more errors than when the intensity was widely different.

The principle of stimulus similarity is often seen in day-to-day life. We confuse for one another people who look alike. Plants and animals that are visibly similar are more difficult to tell apart than those that are very different.

Relationship Between the Training and Goal Stimuli

Stimulus discrimination training is more effective if the training stimuli are more closely matched to the goal stimuli (Stoddard & McIlvane, 1989). By training stimuli, we mean the stimuli used to teach the discrimination and by goal stimuli, we mean the stimuli used to assess whether the discrimination has been acquired. For example, suppose a teacher is training students to recognize giraffes and to say "giraffe" when shown a picture of a giraffe.

One procedure would be to use a giraffe picture as an S+ for the response and very different pictures as the S–s (e.g., pictures of cars, furniture, landscapes, and so on). This would be fine if the goal of discrimination training were to teach the students to discriminate giraffes from widely different stimuli, a broad discrimination that most children learn easily.

However, if the goal of training was for the students to discriminate giraffes from other four-legged animals, then the training stimuli should include giraffes along with mules, horses, zebras, and llamas, for example. These S–s have many more features in common with the S+ and, as a result, the discrimination problem becomes more difficult. At the same time, it becomes more useful in everyday life. A child who does not call a fire engine a giraffe is not readily admired, but a child who does not call a llama a giraffe may well be.

Williams (1969) studied the relationship between the training and goal stimuli in stimulus discrimination training. She gave kindergarten students matching-to-sample discrimination training in which a letter-like form shown in Figure 7.3 was the S+. For one group of children, the S–s, shown in Figure 7.3, were right-left reversals of the S+ and 180° rotations of the S+. For another group of children, the S–s were letterlike forms completely different from the S+. Some examples of the training stimuli are shown in Figure 7.3.

As you can see, the training stimuli for the first group of children were much more similar than for the second group. In keeping with the principle of stimulus similarity, the first group of children made many more errors during discrimination training than the second group. During testing, the children's task was to discriminate the S+s used in training from similar and dissimilar letterlike forms. Those trained to discriminate between similar letterlike forms did much better than those trained to discriminate between completely different letterlike forms.

Rate of Stimulus Presentation

Stimulus discrimination training often consists of a situation in which a teacher presents stimuli to learners, observes the learners' responding, and provides differential consequences. In such situations, the teacher can alter the rate of stimulus presentation by either speeding up or slowing down the process. Carnine (1976a) compared the effects of fast and slow rates of teacher presentations of stimuli on the behavior of two first-grade students. The teacher had described the students as being off-task too often. A fast-presentation rate caused the students to participate and respond correctly more often. In addition, both students were off-task less often when the

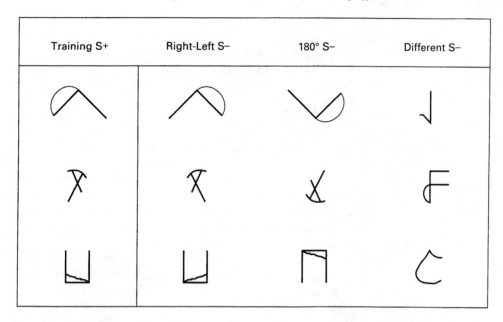

Training S+	Right-Left S–	180° S–	Different S–

Figure 7.3   *Experimental Stimuli Used in Williams's (1969) Experiment*

One group of children was trained to discriminate between the training S+s and S–s that were right-left reversals of the training S+s. A second group of children was trained to discriminate between the training S+s and S–s that were 180° rotations of the training S+s. As such, for these two groups, the S+s and S–s used in training were similar. A third group of children was trained to discriminate between the training S+s and S–s that were dissimilar. Following discrimination training, the three groups of children were tested in their ability to discriminate the S+s from S–s similar and dissimilar to the S+s. The two groups trained to discriminate between the similar stimuli did much better on the test than the children trained to discriminate dissimilar stimuli.

teacher used the fast-rate presentation.

In discussing his data, Carnine cautions against using too fast a rate of stimulus presentation to enable students to attend properly to the stimuli being presented. Using autistic children as subjects, Dyer, Christian, and Luce (1982) compared a procedure in which the subjects could respond immediately after presentation of the S+ to one in which subjects were required to wait 3 seconds before responding. The required delay condition improved the children's level of correct responding. This response-delay procedure was thought to be desirable in inducing the children to attend to the characteristics of the S+. This procedure is suggested for learners who appear to be responding impulsively without paying attention to the stimuli.

Order of Stimulus Presentation

Multiple-stimulus multiple-response discrimination is generally more effective if each type of discrimination problem is presented cumulatively, in which each individual member of the discrimination is learned before new ones are taught. For example, when Carnine (1976b) taught the names of six letters to preschool children, the children were initially taught to say the name of one letter. After this, another letter was added to the discrimination and the children were taught to discriminate between the two. This process continued until all six letters were included. This cumulative-introduction method of discrimination training was compared to a simultaneous-introduction method in which the children could be required to respond to any one of the six letters from the beginning of training. On a discrimination test given after training, children trained using the cumulative-introduction method responded correctly much more often than children trained using the simultaneous-introduction method.

As a general rule, discrimination problems should be presented in a sequence from easy to more difficult. The use of cumulative-introduction as a method of discrimination training is a means of doing just that.

Another useful procedure in discrimination training is to re-present the missed discrimination problems to the learners shortly after the errors have been made. For example, Van Houten and Rolider (1989) used flash cards to teach arithmetic problems to second- and fourth-grade students. In the sequential presentation method, the students were required to respond to 10 flash cards in order, whether they made errors or not. In the rapid re-presentation method, the missed problems were re-presented to the students after they had responded to one intervening problem. The students learned the correct answers to the problems more rapidly when using rapid re-presentation than when using sequential presentation.

Stimulus-Specific Reinforcement

Stimulus discrimination training can be improved if a different reinforcer is made dependent on responding to different discriminative stimuli. Litt and Schreibman (1981) worked with six autistic children ranging in age from 5 to 13 years. Stimulus discrimination training consisted of teaching the children labels for several common objects including a file, a nail, and a compass. The experimenter asked the child to give her one of the objects. A child responding correctly was given an edible reinforcer (e.g., tortilla chips, fruit juice, raisins) that was specific for the object requested. For example, if a child responded correctly by giving the experimenter a nail, she would always receive fruit juice as a reinforcer. The reinforcers used were tested with the children to ensure they were about equal in effectiveness. The children learned the labels for the objects more quickly with this type of stimulus-specific reinforcement than when the same reinforcer was used for all correct responses or when a variety of reinforcers that were not specific to the S+s were used.

The experimenters suggest that the reason for the effectiveness of stimulus-specific reinforcement was that the children had greater control over their environment when different correct responses produced different reinforcers.

Summary

In this chapter we introduced the concept of stimulus discrimination training, which refers to a variety of procedures that teach people to respond selectively to different stimuli. During stimulus discrimination training, a response-strengthening procedure is used to increase the level of a response in the presence of one stimulus, called an S+, and a response-weakening procedure is used to decrease the level of the response in the presence of another stimulus called an S–. In a basic form of stimulus discrimination training, in the presence of an S+ a response is strengthened by reinforcing that response, while in the presence of the S– the response is weakened through extinction.

A related concept is stimulus control, said to exist when presention of a stimulus causes some measure of behavior to change. Excitatory stimulus control exists when presenting a stimulus strengthens some measure of behavior, while inhibitory stimulus control exists when presenting a stimulus weakens some measure of behavior.

We went on to examine several different types of stimulus discrimination and stimulus control procedures. These included simultaneous discrimination, successive discrimination, social discrimination, verbal discrimination, multiple-stimulus, multiple-response discrimination, matching-to-sample discrimination, and multiple-cue discrimination.

We also examined the conditions that make stimulus discrimination effective. In part, the effectiveness of stimulus discrimination will depend on the effectiveness of the procedures used to strengthen the response in the presence of the S+ and to weaken the response in the presence of the S–. Apart from these factors, we examined how several conditions can influence the effectiveness of stimulus discrimination training. These conditions included instructions, active learner responding, pretraining procedures, the similarity of the stimuli, the relationship between the training and goal stimuli, the rate of stimulus presentation, the order or stimulus presentation, and stimulus-specific reinforcement.

Conceptual Exercise   *Stimulus Discrimination Training*

For each of the following items, decide if the item is an example of stimulus discrimination training. If it is, identify the S+ and the S–. Also indicate whether it is an example of simultaneous or successive discrimination, social discrimination, verbal discrimination, multiple-stimulus multiple-response discrimination, or matching-to-sample discrimination. Justify your decisions with a brief explanation. Confirm your decisions by reading the analyses provided in the back of the book.

Note: In some types of discrimination training, the consequence for responding is to tell the learner the correct answer, and this is done whether the learner responds correctly or incorrectly. In this kind of discrimination training, the consequences may not appear to be differential because the same type of consequence, the correct answer, is used for correct and incorrect responses. However, the relationship between the learner's response and the correct answer does differ for correct and incorrect responses. Discrimination training procedures that make use of correct-answer consequences may therefore be judged to make use of use of differential consequences.

1. Undergraduate students at a university in the United States were participating in a psychology experiment. The students were shown photographs of the faces of 30 Japanese people. Each photo was paired with a number. The students' task was to learn which number went with which face so that they could say the number when shown the photo alone. When a student identified a face photo correctly by number, the student was told she was correct. When a student responded incorrectly or did not respond at all, the student was told the correct response. At first, the students were relatively poor at this. However, as the procedure continued, the students learned to recognize the Japanese face photos correctly and were also better at recognizing previously unseen Japanese face photos.

2. Dr. Blake had set up a program at a university counseling department designed to teach shy students to interact with others more often. As a part of the training program, Dr. Blake had her staff interact with the students and reinforce the students' self-disclosures that provided personal information about themselves. As a result, the students increased their frequency of self-disclosures.

3. Two pigeons were subjects in a psychology experiment. When J. S. Bach's Prelude in C Minor for Flute was played for the pigeons, their pecks at a disc in a chamber were reinforced with food on fixed-ratio and fixed-interval reinforcement schedules. When Hindemith's Sonata, Opus 25, a viola piece, was played for the pigeons, pecks at the disc were unreinforced. As a result of these methods, the pigeons came to peck at the disc much more frequently during Bach music than during Hindemith music.

4. Bill was learning the names of different letters of the alphabet. One problem was that, while he would say "a" when shown an A in standard typewriter typeface, he would fail to say "a" when shown an A in italics or in other typefaces. In order to solve this problem, Bill was given training to learn to say "a" to different types of typefaces. Correct responses were reinforced with praise, and incorrect responses were given corrective feedback.

5. Twenty infants, all about a year old, were subjects in a study. They were seated at a panel at which there were two square panels on the left and right. Sometimes the left panel was purple and the right panel was green; at other times the left panel was green and the right panel was purple. If the infants touched the green panel, a delightful peal of recorded laughter would sound. If they touched the purple panel, nothing happened. As a result of this procedure, the infants learned to press the green panel much more often than the purple panel.

6. Trainees at a sheltered workshop were learning how to recognize defective beverage cans in preparation for work at a can factory. As a part of the training procedure, the

instructor gave the students a lecture in which she used a large demonstration can to point out typical defects in can manufacture. As a result, the trainees learned something about how to recognize defective cans.

7. Five infants, 6- to 12-weeks old, were subjects in an experiment. During the experiment, the infants were shown three stimuli, a pattern of black and white stripes, a black and white checkerboard, and a large black circle on a white background. When the stripes were shown to the infants, praise, smiles, and rattle and bell sounds were dependent on left head turns. When the checkerboard was shown to the infants, the consequences were dependent on right head turns. When the black circle was shown to the infants, head turns were extinguished. As a result of this procedure, the infants learned to make left head turns to the stripes, right head turns to the checkerboard, and not to make head turns to the black circle.

8. Preschool children sat in front of a display panel. In a top window of the panel was a letterlike form. When the child pressed this window, four additional letterlike forms would appear in four windows beneath the top window. One of these four forms was the same as the one shown in the top window. If the child pressed the window that contained the form that was the same as the top window, a chime would sound, a red light would flash, and a bead would be dispensed. The beads could be traded in for raisins, candy, and a variety of small toys. As a result of this method, the children learned to choose the correct window. The children also learned to tell the difference between real letters.

9. Professor Keller was teaching his students to receive Morse code signals. In Morse code, each letter of the alphabet is represented by "dots" and "dashes," sound impulses of different lengths. During training sessions, the students would listen to 100 signals. Included in the group of 100 signals were all the letters of the alphabet and the digits from 0 to 9. One signal was presented every 3 seconds. After hearing the signal, the students wrote down what they thought they had heard. After they had written down their answer, the instructor would tell them the correct answer, thereby indicating to the students whether their answer was correct or incorrect. In this fashion, most of the students learned all 36 signals within 12 hours of training.

10. Several children who attended a day-care center were unruly and fought a great deal. In order to solve this problem, a behavior analyst was consulted. The behavior analyst put a program into effect in which four problem children were given tokens exchangeable for toys, free play, and edible treats for every 20 minutes that passed without their touching another child. In addition, when the problem children did strike another child, they were given a 5-minute chair timeout.

11. Two retarded boys were participating in an experiment wherein they were shown pictures of objects. If the child correctly identified the pictured object, he was given a token that could be exchanged for candy, nuts, or the opportunity to look at a picture book. If the child responded incorrectly or did not respond at all, he received an electric shock. In this way the children learned to name the pictured objects.

12. A group of introductory psychology students were participating in an experiment concerned with artistic taste. On each trial, one group of students was shown two pictures, one of which was given a higher evaluation by experienced artists than the

other. The student's task was to indicate a preference. After the student had chosen one of the pictures, a white light would flash if the student's selection disagreed with the artists' and a red light would flash if the student's choice agreed. However, the students were falsely told that the white light indicated agreement with the artists' preference and that the red light indicated disagreement. As a result, the students learned to choose the picture that the professional artists had selected as poorer than the other.

13. Students in a high school science class were learning to distinguish between different types of rocks and minerals. At the direction of their teacher, the students spent 90 minutes examining 30 different rock and mineral specimens in a display case. Because of this, the students became better at recognizing different types of rocks and minerals.

14. Sixteen second-grade students were taught 30 vocabulary words. The students were shown the words on individual cards. If the student said the word correctly, she was given a token in a dish in front of her. If the student was incorrect, she was told the correct answer and no token was provided. The tokens were exchangeable for pennies. Using this method, the students learned all 30 vocabulary words.

15. Four 7- and 8-year-old girls were learning ballet. The students were told which one of four ballet exercises to perform (e.g., dégagé, frappée, développé, and grand battement). If the exercise were performed correctly, the instructor praised the student. If incorrectly, the student would be told to freeze her movements and told what she was doing incorrectly.

16. Children enrolled in a preschool program spent 30 minutes each day learning reading skills. Teachers prepared two cards, one with a word to be learned and the other with a sentence containing the word to be learned. The child was presented with the word card and required to show where in the sentence the word appears. Praise reinforced correct responses and incorrect responses were given corrective feedback.

17. Students in a second-grade class were learning about different forms of transportation. They correctly identified pictures of cars and airplanes as forms of transportation, but failed to identify pictures of skateboards, wheelchairs, and rickshaws as such. Teachers showed the students pictures of skateboards, wheelchairs, and rickshaws and reinforced the students' identification of these as forms of transportation or corrected them when appropriate.

18. Several third-grade children were having difficulty reading sight words. To help their reading problem, near the end of the school day the students would play a bingo game wherein the teacher read a word aloud. When the teacher read the word, the students' task was to look at bingo-type cards to see if they had that word on their card. If they did, they were to place a poker chip over the word. If the students had a row of words covered horizontally, vertically, or diagonally, they were to say "Bingo" and win the game. Using this method, the students learned to identify the written versions of the spoken words.

Conceptual Exercise   *Making Stimulus Discrimination Effective*

In each of the following items, something should be altered to make the stimulus discrimination procedure more effective. Describe what should be altered and explain why.

1. In a tenth-grade typing class, the students were learning to tell the difference between serif and sans serif typefaces. The teacher was using a stimulus discrimination procedure in which students were given examples of different typefaces and were required to check all the examples of serif letters. For each correct response the students received points that they could exchange for a variety of special privileges. The teacher didn't want to influence the students by given hints, so each student was simply given the sheet with the examples and asked to check the serif typefaces. The teacher used examples of serif typefaces different from the examples of sans serif typefaces and varied the style—italics, capitals, lowercase, boldface, and so forth. Although the students seemed to answer randomly, when the teacher looked more closely at the answer sheets, she realized that some of the students picked italic faces, others picked boldfaces and others picked all capitals.

2. A third-grade teacher was using a stimulus discrimination procedure to help her students learn the difference between rectangles and squares. She would present two flash cards, one with a square on it and the other with a rectangle. Her favorite student, Barry, was the demonstration learner. If Barry picked the card with the square on it when asked, the teacher would praise him. If he picked the other card, the teacher said nothing and went on to the next trial. The teacher was careful to give instructions to the class about the important differences between squares and rectangles and to explain that correct answers would be praised and incorrect ones would not be praised. She did not use rectangles that were similar to squares. After the demonstration the teacher gave the whole class a quiz. Correct answers received points that could be traded in for special treats. Although Barry did very well on the quiz, the rest of students did poorly.

3. A 5-year-old retarded girl was learning the difference between "on top of" and "underneath." The trainer would give two objects, such as a red block and a blue block to the girl. The trainer would say, "Put the red block on top of the blue block." If the girl did so, she was given some raisins. If she put the red block underneath the blue block, she was not given any raisins. Then two more blocks would be given to the girl, perhaps a green block and a yellow block. The trainer would say, "Put the green block on top of the yellow block." The trainer was careful to be clear about the differences in instructions and about the consequences of correct responding. The trainer did not go too fast, but the girl was not successful. The trainer overheard another staff member ask the girl what color her sweater was and the girl seemed confused about the question.

4. An English teacher was teaching her class the meaning of "abstract" and "concrete." She would present two words, one more abstract than the other. Each student had an answer sheet and was required to write down the more abstract word for each pair presented. The teacher carefully explained that abstract concepts are more difficult to

picture in your head than concrete concepts and she also said her students would receive 1 minute of extra gym time for each correct answer. The teacher had used this kind of procedure with her students before. She began with a short pretraining procedure and intended to follow this with a longer, more complex procedure. She presented the following pair of words:

Abstract	Concrete
justice	fire
reality	volume
truth	hatred
honor	instrument

She was surprised to find that her students did poorly on the pretraining task, because a colleague had used the same procedure successfully with his class. His word list follows:

Abstract	Concrete
justice	fire engine
reality	radio
truth	automobile
honor	violin

5. Corey was a 2-year-old who hadn't seen his dad for so long he couldn't recognize him. His dad had been away on a job in another country since shortly after Corey's birth. Corey's mom wanted to teach Corey to recognize his dad before he got home so she got a recent photograph of her husband. She explained to Corey that she would show him two pictures, one of his dad and one of someone else. If Corey picked the picture of his dad, he would receive a treat. She explained to Corey that his dad had dark hair and wore glasses. She used the same photo of Corey's dad but presented various photos of her sisters, her mother, her aunts, and Corey's day-care mates. Some of these people had dark hair and some had glasses. Corey did very well at this task. When Corey's dad got home he was pleased that Corey recognized him. He was less pleased when he took Corey on an outing and Corey called every man he saw "Daddy."

6. Davis was to start preschool in the fall. One of the requirements was that each child had to be able to recognize his or her first name, middle name, and surname when it was printed, because the children's cubbyholes, lockers, and artwork storage areas were labeled with their names. Because sometimes the children had the same names, they had to recognize all their names. So that he could start school, Davis's mom worked with him, by showing him two cards, one with his full name (Robert Davis Baker) printed on it, and the other with a different name. She was careful to tell Davis the important things to look for to identify his own name and he knew that he would get his favorite jelly beans each time he succeeded. Davis's mom was careful to use S– names that were not too similar to Davis's own name, but close enough so that he would learn the relevant differences. She didn't go too fast and she was careful to re-present to Davis an item soon after he had made an error. Davis did fine when the S– did not include the name "Robert," but when it did, Davis had trouble.

7. Cindy was learning her alphabet. The teacher had each letter of the alphabet printed on flashcards that she would shuffle and then hold up one at a time. Cindy was supposed to say aloud the letter she saw. If she was correct, she would earn a point that could be traded in later for special treats and privileges. Using a progressive sequence procedure, the teacher started with just five letters that were not too similar looking and whose names were not too similar in sound. The teacher explained the important differences between the letters. Once Cindy had mastered these five, five more would be added to the group. The teacher became quite frustrated because Cindy would blurt out all sorts of letter names almost before the card had been presented.

8. Mr. Johnson was training his 3-year-old the names of the four suits in a deck of playing cards by presenting each symbol on a card and asking Jimmie to name the suit. If Jimmie said, "Clubs" when a ♣ was presented, his father gave him a clicker toy. If Jimmie said, "Diamonds" when a ♦ was presented, his father gave him a dime. If Jimmie said, "Hearts" when a ♥ was presented, his father gave him a happy face sticker and if Jimmie said, "Spades" when a ♠ was presented, he got a sparkly sticker. Mr. Johnson followed all the principles that make stimulus discrimination effective and Jimmie learned very quickly to name all four suits. When Mr. Johnson told his co-workers about this, Ms. Farlane bet him that she could train her daughter Barbara faster than Mr. Johnson had trained Jimmie. She followed a similar procedure to Mr. Johnson's except she rewarded her daughter's correct responses with Barbara's favorite treat, a licorice jelly bean. Barbara did well, but she didn't learn as quickly as Jimmie had. When you decide what Ms. Farlane could have done better, assume that her daughter and Mr. Johnson's son were equally capable of learning the task.

chapter 8

Prompting, Fading, and Chaining

For most children a visual acuity test is a simple procedure. The child responds to the examiner's instructions to read a letter or to indicate to which direction a figure is pointing. However, for children who can neither speak nor follow complex instructions, vision testing is difficult indeed. In the past, few nonverbal children with poor vision have been accurately prescribed corrective lenses because of the difficulties in testing their vision. Such children, then, are doubly challenged. Their poor vision and their lack of verbal behavior makes learning a wide variety of visually oriented tasks extremely burdensome and, as a result, their behavior problems often escalate.

The problem of testing the vision of nonverbal children was a concern of two psychologists, Crighton Newsom and Karen Simon, who were experts in behavior analysis stimulus discrimination techniques. Eleven children, who had been labeled as either autistic or schizophrenic, were selected to participate in the project. The children, most of whom lived at the Children's Treatment Center at Camarillo State Hospital, ranged in age from 5 to 16 years old. Four of the children could make simple one- or two- word requests, but the remaining seven made unintelligible sounds or no sounds at all.

Building upon the earlier work of Joel Macht (1970), Newsom and Simon decided to use a visual acuity test in which the children would be required to discriminate between "E" shaped figures in which the prongs of the E pointed either downward or to the left. The downward-pointing E was selected as the S+ and the leftward-pointing E was selected as the S–.

These S+ and S– stimuli are shown in Figure 8.1. By using cards on which different sized E-shaped figures were displayed, the experimenters planned to test how well the children could see by determining the minimum-sized E-shapes they could discriminate when those shapes were viewed at a distance. The S+ and S– are shown in Figure 8.1a.

Before their visual acuity could be accurately tested, the children had to be able to discriminate between the vertical lines and horizontal lines that distinguish a downward-pointing E from a leftward-pointing E. The experimenters decided to use a fading procedure to teach this discrimination.

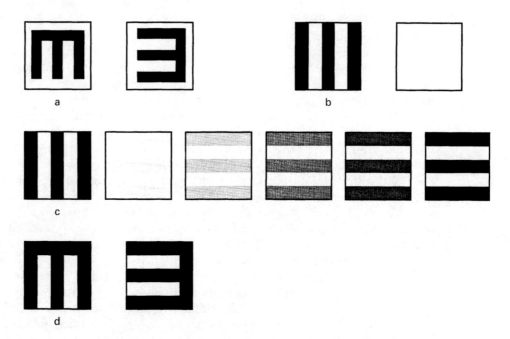

Figure 8.1   *Experimental Stimuli Used in Newsom and Simon's (1977) Study*

The stimuli used to train the discrimination between downward- and leftward-pointing Es began with training vertical and horizontal stripe discrimination. Figure adapted from Newsom and Simon (1977).

In a fading procedure, the discriminative stimuli for a response are gradually changed so that they become increasingly like the goal stimuli to be discriminated. Newsom and Simon wanted the children to discriminate downward-pointing Es from leftward-pointing Es. These, then, were the goal stimuli to be discriminated. Because the children could not discriminate between vertical and horizontal lines, the plan was to start with stimuli that the children could discriminate and gradually change those stimuli so that they were increasingly like the goal stimuli.

The experimenters began by selecting a card with black and white vertical lines as the S+ and a blank card as the S–. These stimuli are shown in Figure 8.1b. The training took place in a long room, down the center of which three long tables were placed end to end. This arrangement formed two aisles, one on either side of the tables. At one end of the room was a blackboard where the experimenters placed the stimulus cards. Two stimulus cards were always placed on the blackboard at the end of each aisle, and the child stood at the end of the room opposite the blackboard.

During training trials, the experimenter placed two cards on the blackboard and, after ensured that the child had looked at each one, gave the child the *verbal prompt,* "Come and get it." Initially, if the child then walked down the aisle that had the vertically striped S+ card at the end, this response was reinforced with praise and either candy, soda pop, or ice cream. If the child began walking down the aisle with the blank S– card at the end, she was told, "No, wrong one," and was instructed to sit down. On the first few trials, some of the children had to be given *physical prompts* to walk down the correct aisle. These physical prompts consisted of manually guiding the child to stand and walk. The position of the S+ and S– cards was randomly changed from trial to trial to prevent the children from forming a position discrimination. Using this method, all the children learned to discriminate between the vertically striped S+ card and the blank S– card within seven trials.

The next step was to begin gradually changing the S– card. Rather than using the blank card as the S–, the experimenters used a card with very light grey horizontal stripes on the white background, as Figure 8.1c shows. The new S– card was only a slight change from the blank card, but it was a change in the direction of the goal S–, a card with dark horizontal stripes on a white background. If the child selected the S+ card rather than the new S–, the child's selection was reinforced and on the next trial another new S– card was presented, one with slightly darker horizontal stripes than on the previous S– card, as shown in Figure 8.1c. However, if the child selected the S– card, on the following trials, the S+ and S– remained the same until the child had selected the S+ on five consecutive trials.

The experimenters used 15 different S– cards in the fading procedure. Each of these cards, several of which are represented in Figure 8.1c, had increasingly darker horizontal stripes. In this way, the children gradually learned to discriminate between horizontal and vertical stripes. After the children had successfully learned to discriminate the S– card with the darkest stripes from the S+, the S+ and S– cards were changed such that the S+ card pointed down and the S– card pointed to the left, as shown in Figure 8.1d. The children were required to make five correct responses to these stimuli before proceeding. Some of the children made either no errors or very few errors during the fading of the stimuli. Although other children had more difficulty, most of the children learned to discriminate between the vertical and horizontal lines.

Once the children had mastered the discrimination between the down- and left-pointing Es, vision testing could begin. During testing, the children were required to discriminate between the S+ stimuli, the down-pointing Es, and the S− stimuli, the left-pointing Es. Testing began with very large letters, which were gradually reduced in size on each trial as long as the child continued to respond correctly. When a child made an error during testing, she was given seven additional trials with the same-sized letters. If the child made five correct choices in a row on these trials, the letter size was again reduced on the next trial. After a single error was made during testing, the testing procedure became more strict: The child was required to choose all new S+ stimuli on five trials in row. Whenever a child failed to meet the five-correct-choices criterion, the child was tested using S+ and S− cards that were one step larger. A child's visual acuity was determined by determining the smallest letter size at which she could meet the five-correct-responses criterion.

Of the 11 children, 8 successfully learned the discrimination between the vertical and horizontal lines and were able to have their vision tested. Two of the eight children were found to have vision impairments that were previously unknown to anyone. The training and testing procedures were completed within one or two sessions, showing that these methods were of practical use in testing the vision of nonverbal children.*

In this chapter, we will examine three specific behavior analysis techniques for teaching skills: *prompting, fading,* and *stimulus response chaining.*

Prompting

One stimulus control procedure that is important in behavior analysis is called *prompting.* A prompt is a discriminative stimulus for a response that is used to induce a desirable response or to discourage an undesirable response. When a behavior analyst uses a prompt, she presents a previously established S+ in order to encourage a correct response, or she presents a previously established S− in order to deter a response. For example, in Newsom and Simon's work with vision testing, the verbal command, "Come and get it," was used to prompt the children to select the S+ used in the training procedure. This prompt was an S+ for the selection task. An example of an S− prompt would have been "Don't come and get it yet," because this would be a discriminative stimulus for not engaging in the selection task.

Prompts differ from other types of discriminative stimuli because they are extra S+s and S−s that are used in order to induce a desired response. For example, if you see a tree fallen on the path during a hike, this is an S+, a discriminative stimulus, for walking around the log and an S− for walking through the log. The tree is not a prompt, however, because it hasn't been placed on the path to deter walking. In

*Based on Newsom and Simon (1977)

contrast, if you see a cord stretched across the path with a sign saying "Avalanche Danger," this is a discriminative stimulus, an S−, that is also a prompt because it has been added to the environment in order to deter walking. As you can see, prompts are defined not by their physical nature, but by the reason for their presentation.

Varieties of Prompting

Behavior analysts make use of several types of prompts including verbal prompts, gestural prompts, picture prompts, physical prompts, and modeling prompts.

Verbal prompts are spoken or written words that are intended to induce a desired behavior. Verbal prompts are often classified as direct or indirect. A direct verbal prompt is a command to engage in a specific behavior (e.g., "Look at the blackboard"). An indirect verbal prompt is used to indicate that something should be done, but it does not specify what the desired behavior is. For example, the question, "Do you remember what you do now?" is an indirect verbal prompt because it encourages behavior to occur, but it does not specify what behavior is required.

Gestural prompts consist of physical movements that have previously been established as discriminative stimuli for specific behaviors. Pointing to an object is a gestural prompt for paying attention to that object. Waving a hand, depending on how it is done, can be a prompt for us either to come or go.

A third type of prompt is a *picture prompt*. A picture prompt is a drawing, painting, photograph, or video image that either illustrates a behavior to be performed or otherwise acts to induce behavior. Picture prompts can be detailed and elaborate. For example, in encouraging sequences of behavior, some behavior analysts have developed picture-prompt books that show in step-by-step fashion, how a task is to be performed.

A fourth type of prompt is called a *physical prompt,* which induces correct responding by manually guiding the person's movements. We saw an example of the use of physical prompts in Newsom and Simon's vision testing procedure in which on the first few trials, the children were physically guided to stand up and walk toward the S+. Physical prompting can also be used in training verbal behavior, as when a speech therapist physically forms a child's lips in order to help the child make a specific sound. Physical prompting is sometimes called *physical guidance* and *manual guidance.* You may recall that physical prompting is sometimes used to induce a response in overcorrection procedures.

Note that a physical prompt is not a pure S+ for a response because when a response is manually guided, the response is not being controlled by an S+, a discriminative stimulus established through prior training. However, in most uses of physical prompting, the manual guidance of the response is only partial and this partial guidance comes to serve as an S+ for the response. One method of partial physical prompting is called *shadowing.* When using shadowing, the behavior analyst guides the learner's movements by keeping her hands a few inches away from the learner, and touching the learner only when necessary.

A fifth type of prompt is called a *modeling prompt*. A modeling prompt is a demonstration of the response for the learner, whose task it is to imitate the response. Modeling prompts, covered in detail in Chapter 10, are an excellent way to teach new responses.

The Purposes of Prompting

Prompting is used for two different purposes. First, sometimes prompting is used to teach a new *discrimination*. For example, suppose in teaching to discriminate between red and pink, our goal is to teach the child to touch a red card and not a pink one. In order to encourage correct responding, we might at first use a gestural prompt by pointing to the red card, or a modeling prompt by touching the red card ourselves, then asking the child to do so. In this way, prompts can be used to help teach the child to tell the difference between red and pink.

Second, prompting is also used to teach new *behavior*, to encourage the learner to make a response topography she has not made before. For example, Luyben, Funk, Morgan, Clark, and Delulio (1986) used prompting to train severely retarded children to use a side-of-the-foot soccer pass. At first, the children were physically prompted: Their legs were guided through the soccer pass movements. Over time, the children learned to respond to imitative prompts, then gestural prompts, then verbal prompts. Eventually, after the children learned to do the soccer pass without balance aids (i.e., a walker, a quad cane, or a normal cane), the children were able to pass the ball without any prompts.

Many uses of prompting in behavior analysis combine the teaching of new discriminations with the teaching of new behaviors. For example, in teaching the children to pass a soccer ball, some discrimination learning was also a part of the procedure, because kicking a soccer ball demands that the position of the ball be discriminated.

Advantages and Disadvantages of Prompting

This use of prompting to teach a new behavior is commonly seen in everyday life. By using a prompt, desired behaviors can be quickly induced with relatively little effort. For example, in preparing a meal you haven't cooked before, your chances of success are good if you follow a printed recipe, which is a set of verbal prompts. Lacking those prompts, however, your chances for a palatable meal drop considerably. But, with repetition, even the most hopeless chef may eventually do without the prompts.

Prompting is very effective when people are required to engage in many different behaviors. Most parents prompt their children to do homework and household chores. Most charitable and political organizations prompt donations through direct mail and phone campaigns. Advertising is essentially an elaborate system of prompting consumers to buy products and services. Most people also use prompts to manage their own behavior, as when you mark an appointment on a calendar so that it will act as a prompt in the future.

Although prompting can be highly effective in inducing behavior, it has disadvantages. Prompting requires that someone prompt the response, which takes up time and energy. For example, it is desirable for children to do their chores without prompting from their parents. In general, a hallmark of a competent performer in any field is that she is able to engage in worthy activities without being prompted to do so. For example, we admire the physician who can diagnose an illness without having to consult pictures in a medical guidebook and we admire a mechanic who can repair an engine without calling a co-worker over for advice. As such, it is often desirable to eliminate prompts once they have enabled the learner to acquire a discrimination or a behavior. One means of eliminating prompts is through the use of fading procedures, described later in this chapter.

Making Prompting Effective

As we have seen, prompts are a special kind of discriminative stimuli. Therefore, the same principles that make discriminative stimuli effective, covered in Chapter 7, make prompting effective. Apart from these principles, one additional factor that makes prompts effective is whether the prompts are *personal* or *impersonal*.

In general, prompts that are delivered in person are more effective than those that are not. For example, Williams, Thyer, Bailey, and Harrison (1989) used signs at parking lot exits to prompt users of cars to buckle their seat belts. Signs were more effective in promoting seat belt use when a person held them than when they were simply posted beneath existing stop signs. Further, the conventional posted signs were more effective when they had been preceded by use of the person-held signs than when not.

Similarly, Reitz and Hawkins (1982) compared personal and impersonal prompts to encourage nursing home residents to attend recreational activities. They found that large signs and loudspeaker announcements were much less effective in getting the residents to attend the activities than written personal invitations or personal prompts from the nursing home staff. Likewise, Jacobs, Bailey, and Crews (1984) found that handbills delivered door-to-door were more effective in increasing participation in a waste-recycling program than newspaper ads.

Fading

Many discriminations are too difficult to be acquired simply by providing differential consequences for responding to the S+ and S–. In addition, many behaviors are impossible to learn through shaping procedures. When behavior analysts are faced with the task of teaching discriminations and behaviors that are difficult to learn, they often turn to fading procedures.

Fading is a stimulus discrimination procedure in which the discriminative stimuli for a response are gradually changed so that they become increasingly like the goal discriminative stimuli. Fading is used when the person being trained cannot respond correctly to the goal S+ and S–. For example, in Newsom and Simon's work in training nonverbal children to discriminate between vertical and horizontal lines, the children were at first unable to make the vertical-horizontal discrimination. The experimenters decided to give the children something easier to do, to discriminate between a blank card and one with vertical lines, a task that most of them could learn. Then they used the fading procedure by gradually changing the S–, the blank card, to make it more and more like horizontal stripes, the desired S– for the response. The similarity of the S– cards to the goal S– was determined by the darkness of the horizontal stripes. The feature of the discriminative stimulus that is gradually changed during a fading procedure is called the *fading dimension*. In this example the fading dimension was the darkness of the horizontal stripes, which were changed from very light grey to black.

When fading procedures are used, stimulus control is often *transferred* from one set of easy-to-discriminate stimuli to another set of difficult-to-discriminate stimuli. For example, in Newsom and Simon's procedure, the stimulus control exerted by the easy-to-discriminate stimuli, the blank and horizontal-striped card, was transferred to the difficult-to-discriminate vertical- and horizontal-striped cards.

The use of fading techniques is sometimes called *errorless discrimination* (Terrace, 1963). When the discriminative stimuli are altered very gradually, correct responses continue to occur to the S+ and incorrect responses continue not to occur to the S–. If this is done gradually enough, incorrect responses may never occur; hence the term *errorless discrimination*. Although the occasional incorrect response may occur during fading, these instances are rare compared with those seen in trial-and-error stimulus discrimination techniques. Errorless learning is desirable, because once an error is made it tends to be repeated and must be unlearned before the correct discrimination or response can be acquired. By reducing errors, fading procedures generally result in more effective and more rapid learning than trial-and-error procedures (e.g., Sidman & Stoddard, 1967; Touchette, 1968; Zawlocki & Walls, 1983).

Fading is similar to shaping and to the thinning of a reinforcement schedule, because all three procedures make use of gradual change techniques. However, fading is different from both shaping and reinforcement schedule thinning. In fading, the *discriminative stimuli* for a response become increasingly like the goal discriminative stimuli. In shaping, *responses* that are increasingly like a goal response are reinforced until the goal is reached. In thinning of a reinforcement schedule, the *frequency of reinforcement* for a response is gradually reduced. While fading involves gradual changes in the *stimuli*, shaping involves gradual changes in the response, and thinning involves gradual changes in the *frequency of reinforcement*.

Prompt Fading Strategies

Prompts differ in their capacity to cue the correct response. A physical prompt is normally considered the strongest type of prompt, because the physical guidance of the response often ensures correct responding. Modeling and picture prompts are considered intermediate-strength prompts, because the response is shown to the learner, who is only required to engage in the demonstrated behavior. Verbal and gestural prompts are considered a weaker type of prompt, because they require that the learner can at least perform the response when instructed or signaled to do so.

When prompting procedures make use of more than one type of prompt, the behavior analyst is faced with a decision about whether to use weaker prompts first, and then move to stronger ones as necessary, or to begin with strong prompts and gradually fade in weaker ones as correct responding continues to occur. The first technique is known as the *increasing assistance method* (also called the least-to-most prompts method, or the system of least prompts). In the increasing assistance method, strong prompts are used only when necessary, ensuring that the learner will not become dependent on strong prompts. The second method is known as the *decreasing assistance method* (also known as the most-to-least prompts method or graduated guidance). In the decreasing assistance method, strong prompts help promote the correct response without errors.

Horner and Keilitz (1975) used the increasing assistance method to teach eight mentally retarded children to brush their teeth. Toothbrushing was divided into a sequence of 15 steps. If a child did not perform a step within 5 seconds of the beginning of a trial, an *indirect verbal prompt* was given, which consisted of saying "Go ahead" or "What's next?" If this prompt did not induce the correct response, the trainer used a *direct verbal prompt,* a command specifying what was to be done (e.g., "Wet the toothbrush"). If this prompt did not work, the direct verbal prompt was repeated. If the repeated prompt failed, the trainer gave a modeling prompt by demonstrating the desired response to accompany the direct verbal prompt. If this also failed, the child was given a physical prompt, guiding the hands through the response, as well as the direct verbal prompt. This is an example of the increasing assistance method because the weakest prompt, the indirect verbal prompt, was used first and increasingly stronger prompts (direct verbal prompts, modeling prompts, and physical prompts) were used only if all the weaker prompts had failed. This method was successful in teaching all eight children to brush their teeth without prompts. In the increasing assistance method, prompts are gradually faded as the learner comes to respond correctly to progressively weaker prompts.

The decreasing assistance method of fading prompts has also been used to teach a variety of tasks. For example, McDonnell and Ferguson (1989) used the decreasing assistance method to teach retarded high school and junior high school students to cash checks and use an automated teller machine. Each of the tasks was divided into a series of steps. In addition, four types of prompts were identified. From strongest to weakest, these prompts were:

- a direct verbal prompt plus physical assistance (e.g., prompting, "Write the word 'Cash' on the check" and physically assisting the writing response);
- the direct verbal cue and either pointing (e.g., to the line on the check) or modeling (e.g., the trainer writing "Cash" on the correct line);

- the direct verbal cue alone; and

- a gesture (e.g., pointing to the correct line on the check).

After an initial assessment of the individual's skills, training began with the strongest prompts needed to induce correct responding. If the student responded correctly with this strong prompt on two trials, the next weakest prompt was used on the following trial. In this way the students learned how to perform the two skills. Note that with the decreasing assistance method, prompts are faded: If the learner performs correctly to a stronger prompt, a weaker prompt is used on the following trials.

Of the two prompting strategies, the increasing assistance method has been used more often than the decreasing assistance method. Relatively little research has compared the two methods (see Demchak [1990] for a review).

Making Fading Effective

The effectiveness of fading is influenced by several factors including step size, fading the S+ rather than the S−, using distinctive feature prompts, and using within-stimulus rather than extra-stimulus prompts.

In fading procedures, the discriminative stimuli for a response are gradually changed in small steps. Sometimes the discriminative stimuli for a response can be changed too rapidly. If step size is too large, stimulus control may be lost and incorrect responding may result. For example, Waranch, Iwata, Wohl, and Nidiffer (1981) used fading to treat H.A., a 21-year-old retarded man who was afraid of mannequins. This problem made it impossible for H.A. to accompany his family on shopping trips. The goal of treatment was for H.A. to touch a full-size mannequin. At first, whenever H.A. touched a small 46 cm mannequin, this behavior was reinforced with praise and the opportunity to play checkers. When he was doing this, reinforcement was dependent on H.A. touching a larger 64 cm mannequin. Once H.A. was doing this without problems, a full-size mannequin was presented. As soon as he saw this large mannequin, however, H.A. became fearful and covered his eyes with his hands as long as it was in the room. Clearly, the step size in the fading process was too large. The therapists recognized what had happened and immediately took steps to rectify the situation. They draped the full-size mannequin with a sheet. Over time, the sheet was removed and the large mannequin was placed closer and closer to H.A. until he was able to touch it without distress. In spite of the setback, this procedure was a great success and H.A. soon was able to accompany his family on shopping trips.

Another factor that can influence the effectiveness of fading is whether the feature being faded is a dimension of the S+ or the S−. Recall that in the study in which Newsom and Simon used fading to assess the vision of nonverbal children, the horizontal lines on the cards were the S− because if the children selected them, their behavior was not reinforced. Newsom and Simon used fading by gradually darkening the horizontally striped cards the children saw while using the same vertical striped cards for most of the procedure. For this reason, Newsom and Simon faded a feature of the S–s. Had they gradually darkened the vertical stripes, the card for which the children's selections were reinforced, they would have been fading along an S+ dimension.

Some evidence indicates that it is better to fade the S+ than the S–. For example, Schreibman and Charlop (1981) taught eight autistic children to discriminate between two geometric figures that differed in only one small way. In one condition, the S– was held constant while the S+ was gradually faded in; in another condition, the S+ was held constant while the S– was faded in. Seven of the eight children learned the discrimination more rapidly when the S+ was faded in first, than when the S– was faded in first. The experimenters believed that the reason for this result was that the children paid more attention to the stimulus that was changed, because people generally pay more attention to novel, changing stimuli than stimuli that remain the same. Therefore, when the S+ was faded, the children learned to pay more attention to it than the S–, which helped the children to choose the S+.

In contrast, when the S– was faded first, the children learned to pay attention to it and this impaired learning, because the S– is the incorrect stimulus. Stella and Etzel (1986) confirmed this interpretation by studying children's eye movements while either an S+ was faded with the S– held constant or vice versa. As shown in Figure 8.2, when the S+ was faded, the children looked at it more often than they

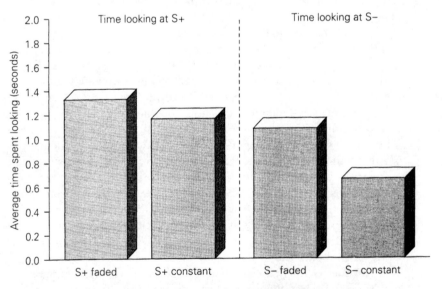

Figure 8.2   *The Influence of Fading a Stimulus on Attending to the Faded Stimulus*

The children spent more time looking at the S+ when it was being faded than when it was constant. They spent more time looking at the S– when it was being faded than when it was constant. Figure adapted from Stella and Etzel (1986).

did when it was constant. Likewise, when the S– was faded, they looked at it more often than they did when it was constant. Essentially, fading a stimulus promotes more attending behavior directed at the stimulus being faded. All these considerations suggest that when using fading methods, the S+ should normally be the stimulus that is faded rather than the S–.

Another factor that contributes to the effectiveness of fading is selection of a fading dimension that is a *distinctive feature* of the S+. By distinctive feature (also called a *relevant feature*), we mean a feature of the goal S+ that distinguishes it from the goal S–. For example, suppose we wish to teach children to discriminate between the uppercase letters R and P (cf., Egeland, 1975). The distinctive feature in this discrimination is the diagonal stem on the R, because it is what distinguishes the an R from a P. In contrast, *nondistinctive* or irrelevant features are features that are the same in the S+ as they are in the S–. For example, in an R-P discrimination, nondistinctive features include the upright line on the left side of the letter and the loop on the top half of the letter; these stimuli fail to distinguish an R from a P. In training discrimination, it is important to focus the learner's attention on those features that reliably differentiate an S+ from an S–.

Rincover (1978b) showed the importance of fading distinctive features in a study in which autistic children were trained to discriminate between three-letter words; for example, between JAR, the S+, and SON, the S–. The two words were presented simultaneously and the children's touches to the JAR card were reinforced with praise and candy, while touches to the SON card were ignored. In one fading condition, as illustrated in Figure 8.3, the top horizontal bar of the J in Jar was exaggerated by making it thicker than the lines used to compose the rest of the letters. This was a distinctive feature prompt because the horizontal line in the J in JAR distinguished it from the S–: The horizontal line is not present in the S in SON.

In a second fading condition, the bottom curve of the J was exaggerated. This was a nondistinctive feature because it is shared by the S–: The bottom of the S in SON is curved in the same way that the bottom of the J in JAR is. Fading proceeded by using the exaggerated features during early trials and then fading them out over time. It was found that fading using the distinctive feature was more effective than fading using the nondistinctive feature. As Gibson (1969) discusses, cartoonists often exaggerate the distinctive features of famous people. Such exaggeration makes it easier for us to identify the individual being portrayed. Have you ever seen a cartoon of David Letterman in which the gap between his front teeth is not emphasized? A sketch of Ronald Reagan without a grossly exaggerated pompadour might go unnoticed. Of course, cartoonists do not fade the features once they have exaggerated them. Often, the exaggerated distinctive features add visual interest and humor to drawings as well as making the subjects of the drawings clearly discriminable.

In general, the more distinctive the feature to be faded, the more effective the fading procedure will be. In this way, the learner will be trained to pay attention to the relevant part of the S+; the part that distinguishes it from the S–.

Another factor that contributes to the effectiveness of fading is whether *within-stimulus* or *extra-stimulus* prompts are faded. The difference between within-

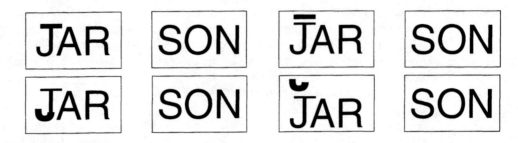

Figure 8.3   *Experimental Stimuli Used in Rincover's (1978b) Study*

The children learned to discriminate between the words more quickly when the fading dimension was a distinctive feature that distinguished between the two letters than when the fading feature was nondistinctive. In the first set of stimuli, the distinctive horizontal bar on the J was faded, but in the second set, the nondistinctive rounded bottom was faded. The first column uses within-stimulus features and the third column uses extra-stimulus features. Figure adapted from Rincover (1978b).

stimulus and extra-stimulus prompts is based on whether the prompt is a part of the goal-discriminative stimulus, the stimulus the learner is being trained to discriminate. A within-stimulus prompt is a part of the goal-discriminative stimulus, whereas an extra-stimulus prompt is not. For example, Rincover (1978b), in his study comparing the effects of distinctive and nondistinctive feature prompts, also compared the effects of within-stimulus and extra-stimulus prompts. As illustrated in Figure 8.3, he used a within-stimulus prompt to teach autistic children to discriminate between the words JAR and SON by exaggerating the horizontal bar in the letter J. This was a within-stimulus prompt because the horizontal bar is part of the letter J, the goal-discriminative stimulus. As also illustrated in Figure 8.3, an extra-stimulus prompt was used by placing the horizontal-bar prompt above the letter J. This was an extra-stimulus prompt because the prompt, the thickened horizontal bar, was not a part of the goal discriminative stimulus, the word *JAR*. The results of the study showed that the within-stimulus prompt was more effective than the extra-stimulus prompt. This result has also been found in studies in which the effect of a within-stimulus prompt has been compared with a gestural prompt, pointing to the S+ (Schreibman, 1975; Wolfe & Cuvo, 1978).

One explanation of why within-stimulus prompts are more effective than extra-stimulus prompts is that extra-stimulus prompts make discriminations more difficult, because the learner must attend to both the extra prompt and the stimuli to be discriminated, a more complex task. In contrast, when within-stimulus prompts are used, the learner need only attend to the main discriminative stimuli, because the prompts are "built-in" to these stimuli. As discussed in Chapter 7, learners such as autistic children and the mentally retarded have difficulty attending to multiple cues, a problem known as *stimulus overselectivity*. Stimulus overselectivity poses special difficulties for autistic children when stimuli to be discriminated are at different spatial locations, as is the case with extra-stimulus prompts (Rincover & Ducharme, 1987).

Note that physical prompts, gestural prompts, verbal prompts, and modeling prompts are all types of extra-stimulus prompts, because they are not normally a part of the stimuli the learner is required to discriminate. Although researchers have shown extra-stimulus prompts to be less effective than within-stimulus prompts, extra-stimulus prompts have the advantage of being easy and convenient to present to the learner and to remove gradually from the learner during fading. In contrast, the use of within-stimulus prompts often requires the development of special training materials in which the prompts are built into the training stimuli. Therefore, using within-stimulus prompts often requires more time and effort on the part of the teacher or trainer than using extra-stimulus prompts.

Other Applications of Fading

Most of the examples of fading we have examined focused on teaching discriminations and behaviors to learners with special training needs. Because so much work in behavior analysis has been conducted in this area, students sometimes get the impression that fading procedures are limited to this type of application. Not so. Let's see how fading can be used to treat irrational fears and the role it might play in persuasive communication.

Phobias are irrational fears some people have that cause them to resist engaging in certain behaviors. In behavior principles, we would say that there is a powerful S− for a response.

Fading principles have been used in such situations. For example, Wulbert, Nyman, Snow, and Owen (1973) used fading to treat a 6-year-old girl named Emma. Emma spoke often to her mother, but had never spoken in kindergarten, preschool, or Sunday school. Fading began by having Emma engage in various number and alphabet tasks while alone with her mother in a clinic playroom. An experimenter was faded in by first having her say things over a radio that Emma could hear in the playroom. Then the experimenter would stand out in the hall where Emma could see her. Later she would stand in the doorway to the playroom with her back to Emma and gradually she would face Emma directly. During the time the experimenter was faded in, Emma continued to perform the tasks with her mother. Emma was praised and given treats any time she spoke to the experimenter. This procedure was combined with avoidance training where Emma was timed-out for failure to interact with the experimenter. These procedures were so successful that the experimenter eventually took over the role of Emma's mother in the playroom. Several different experimenters were faded in to interactions with Emma, while Emma's mother was faded out. Eventually, Emma's first grade teacher was faded in to the task, as were several of her first-grade classmates. This creative use of fading helped Emma learn to communicate with a variety of people, allowing her to interact with other people normally.

Persuading others to conform to our point of view is something we all attempt from time to time. The ancient Greek philosopher Socrates was a master of persuasion. If we examine his techniques closely, we can see that his judicious use of fading was a key to his success. When faced with an opponent in a debate, Socrates would avoid confronting a contentious issue directly. Rather, he would first get his opponent to agree to a general principle. For example, debating whether it is just to injure one's enemies, Socrates would begin by convincing his opponent to agree to something related to the goal: that it is harmful to injure animals because they are made worse by injury. This step accomplished, Socrates would next persuade his opponent to agree to a statement more similar to the final goal; that people, like animals, are made worse by injury. Finally, the opponent had no option but to concede that because one's enemies are people, it must be unjust to injure them. This is an example of fading, because Socrates gradually changed the verbal stimuli that acted as S+s for the "I agree" response.

Perhaps you can see how, in our day and age, fading could be used just as effectively in a debate about free speech. We might begin by getting our opponent to agree that it is acceptable for people to speak freely even if they have views that are *slightly* different from ours. After this, we might succeed in convincing our opponent that it is acceptable for those with whom we disagree *moderately* to express their views. Relentlessly we approach our goal of hearing our opponent agree that it is permissible for people to voice *radically* unpopular opinions.

In general, using the principle of stimulus fading in persuasion involves getting an opponent in a debate to agree to some general principle or concept you have in common, and then gradually moving from there to areas of increasing controversy.

Delayed Prompting

Another errorless learning technique using prompts is called delayed prompting. This method, devised by Touchette (1971), is illustrated in Figure 8.4.

At first, correct responses are prompted and reinforced. Over time, as the learner continues to respond correctly to the prompt, trials are introduced in which the prompt is delayed, giving the learner an opportunity to respond correctly without the prompt. If the learner fails to respond correctly in time, the delayed prompt will cue the correct response, which will then be reinforced. In a *progressive* delayed prompting procedure, the delay between the beginning of a trial and the presentation of the prompt is made longer and longer over learning trials. In a *constant* delayed prompting procedure, the length of the delay remains the same throughout the session. Eventually, if all goes well in delayed prompting, the learner comes to make the correct response before the prompt is presented, and the prompt is no longer needed.

Walls, Haught, and Dowler (1982) used delayed prompting to teach retarded adults several job skills, including assembling a lawn mower engine, a bicycle brake, and an electric drill. Each of the three tasks was broken down into 10 subtasks. At first, the experimenter gave the trainees a modeling prompt: The trainees were shown how to do the subtask and then immediately required to imitate the experimenter.

No delay between S+ and prompt on first trial

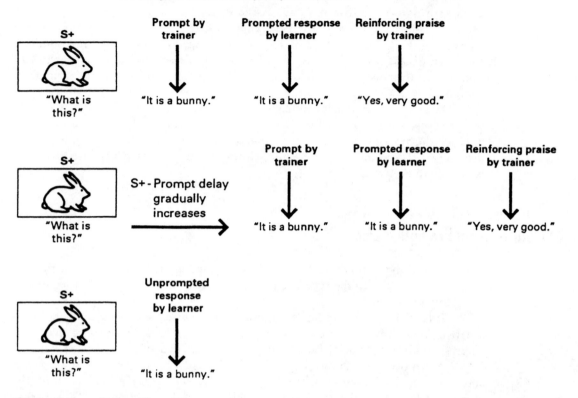

Figure 8.4   *Delayed Prompting*

In delayed prompting at first the prompt "It is a bunny" is given immediately after the stimulus is presented. Gradually the delay is increased until the response "It is a bunny" comes to occur before the prompt is given, demonstrating transfer of stimulus control from prompt to S+.

With the help of the modeling prompt, the trainees responded correctly. At this point in the procedure, a zero-delay was used because there was no delay between the start of the trial and the modeling prompt; they occurred at the same time. On the next trial, a 1-second delay was introduced: The learner had 1 second from the beginning of the trial to do the subtask on her own. If no correct response was in progress after 1 second, the modeling prompt was given and the trainee imitated it again. When the trainees responded correctly on a trial, the delay on the following trial was increased by 1 second. When the trainees responded incorrectly on a trial, the delay interval on the following trial was decreased by 1 second. This procedure was in effect over 10 trials for each subtask. The trainees were judged to have learned the assembly tasks when they began to respond correctly without requiring the modeling prompt. Using this method, the learners acquired the assembly skills.

A key notion in delayed prompting is that the opportunity for the learner to engage in unprompted responding assists in the learning process (Touchette & Howard, 1984). As shown in the Walls et al. (1982) study, with delayed prompting, learners can be given more and more time to engage in unprompted responding as they continue to respond correctly with prompts. These conditions appear to support a smooth transfer of stimulus control from prompts to the goal discriminative stimuli.

Delayed prompting is similar to fading because both procedures initially use prompts, which are eliminated later. However, in fading, the discriminative stimulus for the response is gradually changed over time. In delayed prompting, the discriminative stimuli do not change, although the time at which the prompt is presented does.

Making Delayed Prompting Effective

Research into the factors that make delayed prompting effective has shown that the length of the delay and the schedule of reinforcement contribute to the effectiveness of delayed prompting.

Walls et al. (1982) used delayed prompting to teach several assembly tasks. As a part of the study, these researchers compared three different progressive delay lengths, increasing the delay by 1, 3, or 5 seconds after each trial on which a correct response had occurred. It was found that the 1-second delay produced fewer errors and more rapid learning than the longer delays. The length of time it took the trainees to learn the tasks is presented in Figure 8.5. Walls et al. (1982) observed that the use of a 1-second delay enabled training to proceed quickly without providing early opportunities for incorrect responding.

Touchette and Howard (1984) studied the role of schedules of reinforcement in delayed prompting in teaching letter and word discriminations. On each trial, retarded children were told to point to a named letter or word. During early trials, the experimenter pointed to the correct letter or word at the same time the prompt was given. On later trials, as the children responded correctly, the experimenter's gestural prompt was delayed by increasingly longer time intervals. In one condition, the children's unprompted and prompted correct responses were reinforced on a continuous schedule, with plastic tokens exchangeable for food, toys, and privileges. In a second condition, unprompted correct responses were reinforced on a continuous schedule, whereas prompted correct responses were reinforced only on a fixed-ratio 3 schedule. This condition, then, gave the children extra payoffs for unprompted responding. In a third condition, unprompted responses were reinforced on an FR 3 schedule of reinforcement, whereas prompted responses were reinforced on a continuous schedule. This arrangement gave the children extra payoffs for prompted responding, for waiting for the prompts instead of responding without the prompt. Although the children learned the names of the letters and words using all three procedures, the condition that gave a greater payoff for unprompted responses produced more rapid learning.

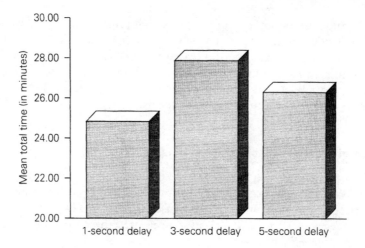

Figure 8.5   *The Influence of the Length of the Delay of the Prompt on the Effectiveness of Delayed Prompting*

The trainees in the 1-second delay group took less time to learn than the subjects in the 3-second or the 5-second delay group. Figure drawn from the data of Walls et al. (1982).

Comparisons Among Procedures

An increasing number of studies have investigated the effectiveness of various fading and delayed prompting procedures. The results as a whole do not clearly support one method over another. (See Demchak [1990] and Handen and Zane [1987] for reviews.) However, individual experiments have suggested that a particular method can be more effective than another under certain conditions. (See Demchak [1990] for a discussion of tentative findings.)

Stimulus-Response Chaining

The methods of prompting and fading we have examined are stepwise procedures. They allow the learner to acquire individual parts of a skill, one at a time. Another stepwise procedure that behavior analysts use is called *stimulus-response chaining*. A *stimulus response chain* (also called a behavior chain) is made up of a series of S+s and responses such that each response produces the S+ for the next response. Normally, the final response in a stimulus-response chain produces a reinforcer, and the reinforcer defines the end of the chain. Stimulus response chains are a familiar part of day-to-day life. For example, in making a cup of tea, filling the kettle with water is the first response, which produces a filled kettle, an S+ for the response of putting the kettle on the stove, which is in turn an S+ for the next response, turning on the stove. Turning on the stove is an S+ for waiting until the tea kettle whistles, which is an S+ for turning off the stove. Turning off the stove is an S+ for removing the kettle from the stove and pouring the tea into a pot. The filled pot is an S+ for adding tea and waiting a few minutes. Eventually the stimulus-response chain ends in a reinforcer, a cup of tea. As this example suggests, many cooking skills and other routines of daily life consist of stimulus-response chains.

Methods of Teaching Stimulus-Response Chains

Because stimulus-response chains are so familiar to us, we often take these skills for granted. We often fail to consider that stimulus-response chains can involve long and complex sequences of stimuli and responses that originally required a considerable amount of learning. Behavior analysts have devised three main methods for teaching stimulus-response chains.

Walls, Zane, and Ellis (1981) taught several stimulus-response chains to retarded people in a study of vocational training. The trainees learned stimulus-response chains involved in the assembly of a bicycle brake, a truck carburetor, and a meat grinder. The experimenters tested the effectiveness of three methods to teach the chains: the whole-task method, forward chaining, and backward chaining. In the *whole-task method,* which is also called the *total-task method,* the experimenters gave the subjects the parts of the devices and told them to put them together. Incorrect responses were corrected using verbal and physical prompts. Using the whole-task method, learners perform the entire task from start to finish and continue practicing in this way until the skill is learned. The task is not broken down into steps and learners are not required to learn one step before advancing to another one.

In the *forward chaining* method, the task was broken down into a sequence of steps. The experimenter required the trainees to learn to assemble the first two parts first, then parts 1, 2, and 3, then parts 1, 2, 3, and 4, and so forth. For example, in teaching the trainees to assemble the meat grinder, the subjects were first trained to fit a part called the auger into the main body of the meat grinder. When they did this correctly, the experimenter disassembled the parts and required the trainees to assemble the two parts again, and then add the third part, the handle of the meat grinder. This method continued until the trainees could assemble all the parts of the device correctly. Incorrect responses were corrected using verbal and physical prompts. As you can see, in the method of forward chaining, the learner gets a great deal of practice in engaging in the beginning "links" of the stimulus-response chain when the method of forward chaining is used. In forward chaining, the task is broken down into a series of steps, and the first step is learned first. Once each step is learned, the following step is added to the training, and this process continues until all the steps had been added in the order from first to last.

The third method Walls et al. (1981) used to teach the stimulus-response chain was backward chaining. In *backward chaining,* the task was also broken down into a sequence of steps. The experimenter required the trainees to learn to assemble the last part first. For example, in teaching assembly of the carburetor, the experimenter gave the trainees the carburetor fully assembled except for one bolt, which the trainees were required to add to the device. When they did this correctly, the experimenters removed the two final parts from the carburetor, the bolt and the top half of the shell of the device. The trainees were then required to add these two parts to the device in the correct sequence. This process continued until the trainees correctly assembled all the parts of the device when presented with the unassembled parts. Backward chaining gets its name because the learner is required to learn the last links of the chain first. When using backward chaining, the learner receives the most training in the final links of the chain.

Walls and his co-workers found that overall, the trainees learned the stimulus-response chains in about the same amount of time using each method. However, the trainees made fewer errors using the forward and backward chaining procedures than the whole-task method. At this time, no clear consensus has emerged among behavior analysts about which of the three methods of teaching stimulus response chains is best. Some researchers have found that forward chaining works best (e.g., Ash & Holding, 1990), some have found that backward chaining works best (e.g., Wightman & Sistrunk, 1987), and some have found that the whole-task method works best (e.g., Wilcox, 1974). It may be that certain types of chains are best taught using one method rather than another. For example, if the final link of a stimulus-response chain is the most difficult link, a backward chaining strategy, which provides the most training on the final link, may be the best one (Ash & Holding, 1990).

Chaining and Other Gradual-Change Procedures

Chaining, like shaping and fading, is a stepwise procedure that is a gradual-change technique. However, the three procedures are all different. Generally speaking, shaping can be considered a response-change technique, while chaining can be considered a response-addition technique. In shaping, behavior that is more and more like a goal response is reinforced along a topographical, qualitative, or quantitative shaping dimension. In contrast, in chaining there is no use of a shaping dimension. Instead, individual behaviors, the links in the chain, are trained individually and added to the chain one by one. In shaping, the duration of a behavior can sometimes be lengthened, but this differs from stimulus-response chaining, in which different behaviors are added to a behavioral sequence.

Stimulus-response chaining also differs from fading. Fading is a stimulus-change procedure, while chaining is a response-addition procedure. In fading, the stimulus for a response is gradually changed so that it becomes more and more like a desired goal stimulus for a response. In contrast, in chaining, a sequence of different behaviors are taught by adding each behavior to the sequence.

Shaping, fading, and chaining procedures are often used together in teaching skills. Shaping and fading procedures can be used to establish individual links of a stimulus-response chain. Shaping can be used to bring about the correct-response topography or other quantitative features of the response, while fading is used to bring the response under proper stimulus control. Once a link in a chain is established, chaining can be used to add extra links to the sequence of behavior being taught.

Making Stimulus-Response Chaining Effective

Generally, procedures to teach stimulus response chains make use of behavioral principles we have already covered in discussing positive reinforcement, shaping, discriminative stimuli, and prompting and fading. For example, if the learner has not acquired a response in a stimulus-response chain, methods like shaping or prompting can be used to bring about the desired behavior. In particular, the use of modeling prompts often helps to teach stimulus-response chains. If the learner has difficulty responding to the stimuli involved in the stimulus-response chain, the methods of fading or delayed prompting can be used to induce correct responding with assistance, and eventually continue to get correct responding without assistance (e.g., Walls, Dowler, Haught, & Zawlocki, 1984; Zane, Walls, & Thvedt, 1981).

Nonetheless, in making stimulus-response chaining effective, a couple of considerations are special, mainly because of the extended length of behavioral chains. First, because chains are long sequences of behavior, specifying the target behaviors can be more difficult and time-consuming. As opposed to the simple definition of a target behavior, defining a chain becomes a process of task analysis, in which the stimuli and responses in the chain are specified. For example, Engelmann and Carnine (1982) have had considerable success in doing task analyses of the precise chains of behaviors students must engage in to solve various types of mathematical operations.

Second, the principle of weak early links specifies that the beginning links in a stimulus-response chain are likely to be weaker than later links in the chain. Stimulus-response chains are extended sequences of behavior in which only the last behavior in the chain is immediately reinforced. As such, both the principles of response energy and immediate reinforcement are at work against the early links in the chain. For example, in discussing the factors that make punishment effective in Chapter 4, we saw that punishers delivered early in a chain are more likely to be effective than those delivered later (e.g., Abramowitz & O'Leary, 1990). In general, in building and maintaining behavioral chains, the principle of weak early links specifies that behavior analysts must pay close attention to the beginnings of behavior chains to ensure that problems do not arise. If there are difficulties, various response-strengthening procedures can be temporarily added to the early links of the chain. These procedures can include social reinforcement, prompting, and decreasing the response energy required in the early links of the chain.

The principle of weak early links has various practical applications. For example, Youdin and Hemmes (1978) have interpreted overeating as a chain of behaviors that begins with urges or thoughts about eating. By reducing people's thoughts of food, the first link in a chain that ends in overeating, these researchers were able to help the people in their program lose weight. It is also possible to promote desirable chains of behavior by strengthening the early links. For example, students who set up a pleasant and attractive study space promote chains of studying behavior by encouraging the behaviors in the initial links in the chain.

Summary

In this chapter, we have examined prompting, fading, delayed-prompting, and stimulus-response-chaining procedures. A prompt is a discriminative stimulus for a response that is intended to alter a behavior. Prompts differ from other types of discriminative stimuli because they are intentionally added to the situation as cues for correct responding. Prompts are presented by other people because their goal is to change the behavior of the person being prompted. Behavior analysts make use of several types of prompts including verbal prompts, gestural prompts, modeling prompts, picture prompts, and physical prompts.

Prompting is used either to teach people to discriminate between two or more stimuli, or it is used to teach a new behavior. Many behavior analysis procedures combine these two goals by teaching new discriminations at the same time that new behaviors are taught. Prompting techniques are effective in getting a response to occur quickly and require relatively little effort on the part of the behavior analyst. However, prompting often has a key disadvantage. Unless prompting is combined with other procedures, it may be necessary to continue to use prompts to get a response to occur. Prompts that are personalized are generally more effective than impersonal ones.

In this chapter we also examined fading. Fading is a stimulus discrimination procedure in which the discriminative stimuli for a response become more and more similar to a set of goal discriminative stimuli. Fading is often used to induce a behavior by presenting prompts which then are eliminated gradually, leaving the behavior under the stimulus control of a set of correct goal discriminative stimuli.

Fading is an errorless learning procedure, because by gradually changing the discriminative stimuli for a response, it is possible for the learner to continue to respond correctly as the stimuli are being changed. Errorless learning has been generally shown to be more effective than trial and error learning, in which there is no gradual change in the discriminative stimuli for a response.

Two methods are used to fade prompts. In the increasing assistance method, the learner is given the weakest prompt necessary to get the correct response to occur. In this way, the learner is encouraged to engage in unprompted responding. In the decreasing assistance method, the learner is first given strong prompts to respond, and over time weaker and weaker prompts are substituted until the learner is able to respond without prompting. The decreasing assistance method helps to minimize the number of errors the learner makes while prompts are being faded.

Several variables enhance the effectiveness of fading. These include choosing fading steps of the appropriate size, fading some feature of the S+, fading a distinctive feature of the S+, and using within-stimulus prompts when possible.

We also examined the use of fading to alter different types of behaviors. Fading has many applications in behavior change. To illustrate, we examined the use of fading to induce people to engage in behaviors they are fearful or reluctant to perform and the use of fading in persuasive communication.

Another errorless learning procedure is called delayed prompting. In delayed prompting, the learner initially is prompted to engage in a behavior. Over time, the prompt for the response is delayed little by little, giving the learner the opportunity to engage in unprompted responding, the goal of the technique. The effectiveness of delayed prompting is influenced by the length of the delays selected and by the reinforcement schedules.

Finally, we discussed stimulus-response chains, sequences of behavior in which each behavior produces a discriminative stimulus for the next response and in which the final response is reinforced. Three methods of teaching stimulus-response chains are the whole-task method, forward chaining, and backward chaining. In general, the factors that make stimulus-response chaining effective are the same factors that make reinforcement and stimulus discrimination training effective. Two special considerations in making stimulus response chains effective are doing a thorough specification of the target behaviors in the chain and ensuring that the early links in the chain are sufficiently strong.

Conceptual Exercise   *Prompting*

For each of the following items, decide if the item is an example of prompting. If it is, also specify whether it is an example of a verbal prompt, a gestural prompt, a physical prompt, a picture prompt, or a modeling prompt. In each case, the target behavior is highlighted. Justify your decision with a brief explanation. Confirm your decisions by reading the analyses provided in the back of the book.

1. Harvey was interested in encouraging people to recycle their waste products. One of the many imaginative things he did to get people in one subdivision to recycle was to distribute brochures door-to-door. The brochures informed people about the recycling program. The brochures caused the people to **participate in the recycling program.**

2. Janice had begun an exercise routine. The first day she worked out too hard. The next day, the hard workout made her muscles so sore she **stayed in bed** longer than she did normally.

3. Litter receptacles were placed in a football stadium during four games of the gridiron season. When the receptacle had a plywood "hat" on it, twice as much **trash was put in the receptacle** as when it did not have the hat on.

4. In a project designed to increase the safety of pedestrians, a sign saying "Extend arm to cross" was placed at either end of a crosswalk. This sign caused an increase in the number of pedestrians who **signaled their intention to use the crosswalk** by extending their arms.

5. In an automobile factory where large machines cut out pieces of sheet metal, a new machine had been installed and several workers were watching it operate. The man demonstrating the machine was careless and lost two fingers in the machine as the men watched. As a result of this, the men who watched **took extra care in using the machine and they never had any kind of accident** while using it.

6. A group of experimenters wanted to see if their could encourage people to select low-fat foods in a cafeteria. In order to do this, they placed a poster that highlighted the advantages of a low-fat diet and identified low-fat foods the cafeteria was serving. Use of the poster increased the eaters' **selection of low-fat food items.**

7. In a project intended to get people to **buckle their seat belts,** a woman stood at the exit of a parking lot with a sign that said, "Fasten Safety Belt." She displayed it to drivers as they came toward the exit of the parking lot. This method increased the number of drivers who bucked their seat belts.

8. A study was conducted with 250 female college students at Colorado State University. The goal of the study was to get the women to do monthly breast self-examinations in order to detect cancers at an early and treatable stage. One method was to mail the women monthly reminders that stated: "Remember to practice a breast self-examination this month." As a result of this method, the women **conducted breast self-examinations** more frequently than they had before.

9. Residents of a small rural town seldom used a road that went from the town to the main highway because the road was longer than a shorter road that also was connected to the main highway. One year the world's largest pulp mill was built near the shorter road. The mill emitted such a terrible stench that no one wanted to use the shorter road anymore. This greatly increased **use of the longer road.**

10. The goal of a project at a North Carolina hospital was to get physicians to **perform preventative health procedures** more often. These procedures included flu shots for senior citizens, breast exams for women over 50, and pap smears. In order to get the physicians to do these procedures more often, two methods were used. One method was to have nurses remind the physicians to conduct the procedure by putting notes on the patients' charts. A second method made use of a computer to issue an encounter form each time one of the patients visited a physician. The encounter form identified the preventative procedures that should be conducted. It was found that the nurse-reminder system increased use of the procedures from 38% to 43%, while the computer-reminder system increased use of the procedures from 38% to 53%.

11. A group of adults were recruited to take part in a study of television advertising. The goal of the study was to get the people to **study the labels** of advertised medications. The subjects were told that the purpose of the study was for them to provide ideas about what made a television program, "The Mary Tyler Moore Show," a success. The subjects watched a 30-minute videotape episode of the program on which there were ads for antacid medications. Some of the ads (a) urged the viewers to read the labels of the antacids before purchasing them and (b) showed shoppers in a store reading the ads for the product. The subjects were given coupons for antacids as payment for their participation in the study, and later were secretly

observed at a drug store where they redeemed the coupons. Ad messages urging the viewers to read medication labels and showing people reading labels caused the viewers to spend more time actually reading the antacid labels before buying the products, but only if they bought the products soon after they saw the television program.

12. Several kindergarten and first-grade children participated in a study in which the goal was to get the children to be more helpful to other children. The children played a game in which they earned pennies for dropping marbles in a hole. Sometimes during the game, a yellow light would go on, indicating that another child playing the game could continue only if the child donated a penny. Sometimes the experimenter suggested that it would be nice if the child occasionally donated a penny to help another child play the game. This suggestion caused the children to **donate pennies** to enable other children to play the game.

13. Ned was working with the management of a Swedish department store, trying to use methods that might reduce **shoplifting**. In order to accomplish this goal, he put red circles near certain items of merchandise and posted signs that told shoppers that shoplifters frequently stole items marked with red circles. This method decreased the amount of shoplifting of the marked items.

14. Susan was a retarded child who was learning how to **use a spoon**. Her trainer would give Susan her supper in a bowl with a spoon beside it. At first the trainer would point to the spoon. If Susan failed to pick it up and began eating with her fingers, the trainer would then say "Susan, use your spoon." If Susan again failed to use the spoon, the trainer would place the spoon in Susan's hand. If this didn't work, the trainer would hold Susan's hand with the spoon and guide the spoon to Susan's food and then to her mouth. After a few trials Susan began using her spoon as soon as her bowl and spoon were put in front of her.

15. The University of Elusive Curriculum's (UEC) mainframe computer had an electronic mail system that faculty could use to communicate with each other. When a user contacted the e-mail system, a buzzer sounded indicating that the user should type in the kind of service needed. If the user did not type anything in within 3 seconds of the buzzer, the word "SERVICE?" appeared on the screen. If the user still failed to type in the name of the service needed, a list of available services would appear on the screen and the user was expected to pick one. Dr. Obtuse, a new member of UEC's faculty, eventually learned to **type in the service he needed** at the sound of buzzer, although at first he often had to wait until the list of services was presented.

Conceptual Exercise   *Fading and Delayed Prompting*

For each of the following items, decide if the item is an example of fading, delayed prompting, or neither delayed prompting nor fading. If it is an example of fading, specify which fading dimension was used. If it is an example of either fading or delayed prompting, specify whether the procedure made use of within-stimulus prompts or extra-stimulus prompts. Justify your decision with a brief explanation. Confirm your decisions by reading the analyses provided in back of the book.

Note: The distinction between within-stimulus prompts and extra-stimulus prompts is based on whether the prompt is a part of the goal discriminative stimulus. In some cases, a prompt is superimposed on a goal discriminative stimulus. For our present purposes, when a prompt is superimposed on a goal discriminative stimulus, consider it to be an extra-stimulus prompt rather than a within-stimulus prompt. Our reasoning here is that when a prompt is superimposed on a stimulus, it is not really part of the stimulus even though it shares the same space as the goal discriminative stimulus.

1. Preteen and teenage retarded boys were learning to tell the difference between circles and ellipses. The boys were seated in front of an eight-panel display. Each panel was 2" square. During part of the training, when the boys touched the panel with a circle projected on it, chimes sounded and candy was dispensed. When they touched a panel without a circle, nothing happened and they were required to then try again. At first, one of the panels had a dark and distinct circle on it and the other seven were blank. Then, very faint ellipses replaced the seven blank panels. Over trials, the ellipses became darker and more distinct until they were eventually as distinct as the circle. Many of the boys continued to select the circle, even as the ellipses grew darker and more distinct.

2. Henry was studying too little, so his father, Ralph, consulted a behavior analyst, Dr. Thomas, who set up a system to encourage Henry to study more. At first, Henry was required to study 15 minutes per day before he was permitted to play video games. Each day, Dr. Thomas increased the study time by 5 minutes until Henry was studying 75 minutes per day. In a few weeks, Henry was studying 75 minutes per day and had become an excellent student. Both Henry and Ralph were pleased with the way the plan worked.

3. Two preschoolers were participating in a study of color discrimination. The experimenters wanted to teach the children to distinguish red-orange from red. If the children pressed a lever when a red light was on, they received marbles that could later be traded for candy and toys. If the children pressed the lever when another color of light was on, they received no marbles. During part of the training, a yellow light was used. Later in training this yellow light was changed to pink, and then finally to red-orange. In this way, the children learned to discriminate between the red and red-orange lights.

4. Gail was a 16-year-old deaf girl who was learning to recognize the ASL (American Sign Language) signs for 10 different colors. Gail sat at a table that held 10 cards, each a different color. At first, the trainer showed Gail a color card and asked her to point to the card of the same color from the ones in front of her. As Gail continued to respond correctly, the trainer presented the color card with one hand and the ASL sign for that color with the other hand. As Gail continued to respond correctly, the trainer began to delay the presentation of the color card. The delay increased as Gail continued to respond correctly by pointing to the proper color card before the trainer showed her the color card. Eventually, Gail was able to point to the correct color cards when given any of the 10 color signs.

5. Eighteen retarded children, 13 boys and 5 girls, attended a special school. None of the children could read. They were trained to identify 16 pictures of objects including a pie, a bus, and an apple. Then, the children were shown the pictures with the name of the object printed just below the picture. If the children responded correctly by saying the name of the pictured object, they were given candy and praised. If the children failed to name the object correctly, they were told "No." At first, the pictures were clear and distinct. Over trials, however, the pictures became fainter and less distinct until they were eventually barely visible. However, the printed names remained clear and distinct. Finally, the printed names were presented in the absence of the pictures and the children were required to read them. In this way, the children learned to read some of the words.

6. Lottie was learning how to read short sentences. As reinforcers, her tutor used plastic tokens exchangeable for small prizes and trinkets at the end of each daily reading class. At first, the tutor gave Lottie plastic tokens for every sentence Lottie read correctly, but as Lottie became a better reader, she earned a token only for every other sentence, then for every third sentence, then for every fifth sentence. Using this method, Lottie's reading continued to improve.

7. Dr. Baker was working as a consultant to a project in which several retarded children, ranging in age from 6 to 9, were being taught to improve their handwriting. Each day, the children practiced copying several letters. If the children's writing of any of the letters had improved from the previous day's work, that child was awarded five tokens good for a reward. This method enabled the children to improve their handwriting significantly.

8. A group of university students were participating in a project in which the goal was to teach them to identify the letters represented by braille patterns. On a screen, the students were shown a braille pattern on which was superimposed the letter represented by that pattern. The students' task was to identify the letter. Correct responses were awarded points, which were displayed on a counter. Incorrect responses did not earn points. During one part of the procedure, if the students continued to respond correctly to the letter patterns, the letters would go increasingly out of focus, although the braille patterns would remain in focus. Eventually, with continued correct responding, the letters went out of focus so much that they were illegible. If the students responded incorrectly, the letters would come back into better focus. In this way, the students learned to identify letters represented by the braille patterns.

9. Three autistic children were being taught to identify the occupations (e.g., dentist, soldier, plumber) of people shown in pictures. During one part of the training, the experimenter showed an occupation picture and asked the children, "What is this?" During the first session, the experimenter prompted the children to identify the occupation by telling the child what it was immediately. During the second session, if the child did not respond correctly, the experimenter gave the prompt 1 second after presentation of the picture. In later sessions, the delay between picture presentation and the experimenter's prompt increased by 1 second per session. Whenever the children responded correctly before the experimenter's prompt, they were praised

and given edible treats. In this way the children learned to identify the occupations shown in the pictures without prompts.

10. Four mentally retarded men ranging in age from 18 to 22 were being trained to read some words. At first, the words were shown on a screen superimposed on picture prompts of the things the words represented (e.g., shoes, cat, fork). The trainees' task was to say the word shown to them. Correct responses were reinforced on a continuous schedule with a light flash and on a VR 3 schedule with tokens tradeable for various canteen items. After each correct response, a 1-second delay was added to later trials. If a response was incorrect, the delay between the word presentation and the picture prompt was reduced by 1 second on later trials. Using this method, the trainees learned to read the words.

11. Several high school students who were having problems studying signed up for a special study hall in which study behavior would be encouraged. Two teachers moved randomly about the room looking at each of the students on a prearranged schedule. If a student was studying at the exact moment the teacher looked at that student, the teacher would award that student a token. The tokens could be exchanged at several local businesses for various discounts on foods and merchandise. At first, the teachers awarded each student tokens at an average top rate of 1 token every 4 minutes. As time went on, however, the tokens were gradually awarded less frequently, eventually, at a maximum rate of 1 every 20 minutes. In this way, the students studied more diligently than they had before and their grades improved.

12. During a work break, Ted, an employee at a sheltered workshop, was learning how to operate an audiotape player without assistance. At first, the trainer showed Ted how to insert and play a tape using model prompts. Ted was also given instructions (e.g., "Press this button"), and his hands were physically guided through the motions needed to operate the machine. As Ted became better at the task, the model prompts, the instructions, and the physical guidance were gradually omitted until eventually, Ted was operating the tape recorder completely on his own.

13. John was a 12-year-old boy who had been identified as autistic. One problem he had was in copying handwritten letters properly. To solve this problem, a set of lessons were prepared in which John was required to trace the dotted outline of a letter. If he did this correctly, he was required to repeat the exercise with fewer dots, making it necessary for John to do more work on his own. When he did this correctly, he was given a letter and required to copy that letter. Using this method, John's handwriting improved a great deal.

14. Maria was a 4-year-old girl who attended preschool. Her problem was that when her mother left her at the preschool, Maria threw tantrums that continued until her mother returned. The goal of treatment was for Maria to engage in "happy" behaviors in her mother's absence. To solve the problem, Maria's mother would leave for only a few minutes at first. Then, as Maria continued to engage in happy behaviors, Maria's mother would leave for progressively longer intervals of time until she was gone for 3 hours. In this way, Maria learned how to be happy at the preschool without her mother.

15. Two researchers were studying the problem of myopia, a vision disorder in which nearby objects can be seen clearly, but distant objects appear blurred. The goal was to get the subjects to identify correctly stimuli presented at a distance from them. At first, the 48 subjects were required to identify capital letters that were presented close up. If a subject identified 10 consecutive letters correctly, the distance between the subject and the letters was increased by 23 cm. If a subject failed to get 10 consecutive correct responses after 50 trials, the distance between the letters and the subject was reduced by 11.5 cm. When the subjects responded correctly, they were told "Good" or "Correct" and when they responded incorrectly they were told the correct response. In this way, the subjects learned to focus on letters that were presented further and further away. In addition, the trained subjects were able to play video games when the screen was presented at a distance from them.

Conceptual Exercise   *Stimulus-Response Chaining*

For each of the following items, decide if the item is an example of a procedure used to teach a stimulus response chain. If the item is an example, specify whether it is an example of forward chaining, backward chaining, or the whole-task method. Justify your decision with a brief explanation. Confirm your decisions by reading the analyses provided in the next section.

1. Several retarded people were being trained to assemble two plumbing devices, a drain and a gate valve. The experimenter presented the trainees with the devices in unassembled form. The trainees were required to put the devices together. When they made a mistake, the experimenters used verbal, gestural, and physical prompts to correct errors. After an error was corrected, the learner continued with the assembly task. The trainees continued working until the devices were assembled, and then they started over again from the beginning. Eventually, as a result of this method, the trainees learned to assemble the devices by putting the parts together in the correct order.

2. Male university students were learning how to land an airplane on an aircraft carrier through the use of a flight simulator. During the first set of trials, the students were trained in the final approach skill, from 2,000 feet until landing. After mastering this, the students were given training in flying and landing from 4,000 feet until landing. Next, they were trained from 6,000 feet until landing. Using this method, the students learned in the proper order the sequence of skills required for landing.

3. Lois was learning handwriting skills. One problem she was having was that she pressed her pencil only very lightly on the paper, producing light handwriting that was difficult to read. In order to correct this problem, Robert, Lois's father, praised Lois when she began pressing more firmly with her pencil, making darker handwriting. Lois's dad continued praising her for pressing more firmly, and gradually Lois's printing became sufficiently dark to be legible.

4. Three handicapped students were being trained in microcomputer-use skills. The students were given materials such as floppy disks that they needed, and were told to

operate the computer. The task involved a sequence of responses including putting disks in the disk drive and turning the computer on. When the students made an error, the trainers used verbal and physical prompts. The students were required to engage in the entire sequence of behaviors repeatedly until they learned the skills.

5. Four retarded adults were being trained to buy snack foods at a McDonald's fast-food restaurant. The task involved a sequence of behaviors including entering the restaurant, going to the counter, ordering two items, paying for the items, finding an empty table, eating the food, throwing away the trash, and leaving the restaurant. At first, trainees were taught to leave the restaurant. When they did this correctly, they were trained to throw away the trash, and then leave the restaurant. This procedure continued until the trainees had learned the entire sequence of behaviors.

6. Amanda was a retarded girl who was learning how to tell the difference between uppercase and lowercase letters. On each training trial, Amada was shown one of each, and was asked to point to the uppercase letter. At first, the uppercase letter on each trial was placed on a grey background, while the lowercase letter was on a white background. During training, the experimenter gradually changed the grey background to white. Despite this, Amanda continued to respond correctly to the uppercase and lowercase letters.

7. Four retarded adults attended a day activities program at a regional center where they were being trained in how to pay their bills. This task involved writing checks, recording the checks, and mailing the bills. Each task was divided into a series of steps (behaviors) that had to be performed in the correct order. For example, the check-writing steps included writing the date on the check, writing the payee on the check, entering the amount of payment correctly, and signing the check. The trainees learned the skills by performing the first behavior correctly, and then doing the first and the second behaviors in the sequence until the trainees had learned all the steps in the sequence.

8. Introductory psychology students participated in an experiment in which they were learning to play a short melody on an electronic piano. Playing a melody involves engaging in a set of behaviors in the proper sequence. The melody was made up of 24 quarter notes, broken down into three groups of eight notes. One group of students were first trained on the first set of eight notes in the melody. When they had learned these notes, they were required to play them, followed by the second eight notes. Finally, the students were required to play all 24 notes until they played well.

9. A group of female college students participated in tasks in which they learned how to fold paper to make a fish, a bird, and a cardinal's hat. In order to do these things correctly, it is necessary to perform the proper paper-folding responses in a specific order. The paper-folding task was broken down into a series of steps. The students were trained by first giving them one of the paper items that had been completely folded except for the last step. The students were required to do the final step. When the students were doing this correctly, they were given the paper folded except for the last two steps, and the students' task was to do the last two steps. This continued until the students were given an unfolded piece of paper and were required to perform all the steps.

10. A group of patients who had experienced leg injuries were in a program of physical therapy. As part of the program, the patients had to remain in an upright position (i.e., standing or walking) for a certain amount of time per day. Any time a patient increased the amount of time upright by 5 minutes or more, that patient was allowed to go home early that day. As a result of this method, the patients remained in upright positions for increasingly longer periods of time.

11. Ted was a 30-year-old man who was blind, retarded, and physically handicapped. He was being trained to respond to fire alarms so that in case of a fire, Ted could get out the building safely. Responding to a fire alarm was broken down into a series of steps that he had to follow one after the other, including walking to the door of his apartment, walking down the hall, turning at the proper corridors, and going out the exit door. During training, Ted was first taught step one. When he did this correctly, he was required to perform step one, followed by step two. This process continued until Ted learned the entire skill.

12. A group of retarded people participated in an experiment designed to examine how people learn vocational skills. As part of the experiment, the trainees were provided with 12 parts of a disassembled lawn mower engine and told to put the parts together. To succeed, the trainees had to put the parts together in the correct order. When they made an error, correct responses were prompted using modeling prompts. The trainees practiced the assembly task from start to finish several times until they learned how to do it.

Conceptual Exercise   *Making Prompting and Fading Effective*

In each of the examples below, a principle of prompting or fading effectiveness has been violated. Indicate what the violation is and how the item could be altered to be more effective.

1. Athabasca University desperately needed donations to build a new athletic complex for the students. The director of fund-raising put an advertisement in the newsletter sent to alumni asking for donations. She was disappointed at the lack of response of the alumni. How and why should this method be altered?

2. Lulu was a 3-year-old who was joining a day-care center in the fall. One of the requirements of the center was that all children had to be able to use the toilet facilities without help. Although Lulu was toilet trained, she needed prompting from her mother. When Lulu had to go to the bathroom, she first went to her mother and told her. Then her mother would take her by the hand to the bathroom, help her take down her panties, sit her on the toilet, and stay until Lulu was finished. Lulu's mother decided to use a fading procedure to train Lulu to go to the bathroom by herself so that she could join the center in the fall. Her mother began by leaving the bathroom after she had put Lulu on the toilet. Lulu had no problem with this step, and her mom praised her. Then her mother simply told Lulu to get on the toilet (instead of helping her) and then left the bathroom. Again, Lulu was praised when she finished. Her mother was so pleased with these results that the next time Lulu had to go to the

bathroom, she simply said, "Go ahead by yourself, Lulu." Her mother was disappointed when Lulu had her first toileting accident since she was 2. How and why should this procedure be altered?

3. Laurie couldn't tell the difference between cats and dogs. Laurie's mom decided to teach Laurie by using pictures. At first, she showed Laurie a picture of a dog on a big leash and a picture of a cat without a leash. She intended to decrease the size of the leash little by little. Laurie did well, and was praised for her behavior. The next-door neighbor was amused when she was out walking her 2-year-old in his harness, and Laurie approached and said, "Nice doggie." How and why should this procedure be altered?

4. Molly was a retarded child who was learning the difference between red and white. She was shown a card with a small red square and with black and white pictures of cherries, apples, and fire engines at the bottom of the card. The white card had a small white square and pictures of snow, clouds, and pillows on the bottom. She was asked to identify the correct color. The trainers intended to fade out gradually the pictures one at a time until Molly was identifying the color without the prompts. The trainers made sure to vary the position of the card and the order, so that Molly was attending to the relevant color dimension. Molly had difficulty learning the difference, even though the trainers were careful to use small steps. How and why should this procedure be altered?

5. David was learning to subtract, with his mother's help. She would give David a subtraction problem such as 15 minus 9. If David didn't respond within 10 seconds his mother would say, "Well, what if it was 15 minus 10?" If David couldn't answer, his mother would say, "15 minus 10 is 5, and so if we take away 1 less than 10, what would we have?" This system wasn't working very well. As soon as David was given a problem, he would randomly respond until the prompt was given. How and why should this procedure be altered?

6. Jeannie couldn't tell the different between dogs and cats. Her teacher would hold up a stuffed toy dog and toy cat and ask Jeannie to point to the dog. If Jeannie failed to do so within a second, the teacher would pull a string on the cat and it would purr. If Jeannie still failed to point to the dog, the cat would purr again and say, "I like mice and cheese. I am a __." If this step didn't work, then the cat would say, "I am a cat." In the beginning, Jeannie didn't point to the dog until the toy cat said, "I am a cat," but eventually Jeannie was able to identify the toy dog without prompts. This procedure, however, took a long time, even though the delay was not too long and the step size was not too large. How and why should this procedure be altered?

7. Charlie was afraid of the dark and could go to sleep only if his overhead light was on. His father decided to use a fading procedure, and bought a rheostat for Charlie's overhead light. For one week, his father turned the light down very slightly and Charlie had no problem going to sleep. The next week, his father again turned it down very slightly with the same result. Charlie's father was so pleased that the third week, he turned the light off. Charlie became very upset and couldn't get to sleep until his father turned his light completely on. How and why should this procedure be altered?

8. Kerry was learning the difference in pronunciation between the broad "a" and the long "a." At first his teacher would show Kerry a broad "a" word such as "cat," or a long "a" word such as "cake." The letter "a" was in bold print. Kerry was asked to say the word aloud and if he pronounced it correctly, he was praised and received a small treat. The highlighted letters were gradually faded until they were the same as the other letters in the words. The teacher was careful to fade with small steps and explained to Kerry that the final "e" was what made the long "a" sound. Kerry learned the difference, but not as quickly as he might have. How and why should this procedure be altered?

9. Bill, an autistic child, was learning his colors. Two color patches were placed on his desk and Bill was asked to point to the red one. At first, the teacher would give Bill some hints. If the correct patch was on the left side of Bill's desk, then a picture of a typical red object, such as an apple, was placed on the left side of the blackboard in the front of the room. If the correct color was on the right side of Bill's desk, then the picture hint would be placed on the right side of the blackboard. The teacher intended to fade out the picture hints gradually, using small steps. How and why should this procedure be altered?

chapter 9

Generalization

The mothers of four autistic children wanted to learn how to help their children acquire the skills they would need in order to lead productive and happy lives. All four children had difficulty communicating; sometimes they wouldn't speak at all. Tantrums were commonplace as were self-stimulatory behaviors. The mothers realized that they needed some professional advice—they wanted to be trained in behavioral techniques in order to manage and teach their children more effectively. These women approached Robert Koegel and two of his colleagues, R. J. Glahn and Gayla Nieminen, for help.

Dr. Koegel and his colleagues met with each mother to determine the specific abilities and needs of her child. Together, the mother and the behavior analysts listed target behaviors for the child to learn. Some of these behaviors were standing up, and making discriminations between first and last, long and short, and blue and yellow. The mothers were given instruction in teaching, according to behavioral analysis principles. If the mother was successful at teaching her child the first target behavior, she was given another behavior or discrimination to teach. If she did not succeed, she was given a 10 to 15 minute demonstration of how to teach that particular behavior.

The team of researchers found the brief demonstrations very helpful in training the mothers to teach specific target behaviors. Unfortunately, the demonstration training was effective only with the specific behavior demonstrated: It did not generalize to new situations.

Generalization is an important term in behavior analysis. It occurs when the effects of a procedure that was used to change a target behavior spreads, such that the behavior changes in other situations—other behaviors are altered, the behaviors of other people are changed, or the effect endures over time after training has ceased (Stokes & Baer, 1977). Although the mothers became very good at teaching specific behaviors to their children, they were unable to apply their newly learned skills in new situations.

Dr. Koegel and his colleagues were not especially surprised that the training the mothers received in teaching specific skills did not generalize to new situations. A procedure designed to teach the mothers to train their children to do many things, rather than just one, was the next step. This parent-training phase included lectures about shaping, stimulus discrimination training, and the use of prompts in teaching new behavior. Videotapes showed models demonstrating correct and incorrect training methods.

This strategy was a great success. The mothers acquired teaching techniques that can be used to teach almost any behavior or skill. Once they learned these skills, they were able to adapt their teaching strategies to the areas their children most needed—a demonstration of the real-world benefits of generalization training.

For behavior analysis to reach its full potential, it is important that laypeople learn how to use behavior change procedures. Thus, the results of the above study have important implications. Some people view behavioral techniques as a "bag of tricks" useful to change only specific behaviors. As Dr. Koegel and his colleagues demonstrated, when people are taught general, rather than specific, behavior analysis principles, they are able to apply these procedures successfully to new behaviors and new situations. Teaching people to apply the principles and procedures of behavior analysis to solve behavior problems in everyday life is a challenge that behavior analysts must meet.*

In most applications of behavior analysis, the learner receives training in which behavior principles are used to teach and strengthen desirable behaviors and weaken undesirable behaviors. This training is usually intensive because it is necessary for the behavior analyst to present stimuli to the learner, to observe responding, and to provide differential consequences. At some point, however, the teacher must allow the learner to behave on her own in environments other than the training situation. Generalization, defined most broadly (Stokes & Baer, 1977), focuses on ways to ensure that the behavior learned in the training situation transfers to nontraining situations once training has ended.

Generalization is of central importance to behavior analysts. When a behavior

*Based on Koegel, Glahn, and Nieminen (1978)

change prevails outside the training situation and lasts into the future, the behavior analyst has accomplished something worthwhile. For example, the parents whom Koegel, Glahn, and Nieminen trained learned skills that would enable them to teach their children an unlimited variety of behaviors and discriminations for years to come. In contrast, training the parents to teach specific behaviors to their children was of little use once those specific behaviors had been learned. It is not difficult to use behavioral principles to change a variety of behaviors. Making those changes last beyond the training situation, however, is. Several procedures will help to ensure that training does generalize beyond the training situation. Before we examine these procedures, we will discuss several specific types of generalization.

Types of Generalization

Although the word *generalization* is sometimes used in the broad sense as we stated earlier, it includes several more specific forms including stimulus generalization, response generalization, subject generalization, behavior maintenance, receptive-expressive generalization, and expressive-receptive generalization.

Stimulus Generalization

Stimulus generalization (also called stimulus induction) is the spread of effect of stimulus discrimination training to stimuli that are similar to either the S+ or the S–. *Excitatory stimulus generalization* occurs when the training that caused a response to be strengthened in the presence of an S+ also causes that response to occur in the presence of other similar stimuli. *Inhibitory stimulus generalization* occurs when the training that caused a response to be weakened in the presence of an S– also causes that response to be weakened in the presence of other similar stimuli.

Baron (1973) demonstrated stimulus generalization with university students. Twelve women were trained to discriminate between a high-pitched 1300 Hz tone, the S+, and a lower-pitched 1000 Hz tone, the S–. If they pushed a button when the 1300 Hz tone sounded, a green light turned on, indicating a correct response. If they pushed a button when the 1000 Hz tone sounded, a red light turned on, indicating an incorrect response. This discrimination training continued until the students had responded correctly on eight consecutive presentations of the S+ and S–.

After the students had completed discrimination training, they were given a generalization test. On the test, the students were presented with the original training tones, as well as with several other tones ranging from 1100 to 1600 Hz. The purpose of the generalization test was to see how the students would respond to stimuli that were slightly different from the S+ and S–. Figure 9.1 on the next page shows the results of the experiment.

As you can see, the students responded most frequently to the 1300 Hz tone, the S+. However, they also responded to the other tones, indicating that stimulus generalization had, indeed, occurred. They responded most often to tones that were

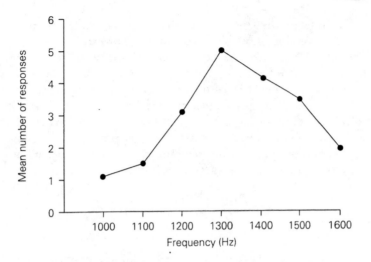

Figure 9.1   *A Stimulus Generalization Gradient Showing the Effects of Stimulus Discrimination Training on Responding to Trained and Untrained Stimuli*

Subjects responded most frequently to the 1300 Hz S+ and progressively less frequently to stimuli increasingly dissimilar to the S+. The subjects responded least frequently to the original S–, the 1000 Hz tone. Figure adapted from Baron (1973).

similar in frequency to the training tone and least often to tones that were dissimilar. The discrimination training that had strengthened responding in the presence of the S+ had also strengthened responding in the presence of stimuli similar to the S+.

Certain usages apply to stimulus generalization. We call the stimuli that have been used in stimulus discrimination training the *training stimuli*. For example, in Baron's study the training stimuli were the 1300 Hertz tone (the S+) and the 1000 Hertz tone (the S–). We call the stimuli that are used to assess the amount of generalization the *generalization test stimuli* or simply the *test stimuli*.

Stimulus generalization occurs often in everyday life. For example, school children learn to read cursive writing though stimulus discrimination procedures. Because everyone's handwriting is different, however, it is important to learn to generalize across different styles; to respond to them in the same way. Being able to recognize that both α and **a** are *a*'s is a skill that children must acquire to be effective readers. There are limits to our ability to generalize across stimuli, as seen when we find another person's handwriting illegible.

Baron's study of tone generalization illustrates excitatory stimulus generalization because the tendency to *respond* to the S+ generalized to stimuli similar to the S+. In contrast, inhibitory stimulus generalization is seen in situations in which a tendency *not to respond* to an S– generalizes to stimuli which are similar to the S– (Rilling, 1977; Honig, Boneau, Burstein, & Pennypacker, 1963).

Rollings and Baumeister (1981) showed inhibitory stimulus generalization in a study in which two retarded men served as subjects. These men engaged in several types of self-stimulatory behavior including head nodding, body rocking, and hand waving. During training, the two men sat in front of a panel mounted with a row of five red Christmas tree bulbs. The bulbs were numbered 1 through 5 from left to right. When light 1 (the light on the far left of the panel) was lit, self-stimulatory behavior was intermittently punished through an activity punisher. The men were required to sit back, look at the experimenter, and perform head turns for one minute. The researchers used manual prompting if the men did not obey the command to engage in head turning. When light 5, the light on the far right of the panel, was lit, the activity punisher was not dependent on the self-stimulatory behaviors: The men could freely engage in self-stimulation without penalty.

The stimulus discrimination procedure was successful in producing stimulus control: When stimulus 1 was on, the men seldom engaged in self-stimulation, but when stimulus 5 was on, the men freely engaged in these behaviors. At this point, the men were tested for generalization to see if the effects of discrimination training would spread to the other three lights on the panel. The five lights were turned on one at a time in a random order and the experimenters recorded the amount of self-stimulation that the men engaged in. The results of the generalization test are shown in Figures 9.2a and 9.2b.

These graphs are *inhibitory generalization gradients*. As you can see, responding was very similar to each of the lights during a pretraining test. After training, however, the effects of punishing the response to the S–, light 1, generalized to light 2 and light 3 for each subject. Light 2 and light 3 were similar to light 1 because

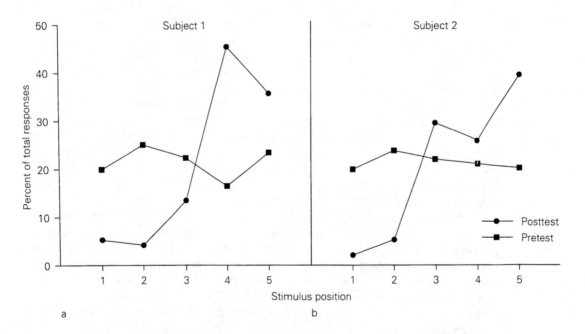

Figure 9.2a and b *Inhibitory Generalization Occurred to Lights That Were Closer to the S– During Training*

See text for explanation. Figure adapted from Rollings and Baumeister (1981).

they were close to it. In contrast, there was no generalization to light 4, which was further away and therefore dissimilar to light 1.

Inhibitory stimulus generalization is commonplace in the natural environment. For example, suppose you had an unpleasant experience with a policeman. If this experience caused you to avoid interacting with anyone in uniform, it would be an example of inhibitory stimulus generalization. Inhibitory stimulus generalization is the spread of effect of extinction, punishment, or some other response-weakening procedure. In contrast, excitatory stimulus generalization is the spread of effect of reinforcement or some other response-strengthening procedure.

The research we have examined demonstrates that stimulus generalization can occur after stimulus discrimination training, in which a learner is taught to respond to specific S+ or S− stimuli. Another form of stimulus generalization is called *setting generalization* or *generalization across settings.* In this type of generalization, training that strengthens (or weakens) a response in one setting causes that response to be strengthened (or weakened) in another setting. A setting or environment is a group of common stimuli that exist in one location. In basic stimulus generalization, strengthening a response in the presence of a training stimulus also serves to strengthen responding to similar test stimuli. Setting generalization follows this pattern, except that responding is strengthened in one environment called a *training situation* or *training setting,* and this serves to strengthen the response in another environment, called a *generalization setting, test situation,* or *test setting.*

Liberman, Teigen, Patterson, and Baker (1973) studied setting generalization in a project designed to increase the rational speech of four adults who had been diagnosed as paranoid schizophrenics and who had been living in mental hospitals for many years. The patients had a variety of delusions about stolen possessions, poisoned food, noble birth, work as a secret agent, and space aliens directing laser beams. Nurses interviewed the patients four times a day. If a patient began speaking delusionally, the nurse ended the interview immediately. In addition, the length of time the patients spoke rationally during the interviews earned them that same amount of time to chat with a therapist or enjoy coffee and snacks later in the evening. During the evening activity reinforcer sessions, rational speech was encouraged and irrational speech was punished by termination of social reinforcement. The patients' speech was also measured during their chats with the therapist and when they were on the ward. In both of these settings, however, no special consequences were dependent on rational and delusional speech.

These procedures increased the level of the patients' rational speech during the daily interviews by 200% to 600%. For three of the four patients, rational speech also improved when they were chatting with the therapist. This is an example of setting generalization because the procedures that caused improvement in the patients' speech in one setting, the interview, also acted to improve rational speech during the second setting, chatting with the therapist. However, setting generalization was not totally successful: The training effects did not generalize to the third setting, the hospital ward.

Setting generalization is important in behavior analysis because many behavior change procedures are used in a special setting such as a clinic, hospital ward, or observation area, and a key goal of the procedure is generalization of the behavior to other settings, those in the person's natural environment.

Another type of stimulus generalization similar to setting generalization is *generalization across experimenters* or *generalization across trainers*. In many behavior change programs, the same trainer works with the learner in every session. Generalization across trainers occurs when the learner is able to engage in the target behaviors in the presence of someone else. A child trained to comply with the commands of one teacher demonstrates generalization across trainers if she also complies with the commands of another teacher. Generalization across trainers is important because the effects of training are of considerably less value if they are specific to a single individual.

Response Generalization

Response generalization (also called response induction) is the spread of effect of a response-strengthening procedure to other responses that are similar to the target behavior. Response generalization has occurred if a procedure that strengthens a target response causes a strengthening of other responses that are similar to that response.

Like many other behavior analysis concepts, response generalization was initially studied in animal research. For example, in one experiment, MacFarlane (cited in Keller & Schoenfeld, 1950) trained one group of rats to run through an ordinary maze and another to swim through a water-filled maze. Then, the maze-running rats were required to swim through the maze and the maze-swimming rats were required to run through the maze. Both groups of rats went through the maze under the second set of conditions as well as they had done it the first time indicating that training in swimming had generalized to running, and training in running had generalized to swimming. This was response generalization because, for example, strengthening maze running also strengthened maze swimming, a response similar to running insofar as both are forms of movement.

Response generalization occurs often in verbal learning. For example, one of the authors of this book frequently gets calls from people trying to reach a popular cafe with a similar telephone number. When people make errors in dialing phone numbers, the number they dial is usually similar to the correct number. This is response generalization because learning to dial a phone number strengthens that dialing pattern and also strengthens similar dialing patterns to some extent. In a verbal learning experiment, Underwood and Hughes (1950) had undergraduate students learn a multiple-stimulus, multiple-response task in which the stimuli were three letter nonsense syllables (e.g., xan, ceg, fov) and the responses were adjectives (e.g., musty, horrid, toilsome). The students were trained to give a specific adjective as a response when presented with a specific stimulus word (e.g., stimulus: "xan"; response: "musty").

When Underwood and Hughes analyzed the errors the students made during training and those made during a recall task a week later, they found that the students' incorrect responses were generally similar to the correct responses. These incorrect responses included homonyms (i.e., words that sound like the correct response) and synonyms (i.e., words having the same meaning or function as the correct response). For example, when the correct response was *toilsome,* the students often gave the incorrect response *tiresome.* This pattern of errors illustrated response generalization because the training that strengthened correct responses also strengthened similar incorrect responses.

Response generalization also often occurs during children's language learning. For example, in referring to the past in English, *ed* is added to verbs, and much of the time when children say words in which the *ed* has been added (e.g., *worked, played, lifted, opened*) the response is correct and is reinforced. However, in the case of irregular verbs, response generalization produces incorrect responding. As such, as a result of reinforcement for the *ed* ending, children often respond incorrectly using words such as *runned, swimmed, speaked,* and *sitted.* This exemplifies response generalization because the language-learning training in which *ed* endings are strengthened in regular verbs also strengthens those endings in irregular verbs. Critics of behavior analysis sometimes use this phenomenon as an example that shows that reinforcement is not important in children's language learning. They argue that the fact that the incorrect *ed* endings (e.g., *swimmed)* appear without being reinforced is evidence that children learn to speak without reinforcement. However, the principle of response generalization accounts for this feature of children's language. The effects of reinforcement in strengthening the *ed* endings in regular verbs generalize to irregular verbs.

Ludwig and Geller (1991) found response generalization in a study in which pizza delivery drivers were trained to wear their seat belts more often. Training consisted of holding meetings with the drivers in which the importance of wearing seat belts was emphasized, having the drivers make a personal commitment to use their seat belts, and providing information to the drivers about how often they were buckling their seat belts. This training in seat-belt use substantially increased the frequency of use among the drivers. Ludwig and Geller also found that, as a result of the training, the drivers began using their turn signals correctly more often. Training in seat-belt use had generalized to turn-signal use, an example of response generalization. The two responses are similar in that both are safe-driving practices.

Like stimulus generalization, response generalization can be classified into excitatory-response generalization and inhibitory-response generalization. In the former, a procedure that strengthens one response also causes another response to be strengthened. In the latter, a procedure that weakens one response also weakens another. In Chapter 4, we examined an experiment that demonstrated inhibitory-response generalization. You may recall that Zeilberger, Sampen, and Sloane (1968) made timeout dependent on a 5-year-old boy's physical aggression and noncompliance with instructions. The timeout procedure not only reduced aggression and noncompliance, but also the boy's screaming, a behavior that was not punished during training. It is an example of inhibitory response generalization because the procedure that weakened one set of behaviors also weakened another.

Stimulus and Response Generalization

In behavior training and in everyday life, it is often desirable for the effects of learning to generalize to both similar stimuli and similar responses. For example, consider someone who has learned to drive one type of car and is now required to drive another. In the new "generalization" car, stimuli such as the steering wheel, the speedometer, gauges, and pedals are likely to be different from, though similar to, those in the old training car. In addition, responses in the new car such as turning the wheel, shifting gears, and depressing pedals are likely to be somewhat different from those made in the old car. Because of these variations in both stimuli and required responses, the driver's ability to drive the new car well depends on how much stimulus and response generalization occurs. There are many differences in both the stimuli present and the responses required in the two cars and so it is difficult to say which type of generalization is more important. In such cases, it is possible only to say that both processes may have been at work. Generalization is not always helpful to the learning process. Have you ever had the experience of hopping into an automatic vehicle after driving a manual shift for years? Did you find yourself searching madly for the clutch and trying to change gears? When stimuli are similar, but correct responses are different, learning is more difficult. This is called negative transfer.

Subject Generalization

Subject generalization occurs when a procedure used to change the behavior of one or more *target subjects* also causes changes in the behavior of other *nontarget subjects* to whom the behavior change procedure was not applied directly.

Broden, Bruce, Mitchell, Carter, and Hall (1970) demonstrated subject generalization in work with two boys named Greg and Edwin and their second-grade teacher. These boys sat next to each other and were the worst behaved students in the class. The teacher, acting as the trainer, began by praising and paying attention to Edwin only when he was on-task; she ignored off-task behavior. This procedure increased both Edwin's and Greg's on-task behaviors even though no consequences were dependent on Greg's behavior. This is an example of subject generalization because the procedures that altered the behavior of Edwin, the target subject, also altered the behavior of his friend, a nontarget subject to whom the procedure was not applied directly. Later, the procedures were reversed: Greg received praise and attention for on-task performance; misbehavior was ignored. Now it was Edwin whose behavior resulted in no special consequences. This procedure increased the level of both boys' on-task behavior again showing subject generalization.

Broden et al. (1970) speculated about possible causes of the generalization they saw with the boys, noting that the teacher needed to be near the boy she was training in order to quickly reinforce on-task behavior. Because the boys sat next to each other, this meant the teacher was also close to the other, nontarget boy. Broden et al. (1970) suggested that the teacher may have served as an S+ for being on-task. Another possibility is that the target boy, who was busy being on-task, did not distract his friend as much as he had in the past. A third possibility is that the on-task boy served as a modeling prompt for the nontarget boy. As you can see, subject generalization may occur as a result of the operation of several different behavioral processes.

A special case of subject generalization occurs when someone who has been trained to do something then trains someone else. In a clever use of this form of subject generalization, Jones, Fremouw, and Carples (1977) taught elementary school teachers several classroom management skills and also trained them to teach those skills. In turn, these teachers taught other teachers the skills that they themselves had learned. After observing the classrooms of teachers who had been trained by the experimenters and teachers who had been trained by other teachers, Jones et al. (1970) concluded that classroom environments had improved in both cases. These results tell us that subject generalization can be encouraged by training subjects to teach the behaviors they themselves have learned.

Behavior Maintenance

Behavior maintenance refers to the durability of behavior change; how long the change in behavior lasts. Behavior maintenance is sometimes called *generalization of the response over time*. Behavior maintenance is an important consideration: Even a significant improvement in productive, desirable behavior is of little benefit to anyone if this behavior occurs only for a short time. Short-term behavior change may be valuable on occasion, but in most situations, long-term change is the goal. Losing 5 pounds for a specific modeling assignment, for example, may be a goal that does not need to be sustained. But for many people, such short-term weight losses can be more harmful than no weight loss at all.

A study by Lovaas, Koegel, Simmons, and Long (1973) illustrates how important lasting change in behavior can be. These researchers worked with 20 autistic children who had severe behavior problems. Most had been expelled from special schools for retarded and emotionally disturbed students because their behavior could not be managed. The behavior analysts developed training programs using a variety of behavioral procedures including reinforcement, punishment, extinction, shaping, discrimination, and prompting. The focus was on reducing undesirable behaviors such as self-stimulation, and strengthening desirable responses such as speech, play, displays of affection, socializing, and self-help skills. The training was successful in increasing the children's desirable behaviors as well as decreasing their undesirable behaviors. They learned to interact better with others and to initiate conversation in social situations. Measures of intelligence and social maturity indicated that these children had improved.

Near the end of the intensive training period, some of the children were placed in their homes with their parents, who were trained in using behavioral procedures. Other children were placed in institutions. The experimenters made follow-up observations 1 to 4 years later. These data indicated that, in general, children whose parents were given training in behavioral techniques tended to retain the learned behaviors: The changes in the children's speech and social skills were sustained over time.

In contrast, the behavior changes of the children who were institutionalized did not persist over time. These initial gains were not totally lost, however. Additional training was successful in reestablishing some of the behaviors that the children had learned. As a result of these findings, Lovaas and his colleagues changed their approach to therapy. Rather than treating the children as inpatients in a hospital with the parents as observers, they began treating the children on an outpatient basis, and using the parents as therapists.

Behavior analysis techniques are most impressive to people when they see the behavior as it occurs both before and after treatment. For example, we are impressed when a child, who previously did little other than throw tantrums, displays good manners due to behavioral training. Indeed, during the early years, behavior analysts often were guilty of overly emphasizing the value of immediate improvements in behavior: They sometimes failed to be interested in long-term benefits, behavior maintenance. Behavior analysts today are more aware of such concerns. The newly polite child, the just slimmed-down dieter, the excessive drinker who is recently abstinent, and the person who has just adopted a set of New Year's resolutions are all merely the beginnings of possible successes and no more.

Receptive-Expressive and Expressive-Receptive Generalization

Sometimes stimuli and responses have dual identities. For example, suppose you are teaching a student the locations of the countries of the world. One way to do this would be to tell the student the name of the country and ask the student to point to the country on a world map (e.g., "Where is Cambodia?"). In this kind of *receptive* or *comprehension task*, a verbal stimulus acts as a discriminative stimulus for the student's response of selecting the correct response from a number of alternatives. Another way to do this would be to point to the country on a world map and ask the student to state the name of the country (e.g., "What is the name of this country?"). In this kind of *expressive task*, the student is required to state the correct label for a specified stimulus. In the first case, the label is the stimulus and pointing is the response; in the second case, pointing is the stimulus, and the label is the response.

When stimuli and responses are reversible, as seen in receptive and expressive tasks, how does training in one kind of task affect the other? This is a question of generalization from one type of training to another. If training in the receptive task helps the subject learn the expressive task, receptive-expressive generalization (or transfer) has occurred. Conversely, if training in the expressive task helps the subject learn the receptive task, expressive-receptive generalization has occurred. These questions are of practical importance because teaching will be most efficient if the task that generalizes best is taught first. Figure 9.3 on the next page illustrates receptive-expressive and expressive-receptive generalization formats.

Training in either receptive or expressive tasks will not always generalize to the other, but it sometimes does. For example, Cuvo and Riva (1980) taught both

Receptive-Expressive Generalization Training

Teacher: "Point to the quarter."

Student correctly selects the quarter.

Receptive-Expressive Generalization Test

Teacher: "What is the name of this coin?"

Student: "It is a quarter."

Expressive-Receptive Generalization Training

Teacher: "What is the name of this coin?"

Student: "It is a quarter."

Expressive-Receptive Generalization Test

Teacher: "Point to the quarter."

Student correctly selects the quarter.

Figure 9.3   *Receptive-Expressive and Expressive-Receptive Forms of Generalization*

In receptive-expressive generalization, training is given on a task in which the learner is required only to respond to a stimulus, and the student learns to emit the corresponding verbal response (i.e., the name or label for the stimulus). In expressive-receptive generalization, the learner is given training in saying the name of a stimulus, and the learner also learns to discriminate the stimulus from among alternatives.

retarded and nondelayed children the names of coins using receptive and expressive training procedures. In the receptive task, the children were required to pick out a specified coin from a set of five. In the expressive task, the children were required to name the specified coin. The results of the study showed that generalization was *bidirectional* across the two tasks: Training in the expressive task improved receptive responding, and training in receptive responding improved expressive responding.

Generally, receptive-expressive generalization is more common than expressive-receptive generalization. However, as Cuvo and Riva's experiment illustrates, expressive-receptive generalization may sometimes occur.

Making Generalization Effective

In studying the conditions that make generalization effective, behavior analysts have discovered several important factors including (a) selection of appropriate target behaviors, (b) the similarity between the training and generalization test stimuli, (c) using multiple training exemplars, (d) using intermittent reinforcement, (e) using delayed reinforcement, (f) using natural reinforcers, (g) using self-control procedures, and (h) behavioral contrast effects. (See Stokes and Baer [1977] and Stokes and Osnes [1989] for reviews of research.)

Selection of Appropriate Target Behaviors

Behavior maintenance is better if the target behaviors are likely to continue to occur and be reinforced once training has ceased (Ayllon & Azrin, 1968). It is important for trainers to be sensitive to the long-term outlook for the behaviors they teach. For example, the focus of many programs for retarded people has been on independent living skills, including vocational skills, money management, self-care skills, and social skills. These useful behaviors are critical to success in independent living.

Sometimes target behaviors are selected that are not likely to be maintained in the long term. For example, some foreign aid programs to underdeveloped countries have taught skills that were more appropriate to a highly mechanized culture, when simpler technologies were needed. Similarly, educational institutions often train people in obsolete skills or in areas for which there is no demand in the marketplace. In selecting appropriate target behaviors, one must be able to predict whether the future environment will support the behavior.

Similarity Between the Training and Test Stimuli

In Chapter 7, we discussed the conditions that make stimulus discrimination effective. One of the important principles was stimulus similarity: The greater the similarity between the stimuli to be discriminated, the more difficult the discrimination will be. This principle also applies to stimulus generalization, but in the opposite fashion: The greater the similarity between the training and test stimuli, the more effective stimulus generalization will be. We saw a demonstration of this principle earlier in this chapter. Baron's research with auditory generalization showed that generalization to the test tones was greatest when they were similar to the training tone.

Dixon (1981) conducted another study of the similarity principle in stimulus generalization. She trained severely retarded students to match photographs of objects with real objects using a matching-to-sample procedure. At first, the students were poor at this task. For example, the students were unable to match a photograph of a banana with a real banana. In other words, the response of identifying a banana had failed to generalize from a real banana to a picture of one. In order to promote generalization, Dixon made the photographs of the objects more similar to the real objects by cutting out the photographed objects from the background of the photographs. This increased the similarity between the photographed objects and the real objects because both stimuli now had the same shape. As Dixon expected, there was much more stimulus generalization between the real objects and the cutouts than there had been with the standard photographs.

The principle of similarity between training and test stimuli has important implications for setting generalization. If a goal of training is that the behavior change generalizes to the natural environment, then the training situation should be made as similar as possible to the natural environment. One way to do this is to train the behavior in the natural environment; another way is to use stimuli in the training situation that are also present in the natural environment.

Training the behavior in the natural environment has a great advantage in that the training and test situations are identical. Behavior analysts often do work in the natural environment: In the home, the classroom, and the workplace. When training occurs in the natural environment, of course, no setting generalization needs to take place, because the behavior is directly trained in the setting in which it is desirable for the behavior to occur. The behavior analyst, freed from the problem of setting generalization, can then concentrate on methods to maintain the behavior change in the natural environment setting. Conducting treatment in the natural environment is one of the practices that distinguishes behavior analysts from many other therapists, who practice exclusively in an office setting (Knapp, Crosby, & O'Boyle, 1978).

Sometimes it is not possible to train behavior in its natural setting. If this is the case, programming common stimuli, using the same stimuli in the training setting that exist in the test setting, will help to make the two settings more similar.

Rincover and Koegel (1975) did just this in their work with ten autistic children. They trained the children to imitate various behaviors of the experimenter (e.g., touching their chin when the experimenter demonstrated the response and told them to do so). To train the imitative behaviors, the experimenters used physical prompts, together with food and praise reinforcers. Once the children had learned the imitative behavior in a small treatment room, a new trainer took them outdoors. There, the new trainer prompted the child to engage in nonverbal imitation. Although six of the ten children engaged in some imitation in the outdoor generalization setting with the new trainer, four did not respond at all.

At this point, the experimenters began to suspect that specific stimuli that were present during original training, but not in the outdoor generalization setting, had come to act as discriminative stimuli for imitative responding. For one boy named John, they found that the original trainer's hand movement acted as an S+ for imitation. When the hand movement was used outdoors, John began imitating. For another child named Cliff, the experimenters suspected that the furniture in the treatment room had somehow become discriminative stimuli for imitative responding. When the table and chairs from the treatment room were moved outdoors, Cliff began responding correctly. As you can see, generalization from the original training setting to the outdoor generalization setting was improved by programming common stimuli, by placing key stimuli in the generalization setting that had been present in the original training setting.

Ayllon, Kuhlman, and Warzak (1982) inventively applied the principle of programming common stimuli in work with eight elementary school students. The students did some of their work at a school resource room, where they usually did a good job on their assignments. The students also worked in a regular classroom where they did not perform nearly as well on the same kinds of assignments. The researchers developed a plan that they hoped would produce generalization of the desirable resource-room performance to the classroom. They asked the students to bring a personal "lucky charm" to the resource room, and to do their work with the lucky charm on their desks. The children brought a variety of items including lipstick, family photos, a medal, and trinkets. After a time, the experimenters had the students bring the lucky charms to their regular classrooms, and to use them as a reminder to work hard. This plan worked very well. Performance in the regular classroom improved substantially with the help of the lucky charms.

Programming common stimuli is a technique also used as a part of some fading procedures when the goal is for the learner to respond correctly in a different setting. We saw an example of such an application in Chapter 8 in the case of Emma, who would not speak in kindergarten, preschool, or Sunday school. At first, Emma performed a variety of activities in a playroom with only her mother present. Gradually, the experimenter was faded in by having her voice come over a radio, having her stand outside the playroom, and gradually having her move closer to Emma. This fading procedure programmed many common stimuli: The same room was used, Emma's mother remained in the room, and Emma worked on the same activities. Keeping these stimuli constant during the fading procedure helped Emma learn to interact with a number of different experimenters.

We often see programming common stimuli in everyday life, when people find themselves in new settings. When forced to move away from loved ones, people often take photographs, paintings, and personal mementos. These provide current stimuli that can to some extent allow their positive behaviors toward the people they miss to generalize to the new setting. Immigrants to new lands retain various features of their old culture because they act as discriminative stimuli for positive behaviors acquired in a former homeland. Of course, they may not describe their behavior in quite these same terms.

Using Multiple Training Exemplars

In general, the greater the number of different training stimuli, the greater the generalization to new stimuli. Stokes, Baer, and Jackson (1974) showed this principle in their study of generalization across trainers. Four retarded children were learning to wave their hands in greeting. Training techniques included physical prompting, reinforcing correct responses with food, physical contact, and social reinforcement. At first, a single experimenter worked with the children but the behavior they learned did not generalize when they met other members of the institution's staff. However, after a second experimenter also trained the greeting response, generalization was more successful: The children began greeting other staff members appropriately.

Neef, Lensbower, Hockersmith, DePalma, and Gray (1990) demonstrated the importance of using multiple exemplars in training four retarded adults to use washing machines and dryers. In one condition, the trainees learned to use only one type of washer and dryer. In a second condition, the trainees learned to use four or five different machines. Generalization was tested with machines the trainees had not encountered before. The trainees who had learned to operate several different types of machines were much more successful in the generalization test than those who had learned to use only one machine. The group trained to use several different machines produced average gains in correct responding of 12% for washing machines and 18% for dryers over performance levels by the group trained to use only one type of washer and dryer.

Another way to improve generalization is to use exemplars in less restricted circumstances, as well as in the training conditions. For example, Campbell and Stremel-Campbell (1982) trained two retarded boys, 10 and 12, to ask "wh-is/are" questions (e.g., "What are you doing?"; "Where is my pen?"), "yes/no reversal" questions (e.g., "Is this mine?") and statements (e.g., "These are mine"). At first, the experimenters trained the boys in a structured academic setting in which the teacher would present the boys with stimuli, prompt correct responses, and observe and provide differential consequences for correct and incorrect responding. These 15-minute formal training sessions were held twice a day.

These methods were effective in teaching the boys the target behaviors when they were in the structured academic setting. The boys were also observed in a free-play environment to see if they would engage in the target behaviors there. And, indeed, they did. The investigators had used an additional technique called *loose-training* to enhance generalization of the target behaviors to the free-play setting. They reinforced unprompted target behaviors when the boys were in a less structured situation. Reinforcement was on a VR 3 schedule. For example, if one of the boys used a wh-is/are question correctly (e.g., "Where are you going?") this response was intermittently reinforced. This is called loose training because the use of additional stimuli outside the structured training setting expanded the range of stimuli that were trained, and thereby loosened the stimulus control achieved in the structured academic setting.

The desirability of using a broad range of stimuli, in addition to stimuli presented in structured settings, is important in many academic contexts. Consider a student learning French vocabulary by flash card in a classroom setting. Although considerable progress can be made in this way, the true test will come when the student is conversing with other French-speaking people.

Intermittent Reinforcement

In Chapters 3 and 6, we discussed an important effect of intermittent reinforcement: Behavior that has been intermittently reinforced is more likely to persist during extinction than behavior that has been continuously reinforced. This feature of intermittent reinforcement has important implications for behavior maintenance. In the natural environment many desirable behaviors undergo periods of nonreinforcement. Therefore, a behavior to be maintained in the natural environment must be resistant to extinction. As discussed in Chapter 6, during the early stages of teaching a behavior, the behavior should be reinforced continuously. Later in training, the reinforcement schedule for the response should be gradually thinned in order to increase resistance to extinction.

Delayed Reinforcement

Although the role of delayed reinforcement in improving generalization is not well understood, there is increasing evidence that it may be an important one. Fowler and Baer (1981) studied delayed reinforcement with seven preschool children. For each child, one behavior was selected for change on the basis of the child's individual needs. Behaviors included offering to share and play cooperatively with other children, positive statements about activities (e.g., "Painting is fun"), good posture while seated, and conversations with other children.

One method used to encourage the target behaviors was an *early reinforcement* procedure. In this condition, the children rehearsed their target behavior with the experimenter for a few minutes prior to a daily classroom observation period. The experimenter told the children how many times they were expected to engage in the target behavior in the classroom. After the children had been observed in the classroom, they met with the experimenter again. If the child had met the criterion by engaging in the target behavior the specified number of times, the child received a sticker or a point, which could be exchanged for toys. Later in the day, the children were observed in the classroom again. This second session was a generalization session because reinforcement was not dependent on the children's behaviors during this time.

As well as this early reinforcement procedure, the experimenters also used a *late reinforcement* procedure. This was identical to the early reinforcement method, except that the experimenter met with the children and awarded stickers and points at the end of the school day. As a result, the generalization session occurred before rather than after the meeting with the experimenter, the time at which the reinforcers were awarded. The results are illustrated in Figure 9.4 on the next page.

Fowler and Baer were particularly interested in target behavior frequency during the generalization session. In general, they found that generalization was stronger when they used the late reinforcement method. Apparently, that method increased generalization because the children were not able to discriminate the reinforcement dependency. Although the children's reinforcers depended entirely on their behavior during the first session, the children were not sure if reinforcement was dependent on their performance in the generalization session. For example, two of the children in the late reinforcement condition asked, "Do I need to share all day?"

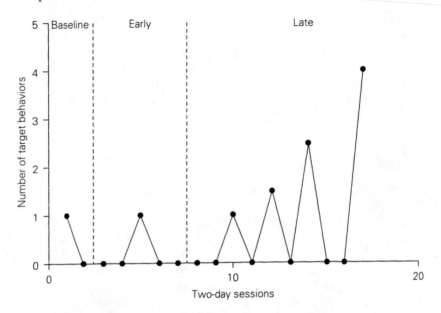

Figure 9.4   *The Influence of Immediacy of Reinforcement on Generalization*

Generalization of behavior was promoted more through delayed reinforcement than immediate reinforcement. Figure adapted from Fowler and Baer (1981).

Fowler and Baer's study showed that delayed reinforcement can produce generalization across settings. Mayhew and Anderson (1980) found that delayed reinforcement can improve behavior maintenance as well.

Because delayed reinforcement is effective in promoting generalization, it should be considered in applications of behavior analysis. Keep in mind, though, that delayed reinforcement should not be used early in the learning process; at this stage, the goal should be to strengthen the behavior in one setting. Once the behaviors have already been learned, however, delayed reinforcement may be an excellent method for promoting both generalization of the behavior to new settings and behavior maintenance.

Natural Reinforcers

Behavior maintenance is more effective if the target behavior is maintained by natural reinforcers rather than contrived reinforcers (Ferster, 1967). As we discussed in Chapter 2, behavior analysts often use contrived reinforcers to encourage desirable behaviors at the time that the behavior is being strengthened. However, once the training is over, long-term maintenance of the behavior will depend on the effectiveness of natural reinforcers for the response. For example, in learning a foreign language in a classroom, contrived reinforcers are used to improve correct responding.

However, once the student's course of study is completed, maintenance of the foreign language responses will be dependent on the natural reinforcers, such as communicating with speakers of the language and reading material written in the language.

Because natural reinforcers are so important in maintaining behavior, anything that can be done to help ensure that behavior is reinforced by natural reinforcers will be desirable. Two things that can be done are to use natural reinforcers that predict other reinforcers and to teach people to recruit natural communities of reinforcement.

As discussed in Chapter 2, conditioned reinforcers are more effective when they predict that other reinforcers are on the way. This principle of reinforcer effectiveness applies to natural reinforcers such as praise. For example, in Lauten and Birnbrauer's study, the effectiveness of the natural social reinforcer "Right," was enhanced when it had predicted candy delivery compared to when it did not. Behavior analysts often apply this principle in token economies by accompanying token delivery with words of praise (Kazdin & Bootzin, 1972). This makes praise more effective as a reinforcer later, when the contrived token reinforcers are discontinued. In turn, this helps to maintain desirable behaviors acquired through token reinforcement.

Praise, positive comments, and recognition from others are powerful reinforcers for most people. Aside from being highly effective, all these natural reinforcers are free. Unfortunately, for various reasons, people often fail to use these reinforcers. As a result, desirable behaviors undergo extinction. You probably can recall an instance in which you did something worthwhile that you thought would be recognized as an achievement, only to find that your behavior was ignored.

Another way to increase the likelihood that natural reinforcers will maintain behavior is to teach people to induce others to provide these reinforcers. For example, Seymour and Stokes (1976) worked with four girls who lived in the maximum security unit of a correctional center. The girls had repeatedly broken the law. At the institution, they were disruptive, noncompliant, and had low rates of performing academic and work tasks assigned to them. These tasks included learning living skills such as reading bus timetables, making bank transactions, assembling tote bags, typing and doing other office work, and preparing food. Treatment for these problem behaviors included the use of a token economy to reinforce desirable behaviors, and the use of response cost and timeout to reduce undesirable behaviors. The girls also recorded their work behaviors. These procedures were successful in improving the work of three of the four girls.

Although the girls' work output had improved, they were not obtaining more praise for their behavior from staff who worked at the institution. To induce the staff to praise the girls more, the experimenters taught the girls to use a cuing procedure. The cuing method consisted of having the girls point out their performance improvements to the institutional staff, who had not been told about the cuing procedure. This cuing procedure had its intended effect: The staff began praising the girls more for their improved performances. In subsequent work, cuing praise has been used successfully with preschool children (Stokes, Fowler, & Baer, 1978) and severely disabled people (Mank & Horner, 1987). In one form or another, it may be useful for virtually all subject populations.

Seymour and Stokes' cuing method is an example of *training people to recruit natural communities of reinforcement*. The main idea behind this technique is that natural reinforcers are often available, but the person whose behavior requires reinforcement must be taught how to get those reinforcers. Of course, behavior analysts who work in this area must be careful not to train people to boast of their accomplishments too much. People who are perceived as constantly blowing their own horns are not likely to be admired and praised by others. However, use of subtle methods of evoking praise in others appears to be a useful way to help natural reinforcers maintain newly-learned skills.

Self-Control Techniques

Another method to enhance generalization, especially behavior maintenance, is with the use of self-control procedures. A self-control procedure is a method in which a person engages in one behavior called a *controlling* response that alters or maintains the level of another behavior called the *controlled* response (Skinner, 1953). For example, consider the response of marking the date of a friend's birthday on a calendar and the response of noticing that it is your friend's birthday on the marked day and sending a card. Marking the calendar is the controlling response because it causes the later responses, noticing the date and sending the card. This is a self-control procedure because *you* engaged in both the controlling and the controlled responses. Self-control is perceived by some people as contradicting behavior analysis principles in some way, but as you can see, self-control is a special case of behavioral principles at work.

Self-control skills must be learned but once they are, people can manage the levels of their own behaviors by engaging in controlling responses. Many university students have learned to improve their study habits with the use of self-control techniques. For example, Richards, McReynolds, Holt, and Sexton (1976) trained introductory psychology students in a self-control technique known as self-monitoring. Self-monitoring includes measuring some aspect of your own behavior, recording it on a chart or graph, and observing changes over time. In Richards's et al. (1976) study, students recorded and graphed the number of pages they read each day. In other applications of self-monitoring, students have recorded the duration of study time. Results of self-monitoring experiments have shown that the method can improve students' final exam grades.

Self-monitoring has been shown to be effective in strengthening a variety of desirable behaviors and weakening a variety of undesirable behaviors. Stop smoking, weight control, and controlled-drinking programs often use self-monitoring as an important part of the therapeutic process. Self-monitoring is a self-control method because the controlling response, recording the level of some target behavior, appears to be effective in altering the controlled response, the behavior that is being recorded. Like other self-control procedures, self-monitoring can improve behavior maintenance because the technique enables learners to manage their own behavior without the day-to-day help of other people. For example, after students have learned how to self-monitor their behavior in one course, they can continue to use the technique throughout their academic careers and beyond. Indeed, many behavior analysts have accumulated years and years of data by self-monitoring their own on-task behaviors. Essentially, once training in self-monitoring is completed, the method can continue to be used and continue to maintain behavior at desirable levels.

Behavioral Contrast Effects

One factor that can reduce the effectiveness of generalization across settings is called behavioral contrast. In behavioral contrast, a procedure used to increase or decrease the level of responding in one stimulus situation causes an opposite change in the level of responding in another stimulus situation. For example, Koegel, Egel, and Williams (1980) found behavioral contrast in work with autistic children ranging in age from 5 to 10 years old. The experimenters selected several target behaviors based on the individual needs of each child including compliance with instructions and visual orientation to objects to be grasped. The target behaviors were measured in a therapy setting in which the behavior was reinforced, and a nontherapy setting, a physically different location where the behavior was not reinforced. As you might expect, reinforcement of the target behavior in the therapy setting caused an increase in the percentage of correct responding in the therapy setting. However, the strengthening of correct responding in the therapy setting had another effect: The percentage of correct responses decreased in the nontherapy setting. This was an example of behavioral contrast because reinforcing the target behavior in the therapy setting caused a decline in the level of the target behavior in the nontherapy setting, in which the behavior was not reinforced.

Koegel et al. (1980) found that they were able to eliminate the behavioral contrast effect by using the method of programming common stimuli, as described earlier. By using certain aspects of the reinforcement procedure in the nontherapy setting, they found that the undesirable decrease in the target behavior no longer occurred.

Although behavioral contrast effects have been shown in applied settings, they have not been studied extensively and it is difficult to say to what extent they occur. Nonetheless, the possibility of such effects poses some interesting problems. For example, if one parent begins reinforcing a child's desirable behaviors, does this mean that the level of the child's desirable behaviors will diminish in the presence of the opposite parent? If a teacher reinforces correct academic responding in her classroom, does this mean that her students' correct responding will diminish in their other classes? If a person takes a lover who systematically reinforces his or her laughter, does this mean that laughter will decline in the presence of the person's spouse? Because the operation of behavioral contrast in human environments is not well understood, we can only speculate about the answers to these questions.

Summary

Generalization is broadly concerned with the problem of how changing target behaviors in the training situation will influence behavior in nontraining situations, after training has ended. Behavior analysts are interested in these generalization processes because the goal of most behavioral procedures is to produce behavior changes that (a) spread to stimulus conditions other than the training conditions (i.e., stimulus generalization), (b) spread to other desirable behaviors (i.e., response generalization), (c) spread to people other than the ones directly trained (i.e., subject generalization), and (d) endure even after training has ended (i.e., behavior maintenance).

We considered several specific types of generalization. Stimulus generalization occurs when the effect of a discriminative stimulus spreads to stimuli that are similar to it. As similarity between test and training stimuli increases, so does generalization.

In excitatory stimulus generalization, the strengthening of a response in the presence of one stimulus causes a strengthening of that response in the presence of similar stimuli. In inhibitory stimulus generalization, the weakening of a response in the presence of one stimulus causes a weakening of that response in the presence of similar stimuli. Excitatory and inhibitory stimulus generalization gradients are graphs that illustrate the spread of effects of excitatory and inhibitory discriminative stimuli.

Two specific types of stimulus generalization of particular interest to behavior analysts are setting generalization, in which behavior generalizes from one setting to another, and experimenter generalization, in which behavior generalizes from one trainer to another.

Another type of generalization we examined is called response generalization, in which behavior generalizes to other similar behaviors. In excitatory response generalization, the strengthening of one response also strengthens a similar response. In inhibitory stimulus generalization, the weakening of one response also weakens a similar response.

Although stimulus and response generalization are separate behavioral processes, they work in parallel in many learning situations. Often we are required to respond in a situation in which both the stimuli and the responses required are similar to those we have previously encountered.

Another type of generalization is called subject generalization, in which the behavior of one person generalizes to the behavior of someone else. This type of generalization can be encouraged by teaching trainees how to teach others the behaviors they have learned.

We also examined behavior maintenance, a type of generalization crucial to the success of behavior change projects. Behavior maintenance occurs when the training procedures produce behavior changes that endure even after training has ceased. In general, experienced behavior analysts do not have great difficulty changing behavior for a limited time under training conditions. A more difficult challenge is to ensure that those changes persist after training has ceased.

Two other types of generalization are called receptive-expressive generalization and expressive-receptive generalization. In receptive-expressive generalization, learners are given discrimination training in which they are presented with a stimulus such as a word and are required to select a corresponding object or item from a group of alternatives. Later, the learners are presented with the object or item and are required to say the corresponding word. If the receptive task helps the learners do better on the expressive task, we say that receptive-expressive generalization has occurred. Conversely, in expressive-receptive generalization, the learners first engage in an expressive task in which they are required to say a word that corresponds to an object presented to them. After training in this task, they are given a task in which they are provided with a word and required to select a corresponding object. If the training in the first task aids correct responding in the second task, we say that expressive-receptive generalization has occurred.

Finally, we also examined several factors that influence the effectiveness of generalization, including selecting appropriate target behaviors, maximizing the similarity between the training and test stimuli, using multiple training exemplars, using intermittent reinforcement, using delayed reinforcement, using natural reinforcers, using self-control procedures, and behavioral contrast effects.

Conceptual Exercise   *Types of Generalization*

For each of the following items, decide if the item is an example of (a) stimulus generalization, (b) response generalization, (c) both stimulus and response generalization, (d) subject generalization, (e) behavior maintenance, (f) receptive-expressive generalization, or (g) expressive-receptive generalization. Some of the items are examples of more than one type of generalization. Justify your decision with a brief explanation. Confirm your decision by consulting the analysis section in the back of the book.

1. Two behavior analysts were working with five swimmers on the Manitoba Marlin Swim Club. The behavior analysts broke down three swimming strokes (i.e., backstroke, breaststroke, and freestyle) into several components. They found that when they trained the swimmers to respond correctly in one component of a stroke, that other components of that same stroke also showed an increase in correct responding, even though those other components had not yet been the focus of training.

2. Three fourth-grade students, who had been labeled as learning-disabled, seldom asked questions in their math class and were not learning as much as their classmates were. Their teacher said that the problem was that the students were not participating in class. The students learned how and when to ask questions through lessons that included videotaped modeling practice, and praise for correct responding. This training took place in a learning resource room. As a result of this training, the students' frequency of question asking increased in math class and in the regular classroom. The training that the students received also increased the students' accuracy in solving math problems that were assigned to them every day.

3. Dan, Hank, and Ricky were three boys who attended a preschool for children with behavior problems. They seldom engaged in appropriate social behavior. In order to

solve these problems, the children's teacher used prompts and praise to encourage appropriate social behaviors such as playing with other children and sharing. As a result of these procedures, Dan, Hank, and Ricky engaged in appropriate social behavior more often. In addition, the appropriate social behavior of several other children who did not receive the behavior change procedures also increased.

4. In a project design to improve the problem-solving skills of a community board, three behavior analysts taught the board members (a) how to state problems they encountered, (b) how to generate solutions to the problems, and (c) how to take action to implement the solutions. As a result of this training, the board members engaged in the three problem-solving behaviors more often than they had before training. In addition, follow-up observations made 1 week to 2 months after training showed that the board members continued to use the problem-solving skills they had been taught.

5. Leonard was learning French vocabulary on his computer. An object would appear on the screen and Leonard's task was to say the French name for the object. If he failed to say the French word within 5 seconds, a voice said the word over the computer's speaker. In this way, Leonard learned the French names of 20 objects. Then, the computer's speaker said the French word and Leonard's task was to select the correct object from among several alternatives. As a result of his training on the first task, Leonard did better on the second task.

6. Two 4-year-old children, who attended preschool, were participating in an experiment. The children were told the name of an object and were required to point to the named object from two objects sitting on a table. Correct pointing responses were reinforced with poker chips that could later be exchanged for toys. As a result of this training, the children learned to point to the named objects. Later, the children were tested to see if they could say the name of objects that the experimenter pointed to. As a result of the training in pointing to the objects, it was also found that the children could say the names of the objects.

7. Two fourth-grade teachers were being taught to praise their students by specifying the behavior the student had performed correctly (e.g., "You solved that problem correctly Ashley"). This was done through the use of several training techniques, including teacher self-recording of the amount of praise they delivered. At first, the teachers were trained to use praise during reading lessons, and the training increased the amount of praise the teachers gave during these lessons. However, this training did not affect the amount of praise the teachers gave during language arts lessons or math lessons.

8. Five mentally retarded youths ranging in age from 9 to 19 years had never learned to pour liquids with a pitcher. The trainees practiced pouring with eight different training pitchers that differed in size, the amount of liquid used, the size of the opening, whether the pitcher had a handle or a lid, and so forth. Training methods included the use of praise for correct responding and physical prompting, if necessary. As a result of this practice, the trainees were able to pour correctly using 16 different pitchers that had not been used during training.

9. First- and second-grade children participated in an experiment. During training trials, the experimenter told the children the name of an object in Spanish, and the children's task was to place a poker chip over the picture of the named object from among a group of eight different pictures. In this way the children learned to respond to eight Spanish words. Later, the experimenter showed the children pictures of the objects and the children's task was to say the Spanish name for the pictured object. The children did well on this task because of the training they had received on the first task.

10. Susan, and Mark were autistic 20-year-olds. They were trained to purchase food items at their school cafeteria through the use of prompting and fading, praise for correct responding, and videotaped modeling prompts. After this training, Susan and Mark were observed to see if they could correctly purchase items at a grocery store, a drug store, a convenience store, and a bookstore. They were successful at purchasing items at these stores, and they continued to use their new skills correctly two weeks after training.

11. Two behavior analysts trained four retarded children to name objects. For some of the objects, the name training used real objects. For other objects, name training used picture cards. And for some of the objects, the trainers used photographs. After this training, they tested the children to see if they would name the objects correctly in the natural environment. Three of the children were able to correctly name objects in the natural environment only when the real objects had been used in training. The fourth child was able to correctly name objects in the natural environment whether he had been trained using real objects, pictures, or photographs.

12. Charlotte, 10, was the most disruptive pupil in her class. She had no friends among her classmates, who either ignored her or teased her. During treatment, the teacher rated the appropriateness of Charlotte's behavior every 10 minutes and gave her from 0 to 10 points based on how well she behaved. This method was successful in reducing Charlotte's disruptive behavior from 4.17 disruptions per minute to 1.11 disruptions per minute. In addition, this procedure reduced the level of disruptive behavior among Charlotte's classmates, even though the procedure was not applied to them.

13. Four mentally retarded adults who worked at a sheltered workshop were trained in how to cook. Prior to training, the trainees were unable to prepare edible food. Training consisted of separating baking, boiling, and broiling tasks into components, prompting using the increasing assistance method, and reinforcement in the form of praise and food. The trainees learned the skills and were able to do things such as broil hot dogs, bake cornbread, and boil eggs and vegetables. From 7 to 11 days after original training, the trainees were retested to see if they could still cook properly and the testing indicated they could do so.

14. Five black children were students in a first-grade class made up largely of white children. Their teacher was concerned because the children did not play together. In order to promote interaction between the black and the white children, they were trained to eat lunch together through the use of prompting, social reinforcement,

and tokens exchangeable for edible treats. As a result of this training, the children interacted with one another more often during free-play periods. However, once the treatment was discontinued, interactions between the black and the white children did not occur very often.

15. Jenny was an 8-year-old who refused to clean her room. A system was established in which Jenny could earn points exchangeable for toys, privileges, money, and outings. As part of the system, four room-cleaning behaviors were measured: putting dirty clothes in a laundry basket, hanging up clean clothes or putting them in drawers, picking up toys, and making the bed. Of these four behaviors, only picking up the toys was reinforced. Despite this, Jenny also performed the other three tasks.

16. The disruptive library behavior of a class of 25 fourth-grade students was such a problem it had come to the attention of the school psychologist. In order to solve the problem, the "good behavior game" was used, a game in which the class was divided into two teams. The teams were awarded points if all the members of the team were behaving appropriately when they were periodically observed. The winning team had the option of having a story read to them or working on a special art project. The good behavior game was used in the library, where it produced a 21% increase in the percentage of on-task behavior. The good behavior game also improved the level of on-task behaviors in the classroom, even though the good behavior game was not used in the classroom itself.

17. People participated in a program to improve their public speaking abilities, wherein training consisted of demonstrating correct and incorrect speaking behaviors, practice in speaking, examination of videotapes of practice speeches, praise for appropriate speech, and corrective feedback for inappropriate speaking behaviors. During training, speakers practiced speaking in front of a small group of trainees. As a result of these techniques, the trainees improved their ability to speak in front of their own small group and to a larger audience of 18 or 19 people.

18. Ninety-eight inner-city students were enrolled in a program in which they received various types of reinforcers for attendance, completing assignments, and getting good teacher ratings in their math and English classes. As a result of the program, their attendance at English and math classes was much improved. Another effect of the procedure was an increase in the students' attendance at their science and social studies classes, even though these behaviors were not directly reinforced.

19. Five retarded males who also had physical handicaps were being trained in pedestrian safety. At first, training took place using a miniature model street with a "Walk-Don't Walk" sign and a traffic light. The trainees used a doll to simulate crossing a street and other pedestrian behaviors. Pedestrian safety skills were divided into a number of correct and incorrect responses. During training, correct responses were praised and incorrect responses were followed with corrective feedback. After the trainees learned the pedestrian skills on the miniature street using the doll, they were tested on a real city street and responded correctly.

20. An 8-year-old boy named Allan was trained in various home safety skills including safe food preparation, avoiding dangerous weather conditions, interacting with

strangers, and responding to fires, cuts, and burns. Allan learned the skills very well. Allan's 5-year-old brother Bert, who was not trained in any of the skills, was tested to determine if he had also learned the skills. Testing showed that he had.

21. Several men who lived at a veterans' administration hospital had been diagnosed as schizophrenic. They participated in an experiment. They were trained, in a structured interview, to engage in "healthy talk," which consisted of answering questions in a coherent and relevant manner. Training techniques included both positive and negative token reinforcement of healthy talk. The men learned to engage in healthy talk more often as a result of this method. Later, the men were tested on another task in which they were required to explain the meaning of proverbs. It was found that the training that improved the mens' healthy talk also improved their ability to interpret proverbs correctly.

22. Isabel was an 8-year-old girl who was learning the names of various flowers. One morning Isabel and her father sat looking at a picture book. As he showed Isabel a flower, he had her say its name. They did this with seven different types of flowers. Later that afternoon, Isabel's father tested her by saying the name of a flower and asking Isabel to pick out the correct one from pictures of the seven flowers she had learned. As a result of the morning training, Isabel did very well on the afternoon task.

Conceptual Exercise   *Making Generalization Effective*

In each of the following items, something should be altered to make generalization more effective. Describe what should be altered and explain why.

1. Four retarded adults who had poor social skills were learning how to initiate conversation and respond to comments directed toward them. The trainer would approach each person at various intervals during the session and ask a question or make a comment. If the patient responded appropriately or initiated spontaneous conversation with the trainer, the trainer would praise the patient and provide lots of attention. The trainer was careful to ask questions but make comments that were varied and similar to the kinds of questions and comments the patients would experience in the natural environment. The trainer also was careful to reinforce continuously during the beginning sessions. Later, as skills were improved, the trainer used intermittent reinforcement. The training sessions were carried out in the hospital coffee room. The patients improved their social skills a lot during these sessions, but later in the cafeteria the patients did not initiate conversation or respond to comments from people other than the original trainer.

2. Vlasta was a student who suffered from test anxiety. If she had to write a test in school, she would become so anxious she couldn't remember anything that she had learned. She signed up for a relaxation workshop specifically designed for students with test anxiety. In this workshop the trainer used systematic desensitization techniques to help Vlasta relax. The trainer played the role of the teacher and Vlasta was the student. The trainer used several different kinds of quizzes similar to the quizzes

Vlasta would be writing in school. The natural reinforcers of doing well on the quizzes were effective and the trainer praised Vlasta on an intermittent schedule so that her relaxed behavior would persist. As Vlasta succeeded different trainers were brought in. This procedure was very successful but the first time Vlasta entered her regular classroom and saw all the other students working away, she became extremely anxious and did not do well on her quiz.

3. Reg was a retarded teenager who wanted to work on simple carpentry in a sheltered workshop. His father worked with him to prepare him for his new job. His father knew that his own workshop was very similar to the sheltered workshop; he had the same tools and taught Reg to build the kinds of things he would be building at his new job. Every time Reg used a tool correctly, his father rewarded him with a colored token, which Reg collected avidly. His father knew about behavioral principles and was careful to use intermittent reinforcement by giving tokens only some of the time for correct tool use. Sometimes his father had friends over who delivered the tokens, so that Reg became used to dealing with other people. Sometimes Reg's father would delay reinforcer delivery to increase its effectiveness. Nevertheless, when Reg began his job and discovered that tokens were not used in the sheltered workshop, his newly learned skills did not generalize.

4. Lyn was learning to be more assertive on the telephone. Her teachers, who answered her calls, responded appropriately and praised her if Lyn's requests were assertive. The teachers were careful always to praise behavior that was likely to work well in the natural environment, and the natural reinforcers of Lyn's receiving information and praise seemed effective. Unfortunately, when Lyn called the local library, a travel agent, and a theatre box office, the people who answered the phone were rude and unresponsive. Lyn's newly learned assertiveness was quickly lost.

5. Ruth, a developmentally delayed child, was about to start private school. Her mother wanted Ruth to have good dining skills before she left for school. Her mother worked as an etiquette consultant and knew all about the correct utensils, setting a proper table, and so forth. She used behavioral principles to train Ruth about which fork was the shellfish fork and which was the pickle fork, for example. Ruth's mother often invited friends for dinner so Ruth could practice her new skills with other people around. Intermittent reinforcement was used and the natural reinforcers of praise for appropriate dining behavior seemed effective. When Ruth left for school she discovered at lunch that only one glass, one fork, and one spoon were set. Her newly learned sophisticated dining skills did not help much at school.

6. At the Sunny Vale Day-Care Center, the teachers were working on teaching the children social skills such as using "please" when asking for something and saying "thank you" when something was given. The teachers enlisted the aid of the children's parents. At the center, each time a child spoke appropriately, he or she would be awarded a token that could be traded in for a variety of special toys and privileges. Every two days, the children were gathered together and a token trade was conducted. The parents kept track of the behavior of their children when they were at home. Early in the training, continuous reinforcement was used, but later intermittent reinforcement was used to ensure behavior persistence. The parents were delighted to report that polite behavior seemed to generalize when the children were

at home. At the Happy Days Day-Care Center a similar training program was in effect. But at this center the tokens were traded in at the end of each day-care day. The polite behavior of these children increased during the day at the day care center but not at home as much as had been the case with the Sunny Vale Center.

7. Ruth and Elsa were two adult sisters who lived together. Ruth was studying behavior principles at the extension department at a nearby university and decided to use her sister as her subject for her course project. Elsa had several behaviors that annoyed Ruth. Elsa was very forgetful. She would forget to do her share of the chores, would forget items she was supposed to buy at the grocery store, would forget her keys when she left the house and so on. Ruth decided to work on Elsa's forgetfulness when she went shopping. Ruth would make a grocery list for Elsa each week and Elsa was supposed to check off each item at the store. If Elsa returned with all the items, Ruth praised her competent behavior. This plan worked well for grocery shopping, but Elsa's "remembering behavior" did not seem to generalize to other areas. Ruth had been careful to use the natural reinforcer of praise, to begin with continuous reinforcement, and later to use intermittent reinforcement. Ruth had hoped that Elsa would start to use lists to help her remember other things but this didn't happen.

8. Jennifer, a 5-year-old who was soon to start kindergarten, had a few problems still with toilet accidents. Her mother decided to work on this problem so that Jennifer could start school without any embarrassing accidents. Her mother enlisted the aid of friends, Jennifer's dad, and her brother. When Jennifer needed to use the toilet, she asked permission and whoever was around would praise her and hug her immediately after she returned. Jennifer's mother did this to make the home situation similar to what Jennifer would experience in school. In addition, at the end of the day without accidents, the family would gather together and applaud her, something she seemed to really enjoy. When Jennifer started kindergarten, her family would check with the teacher to see whether any accidents had happened during the day. If none had, they would get together and applaud her when she came home from school. Jennifer was in quite a large class of 20 students, and the teacher didn't have time to praise and hug each child when they returned from the bathroom. Jennifer's mother was disappointed to find that her toilet behavior did not generalize very well at kindergarten.

9. Billie had a problem with stuttering and was enrolled in a special class for children with these problems. Several teachers worked with each child to train fluent speech. Each time a child made a fluent utterance that was a complete sentence, request, question, or response, the teacher would award tokens. The teachers used continuous reinforcement at first, and later used intermittent reinforcement. The teachers tested for generalization by having the children use the telephone to call the local library and request information. After the generalization session, the children were allowed to trade in the tokens they had earned for a variety of special treats. Although the children did well during training, very few of them were able to be fluent on the telephone.

10

Modeling

Allan Hayduk faced a tremendous challenge in his first year as a junior high school teacher. He was assigned to teach math and science in a special program designed for students with serious behavior problems. Some of these students had learning disabilities; some were extremely disruptive and aggressive; many had problems at home, and several had had run-ins with the police. The students were so difficult that many teachers and administrators at the school saw the special program as a mere holding tank. They doubted whether any of these students would ever be able to function in a regular classroom situation. The teacher turnover in the special program was high and the dedicated few who stuck with it found the job extremely taxing.

Despite the potential problems, Allan anticipated his first year in teaching to be a challenge. As an undergraduate, Allan had learned about behavior analysis principles and he looked forward to an opportunity to apply these methods. While teaching, he was also learning more about behavior principles, working full-time on a master's degree in educational psychology.

Allan did not have to wait long to get a chance to use behavioral procedures. Early in the school year, many students in the special education program had become discipline problems, engaging in high rates of aggressive behavior and disruptive behavior. Allan realized that unless he was able to reduce these behaviors, the students were unlikely to learn anything worthwhile in his classroom, and, in his own eyes, he would have failed as a teacher. He had been reinforcing desirable behaviors from the first day of school, but this alone had not been completely successful. He also considered using DRO, but because he was working alone with a rather large class and many problem students, he was unable to use a stopwatch to time the behaviors of individual students, as is necessary when using DRO. Allan did not want to resort to punishment, but eventually he did turn to a timeout procedure: He made 10 minutes of timeout dependent on instances of aggressive and disruptive behavior. However, as the baseline data shown in Figure 10.1 illustrate, this was not entirely successful. Among the three worst problem students in the class, outbursts of aggression and disruption occurred several times a day.

At this point, Allan thought he might have to use stronger aversive control methods to maintain order in his classroom. However, as an undergraduate student, Allan had read a book on modeling, which is generally concerned with why and how people come to imitate each other's behavior. He decided that a modeling procedure might be worth trying to stem the tide of aggressive outbursts that threatened to overwhelm his classroom.

To illustrate this method, let's take a detailed look at an event that happened one day in Allan's classroom. John came into class late and slammed his books down on his desk. Then he turned and knocked another student's books from his desk, swearing at the student he had victimized. John then picked up one of the books and sat at his desk with it.

"Can you think of a better way to have handled that?" Allan asked calmly.

"Yes," John replied.

"OK," Allan said, "but before we do it the better way, I'd like you to go back out the door, then come in, and do it again the way you just did." John complied, but performed the actions in a calmer manner this time. Allan then turned to Mike, who was the most popular boy in the class. Although Mike was frequently aggressive and disruptive himself, he held considerable influence with the other students.

"Mike," Allan asked, "if you were the teacher, how would you feel about that?"

"Dumb man, that was pretty dumb," Mike replied. Allan then turned back to John.

"OK, now let's see you do it your better way," Allan told John. John then left the room and returned calmly.

"Gimmie my book or I'll get you at lunch," John told the student he had previously victimized. The student then gave John the book.

"Mike," Allan asked "if you were the teacher, how would you feel about that?" Mike gave a thumbs up sign, approving of the new way of handling the problem. The class resumed. Although Allan thought John's "better way" of handling the problem was far from perfect, the solution was, nonetheless, better than the original behavior. The procedure had taken only 3 minutes to implement.

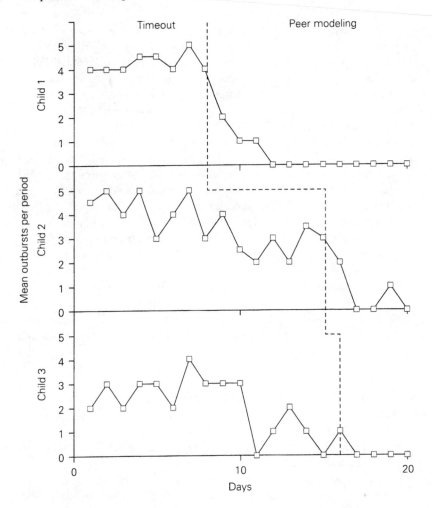

Figure 10.1   *The Influence of Timeout and Peer Modeling on the Reduction of Disruptive Classroom Behaviors*

Ten-minute timeouts produced little reduction in classroom outbursts. The peer modeling procedure was much more effective in eliminating outbursts. Data are displayed from the three most disruptive students in the class. Figure adapted from Hayduk (1978).

Allan's method was to ask the student to reenact instances of disruptive behavior, first as it had originally occurred and then changing the behavior to a more socially acceptable form. By practicing a better way to solve the problem, the student was also modeling appropriate behavior for the rest of the class. Asking Mike, an influential, high-status student, for feedback was a masterstroke. Mike's disapproval of the inappropriate behavior and his approval of the better way would have more impact on his fellow students than any feedback Allan could have given.

On occasion, variations to this basic plan occurred. Sometimes the high-status student suggested that the better way of behaving could have been better still, and in these cases the misbehaving student would behave as Mike suggested. When the misbehaving student could not think of a better way to behave Allan turned to the class for suggestions, and a high-status student modeled the alternative behavior suggested by the class.

You may be thinking that the method wouldn't work if a misbehaving student refused to model a better way of behaving when asked to do so. And, in fact, this was a problem in the beginning. Students typically ignored Allan's request to model a better way of behaving or they became even more hostile. Fortunately, Allan had anticipated this possibility and had a back-up plan. When a misbehaving student refused to model a desirable behavior, a same-gender high-status student was asked to model both the inappropriate aggressive act and an appropriate alternative behavior. Then, the next highest status student of the same gender was asked to comment on the inappropriate behavior and on the alternative behavior. Finally the student who had originally misbehaved was invited to model the better way. Allan found that about as many students accepted this invitation as declined. After this modeling, the class resumed its ongoing activities.

The effectiveness of the procedure is illustrated in Figure 10.1. As shown, the procedure was first used with Student 1, and later used with Student 2 and Student 3. As you can see, when the procedure was used with Student 1, the aggressive behaviors of Students 2 and 3 tended to be reduced as well. These students had the opportunity to observe Student 1 receiving disapproval for inappropriate behavior and approval for modeling a better way of handling the situation. Observation alone served to improve their own behavior. These types of modeling effects, in which the behaviors of the observers are strengthened and weakened simply by observing applications of reinforcers and punishers, are called *vicarious reinforcement* and *vicarious punishment*. Vicarious punishment effects are seen when an observer's behavior is weakened after observing the punishment of a model's behavior. Vicarious reinforcement effects are seen when an observer's behavior is strengthened after observing the reinforcement of a model's behavior.

Allan's modeling strategy was also highly successful with the other five problem students in his class. In only a matter of days, their aggressive behavior was eliminated. Happily the improvements the students achieved in Allan's classroom generalized to their other classes and their home environment as well. Other teachers reported that the behavior of the students was generally improved in their classrooms. Mothers of two of the students remarked that they were much better behaved at home; they seemed to think more carefully about what they were doing instead of "flying off at the handle." The school principal was so impressed with Allan's work that he wrote him a note thanking him for introducing behavioral principles at the school.

Three months later the students continued to demonstrate less aggressive, better ways of behaving. Because of their special problems, learning remained a challenge for many of Allan's students, but the positive, nonpunitive nature of the classroom environment he created gave them opportunities to develop many of the skills they would need to lead successful and productive lives.*

Modeling and Its Advantages

Modeling occurs when one person, the model, performs a behavior, and this performance prompts imitation of that behavior by another person, the observer. As discussed in Chapter 8, the behavior the model engages in is called a *modeling prompt.* Modeling is a stimulus control procedure. The behavior of the model acts as an S+, a discriminative stimulus, for the observer's imitation of the modeled response.

Another term used to describe part of the modeling process is *behavior rehearsal* or simply *rehearsal,* which means to engage repeatedly in a behavior. Normally the purpose of rehearsal is to ensure that the behavior is well-learned. In some types of modeling, it is desirable for the learner to rehearse the modeled response, to continue to perform the imitative response. For example, consider a child who is afraid to dive from a diving board. Modeling the behavior might induce the child to imitate, but it would be desirable for the child to continue to dive several times to replace fully the negative emotional reactions with positive ones.

Modeling has a powerful influence on our behavior. We began this book with the proposition that "We are what we do." Research dealing with the effect of models on behavior indicates that there is also a great deal of truth to the proposition that "We are what we observe." Modeling research indicates that through observation, we acquire the capacity to engage in new forms of behavior, and that we are more likely to engage in behaviors that we have observed.

Much of our knowledge of modeling processes is due to the work of Dr. Albert Bandura, who initiated an extensive program of research in modeling processes during the early 1960s (see Bandura [1969] for coverage of this initial work). Although Dr. Bandura is not a behavior analyst, his work in modeling has influenced many behavior analysts, who share Dr. Bandura's interests in the many practical uses of modeling in teaching skills and altering behaviors.

Modeling is an excellent way to teach new behavior. Of course, shaping can teach new behavior through reinforcement of responses that are more and more like the desired behavior. Shaping is effective but progress can be slow. Modeling, on the other hand, can produce rapid gains: It may take only one modeled instance to learn a behavior. The use of modeling to teach new behavior is therefore sometimes called one-trial learning. Like errorless learning techniques, modeling often has the advantage of allowing the learner to acquire new responses without errors.

Modeling has another advantage: It is a natural method of teaching that occurs regularly in our everyday lives. Through modeling, parents teach their children such things as being honest, handling adversity with logic and reason, and ultimately,

*Based on Hayduk (1978)

how to raise children. Parents, by their examples, teach their children an enormous number of behaviors. We all have the potential to act as models. Any behavior we engage in may be imitated by others. Modeling is one of the major ways by which a society passes on its practices, both good and bad, to successive generations.

Modeling procedures have been used to solve many behavioral problems. Modeling has been used to teach verbal behavior, to teach a wide variety of self-care skills, to reduce unreasonable fears, to improve communication, to prepare children for stressful medical and dental procedures, to promote academic activities, and to promote better employee performance. As you can see, modeling is not just a procedure for training unruly children.

A key advantage of modeling as a behavior modification procedure is that it naturally specifies desirable behaviors to be emulated, and therefore represents a constructional approach to behavior change. When using modeling, it is necessary to define desirable behaviors that are worth engaging in. The world would certainly be a better place if, every time anyone used punishment, that person would at least also use modeling to demonstrate an acceptable alternative to the punished behavior. Note how Allan Hayduk used modeling in this fashion.

Modeling is not a simple matter of two people behaving in similar ways. To qualify as an instance of modeling, the observer must not only engage in behavior like that of the model, but this behavior must be *functionally controlled* by the model's behavior. By that, we mean that the behavior of the observer is due to past reinforcers for imitation, not to other factors. For example, a police officer in pursuit of a fleeing thief is not modeling the running behavior of the thief. The thief's running behavior is not an S+ for imitative running by the police officer, but an S+ for apprehending the thief. In the same vein, when people awaiting their bus all look down the road in anticipation of its arrival, they are not imitating each other to any great extent. Their common behavior is due to the stimulus control of the location from which the bus will appear, not each other's behavior.

Disadvantages of Modeling

Because people often fail to realize how influential their behavior is on others, they underestimate the effects they have when they behave in undesirable ways. Every time an undesirable behavior is modeled, there is a chance that it will be imitated. Parents and educators can serve as models of desirable behaviors, but cannot realistically prevent children from observing models performing undesirable acts. Other procedures, such as discrimination training, must be used to induce learners to distinguish between desirable and undesirable models.

The effects of modeled aggression on observers should be a concern of everyone who wishes to live in a safe society. More than ever before, children, as well as adults, are exposed to acts of violence. This increase in the amount of aggression and violence we see is due largely to the increasing availability of visual mass media, notably television and films, where these behaviors are frequently portrayed. Does the aggression children see on television and in films cause them to be more violent and aggressive? This is the question that four researchers, Jacques-Philippe Leyens, Leoncio Camino, Ross Parke, and Leonard Berkowitz, wanted to answer.

To conduct their investigation, the research team selected a private high school in Belgium for boys with family or school problems and boys who had encountered problems with the law. The school was a good place to study the effects of media violence because the boys lived at the school and their access to television and films was regulated. Generally, the students were allowed to watch only news, sports, and some musical television programs.

The first week of the study was a baseline period during which the students' aggressive behaviors were measured during daily observation periods. The experimenters identified and measured several different categories of aggressive behavior, including physical threats (e.g., shaking a fist at someone else), physical attacks on others that caused pain, and verbal aggression (e.g., cursing at another person). During the second week of the study, the boys in two of the four residential cottages at the school watched violent films, while the boys in the other two cottages watched nonviolent films. The violent films included *Bonnie and Clyde* and *The Dirty Dozen*. The nonviolent films, which were comedies, included *Alexandre le Bienheureux* and *Daddy's Fiancee*. After viewing the films, the boys in both groups rated the films on several dimensions, finding the violent and nonviolent films equally interesting and exciting. They rated the violent films as more brutal, violent, aggressive, and cruel than the nonviolent films, which they rated as funnier than the violent films.

As soon as the violent films were shown, several types of aggressive behavior suddenly increased, including physical aggression. As shown in Figure 10.2, there was little difference between the groups in physical aggression before the films were shown, but after the films were introduced, the group who watched them engaged in much more physical aggression than the group who watched the comedies. This aggression continued during the observation periods over the days when the violent films were shown.

Aside from the main result of the study, the researchers reported three other effects they observed. First, they noticed that the specific types of aggressive behavior the boys engaged in were often identical to the acts shown in the films. Second, there was also some indication that the increase in aggression persisted for at least a week after the violent films were no longer shown. In particular, boys in one of the cottages continued to aggress against one another verbally during the week after they had ceased viewing the violent films. And third, the researchers were surprised to learn that in one of the cottages where the residents saw nonviolent films, some types of aggression, particularly verbal aggression decreased. The researchers speculated that the reason for this finding was that the heroes in the nonviolent films modeled nonviolent forms of conduct.

This study demonstrates that modeling can result in the imitation of undesirable as well as desirable behavior. It is important that we all recognize that our behavior can have a negative as well as a positive influence on the behavior of those around us. People in positions of authority, in particular, must take special care in modeling desirable behavior to those they influence.

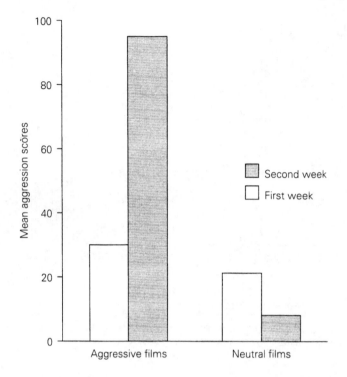

Figure 10.2   *The Effect of Aggressive and Nonaggressive Film Models on Viewer Aggression*

During the week before watching the films (i.e., "first week"), there was little difference in the physical aggression of the boys in the aggressive and neutral film groups. During the week when the films were viewed (i.e., "second week"), aggression increased substantially in the group that watched the aggressive films and declined in the group that watched the neutral films. Figure adapted from Leyens, Camino, Parke, and Berkowitz (1975).

A near-tragic event in which inappropriate behavior was modeled and imitated happened in September of 1975. On the fifth of that month, Lynette Fromme attempted to kill President Gerald Ford. Only 17 days later, on September 22, another woman, Sara Jane Moore, also attempted to kill President Ford. Because Fromme was the first woman ever to attempt to assassinate a U. S. President, it seems likely that she served as a model for Moore. It also seems likely that the violence that both these women modeled influenced many other people as well. The Secret Service records for that period show a large increase in the number of threats against the life of President Ford immediately after the September assassination attempts (Simon, 1979). These data are shown in Figure 10.3.

The people who threatened President Ford were not imitating the assassination attempts. But the models' behavior of aggression with weapons appears to have caused imitation of the *aggressive feature* of the behavior. Simon's data strongly suggest that the modeling of aggression with weapons caused people to engage in verbal aggression against the president.

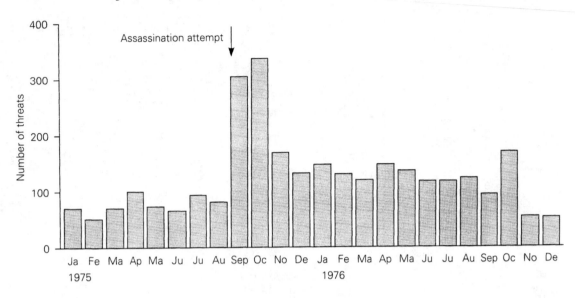

Figure 10.3   *The Influence of a Well-Publicized Act of Aggression on Aggressive Imitation*

After Fromme's assassination attempt on President Ford, the number of threats on his life increased substantially. Drawn from Simón's (1979) data.

Research in the modeling of aggression and other inappropriate forms of conduct, of which the studies we have examined are only a small part, clearly indicates that inappropriate models promote inappropriate behavior in observers. We are not suggesting that every time aggression is modeled, all observers will be compelled to engage in acts of aggression against others. Although modeling is a powerful influence on our behavior, it is only one of many. Nevertheless, research shows that aggression can breed aggression and undesirable behavior can breed more undesirable behavior.

We all can help to improve the human condition by heeding the research in modeling, which shows that aggression can be reduced in at least two ways. First, people's behavior will be improved by increasing people's, especially children's, exposure to admirable and interesting models who are rewarded for interacting with others in an intelligent and nonaggressive fashion. Second, by reducing people's exposure to violent and aggressive models, especially when they are presented heroically and are rewarded for their aggression, people will be less likely to engage in acts of violence and aggression.

Types of Modeling

Among the types of modeling processes are exact imitation and behavior-feature imitation, vicarious modeling processes, generalized imitation, observational learning, peer modeling, covert modeling, self-modeling, participant modeling, and symbolic modeling.

Exact Imitation and Behavior-Feature Imitation

When people think of imitation, the most familiar examples that come to mind are ones in which there is exact imitation of the modeled response, when the observer's behavior is identical to the model's. Modeling processes, however, include imitation of *features* or *properties* of behavior as well as exact imitation. As we have discussed in earlier chapters, behavior is composed of a wide variety of properties or features.

For example, consider the simple response of uttering a sentence. The words in the utterance will be said at a certain rate such as rapidly or slowly. The sentence will have a duration, the total time the utterance takes. The utterance will have a certain pitch, volume, and a variety of other sound properties associated with the speaker's voice. The utterance will have certain grammatical properties such as a subject, a verb, and agreement or disagreement between them. The utterance will have certain emotional and psychological properties: It can be warm or hostile, sophisticated or crude. It is possible for a listener to imitate the exact utterance, matching all the features of the speaker's sentence. However, it is also possible for a listener to imitate various individual features of the utterance without imitating it exactly. For example, a skilled mimic might attend to the speaker's accent, and imitate this feature of the response. Someone else might be influenced through modeling to imitate other features of the utterance, such as its rate or loudness. And others might imitate the emotional warmth or coolness of the utterance. Imitation of specific properties or features of a behavior are examples of modeling, even though they are not examples of exact imitations. When only some of the properties of the model's behavior are imitated, we call this *behavior-feature* imitation. In contrast, when all of the features of the model's behavior are imitated, *exact imitation* occurs.

An example of behavior-feature imitation was Simon's study of the imitation of aggression against President Ford. Clearly, the people who threatened the president were not imitating the specific acts of the assassins. However, Simon's data strongly suggest that those who threatened the president imitated the *aggressive feature* of the models' behaviors.

Behavior-feature imitation can occur even when the modeled response and the imitative response do not share any topographical properties. For example, Harris and Evans (1974) studied the effects of modeling creative responses on university students. Psychologists usually measure divergent behavior, unusual or atypical responding, as an indication of creative behavior. One of the tasks the students were given was to identify uses for a paper cup. For one group of students, "convergent" responses were modeled: The students examined a list of 20 responses to the task that all involved using the cup in its usual way; to hold things (e.g., to hold bobby pins, plants, or juice.). Another group of students examined a list of 20 "divergent" (i.e., creative) responses that consisted of more unusual uses (e.g., as a base for a beehive hairdo, as a base for Christmas bell ornaments, or as building blocks). For a third control group, no modeled responses were provided. Data from the study indicated that (a) the divergent group gave more divergent responses than the convergent and control groups, and (b) the convergent group gave more convergent responses than the other two groups. This study illustrates that modeling can encourage a feature of creative behavior, behavioral divergency. This modeling of the divergent feature of behavior illustrates that behavior-feature modeling can occur even when the imitative responses are defined by their dissimilarity to the modeled responses.

The distinction between behavior-feature imitation and exact imitation is very important, because behavior-feature imitation can account for a great deal of learning, especially language learning by children, while exact imitation cannot. For example, a child saying the word "throwed" for the first time is rarely an example of exact imitation, because "throwed" is an incorrect response uttered only by children who are learning the language; children are clearly not imitating others when they say "throwed." However, Kymissis and Poulson (1990) point out that when a child says "throwed" for the first time, this utterance can nonetheless be explained through behavior-feature imitation. Children can learn the verb "throw" through imitation, and they can also learn the behavior-feature "ed" ending through imitation. When the child says "throwed," as a result of the separate imitation learning of "throw" and "ed," this utterance can be a form of imitation learning. This pattern of behavior-feature imitation is a key means of language learning in children, because it enables children both to learn through imitation and to recombine behavior features to form novel responses. (According to this analysis, behavior-feature imitation may be the basis for response generalizations in children's language learning, as discussed in Chapter 9.)

Vicarious Processes

As we have seen, in the most basic form of modeling, the modeled behavior acts as an S+ for the observer's behavior of imitating the modeled response or some feature of it. Vicarious reinforcement and punishment follow this basic pattern, but are also concerned with the additional influences of observing the *consequences* for the model's behavior on the likelihood that the model will be imitated. In *vicarious reinforcement*, rewarding consequences follow the model's behavior and make observers more likely to imitate the behavior than if the behavior had been modeled without the rewarding consequences. In *vicarious punishment*, punitive consequences follow the model's behavior and make observers less likely to imitate the behavior than if the behavior had been modeled without the punitive consequences.

Vicarious reinforcement and vicarious punishment appeared to be at work in Hayduk's (1978) study that introduced this chapter. You may recall that Allan had a high-status peer disapprove of the undesirable aggressive behavior and approve of the desirable alternative to aggression. The other students observed this and appeared to have been influenced by it because their aggressive behavior weakened and desirable behavior strengthened.

Bandura (1965) studied the effects of both vicarious reinforcement and punishment on the behavior of nursery school children. The children watched a 5-minute film in which a man, an aggressive model, pummeled, kicked, and threw balls at a life-sized bobo doll (a plastic inflatable doll often used to study aggression in children). When struck, the bobo doll bounces back up to be struck again, providing opportunities for repeated aggression. For children in a vicarious reinforcement group, the film ended with another man appearing on the scene with candy and soda pop. The man with the treats told the model that he was a "strong champion," and that he deserved the candy and soda pop he was then given. For children in a vicarious punishment group, the film ended with a man appearing on the scene who reprimanded the aggressive model. The model was told that he was a bully and that his behavior would not be tolerated. The man who had delivered these reprimands then spanked the model with a rolled-up magazine. For children in a control group, the film ended right after the model had attacked the bobo doll.

After viewing the film, the children went to a playroom with a bobo doll. The results of the study, illustrated in Figure 10.4, showed that the children in the vicari-

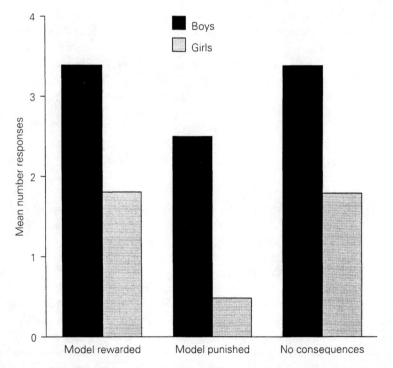

Figure 10.4   *The Influence of Punishing a Model's Aggression on Imitation of Aggression*

Imitative aggression was more frequent when the model's aggression was rewarded or there were no consequences for aggression than when the model's aggression was punished. Figure adapted from Bandura (1965).

ous reinforcement group and control groups engaged in imitative aggression against the bobo doll more often than those in the vicarious punishment group. This effect was more pronounced among the girls than the boys.

Bandura's study illustrates a vicarious punishment effect because the vicarious punishment group imitated the aggression less often than the control group. Vicarious reinforcement was not seen in this study because the vicarious reinforcement group did not engage in imitative aggression more often than the control group.

When first learning of vicarious reinforcement and punishment, many students have difficulty understanding these concepts because they have previously learned that reinforcement and punishment are means of altering behavior through the use of response-dependent consequences. But in vicarious reinforcement and punishment, consequences are not dependent on the behavior of the observer whose behavior is altered. In addition, in order to qualify as an example of vicarious reinforcement or punishment, the model's behavior does not have to be altered; all that is required is that the model receives some consequence that is generally considered desirable or undesirable.

The answer to this puzzle of vicarious reinforcement and punishment is that, in fact, vicarious reinforcement and punishment are not forms of reinforcement and punishment at all, but forms of stimulus control. In vicarious reinforcement, the model's behavior and the reward for it act as an S+ for imitative responding by an observer. In vicarious punishment, the model's behavior and the aversive event that follows it act as an S− for the observer's imitative responding.

In studies of vicarious reinforcement and punishment, there is not normally an attempt to determine if the consequences for the models' behavior do indeed strengthen or weaken that behavior. Recall from Chapters 2 and 4 that to use the terms *reinforcement* and *punishment* correctly, we must demonstrate a strengthening or weakening effect on behavior. As such, the terms vicarious reinforcement and punishment are often used incorrectly because of the absence of a demonstrated reinforcing or punishing effect on the behavior of the model. It would be better to call vicarious reinforcement and punishment vicarious reward and vicarious penalty: The terms reward and penalty are nontechnical terms and do not require a demonstration of a change in some measure or aspect of behavior, as the terms reinforcement and punishment require. However, the labels vicarious reinforcement and punishment have been used for so long they have become accepted.

How are the S+s and S−s in vicarious reinforcement and punishment established? Observing someone else receive a reward for a behavior is often a cue that if you also engage in the behavior, your behavior will also be reinforced. For example, if we see others engaging in an rewarding activity, the chances are that if we join it and engage in the same activity, it will also be rewarding for us; at least this happens much of the time. Similarly, observing punishment of someone else's behavior is often a stimulus situation in which your behavior will also be punished should you engage in that same response. The stimulus situations involved in vicarious reinforcement and punishment have therefore been established as S+s and S−s for imitative behavior in a way much like other discriminative stimuli are established: by reinforcing a response in the presence of the S+ and by extinguishing or punishing a response in the presence of an S–. The only difference is that the S+ and the S– are more complex, consisting of a model's behavior and the consequences of that behavior.

Research has shown that the response-altering effects of vicarious reinforcement are stimulus-control effects that differ from the effects of standard reinforcement. Ollendick and Shapiro (1984) and Deguchi, Fujita, and Sato (1988) showed that vicarious reinforcement elevated children's responding for only a brief time. Deguchi et al. (1988) found that direct reinforcement was necessary to maintain the children's performance. Ollendick and Shapiro found that an additional problem with vicarious reinforcement was that the observer child began engaging in behaviors that interfered with task performance. For example, the children would sometimes call out, "Hey, I can do them too," and, "Look at mine," when the model's response was repeatedly reinforced without also reinforcing the observer child's responding. As you can see, there can be problems if you depend solely on vicarious reinforcement for an extended period.

Vicarious reinforcement, by itself, cannot ordinarily be expected to maintain behavior for more than a brief period of time without some use of direct reinforcement. However, sometimes vicarious reinforcement can be useful even though its effects are temporary. For example, Mansdorf (1977) established a token economy by first training a retarded woman to comply with requests to perform low-frequency behaviors by making tokens dependent on those behaviors. The tokens could be exchanged for candy. Later, this woman served as a model for other residents at the institution, who observed her behavior being reinforced with tokens. Subsequently, the token economy was rapidly introduced because the observers were willing to comply with staff requests as a result of observing the model woman's behavior be reinforced with tokens. Darch, Carnine, and Gersten (1984) used vicarious reinforcement to improve attentive student behaviors. When a student was not paying attention to the teacher, the teacher reinforced other students who were doing so. When the nonattending student began paying attention, the teacher began directly reinforcing the behavior of that student.

Another vicarious process is called *vicarious helplessness*. As described in Chapter 5, learned helplessness is the impairment of performance at a task, due to a history of response-independent aversive consequences. Vicarious helplessness occurs when observing the behavior of a model who encounters response-independent aversive consequences causes an impairment in the observer's behavior. For example, DeVellis, De Vellis, and McCauley (1978) had female university students watch other model students engage in a button-pushing avoidance task. One group of women watched the models engage in the task in which loss of money was dependent on the absence of the correct response, a particular sequence of button pushing. Another group of women watched the models engage in the same task, but token loss occurred independently of responding. A third group, a control group, did not receive any training. Following training, women in all three groups who had previously observed their models' behavior worked at a manual avoidance task in which token loss was dependent on the absence of correct responses.

Results of the study showed that the women who had observed models experience response-independent token loss performed more poorly than women who had observed models experience response-dependent token loss or women who did not observe any models. Essentially, observing models encounter response-independent aversive consequences disrupted the women's performance on a subsequent task in which the women could successfully avoid the aversive consequences.

More broadly, the vicarious helplessness data suggest that there can be times when our own behavior is impaired when we see a helpless model encounter response-independent consequences. Levine (1977) has shown that when people watch television news broadcasts, they observe many instances in which people encounter consequences that are largely response independent. In a survey of evening network newscasts on NBC and CBS, she rated the degree to which people encountered "helplessness," consisting largely of response-independent aversive consequences (e.g., airplane crashes, earthquakes, abused infants, innocent crime victims) and found that over 71% of the broadcasts were devoted to coverage of events in which there was some degree of helplessness. Exactly what effect this has on our own behavior is currently a matter of speculation.

Generalized Imitation and Observational Learning

Another type of imitation that is of great value in teaching is called generalized imitation. Generalized imitation occurs when an observer can imitate many different kinds of new behaviors demonstrated by a model without specific training and without reinforcers dependent on each instance of imitation. Generalized imitation is important in learning because once a learner achieves generalized imitation, it is possible for her to learn a vast array of new behaviors simply by having a model demonstrate those behaviors. For example, you may not know how to solder a joint in metal pipe, but with the proper materials and a good model, a single demonstration would probably be sufficient to enable you to perform this task. You are able to do so because like most people you have a *generalized imitative repertoire,* meaning that you can imitate a large range of behaviors you have never engaged in before, simply by observing someone else.

Although we take our generalized imitative repertoire largely for granted, it is something that must be learned. In a classic study, Baer, Peterson, and Sherman (1967) trained generalized imitation in three severely retarded children aged between 9 and 12 years, including a 12-year-old girl named Marilla. Marilla could follow some simple commands, but did not imitate the actions of others. Many people at the institution where she lived considered her incapable of learning.

At first, training consisted of the experimenter telling Marilla to "Do this," demonstrating a behavior, and seeing if she would imitate the act. This procedure was unsuccessful, so the experimenters turned to shaping and faded physical prompting procedures to induce her to engage in a simple imitative response, arm raising. After Marilla had learned to imitate arm-raising, she was trained to imitate other responses, including table-tapping, chest-tapping, head-tapping, knee-tapping, and nose-tapping. Each of these responses was trained using shaping and faded physical prompting, but with each new behavior, less and less shaping and prompting was required. Finally, when the experimenter told Marilla, "Do this," and tapped the arm of his chair, Marilla also tapped the arm of her chair, imitating the modeled response. This act of imitation is called an instance of *generalized imitation*, because tapping the arm of the chair was an imitative response that had not been previously trained. The training Marilla had received to imitate the other responses had generalized to a new imitative response.

Marilla was given additional training that enabled her to imitate other responses. By the time she had learned 130 imitative responses, she could imitate each new response that was modeled for her. Following shaping of vocal responses, Marilla went on to learn 10 words, including "Hi," "OK," and "Marilla," through the use of modeling techniques. (See Whaley and Malott [1971] for additional information about this study.)

More recently, generalized imitation has been demonstrated in infants. Poulson, Kymissis, Reeve, Andreatos, and Reeve (1991) trained generalized vocal imitation in three infants between 9 and 12 months old. During a baseline period, the infants' parents modeled sounds and the frequency of the infants' imitative and nonimitative responding was measured. During training, the infants' parent continued to model sounds by saying, "[Infant's name], can you say [modeled sound]?" The sounds the parents modeled were divided into training sounds (e.g., *buh*) and test sounds *(dah)*. If an infant imitated a training sound, she was praised (e.g., "Good baby, you said buh"), but no consequences were dependent on imitation of test sounds. After several sessions, the training procedure produced generalized imitation: Each of the children was able to imitate modeled test sounds not previously reinforced. Training the infants to imitate the training sounds had generalized to the test sounds. These researchers suggest that parents and others could use this procedure to accelerate vocal imitation in infants, an especially useful outcome for children who are at risk for language-learning problems.

When generalized imitation has been achieved, many new modeled behaviors can be imitated. When new behaviors are learned as a result of merely observing a model engage in them, *observational learning* has occurred. One feature of observational learning is that it is possible for *learning* to take place through observation on one occasion, but not be demonstrated in observable *behavior* for some time after observation has taken place. This is sometimes called *deferred imitation*. For example, Meltzoff (1988) modeled different types of play behaviors to 14-month-old infants. Each of the modeled behaviors had never been engaged in before by the infants. A week after the behaviors were modeled, the infants were given the play materials and were able to perform the modeled behaviors more often than control infants who did not observe the modeled behaviors.

Peer Modeling

Often modeling procedures make use of an expert model who is distinguished from the learners by skill level or age. A simple example is a mathematics teacher demonstrating how to solve a long division problem. The teacher is distinguished from the students by skill level, age, and status. However, often models are peers, people who are equal in skills, age, or status. When peers serve as models for imitative behavior, peer modeling occurs.

Peer modeling begins to occur at a young age and is a powerful social influence. Many parents and teachers often wish they had as much influence on children as peers do. However, with some imagination, it is possible to put the power of peer influences to work through modeling. For example, in the introduction to this chapter, we saw how Allan Hayduk made use of the power of peer modeling to teach his class to engage in socially acceptable alternatives to aggression.

Birch (1980) also recognized the power of peer modeling and put this influence to work to change preschoolers' food preferences. As parents know, food preferences in young children can be very resistant to change, but what would happen if this resistance was countered by peer modeling influences?

At first, the children were observed to determine their food preferences. Peer modeling took place at lunch. A "target" child who strongly enjoyed one type of vegetable (e.g., beets) and disliked another type (e.g., broccoli) was seated with three or four other children who had the opposite vegetable preferences and who served as peer models for the target child. This seating arrangement was in effect for 4 consecutive weekdays. On the first day, the target child selected her vegetables first. On the other three days, the model children made their selections first. The study took place over a 9 week period, during which children who were target children during some weeks would act as models during other weeks. The results of the study showed that the peer modeling procedure reversed the target children's food preferences. By the 4th day of a given week, the target children were choosing and consuming the vegetable they had initially disliked.

The effectiveness of peer modeling suggests that it is highly desirable for us to have opportunities to observe peers who are skilled, especially in areas in which we are deficient. For example, peer modeling influences suggest that it is desirable for retarded children to be able to observe the academic skills of average children (e.g., Egel, Richman, & Koegel, 1981; Barry & Overmann, 1977). The effectiveness of peer modeling has therefore become one of the arguments in favor of *mainstreaming*, a word that refers to the practice of placing retarded children in regular classrooms rather than in special classrooms.

More broadly, the effectiveness of modeling suggests that there are harmful consequences of isolating any group of people who are disadvantaged in some way because this prevents the learning of useful skills through modeling. For example, often the poor and the educationally disadvantaged live in isolated slums where they have limited opportunities to meet and observe skilled people. In this case, modeling influences suggest that it is desirable to plan neighborhoods in which disadvantaged people live together with wealthier and better educated peers.

Covert Modeling

The basic pattern of modeling consists of the model's performance, followed by the observer's imitation of the performance or some feature of it. A procedure called *covert modeling* is a variation of this pattern. Instead of actually watching a model engage in a behavior, the learner imagines a model performing a behavior.

In one of the first studies of covert modeling, Cautela, Flannery, and Hanley (1974) used the method to reduce the fears that 30 female university students had of laboratory rats. At first, none of the students could bring herself to hold a rat. Two managed to touch the rat, but ran out of the laboratory immediately afterward in a state of fear. One group of students given an *overt modeling* treatment watched the experimenter encounter a rat in six 2-minute scenes that had been scripted and rehearsed. In these scenes, the experimenter talked to the rat, let it wander out of its cage, and stroked and held the rat. A second group, given covert modeling, were asked to sit in a chair and vividly imagine scenes that the experimenter read to them. The scenes were descriptions of the same six 2-minute scenes the women watched in the overt modeling group. However, instead of actually watching, the covert modeling students imagined they were watching the scenes. Finally, a third group of students, a control group, discussed their fears of laboratory rats with the experimenter in an attempt to gain insight into the nature of their fears.

Following treatment, the students were tested to see if they would approach a real rat. Almost all the students who had received the modeling procedure, either overt or covert, could now stroke the previously feared rat. Over half the subjects who received modeling could now even hold a rat in their hands. Students in the control group, however, fared less well; only 3 of the 9 control students were able to stroke the rat and none was able to hold a rat. The effectiveness of the overt and covert modeling treatments did not differ. In this study, imagining the model engage in the behavior was as effective as watching a model.

Like overt modeling, covert modeling has been used in a variety of ways including assertiveness training, in which people who are normally not sufficiently assertive imagine others responding assertively in situations where it is appropriate to do so. One advantage of covert over overt modeling is that it is possible to engage in covert modeling at almost any time in situations where the use of overt modeling is not possible, such as riding in a bus or car. One possible disadvantage of covert modeling is that sometimes, with difficult-to-learn responses, it is necessary for the learner actually to engage in the modeled response in order to determine if it has been correctly imitated; covert modeling does not allow for this. Kazdin (1982c) found that a combination of covert modeling of assertive behaviors with overt rehearsal of the behaviors was more effective than either procedure by itself.

The extent to which people benefit from (or are disadvantaged by) covert modeling in informal day-to-day situations is unknown. However, in daydreams and other leaps of the imagination, we do conceive of all sorts of situations in which imaginary models behave in various ways, a process that occurs with rich detail among children (Winner, 1982). When we imagine admirable, heroic models, does it encourage similar future behavior on our part? Does imagining inappropriate models worsen our behavior? In any case, the data showing that covert modeling can be effective suggests that the realm of imagination is not an island within us, but is closely linked to what we actually do.

Self-Modeling

Advances in audiotape and videotape technology have given people opportunities to observe themselves in ways that were previously not possible. This has made *self-modeling* possible, a procedure in which an instance of a person's desirable behavior is taped and later replayed by that person, causing the individual to imitate her own behavior. Research has shown that self-modeling can be useful in improving performance.

For example, Dowrick and Hood (1981) showed the value of self-modeling in a study conducted at a sheltered workshop for young adults with moderate or severe physical handicaps. The workers were engaged in activities such as assembling cigar boxes. Videotapes of work performances in one group were made in which mistakes and hesitations in work were edited from the film. As a result, the edited videotaped showed the workers working at a rate six times more rapid than their normal pace. At midday, the workers watched the film, in which each worker was shown performing for 60 seconds. During the study, the group of workers who used self-modeling improved their assembly rates by 15%. In contrast, a group given cash bonuses for performance improvements improved their assembly rate by only 3%, while the assembly rate of a group that discussed their performance with the experimenter every day declined by 3%. A 4-month follow-up observation indicated that the self-modeling group continued to improve while the other two groups did not.

We see a widespread application of self-modeling in professional and amateur sports (Hosford, 1981). Athletes who seek to improve their performance often view their own desirable performances on videotapes in order to emulate these behaviors in the future. Self-modeling can be combined with covert modeling, such as a basketball player imagining herself shooting perfect free throws before actually attempting one in the game.

Participant Modeling

One type of modeling that has been used primarily to treat people with unreasonable fears is called *participant modeling*. In participant modeling, the modeled behavior is broken down into steps. At first, the model demonstrates a response the learner can engage in relatively easily, and the learner is required to do so. The model then demonstrates behaviors that are increasingly more difficult for the learner, who is prompted and encouraged to imitate the model's behavior at each stage of the process.

Speltz and Bernstein (1979) used participant modeling to treat a man who was afraid to be in enclosed spaces. It was believed that his claustrophobia began with a childhood asthma attack. He was extremely uncomfortable in elevators, shower stalls, and even under his bed covers, and he had a panic reaction when a scarf or mask was placed over his face.

The therapists first made up a list of 28 behaviors that ranged from very easy to very difficult. The least stressful behavior on the list was the man holding his hand over his mouth in a lighted room. The most stressful behavior was the man wearing a surgical mask while enclosed head-first in a zipped bag with his hands and feet tied. During therapy sessions, the desired responses were demonstrated and the man imitated the response, rehearsing the behavior several times before going on to the next behavior on the list. The man was also given homework assignments in which he continued to rehearse the modeled responses at home. If the man became uncomfortable at any point, he relaxed through deep breathing and repeated the last step he had successfully completed. The therapists encouraged imitative responding through the use of encouraging verbal prompts and gentle physical prompts. These prompts were faded as they were no longer required.

Eventually, these methods eliminated the man's fears of enclosed spaces and breathing restrictions. The man began enjoying his morning shower, and no longer panicked in the way he formerly had when the dentist used a rubber dam. Nearly 3 years after treatment, the man experienced no discomfort during tests using an enclosed chamber and an oxygen mask. He felt his problem was entirely solved.

Participant modeling is similar to shaping because in both procedures there is a gradual progression toward a goal response and because the learner's behavior is reinforced as it becomes more like the goal response. However, in participant modeling, the model demonstrates each required response at each step of the process; in shaping, the behavior analyst must wait until the desired behavior occurs. Essentially, participant modeling can be considered as a form of shaping in which modeling prompts are added to the shaping procedure.

Symbolic Modeling

Many instances of modeling make use of a real live model. Use of a live model is sometimes called *in vivo* modeling. However, as you have seen from the examples of modeling we have examined, modeling also can use filmed models, videotaped and audiotaped models, puppet and doll models, and prose descriptions of modeled actions. These instances of modeling in which the model is not live are collectively referred to as *symbolic modeling*. Generally, live models are considered more effective than symbolic models (Bandura, 1969). However, the decision whether to use live or symbolic models will often depend on the nature of the response, the learners being taught, and practical considerations. For example, a videotaped model can be shown repeatedly to learners without having to repeatedly reenact the response through *in vivo* modeling.

Making Modeling Effective

Modeling is a special type of stimulus discrimination procedure in which the model acts as a discriminative stimulus for engaging in the modeled response. As such, the principles that make stimulus discrimination effective will also make modeling effective. For example, as with stimulus discrimination, with modeling it is necessary that the learners attend to and actively respond to the appropriate stimuli. If the learner does not have these skills, pretraining in them will make modeling more effective (Luciano & Polaino-Lorente, 1986). In addition, when possible, instructions should be used to explain the task to the learner and to encourage imitative responding. Also, like other desirable behaviors, imitative acts should be encouraged through reinforcement.

Because modeled behaviors are a type of prompt, the principles that make prompting and fading effective also apply to the use of modeling prompts. For example, it is often desirable to eliminate modeling prompts as the learner becomes more skilled, and the methods of prompt fading and time delay can be used to eliminate modeling prompts gradually.

Certain conditions are of special importance in making modeling effective. These include (a) selection of the modeled behaviors; (b) rewarding the model's behavior; (c) rehearsing and practicing the modeled response; (d) the characteristics of the model; (e) the use of multiple models; and (f) the use of appropriate mediating responses.

Selection of the Modeled Behaviors

Two considerations that should go into the selection of the modeled response include breaking down difficult responses into smaller components to be modeled and focusing on one response at a time when the goal is to teach several related responses.

Sometimes target behaviors are too long, too complex, too unfamiliar, or otherwise too difficult to be imitated after a single demonstration. In such cases, the target behavior should be broken down into smaller parts that the learner can imitate (Bandura, 1969). For example, students who are learning a foreign language often are not able to imitate entire sentences with unfamiliar words. However, by breaking down the sentence into small phrases and having the student imitate one phrase successfully before moving on to the next phrase, it is possible for students to imitate entire sentences by gradually increasing the length of the utterance. This technique is part of a method of foreign language learning called *guided imitation* (e.g., Stockwell, Bowen, & Silva-Fuenzalida, 1985). Lovaas (1966, cited in Bandura, 1969, p. 142) used a similar method in teaching an autistic child to say the word *baby*. When the child could not imitate the entire word initially, the component sounds were individually modeled and imitated, leading to eventual imitation of the entire word. Another example of this principle is seen in participant modeling, in which the therapist breaks down the goal target behavior into steps the learner can perform much more easily than the goal response.

Sometimes the complex modeled behaviors will incorporate several desirable features, and in such cases it is useful to employ modeling procedures that focus on each feature, one at a time. For example, in training second-grade students in group discussion skills, Borgen and Calder (1980) taught three skills, self-disclosure, staying on topic, and listening to others. They had more success with a segmented modeling procedure in which each skill was modeled individually than with a combined modeling procedure in which the skills were modeled together. Focusing on one type of modeled response at a time is a way of making the goal response more distinctive for the learner, which in turn improves the effectiveness of modeling (Mann & Decker, 1984).

Reinforcing the Model's Behavior

As we discussed in our examination of vicarious reinforcement, providing rewarding consequences to the model can improve the effectiveness of modeling. Especially when peer models are used, it is desirable to reinforce the models' behavior.

Rehearsing and Practicing the Modeled Responses

For some difficult-to-learn behaviors, it is desirable for the learner to continue to engage in the response after it has been imitated. For example, Kazdin and Mascitelli (1982) ran a social skills training program that included instruction in how to act assertively. One group of trainees learned the social skills through covert modeling, in which they imagined scenes in which another person acted assertively. A second group of the trainees received the covert modeling training, but also received an overt rehearsal treatment in which they acted the scenes with the help of the therapist. A third group of trainees received the covert rehearsal treatment along with homework assignments in which they practiced assertiveness skills such as initiating conversations, making requests, giving a compliment, and speaking in a group situation. The trainees were tested in a role-playing situation in which they responded to tape-recorded events as if they were participants. It was found that both overt rehearsal and the homework practice improved the trainees' performances in the role play test.

Because the method of participant modeling incorporates extensive practice of the target behaviors, it will often be more effective than modeling techniques that do not require learner practice. For example, Wurtele, Marrs, and Miller-Perrin (1987) found that kindergarten children learned sexual-abuse-prevention skills better through participant modeling than through modeling in which the children merely observed the experimenter demonstrate the skills.

Characteristics of the Model

A considerable amount of research has been devoted to discovering what characteristics of models make them more likely to be imitated. The following characteristics have each been shown to influence the likelihood that observers will imitate models: (a) competence of the model; (b) status of the model; (c) similarity of the model to the observers; (d) emotional and attitudinal features of the model; and (e) consistency of the model.

Competence of the Model.   People will more readily imitate models who have been successful at a task than those who have been unsuccessful (Baron, 1970; Gelfand, 1962; Landers & Landers, 1973; Mausner, 1954). This general principle also appears to extend to situations in which the model is not actually successful at the task, but makes statements of confidence in his ability to perform the task. For example, Zimmerman & Ringle (1981) found that a model who made optimistic statements about his ability to solve puzzles led to more persistent puzzle-solving in observer children than a model who made pessimistic statements about his ability.

Status of the Model.   Models having high status will be more likely to be imitated than models of low or unknown status (Mausner, 1953; McCullagh, 1986; Thelen & Kirkland, 1976). As seen in Hayduk's study in the introduction to this chapter, using high-status models is a practical procedure that can be useful, especially with peer modeling.

McCullagh (1986) demonstrated this principle of model status in a study in which young girls watched a brief film of a woman performing a rope-climbing athletic activity. In the high-status condition, the woman was identified as a popular cheerleader, while in the low-status condition the same woman was identified as a university student interested in people's ability to learn balance tasks. When given an opportunity to perform the task themselves, the girls who saw the high-status model performed significantly better than those who saw the low-status model.

Naturalistic observations also illustrate the powerful effects model status can have on large numbers of people. When movie actor Clark Gable appeared without an undershirt in two scenes in the 1934 film *It Happened One Night,* undershirt sales fell, apparently due to the influence of this high-status model. The principle of model status is behind the extensive use of popular actors and actresses in advertising, despite the lack of evidence that their high status carries with it any special skills in correctly judging the value of competing consumer products.

Similarity Between the Model and Observers.   In general, models who are similar to the observers are more likely to be imitated (Brown & Inouye, 1978; McCullagh, 1987; Stotland, Zander, & Natsoulas, 1961). We previously examined one special case of this principle in discussing peer modeling. Because they are more similar to the observers, children will often more readily imitate peer models than adult models (e.g., Kornhaber & Schroeder, 1975) or younger models (Brody & Stoneman, 1981). The advantage of using models who are similar to the learner appears to extend to covert modeling. Kazdin (1974) found that when learners imagined models who were similar to themselves in age and sex, covert modeling was more effective than when dissimilar models were imagined.

As we have discussed, competent models are generally more effective than incompetent models. However, in treating fear of snakes, Kazdin (1974) found that a covert *coping model,* who expressed some fear before engaging in the response, was generally more effective than a *mastery model,* who approached snakes with confidence and aplomb. This beneficial effect of a coping model may be due to the model similarity effect.

Emotional and Attitudinal Features of the Model.   In general, people are more likely to imitate models who have positive attitudes and emotional behaviors. Specifically, people will imitate cheerful rather than doleful models (Roberts, Santogrossi, & Thelen, 1977), warm and enthusiastic rather than cold and uninterested models (Yussen & Levy, 1975), sociable rather than unsociable models (Collins, Parks, & Marlatt, 1985), and truthful and sincere models rather than dishonest and insincere ones (Klass, 1979). Generally speaking, people imitate models to whom they are attracted (Baron, 1970).

Consistency of the Model.   Models who are consistent in performing a response are more likely to be imitated than models who are inconsistent. For example, Fehrenbach, Miller, and Thelen (1979) had a model make aesthetic-choice responses that second- and third-grade children observed. When the model was inconsistent in modeling the responses by changing her choices, the children imitated the model much less than when the model made the same choices consistently. When modeled behaviors are inconsistent over time, observers may conclude that the model's vacillating behavior is weak, improperly controlled, and not worth imitating.

Multiple Models

In general, the greater the number of models performing a response, the more likely observers are to imitate the response (Bandura & Menlove, 1968; Fehrenbach et al., 1979; Kazdin, 1975, 1976). In some situations, the use of multiple models serves to encourage generalization through the use of multiple training exemplars, as discussed in Chapter 9. For example, through modeling training, Bandura and Menlove (1968) taught 3- to 5-year-old children not to fear dogs. One group of children watched a film showing a 5-year-old model interact with a dog in gradually more threatening situations. Another group of children watched a film of the same length showing a variety of model children interact with a variety of dogs, also in progressively more threatening situations. To assess the effects of the modeling treatments, the trainers tested the children with real dogs, including one task that assessed the children's ability to remain with a dog in a playpen. The benefits of the multiple-model treatment were shown in a one-month follow-up test, in which more than twice as many of the multiple-model children were able to interact with dogs than were the single-model children.

In other situations, multiple models appear to encourage imitative responding due to social pressure. This type of multiple-modeling effect may occur when live models are used who have the potential to provide social reinforcers and punishers for imitative and nonimitative behavior. However, Kazdin (1975, 1976) found that multiple covert models (i.e., imagining several models engage in a response) also contributed to the effectiveness of modeling, suggesting that direct social pressure is not the only factor involved in the effectiveness of multiple models.

Use of Mediating Responses

The effectiveness of modeling, especially deferred imitation, will be improved if the learner acquires appropriate mediating responses or verbally summarizes at the time the modeled behavior is observed (Bandura & Jeffery, 1973; Gerst, 1971; Kazdin, 1979). Gerst demonstrated this principle in an experiment in which sign-language hand movements were modeled to learners. One group of learners was required to described the modeled responses with short summary labels, one group was required to imagine them in visual form, one group was required to describe verbally the specific movements that comprised the hand signs, and a control group engaged in none of these activities. When the learners were tested to see if they could imitate the modeled responses after 15 minutes had passed, the group that responded to the hand signs using summary labels recalled more of the signs than did learners in the other groups.

Using summary labels can improve performance on deferred imitation tasks because often the physical responses involved in modeling can be complex and difficult to recall. However, when the learner acquires a summary label to describe the modeled response, it is possible for the learner to recall the label later, which can in turn act as a discriminative stimulus for recalling the original modeled response.

Summary

In this chapter we have examined modeling, a topic concerned with how and why people come to imitate each other's behavior. A model demonstrates a response, which is then imitated by an observer. The modeled behavior is called a modeling prompt. Modeling is a form of stimulus control in which the model's behavior serves as a discriminative stimulus for an observer's imitation of that response.

Modeling is an excellent means of teaching new behavior. To use modeling, the behavior modifier must define and demonstrate desirable behaviors to be encouraged, and is therefore compelled to adopt a constructional approach to behavior change. In addition, once the skill of imitation has been acquired, it is possible for the learner to acquire many responses errorlessly through a single demonstration of the response to be learned. Also, modeling is a natural process that does not require a formal instructional setting, for we learn from models all the time simply by observing the behavior of other people.

Because modeling is such a powerful influence on human behavior, a great deal of undesirable behavior is both acquired and strengthened through modeling. For example, research has clearly shown that violent and aggressive models promote imitative responding in observers. For this reason, people concerned with reducing the amount of violence and aggression within their society should be concerned about the models to which people, especially children, are exposed.

We examined several different types of modeling processes including exact imitation and behavior-feature imitation, vicarious reinforcement, vicarious punishment, and vicarious helplessness, observational learning, peer modeling, covert modeling, self-modeling, participant modeling, and symbolic modeling. Through modeling, observers can be influenced either to exactly match the modeled response or, in behavior-feature imitation, to imitate specific features of the modeled response. Behavior-feature imitation is very important in children's learning, especially the learning of verbal behavior.

In vicarious reinforcement, a model is rewarded for engaging in a response and the rewarding consequence strengthens imitative responding in an observer. In vicarious punishment, the model is penalized in some way for engaging in a response decreasing the likelihood that an observer will imitate the response. In vicarious helplessness, the model's behavior is penalized in response-independent fashion, which impairs the behavior of observers who view the model.

Generalized imitation is the ability of a learner to imitate responses she has not previously learned and without reinforcers dependent on each instance of imitative responding. By building a repertoire of generalized imitation, learners can acquire a vast array of new behavior rapidly, as startling demonstrations show in which formerly mute children learn to acquire verbal responses quickly once they learn the skill of generalized imitation. Observational learning, a product of generalized imitation, occurs when the learner acquires new responses simply by observing those responses be performed.

We next examined peer modeling and self-modeling. Much behavior is learned from peers, prompting many parents and teachers to feel that they cannot compete with peer influences on behavior. However, we examined ways in which the powerful influence of same-age peers can be put to work in a creative ways to encourage desirable behaviors through peer modeling. In self-modeling, one person takes on the roles of both model and observer. Research has shown that observing ourselves perform especially well on one occasion can strengthen imitations of our own desirable performances.

Two additional techniques we examined that have been used extensively in behavior therapy are covert modeling and participant modeling. In covert modeling, the model's behavior is not observed but imagined by the learner, a technique sometimes as effective as observing a live model. In participant modeling, the learner is unable to perform the desired modeled response, so the modeling task is broken down into steps ranging from easy-to-imitate to difficult-to-imitate. Each step is individually modeled and imitated, enabling the learner to progress gradually toward the final goal response.

We considered one final type of modeling, symbolic modeling, which consists of using alternate presentation modalities to live modeling. For example, when a videotaped model is shown, the model is presented in symbolic form in the sense that the screen image of the model symbolizes a real model. Similarly, when we read a biography of a famous person, the individual's behavior is modeled through written words, not direct observation.

We looked at a variety of conditions that can make modeling effective. Modeling is improved if the modeled behaviors are selected properly for the learner, if the learner practices and rehearses the modeled responses, if the model we select has the appropriate characteristics, if more than one model is used, and if appropriate mediating responses are selected.

Conceptual Exercise   *Modeling and Related Processes*

For each of the following items, decide if the item is an example of (a) modeling, (b) vicarious reinforcement, (c) vicarious punishment, (d) generalized imitation, (e) peer modeling, (f) covert modeling, (g) self modeling, (h) participant modeling, or (i) symbolic modeling. Some of the items are not examples of any of these concepts and most of the items are examples of more than one of these concepts. Indicate your choice and briefly explain why. Confirm your decisions by consulting the analyses provided in the back of the book.

1. Twenty-four girls between 6- and 7-years-old were participants in an experiment. During the first part of the study, the experimenter had an adult woman view 12 slides showing two objects of approximately equal value and select the object she preferred. For example, two objects on one slide were binoculars and a radio while on another slide the two objects were red and blue wooden spools. The girls watched as the woman viewed the slides. For one group of girls, the experimenter approved of the woman's selection of preferred objects, while for a second group, the experimenter disapproved of the woman's selections. For a third group of girls, the experimenter neither approved nor disapproved of the selections. After watching the woman select the objects, the girls were required to indicate which of the objects on the same slides they preferred. The girls who watched the woman whose selections the experimenter approved imitated those selections more often than control-group girls did. Also, the girls who watched the woman whose selections were disapproved of imitated those selections less often than the control-group girls.

2. Dan and Phil, 6 and 8, were two boys who attended a special education class for retarded children. As part of an experiment, the teacher began approving of Dan's attentive behavior, which made it more likely to occur. This procedure also caused an increase in the likelihood of Phil's attentive behavior, even though the teacher did not reinforce it. However, Phil could observe Dan's behavior and the teacher's approval of it.

3. Third-grade children were shown a short film of a model child who played a beanbag toss game. One group of children saw the model aim only at a distant, difficult target while another group observed the model aim only at a close, easy target. A control group did not watch the model child playing the game. Three weeks following this modeling training, the children were brought to a different classroom and with a new

experimenter in charge, played a spelling bee game in which they were given the option of trying to spell words of four different levels of difficulty. Children who had originally watched a model choose the difficult beanbag task chose to try to spell more difficult words than either control children or children who observed the model select the easy task.

4. A group of people who feared spiders and snakes had volunteered for a project designed to reduce their fears. In order to solve the problem, the experimenter demonstrated approach responses toward the spiders and snakes, and the fearful people would then imitate the experimenter, who encouraged their imitations. At first, the experimenter demonstrated responses that provoked little fear, such as moving nearer to the animals in a cage, but still remaining a distance away. Gradually, the experimenter modeled closer and closer approach responses, culminating in a demonstration of picking up and holding the animal. This method substantially reduced the subject's fears of snakes and spiders.

5. Students in a third-grade classroom usually arrived at the classroom before their teacher did. Before he entered the room, the children were normally noisy, but as soon as he entered and said, "Good Morning," all the students in the class immediately quieted down because he had entered. However, observations taken on days when substitute teachers were present indicated that the students did not quiet down when they entered the classroom.

6. Pete and Nancy were two 8-year-olds who had been identified as learning disabled. During baseline conditions, the children read a required passage every day. Following this, a modeling procedure was used in which the teacher read the passage for 1 minute, after which the child was required to read, picking up from the point where the teacher left off. This method improved each student's rate of correct reading responses.

7. In an experiment, patients who were suffering from hypertension watched a videotape of model patients who appropriately divulged relevant information to their doctors and posed appropriate questions. Compared to a control group of patients who did not watch the videotapes, the experimental patients communicated with their doctors better by disclosing relevant information and asking appropriate questions.

8. Cynthia was a swimming instructor who was teaching three children who had spina bifida, a spinal cord disorder that causes paralysis below the waist. As part of the teaching procedures, videotapes were made when the children showed a noticeable improvement in their swimming technique. Then, the children repeatedly watched themselves on the videotape swimming in the improved way. As a result of watching themselves on the videotapes, each of the children engaged in more correct swimming behaviors.

9. Three boys aged between 6- and 8-years-old who had been identified as autistic participated in a project designed to teach them conversational skills. As part of the training, the boys watched videotapes of adults conversing with one another about toys that the boys liked. After watching the videotapes, the boys held the same conversation they had seen in the videotape with the experimenter. After this type of training, it was found that the boys could carry on conversations in different settings, with different people, and about different toys.

10. Two boys, 11 and 13, were participating in an experiment, in which the experimenter told them English words (e.g., window, night, soap), and reinforced the boys' imitations of the word with tokens, smiles, and praise. The experimenter also mixed Spanish words (e.g., traje, noche, ave) with the English words, but did not reinforce the boys' imitations of the Spanish words. Both boys nonetheless continued to imitate the Spanish words. Assume that the boys had never spoken the English and Spanish words before the experiment.

11. In Prairieville, there was a sharp drop in housing prices because during the past two years, builders had built too many new houses, flooding the market for new homes. This drop in housing prices caused a large increase in new home sales.

12. A group of boys and girls between 6- and 8-years-old were all attending a summer camp for diabetic children. Half the children watched a film in which other children learned to self-inject insulin, a substance that helps people who have diabetes regulate their blood sugar levels. The rest of the children watched a film about nutrition. After watching the film, all the children were taught how to self-inject insulin. The researchers found that the older girls in the group who had seen the film about self-injection were able to inject insulin with more skill.

13. Two researchers, interested in encouraging women to conduct breast self-exams in order to detect breast cancers, conducted an experiment with 60 female university students who had never conducted breast self-exams. One group was shown a videotape in which the experimenter demonstrated a breast self-exam. A second group was shown a videotape in which the experimenter demonstrated a breast self-exam using synthetic breasts on a life-sized half-torso model. A third group watched a videotape about breast self-exams, but the technique was not demonstrated. After one month, data indicated that more of the women who were given either an actual demonstration or the demonstration with a synthetic model were conducting self-exams more often than women who were not given a demonstration. However, this benefit did not persist after 3 months.

14. Billy, a 6-year-old boy, had been identified as autistic and had never spoken. Using an intensive training program, an experimenter reinforced his vocalizations, and used shaping and fading procedures to get Billy to repeat the word *baby* after the experimenter had said it. After this training, Billy learned more words and was able to imitate new words the experimenter presented. Billy was also sometimes presented with Norwegian words that he correctly imitated even without reinforcement.

15. A group of female university students who were unassertive had volunteered for an assertiveness training program. For some of the students, treatment of their problem consisted of reading scenes that described people who were appropriately assertive. The student's task was then to imagine a similar situation in which the person was appropriately assertive. Example scenes included expressing criticism of a friend's artwork, politely asking a classmate to cease loud gum chewing, and approaching an attractive unfamiliar man at a party to initiate a conversation. Data

from the study indicated that the women became more assertive as a result of the treatment procedure.

16. At a nursing home for the elderly, one problem was that the patients would resist bathing both by physical means and by verbally abusing the staff whose job it was to bathe them. In order to solve the problem, the bathing task was broken down into a series of steps, beginning from entering the bathing area and ending with getting out of the bath tub. The experimenter demonstrated each step to four female patients at a time, and then the residents were asked to do as the experimenter had done. The experimenter provided prompts and reinforcers for engaging in the behaviors at each step of the process. When one step was completed, the experimenter went on to the next step. Eventually, this method resulted in the women becoming much less resistant to bathing.

17. A group of university students volunteered to be treated for test anxiety. During the first session of the treatment program, they listened to audiotapes of students describing high levels of test anxiety. In subsequent treatment sessions, the students listened to tapes in which the students emitted fewer and fewer test-anxious behaviors, until at last they engaged in none of these behaviors. As a result of this treatment, the students' test-anxious behaviors were reduced substantially.

18. Vikka, a young Russian girl who was attending kindergarten, seldom received affection and was often mistreated. One day one of her classmates cut his finger on a toy. When the teacher noticed this, she gave him a big hug, dressed his wound, and treated him kindly. Because Vikka saw the boy receive affection, she deliberately cut her toe with a sharp stone. By doing so, Vikka was then fussed over by the teacher too.

19. Children between the ages of 3- and 6-years were in an experiment. One group of children watched a woman engage in several types of aggressive responses directed at toys. Another woman, the experimenter, praised the acts of aggression eight times. Another group of children watched the woman engage in several types of aggressive responses, but the aggression was reprimanded eight times. For a control group, the aggressive responses were neither praised nor reprimanded. In order to test the effects of these treatments, the children then were observed in a playroom. The children who had watched the aggression be rewarded engaged in more aggression than children in the control group. Among the younger children, those who had watched the aggression be reprimanded engaged in less aggression than children in the control group.

20. Several people had responded to advertisements about a program for people with a fear of heights. At first, the therapist broke the task down into several stages ranging from standing on the bottom rungs of a wooden ladder to climbing up a ladder attached to a structure on the roof of a seven-story building. Then, the therapist demonstrated each step from easiest to most difficult, after which the learner was required to imitate the therapist's demonstration. The therapist gave the learners encouragement as they performed the responses. In this way, the people were able to climb much higher than they had previously, and with less fear.

21. Workers in a tall office building with westward facing windows were monitored to see whether they closed the shades in the windows. By midafternoon, when the sun began to shine brightly through the windows, shades in 75% of the office windows were closed.

22. Chuck, a 10-year-old, lived in a hospital where he was being treated for severe asthma. He also had several behavior problems, including staying in bed all morning, whining and crying when other boys taunted him, failing to initiate play with other boys, and jumping on the laps of adults while giggling and trying to tickle them. In order to solve these problems, a trainer made a videotape in which Chuck was told he was going to be an actor. As instructed, Chuck enacted roles in which he (a) arose in the morning and made his bed, (b) defended himself and fended off an attack by two other boys, (c) initiated contact with two other children who were playing a game, and (d) behaved appropriately with an adult in an office setting. Over the next weeks, the trainer showed Chuck this videotape repeatedly, causing him to imitate the appropriate behaviors and engage in the inappropriate responses much less often. Counselors and medical staff noted improvements in Chuck's behavior and Chuck maintained the improvements during the remaining 6 months he lived at the hospital.

23. A group of university students who greatly feared snakes participated in a program designed to reduce their fears. As part of the treatment, the students vividly imagined 15 scenes in which a person similar to themselves gradually approached a caged garter snake. The final scene was one in which for 30 seconds the person held the snake without gloves 10 inches from her face. This method successfully enabled the students to approach snakes to a greater degree than they had before treatment.

24. A 26-year-old prison inmate asked for help with his stuttering problem. Treatment of the problem involved weekly audiotaping the man speaking and editing out instances in which he stuttered. The man then later listened to himself on the tape. This method decreased the frequency of the man's stuttering.

25. A group of boys whose average age was about 6 years were in an experiment. The boys watched a film in which a mother told her child not to play with a set of toys on a table, then left the room. The child in the film then played with the toys on the table. For one group of observer boys, the film ended with the mother returning, taking the toys away, and shaking the child. For another group of boys, the mother did not return after leaving the room. The boys who watched the film were then placed in a room where the experimenter told them not to play with some toys. The experimenter then left the room and the boys were secretly observed to see what they would do. The boys who had watched the film in which the mother had penalized the child for toy play played with the forbidden toys much less than children who had watched the film in which there were no consequences for toy play.

26. Three male university students were subjects in an experiment. In an experimental room decorated to look like a tavern, a university student who was working with the experimenter drank beer with the subjects. It was found that when he increased his rate of beer consumption, it caused the subjects to increase their rate of beer con-

sumption. When he decreased his rate of beer consumption, this caused the subjects to decrease their rate of beer consumption.

Conceptual Exercise	*Making Modeling Effective*

For each of the following items, one of the factors that makes modeling effective has been violated. Identify the problem and briefly explain how the procedure could have been made more effective. Consult with the analyses that are in the back of the book to confirm your decisions.

1. A study-skills training seminar was being conducted for students who had poor study habits. The students watched a videotape of students similar to themselves who demonstrated the behaviors that encompass good study behavior. These models demonstrated how to gather all the needed equipment before sitting down to study, how to select a good study area, the appropriate lighting for a study area, the best time of day for studying, how to summarize, how to read text for maximum learning, and how to practice the behavior required on tests and quizzes. Several models were used in the film and each was praised by a parent figure. The students who viewed the film were then asked to practice the entire sequence of modeled behavior several times. This seminar was not as effective as its leaders had hoped.

2. John was participating in a study of conformity. He was seated with several other people in a room. Unbeknownst to John all the others were confederates of the experimenter. The experimenter would give the group a simple perception task and asked each person to give the correct response, which was quite obvious. All these people gave their answer aloud before John was asked for his answer. Each person chose the same incorrect response with one exception. One other person chose the obvious correct answer. The experimenter wanted to know if John would side with the incorrect majority or with the correct (but lone) dissenter. The dissenting person wore thick glasses and, when all the subjects entered the room, this person had stumbled into things frequently. The experimenters found that John's response matched the incorrect majority rather than the correct dissenter.

3. In an elementary school, a program was mounted in an attempt to reduce drug use of the students. The students viewed a videotape of high school seniors, models who were approached by a drug dealer who tried to interest them in buying illegal drugs. The models refused to buy the drugs. Several other high school students then approached the models and congratulated them on their decisions. The elementary students were then observed in a test situation in which they were approached by a "drug dealer" who tried to convince them to buy drugs. They were required to practice the refusal behavior they had seen in the film. Imitation was not as successful as it should have been.

4. Marly was a severely retarded child who was being taught to retrieve a named object from a group of objects on a table, return to the teacher, and give him the object. The teacher broke down this complex behavior into parts and used children of Marly's

age to demonstrate each step. First a model child would walk to the table and the teacher would ask Marly to imitate this behavior. Then the teachers would place at the table a model child, who would pick up the named object. Marly would be asked to imitate this behavior. Then a model child would walk with the object back to the teacher. The teacher was careful to praise each model for demonstrating each step. Marly was required to practice each step three times before another step was modeled. Sometimes she accomplished the required behavior in the three practice trials and sometimes she didn't, before the next step was modeled.

5. In a ballet class the teacher was demonstrating five different ballet steps to her students. She used students from another class to model the steps. Each girl would demonstrate a particular step and the teacher would praise her. When all five steps had been modeled, the teacher dismissed her class. The next class day, the students were asked to imitate the steps they had seen. One student did very well but the rest did not. When the teacher asked the successful student about this, the student said that as each step was demonstrated she had silently given the step a short name to help her remember it.

6. In a day-care center, the children were learning shape sorting. A child who already knew how to do this would demonstrate by placing a round block in the round hole of the shape sorter. The teacher would praise her. Several demonstration children were used to model the sorting of each of the different shapes. As the model placed the shape in the shape sorter, the teacher would say aloud the name of the shape to provide a label for the learners. Some of the learners were asked to sort the shapes themselves after the models had demonstrated, and some of the learners continued to observe their classmates. Later in the day, all the learners were asked to imitate the shape-sorting models. The children who had been allowed to sort the shapes right after the demonstration were better able to imitate than those who had simply observed.

7. Rory, an autistic child, was in a language learning program where he was learning to say his name. Several speech pathologists worked with Rory, taking turns being the model while another would reward the model with praise and a small edible treat. The model would say, "My name is Susan," and she would receive her reward. Another model would say, "My name is Jim," and so on. After self-naming had been demonstrated, Rory was asked several times to say his name. Although Rory sometimes was able to do so, sometimes he was not.

8. A group of middle-aged women about to reenter the workforce were taking a seminar in how to behave in an interview. All the women were shown a video of an interview where a prospective employer questioned several middle-aged women. These models asked appropriate questions and answered questions in appropriate ways. The prospective employer was very attentive and made several positive remarks to the model throughout the interview. At the end of the interview, the prospective employer said to the woman, "I am very impressed with you and I am pleased to offer you a position in our firm." All the women were then sent out on job interviews. Some of them did very well and imitated the behavior of the models they had seen but some of them did less well. When the women got together to discuss their

experiences, the women who had done well explained that they had gone home after the seminar and practiced with their spouses what they had seen.

9. A group of middle-aged women who were about to reenter the workforce were taking a seminar in how to behave in an interview. All the women were shown a video of an interview where a prospective employer questioned several middle-aged women. These models asked appropriate questions and answered questions in appropriate ways. The prospective employer was cool and seemed inattentive, often gazing out the window. At the end of the interview, the prospective employer escorted the woman to the door. All the women then practiced what they had seen using each other in the role of the prospective employer. The next day the women returned and participated in a simulated interview with a member of the training staff. Although the women imitated some of what they had seen they did not do as well as they might have.

chapter 11

Rule-Governed Behavior

Matt, 10, was doing well in elementary school, where he especially excelled in athletic activities. Although a little on the shy side, Matt was generally well-liked and had lots of friends. He seemed to be a pretty typical, well-adjusted child. Despite the outward indications, Matt had been experiencing recurring nightmares so terrible that he had been unable to sleep alone for 2 years.

One night when Matt was 8 years old and fast asleep in his room, a car went out of control and smashed through a wall of the family house. Fortunately, no one was injured, but Matt began having nightmares and was unable to sleep alone in his room any longer. In the nightmares were bad guys who were trying to hurt him or his friends. Weapons and car chases were frequently a part of the dreams, as was the sound of car tires squealing and then the thud of a collision. Matt's parents recognized that his fears were far beyond the normal fears all children have after a bad dream. Therefore, his parents allowed Matt to sleep in their room with them, either in their bed or on the floor in a sleeping bag.

Matt's problems were so severe that his parents sought professional help, and Matt saw several therapists. One treatment, in which Matt's parents rewarded him for staying in his room, was not successful. Another treatment that made use of drugs also failed. One therapist helped him to the point where he could sleep alone in his room again, though his parents had to accompany him into the room. This might have been the end of Matt's troubles. Unfortunately, a year and a half after the original auto accident, Matt's family was riding together in their car when they had an accident. The family car was demolished and Matt's mother was injured, although not seriously. This incident renewed Matt's fears. The nightmares started again and he was unable to sleep alone.

Matt's parents again sought the help of therapists but nothing seemed to help him: Things were getting desperate. Eventually, they were referred to Dr. Charlotte Johnston, a professor at the University of British Columbia, where she specialized in child psychology. Dr. Johnston had a bright young graduate student named Eileen Palace, whom she assigned to Matt's case.

Eileen interviewed Matt and his parents and administered several tests. She decided that successful treatment for Matt would have to combine a method to treat his fears with a method to alter the way he thought about himself. To treat Matt's fears, Eileen decided to use a technique called *systematic desensitization,* a method in which the therapist first teaches the fearful person to relax. Then, the person learns to remain relaxed while thinking about and picturing the things that frighten her. At first, the person imagines things that aren't very frightening. As she successfully encounters these stimuli, she imagines things that are more fearful, while continuing to remain relaxed. In Matt's case, it was the content of his dreams that scared him (the bad guys who were out to harm him and his friends). Eileen taught Matt to relax, and then had him imagine the parts of his dreams that were not so frightening. As he did this successfully, Eileen had him imagine progressively more fear-provoking parts of the dreams, all the while ensuring that Matt remained relaxed.

Although the systematic desensitization procedure was an important part of Matt's treatment, it is not our primary concern at this point. (We will look at systematic desensitization and related procedures in detail later, in Chapter 13.) After using systematic desensitization for a while, Eileen had Matt list 10 *coping self-statements.* These statements were things Matt could say to himself that would help govern his own behavior. We might call them *self-rules* or *self-instructions.* Examples of the coping self-statements included things such as "I can do it, I know how to relax." "It's just a dream. It's not real." "Think of how proud I will be in the morning. . . ." One of Matt's favorite television cartoons was a show called "The New Centurions," and another one of the coping self-statements was, "If I were a centurion . . .," a statement that encouraged him to think of himself as a brave superhero. As you can see, the coping self-statements were all rules that specified that Matt was in control: His dreams were not a real threat to him.

Figure 11.1 illustrates the effects of these procedures. Clearly, the systematic desensitization procedure was successful in reducing the number of times Matt went to his parents' room to sleep. Adding the coping self-statements reduced the level of this behavior even further. But Matt was still very much afraid, still had nightmares, and still slept in his parents' room some of the time.

Eileen decided to use a method called *guided mastery.* She asked Matt to make up new endings for his nightmares where he was a superhero and defeated the bad

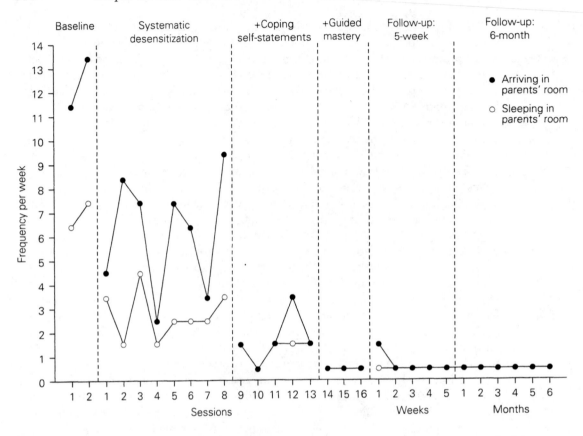

Figure 11.1   *The Effects of Systematic Desensitization, Self-Statements, and Guided Mastery Training on the Frequency of a Young Boy's Nighttime Behaviors*

Matt's rate of arriving and sleeping in his parents room declined considerably after the coping self-statement and guided mastery training were added to the systematic desensitization training. Figure adapted from Palace and Johnston (1989).

guys. The revised endings to the dreams were called *mastery endings* because they cast Matt in control of (or mastering) the dream situation. After the endings were changed, Matt received practice in imagining the changed endings and changed one as follows:

> You and your friend face a man dressed all in black, stealthily approaching you on the street. He wears a black ski mask covering his face with the exception of a hole at the side of the mask revealing a missing ear, and a bruised and bloody hole. As he reaches into the black bag with his deformed hands, and hurls an axe into the air, you transform into Jake Rockwell, who wears a cast iron exoframe armed with artillery. You coolly call Crystal on your wristcom to send down the heavy assault system,

and fire the freeze machine, automatically freezing in space the bad guy and his axes. The intruder is arrested, and placed under surveillance. The onlookers cheer—you, Jake Rockwell, have saved them all (Palace and Johnston, 1989, p. 223).

The guided mastery procedure may be considered a type of covert self-modeling in which Matt imagined himself as Jake Rockwell, challenging and defeating the bad guy. As Figure 11.1 shows, this procedure worked very well. Matt could sleep in his room alone and was no longer troubled by his nightmares. For the subsequent 6 months, Matt neither slept in his parents' room nor had more nightmares. Exactly why the nightmares ended is not known. One possibility is that, combined with the other procedures, rehearsing the mastery endings of the dreams eliminated Matt's fears such that the dreams never occurred again. A second possibility is that one night Matt had the beginning of the nightmare again, confronted the bad guy, challenged him, and defeated him as he had in the guided mastery endings.*

Rule-Governed Behavior

When we tell someone else to do something or when we tell ourselves to do something, we are using a behavior change procedure, even though we might not think in these terms. Instructing someone to do something can change behavior quickly and effectively. In previous chapters, we saw how instructions can make behavioral procedures more effective. For example, in Chapter 2 we examined how instructions that specify the dependency between a response and its reinforcing consequences can improve the effectiveness of positive reinforcement procedures. So, behavior analysts usually give instructions to the people whose behavior they want to change.

Changing behavior with instructions is an example of what behavior analysts call *rule-governed behavior*. In full form, rule-governed behavior is the behavior of following a rule. A rule, in complete form, is a verbal stimulus that specifies three things:

- the stimulus conditions under which a response is to occur or not to occur;
- the response itself; and
- the consequences dependent on the response. (Skinner, 1969).

For example, Abraham Lincoln once provided the rule: "Things may come to those who wait, but only the things left by those who hustle." This is a rule because Lincoln specified:

- the stimulus conditions—the conditions under which we hustle and wait;
- the behaviors—hustling and waiting; and

*Based on Palace and Johnston (1989) and E. Palace, personal communication (1992)

• the consequences—getting first choice of available reinforcers (i.e., things) versus getting reinforcers that have been left over.

If you read and then apply Lincoln's rule, for example by taking immediate action to achieve a goal in your personal life that you had been putting off, it is an example of rule-governed behavior. Your action would be due to the verbal stimuli, the words in Lincoln's rule. An important feature of rules is that they can be applied in novel situations and to novel forms of behavior (Hayes & Hayes, 1989). A person who has learned Lincoln's rule, for example, can apply it to her advantage in every situation in which active responding produces reinforcers. In addition, the behavior of hustling in different situations will take various new forms.

Another term used to describe rules is contingency-specifying stimuli (or dependency-specifying stimuli). As discussed earlier, rules specify contingent (or dependent) relationships among (a) the stimulus conditions under which a response is to occur; (b) the response itself; and (c) the consequences for the response. Lincoln's rule is a contingency-specifying stimulus because it designates the relationships between (a) the stimulus conditions for hustling and waiting; (b) the behaviors of hustling and waiting; and (c) the reinforcing consequences of those behaviors.

Often, rules are incomplete in that they do not specify each of the three components of a "full" rule. For example, "To thine own self be true" is a rule that specifies a behavior, telling yourself the truth, but does not specify the consequences dependent on the response. One rule Matt used to control his nightmares was, "I can do it, I know how to relax." This rule did not specify stimulus conditions, but they did not need to be explicitly specified because the coping rules Matt used were applicable to the nighttime situations in which he felt afraid. The rules "do it" and "relax" both specified that Matt be calm. The consequences were also left unspecified, but these again were implied by the context of therapy, the ending of the nightmares. Note that in the case of the coping statement, "Think of how proud I will be in the morning," the rule specified the consequence, while the stimulus conditions and responses were implied by the context of the therapy. Finally, the rule, "It's just a dream. It's not real," specifies that Matt respond differently to dreams and to reality, but the consequences are not specified.

Life is full of rules, perhaps too many. There are laws, regulations, and guidelines; unwritten codes, taboos, and norms; proverbs, superstitions, and commandments; instruction manuals, textbooks, and recipes. In addition to all the rules our society expects us to follow, we adopt our own personal codes of conduct, rules that we apply to our own behavior. Skinner (1969) distinguishes between rules that are *commands* and rules that are *advice*.

When the rule giver controls the consequences for following and not following the rule, we generally call the rule a *command*. When the rule-giver does not directly provide response-dependent consequences, but merely calls attention to them, we call the rule *advice*. For example, suppose a teacher tells her students that unless they study, she will give them poor grades. This is a command because the rule giver, the teacher, can and does provide response-dependent consequences for following the rule. On the other hand, if parents tell their children that unless they study they will get poor grades, it is advice, because parents do not control the grades their children receive.

Rules are important in logical thinking and in intelligent behavior. For example, imagine that you are planning your vacation. What should you pack? It will be a short vacation and inconvenient to carry excess baggage. You are going to a warm place: You won't need cold-weather clothing. As you go through this sort of process, you are essentially making rules for yourself that govern what you will and will not pack for your holiday. This use of self-rules is an example of logical thinking.

One of the most important decisions in life is choosing a career. Suppose you identify yourself as someone who is good at math and science, someone who enjoys laboratory work, and someone whose behavior is reinforced by the elimination of human suffering. You can use these rules about yourself to govern more specific career-selection responses. These examples illustrate that other people do not always apply rules to us. Often, the rules we follow are ones we devise ourselves to make our behavior more successful (Skinner 1969, 1989). Although there are many different types of logical thinking, the field is broadly concerned with the study and use of rules for manipulating verbal stimuli to enable those stimuli to govern successful behavior (cf., Nisbett, Fong, Lehman, & Cheng, 1987; Terrell & Johnston, 1989).

Another way to categorize rules is on the likelihood that the rule follower will be directly influenced by the consequence of following the rule. Malott (1986, 1989) talks about *direct-acting consequences* and *indirect-acting consequences.* Some rules are based on powerful response-dependent consequences that control behavior effectively. For example, consider the rule, "Don't eat that mushroom, it's poisonous." This rule is based on a direct-acting consequence because the toxic effect of eating a poison is an effective punisher for behavior.

Other rules are not based on powerful response-dependent consequences, but on consequences that are individually weak and only of cumulative significance. For example, consider the rule, "Restrict your consumption of high-fat foods, because they can cause heart disease and cancer." Poor health is a long-delayed consequence of eating high-fat foods. It takes years of eating high-fat foods to produce poor health, and some people who eat high-fat foods beat the odds and never suffer negative consequences for their behavior. For these reasons, poor health is not an effective consequence for eating high-fat foods. It is an indirect-acting consequence, because it does not deter poor eating directly through punishment. Similarly, the rule "Fasten your seat belt before driving" is a rule based on an indirect-acting consequence because most people will not be involved in an auto accident whether they wear seat belts or not. Other rules are based on indirect-acting consequences that are even more remote. For example, rules about not using materials that damage the ozone layer of the atmosphere may not affect us at all within our lifetimes, but will harm future generations.

Rules based on direct-acting consequences are clearly easier to follow than those based on indirect-acting consequences. However, because many rules with indirect-acting consequences are so very important, behavior analysts have become more concerned with finding ways to encourage people to follow them. These procedures generally involve using contrived consequences to make following rules more effective (Malott, 1986, 1989). We can see examples of this today. Recycling is a behavior that will preserve the environment for future generations. Because individuals may not benefit in obvious ways by immediate improvements, people may be less likely to follow rules specifying recycling. By offering contrived, immediate positive consequences such as bottle refunds for recycling behavior, we can increase the likelihood that people will follow these rules.

Rule-Governed Behavior and Contingency-Shaped Behavior

Contingency-shaped behavior is not rule-governed. It is behavior that is directly controlled by its consequences, not by a specified rule. Skinner (1969) illustrates the difference between the two types of behavior in playing the game of pool. Consider a physicist who knows all about the rules (principles) that govern the motion of objects. When she lines up her shots, she places her cue stick according to the rules of physics. This is rule-governed behavior because each shot is governed by the rules of objects in motion. In contrast, consider the behavior of a poolroom hustler who has learned the game exclusively through reinforcement for making good shots and punishment for making poor ones. Her behavior is contingency-shaped because the shots are due to the previous consequences for making similar shots and the stimulus control these consequences have established. We often call rule-governed behavior planned, calculated, and logical, and say that the person whose behavior is rule-governed "knows the rules." We often call contingency-shaped behavior intuitive, natural, and unconscious, and say that the person whose behavior is contingency-shaped "knows how."

Our examples of the two pool players represent two extreme cases. The physicist's behavior of making the first shot would be entirely due to rules, while the hustler's behavior would be entirely due to past shot-making consequences. In the real world, we seldom find such extreme cases. After the physicist made a few shots, the consequences of shot making would begin to influence her behavior. And, our hypothetical hustler is unrealistic because, during her many years in the poolroom, she would have undoubtedly learned certain helpful rules of the game from other players, books, and magazines. Yet, you can see from this example that we can distinguish between the physicist's behavior, more-or-less rule-governed, and the hustler's behavior, which is more-or-less contingency-shaped (cf., Buskist & Miller, 1986). The physicist's behavior is due more to rules, to contingency-specifying stimuli, and the hustler's behavior is due more to the directly encountered consequences of shot-making.

Note that the consequences influence both rule-governed and contingency-shaped behavior. With contingency-shaped behavior, behavior has been directly altered by past consequences for responding. In the example of the poolroom-hustler, the past reinforcers and punishers associated with good and poor shots would be the consequences responsible for the acquisition of skilled performance. With rule-governed behavior, the behavior of following rules can be considered a class of behavior, past instances of which have been reinforced. In the example of the physicist playing pool, the physicist's behavior of following the laws (rules) that govern the motion of objects would have been previously reinforced as well. For example, these laws would have enabled the physicist to make various kinds of accurate predictions about the course of travel of moving objects. Even though making shots in the poolroom would not have been reinforced, the general class of behaviors involved in following the rules of physics would have been reinforced.

Often when we learn something new, our behavior is rule-governed, but with experience it becomes more sensitive to the contingencies. Terrell and Johnston (1989) have described this pattern in learning a foreign language:

> An individual learning a second language may first learn the rules of grammar for that language, and for some time those rules may be meticulously consulted before each utterance. Once fluent, however, the speaker usually no longer consults the rules before speaking. Rather, the verbal behavior comes under the control of the foreign verbal community's reinforcement contingencies (p. 39).

Characteristics of Rule-Governed and Contingency-Shaped Behavior

When we observe someone behaving in a certain way, we usually can't tell if the behavior is governed by a rule or by experience with the contingencies. The behavior looks the same to us. But there are some important differences.

First, behavior can be quickly acquired by rule-governed control, but acquired much more slowly through contingency-shaped control (Ayllon & Azrin, 1964; Danforth, Chase, Dolan, & Joyce, 1990; Pereira & Pérez, 1987; Vaughan, 1985). Suppose you want to spice a dish of food properly. You can do this quickly by following the rules of a good recipe. In contrast, to get a desirable taste through a process of contingency-shaping, it would be necessary to go through a long process of carefully adding small amounts of spices at a time and sampling the results. Even then, it might take several failures before a palatable dish is served. Nonetheless, the person who has learned to spice a dish through contingency-shaping has learned a great deal about the properties of each spice and how they should be combined for maximum flavor. This cook can use his or her knowledge to create other dishes. The rule-following cook, on the other hand, has not really learned much about flavoring foods, notwithstanding the perfect meat loaf.

A second difference between rule-governed and contingency-shaped behavior is that contingency-shaped behavior can sometimes be more sensitive to its consequences than rule-governed behavior. After people begin following a rule, rule-following may persist even when the behavior is less successful than an alternative behavior. (Hayes, Brownstein, Zettle, Rosenfarb, & Korn, 1986; Kaufman, Baron, & Kopp, 1966; Shimoff, Catania, & Matthews, 1981). In this research, people have done button-pushing tasks in which their behavior has been put on certain schedules of reinforcement. A common finding is that when given a rule about how to respond, subjects continue to follow the rule even when it is unhelpful in obtaining the maximum number of possible reinforcers. In contrast, when given no rule, subjects are more successful in discovering response strategies that allow them to get the most reinforcers.

Rule-governed behavior is sometimes insensitive to its consequences, but not always (e.g., Ribes & Martinez, 1990). Behavior analysts are currently studying the conditions that cause rules to overpower the effects of the consequences of rule-following (Joyce & Chase, 1990). For example, LeFrancois, Chase, and Joyce (1988) found that after people have experienced a variety of reinforcement schedules, their rule-governed behavior becomes more sensitive to response-dependent consequences. In this sense, variety of experience can reduce rule-governed control of our behavior.

The insensitivity of rule-governed behavior may be the cause of odd behaviors as well as serious behavior problems. For example, take the case of superstituous rules that specify fictional consequences. Superstitious rules include ones that specify that you must not cross the path of a black cat, and horoscope messages that specify that certain types of your daily behaviors are going to receive reinforcing or punishing consequences. Many people carefully follow superstitious rules even though these rules have no payoffs. When people adopt a faulty rule (e.g., "I am the cause of the troubles of many other people," cf., Beck, Rush, Shaw, & Emery, 1979), these rules may continue to influence maladaptive behavior even when following the rules does not lead to more reinforcers.

A final consideration between rule-governed and contingency-shaped behavior is that of developmental readiness. Because rule-following requires a certain mastery of the language, much of the behavior of young children is contingency-shaped. Only when children grow older does their behavior become more rule-governed (Bentall & Lowe, 1987; Bentall, Lowe, & Beasty, 1985). In fact when people reach adulthood, it is difficult for them to "turn off" rule-governed control. Adults often talk to themselves, and in doing so they provide self-rules that govern their conduct.

Types of Rule-Governed Behavior

As we have seen, rule-governed behavior includes any use of instructions to change behavior. This field is too large to cover it all here. Instead, we will focus on a few selected types of rule-governed behavior that are of special importance in behavior change procedures. These methods include self-instructions, problem-solving therapy, and cognitive therapy.

Self-Instructions

Normally when people think of an instruction, a command, or a rule, they think of something that other people order them to do. Yet, a considerable body of research has shown that people can use self-instructions or self-rules to govern their own behavior. Self-instructions are rules that an individual says to herself, causing the individual to follow the rule. Self-instructions can be said either aloud (overt) or to one's self (covert). For example, in the introduction to this chapter, Matt used coping self-statements, a form of self-instructions, to help him be brave, to remain calm, and to distinguish his nightmares from reality. Matt learned these self-instructions and repeated them to himself at night to control his own fearful behaviors.

Self-instructions are often used for self-control. For example, one self-rule specifies that if you are angry, you should slowly count to 10 before saying or doing anything rash. Following this type of rule allows emotional responses to subside and to be replaced by logical responses.

It is useful to distinguish between two types of self-instructions, *task-specific self-instructions* and *self-instructional packages*. Simple self-instructions are self-rules that pertain to the specific behavior to be changed. For example, the self-instructions Matt used were simple self-instructions because they all pertained to the specific brave behaviors to be increased and the specific fear responses to be decreased. Similarly, the self-rule about counting to 10 when you are angry is also task-specific self-instruction because it pertains to a specific response.

Specific self-instructions can be contrasted with a self-instructional package, originally developed by Meichenbaum and Goodman (1971), which has a sequence of self-instructions: (a) defining the goal or problem by asking yourself, "What do I have to do?"; (b) selecting a means of action to address the goal or solve the problem by asking yourself, "What is my plan?"; (c) following the plan by using task-specific self-instructions; and (d) evaluating your performance and providing self-rewards for correct responses and correcting errors.

Meichenbaum and Goodman used the self-instructional package with second-grade children who were in a special class because of their hyperactive behaviors and poor self-control. The children learned to be less impulsive through the use of the four-step self-instructional package, including the following self-verbalizations that the children learned:

> Okay, what is it I have to do? You want me to copy the picture with the different lines I have to go slow and be careful. Okay, draw the line down, down, good; then to the right, that's it; now down some more and to the left. Good, I'm doing fine so far. Remember go slow. Now back up again. No, I was supposed to go down. That's okay. Just erase the line carefully. . . . Good. Even if I make an error I can go on slowly and carefully. I have to go down now. Finished. I did it (p. 117).

Self-instructions have been used to deal with a variety of behavior problems including impulsivity in children (Kendall & Braswell, 1985), overactivity in children (Bornstein, 1985; Bornstein & Quevillon, 1976); encouraging honesty (Casey & Burton, 1982), children's fears of being alone (Peterson, 1987), teaching counting and arithmetic skills (Murphy, Bates, & Anderson, 1984; Van Luit & Van der Aalsvoort, 1985), improving performance on academic tasks (Bryant & Budd, 1982; Reiher & Dembo, 1984), encouraging attending to tasks (Burgio, Whitman, & Johnson, 1980), coping with pain (Heyneman, Fremouw, Gano, Kirkland, &

Heiden, 1990), and improving the "healthy talk" of institutionalized people diagnosed as schizophrenics (Meichenbaum & Cameron, 1973).

The studies showing the effects of self-instructions suggest that what people say to themselves is an important influence on their behavior. Within limits, people can alter their own behavior to their advantage by providing the proper self-instructions (Kassorla, 1984; Kendall, 1992; Lowe & Chadwick, 1990; Whaley, 1973). The power of positive thinking is, in behavior analysis terms, the effective use of self-instructions and self-talk that specify that you can achieve difficult goals. This principle applies only within certain limits. For example, a person lacking the skills to pass a college entrance examination will not benefit from self-instructions to do well on the exam. However, self-instructions can promote persistence at academic tasks (Reiher & Dembo, 1984) and improve performance quality. In this way, positive thinking can promote skill development and success. Self-instructions appear to be important in making a difference between success and failure in situations where people have the skills to perform well, but might fail to apply them fully.

Problem-Solving Therapy

Problem situations are ones in which people find that they lack a behavior that will be successful in that situation. (D'Zurilla & Goldfried, 1971; Skinner, 1953). For example, consider the plight of an unhappily married couple. Each spouse's attempts to communicate with the other go unreinforced, and it seems as though nothing the partners can do will resolve the situation. When faced with such an impasse, many people either give up or respond automatically by continuing to engage in unsuccessful behaviors.

D'Zurilla and Goldfried (1971) introduced problem-solving therapy as a behavior change technique to solve problem situations. The main idea of problem-solving therapy is to get people to stop responding automatically to problem situations and instead get them to follow a set of problem-solving rules more likely to evoke successful behaviors.

Problem-solving therapy has five stages. First, in a *general orientation* stage, the therapist explains the rationale for problem solving, to teach people to follow problem-solving rules. The therapist also encourages clients to begin looking for problems to solve in their lives. Instead of viewing their difficulties as problems to solve, many people use maladaptive approaches: Ignore problems in order not to confront them, view problems as insoluble, or punish the behavior of other people as an automatic reaction to problems. To make people aware of problems, the therapist asks them to keep a record of the problem situations they encounter in their daily lives.

The second stage of problem solving is *problem definition and formulation*. The purpose of this stage is to get people to follow the rules: (a) Define the problems as specifically as possible, and (b) formulate the problem by identifying goals. For example, as discussed in Chapter 1, many people have difficulties in solving behavior problems because they do not define the problem in specific behavioral terms and instead attribute the problem to explanatory fictions. In addition, many people do not define all the specifics of the problem situation. For example, D'Zurilla and Goldfried worked with a woman named Sally, who was having problems with her husband. At first, Sally defined the problem as her being depressed because her husband was out working late and she was home alone. After working with Sally, the therapists got her to define several aspects of the problem more specifically. It turned out that Sally's husband worked late because the family needed the money, that she enjoyed company and interesting conversation, that she lived on a poorly lit street and was afraid of break-ins, and that her husband's long working hours had interfered with their sex life. Once she specified a problem definition, Sally formulated goals to socialize more during the week, to feel safer at home, and to have more sex.

The third stage of problem-solving therapy is called the *generation of alternatives*. The purpose of this stage is to encourage people to follow the rule: Describe alternative behavioral strategies for solving problems. In Sally's case, she considered several solutions, including visiting with women friends and relatives during the week, initiating sex with her husband, having an affair with another man, and safeguarding her home from break-ins. Some of the potential solutions were flawed, but a key principle of generating alternative solutions is to list many solutions without immediately judging them. Often a flawed alternative can be the springboard for a better idea. But this is not possible if concern with flaws prevents people from having any ideas at all.

The fourth stage of problem-solving therapy is *decision making*. At this stage, the person working on the problem follows the rules: (a) Identify the likely consequences of each alternative behavioral strategy and find the best strategy, the one with the most important reinforcing consequences, and the fewest important punishing consequences; and (b) once the general strategy has been decided, generate ideas about specific behaviors to carry out the strategy. In Sally's case, she considered the personal, social, short-term, and long-term consequences of each alternative she had generated. For example, one of Sally's alternatives was to have an affair with another man. At the decision-making stage, she decided that the likely consequences of this alternative would be good sex, pleasant conversation and socializing, guilt, her husband's learning of the affair, divorce, and problems for Sally's and her husband's child. Sally evaluated all the alternatives in this way and decided which were best for her.

Once Sally had selected the general strategies, she again generated ideas, this time about specific things she could do to carry out her strategies. She considered whom to invite to her home during the week, whether to take a sewing class during the week, whether to initiate sex early in the morning, and whether to have dead bolt locks installed on the doors of her home. Next, she selected the best specific behaviors to engage in, also based on the consequences of the identified alternatives.

The fifth and final stage of problem-solving therapy is *verification*. At this stage, the person who has gone through the previous steps follows a rule to evaluate the success of the decisions made. If success has not been achieved or has been incompletely achieved, the individual returns to an earlier stage and revises the procedure. In evaluating the success of her decisions, the solutions she decided upon worked well, so the verification stage simply involved Sally's confirmation of her success.

Problem-solving therapy is a type of rule-governed behavior because at each stage of the process, the person follows rules that aid in finding a successful behavior that solves the problem. When the problem-solving rules are learned well, problem-solving can be considered as a form of self-instruction in which the individual recalls the problem-solving rules she encountered in problem situations.

Problem-solving therapy shares certain features of Meichenbaum and Goodman's self-instructional package because both methods define problems and evaluate progress. However, problem-solving therapy includes a stage at which a variety of alternative solutions is generated, and this stage is not a part of the self-instructional package. In addition, problem-solving therapy includes a stage at which a decision is made about the best solution, also not a part of the self-instructional package. Discriminating between problem-solving therapy and self-instructional packages is not always simple because self-instructions are sometimes identified as a problem-solving technique.

Problem solving is a particularly useful treatment because once people learn the problem-solving skills, they can successfully apply them to new, unfamiliar problems (Chase & Wylie, 1985; D'Zurilla & Goldfried, 1971; Park & Gaylord-Ross, 1989). In other words, problem-solving is a technique with generalized applicability. Problem-solving is also important because research has suggested that people with moderate-to-severe behavior problems differ from other people in that they lack problem-solving skills (e.g., Platt & Spivack, 1972; Platt, Spivack, Altman, Altman, & Peizer, 1974). Research has also shown that compared to normal children, children with learning disabilities lack the type of self-verbalizations that normally occur during effective problem solving (Harris, 1986b).

As Sally's example illustrates, marital therapies make use of problem-solving techniques (Greer & D'Zurilla, 1975; Jacobson, 1977; Jacobson et al., 1985). Problem-solving also has been used to treat many other disorders, including test anxiety (Mayo & Norton, 1980), unreasonable fears (Kleiner, Marshall, & Spevack, 1987), depression in children (Stark, Reynolds, & Kaslow, 1987), social-skill deficits (Park & Gaylord-Ross, 1989), poor study skills (Richards, 1978), prevention of injuries in the workplace (Martella, Agran, & Marchand-Martella, 1992), conflicts between teenagers and parents (Robin, 1979), anger control (Feindler, Marriott, & Iwata, 1984), and excessive drinking (Intagliata, 1978; Kelly, Scott, Prue, & Rychtarik, 1985).

Maladaptive Rule-Governed Behavior and Cognitive Therapy

Usually, when we think of a rule we think of something that someone has devised that helps us in some way, either by evoking behavior that will be reinforced or by discouraging behavior that will be punished or cause harm. Yet, for various reasons, people adopt self-rules that serve no useful purpose or are self-defeating. Therefore, the goal of some therapies, generally called *cognitive therapies,* is to replace maladaptive rules with helpful rules (e.g., Beck, 1976; Beck, Rush, Shaw, & Emery, 1979; Ellis & Greiger, 1977; Kassorla 1984). Generally, cognitive therapies replace maladaptive rules with helpful rules through procedures like self-instructions and problem-solving, among other procedures. Although behavior analysts did not originate cognitive therapies, their methods can be interpreted in terms of the behavior analysis concepts of verbal stimulus control and rule-governed behavior. Like self-instructions and problem-solving, cognitive therapies have been used to treat a variety of behavior problems.

Beck et al. (1979) give examples of maladaptive rules that affect the behavior of depressed people and suggest that three types of maladaptive rules affect such people: (a) self-rules that specify that the depressed person is defective or inadequate and has characteristics that prevent happiness; (b) self-rules that specify that the external environment is full of obstacles that cannot be overcome; and (c) self-rules that specify that the person's current difficulties will continue into the future and doom future activities. In each case, a goal of therapy is to replace these maladaptive rules with more desirable rules that specify that the individual is adequate and effective, that problems can be overcome, and that success can be attained in the future.

Beck et al. (1979) used cognitive therapy to treat a 36-year-old married woman who was the mother of two boys, 9 and 14. Tracy thought of herself as worthless, unable to do anything right, and a failure as a wife and mother. She considered suicide as a way to rid her family of a burden.

Initially, Tracy's therapist had her keep a record of her daily activities. During the first sessions, the therapist also began emphasizing the relationships among thoughts (self-rules), behavior, and happiness and sadness. In addition, the therapist began trying to get Tracy to cease self-criticism. By the fourth session, Tracy had begun to think that perhaps she should not label herself as an incompetent mother, but instead should consider learning child-training methods to help solve her specific problems. In recording her thoughts at this time, Tracy tried to avoid using negative labels to describe herself. Her therapist encouraged Tracy to begin thinking in terms of "want" statements, things she wanted to do, rather than "should" statements, things she felt compelled to do. The therapist continued to point out errors in the logic of Tracy's negative self-judgment. Part of Tracy's homework assignments was to analyze the faulty logic of her previously automatic self-criticisms.

As treatment progressed, Tracy worked with her therapist to formulate specific goals. Instead of criticizing herself for not being a better mother, she defined specific goals. These included sharing more time with her husband and placing limits on her older son's behavior. As she successfully progressed toward these goals, her depressed behavior began to subside. Over time, Tracy came to realize that her problem stemmed from a defective self rule: That other people would dislike and reject her unless she worked to meet their expectations. This self-rule compelled Tracy to act based on what she *should* do rather than want she *wanted* to do. By the end of the therapeutic process, Tracy had established new self-rules, including her goals and the idea to do things she wanted rather than trying to meet others' expectations. Tracy's therapy took place over the course of 22 sessions in 14 weeks. By the end of that time, she was no longer depressed. She maintained this improvement at follow-up checks of 1, 2, and 6 months.

Making Rules and Self-Rules Effective

Rule-governed behavior is under the control of verbal discriminative stimuli (Galizio, 1979; Skinner, 1969). Therefore, the principles discussed in Chapter 8 that make discriminative stimuli effective also influence the effectiveness of rules. Let us examine three general factors that influence the effectiveness of rules: (a) differential consequences dependent on following and not following rules; (b) the specificity and clarity of rules; and (c) combining rules with reasons. We will then review previously discussed factors that influence the effectiveness of rules.

Differential Consequences

Like other discriminative stimuli, rules and instructions can be made more effective if there are differential consequences dependent on responding to (i.e., following) the rule. For example, Neef, Shafer, Egel, Cataldo, and Parrish (1983) worked with six children ranging in age from 6 to 8. Three of the children had been identified as autistic while the other three had been identified as developmentally delayed. At first, the experimenters observed the children in their classroom and talked to the teachers. As a result of the information they collected, they identified 5 "Do rules" and 14 "Don't rules" that were applicable to the children. "Do" rules included commands such as "Come here," "Sit down," "Bring me (object)." "Don't" rules included such things as "Don't touch," "Don't leave," "Don't climb," and "Don't spit." At some periods during the experiment, the experimenters made consequences dependent on following the Do rules, but not on the Don't rules. At other points in the experiment, this was reversed: Consequences were dependent on the Don't rules but not on the Do rules. Consequences included praise, reprimands, and correcting errors. Figure 11.2 shows some of the results of the study.

The data in Figure 11.2 represent the students' responding to novel Do and Don't instructions, ones that were not used during training. As indicated, when the consequences were dependent on the Do rules but not on the Don't rules, the children followed Do rules but not Don't rules. Conversely, when consequences were dependent on Don't rules but not Do rules, the children followed the Don't rules but not the Do rules. This study shows that consequences influence not only whether a specific rule will be followed, but also govern whether a general type of rule (e.g., Do or Don't) will be followed.

The role of differential consequences in making rules effective also appears to apply to self-rules. For example, in what is called say-do correspondence training, a self-rule specifying that a person is going to do something is used. For example, Israel and O'Leary (1973) had children use self-rules to play with a particular type of

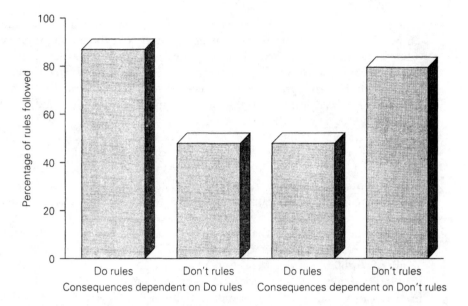

Figure 11.2 *The Effects of Consequences on Compliance With Two Different Types of Rules*

When consequences were dependent only on following the Do rules, the children followed the Do rules more often than the Don't rules. When consequences were dependent only on following the Don't rules, the children followed the Don't rules more often than the Do rules. Figure drawn from table in Neef et al. (1983).

toy (e.g., "I'm going to play with the puzzles."). The children followed the self-rules more often when reinforcers, snacks and praise, were dependent on following the self-rules. Currently, behavior analysts are exploring the use of correspondence training methods to establish self-control and generalized changes in behavior. (See Paniagua [1990] for a review of correspondence-training methods.)

The Specificity and Clarity of Rules

In previous chapters, we have shown how rules that specify relationships between behavior and consequences can improve the effectiveness of behavioral procedures. In addition, the more specific and clear the rule is, the more effective it is likely to be (Moore & Olson, 1969). For example, as discussed in Chapter 5, Miller et al. (1970) showed that the more specific instructions were, the more effective they were (See Figure 5.1).

Vague and ambiguous rules are often characteristic of formal education. Teachers give students only vague rules about what they are expected to learn. A better approach that behavior analysts have actively promoted in education is to provide students with clear and specific instructional objectives, rules about what students are expected to learn (Vargas, 1972). Vance and Colella (1990), for example, showed that when the experimenters assigned specific difficult goals, subjects performed better than when the experimenters simply told them to do their best.

Sometimes well-specified rules become unclear when people are inconsistent in stating them. Stouwie (1971) found that when two experimenters specified a rule that prohibited play with a toy, children did not play with the toy. When the two experimenters were not consistent in specifying this rule, the children were much more likely to play with the toy.

Two cautions apply to the use of rules. When making rules, people tend to specify only what should not be done rather than what should be done. Part of the reason for this may be that "don't" rules can sometimes be more effective than "do" rules (Redd, Amen, Meddock, & Winston, 1974). However, using rules that specify desirable behaviors is a constructional approach to behavior change because it provides a positive goal toward which the learner can strive.

Another problem is that overly specific rules may not produce generalized changes in behavior. Casey and Burton (1982) found that rules specifying the desirability of truthful behavior were more effective in producing generalized truthfulness than task-specific "do" and "don't" rules. For example, telling a child not to steal his brother's bicycle may effectively reduce theft of the bicycle, but not other types of theft. Alternatively, if the rule is to respect the possession of others, rule-governed behavior may reduce other types of theft. Rules that specify general classes of desirable behavior may be useful in producing generalized changes in behavior.

Combining Rules With Reasons

One problem with many rules is that they fail to specify the consequences for following and not following the rules. Rules that provide reasons for following the rule are generally more effective than those that do not. In Chapter 4, we saw an example in Parke's (1969) experiment. In that study, children only instructed not to play with a toy played with the toy more than children given the same instruction accompanied by a rationale, that the toy would wear out or break, and then other children would not be able to play with it. Similarly, Davies, McMahon, Flessati, and Tiedemann (1984) found that children obeyed their mother's instructions when she gave a reason for following them.

A second problem with rules is that many of the rules that specify reasons for rule-following specify consequences that are contrived rather than natural. For example, if a mother tells her child, "Don't wander away from me or else I'll spank you," a reason has been provided, but the reason involves a contrived consequence rather than a natural consequence. Conversely, if the mother gave the rule along with a reason concerning the danger of being lost in crowds, the reason would be a natural consequence for rule-following.

Using rules that specify natural consequences rather than contrived ones is desirable for several reasons. Natural consequences promote generalization and maintenance of behavior more than contrived consequences. Rules that appeal to natural consequences may therefore help bring behavior under the control of those consequences. In addition, the use of reasons promotes the learning of the logical reasoning skills involved in making causal connections between behaviors and natural, often deferred consequences. However, in order to be effectively governed by reasons, children must have certain basic verbal abilities. Some observers have suggested that verbal rationales are unable to act as effective discriminative stimuli for children younger than approximately $4\frac{1}{2}$ years. (See Davies et al. [1984] for a treatment of this issue.)

In general, rules should specify reasons for following the rules and those reasons should concern the natural consequences for rule-following. When specifying the natural consequences for rule-following is ineffective, contrived consequences or other response-strengthening procedures should be used.

Other Factors That Make Rules Effective

In previous chapters, we discussed several additional factors that make rules effective. These include:

- using accurate rules (Chapter 3; Weiner, 1970).
- mixing difficult-to-follow rules with easy-to follow rules (Chapter 5; Mace & Belfiore, 1990).
- using rules to specify what consequences will follow correct and incorrect responses in stimulus discrimination training (Chapter 7; Spence et al., 1969).
- delivering rules personally rather than impersonally (Chapter 8; Williams et al., 1989; Reitz & Hawkins, 1982).

Making Self-Instructions Effective

Research has shown that several specific factors improve the effectiveness of self-instructions, including whether the self-instructions are overt or covert, whether other people know that the self-instructions are being used, and the use of self-reward for following self-instructions.

Meichenbaum and Goodman (1969) compared the effects of overt versus covert self-instruction to do things "faster" and "slower." For kindergarten children, these self-instructions were more effective when said aloud than when said silently to themselves. In contrast, among first-grade children, the self-instructions were more effective when said covertly rather than overtly. These results suggest that the ability to use self-instructions depends on having learned to respond to covert verbal stimuli, and this is a skill young children have not acquired. However, even with adults, it is often desirable at first to have people say the self-instructions aloud to ensure that they are using them. Later, the self-instructions can become covert (e.g., Meichenbaum & Cameron, 1973).

A key factor that influences the effectiveness of self-instructions is whether other people know that someone is using them (Hayes & Wolf, 1984; Rosenfarb & Hayes, 1984; Zettle & Hayes, 1983). Hayes and Wolf studied this factor in an experiment with university students. The experimental task required students to put one hand and part of their arm in ice water. The students then periodically rated how much pain they had on a scale from no pain at all to extreme pain. Two groups of students made use of coping self-instructions. One group made use of instructions that helped them tolerate the cold water (e.g., "I can keep my hand in the water in spite of the coldness."). Another group made use of statements that were designed to alter the subjective experience of pain (e.g., "I don't have to interpret the sensations as unpleasant."). In addition, the task was structured so half the students who used each type of self-statement knew that the experimenter had knowledge of what self-statements the subjects were using. This group was called the public group because their use of the self-statements was public knowledge. The other half of the students was led to believe, falsely, that only they knew what self-statements they were using, and that the experimenter did not know whether they were using self-statements. This group was called the private group. A control group of students did not use self-statements, but merely discussed the topic of pain with the experimenter.

As you can see in Figure 11.3, the self-statements were effective in reducing feelings of pain only among the public group. The private self-statements were of no

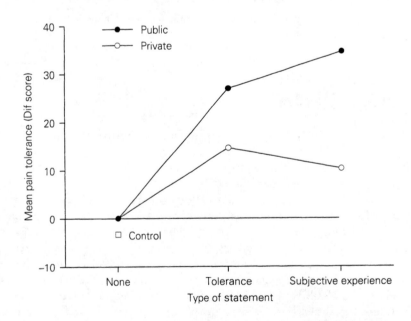

Figure 11.3   *The Influence of Public Disclosure on the Effectiveness of Self-Statements*

The public self-statements significantly reduced the students' reported feelings of pain compared to the control group. The private self-statement group was not statistically different from that of the control group. Figure adapted from Hayes and Wolf (1984).

help in reducing the reported experience of pain. The practical implication of this study is that, if you are using self-statements to alter your behavior, it is desirable to tell other people that you are doing so. If you keep this information to yourself, self-instructions may not be effective at all. Hayes and Wolf suggest that making a public commitment to doing something makes us more likely to be successful at what we seek to do.

Another aspect of Meichenbaum and Goodman's self-instructional package that is useful is self-reward. Nelson and Birkimer (1978) sought to reduce the impulsivity of second and third grade children; they showed that using self-instructions plus the self-reward component of the package was more effective than using self-instructions alone.

Making Problem-Solving Rules Effective

Research has shown that several conditions contribute to the effectiveness of the rules used in problem-solving. These conditions include the number of alternative solutions generated, training in problem definition and in decision-making, providing opportunities to rehearse problem-solving skills, and providing performance feedback for problem-solving rule-following.

D'Zurilla and Nezu (1980) had university students solve two problems: One was the problem of a student who wanted to get a good grade, but felt he could not because many of the other students in the course were cheating on exams. A second problem situation was that of a student who was placed on a university committee assigned the task of reducing the number of burglaries in campus dormitories. One group of the problem-solvers was trained in the *quantity principle,* the notion that the more solutions that are generated, the better the quality of the ultimate solution. Raters who were unaware of the purpose of the study rated the goodness of the solutions the students selected. These data, illustrated in Figure 11.4, show that the solutions of the students trained in the quantity principle were superior to the solutions of other students.

Nezu and D'Zurilla (1981) found that teaching subjects the problem-definition and decision-making rules of problem-solving improved problem-solving. Students worked on problems involving how to avoid fighting with a friend and how to reduce campus crime. Students who learned either the rules of problem-defining or decision-making discovered better solutions than students who did not learn these rules. Cormier, Otani, and Cormier (1986) also showed that training in the decision-making rules of problem-solving is beneficial, especially for the long-term effectiveness of problem solving.

In another study of problem solving, Jacobson and Anderson (1980) worked with couples in troubled marriages. One group of couples received a complete form of marital therapy, consisting of learning problem-solving rules, practicing the rules in videotaped discussions, and providing the couples with feedback about how well they followed the problem-solving rules. A second group received similar marital therapy, but without an opportunity to practice problem-solving rules, though they

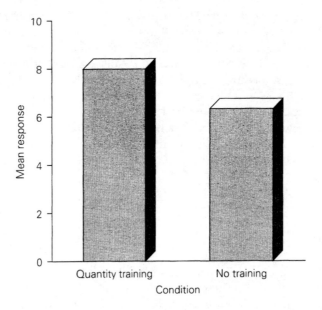

Figure 11.4   *The Effects of Quantity Training on the Effectiveness of Problem-Solving*

Students who received quantity training generated a greater number of superior solutions than students who received no training. Figure drawn from D'Zurilla and Nezu's (1980) data.

did receive extensive feedback on an interaction videotaped before therapy. A third group also received a similar form of marital therapy, except that this group practiced the use of the problem-solving rules, but received no feedback regarding their performance. Data from the study showed that the group that received the complete form of marital therapy, which included practice (rehearsal) and feedback, learned to follow the problem-solving rules better than the other two groups.

Some Advanced Considerations

Most basic concepts of behavior analysis, including reinforcement, schedules of reinforcement, punishment, and extinction, were first introduced by B. F. Skinner in his book *The Behavior of Organisms,* published in 1938. In contrast, Skinner introduced the concept of rule-governed behavior some 30 years later. Because rule-governed behavior is a relatively new behavioral principle, behavior analysts have not studied it as extensively as most of the other basic principles. As a result, rule-governed behavior is a often a controversial topic among behavior analysts. Many behavior analysts have initiated programs of research to settle these controversies and to give us a better understanding of how rules and instructions influence our behavior. At present, however, we must be content to speculate about certain aspects of rule-governed behavior rather than to come to firm conclusions. Three consequences of the newness of the topic of rule-governed behavior are (a) that the concept is often misunderstood, (b) that behavior analysts are not sure about exactly when and when not to use rules in behavior-change therapies, and (c) that some intriguing speculations can be made about the role of rules in promoting optimistic behavior and preventing depressed behavior.

First, rule-governed behavior is an area of behavior analysis that is frequently misunderstood. For example, often observers label the sorts of rule following we see in self-instruction, problem solving, and cognitive therapy as activities different from behavior. However, as we have seen in this chapter, rule-following is behavior that may be analyzed using the same essential principles we use to analyze other forms of behavior. We have emphasized, for example, that rules are verbal discriminative stimuli that govern our conduct. Many observers outside the field of behavior analysis believe that it is concerned only with the effects of reinforcers and punishers on behavior. To the contrary, rule-governed processes are a major area of research and theory within behavior analysis.

One example of rule-governed behavior is the behavior of making and using hypotheses. A hypothesis is a tentative rule about what might be true that can guide subsequent behavior. For example, in reading a murder mystery, people have hypotheses about "whodunnit," and this tentative rule guides the reader's perusal of the story. The reader notes evidence that either confirms or refutes the hypothesis. Hypothesizing of this type occurs all the time, as people hypothesize about who might be romantically interested in them, who is trying to discredit or cheat them, or how other people will fare in new activities. We are constantly constructing tentative self-rules of this sort, retaining and acting upon those that appear to help us, and discarding those that are ineffective.

Hypothesizing has been studied in psychology experiments. For example, during the 1960s, researchers conducted experiments in which people's verbal responses were reinforced. The verbal responses included such things as saying a human noun such as uncle, aunt, Argentinian, or clerk. A common finding in such studies was that when the subjects formulated the rule that specified the relationship between the target response and delivery of the reinforcer, there was a rapid increase in correct responding (e.g., DeNike, 1964). This effect suggested that the hypothesis acted as a rule that successfully governed correct responding. For example, a subject might say, "It seems when I say a human name, I get approval, so that's what I'll do from now on," and this self-rule governed behavior in the experiment. This type of effect is sometimes misinterpreted as showing that behavioral principles such as reinforcement do not work with people. It should instead be considered an example of a way in which rule-governed behavior does work with people (Hineline & Wanchisen, 1989).

Second, another current issue in the area of rule-governed behavior is when rules should and should not govern behavior. In most of the chapters of this book, we have suggested that people should be given instructions about the relationship between their behavior and its consequences. For example, when reinforcing a child's behavior, we have suggested that the child should be given a rule specifying the relationship between performing the behavior and receiving the reinforcer. This advice reflects current practice in behavior analysis.

Are there times, though, when it is better for people's behavior to be contingency-shaped rather than rule-governed? Hayes, Kohlenberg, and Melancon (1989) have suggested that behavior therapies rely too much on rule-governed control of behavior and that behavior analysts should explore therapies based on contingency-shaping methods. Contingency-shaped behavior has the advantage of being considered more natural than rule-governed behavior (Skinner, 1969), a feature that may recommend its use in therapy. In addition, Chase and Danforth (1991) have suggested that some types of learning are improved more though contingency-shaping procedures than through rule-governed methods. As we have emphasized, these effects are not currently well understood. Both Hayes et al. (1989) and Chase and Danforth (1991) have suggested that behavior analysts study the ways in which rules help and hinder learning.

Third, rule-governed behavior may be linked both to behavior we call optimistic and cheerful and to behavior we call pessimistic and depressed. Evidence for this linkage comes from studies that show that nondepressed people's behavior is governed by more self-rules that specify that their ongoing behavior is desirable and will receive reinforcing consequences than by self-rules that specify that their behavior is poor and will be punished or go unreinforced (See Kendall [1992] for a review). Specifically, these studies showed that nondepressed people have about a 2 to 1 ratio of positive to negative self-rules. In contrast, mildly depressed people have a 1 to 1 ratio of positive to negative self-rules and more severely depressed people have a ratio of 1 positive self-rule for every 2 negative self-rules.

An unexpected finding from this line of research is that nondepressed people tend to be governed by inaccurate self-rules that specify an unrealistically high proportion of positive reinforcers will be dependent on their ongoing activities (e.g., Alloy & Ahrens, 1987). In contrast, the behavior of depressed people tends to be governed by self-rules that more accurately specify the true relationships between behavior and reinforcers and punishers. These findings also apply to the use of self-rules that specify the degree of dependency between one's behavior and consequences. Nondepressed people tend to overestimate the degree to which reinforcing consequences are dependent on their behavior, while depressed people more accurately specify the extent of these dependencies (Alloy & Abramson, 1979; Taylor & Brown, 1988). In sum, these surprising findings suggest that it is beneficial to be governed by self-rules that specify that reinforcers are dependent on our behavior and are dependent in greater quantities than is actually the case. These data may be of help in treating depression through altering self-rules and, more generally, point to the value of hope and optimism, even over logic and reason, as useful features of our behavior.

Summary

Much of our behavior is rule-governed. Among the many different types of rules are commands and advice. Some rules are based on direct-acting consequences and others on indirect-acting consequences. Many human problems are concerned with getting people to follow rules based on indirect-acting consequences.

Rule-governed behavior is central to logical thinking. When we think logically, we bring our behavior under the control of rules and apply them to our current situation.

Rule-governed behavior contrasts with contingency-shaped behavior. We say that a person "knows the rules" when her behavior is rule-governed, whereas we say that a person "knows how" when her behavior has been contingency-shaped. In real life, our behavior is seldom exclusively rule-governed or contingency-shaped, because both rules and consequences influence most of what we do.

Three practical behavior change procedures that are based on rule-governed behavior are simple self-instructions, self-instructional packages, and problem-solving and cognitive therapy.

Rules are more effective if consequences are dependent on rule-following and if the rule is clearly specified.

Some behavior analysts have come to question when rules should and should not be used to alter behavior. The answer to this question will depend on future research into the merits of rule-governed and contingency-shaped therapies.

Conceptual Exercise   *Rule-Governed and Contingency-Shaped Behavior*

For each of the following items, decide if the item is an example of either rule-governed or contingency-shaped behavior. Indicate your choice by checking the appropriate box and justify your decision with a brief explanation. Confirm your decisions by consulting the analyses provided in the back of the book.

1. Captain Regulas commanded a navy ship, and it was his duty to recover parts from defunct satellites as they reentered Earth's atmosphere from space. To point his ship in the appropriate direction, Regulas relied on information about the orbit and trajectory of the satellite, wind speed in the atmosphere, the weight of the satellite, and many other factors. Regulas put these data into a computer program that predicted where in the ocean the satellite would come down. In this way, Regulas was able to position his ship to pick up the satellite parts.

2. Having recently graduated from high school, Biff was working as an apprentice blacksmith with Mr. Rune, who had been a professional blacksmith all his life. Among Mr. Rune's interests was poetry, and he taught Biff a poem to get him to operate a bellows that kept the coal fire in the forge burning hot. The proper way to operate the bellows was to use it to push air into the coals slowly and evenly, and then to refill the bellows with air rapidly. This permitted the maximum amount of air to keep the coals burning, while minimizing the time when the bellows was being refilled with air rather than feeding the fire. The following poem, which Biff memorized and recited eloquently, enabled him to operate the bellows properly the first time he used it:

Up high, down low,

Up quick, down slow,

And that's the way to blow.

3. Carol had been driving a standard transmission for several years. Due to her long experience with her present car, Carol could shift gears flawlessly while engaging in other activities, including listening to the radio, singing, or conversing with passengers. Her behavior of shifting gears was due to influences such as the feel of the car and the sound of the engine. These stimuli had been established as cues for her behavior of shifting gears due to the past consequences of correct and incorrect shifting.

4. Mike enjoyed running and riding his bike at night. He always wore white clothing when doing night workouts, adhering to the principle "Wear white at night," because he felt this was safer than wearing dark colors.

5. Chris had been watching a movie in a theater and walked outside into bright sunlight. She pulled the brim of her hat down, which dimmed the brightness of the light. She did this because in the past, pulling the brim of her hat down had dimmed bright lights that caused her discomfort.

6. Martha was writing a letter to a friend. She had stopped writing because she was not sure how to spell the word receive. Then she remembered something she had been taught many years earlier, "I before e except after c." This line allowed Martha to spell receive correctly and continue writing the rest of her letter.

7. Bob Johnson had been an outfielder for the Muskeg Creek Trail Trappers for 10 years. When he had been younger, he had sometimes failed to catch fly balls because he misjudged the ball's trajectory. However, due to the punishers associated with failed catches and the reinforcers associated with successful catches, Bob had learned to judge the trajectory of fly balls correctly. In this way, he could anticipate the spot where the balls would come down and catch them.

8. Wayne was asleep. He had fallen asleep on his left side and had remained on that side for several minutes. The mild discomfort from remaining in one position too long grew, and because of this, he turned over onto his right side. He did this because in the past, periodically changing his body position during sleep had successfully removed the mild discomfort from sleeping in one position for too long.

9. Carol had been reading Dale Carnegie's book, *How to Win Friends and Influence People*. One of Carnegie's suggestions was to call people by name. Carol heeded this advice and began calling people by their names, something she had rarely done before.

10. At first when Vance returned from the navy and married Maria, he shaved only once every few days. However, immediately after he shaved, Maria showered him with kisses and affection, something she did much less often when he had not shaved. As

a result, Vance began shaving every day. One day a co-worker asked Vance why he shaved more often. Vance said that he didn't know, that he hadn't thought about it.

Conceptual Exercise *Rule-Governed Behavior Change Procedures*

For each of the following items, decide if the item is an example of (a) self-instructions; (b) a self-instructional package; (c) problem-solving; (d) cognitive therapy; or (e) not an example of rule-governed behavior. Indicate your choice by checking the appropriate box and justify your decision with a brief explanation. Confirm your decisions by consulting the analyses provided in the back of the book.

1. Children between the ages of 5 and 6 years old who had shown more fear of the dark than other children, were participating in an experiment. The experiment took place in a small schoolroom where the windows had been covered with black plastic to ensure conditions of total darkness. A small lamp that could provide various levels of illumination was in the room. A competence group of children was taught to say, "I am a brave girl [or boy]. I can take care of myself in the dark." A stimulus group of children was taught to say, "The dark is a fun place to be. There are many good things in the dark." A neutral group was taught to say a nursery rhyme, "Mary had a little lamb. Its fleece was white as snow." After this training, the experimenter left the room and over a loudspeaker read some material that elaborated on the special words the children had learned. From time to time, the children repeated the words they had learned. Following these training procedures, the children were tested on their ability to tolerate being alone in the dark. They were told to try to remain in total darkness as long as they could. When they could no longer be in total darkness, they could turn up the level of illumination as little as possible to permit them to remain in the dark. The main finding of the experiment was the superior performance of the competence group. Teaching them to say, "I am a brave girl [or boy]. I can take care of myself in the dark," enabled the children to improve their ability to stay in the dark more than the other two groups could tolerate.

2. A group of kindergarten children at a school in New York was being taught to write letters with a pen. One group of children was taught to say the rules for writing the letters they were learning. These rules were to define the goal by asking "What do I have to do?", to select a plan to attain the goal, to follow the plan by using task-specific self-instructions, and to evaluate the performance and prove self-rewards for correct responses and correcting errors. For example, for the letter "P," the children were taught to say to themselves: "I have to go down, down, slow, stop at the bottom, stop." In addition, when the children made an error they told themselves correction rules, "No, that's not straight; I have to make a straight line, like a stick." Children trained in this way learned better than children who were not taught to give themselves the letter-writing rules.

3. A group of university students who were afraid of public performance had volunteered to be in a project designed to reduce their fears. As part of the project, the students watched skilled, self-assured actors perform in brief skits, which improved the

students' ability to act on stage. This improvement was measured by comparing the experimental students who watched the skilled actor with control group students who did not.

4. A group of agoraphobics, people who fear being outside their homes, was given training to help them overcome their fear responses. Therapists taught the people to recognize problems in their lives, to define their problems specifically, to generate alternative solutions, to select the best solution, and to evaluate the results. As a result of using this method, the people reduced their level of fear responses and could travel in the outside world more than they had before. In addition, in a follow-up check the people continued to improve, suggesting they were continuing to use their problem-solving skills effectively.

5. Female college students of normal weight for their height and frame had a negative view of their bodies. These women were following self-rules that specified that their bodies were inadequate. Treatment of this problem took two main forms. First, the women received discrimination training in which they learned that their body parts were of normal sizes. Second, the women learned to respond to their bodies with more positive statements, and to replace their negative self-rules with positive self-rules. Because of these procedures, the women were able to replace their negative body images with a much more positive view of their bodies.

6. A group of people volunteered to be in a project designed to treat psychological depression. The therapists treated one group of people by (a) teaching them alternative self-rules to replace unhelpful self-rules; (b) teaching them to distinguish between thoughts and facts; (c) teaching them to examine the short-term and long-term consequences of unhelpful self-rules; and (d) to recognize why illogical self-rules are illogical. Because of this training, the people were able to replace their unhelpful self-rules with more helpful ones and this reduced the frequency of the depressed behaviors.

7. People who were having problems volunteered for a project designed to change people's suicidal thoughts. For Group A, therapy consisted of (a) giving the people an overview in which they learned that difficulties are a normal part of life; (b) providing training in defining difficulties in specific terms rather than vaguely; (c) teaching the people to come up with many different ideas about how to overcome difficulties; (d) teaching people to predict and evaluate the likely consequences of different ideas about how to overcome difficulties and selecting a plan of action on this basis; and (e) evaluating the outcome of the selected plan of action. For group B, therapy consisted of training in listening to the therapist and the people sharing their experiences with each other in a support group. After the therapy was over, the people in Group A were less depressed, less lonely, more hopeful, and better able to deal with difficulties than the people in Group B.

8. C.P. was a 29-year-old British man who had been troubled by delusional beliefs. He believed that his wife, whom he had not seen for several years, was reading his mind and controlling his behavior. He also believed that in previous lives he had been Jesus Christ and Leonardo da Vinci. C.P.'s treatment consisted of the therapist challenging C.P.'s beliefs and encouraging him to adopt alternative explanations for

things that had happened to him. In this way, C.P.'s delusions were replaced with more useful beliefs.

9. Much of the time, Andrew, a 15-year-old high school student, engaged in coherent verbal behavior and appropriate social skills. However, he sometimes engaged in talk that didn't make any sense. As a part of his treatment, Andrew met with Dr. Randolph twice a week. During the treatment sessions, if Andrew engaged in sense-less talk or inappropriate social behavior, Dr. Randolph ignored Andrew. If Andrew engaged in sensible talk or desirable social behaviors, Dr. Randolph listened to him with rapt attention. As a result of these methods, Andrew talked sensibly more often and his social skills were much improved.

10. Terry was an adolescent boy who engaged in several inappropriate behaviors, including missing the school bus, requesting to go to the school washroom 13 times per day, and failing to wash himself regularly. To help solve these problems, a teacher taught Terry to deal with problems in a new way, by defining what he want-ed to do, making a plan to do this, following his plan by telling himself specific things to do, and evaluating his behavior and providing self-rewards or correcting errors as appropriate. Terry learned to do this procedure to deal with three prob-lems, getting on the bus to school on time, regulating his trips to the washroom dur-ing school, and maintaining personal cleanliness.

11. West Virginia University students were in a psychology experiment. First, the experi-menters observed the students to see how long they kept their hands in a container of cold water and what they said as they did so. On the basis of these data, the researchers divided the students into catastrophizers, people who engage in nega-tive thinking about problems, and noncatastrophizers, people who do not engage in such thinking. Then, the experimenters taught half the students self-rules (i.e., cop-ing statements) that specified that pain can be reduced by diverting your attention to something else. The experimenters taught the other half of the students self-rules that specified reducing negative thoughts. The experimenters measured the stu-dent's ability to keep their hands in the cold container and the amount of pain the students said they experienced. The students who were catastrophizers benefited from the self-rules that specified reducing negative thoughts, while the noncatastro-phizers benefited from the self-rules that specified thinking about something other than the pain.

12. First-grade children participated in a research project designed to study how to induce children to be honest. One group of children learned to say self-rules that specified that they engage in honest behavior. Another group of children was merely instructed to be honest and did not learn self-rules. After training, the experimenters observed the children engage in activities in which they could cheat. The children trained to use the honesty self-rules cheated less in these activities than the children who were told to be honest.

13. A group of teenagers and their parents who had been having difficulties in getting along with one another enrolled in a training program designed to help them. The teenagers and the parents attended therapy together, and received training in defin-ing problems, thinking of different ways to solve the problems, deciding on the best

way to solve the problem, and then carrying out that solution. This training caused the teens and the parents to become better problem solvers in role-playing situations. There was also some indication that the new skills improved the interactions between the teens and the parents at home.

14. The teachers of student pianists had referred their pupils for therapy. The students were troubled by extreme musical performance anxiety. One problem the musicians had was a high frequency of negative thoughts and self-rules that specified that they were inadequate. Treatment consisted of reducing the musician's negative thoughts and self-rules and replacing them with positive, task-oriented thoughts and self-rules. The musicians themselves developed the positive thoughts and self-rules and rehearsed the new thoughts and rules while they practiced the piano. Compared to a no-treatment control group, the pianists who received the treatment reduced their anxious behaviors during musical performances.

15. Nine first-grade teachers and 57 students participated in a study designed to improve the students' academic skills. The teachers gave the students a variety of academic tasks including identifying words by their context, vocabulary learning, and logically sequencing the parts of a story. The teachers taught an experimental group of students several self-guiding questions to use as they learned the skills. These questions were (a) to ask what should be done; (b) to use a plan to do what should be done, (c) to use specific directions appropriate to the task; and (d) to evaluate performance using self-reward and correction of errors. The teachers did not train a control group of children to use the self-guiding questions. Data from the study showed that the experimental children learned the academic skills much better than the control children.

16. A group of second-grade boys who had a greater frequency of aggressive behaviors than most boys of their age were participating in a study. As a part of the study, the boys learned a variety of techniques: to define problems, to think of different solutions to the problems, to select the best solution and use it, and to evaluate whether the solutions were working. Because of this training, the boys increased their frequency of desirable behaviors.

Conceptual Exercise   *Making Rules Effective*

Each of the following items has violated one of the factors that makes rule-learning effective. Identify what is wrong.

1. David lived in a very close knit neighborhood where everyone watched out for everyone else. As a result, theft, burglary, and so on rarely occurred. When David got a new expensive mountain bike for his birthday, his mother told him he must lock it in the garage every night before he went to bed. She explained to him that if he followed this rule, his bike would be safe; if he did not follow the rule his bike would be stolen. David forgot to lock up his bike one night. It was there in the morning. As a result, David rarely bothered to follow his mother's rule.

2. Nicholas's father explained to him that if he was polite to his friends, they would be polite to him. Nick's dad explained carefully what being polite meant. However, Nicholas soon discovered that being polite rarely resulted in his friends being polite to him and Nicholas soon stopped following his father's rule.

3. Andrew was 2-years-old. His mother sat him down one day and said "Andrew, It is very important for you to be good. Goodness is a virtue. If you are good with me I will give you a special treat. Other people will treat you very well if you are good. If you are not good, people will treat you badly." Andrew listened carefully to his mother and, in fact, whenever Andrew was good he was rewarded with kindness from others. Nevertheless, Andrew frequently sneaked candy from the grocery store and stole frisbees from the little boy down the street.

4. Matti was on a camping trip with his parents. He picked up an ax that his mother had been using to split wood for kindling. Alarmed, his father said "Matti, do not pick up that ax again." Matti was spotted shortly after playing with the ax again.

Conceptual Exercise   *Making Self-Instructions Effective*

From the factors that make self-instructions effective, choose the one that has been violated in each of the following items.

1. Marissa was a preteen girl who was overly concerned with her weight. Her mother was becoming worried. Marissa was not overweight but she thought she was. Marissa and her mother made an agreement that every time Marissa looked in a mirror, she was silently to say to herself, "I am not fat." Marissa's family knew that she was using self-instructions. Every time Marissa looked in the mirror and used her self-instruction, she would put a check mark on a chart near the mirror. These check marks could be traded in for various treats, such as going to the movies. This scheme did not work as well as it could have, and Marissa continued to be concerned about her weight.

2. Lance decided to quit smoking. Whenever he felt like having a cigarette, he would say aloud, "I am a nonsmoker." Each day that he refrained from smoking, Lance would treat himself by purchasing a hockey card for his collection. Lance didn't want other people to evaluate his progress so he kept his plan to himself. He did cut down, but he wasn't as successful as he might have been.

3. Merrilyn hated exercise, but the ski season was coming up, so she announced to her husband and friends that she was going to work out three times a week. She would get up on her workout mornings and announce that she was going to the gym. Off she go would go, and after she finished she would say aloud how good she felt. This procedure worked for a few weeks, but Merrilyn soon abandoned her workouts.

4. Luis's mother told him that he must look both ways before crossing the street. She told him that whenever he came to a crossing he should say to himself, "Look both

ways." Luis's mom would walk slightly behind him to watch if he followed this rule. When he did follow the rule he would clap his hands and his mother would join him as a reward. He was pretty good, but not as good as he could have been, at following his rule.

5. Bernice was small for her age and got picked on a lot. She told her classmates that she was tired of being picked on and that when they started teasing her, she was simply going to walk away. The first time someone picked on her, Bernice said loudly, "I am walking away" and she did so. Most of the time Bernice followed her own rule, but sometimes she didn't.

Conceptual Exercise   *Making Problem-Solving Effective*

In each of the following, one of the factors that makes problem-solving effective has been violated. Identify the factor.

1. Marissa had problems at work because she was not assertive enough. Her colleagues would frequently ignore what she had to say or interrupt her. She decided to take a course in assertiveness training. As a first step, she learned how to define problems and how to make decisions. Then her specific problem was addressed. Her teacher asked her what she could do if she were interrupted by a colleague. Marissa suggested that she could in turn interrupt the person who had interrupted her. Then the teacher played the role of a colleague and interrupted Marissa frequently. Marissa interrupted back and the exchange was videotaped. They watched the video together and the teacher gave feedback about Marissa's performance. Marissa reported that although she had some success at work she was generally disappointed with her level of assertiveness there.

2. Several new employees at a computer software company were given several problems to solve that users of the software had reported. First the employees attended a workshop designed to train them in problem definition and decision-making skills. Then the employees sat down together and addressed each of the problems that the software users had identified. Through brainstorming, the employees came up with many alternatives that might solve the problem. When they settled on a solution to the first problem, they submitted it to their employer and went on to the next problem. Some of the solutions they submitted were in fact implemented and some were not. The employees were not informed as to which solutions were used.

3. A company decided to hold a problem-solving competition. Two groups were formed. Both groups were given instructions in problem definition and decision making. Group A was also given the opportunity to practice their newly learned skills. Each group was given 12 problems to solve and experts in the area judged the solutions to each. Both groups, using a brainstorming approach, generated all sorts of possible solutions, even silly ones. Feedback was provided to each group after each solution was submitted. The second group, Group B, did not do nearly as well as Group A.

chapter 12

Feedback

Edward J. Feeney worked for the Emery Air Freight Corporation, where he had worked his way up from freight agent to vice president. As vice president, he became dissatisfied with the company's sales training methods, which consisted of having trainees watch motivational films and listen to lectures designed to inspire them to sell. Influenced by behavior analysis principles he had read about, Feeney introduced a new sales training program that made use of step-by-step behavior changes and provided the trainees with frequent feedback on their performance. Unlike the motivational films and lectures, the program focused on teaching specific skills the staff needed in order to improve their sales performance. Emery's sales increased from $62 million to $80 million in the first full year of the new program's operation.

Feeney's success with using behavior analysis methods in the sales training program convinced him that these methods might be useful elsewhere in the company. He became interested in the customer service area of the company and convinced Emery's top executive officers to allow him to try some behavior analysis techniques there.

Emery's Chicago office became Feeney's experimental project. There, the customer service representatives had set a goal of responding to customer inquiries within 90 minutes of the inquiry. An initial survey of employees and managers showed that they thought they were meeting the 90-minute goal about 90% of the time. However, more careful observations showed that in fact the employees were achieving the goal only 30% of the time. As part of a program to solve this problem, the representatives kept daily records of how long it took them to reply to each customer inquiry. This feedback method, in which people measure their own behavior and often record it on a chart, is called *self-monitoring*. In this case, the employees' self-monitoring was combined with managers' feedback about the level of callbacks. The program emphasized the value of giving employees praise whenever possible. As a result of these self-monitoring and feedback procedures, the percentage when the employees achieved the 90-minute performance goal increased from 30% to 90% to 95%. Over time, the managers cut back their feedback, but when they cut back too far, performance deteriorated. According to Feeney, "We found that when we provided daily feedback only one week out of four or one out of five, performance reverted to the previous level or was almost as bad" ("At Emery," 1973, p. 45).

Buoyed by his success in the customer service department, Feeney brought in a group of behavior analysts who worked at a business consulting company called the Praxis Corporation. The Praxis consultants convinced Feeney that rather than jumping from one part of the company to another in applying behavior analysis, he should make use of *performance audits*. In a performance audit, management surveys the performance problems that exist within an organization and decides what problems to solve based on where the most money can be saved. For example, a performance audit might show employee tardiness as a problem, but of low priority because solving other problems could save more money.

One performance audit revealed a key problem. Shipping small items in one container is much cheaper when they are going to the same place than shipping the items individually. Company executives thought that the containers were being used properly 90% of the time. However, the performance audit revealed that shippers were using the containers only 45% of the time that they could have been. The problem was not due to training, because the workers knew how to use the containers. Instead, the problem was that the workers did not have a good idea of how they were performing and did not realize the relationship between container use and costs.

To solve this problem, Feeney set up a system in which the employees received daily *feedback* from their managers about appropriate use of the containers: Managers told the employees to what extent they were using containers when they should. The managers also regularly praised employees for good performance. The result? Appropriate use of the containers rose from 45% to 95%, and in most of the company's customer service offices, this increase occurred in a single day. This use of feedback and praise produced an annual saving of $650,000 for the company. After the program started, feedback ceased a few times because managers changed jobs, for example. During these periods, appropriate use of the containers dropped off to only 50%. However, once feedback resumed, performance returned to 95%.

As Feeney observed his program in action, he gained some insights into what types of praise worked best. In particular, he found that a type of positive feedback called *labeled praise* was highly effective. Rather than simply saying, "Tremendous job, Joe," an example of labeled praise might be "Joe, I liked the ingenuity you showed just now in getting those crates into that container. You're running pretty consistently at 98% of standard. And after watching you, I can understand why" ("At Emery," p. 43).

Feedback and praise were applied to other types of performance too. Some employees kept daily records of the number of damaged cartons and received daily feedback about their level of performance reducing instances of damage.

How did the Emery Air Freight employees themselves feel about this use of behavior analysis? According to Feeney, combining feedback and praise worked well with 9 of every 10 employees. In a few cases, the program saved the jobs of workers who would have been fired for poor performance without the advantage of intensive feedback to help them do their jobs better. Some managers who didn't want to use feedback and praise with problem employees left the company. One indication that the employees responded positively to the program occurred at the Chicago office where Feeney had worked with the customer service representatives. After working with the program, the representatives began establishing for themselves new goals that were higher than they had formerly used.

All totaled, Emery Air Freight's use of behavior analysis principles, feedback and praise, produced savings of $3 million dollars in three years. Other companies took notice of Feeney's application of behavior principles at Emery. Today, several graduate programs specialize in training students to use behavior analysis in managing organizations and many behavior analysts work as consultants to corporations.*

Feedback: A Behavioral Consequence

Our behavior constantly produces *feedback,* consequences of our behavior that our behavior causes. A simple turn of your head produces a change in scenery, a letter to a friend asking for advice produces counsel, writing an essay at school produces comments from the instructor. A child's grammatical error in speaking results in a parent's repeating the utterance in grammatically correct form. In these cases, feedback consists of response-dependent consequences of behavior. We call praise, compliments, congratulations, and other approving consequences *positive feedback*. We describe criticism, disapproval, and error correction as *negative feedback.*

In general, behavior analysts use the term feedback in situations where they cannot be specific about the functions of behavioral consequences. Feedback differs in two ways from other behavioral consequences such as reinforcement, punishment, and extinction. First, feedback is not defined by a change in behavior caused by the response-dependent consequences. For a reinforcer to be properly called a rein-

*Based on "New Tool" (1971), and "At Emery" (1973)

forcer, it must strengthen some measure of behavior. Feedback, however, need not have any effect on behavior to be called feedback. Feedback refers to any response-dependent changes in the environment.

Second, feedback that is effective in changing behavior can be made up of different types of consequences, including reinforcers and punishers. Sometimes it is convenient to refer to the joint action of reinforcers and punishers without specifying which is responsible for behavior change; use of the term *feedback* allows for this. Feedback is also a useful term because it allows us to describe behavioral consequences that act as reinforcers and prompts at the same time. For example, suppose we are teaching a child a color-naming task. We point to a green object, the child says "green," and we agree, repeating "green." Our saying "green" may reinforce the child's response, but it is also a modeling prompt. As such, we are strengthening the child's "green" response in two ways, through reinforcement and prompting. We can't clearly say to what extent the consequence is a reinforcer or a prompt, so we call the consequence feedback to refer generally to both reinforcement and prompting.

A similar analysis applies if the child responds incorrectly in our color-naming task. If the child responds "blue" to a green object, we might correct the child by saying "green." Here, the consequence we provide might act as a mild punisher for the child's error as well as a modeling prompt for future correct responding to green objects. Describing the consequence as feedback again allows for the possibility that both punishment and prompting processes are involved in our correction procedure. Generally, feedback strengthens behavior through a combination of both reinforcement (and punishment) and prompting (Duncan & Bruwelheide, 1986).

Sometimes behavior analysts may wish to separate the reinforcing, punishing, and prompting effects combined in feedback messages. At other times, the behavior analyst is concerned mainly with the practical matter of producing a change in behavior, not with whether the change was due more to reinforcement than to prompting, for example. In any case, if the behavior analyst is curious about the degree to which a feedback message acts as a reinforcer, a punisher, or a prompt, additional research can often satisfy her curiosity, despite frequent practical problems in separating the functional properties of behavioral consequences.

In any case, recognize that feedback is not a new principle of behavior. Instead, it may be presumed to involve the joint action of principles we have examined in earlier chapters including positive reinforcement, punishment, escape conditioning, avoidance conditioning, shaping, schedules of reinforcement, stimulus control, prompting and fading, and so forth.

Advantages and Disadvantages of Feedback

Among the several advantages to using feedback as a behavior change strategy, one important one is that it allows the behavior analyst to concentrate efforts on correcting problems rather than anticipating problems that do not exist. For example, in teaching social skills, we might spend a lot of time providing rules for social behavior: how to greet people, use their names, make eye contact, respond to utterances in a timely fashion, stay on the topic of conversation, and so forth. However, the trainees may already have many of these skills. By allowing the trainees to engage in social interaction and providing appropriate feedback, it is possible to concentrate on changing those social behaviors most in need of change. In addition, in teaching some types of skills, feedback can be more effective than providing instructions (e.g., Rosenfarb, Hayes, & Linehan, 1989) or other types of prompts (Haught, Walls, & Crist, 1984).

Feedback, used effectively to change behavior in various types of organizations, has several advantages (Prue & Fairbank, 1981). First, a key advantage of using feedback is that it is an inexpensive way of producing behavior change. For example, Emery Air Freight's costs of using feedback were low. Second, use of feedback often makes aversive control techniques unnecessary: One Emery employee on the verge of being fired was able to make use of intensive feedback to improve his performance. Third, in many organizations union contracts and other laws and rules prevent the use of reinforcing incentives to change behavior. In these situations, feedback strategies that provide people with information about the quality of their performance can be used.

One disadvantage to using feedback is that once an incorrect response has occurred, there is a tendency for that response to continue to occur. This is called *error perseveration* or the stubborn-error effect (e.g., Kim, Marx, & Broyles, 1981). As such, overdependence on the use of feedback can lead to an initially high error rate and persistence of those errors, a problem that can be solved by combining feedback procedures with prompting methods. For example, errorless discrimination methods such as delayed prompting use prompting to minimize errors, and feedback to correct those that do occur.

Types of Feedback

In this section, we will look at several different types of feedback commonly used in diverse applications of behavior analysis, including publicly posted feedback, individual feedback, automated feedback, self-monitoring, labeled praise, correct-response feedback, corrective feedback, outcome feedback and why-feedback, and biofeedback. In addition, we will consider the idea of feedback-seeking.

Publicly Posted Feedback

Behavior analysts have made extensive use of a type of feedback called public posting, in which a chart or graph that displays performance is posted in a prominent place.

Public posting has been used very effectively to reduce speeding. We saw the impact of speeding on traffic deaths in the 1970s, during the energy crisis, when the U.S. Congress reduced the speed limit to 55 miles per hour. The driver speed reductions that followed saved thousands of lives (Labrum, 1976).

In a series of experiments, Van Houten and his colleagues have shown that publicly posted feedback about driving behavior can improve safe driving (Van Houten, Malefant, & Rolider, 1985; Van Houten & Nau, 1981, 1983; Van Houten, Nau, & Marini, 1980; Van Houten, Rolider, Nau, Friedman, Becker, Chalodovsky, & Scherer, 1985). Using a concealed radar device, Van Houten et al. (1980) measured the speeds of cars on a street where there was a 50 kilometer per hour speed limit. During baseline conditions, 90% of the drivers were over the speed limit. The experimenters then posted a sign that showed the percentage of drivers who were not speeding on the previous day and the best percentage performance of the drivers on all the days the researchers had measured speeding. The sign reduced to 78% the number of drivers who were speeding, and it also reduced the speeds of over-the-limit drivers. These improvements continued even when the researchers altered the sign to show the percentage of drivers who had not speeded the previous week.

In this and subsequent research, Van Houten and his colleagues have shown that public posting is cost-effective and works better than increased police surveillance. Public posting is effective even when many signs are in use in the same city and its speed-reducing effects persist as far as 6 kilometers beyond the sign. Van Houten, Malenfant, and Rolider (1985) showed that public posting also works to increase the percentage of drivers who yield to pedestrians.

Other desirable behavior changes that public posting has produced includes promoting industrial safety (Karan & Kopelman, 1986; Komaki, Collins, & Penn, 1982), improving performance in a small business (Komaki, Waddell, & Pearce, 1977), improving academic performance of grade school children (Van Houten and Van Houten, 1977), and improving performance of behavior analysts (Duus, 1988). (See Nordstrom, Lorenzi, and Hall [1990] for a review of public posting.)

One advantage of public posting is that it is inexpensive (Prue & Fairbank, 1981). For example, a supervisor can influence the performance of dozens of employees using a single graph or chart. Like other behavioral procedures, publicly posted feedback may sometimes have disadvantages. When performance is very poor, it may embarrass people and produce emotional reactions that interfere with behavior change. Likewise, undesired emotional behaviors can result if public posting induces an overly competitive environment. In these cases, privately delivered feedback may be more desirable.

Individual Feedback

Public posting enables feedback in a public place where performers and anyone else who happens to look can see it. In contrast, individual feedback (also called private feedback) goes to each person more-or-less privately, either in written or spoken form.

Individual feedback is useful when it would not be tactful to make people's performances public knowledge. In addition, individual feedback is necessary in situations where the behavior has many different features, making it possible for learners to make many different types of errors. Individual feedback can be keyed to the specific errors each learner is making.

Written Feedback.   Teachers often give written feedback in marking students' homework assignments. Although many teachers wonder whether the time and effort in providing written comments has any effect on students, research has shown that written comments are clearly valuable. For example, Elawar and Corno (1985) studied the effects of giving feedback on the math homework of sixth-grade Venezuelan students.

A teacher in one class randomly selected 14 students to be in a feedback group and 14 students to be in a control group. For the control group, the teacher graded the homework in the usual fashion, marking each problem correct or incorrect and giving a total score. For a second group of students, the teachers constructively criticized students' errors and suggested ways to improve. The teachers also gave at least one positive comment about something the student had done well. For example, one such comment was, "Juan, you know how to get percentage but the computation is wrong in this instance . . . Can you see where? [teacher has underlined the location of errors]" (p. 164). In giving the written feedback, four questions guided the teachers: "What was the student's key error? "Why did the student make the error? What can the student be told to avoid the error in the future? What did the student do well that can be praised?"

Some results of the study are shown in Figure 12.1. As you can see, there was little difference between the feedback and control groups on a pretest of math achievement, but on a posttest, the experimental group scored much higher. In addition, students who received the enriched feedback came to enjoy math more than the control students did.

Written feedback has the advantage of being a permanent product: When we have written feedback, we can refer to it for guidance when we need it. In addition, written feedback can be given and received at times most convenient to the giver and receiver. Written feedback has the disadvantage of taking longer to create that spoken feedback: We write more slowly than we can speak. In a study of written feedback in a hospital setting, Babcock, Sulzer-Azaroff, and Sanderson (1992) speculated that the response energy written feedback required discouraged its use among a group of nurses. An additional problem with written feedback is that people often ignore written messages more often than spoken ones unless there are very good reasons to read them.

Spoken Feedback.   An important use of spoken feedback is in language learning. At one time, some psychological research indicated that parents do not correct their children's errors in speech. This finding led some authorities to believe that the ability to speak correctly is not a learned skill, but is present at birth.

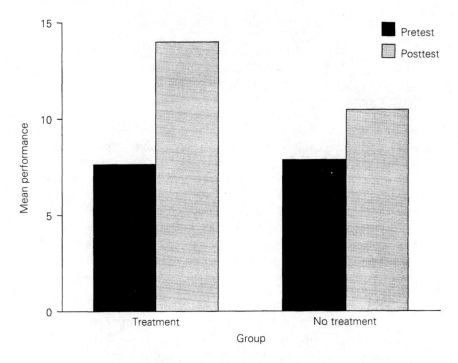

Figure 12.1   *The Effects of Enriched Feedback on Mathematics Achievement*

The treatment group who received enriched feedback improved more on the mathematics achievement posttest than the control group who did not receive feedback. Figure drawn from Elwar and Corno's (1985) data.

Recent research has shed more light on the issue. Bohannon and Stanowicz (1988) observed adults who were both parents and nonparents interact with children. They measured the children's instances of correct speech and errors of grammar and pronunciation. They also observed what adults said after the children's correct and incorrect instances of speech.

Data from the study showed that the adults did provide differential consequences for correct and incorrect child speech with subtle types of feedback, not blunt feedback (e.g., "You said that wrong"). First, Bohannon and Stanowicz found that when a child spoke correctly, adults were more likely to give feedback in the form of an *exact repetition* of the child's sentence. In contrast, when a child spoke incorrectly, adults were more likely (a) to *recast* the child's speech by saying the same thing correctly; (b) to give an *expanded repetition*, recasting the child's sentence and adding additional information; and (c) to pose questions related to what the child had said. For example, if the child said "That be a tiger," the adult might recast the sentence by saying "That is a tiger." If the child said, "Tiger growling" the adult might give an expanded repetition by saying, "The tiger is growling at the lion." If the child said, "That Duke," the adult might pose the question, "Is that his name?"

These researchers also found a difference between parent and nonparent adults in the way they reacted to children's speech. Parents were much more likely to provide differential feedback for correct and incorrect responding than nonparent adults. These considerations suggest that children make use of spoken feedback from adults, especially parents, in learning to speak correctly.

When we hear the word *feedback,* we sometimes think of blunt and simple evaluative messages such as "That's right," or "You're wrong." However, Bohannon and Stanowicz's work shows that feedback can consist of subtle differences in the way people respond to correct and incorrect responses. In day-to-day life, people are constantly providing each other with different feedback for different responses, and only sometimes is this feedback in blunt right-wrong messages. Sometimes, indirect cues such as the length and tone of voice of the message are important. (See Bohannon, MacWhinney, and Snow [1990] for a further discussion of these issues.)

Spoken feedback has also been examined in many other areas of behavior analysis. Many studies of training through stimulus discrimination and prompting described in Chapters 7 and 8 made use of spoken feedback from trainers or teachers. Like other types of feedback, spoken feedback has been used extensively in organizational behavior management (Prue & Fairbank, 1981; Balcazar, Hopkins, & Suarez, 1986).

Among several advantages of spoken feedback are that it can be delivered quickly, it can be personal, and ambiguities about the feedback message can be clarified through interaction between giver and receiver. Perhaps for these reasons, Babcock et al. (1992) found that nurses preferred spoken feedback over written feedback in a project designed to minimize the transmission of infections such as AIDS. However, the effectiveness of spoken feedback will depend on the social skills of the feedback giver and the relationship between the feedback giver and receiver. Sometimes feedback givers who have poor social skills can make even positive feedback seem inappropriate (Prue & Fairbank, 1981). If there is a poor relationship between the feedback giver and receiver, even mild negative feedback can further worsen the relationship. These considerations may be why computer-delivered feedback can sometimes be more effective than a supervisor's spoken feedback (Earley, 1988).

Automated Feedback

Another way to provide feedback is through automated devices. *Automated feedback* is provided, at least in part, automatically by a machine. Videotaped feedback is the most commonly used type of automated feedback. Behavior analysts have used it to teach a variety of skills. Typically, a person's behavior is videotaped and later viewed by that person. During viewing of the tape, the trainer can point out good and poor features of the individual's performance, so that videotaped and spoken feedback are combined.

Speas (1979) made use of videotaped feedback in training people, about to be released from prison, to present themselves well in a job interview. Target behaviors included explaining skills, answering problem questions, showing enthusiasm, having an appropriate appearance, and opening and closing the interview properly. One group of inmates saw videotaped models being interviewed and practiced being interviewed themselves. A video group saw the models, practiced interviewing, and also watched their practice interviews on videotapes. As they watched the videotapes, the instructor and the other inmates provided feedback about the interview performance. After training, judges who watched the inmates in test interviews rated both groups of subjects better than a no-treatment control group. Results favored the video group in several respects. For example, the judges rated inmates in the video feedback group as more likely to be hired than those who did not receive any training.

There are other varieties of automated feedback. Entertainers who mimic the voices of famous people learn to do so with the help of audiotaped feedback. Voting machines provide feedback from the electorate. Ratings of television programs are determined by devices that assess which channels samples of viewers are watching. Various types of scientific instruments measure pollution, depletion of the ozone layer, increases in carbon dioxide in the air, accidental radiation emissions, and so forth and thereby provide feedback about the harmful effects of various human behaviors on the physical environment.

In social situations, it is often difficult to infer what other people think of what we say and do. Gear, Marsh, and Sergent (1985) explored the use of automated feedback in group discussion. A group of five men discussed the design of a new university. Every 7 minutes during the discussion, each man turned a knob on a panel in front of him to rate the performance of the group and his feelings about the discussion. As shown in Figure 12.2, dials presented a summary of the feedback, showing both how good the ratings of performance and feelings were, along with displays showing how much the men agreed with one another in their ratings. Although further testing is needed, the feedback machine holds great promise for making university faculty meetings much shorter.

Although many devices give us automatic feedback in day-to-day life, many of them could be improved to provide more effective feedback. For example, Weber (1980) has pointed out that car gas gauges could be designed to provide better feedback about fuel usage, such as information about the cost of driving and immediate feedback about the cost of rapid acceleration.

Self-Monitoring

Self-monitoring, sometimes called self-recording, is a procedure in which one measures some feature of one's own behavior and displays it in a chart or graph. In the introduction to this chapter, we described how the Emery Air Freight customer service representatives used self-monitoring to ensure that employees returned phone calls within 90 minutes of receiving them. In addition, in Chapter 9 we exemplified the use of self-monitoring in improving study behavior.

B. F. Skinner, in great demand as a speaker, used self-monitoring to maintain his writing. To help ensure that he was not distracted from his work, he attached a

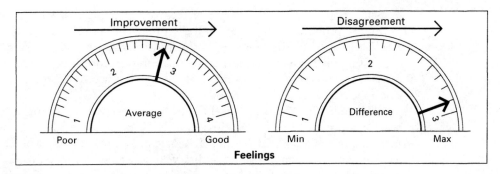

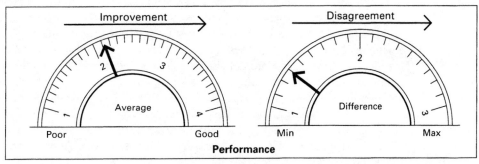

Figure 12.2 *A Feedback Machine*

Members of a group engaged in a problem-solving discussion received feedback from a machine about aspects of the discussion. Group members periodically rated their feelings about the discussion and the performance of the group. These ratings were averaged and displayed on the meters illustrated. Separate meters also indicated the extent to which the group members agreed among themselves in their ratings. Figure from Gear, Marsh, and Sergent (1985).

clock to the light at his desk. When the light was on, so was the clock. When he worked at his desk, the clock ran and recorded the time he worked. Every time the clock passed the 12-hour mark, Dr. Skinner put a point on a graph he kept. In this way, he received clear feedback about whether he was spending enough time writing. When his graph showed that he was not writing enough, he cut back on his speaking schedule.

Another person who made effective use of self-monitoring was Benjamin Franklin (Knapp & Shodahl, 1974), who divided his behavior into several categories such as temperance, order, resolution, frugality, industry, sincerity, chastity, and humility. He kept a notebook in which he recorded incorrect responses within each behavioral category. Although he was surprised to learn that he engaged in more incorrect responding that he imagined he would, he was satisfied by watching the frequency of his incorrect responding decrease over time. Franklin found this method to be so effective that he hoped that virtuous people of all the world's nations might someday use it as a part of a program to encourage good behavior.

Self-monitoring is an example of feedback because charts or graphs of one's behavior are probably effective as both discriminative stimuli and as reinforcers. For example, in Dr. Skinner's case, his graphs showing that he was engaging in high levels of writing probably served to reinforce writing. In addition, especially when they showed that his writing was insufficient, the graphs acted as prompts to do fewer public appearances and more writing.

Self-monitoring has been used to encourage many desirable behaviors. Among these are expressive speech (Schloss, Smith, & Schloss, 1988), improved performance in sports (Critchfield, 1989; McKenzie & Rushall, 1974), worker productivity (Ackerman & Shapiro, 1984), accuracy in solving arithmetic problems (Fink & Carnine, 1975; Dunlap & Dunlap, 1989), parenting techniques (Herbert & Baer, 1972), energy conservation (Winett, Neale, & Grier, 1979), fiction writing (Wallace & Pear, 1977), on-task behaviors of staff (Calpin, Edelstein, & Redmon, 1988; Richman, Riordan, Reiss, Pyles, & Bailey, 1988), study behaviors (Richards, 1975), learning to read new words (Lalli & Shapiro, 1990), problem solving (Delclos & Harrington, 1991), managing diabetes (Gilden, Casia, Hendryx, & Singh, 1990), social skills (Schloss & Wood, 1990), job interviewing skills (Schloss, Schloss, & Smith, 1988), treating speech disfluencies (Whitney & Goldstein, 1989), pursuing career goals (Herren, 1989), independent student behaviors (Rooney & Hallahan, 1988), and insomnia (Bayes, Masvidal, & Moros, 1982). As you can see this technique has had wide applicability.

Although self-monitoring can effectively change behavior, people who use it are often inaccurate in measuring their own behaviors (Lipinski & Nelson, 1974). If you have ever tried to monitor your own behavior, you may have some insights about why this is so. Observing and recording a specific response that you engage in is difficult to do accurately while performing the other activities of day-to-day life. Nonetheless, even if you record inaccurately, self-monitoring will often be effective as a behavior-change technique.

Self-monitoring is said to be a self-control technique because the person who is using the behavior change procedure is the same person whose behavior is being changed. As discussed in Chapter 8, self-control methods are often useful in encouraging the generalization of behavior change. For instance, Kelly et al. (1983) taught behaviorally disordered youths social skills, but the skills did not generalize beyond the training environment. However, when self-monitoring was added, rapid generalization occurred. Other researchers have also found that self-monitoring aids in generalization (e.g., Ackerman & Shapiro, 1984; Leal, Crays, & Moely, 1985). In a review of the generalization of parent training, Sanders and James (1982) found more support for self-monitoring than for other generalization-producing methods.

One can use considerable imagination in applying self-monitoring techniques. Many behavior analysts have made use of wrist counters designed for keeping score in golf, to self-monitor their behavior. One enterprising student self-monitored her writing behavior by using a fountain pen with liquid ink cartridges. By tracking how quickly each ink cartridge was spent, she measured the rate of her writing behavior. If you are considering a behavior-change project, experimentation with self-monitoring is a good place to start. You can use yourself as a subject and gain insights into the process of behavior change.

Labeled Praise

Labeled praise, also known as *descriptive praise,* is praise that specifies the behavior or features of behavior that are desirable. Bernhardt and Forehand (1975) studied labeled praise in an experiment with 20 preschool children and their mothers. The children played a game, the object of which was to drop marbles into either a red or a green hole. The specific hole selected for each child as the correct response was the hole the child used least during baseline observations. In an unlabeled praise condition, the mothers praised correct responses by saying things like "Good girl," "Way to go," or "You're good at this game." In a labeled praise condition, the mothers praised correct responses by saying things such as "What a good boy you are for putting a marble in the red [green] hole," and "Way to go, you put another marble in the red hole." The labeled and unlabeled praise conditions differed because the labeled praise specified the praised response, while the unlabeled praise did not. As Figure 12.3 shows, labeled praise was more effective than unlabeled praise in strengthening correct responding. Bernhardt, Fredericks, and Forbach (1978) found similar benefits for labeled praise.

Like many other types of feedback, labeled praise strengthens responding in two ways. First, it makes use of praise, a reinforcer. Second, it makes use of discriminative stimuli: The words in the praise message that describe the correct response serve as an S+ for continuing to engage in the specified response. Because we often don't know to what degree labeled praise is effective as a reinforcer or a discriminative stimulus, it is useful to talk about labeled praise as a form of feedback.

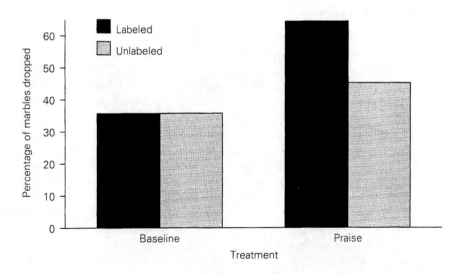

Figure 12.3   *The Effects of Labeled Versus Unlabeled Praise on the Effectiveness of Praise Feedback*

Correct responding improved more from baseline when labeled praise was used than when unlabeled praise was used. Figure drawn from Bernhardt and Forehand's (1975) data.

Correct-Response Feedback

One type of feedback that is often used in written exercises, flash-card drills, and computer-assisted instruction is *correct-response* feedback, also known as *knowledge-of-the-correct-response* feedback (KCR). Correct-response feedback consists of the correct answer to a question or problem. For example, in the conceptual exercises in this book, we have encouraged you to try to answer each item, and then to look at the correct answer. This is correct-response feedback because you find out what the correct answer is after responding to the item in the exercise. In the exercises in this book, you get the correct-response feedback and also additional information about why each item is an example or not.

In the past, some observers have considered correct-response feedback to be a type of positive reinforcement for correct answers. Although correct-response feedback may reinforce correct answers, it also provides discriminative stimuli. For example, suppose a tutor is quizzing students on a group of spelling words using flash cards. If the students get an answer correct or incorrect, they receive the correct spelling. The correct answer may act to reinforce correct answers and punish incorrect answers, but the correct answer is also a discriminative stimulus that strengthens correct spelling through prompting. The correct spelling may be considered as a type of modeling prompt. In general, correct-response feedback combines reinforcing consequences with modeling prompts.

Correct-response feedback is often used in training and teaching. For example, the methods of stimulus discrimination, prompting, and fading we discussed earlier all make use of correct-response feedback.

Corrective Feedback

Some people believe the most important role of feedback is to correct the learner's errors. Sometimes procedures like correct-response feedback or simply praising good performance can correct errors. Correct-response feedback can correct the learner's errors by modeling the correct response. Praising good performance can correct errors by extinguishing poor performance. At other times, however, behavior analysts make special consequences dependent only on incorrect responses. When these consequences prompt or otherwise strengthen the correct responses, we may call these consequences *corrective feedback*.

Hayes and Marshall (1984) used corrective feedback in training public-speaking skills. People who had volunteered to receive training to help them with public-speaking problems were videotaped giving speeches. The therapist provided positive feedback using labeled praise for what the speakers had done well. Corrective feedback was also provided: The therapist pointed out inappropriate speaking behaviors, described why the behaviors were inappropriate, and the therapist and the group suggested other, more desirable behaviors that should replace the inappropriate responses. This procedure is an example of corrective feedback because the feedback for the incorrect responses was dependent only on incorrect responses, and served as prompts for other desirable behaviors.

In Chapter 8 we discussed the increasing assistance method in prompting, another example of corrective feedback. If an error occurs it is corrected by prompting a correct response using a relatively weak prompt. If the error continues to occur, stronger and stronger prompts are used until the correct response occurs, even if it must be physically guided. The increasing assistance method is corrective feedback because:

- the prompts are consequences dependent on incorrect responses, and

- the prompts act as discriminative stimuli for correct responding (and perhaps also as mild punishers for incorrect responding).

We examined other forms of corrective feedback when we discussed positive-practice overcorrection methods in Chapters 4 and 5. These can be considered forms of corrective feedback in which the feedback is coupled with learner practice of the correct response. Engelmann and Carnine (1982) recommend that drill and practice of correct responses accompany corrective feedback. They also suggest that only one type of error be corrected at a time.

Outcome Feedback and Why-Feedback

Most feedback messages include *outcome feedback:* information about whether performance is correct or incorrect; this may include correct-response feedback as well. However, providing feedback messages that include only outcome feedback is often not enough. Sometimes we need to add *why-feedback.*

Why feedback includes information about the reasons for the correctness or incorrectness of the response. It can explain why correct responses are correct (correct-response why-feedback), why incorrect responses are incorrect (corrective why-feedback), or both.

Grant, McAvoy, and Keenan (1982) studied why-feedback with students in an introductory psychology course. The students studied conceptual exercises much like those you are using in this textbook. For some concepts, the students received only outcome feedback: The feedback specified only whether the item was an example of a particular concept (e.g., "Yes, this is positive reinforcement"). For other concepts, the students received why-feedback: The feedback described why the items were examples or why they were not (e.g., "No, this is not an example of positive reinforcement because there was no increase in the level of the target behavior"). As Figure 12.4 illustrates, students learned better on unit quizzes when they received why-feedback than when they received only outcome feedback. Why-feedback also improved their performance on the final exam more than outcome feedback.

Researchers have also compared the effectiveness of outcome feedback to other forms of more detailed why-feedback. For example, Wigton, Patil, and Hoellerich (1986) trained medical students to diagnose urinary tract infections. Working at a computer, the students read case material about patients that described the patients' history and symptoms. The lesson focused on teaching the students to focus on several key patient symptoms that indicate urinary tract infections. These symptoms

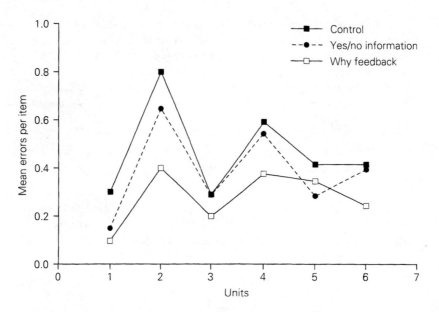

Figure 12.4   *The Influence of Why-Feedback on the Effectiveness of Feedback*

Students made fewer errors when they were given an analysis of why items were examples or nonexamples than when they were only given yes/no feedback or no feedback. Figure adapted from Grant, McAvoy, and Keenan (1982).

included painful urination, back pain, white blood cells in urine, red blood cells in urine, and bacteria in urine. The presence of these symptoms means that there is a certain chance of a urinary tract infection. Some symptoms are more indicative than others, such as the presence of white blood cells in urine being more predictive of an infection than the presence of red blood cells. Also, when the symptom is more severe, it is more predictive of infection. To diagnose these infections correctly, the students must be trained to weight certain symptoms more than others, and to pay attention to their severity. After reading each patient history, the students estimated the likelihood that the patient had a urinary tract infection.

After doing 18 patient case histories, students in a control group received out-come feedback: For each patient, the computer told the likelihood of an infection, given the symptoms. Students in an experimental group received this feedback, and they also received bar-graph feedback about how much they were overweighting or underweighting specific symptoms in making their estimates. This was an example of why-feedback because the feedback messages informed the students of why they were making incorrect diagnoses. For example, if a student put too much emphasis on back pain and not enough on bacteria, the why-feedback indicated this. Data from the study showed that the why-feedback was much more useful in training the students than the outcome feedback. Other researchers have studied the value of why-feedback in similar judgment tasks. (See Balzer, Doherty, & O'Connor [1989] for a review.)

Why-feedback is beneficial in many situations. If you sense that a loved one is unhappy with what you have done, ordinarily you want to know why, so that you can correct the problem. When a student does poorly on an essay, it is more helpful to know why an instructor has criticized her performance. When an employee perceives that a supervisor is displeased with her work, it is useful to receive why-feedback rather than simple correct-incorrect feedback. Kim and Phillips (1991) found that the use of why-feedback produced more favorable student attitudes toward a lesson as well as improved learning. In a survey of university students, Geis (1974) found that why-feedback from instructors was a frequently cited feature of good teaching.

Why-feedback is known by several different names, including *analysis statement feedback, complex feedback, descriptive feedback, elaborated feedback, diagnostic feedback,* and *cognitive feedback.* All these types of feedback generally refer to feedback messages that provide specific reasons for the correctness or incorrectness of a response.

Biofeedback

Another important type of feedback used in behavioral medicine is biofeedback, which provides feedback about people's physiological state, such as heart rate, blood pressure, muscle tension, brain wave patterns, and skin temperature. Because various instruments measure and provide the feedback about physiological processes, biofeedback is also usually a form of automated feedback.

Blanchard et al. (1986) used biofeedback to treat patients who suffered from hypertension (high blood pressure). The patients, who averaged about 50-years-old, all were taking two types of medication to reduce high blood pressure, medications that are expensive and have undesirable side effects. During treatment, each patient sat in a comfortable reclining chair. The experimenter attached a temperature-sensing device to the patient's index finger to indicate the temperature either on a meter or through an audible signal, whichever the patient preferred. The patient's task was to try to increase her temperature by using the feedback, the temperature meter, or the audible signal provided. At home, the patients also practiced trying to warm their hands. Biofeedback therapy occurred twice a week for 8 weeks, and data from the study showed that the treatment was more successful in reducing high-blood pressure than another therapy that taught the patients to relax. Many patients who received biofeedback training were able to stop taking one of the medications they were using.

Biofeedback is classified as a form of feedback because it is suspected that the effects of the method are due to (a) reinforcement of responses that produce desired bodily changes and punishment of responses that do not; and (b) prompting of desirable changes in physiological responses. In many applications of biofeedback, therapists do not tell patients to do anything specific to alter the feedback they receive, just to try to change in the desired direction. When biofeedback works, it is often not known what the patients are doing to produce the desirable changes. Indeed, because physiological changes are not easily observed, much is unknown about the specific ways biofeedback acts to alter physiological responses.

Feedback Seeking

Most of the types of feedback we have examined are ones in which a trainer, manager, or teacher gives feedback to a trainee, employee, or learner. Self-monitoring is an exception to this. In self-monitoring, people record their own behavior and use this information as feedback to manage their ongoing behavior. In this respect, self-monitoring is an example of *feedback seeking,* behavior engaged in the goal of getting feedback in order to improve one's performance.

Feedback seeking is a very important process. Research has shown that people who actively seek feedback are more effective than those who do not. For example, Komaki (1986) compared the behaviors of two groups of 12 managers whom supervisors had rated highest and lowest in motivating others. Komaki observed each of the managers during their daily activities at a medical insurance firm. The key difference between the two groups of managers was in seeking feedback: The best managers spent more time collecting performance information than the poorest managers.

Feedback seeking is also important in sports. Komaki, Desselles, and Bowman (1989) observed the behavior of sailboat racers at a regatta during the competition. Data from the study showed that the skippers who more often told their crews what they were doing right and wrong were more likely to win races than skippers who did not do this. Feedback seeking was also important: The skippers who sought out the most performance information were the ones most likely to win races. Skippers who didn't seek as much information tended to lose races. Some people think that champion athletic performance requires mysterious inner qualities. This study suggests, however, that feedback seeking and feedback giving may be the real secret to a winning performance.

Feedback seeking is often the reason behind success as a student. We have found that when students use the structured conceptual exercises that we have included in this book, most students learn the material well as long as they get enough practice. This result is mainly because the exercises promote active responding and provide frequent feedback. When students study a reading assignment from a more typical college textbook, often they simply read and reread the material, failing to seek feedback about how well they are learning. A more effective strategy is to read, later to try to recall what they read, and then to look at the text again to get feedback about how well they have recalled (Grant, Keenan, & Hursh, 1980; 1982). When using this method, students are arranging the study task such that they can take advantage of the power of feedback to enable them to learn better. Leal et al. (1985) used a similar self-testing method to improve children's recall.

Feedback-seeking strategies also appear to be important in producing behavior maintenance, long-lasting behavior changes. In Chapter 9 we saw how Seymour and Stokes (1976) taught girls in a correctional institution to use a cueing procedure to recruit praise for their behavior from the staff members. The experimenters reasoned that if the girls received positive feedback for the new desirable behavior they had learned, these behaviors were more likely to continue. Often, desirable behaviors do not last over time because people have never learned appropriate feedback-seeking skills.

Although seeking positive feedback is important, it is also essential to seek out negative feedback. In a study of hundreds of managers, Ashford and Tsui (1991) found that employees rated managers who actively sought out negative feedback as more effective than other mangers. In addition, the managers who sought out negative feedback tended to have more accurate information about how their colleagues evaluated them than did the other managers.

Seeking negative feedback may seem like a contradiction of behavior analysis, which highlights the power of positive reinforcement. However, negative-feedback seeking may be seen as a special case of reinforcement. For effective individuals, the discovery of negative feedback may function as a reinforcer in the sense that it provides opportunities to solve problems and thereby provides for longer-term reinforcement.

Unfortunately, little is known about why some people actively seek out feedback and improve their behavior and other people fail to do so. Possibly people who fail to seek out feedback do so because their previous efforts to seek out feedback have been punished. As we have emphasized, our society relies extensively on aversive control (Sidman, 1989) and one consequence may be the failure to seek out feedback that would be helpful in improving performance. The evidence that indicates that feedback-seeking is useful also suggests that programs that teach people how to seek feedback, tolerate negative feedback, and turn negative feedback to one's advantage would be of value. However, at the same time, behavior analysts generally emphasize changing our cultural practices so that feedback is constructive and based on positive reinforcement rather than aversive control.

Making Feedback Effective

Conditions that contribute to the effectiveness of feedback include the immediacy of feedback, the use of response-dependent feedback, the specificity of feedback, the frequency of feedback, the predictability of feedback, the source and credibility of feedback, combining feedback with goal setting, drill and practice, and adding contrived reinforcers to feedback.

Immediacy of Feedback

In general, the more quickly feedback is given, the more effective it will be. Under realistic learning conditions, research has shown there is a distinct advantage to pro-

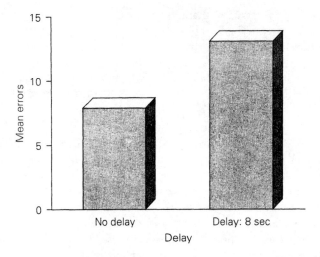

Figure 12.5   *The Relation Between Immediacy of Feedback and the Effectiveness of Feedback*

In learning from a self-instructional lesson, students made more errors when feedback was delayed by 8 seconds than when it was immediate. Figure adapted from Boersma (1966).

viding feedback as soon as possible after a response (Barbetta, Heward, Bradley, & Miller, 1992; Kulik & Kulik, 1988). For example, Boersma (1966) found that under certain conditions, a delay in correct-response feedback of only 8 seconds can impair student learning, as illustrated in Figure 12.5.

In some respects, providing immediate feedback is more important than providing immediate reinforcement. As we discussed in Chapter 2, delays in the delivery of reinforcers are not necessarily harmful if the learner receives immediate feedback that she has done well and that reinforcers will be forthcoming. However, without immediate feedback, it is difficult to bridge the delay between response and reinforcer.

Response-Dependent Feedback

Feedback should be dependent on the learner's attempt to respond to task (Bangert-Drowns, Kulik, Kulik, & Morgan, 1991; Kulhavy, 1977). This principle of *response-dependent feedback* is also known as the *principle of presearch availability*. In using the conceptual exercises in this book, you would be following this principle if you tried to answer each item before looking up the answer to the item. In contrast, if you peek ahead at the answer and copy it, you will not learn as much as when feedback is dependent on an attempt to respond (Anderson, Kulhavy, & Andre, 1972).

An advantage of using computers to teach is that the computer can provide feedback only after the learner has made a response, a feature computers share with earlier mechanical teaching machines (Skinner, 1968). Because computers ensure that feedback is response-dependent, computer-aided learning can often be more effective than learning through books that cannot ensure that feedback is indeed response-dependent (Bangert-Drowns et al., 1991).

Specificity of Feedback

Generally, specific feedback will be more effective than general feedback. We have already seen examples of this principle in the cases of labeled praise and why-feedback. Labeled praise is more specific and effective than unlabeled praise, and why-feedback is more specific and effective than outcome feedback. Feedback messages should clearly specify the target behavior rather than referring globally to areas of performance (Coon, Lipscomb, & Copple, 1982; Fredericksen, Richter, Johnson, & Solomon, 1982; Till & Toye, 1988; Tziner & Latham, 1989).

Frequency of Feedback

In general, the more frequent the feedback, the more effective the feedback will be in improving performance. Frequent feedback permits correction of performance problems before they can become established.

Alavosius and Sulzer-Azaroff (1990) studied the performance of employees at a medical facility for the mentally retarded. Many patients with physical disabilities had to be lifted, moved, and fed by staff members. These disabled people sometimes receive injuries when positioned for feeding. Alavosius and Sulzer-Azaroff wanted to see if they could train the staff to use safe techniques. During a low-frequency feedback condition, the experimenter stopped at the facility once a week and gave the employees oral and written feedback about their performance on three of the selected tasks. During a high-frequency feedback condition, the experimenter gave the staff written and oral feedback many times per day until they were doing the lifting, moving, and feeding tasks properly. Data from the study showed that the low-frequency feedback enabled the staff to learn the skills in about 3 to 4 weeks, but the high-frequency feedback enabled them to learn the skills in only 2 or 3 days. In their review of research, Balcazar et al. (1986) found that both daily and weekly feedback were more effective than monthly feedback.

Frequent feedback through quizzing also improves the academic performance of university students. Semb (1974) found that when students received frequent quizzes in a child development course, they learned the material more efficiently than when they got infrequent quizzes. For this reason, systems of behavioral instruction (Keller, 1968; Johnson & Ruskin, 1977) make use of frequent quizzing of students instead of merely using, for example, a midsemester and a final exam. Through frequent quizzing, students receive more feedback about how well they are learning, allowing more correction for errors and misconceptions.

The need for frequent feedback can vary from one situation to another. Because it costs time, energy, and money to give feedback, less frequent feedback is preferable if performance remains good. For example, Chhokar and Wallin (1984) found that providing feedback every two weeks about safe practices at a factory was as effective as providing weekly feedback. As such, one challenge for behavior analysts is to determine the appropriate frequency of feedback for effective performance. Spencer and Semb (1978) explored a clever way to do this. Students in a university course took frequent quizzes, but students who did well on these quizzes could opt to take less frequent quizzes that covered more material. Essentially, this method adjusted the frequency of feedback to the needs of individual students.

Predictability of Feedback

The principle of feedback predictability is that when feedback is intermittent, unpredictable feedback is more effective than predictable feedback. Saudargas, Madsen, and Scott (1977) demonstrated this principle in their work with third-grade students. The students took home reports that provided both students and parents with feedback about the amount and quality of the students' work. Under one condition, the teacher gave the students the reports on an unpredictable schedule. Thirty minutes before the end of the day, the teacher identified those students who would receive reports for that day. This was a *variable-time* feedback schedule because the feedback messages about the students' work occurred on a schedule that varied from report to report. Under another condition, the teacher gave the students the home reports every Friday (a *fixed-time* feedback schedule). Data showed that under the variable-time feedback schedule, the students completed much more of their assigned work as well as more extra work that they voluntarily took on. Another advantage of the variable-time schedule was that on any given day the teacher had to do no more than seven reports. With the fixed-time schedule, she had to prepare reports for the entire class every Friday.

The principle of feedback predictability applies only when feedback is intermittent. For example, if a student is receiving more-or-less continuous feedback from a tutor about performance on long-division problems, feedback is predictable because it follows each student response. In this kind of learning situation, it is not desirable to make feedback intermittent. However, there are times when feedback must be intermittent due to limited time and energy of the feedback-giver or because the learner is being taught to maintain the behavior in the absence of feedback. Under these conditions, unpredictable feedback is generally more desirable than predictable feedback.

The Source and Credibility of Feedback

The effectiveness of feedback will be influenced by the status of the feedback-giver and by how accurate and credible people judge the feedback to be. In their review of studies of feedback, Balcazar, Hopkins, and Suarez (1986) found that when managers or supervisors provided feedback, it was more often effective, probably because managers can provide back-up reinforcers and punishers for good and poor performance. As such, whenever possible, it may be desirable for the person who is providing feedback to be a manager or supervisor, permitting extra feedback to become a natural part of a working relationship.

Another factor that can make feedback more effective is its credibility, how accurate people judge it to be. Podsakoff and Farh (1989) studied the effect of this variable with university students, who were given a list of adjectives. Their job was to think of as many things as they could that each adjective could describe appropriately. Later, the students received feedback about how well they had done. One group of students received low-credibility feedback: The experimenter told them that she had based her performance evaluation on her experience. Another group of students received high-credibility feedback: The experimenter told them that she had based her evaluations on performance of 300 other university students who had taken the same test. After receiving the feedback, the students engaged in the task a second time, which allowed the effects of the feedback to be judged. When students received high-credibility negative feedback, they set higher goals and did better than when they received low-credibility negative feedback.

Other research has found the credibility of feedback to be influenced by its consistency. Stone and Stone (1985) found that consistent feedback was judged to be more accurate than inconsistent feedback. As with other types of behavioral consequences, consistency is very important for the effectiveness of feedback and inconsistent feedback can produce harmful effects.

Combining Feedback With Other Procedures

In their review, Balcazar et al. (1986) found that feedback was often more effective when combined with other procedures than when used alone. Three methods that are effective in combination with feedback are *goal-setting, drill and practice,* and *the use of contrived reinforcers.*

Goal-setting.   An excellent way to use feedback is to combine it with goal-setting. Receiving performance feedback allows people to use information about their current level of performance to set realistic goals for improvement.

Pritchard, Jones, Roth, Stuebing, and Ekeberg (1988) examined the value of goal-setting to increase the productivity of five air force units that were responsible for repairing electronic equipment and storing and distributing materials. Five months of feedback to staff had produced an increase in productivity of 50% over baseline. The goal-setting treatment consisted of training the supervisors to set realistic goals based on the feedback they were receiving. The training in goal setting increased productivity to 75% over baseline levels. In another study with airport employees, Tziner and Latham (1989) found the use of goal setting was also associated with improved job satisfaction and morale.

Goal-setting should be combined with feedback about whether people are attaining the goals (Erez, 1977; Kim & Hammer, 1976). For example, Reber and Wallin (1984) found that feedback and goal setting work together: Goal-setting without feedback improved safe practices at a factory, but in general, feedback was also needed to achieve the goals. (See Mento, Steel, and Karren [1987] for a review of goal-setting procedures.)

Drill and Practice.   The effects of feedback are generally improved when learners are required to practice the correct response, an application of the principle of active responding, previously discussed in Chapter 7. For example, Sterling, Barbetta, Heward, and Heron (1992) taught health education to students with learning disabilities. The teacher had the students answer several questions about health education by providing correct-response feedback. In one condition, the students were required to respond actively by repeating the correct answer after the teacher had provided it. In a second condition, the students were praised merely for attending to the correct response. Tests given at the end of each day and 2 weeks following learning showed the superiority of the performance of the students who were required to respond actively.

Corrective feedback has also been usefully combined with various types of drill and practice (Engelmann & Carnine, 1982). For example, when teaching children to read, most teachers give students correct-response feedback when they make an error in reading a word and then require the student to say the word correctly (Jenkins & Larson, 1979). In reading instruction, this method of giving correct-response feedback for errors is called *word supply*. Some research has explored alternatives to the word supply method (O'Shea, Munson, & O'Shea, 1984; Rosenberg, 1986; Singh, 1990). For example, Singh (1990) worked with three mentally retarded 13- to 15-year-olds. Sometimes, the teacher corrected the students' reading errors using the word supply method. At other times, the teacher corrected the errors using a *sentence-repeat procedure:* After making an error, the teacher gave the student the correct response, required the student to say the word, and further required the student to repeat the entire sentence in which the error occurred. The sentence-repeat method produced fewer errors than either the word-supply method or no feedback.

Essentially, the benefits of the sentence-repeat method reflect the value of coupling feedback with required practice of the correct response. Other studies have shown that flash-card drilling over misread words is also a more effective procedure than word-supply alone (e.g., O'Shea et al., 1984; Rosenberg, 1986).

In general, the research showing the value of combining drill and practice with feedback illustrates that, often, providing information about the correctness or adequacy of performance is not enough. There also must be opportunities to practice difficult-to-learn responses.

Contrived Reinforcers.   Feedback may be ineffective in changing behavior unless it is combined with reinforcers for improved performance. Wincze, Leitenberg, and Agras (1972) worked at a mental hospital with 10 patients who had been diagnosed as paranoid schizophrenics. The therapists asked questions that tested the patients' delusional responding and gave them correct-response and why-feedback for their responses. For example, a therapist asked one patient if he were Jesus Christ. The patient said, "yes," so the experimenter told the patient that he was incorrect and gave why-feedback: "Jesus Christ lived nearly 2,000 years ago. Your name is Mr. M. and you are 40 years old." This kind of feedback procedure was effective in reducing the delusional speech of five of the patients, but the other five patients' delusional speech diminished only when tokens exchangeable for food, privileges, cigarettes, and recreational activities were made dependent on nondelusional speech.

Salzberg, Wheeler, Devar, and Hopkins (1971) found a similar effect. They used correct-response feedback to encourage kindergarten children to improve their printing responses. This method did not improve the children's printing, but accuracy improved when an activity reinforcer, access to play, was made dependent on accurate printing.

The ways in which feedback and reinforcers should be coupled have not been thoroughly explored but we offer two speculative observations. First, feedback should be used by itself before contrived reinforcers are made dependent on the target behavior. Feedback is a more natural behavioral consequence than additional incentives and is often cheaper and easier to provide. Second, when contrived reinforcers are introduced, feedback, especially why-feedback, should continue to be provided. For example, in the Wincze et al. (1972) study, using tokens to reinforce the absence of delusional speech might not by itself enable the patient to develop the logical reasoning skills necessary for a generalized reduction in delusional speech. Providing why-feedback might better serve this purpose.

Summary

Feedback consists of those consequences of our behavior that our behavior causes. It includes consequences that alter behavior, such as reinforcers and punishers, as well as consequences that have no effect on behavior. Feedback also includes consequences that act as discriminative stimuli. As such, many feedback messages both reinforce and prompt desirable behavior. Feedback is a convenient term because it allows us to talk about behavioral consequences without specifying their exact role in behavior change.

Feedback can help to correct behavior quickly, is inexpensive, is unintrusive, and often precludes the need for any kind of aversive control. Behavior analysts often combine techniques such as prompting with feedback, especially when teaching difficult skills.

Feedback can be presented in a variety of ways and has been used to modify a wide range of behaviors. Our personal effectiveness is often enhanced when we actively seek out feedback rather than waiting for it to come to us.

Feedback should be delivered as soon as possible after the response has occurred and it should be delivered only after the learner has attempted to respond. It should specify the behaviors of concern and should occur relatively frequently. Observation of the learner's performance and associated feedback should occur unpredictably so that performance quality is always high. Respected individuals in positions of authority can deliver more effective feedback, particularly when the feedback is perceived to be credible and accurate. Feedback should be combined with other techniques such as goal-setting and drill and practice. When feedback itself is ineffective or only partially effective, contrived reinforcers may be used to enhance the effects of feedback.

Conceptual Exercise   *Types of Feedback*

For each of the following items, decide if the item is an example of feedback. If it is an example of feedback, then also specify which of the following types of feedback it is: Publicly posted feedback, written feedback, spoken feedback, automated feedback, biofeedback, labeled praise, self-monitoring, correct-response feedback, corrective feedback, and why-feedback. In each item, the stimuli in question are highlighted. Examples may contain more than one type of feedback. Check your decisions with the analyses in the back of the book.

Note: In this exercise, corrective feedback refers to response-dependent consequences for incorrect responses that prompt correct responses. Feedback must be dependent only on incorrect responses for it to be an example of corrective feedback.

1. An old house on the campus of a midwestern university had been turned into a bar for students. The students who worked at the bar didn't clean it regularly. Garbage was littered about. Sticky grease covered many of the surfaces. The State Board of Health had threatened to close the bar. The Dean of Students told the general manager of the bar either to clean the place up or it would be closed down. The general manager consulted with a behavior analyst, Professor Anderson, who taught at the university. He organized a team project in which the team broke cleaning tasks down into subtasks. After a baseline period of observation, the behavior analysts put up **graphs for each bar employee on a wall near the general manager's office** showing the percentage of the cleaning tasks the employees had done. Putting the charts on the wall increased the amount of cleaning tasks they did. After the program had been in effect for awhile, the Dean of Students visited the bar. He was pleased to see such a dramatic improvement and promised that the bar could stay open.

2. Several behavior analysts were working at a large state psychiatric hospital where they were using several techniques to improve treatment activities at the hospital. One method was to have the clinical director of the hospital hold a **weekly meeting with the unit treatment coordinators.** At the meeting, the clinical director discussed and evaluated how well the units were performing the treatment activities. As a result of this technique, there was an improvement in treatment activities.

3. A key reading skill is understanding the main idea of reading material. A group of university students with poor reading skills participated in an experiment wherein they read brief essays. During a period of baseline observations, for every five lines the students read, they underlined a few words that represented the main idea of the lines. Later in the study, after they had underlined, the students peeled off a piece of sticky-backed paper from their materials that showed the **correct words that they**

should have underlined. As a result of this procedure, the students improved their ability to underline the main ideas in new material they read.

4. Behavior analysts were teaching four retarded children to swim the sidestroke and the elementary backstroke. One training method was **to provide approval when the children performed the strokes well, and to tell them specifically what aspect of the strokes had earned the approval.** This method worked much better than only congratulating the children.

5. Staff at a factory that manufactured electrical circuits were training new employees at the factory to inspect circuits for faults. Before they did any inspections, **employees were shown a videotape that illustrated typical faults in electrical circuits and how to identify them.** As a result of viewing this videotape, the new employees became better at inspecting the circuits for faults.

6. Five men had received spinal cord injuries that resulted in their being quadriplegics, paralyzed from the neck down. Researchers attached instruments to sites on paralyzed areas that measured electrical impulses due to activity in the patients' nervous systems. As the patients **watched a microcomputer screen that showed the amount of nerve activity that was occurring,** the experimenter told them to try to increase the amount of activity. Using this method, the patients were able to increase certain types of electrical nerve activity in their bodies.

7. University students were learning to identify a crystal called RX_2. The students looked at pictures showing different molecular structures. For each picture, the students' task was to write down whether the picture was an example of an RX_2 structure or not. After some of the students responded to each item, they received **written information explaining the reason the picture was or was not an example of the RX_2 structure.** These students learned better than students who, after responding to each picture, received information only about whether the picture was an example of the RX_2 structure.

8. A group of researchers wanted to see if they could promote energy conservation. They had one group of residents of townhouses **read their electricity meters, record the results on a chart, and plot the daily use of electricity on a graph.** As a result of these methods, the residents reduced their electricity use 7%.

9. Instructors were teaching reading to third-grade students who had been identified as learning-disabled. When the students read correctly, the instructor did nothing. When the students made an error, the instructor would do the following things as long as the child continued to respond incorrectly: **(a) point to the missed word and ask the student to try again; (b) try to get the student to sound out groups of letters in the word; and (c) tell the student the word.** This procedure helped the students improve their reading skills.

10. Ned and his valiant team of crime-fighting behavior analysts were out to curtail shoplifting. In this project, the team wanted to discourage shoplifting by grocery store employees in Sweden. The team identified the most frequently stolen items in

the store: candy, personal hygiene products, and trinket jewelry. After baseline observations, the team posted a list of the frequently stolen items in the store lunchroom. They also put up a **diagram showing how many items of each type were stolen**. The researchers updated the diagram twice a week with the most recent data. As a result of this method, losses fell from eight per day to only two per day.

11. Two 10-year-old boys who had severe behavior problems attended an in-patient school at a psychiatric hospital. During baseline observations, the boys' behavior was often inappropriate in class. The boys were often out of their seats, arguing with others, and inattentive to their work and the teacher. They seldom engaged in appropriate behavior such as being on-task and interacting positively with the teacher or other students about academic work. To try to solve these problems, the researchers videotaped the boys in class and later **showed segments of the videotapes to the boys**. As a result of this method, the levels of the boys' appropriate classroom behavior increased substantially.

12. Two behavior analysts wanted to prevent industrial accidents in a small factory with six supervisors. Every day the experimenters observed several departments to see if any of 18 identified hazards were present. These hazards included obstructions, hazardous materials storage, and dangerous electricity. Twice a week, the experimenters prepared **a form. The form included the number of hazards in a department, their locations, suggestions for improvement, and positive comments about a safe workplace, as appropriate**. The forms were provided at a meeting between the production manager or personnel manager and the departmental supervisor. Sometimes a company vice president read aloud the positive comments on the form at the meeting. These methods reduced hazards substantially in all six departments at the factory.

13. A group of people who had diabetes were learning basic things about how to manage this disorder. They learned the lesson while working at a computer. The computer drills required them to respond to items of information. For one group, the computer told them only the correct response to each item. For another group, the computer **told them this and explained why the correct answer was correct**. The group given the explanations did better than the group given only the correct answers.

14. Each day a teacher who taught a class of fifth-grade students set aside 30 minutes to discuss stories that the class was reading. In addition the teacher set aside 20 minutes in the afternoon to discuss social studies lessons. The teacher used a point system to get the students to ask many questions during discussion periods. The teacher wanted to get the students to ask more complex questions rather than simple ones. Complex questions were ones that required answerers to apply abstract information, break down information into components, and combine facts in new ways. The teacher encouraged complex questions by **commending students who asked such questions and telling the students exactly what they had done well**. This method produced a large increase in the number of complex questions the students posed.

15. In a preschool, each time a new child was enrolled, one of the aides took the new child aside and **described a few simple rules for behavior in the preschool, and also**

explained the reasons for following each rule. For example, the new children were asked to listen to the teacher so that the teacher would not have to repeat instructions. Only after the aide had taken the child aside was the child permitted to enter the classroom and meet the teacher. Use of this method caused new students to behave well.

16. Twenty-three patients who suffered from migraine headaches were receiving treatment for their problem. During therapy, the experimenters attached a blood flow sensor to the patients' heads. The sensor measured the amount of blood pumped into the patients' brains through their temporal arteries. With each heartbeat, **a video screen displayed the amount of blood pumped. On the screen, a horizontal bar grew longer when blood flow increased and shorter when it decreased. When blood flow reached a desirable level, the word "GOOD" also appeared on the screen.** As a result of using this method, the patients' headaches declined 50%.

17. A researcher wanted to prevent heat loss from buildings at night in order to conserve energy. Therefore, he wanted to encourage people who worked at university offices to "drop and tilt" their venetian blinds at the end of the day: To lower the blinds and tilt the slats to deflect heat back into the offices. At one point in the study, the university president encouraged university staff to use the drop and tilt method in bulletins distributed to all staff. The researchers compared this method to a method in which the cleaning staff left **small notes on the desks of people who had not dropped and tilted.** The notes asked that the person use the drop and tilt procedure and included a drawing illustrating the correct positioning of the blinds. The use of the notes on the desk improved correct responding to 65% in one building and 69% in another. In contrast, the president's message improved correct responding only to 14% and 45% in the two buildings.

18. A midwestern university hockey team had a problem. The players were not body-checking their opponents. A body check is a play in hockey in which a player bashes into an opponent, taking the opponent out of play. To increase the number of body checks, **graphs were posted in the entryway to the team locker room,** showing the number of "hits" (body checks) for each player. As a result of the graphing procedure, the number of bodychecks per player increased. While previously other teams had soundly beaten the team, the graphing procedure made the team one of the more respected opponents in their league.

19. A man who worked as a draftsperson for an engineering firm was often late for work and spent much of his time at work goofing off. To try to solve the problem, a researcher worked with another employee at the firm. They had the man who was a problem **fill out a chart every day.** The chart showed work start and stop times at the beginning of the day and during the day. During a work day, the man always had this chart in front of him. This method improved both the man's promptness and his time on-task. His average arrival time before treatment was 10:45 AM, and after treatment this improved to 8:10 AM. The average percentage of time spent working per day increased from 51% to 88%.

20. A researcher was working with two university professors to see if student ratings of the professors' classes could be improved. Every day after class, the students filled

out a form on which they rated various features of their instructors and explained why. During part of the study, the professors received only a written summary of the students' ratings without the reasons the students gave. During another part of the study, the professors received **the summary of the ratings plus a written list of the students' reasons for the ratings.** Data showed that when the professor received the reasons, student ratings of the class improved more than when the professors received only a summary of the ratings.

21. A team of behavior analysts was trying to improve the social behaviors of department store salespersons toward customers. Target behaviors included appropriately opening communication with the customer, making courteous conversation, and appropriately closing the interaction. One method that was effective was for the researchers to **show the salesperson a graph of her daily performance and to discuss how that performance** compared to previous performance.

22. An experimenter was training preschool children to use novel combinations of words in sentences. The children watched puppets perform and the children's task was to describe what had happened. Tokens and praise were dependent on correct responses. **If an incorrect response occurred, the experimenter modeled the correct response and asked the child to imitate it. If the child could not imitate the entire sentence, the experimenter broke down the sentence into components. The child then imitated the components until she could utter the entire sentence correctly.**

23. During practice of a basketball team, the coach showed the players how to shoot a fade-away jump shot (or jumper) in which the shooter jumps slightly backward and then releases the shot. **The coach gave a clear demonstration of the technique and explained some of the details of how to execute the shot properly.** Afterward, each player tried out the shot and all of them executed it more or less correctly.

24. Casey, Billy, and Carrie were fifth and sixth grade students who had been identified as having learning disabilities. Each of them was unable to solve subtraction problems that demanded regrouping. These problems included those in which the numeral in the number being subtracted is larger than the numeral in the number from which subtraction occurs. The children received points for correct answers to the problems, but this method increased correct responding only somewhat. After this, the teacher began analyzing the children's errors every day and on the next day gave the **children personalized checklists that listed errors to avoid.** Then, while working on each new problem, the children had to check off each item on a list to ensure they had avoided the errors they had made previously. Through this method, all the students learned how to do the subtraction problems.

25. Seven patients had problems with fecal incontinence, soiling themselves by having bowel movements at inappropriate times. These problems were thought to be due to lack of their control of the sphincter muscles that induce bowel movements. In an attempt to solve this problem, a special balloon was inserted into the patients' rectums. The balloon was attached to a device that changed movements of the balloon into electrical impulses, **which in turn produced movements of a pen on a polygraph machine. With the balloons inside them, the patients watched the polygraph pen.**

The experimenter told them how their polygraph readings were different from normal people's. The experimenter told the patients to try to produce normal readings and praised them when they achieved these readings. When the patients got control over their sphincter muscle responses, the polygraph pen was covered to ensure they could achieve control without watching the pen. The experimenter urged the patients to practice what they learned outside the laboratory setting. One patient who had other anal problems stopped the therapy due to pain, but this patient was the only one who reported any pain. Four of the patients achieved complete success in solving their problems, one patient reported only very minor continuing problems, and one patient reported problems only during waking hours.

26. A group of behavior analysts was working with a 28-year-old mother of a 7-year-old boy named Mark. Mark's mother had often left him unattended, and he told a social worker his mother didn't like him and that he feared that she was going to abuse him. As a result, Mark's mother was referred to the behavior analysts to train her in child management. The behavior analysts taught Mark's mother **to say positive things to Mark when he did something well, and to tell him exactly what it was that he had done well**. The training program produced an increase in the frequency of these behaviors, a decrease in criticisms of Mark, and an increase in the percentage of her commands that Mark obeyed. Before training, Mark's mother disliked him, but after training, she came to enjoy her role as a mother. Neglect and potential abuse of Mark were no longer a concern.

Conceptual Exercise   *Making Feedback Effective*

In each of the following items one of the factors that makes feedback effective has been violated. These factors include the immediacy of feedback, the use of response-dependent feedback, the specificity of feedback, the frequency of feedback, the predictability of feedback, the source and credibility of feedback, and combining feedback with goal setting, drill and practice, and adding contrived reinforcers to feedback. In each item, identify the problem and consult the analyses in the back of the book to confirm your decisions.

1. Johnny was learning his multiplication tables with flash cards. The teacher had set specific goals for Johnny's improvement in this skill. The teacher held up a flash card that had a multiplication problem on it and Johnny gave his answer to the problem out loud. Only after Johnny had responded was the next problem presented. When Johnny had completed five problems, the teacher would go through each one and tell Johnny if his answer was correct. If the answer was incorrect the teacher would carefully explain how to solve the problem and give Johnny additional drill and practice. Then five new problems would be given.

2. At a factory that made blue jeans, the managers wanted to improve product quality. They gave the blue-jean inspectors feedback about how many defective pairs of jeans passed through the inspection process undetected. The feedback was immediate, unpredictable, and frequent. An adequate worker-incentive plan was in effect for

detection of defects. Part of worker training included extensive drill and practice in detection of defective jeans. Workers who were having problems could receive additional drill and practice of this type. Despite these measures, the company president still was not satisfied with the percentage of defective blue jeans that passed the inspection process. Although the employees appreciated receiving the performance feedback, they were confused because they didn't know what performance goals the company had set.

3. Peter was learning French pronunciation. After his teacher presented a French word, Peter had to pronounce it out loud into his microphone. Peter never knew for sure when his teacher was listening, but quite often she would immediately follow Peter's response with, "That's correct" or "That's not correct." Peter had been assigned specific goals for improvement in this skill, and he was given extra drill and practice over items with which he was having difficulty.

4. June's class was learning the multiplication table. As the teacher held up a flash card with a problem, each child was expected to write down the answer. Then the teacher would give the answer immediately and explain how the solution was found. The teacher made sure that she gave feedback frequently and on an unpredictable schedule. Sometimes June wrote down answers but not always. The students were given specific goals for learning the tables as part of the math curriculum and were given drill and practice over types of problems they had trouble learning.

5. Employees at a tire factory were encouraged to submit suggestions to a suggestion box. Each time a worker submitted a suggestion, management gave her immediate feedback that specifically answered the worker's suggestion. If an employee submitted a suggestion that management accepted and the suggestion made the company a lot of money, the employee received a letter of thanks from a vice president in charge of suggestions. The company practiced goal setting with its employees.

6. David was learning to ride his bicycle safely on the streets. He was in a special program led by a policeman. The policeman asked David many questions about road safety. When David gave the right answer the policeman praised him immediately and frequently. When David was incorrect, the policeman gave him specific information about the proper rule and extra drill and practice. The policeman made sure that David always tried to answer the question before he gave any feedback. The program had specific goals to be attained and was very successful. David was so pleased with himself that he decided to teach Aaron, his friend, the same things he had learned. Although he copied the way his teacher had taught him, he was not as successful in teaching Aaron.

7. Students in a second-grade class were learning handwriting. Their teacher, Mr. Ramirez, frequently walked from one student's desk to another, examining the quality of each student's letters. He managed to do this so that it was not predictable when he might show up at any one student's desk. If the students were having a problem, Mr. Ramirez specifically explained the problem and then went off to the next student. All the students were given goals for good handwriting, as a chart of perfect letters at the front of the classroom indicated. Grades provided adequate incentives for the students.

8. Government inspectors visited a fish packing plant every Tuesday and Friday. At those times, the inspectors gave the plant managers feedback about sanitary conditions at the plant and about other factors that affected the quality of the products. The inspectors gave very helpful and specific comments about the conditions at the plant and specified clear product-quality guidelines to the plant managers. If necessary, the inspectors could provide the managers with training manuals that provided information and practice in product-safety techniques.

9. A group of government auditors visited savings and loan companies to audit them and to ensure that the companies were in good financial health. They visited each savings and loan company on an unpredictable schedule once during any 5-year period. During the visit, they gave the company officers detailed and specific feedback about the company's accounting practices and other relevant aspects of operation. The auditors had clear goals that they communicated to the company officers. If necessary, the auditors provided the company officers with manuals that trained them in proper accounting practices. Avoiding fines provided an incentive for the savings and loan companies to comply with the auditors' feedback. Despite these procedures, many of the savings and loan companies went bankrupt.

chapter 13

Pavlovian Conditioning

Terry was a 27-year-old sales manager who had moved to Canada from his native England to try to escape from a debilitating problem, an intense and consuming fear of nuclear war. At the time, during the late 1950s and early 1960s, many people were profoundly affected by similar problems. However, Terry's case was so difficult that he could not bear to listen to the radio, read a newspaper, watch a movie, or converse with other people. Doing any of these things might bring bad news about the international situation, something he could not tolerate. Terry recognized that his problem was interfering with his daily life, and had consulted a psychiatrist for 2 years. However, the therapy he received was ineffective. His fears grew more intense. Terry began drinking heavily to reduce his fears. He consumed as much as 26 ounces of rye whisky or vodka every day, a habit that eventually cost him his job. Unemployed, he avoided all contact with other people and spent much of his day at home, his head under the covers of his bed. Terry's thoughts turned to suicide. He took an overdose of sleeping pills, survived, and was committed to a mental hospital.

In the hospital, he received six electroconvulsive shock treatments, a drastic form of therapy that did not solve his problems. He spent one weekend at home and became so frightened that he began drinking again. At the hospital, he continued to avoid listening to the radio or watching television. He began to fear losing his wife, on whom he had grown increasingly dependent. In this regard, Terry's fears were very real. Because of the understandable stresses Terry's problems had placed on her, Terry's wife was considering a separation.

Terry's problems came to the attention of Beatrice Ashem, a staff psychologist at the hospital where Terry had been placed. Beatrice had read a lot about a new therapy designed to treat phobias, intense maladaptive fears. Dr. Joseph Wolpe had introduced the therapy, called *systematic desensitization,* only a few years before and had been successful in treating phobias. At the hospital where she worked, Beatrice had found none of the existing treatments to be helpful to patients who had severe phobias. She attended a workshop that Dr. Wolpe conducted and although she had not used systematic desensitization before, she thought it was worth a try with Terry, with whom other therapies had failed.

During relaxation training, preparatory to systematic desensitization, the therapist has the patient relax each muscle group. Through gentle and soothing verbal instructions, the patient is brought to a state of calmness and serenity. For the first three sessions, Beatrice trained Terry in deep muscle relaxation and had him practice every day. Beatrice then constructed anxiety hierarchies, lists of things that elicited Terry's fears, ranked from the least to the most fearful stimuli. In Terry's case, three different anxiety hierarchies were constructed.

One hierarchy was for his fear of reading a newspaper, one was for his fear of radio and television news, and one for his fear of knowledge of world events. The anxiety hierarchy to treat Terry's fear of radio and television news was as follows, with the stimuli ranked from least to most fearful:

1. Seeing radio and television sets in a store.
2. Hearing a musical program.
3. Seeing a play on television.
4. Hearing "This is the Metro News."
5. Hearing on the radio: "We interrupt this program to bring you a special bulletin."
6. Hearing "This is the CBC News."
7. Going to a movie with his wife, knowing there is to be a newsreel.
8. Turning on the radio to hear the news. (Ashem, 1963, p. 83)

During therapy, Terry was instructed to relax. When he had achieved a state of deep relaxation, Terry was asked to imagine the least fearful event in the anxiety hierarchy. If he felt any fear responses to the scene he imagined, he was to raise his finger, signaling Beatrice to instruct Terry to stop imagining the scene. She then again asked Terry to relax. When a state of relaxation had been reestablished, Terry imagined the same scene again. If Terry were successful in imagining a scene twice without any fear responding for at least 10 seconds, he proceeded to the next most fearful item in the anxiety hierarchy.

This process continued until Terry could imagine the most fearful scenes in the hierarchy while remaining completely relaxed. Some steps in the anxiety hierarchies were more difficult than others. For example, imagining seeing a radio or television set in a store required only the minimum of two presentations for Terry to respond without feeling anxious. However, imagining hearing "We interrupt this program to bring you a special bulletin" required 25 presentations before Terry could remain relaxed.

After 13 desensitization sessions, Terry could listen to the radio and watch television without anxiety. The hospital staff permitted him to go home one weekend and he was able to go to a movie with his wife. After 19 therapy sessions, Terry could turn on a radio and listen to a news broadcast without fear. Terry's wife said that he was a changed man. He could now go to movies and visit with friends.

Three months after the end of therapy, Terry's improvement continued. He was in good health, living without the fear and depression that had almost ruined his life. For her part, Beatrice went on to get a doctoral degree and practice behavior therapy, and Dr. Ashem specialized in the treatment of anxiety disorders.*

Pavlovian Conditioning

People are born with certain stimulus-response relationships that are built-in to our bodies. These stimulus-response relationships are called *unconditioned reflexes*. Table 13.1 shows several unconditioned responses. Unconditioned reflexes are familiar to everyone. Peeling onions causes us to cry. A loud noise elicits crying and other fear responses in infants and a startle response in adults. These reflexes are called unconditioned because they have not been learned.

Sometimes, behavior analysts have made use of unconditioned reflexes to induce certain desirable behaviors. For example, Babbitt, Hoch, Krell, and Williams (1992) worked with two girls, 16 months and 23 months, who did not swallow. The girls had been fed through tubes since they were only a few weeks old. Fortunately, the experimenters found an unconditioned reflex involving the swallowing response. They used an oral stimulator on each girl's tongue, applying it first to the back of the tongue and then bringing it forward while applying a small amount of pressure. When they did this, both girls swallowed. This was an unconditioned reflex because the tongue pressure caused swallowing and because this stimulus-response relationship was unlearned. Once swallowing was elicited in this fashion, the experimenters used other procedures to encourage the swallowing response in the absence of the oral stimulator. For one girl, tube feedings were eliminated completely and for the other, tube feedings were reduced by half.

Certain usages apply to unconditioned reflexes. We call the stimulus that causes the response an *unconditioned stimulus* (US). We call the response caused by the unconditioned stimulus an *unconditioned response* (UR). We say that the unconditioned stimulus *elicits* the unconditioned response.

*Based on Ashem (1963), personal communication (1992)

Table 13.1 *Examples of Unconditioned Reflexes*

Unconditioned Stimulus	Unconditioned Response
Puff of air to the eye	Eye blink
Light to the eye	Pupil contraction
Food in the mouth	Salivation
Cold temperature	Shivering
High temperature	Perspiration
Spoiled food	Sickness, vomiting
Onion vapors	Crying
Tap to knee (patellar tendon)	Knee jerk
Foreign matter in nose	Sneezing
Foreign matter in throat	Coughing
Pressure to baby's lips	Sucking
Stimulating sex organs	Erection, glandular secretions
Startling noise	Heart rate increase, pupil dilation, tense muscles

Pavlovian conditioning is a type of learning that builds on unconditioned reflexes and is named after the Russian physiologist who did much of the original research in the area, Ivan Pavlov. He described his extensive work in his impressive book, *Conditioned Reflexes* (Pavlov, 1927/1960). In the most basic demonstration of conditioning, Pavlov worked with dogs, using food as a US and salivation as a UR. Just before Pavlov put food in a dog's mouth, he sounded a metronome. Pavlov set up a predictive relationship between the sound of the metronome and the US, the food. The metronome sound predicted the food because (a) whenever the metronome sounded, food came soon afterward; and (b) whenever the metronome was silent, no food was delivered. For these reasons, we can say that the metronome sound predicted the food. Pavlov found that after the animal had had some experience with the predictive relationship between the metronome and the food, the dog began to salivate to the metronome alone.

We say that before conditioning took place, the metronome sound was a neutral stimulus (NS) because it had no effect on salivation. After conditioning, we say that the metronome sound became a conditioned stimulus (CS) for salivation. We call the response that a CS elicits a conditioned response (CR). Here, the salivation to the metronome was the CR. Pavlov's entire procedure can be summarized in a word diagram. (Grant [1989] found word diagrams of the following type help students learn about Pavlovian conditioning.)

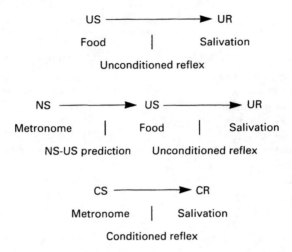

Pavlovian conditioning is an important form of learning that affects many different behaviors. Among these behaviors are many of our emotional behaviors. For example, English (1929) observed Pavlovian conditioning in Joan, a 28-week old infant. One day Joan's mother held a stuffed black cat out to her. Seeing this, Joan's older sister let out a loud howl, apparently because it was her cat and she didn't want Joan to play with it. Joan, in turn, wailed in fearful response to her sister's howl. Over a 10-minute period, the cat was presented to Joan several times. Each time, Joan responded fearfully to the cat. Her eyelid quivered, her lower lip trembled, and she cried. In this case, Joan's older sister's howl was a US for Joan's fear responses, the UR. The stuffed black cat predicted the howl because it was presented just before the loud howl. Because it predicted the howl, the cat became a CS for Joan's fear responses, the CR. We can illustrate this in another word diagram:

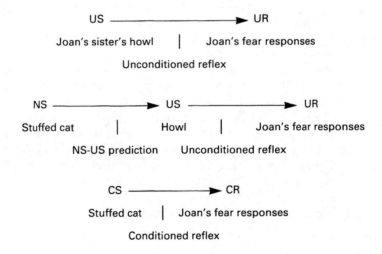

In Pavlovian conditioning, an NS (e.g., stuffed cat) predicts a US (e.g., loud howl) and, as a result of that predictive relationship, acquires the ability to elicit a CR (e.g., crying and fear). An important defining feature of Pavlovian conditioning is therefore the relationship between the NS and the US.

People, of course, are always responding to stimuli, often for reasons other than Pavlovian conditioning. Consider for a moment, the eye-blink reflex. Suppose we repeatedly elicit the eye-blink reflex by presenting puffs of air to our subject's eye. Suppose then that we sound a tone and our subject immediately blinks. This would not be an example of Pavlovian conditioning.

Because the tone has never predicted the air puffs in the past, blinks to the tone now are not examples of Pavlovian conditioning. Instead, blinks to the light would be examples of responding that is due to factors other than the predictive relationship between the NS and the US. One of these factors is pseudoconditioning, which refers to the ability of the CS (or NS) to elicit a response due to the prior presentation of the US rather than to a predictive relationship between the CS and US.

Pavlovian and Operant Conditioning Compared

When behavior changes as a result of response-dependent consequences, we say that the change occurred through operant conditioning. Positive reinforcement, punishment, and escape and avoidance are all examples of operant conditioning procedures. In contrast, when behavior changes as a result of setting up a predictive relationship between a neutral and an unconditioned stimulus, we say that the change occurred through Pavlovian conditioning. Specifically, in Pavlovian conditioning the neutral stimulus becomes a conditioned stimulus that can elicit a conditioned response.

A key distinction between operant and Pavlovian conditioning is the role of response-dependent environmental consequences. These consequences are essential in operant conditioning but are not involved in Pavlovian conditioning. In Pavlovian conditioning, the US is presented dependent on the occurrence of the NS. In this sense, the US is presented on a stimulus-dependent basis: The US is presented only if the NS has been presented. In contrast, in operant conditioning, consequences are presented on a response-dependent basis: If the response occurs, the consequence occurs and if no response occurs, no consequence occurs.

Another difference between the two types of conditioning is in the general types of behavior they alter. Pavlovian conditioning most readily influences the responding of the autonomic nervous system, which controls the actions of glands and behaviors we normally label as involuntary. Blushing is an example of a response we label as involuntary. In contrast, operant conditioning most readily influences complex movements made by the skeletal muscles, behaviors we normally label as voluntary. For example, actions such as walking and writing are performed by the skeletal muscles.

Table 13.2	*Differences Between Operant and Pavlovian Conditioning*	
	Pavlovian	**Operant**
Procedure	Neutral stimulus predicts an unconditioned stimulus.	Stimulus consequence is dependent on the occurrence of a response.
Outcome	Neutral stimulus becomes a conditioned stimulus that elicits a conditioned response.	Response level increases or decreases in strength.
Stimulus	Stimulus elicits response.	Stimulus sets the occasion for a response or signals that consequence will follow a response.
Responses Affected	Most readily affects responses controlled by the autonomic nervous system.	Most readily affects skeletal muscle responses.
Usage	Response is said to be elicited by a stimulus. Response is said to be involuntary	Response is said to be emitted by the organism. Response is said to be voluntary

Many of the practical applications of Pavlovian conditioning have been concerned with emotional behaviors, while operant conditioning applications have been concerned with teaching complex skills. This difference between the two types of conditioning is only a rough guideline. Both types of conditioning have been used to alter autonomic responses and responses made by the skeletal muscles. You may recall the use of biofeedback, an operant procedure, to alter responses we usually call involuntary such as blood pressure and heart rate.

Differences between operant and Pavlovian conditioning are summarized in Table 13.2. (For more extensive discussions of the differences between the two types of conditioning, see Catania [1984] and Millenson and Leslie [1979].)

Another difference between operant and Pavlovian conditioning is in the words we use to describe these methods. When speaking of operant behavior, we say responses are *emitted* or *engaged in*. When speaking of Pavlovian conditioning, we say that responses are elicited, either by a US or a CS.

Pavlovian Extinction

Conditioned responses acquired through Pavlovian conditioning are subject to extinction. Pavlovian extinction will occur if the CS no longer predicts the US. For example, if Pavlov's dogs were exposed to the metronome many times with no food forthcoming, eventually they would stop salivating, and the CR would extinguish. Often Pavlovian extinction occurs when the CS is repeatedly presented without being followed by the US.

Remember Joan, the baby whose fear responses were conditioned to a stuffed black cat, the CS. Joan's fear responding might have been extinguished through repeated presentations of the cat without the US, the howl, occurring. In this situation, the cat would no longer predict the loud howl. If Joan's fear responses diminished to the cat because the cat no longer predicted the howl, we could say that extinction of the conditioned response had taken place. Often, the CS must be presented for a considerable period of time before the CR undergoes extinction. Extinction of conditioned fear responding is improved by prolonged exposures to the feared stimuli (Marshall, 1985).

Pavlovian extinction occurs in everyday life and we can often use it to our advantage. For example, for someone who has been in an auto accident, car and traffic stimuli are neutral stimuli that have "predicted" the stimuli associated with an accident, which are USs for fear and other emotional responses. Often, the best strategy for handling this problem is for the individual to drive again soon after the accident. In this way, car and traffic stimuli will occur, but will not predict an accident, provided none occurs. Because the car and traffic stimuli do not predict the USs involved in an accident, the conditioned emotional responses to the car and traffic stimuli are likely to undergo extinction. This strategy of extinction of conditioned responses through the give-it-another-try method is useful, especially when the presentation of the US is a rare occurrence.

Types of Pavlovian Conditioning Therapies

Several varieties of behavior therapies are based on Pavlovian conditioning, including counterconditioning, systematic and *in vivo* desensitization, aversion therapy, and flooding and exposure treatment.

Counterconditioning

Counterconditioning is a method of Pavlovian conditioning in which an undesired CS-CR relationship is weakened or eliminated by setting up a new CS-CR relationship in which the new CR is opposite to or incompatible with the old CR. The concept of counterconditioning is fundamental to several different types of behavior therapies based on Pavlovian conditioning.

Smith (1973) provides an example of counterconditioning in which a therapist counterconditioned anger responses with humor. A 22-year-old woman who behaved angrily toward her husband and her 3-year-old son sought help to control her anger. When angered by her son, she had screamed as loud as she could, jumped up and down, smashed objects, and even physically attacked him. She behaved in a similar fashion toward her husband when he made her angry. She considered her reactions automatic and beyond her control. The problem had become so bad that she had considered suicide. She had become depressed because she realized that "my temper makes everyone, including me, miserable" (p. 577).

To treat the problem, the therapist developed several scenes of situations ranging from least to most anger-provoking. These scenes included interactions with both the husband and the son that provoked the woman's anger. The therapist put humorous content into each of the scenes because he felt that by making Nora laugh she would not become angry. In many cases the humor was in the form of slapstick comedy portraying, for example, the humorous elements of her son's mischievous behavior. The therapist read the scenes to Nora, if she became angry, the therapist reemphasized the humorous content of the scene. Nora moved on to new scenes only when she was able to imagine the less anger-eliciting scenes successfully. In this way, Nora learned to respond to the former anger-eliciting stimuli without becoming angry. After three sessions of treatment, Nora's relatives noted that she had improved control of her temper. Over time, she continued to improve and was no longer depressed. We can diagram the treatment as follows:

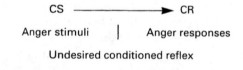

Counterconditioning procedure:

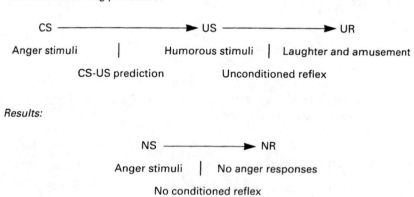

Results:

Counterconditioning works through the conditioning of opposite CRs to a single CS. Once an incompatible response is conditioned to a stimulus originally established as a CS for one response, the CS may lose its ability to elicit the original response. In Nora's case, conditioning humorous responses to the anger-provoking stimuli caused those stimuli to lose their ability to act as a CS for anger responding. In this case, anger and humor were incompatible responses.

Smith (1973) originally interpreted this case study as an example of the counterconditioning of anger using humor. However, there are other possible ways to account for the effectiveness of the therapy. For example, when we are able to see the humor in situations, we attend to certain discriminative stimuli, the funny things, rather than others. In this example, the therapy may have functioned like a discrimination training procedure in which the therapist taught Nora to attend to the humorous aspects of the stimuli in her daily life. This new pattern of discriminative responding may have had a more important role in the success of the therapy than counterconditioning, though the two processes could have worked together. As you can see, case studies in behavior therapy such as this one can often be interpreted in different ways.

Therapists have used a variety of incompatible responses in counterconditioning. Nevo and Shapira (1988) described how pediatric dentists countercondition children's fear of dental procedures through humor. Croghan and Musante (1975) have shown how the positive emotions elicited by playing a game can countercondition a child's fears. Jones (1924) used the positive emotional responses that candy and pleasant conversation elicit to countercondition a child's fear of animals. Similarly, Rovetto (1983) used the positive emotional responses that conversation elicited to countercondition a man's fear of driving a car, while Houlihan and Jones (1989) used conversation in a similar fashion to countercondition a child's school phobia. Liked and disliked music can alter emotional responding to neutral stimuli (e.g., Eifert, Craill, Carey, & O'Connor, 1988) and also may be useful in counterconditioning.

Like many other therapies based on Pavlovian conditioning, counterconditioning can make use of both real or imagined stimulus elements. When the therapist makes use of actual stimuli, we say it is *in vivo* therapy. When the therapist makes use of imagined stimuli, we say it is an *imaginal* procedure. In the case of the woman beset with excessive anger, both the anger-provoking stimuli and the humorous stimuli were imagined. The therapist might have incorporated *in vivo* elements by presenting actual anger-provoking stimuli and having the woman imagine the humorous content. There are many ways to combine *in vivo* and imaginal stimuli in counterconditioning therapies.

Counterconditioning occurs naturally in nontherapeutic contexts. For example, by simply talking to ourselves, we can often set up predictive relationships that permit counterconditioning. Eifert (1984), for example, showed how self-verbalizations, such as "This pretty snake lies peacefully in the sun," can countercondition fears with pleasant emotional stimuli. This suggests that our self-talk, if properly arranged, can serve the purpose of counterconditioning. Counterconditioning frequently occurs in the course of daily life. We learn both pleasant and unpleasant emotional responses toward stimuli at one time, but later opposite responses replace those originally conditioned. The emotional responses of many happy newlyweds, for example, are counterconditioned during marriage such that when they divorce, often they have acquired completely opposite emotional responses. In political campaigns, those interested in promoting a candidate often seek to countercondition the voters' positive emotional responses toward an opposing candidate through counter-conditioning of fear and anger. Salespersons and advertisers similarly make extensive use of counterconditioning. Saper (1988) has discussed the potential uses of counterconditioning to prevent acts of political terrorism.

Systematic and *In Vivo* Desensitization

One of the most widely used behavior therapies is systematic desensitization. In the introduction to this chapter, we saw how Beatrice Ashem used systematic desensitization to treat a man's fear of a nuclear disaster. Systematic desensitization can be viewed as a form of counterconditioning in which (a) deep muscle relaxation is the response that replaces an undesired CR (often some type of fear responding) and (b) the therapist introduces the CS for the undesirable CR gradually and in imaginal form.

Looking back at the case of Terry, who feared a nuclear disaster, there was an undesirable CS-CR relationship, because world news was a CS that elicited Terry's fear responding. During therapy, world news became a CS for relaxation responses by gradual introducing of the CSs in imaginal form while ensuring that Terry remained relaxed. The outcome of this therapy was to replace Terry's fear response to the CSs of world news with relaxation. We can diagram the procedure in the following way:

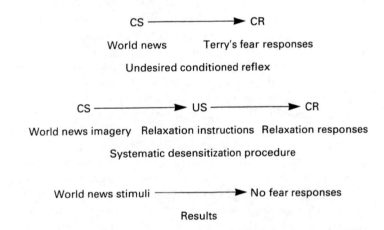

Systematic desensitization has been successful in treating a variety of problems, mainly those involving fear responding and other types of anxious behavior. In systematic desensitization, the therapist presents the stimuli in the anxiety hierarchy in imaginal form: The therapist tells the person being treated to imagine the fear-provoking stimuli.

A variant of this method is *in vivo* desensitization, in which the individual encounters the actual fear-eliciting stimuli. For example, if the therapist had used *in vivo* desensitization with Terry, she would have brought Terry to a state of deep relaxation, and then confronted him with the first item in the anxiety hierarchy, seeing a radio or television in a store window. Other than the use of actual rather than imaginal stimuli, *in vivo* and systematic desensitization are very similar. Both methods make use of relaxation, an anxiety hierarchy, and removal of a feared stimulus if the patient encounters discomfort. In both methods, progression to more fearful stimuli occurs only when the person can remain relaxed when confronting less fearful stimuli in the hierarchy.

Grings and Schandler (1977) conducted an experiment that provides insight into the way in which counterconditioning and systematic desensitization function. For an experimental group of volunteer students, they established a yellow disc as a CS by having it predict shock. The CR in the experiment was the ability of the subject's skin to conduct electricity. Change in skin conductance, also known as galvanic skin response (GSR), is a UR for the US of electric shock, among other things. Experimenters often use the skin conductance response as a measure of fear conditioning. The experimenters also established a triangle as a stimulus for relaxation by training the subjects to relax through biofeedback in the presence of the triangle. The experimenters were interested in how the subjects would respond to the yellow disc alone and the yellow disc superimposed on either the triangle or a column of vertical dots, an untrained stimulus. The results of the study are shown in Figure 13.1.

As you can see, the yellow disc elicited the strongest skin conductance response, showing the effects of the CS. The yellow disc superimposed on the triangle produced the least skin conductance response, showing that the relaxation training acted to reduce the effects of the CS. Finally, superimposing the dots on the yellow disc produced some reduction in the skin conductance response, but not nearly as much as superimposing the triangle, the relaxation stimulus, on the yellow disc. Heart-rate measures showed similar effects. This experiment suggests that relaxation training in systematic desensitization works actively to countercondition learned fears.

Aversion Therapy

In aversion therapy, Pavlovian conditioning is used to establish a conditioned aversion to an inappropriate stimulus that normally elicits good feelings and acts as a positive reinforcer. A conditioned aversion occurs when a person has learned a set of unpleasant responses, such as those involved in nausea or fear, that are elicited by a stimulus. Rush (1789, cited in Elkins, 1991a) pointed out that Moses, the Biblical prophet, made use of aversion therapy. Returning to his people, the Israelites, after an absence, Moses found them worshiping a golden calf, something that he had prohibited. Rush gives the following account:

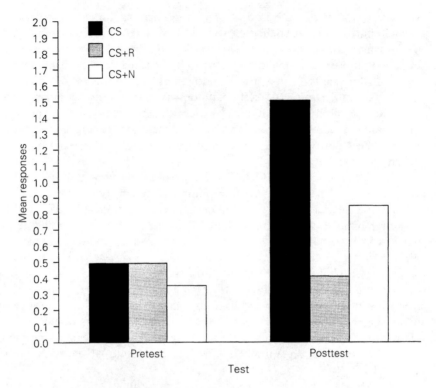

Figure 13.1   *The Conterconditioning Effect of Relaxation*

Subjects' skin conductance responses were conditioned to a CS, a yellow disc, that predicted shock. Subjects were also trained to relax in the presence of another stimulus, a triangle
(R), but were not trained to relax in the presence of a third stimulus, a column of vertical
dots (N). After conditioning when the CS was presented alone or superimposed on the
untrained stimulus (CS + N), strong conditioned responses were obtained. However, when
the CS was presented superimposed on the relaxation stimulus (CS + R), the conditioned
response was weak, illustrating the effects of relaxation counterconditioning. In pretesting
before conditioning, there was little difference in the effects of the stimuli. Drawn from
Grings and Schandler's (1977) data.

This (type of) appeal to that operation of the human mind, which obliges it to
associate ideas accidentally or otherwise combined, for the cure of vice, is very
ancient. It was resorted to by Moses, when he compelled the children of Israel
to drink the solution of the golden calf (idol) . . . in water. This solution, if
made, as it most probably was, by means of what is called hepar sulphuris [sul-
furated potash], was extremely bitter, and nauseous, and could never be recol-
lected afterwards, without bringing into equal detestation the sin which subjected them [the children of Israel] to the necessity of drinking it (Elkins,
1991a, p. 387).

We may illustrate this instance of conditioning as follows:

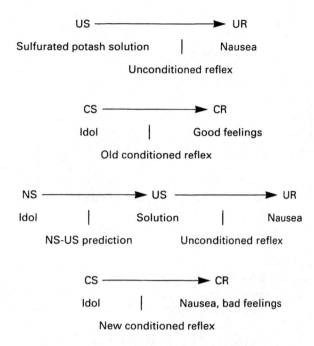

Aversion therapy, a type of counterconditioning, has been used to establish conditioned aversions to such things as alcoholic drinks, cigarettes, and inappropriate sexual stimuli. In counterconditioning, an undesired CS-CR relationship is weakened or eliminated by conditioning a new CR to the CS that is opposite to the original CR. In aversion therapy, the original CR is one that is pleasurable, while the new CR is one that is unpleasant, such as fear responding or nausea.

Aversion therapy has been used with some success in the treatment of alcoholism (Bandura, 1969; Elkins, 1991a; Wiens & Menustik, 1983). Therapists in private hospitals in the United States have used this treatment extensively since 1935 and have achieved a 60% rate of abstinence among former patients (Smith, 1982). This level of success is very good for alcoholism, a difficult disorder to treat. In an experimental study, Boland, Mellor, and Revusky (1978) worked with 25 alcoholic men who ranged in age from 25 to 55 years. The men began sessions by tasting an alcoholic drink. The experimenters then gave the men a lithium-based drug that induces nausea and vomiting. While the drug took effect the men continued to taste and sip their drinks. They stopped drinking 15 minutes after the first signs of sickness appeared, or sooner if they were about to vomit. Each man had six aversion therapy sessions, one every other day.

Although most of the men became very sick due to the procedure, none of them suffered any dangerous side effects. After 6 months, 36% of the experimental group remained abstinent from alcohol. However, eight of the men did not become sick from the drug, even though the experimenters increased their dosage to induce sickness. If we consider only the men who became sick, the aversion therapy produced 47% abstinence after 6 months. A control group treated with another drinking deterrent achieved only a 12% abstinence rate.

Another type of aversion therapy is covert sensitization, in which a conditioned aversive CS is established by having someone imagine associations between the CS and aversive stimuli. Cautela (1967), who devised covert sensitization, described its use in treating several disorders, including obesity. Treatment consisted of having the person imagine eating high-calorie desserts like apple pie, feeling queasy in the stomach, and vomiting over the table and other people's food. The therapist used 10 repulsive scenes per session, using different high-calorie foods. In addition, whenever the individual felt an urge to eat a high-calorie food, that food was to be imagined with vomit all over it. Cautela described covert sensitization as generally effective in treating overeating. Effects of the treatment were specific to the foods used in the imaginal scenes. The people continued to enjoy eating other high calorie foods.

Like other behavioral procedures using aversive stimuli, aversion therapy is sometimes controversial. (See Elkins [1991a; 1991b], Howard and Jenson [1990], and Wilson [1991] for some current perspectives.) Many of the same problems we discussed about punishment also apply to aversion therapy. When used inappropriately, aversion therapy is a dangerous procedure with the capacity to do much harm. Aversion therapy techniques are very intrusive and many require specialized skills. They should be used only by qualified professionals. When using aversion therapy, the therapist should take a constructional approach to behavior change by teaching the individual new skills to replace those behaviors eliminated through aversion therapy.

Flooding and Exposure Treatments

As discussed earlier, extinction of Pavlovian conditioning consists of setting up a situation in which the CS no longer predicts a US. Over time, this can weaken the ability of the CS to elicit the CR. Note that in counterconditioning, including systematic desensitization, the CS occurs without predicting a US, so part of the effectiveness of these procedures may be due to extinction. For example, in the story of Terry in the chapter introduction, the therapist exposed Terry to the CSs that elicited fear and, of course, none of these CSs predicted a US for fear responding. As such, part of the effectiveness of counterconditioning procedures may be due to extinction because of the unpredictiveness of the CS. However, in counterconditioning the individual learns a new CR to an old CS, so relearning a new response is part of the procedure, besides extinction of the old CR.

Many therapists believe that part of the reason people maintain phobic behavior for years is that they learn to avoid the phobic CS diligently. Therefore, the CR never has a chance to undergo extinction. One solution to this problem is *flooding,* which is presenting the CS for undesirable responding in intensive, maximum form in a situation in which it does not predict a US. Originally introduced by Stampfl and Levis (1967), flooding is also known as *implosion* or *implosive therapy.* The rationale for this approach is extinction: By presenting the CS for the undesirable response in intensive form with no US predictiveness, the CR will undergo extinction.

Boulougouris, Marks, and Marset (1971) used flooding with 16 patients. Nine had agoraphobia, fear of becoming panicked and incapacitated in the world outside their living spaces, and 7 had other phobias. During the first flooding session, the therapists trained the patients to imagine vivid scenes. During five 50-minute flooding sessions, the therapist described anxiety-provoking scenes to the patients, who imagined the scenes. The experimenters provide the following example of one scene: ". . . an agoraphobic might hear the therapist describe that he went out into the street, became anxious, felt like fainting, was bathed in sweat, screamed in despair, tried to run back home but fainted and was taken by ambulance to a mental hospital, where he woke up feeling he was going mad" (Boulougouris et al., 1971, p. 8). Physiological measures, along with therapist and patient ratings, showed that the flooding procedure helped the patients more effectively than a systematic desensitization procedure.

As with other therapies based on Pavlovian conditioning, in flooding, the CSs may be either imaginal or *in vivo* (e.g., Emmelkamp & Wessels, 1975; Kandel, Ayllon, & Rosenbaum, 1977). When therapists use imaginal flooding they often present the phobic stimuli in exaggerated form, but when they use *in vivo* flooding, the fearful person is typically brought into contact with normal, unexaggerated stimuli. For example, Emmelkamp and Wessels's use of *in vivo* flooding for agoraphobics consisted simply of having the people take a 90-minute walk through town. Therapy making use of prolonged *in vivo* contacts with typical fear stimuli has come to be described as exposure treatment (e.g., Booth & Rachman, 1992; Watson, Gaind, & Marks, 1971; Watson, Mullett, & Pillay, 1973). (See Thyer, Baum, and Reid [1988] for a review of exposure therapy.)

In flooding, there usually is an attempt to maximize fear responding through the use of intense and often exaggerated fear stimuli, whereas in exposure treatment, the therapist simply brings the individual into contact with normal fear stimuli that elicit more moderate levels of anxiety (Watson et al., 1971). Exposure therapy is the most favored treatment for anxiety disorders (Barlow & Wolfe, 1981). Because flooding presents the phobic individual with maximally aversive stimuli, it often causes considerable discomfort. Rudestam and Bedrosian (1977) treated university students for different types of phobias with both systematic desensitization and flooding and found that flooding produced more desirable physiological changes than systematic desensitization. However, both the therapists and the students rated systematic desensitization as more effective than flooding.

Similarly, Horne and Matson (1977) treated university students for test anxiety using flooding, modeling, systematic desensitization, and study-skills training. Although flooding eliminated the student's test anxiety, the students could not recommend the procedure because of the discomfort it caused them. King and Gullone (1990) had a sample of high school students, parents, professionals (teachers and nurses) rate the acceptability of several behavioral procedures used to treat a child's extreme fear of dogs. These procedures included flooding, relaxation, systematic desensitization, emotive imagery, modeling, contingency management (reinforcement and punishment), and positive self-statements. Flooding was by far the least acceptable procedure for each of the three groups.

The lack of acceptability of flooding is a disadvantage of the technique and must be considered when making decisions about behavioral programs. Because of possible side effects associated with aversive stimuli, aversive procedures such as flooding should be used only by certified professionals who are fully aware of the benefits and risks of the method compared to other treatments.

Therapists have successfully used flooding to treat various phobias, fears, and other emotional disorders. Among other problems, flooding has been effective with Vietnam veterans who suffer from posttraumatic stress disorder (PTSD). Individuals who have this disorder are often troubled by nightmares, thoughts of horrific battle scenes, anxious behaviors, and depressed behaviors (Cooper & Clum, 1989; Keane & Kaloupek, 1982; Keane, Fairbank, Caddell, & Zimering, 1989).

Graduated extinction (Bandura, 1969) is another procedure that relies on extinction of Pavlovian conditioning. In graduated extinction, the therapist repeatedly presents the CS for the undesired CR, first in muted form and then in increasingly stronger forms. Graduated extinction is like flooding, but instead of presenting the CS at maximal strength from the outset, the therapist introduces the CS at low intensity at first and increases it over time. Graduated extinction is like systematic desensitization in that the therapist presents the fear-provoking CS in the graded steps of an anxiety hierarchy. However, graduated extinction does not make explicit use of relaxation training and, in this respect, is not a counterconditioning procedure. Graduated extinction is often referred to as graduated exposure.

For example, Michelson, Mavissakalian, and Marchione (1988) used this method to treat agoraphobic people. The therapist accompanied the people in gradually longer exposures to the outside world. Saul, Rome and Leuser (1946) used graduated extinction to treat U. S. Navy sailors suffering from combat fatigue as a result of World War II battle experiences. Due to battle site conditioning experiences, the sailors had developed severe startle reactions and conditioned aversions to loud noises, which in some cases had generalized even to music. The therapists treated these problems by showing a film of a naval battle in which warplanes were bombing a ship. They made the following observations of the men's reactions to the film:

> It was readily observed that the men are hypersensitive to very specific sights and sounds. For example, Number 9 did not mind the plane crashes or the general quarters gong, but could not stand the flashes of the big guns. Number 14 did not mind the flash of the guns but was at first panic-stricken by the explosion of depth bombs and near misses in the water. This was because he had dropped many depth charges while on anti-submarine duty (Saul et al., 1946).

At first, even though the volume of the films was kept low, the men had difficulty watching. Some could only stand in the doorway of the room and peek at the film. However, over time the volume of the film was gradually increased, sometimes by the therapists but sometimes by the men themselves. This treatment benefited 13 of the 14 men treated, as shown by the weakening of the startle responses and fear of loud noises.

Graduated extinction is probably an important means by which undesirable fears and emotions are weakened in the course of daily life. After an unpleasant emotional experience with another person, for example, people often interact with one another only tentatively at first and gradually increase contact over time. This minimizes the elicitation of unpleasant emotional responses while permitting extinction of emotional responding to occur.

Other Types of Pavlovian Conditioning Processes

Of the several varieties of Pavlovian conditioning, conditioned aversions and attractions, second-order conditioning, and conditioned suppression are particularly important to human behavior in day-to-day life.

Conditioned Aversions and Attractions

In our discussion of aversion therapy, we described how aversive stimuli can be deliberately used to condition aversions to undesirable stimuli. In everyday life, aversions are conditioned unintentionally. For example, at one time or another, you have probably had the experience of eating some food you liked, becoming ill, and afterward not liking that food anymore. This is a type of Pavlovian conditioning known as taste-aversion conditioning. Logue, Ophir and Strauss (1981) gave a questionnaire to over 500 undergraduate students and found that 65% of them had a food aversion. In most of these cases, the students reported they had eaten the food and later become sick. We can diagram this pattern of conditioning as follows:

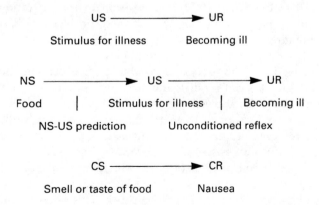

Logue et al. (1981) found that taste aversion conditioning was most effective when the food was novel and had a distinctive taste. In about 20% of the cases, the students formed a taste aversion to a food even when they attributed the cause of their sickness to something other than the food, such as the flu.

One group of people who frequently acquire taste aversions are cancer patients who receive chemotherapy treatments. Side effects of these treatments include nausea and vomiting. Bernstein and Webster (1980) studied this process by giving adults one of two distinctive flavors of ice cream, Maple Nut or Hawaiian Delight, before a chemotherapy treatment. Flavor preference tests given to the patients after chemotherapy showed they had developed taste aversions to the flavor of ice cream they had eaten before chemotherapy. This was true for the patients even though each of them was aware that the sickness they encountered after their treatment was due to chemotherapy and had nothing to do with the ice cream.

Bernstein and Webster also found that taste aversion conditioning occurred even among those patients who reported no nausea due to the chemotherapy. Since Bernstein and Webster's work, considerable research has been devoted to understanding the process better and to preventing and removing taste aversions conditioned through cancer chemotherapy. This prevention is important because cancer patients have problems in consuming sufficient amounts of food. Anything that can be done to prevent or remove taste aversions can therefore help the patient receive proper nutrition to fight the disease. [See Carey and Burish (1988) for a review.]

Taste aversions are only one type of conditioned aversion. People develop aversions, fears, and phobias to all sorts of things, often due to Pavlovian conditioning. For example, in a survey of driving phobias, Munjack (1984) found that 70% of people who had driving phobias said that the problem was due to a bad driving experience. Öst and Hugdahl (1985) found that 61% of patients who had blood or dentist phobias reported that their problems developed through an unfortunate experience in which blood or dentist stimuli predicted an aversive event. McNally and Steketee (1985) studied people who had animal phobias. Among those patients whose fear sources could be traced, most were due to bad childhood experiences with animals that conditioned the fear responses. Similarly, Merckelbach, de Ruiter, van den Hout, and Hoekstra (1989) studied people who had various types of fears of social situations. They found that 78% of these problems were reportedly due to direct conditioning experiences.

Fears and phobias are sometimes learned through means other than direct conditioning. In vicarious classical conditioning, observing another person's CR being elicited by a CS can produce the same response in an observer. For example, Venn and Short (1973) showed that nursery school children could acquire fears and positive emotional responses to an NS if a model behaved fearfully or with positive emotional responses to the NS. In addition, conditioned emotional responses can be acquired through rule-governed means. For example, Cook and Harris (1927) established conditioned emotional responding to a green light, as measured by skin conductance responding, simply by instructing subjects that the appearance of the green light would be followed by a shock. This rule-governed conditioning may, for example, be responsible for fear of snakes among people who have never been harmed by a snake, but who have been told that snakes are dangerous. In any case, although people can acquire severe fears and phobias through a variety of means, surveys tend to show that people acquire most of them through direct conditioning.

The opposite of conditioned aversion might be called conditioned attraction, the Pavlovian conditioning of pleasant CRs to a CS. Pleasant CRs can include positive emotional responses and sexual responses. Experimenters have not studied conditioned attractions as much as conditioned aversions. However, they have been the focus of attention in research in marketing and advertising, which seeks to examine how Pavlovian conditioning can be used to get people to prefer and purchase commercial products (e.g., Gorn, 1982; Bierley, McSweeney, & Vannieuwkerk, 1985).

Some observers suspect that conditioned attractions are the basis for sexual fetishes. For example, Rachman and Hodgson (1968) used a device that measured the level of sexual arousal of male subjects. The experimenters gave the men conditioning trials in which the NS, a pair of knee-length boots, was shown for 30 seconds, followed by a 10-second presentation of 40 different slides of nude or scantily dressed women, a US that elicited the UR of sexual responding. As a result of this method, the boots presented alone became a CS that had the ability to elicit the CR of sexual responding.

Conditioned attractions are probably the basis for much of the friendship and affection we feel for people as well as other things in life we value and enjoy. One of the puzzles of human behavior is expressed in the statement "There is no accounting for taste." Conditioned attractions may provide part of the answer to this puzzle. As Rachman and Hodgson's data suggest, the odd attractions people have to many things may be due to happenstance predictive relationships between NSs and USs. Because Pavlovian conditioning can occur in as little as a single trial (Seligman, 1971; Stuart, Shimp, & Engle, 1987) odd tastes can sometimes be due to rapid Pavlovian conditioning of strange NS-US combinations.

Second-Order Conditioning

In Pavlovian conditioning, the CS acquires the power to elicit a CR because it predicts a US. In second-order conditioning, a neutral stimulus predicts an effective CS, and gains the ability to elicit a CR. Second-order conditioning is effective in establishing verbal stimuli as CSs (Staats & Staats, 1957; Moran, 1981). Many words we use are CSs for our emotional and evaluative responding. We respond with positive emotions to words such as *happy, baby,* and *love* and respond with negative emotions to words such as *murder, rape,* and *wicked.* The emotional reactions these words stir in us are established through previous learning: Very young children do not respond emotionally to words in the way that adults do.

Staats and Staats showed that words with positive and negative referents can be used to change people's evaluations of neutral stimuli. They showed university students nonsense syllables (e.g., *xeh, yof*) paired with either positive (e.g., *beauty*) or negative (e.g., *thief*) referents. When the nonsense syllables were paired with (predicted) negative words, the students came to evaluate the nonsense syllables as relatively unpleasant. Conversely, when positive words were paired with the nonsense syllables, the students came to evaluate the nonsense syllables as more pleasant. This use of second-order conditioning may be illustrated as follows:

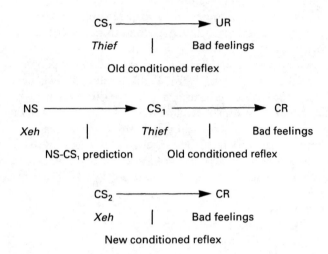

Essentially, second-order conditioning builds new CSs by having neutral stimuli predict old CSs, and in this way changes the neutral stimuli into new CSs.

Several experimenters have explored practical applications of second-order conditioning using word CS_1s. For example, Early (1968) worked with fourth and fifth grade pupils to try to improve the popularity of four students who had been shunned by their classmates. This problem of children being rebuked by their peers is often a perplexing one for parents, teachers, and the children themselves. The experimenter prepared cards on which she put the names of the rebuked children directly above positive adjectives, and put the names of popular students above neutral words:

    Adele   Karen

    Neat   Table

The names of the students predicted the positive adjectives and neutral words in the sense that the students read the names first. The experimenter told the students that she was conducting memory research in which they would memorize word pairs. For students in a control group, the unpopular students' names predicted neutral words rather than positive adjectives. The most striking result of the study, shown in Figure 13.2, was an increase in the number of interactions the unpopular students had with their peers.

The experimenter noted that before treatment, the four unpopular children seldom spoke to their peers and interacted mainly with younger children when they made contact at all. After treatment, the less popular children became more lively and played games with children of their own age for the first time. Observations showed that the formerly shunned children interacted with their peers because their

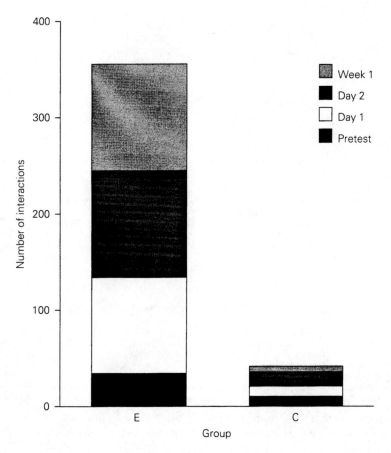

Figure 13.2   *The Influence of Second-Order Conditioning in Improving Acceptance of Rebuked Children by Their Classmates*

For an experimental group, the names of shunned children were established as CSs that predicted positive adjectives, but for a control group the shunned children's names predicted neutral adjectives. After conditioning, children in the experimental group interacted with their classmates much more frequently, but control children's interaction levels did not change. Figure drawn from Early's (1968) data.

approach responses, formerly punished, were now socially reinforced by peers.

Second-order conditioning using word CS_1s has been successful in solving several behavior problems. Experimenters have used it to treat phobias, to discourage children's cigarette, alcohol, and drug use (Moore, Moore, & Hauck, 1982), to reduce children's test anxiety (Parish, Buntman, & Buntman, 1976) and to reduce racial prejudice (Parish, Shirazi, & Lambert, 1976). These applications represent second-order conditioning because a new incompatible CR replaces an old one. For example, in Early's study we can diagram the counterconditioning procedure as follows:

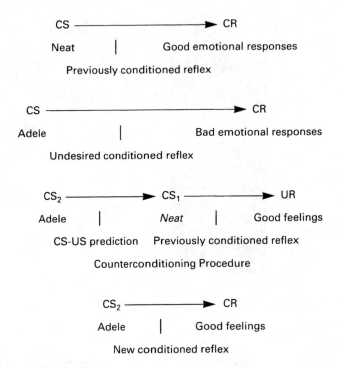

CS ——————————————→ CR

Neat | Good emotional responses

Previously conditioned reflex

CS ——————————————→ CR

Adele | Bad emotional responses

Undesired conditioned reflex

CS_2 ————→ CS_1 ————→ UR

Adele | *Neat* | Good feelings

CS-US prediction   Previously conditioned reflex

Counterconditioning Procedure

CS_2 ————→ CR

Adele | Good feelings

New conditioned reflex

If second-order conditioning works, is it possible to go further, for example to third-order conditioning in which a neutral stimulus becomes a CS_3 because it predicts a second-order CS_2? For example, in Staats and Staats's work, third order conditioning would have consisted of having a new NS nonsense syllable predict the freshly established CSs, *xeh* and *yof*. Tests of third-order conditioning of this sort have not been especially successful (Cicero & Tryon, 1989; Tryon & Cicero, 1989). Apparently, the power of CSs weakens the further removed they are from directly predicting the original USs.

Studies of evaluative conditioning, which include the second-order conditioning studies we have looked at, make for excellent projects for student experiments. They are relatively safe, not intrusive, and as you can see in studies like Early's, have important practical applications. However, as Bierley, McSweeney, and Vannieuwkerk (1985) have noted, some of these studies have not made use of proper control groups. Consult Bierley et al. (1985) for a helpful discussion of these issues if you are interested in doing a Pavlovian conditioning experiment.

Pavlovian-Operant Interactions and Conditioned Suppression

Pavlovian and operant conditioning often work together to influence behavior. For example, if you have a conditioned aversion to a food, Pavlovian conditioning has established the smell of the food as a CS for unpleasant nauseous feelings. In addition, operant processes are likely to be involved. The smell of the food can act as a punisher for responses that produce it and act as a reinforcer for responses that remove the smell. Similarly, a loved one can serve as a CS for pleasant emotional responses established through Pavlovian conditioning. At the same time, that person probably will act as a positive reinforcer for the operant approach behaviors.

There are many other instances in which the same stimulus has multiple functions, acting as CSs, reinforcers, and discriminative stimuli. Pavlovian and operant conditioning interact in conditioned suppression. In conditioned suppression, presentation of a CS that predicts an aversive US such as shock causes operant behavior maintained by reinforcers to be weakened or eliminated until the CS is removed. The suppression of responding to the CS produces conditioned emotional responses (i.e., fear responding) that interfere with operant behavior.

Conditioned suppression was originally studied in rats. A tone is established as a CS for conditioned fear responding by having the tone predict shock. Later, the rat's lever-pressing behavior is maintained at a steady rate on a schedule of reinforcement. Then, the tone CS is introduced, which produces a reduction in the rate of the lever pressing response.

Reiter and DeVellis (1976) showed that conditioned suppression can work with people when the CS is a social stimulus. Student subjects completed an interest survey. For students in an experimental group, the experimenter came in at one point and expressed shock and displeasure because the subject had used a pen to fill out the survey rather than a pin punch. The experimenter was the CS, his shocked reaction was the US, and the student's emotional responding was the UR. After this, the students engaged in a second activity, solving subtraction problems. While they were doing this second activity, the experimenter returned to the room and pretended to be searching for a book. The researchers measured the time the students spent to solve the subtraction problems.

As shown in Figure 13.3, when the experimenter entered the room, the rate of problem solving decreased for students in the experimental group. For students in a control group, for whom the experimenter was not established as an aversive CS, there was no reduction in response rate due to the experimenter's presence. Among other things, the principle of conditioned suppression suggests that when you study, you should keep your study area clear of disagreeable people, mementos of unpleasant experiences, and any other stimuli apt to elicit strong emotional responses. We can diagram conditioned suppression in the following way:

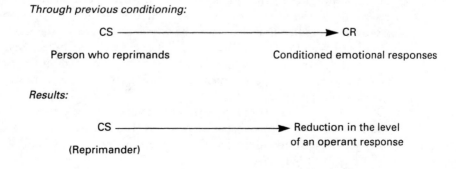

Through previous conditioning:

CS ————————————————————▶ CR

Person who reprimands   Conditioned emotional responses

Results:

CS ————————————————————▶ Reduction in the level
                                          of an operant response
(Reprimander)

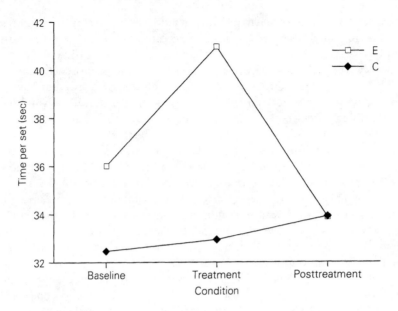

Figure 13.3 *The Effect of Conditioned Suppression Using a Human CS*

After human stimulus was established as a CS that predicted an aversive event, appearance of that stimulus produced a conditioned suppression effect, a decline in the rate of an operant response. For a control group, a human stimulus did not predict the aversive event and had no effect on the rate of the operant response. During a posttreatment phase, the human stimulus no longer predicted the aversive event, and differences between the experimental and control groups were eliminated. Figure adapted from Reiter and DeVellis (1976).

More recently, Scotti, Vittimberga, Ridley, and Cornell (1992) studied conditioned suppression in Vietnam veterans who had been identified as having posttraumatic stress disorder (PTSD), a problem we described earlier. The veterans were equipped with a set of headphones. They were then given the difficult task of listening to spoken words presented through one ear while different words were presented at the same time to the other ear. The subjects were instructed to "shadow" or repeat aloud the words that were presented to their right ear and to ignore the words presented to their left ear. The words presented to the right ear were called target words and the words presented to the left ear were called the distractor words. This task in which the subjects must listen to two messages in this fashion is called a dichotic-listening task; experimental psychologists often use it to study various types of behavioral processes.

Scotti et al. (1992) presented both combat-related words (e.g., *ambush, recon,* and *overrun*) and noncombat-related words (e.g., *prize, pencil,* and *upon*) as distractor words, the words presented to the subjects' left ears. Results of the experiment showed that the Vietnam veterans with the PTSD disorder made more errors in repeating to target words when distractor words were combat-related words than when the distractor words were noncombat-related words. Further, for the Vietnam veterans with the PTSD disorder, the combat-related words caused more listening errors than for two other groups of veterans: One with Vietnam combat experience but without PTSD, and a group of veterans without combat experience. In this study, the CSs were the combat words, and the operant responses were the correct listening responses to the target message. This was a conditioned suppression procedure because the CSs the combat words, reduced the rate of correct listening responses, the operant behavior.

Conditioned suppression is sometimes responsible for the disruption of ongoing behavior in day-to-day life. Persinger (1985) has suggested that death anxiety is a form of conditioned suppression in which stimuli that predict death cause emotional responding and reduction in the rate of operant behavior. Brasted and Callahan (1984) have suggested that conditioned suppression occurs during grieving for the loss of a loved one. Similarly, hearing news that foretells economic or political aversive stimuli can depress the rate of ongoing performances.

Other Work in Pavlovian Conditioning

Pavlovian conditioning is currently such an active area of research that it is not possible to discuss all the different types of Pavlovian conditioned responses here in any detail. However, we can briefly mention some promising approaches. Work in evaluative conditioning is currently experiencing a resurgence of interest and, as we have seen, has many practical applications. (See Jaanus, Defares, & Zwaan [1990] for a review.) Pavlovian conditioning is useful in assessing the hearing of people with multiple handicaps (Lancioni, Coninx, & Smeets, 1989). Placebo effects, the beneficial effects of taking an ineffective substance that is believed to be effective, have been interpreted as a Pavlovian conditioning process. Alterations of the responsiveness of the immune system are also believed to be influenced by Pavlovian conditioning. (See Turkkan [1989] for an extensive review of these effects.)

Making Pavlovian Conditioning Effective

The effectiveness of each of the therapies we have discussed is influenced by many different therapy-specific factors that we will not cover here. In this section, we will examine general factors that influence the effectiveness of Pavlovian conditioning including the effectiveness of the US, the timing of the NS and US, the number of conditioning trials, the intensity-vividness of the CS, Garcia effects, CS preexposure, and overshadowing and blocking effects.

Effectiveness of the US

In general, the greater the effectiveness of the US in eliciting a UR, the greater the effectiveness of the CS in eliciting the CR. Maltzman, Langdon, Pendery, and Wolff (1977) showed this principle in an experiment in which three different noise volumes served as the USs for the UR of the skin conductance response. Figure 13.4a shows that a 110 decibel noise produced a stronger UR than a 95 decibel noise, which in turn produced a stronger UR than an 80 decibel noise. As such, Figure 13.4a shows that the greater the magnitude of the US (the louder the noise), the more effective the noises were in producing URs.

The CS in the experiment was the word *plant*, which predicted the US, the noise. Conditioning took place over 10 trials in which the spoken stimulus *plant*, occurred 10 seconds before a noise, which lasted 1 second. The long interval between the CS and the US allowed the experimenters to measure the strength of

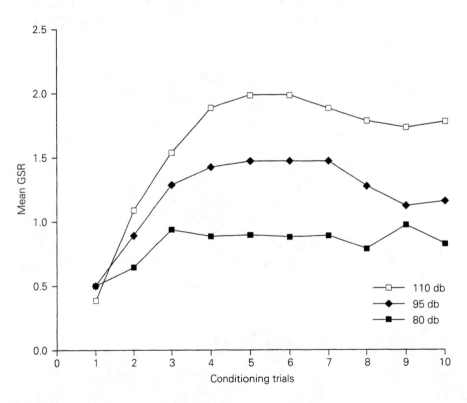

Figure 13.4a *The Effect of the Strength of the US on Pavlovian Conditioning*

Conditioning was more effective when a stronger (louder) US was used than when weaker USs were used. Figure adapted from Maltzman, Langdon, Pendery, and Wolff (1977).

the CR to the CS on each of the 10 conditioning trials. As shown in Figure 13.4b, the effectiveness of the CS in eliciting the CR depended on the effectiveness of the US predicted by the CS. The CS was most effective when it predicted the loudest US, the 110 decibel noise, and least effective when it predicted the quietest US, the 80 decibel noise. The CS was of moderate effectiveness when it predicted the medium US, the 95 decibel noise.

Erickson, Tiffany, Martin, and Baker (1983) demonstrated the principle of US effectiveness in their study of aversion therapy. They compared a rapid-smoking method, in which smokers inhaled cigarettes at a rapid pace, with a rapid-puffing method, in which the subjects smoked cigarettes without inhaling. The rapid-smoking stimuli were more effective USs than the rapid-puffing stimuli. Rapid smoking caused more unpleasant URs of feeling sick and nauseous. The rapid-smoking treatment produced more abstinence from cigarettes than the rapid-puffing treatment This suggested that the more aversive USs associated with rapid smoking caused greater conditioned aversions to cigarette stimuli that the less effective USs associated with rapid puffing. Although it is desirable to minimize the discomfort people have during therapy, the principle of US effectiveness indicates that the effectiveness of aversion therapy increases as discomfort increases. More happily, in applications where the US elicits pleasant responses, more effective USs will produce better conditioning.

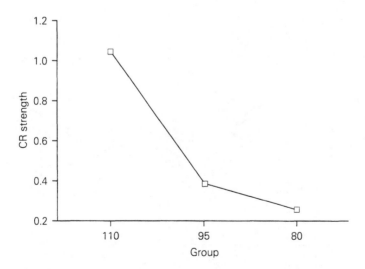

Figure 13.4b *The Effect of the Strength of the US on Pavlovian Conditioning*

When a stronger US was used, skin conductance conditioning was more effective than when weaker USs were used. Figure adapted from Maltzman, Langdon, Pendery, and Wolff (1977).

Timing of the NS and US

The principle of NS-US timing is that conditioning will be most effective if the NS precedes the US by less than a second. Moeller (1954) demonstrated this principle in conditioning the skin conductance response of university men. White noise, noise that sounds like a television set tuned to an inoperative channel, was used as the NS. For one group, a short burst of white noise predicted shock that occurred 250 milliseconds (a quarter of a second) after the white noise went off. For three other groups, the shock was delivered 450, 1000, or 2500 milliseconds after the white noise stopped. The results of the experiment are shown in Figure 13.5, which shows the strength of the CR for each group. As you can see, conditioning was most effective when the NS preceded the US by 450 milliseconds. At the shorter 250 millisecond interval, conditioning was less effective. Similarly, at the intervals greater than 450 milliseconds, conditioning became progressively worse.

Although the effectiveness of conditioning deteriorates with longer NS-US intervals, it is possible to obtain conditioning at relatively long intervals. Conditioning using long NS-US intervals is known as *trace conditioning*. In general, when using the Pavlovian conditioning therapies, short NS-US intervals should be used to make conditioning maximally effective.

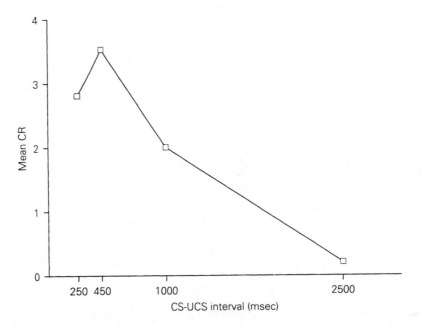

Figure 13.5   *The Relation Between the NS-US Time Interval and the Effectiveness of Pavlovian Conditioning*

Conditioning is most effective when the time interval between the CS and US is approximately .5 seconds. Figure adapted from Moeller (1954).

Backward conditioning is a procedure in which the order of the NS and the US is reversed, such that the US precedes the NS. The effectiveness of backward conditioning is a controversial topic (Hall, 1984; Spetch, Wilkie, & Pinel, 1981). When it does work, it is generally less effective than standard (i.e., forward conditioning) Pavlovian conditioning (e.g., Stuart, Shimp, & Engle, 1987).

Inappropriate NS-US timing has been a problem in aversion therapy. As Elkins (1991a) discusses, there have been many failures of alcohol-aversion therapy because the experimenters gave subjects alcohol only after they had reached a state of drug-induced nausea. This method was much less effective in establishing abstinence than other procedures with appropriate NS-US timing.

Number of Conditioning Trials

In general, the greater the number of trials in which the CS predicts the US, the more effective conditioning will be (Baeyens, Eelen, Crombez, & Van den Bergh, 1992; Sachs, 1975; Stuart, Shimp, & Engle, 1987). Stuart et al. (1987) illustrated this principle in a study of evaluative conditioning. University students watched a slide presentation in which presentations of a tube of Brand L Toothpaste were NSs that predicted USs, pictures that elicited positive emotional responses. The pictures included a mountain waterfall, two attractive sunsets, and clouds in a blue sky seen with a mast of a sailboat in the foreground. The experimenters selected attractive pictures as USs because they are so frequently used in advertising. Four different groups of students received different numbers of conditioning trials. For one group, the tube of toothpaste predicted the pleasing pictures only once on a single trial, while for the three remaining groups, the CS-US prediction occurred over 3, 10, or 20 trials. On each trial, a 5-second presentation of the toothpaste was followed by a 5-second picture presentation, followed by a 5-second presentation of the toothpaste tube superimposed on the picture. In addition, the experimenters included trials in which other brands of products (cola, detergent, and soap) predicted neutral pictures that elicited no positive emotional responses. The purpose of these trials was to distract the students' attention from the NS-US trials and in this way discourage the subjects from guessing the purpose of the experiment.

Figure 13.6 shows how the students rated, on a 1 to 7 semantic differential scale, the goodness, quality, likability, superiority, and attractiveness of Brand L Toothpaste. As you can see, more conditioning trials seemed to produce more positive attitudes toward the CS. However, although suggestive of other relationships, the difference between only the 20-trial group and the 1-trial group was statistically significant.

The influence of the number of trials on conditioning indicates that behavior therapies using Pavlovian procedures should make use of repeated NS-US trials. For example, as you have seen in our discussion of aversion therapy and in the studies in the conceptual exercise in this chapter, successful uses of aversion therapy have tended to use many conditioning trials. The effectiveness of conditioning trials, as shown in the experiment of Stuart et al. (1987), also suggests that television commercials

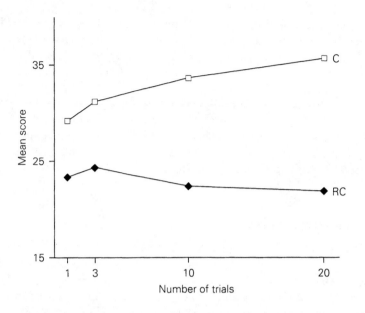

Figure 13.6   *The Effect of the Number of Conditioning Trials on the Effectiveness of Pavlovian Conditioning*

The number of conditioning trials improved the effectiveness of conditioning for a conditioning group (C) for whom the NS, a tube of toothpaste, predicted the US, attractive pictures. For a random control group (RC), the appearance of the tube of toothpaste did not predict the appearance of the attractive pictures. Figure adapted from Stuart, Shimp, and Engle (1987).

and print-based ads are more effective if they are repeated often. Although advertisers violate many behavior principles, this is not one of them.

There may be a limit beyond which conditioning trials are no longer effective or are counterproductive. For example, although Baeyens et al. (1992) found that the effectiveness of conditioning positive evaluative responses increased from 1 to 10 trials, at 20 trials subjects had come to respond more negatively to the CS. However, this loss of effect with increasing trials was not seen when negative evaluative responses were conditioned.

It must be emphasized that the effectiveness of the CS is influenced by the degree to which the CS predicts the US and not exclusively by the number of trials on which the CS occurs before the US. For example, in Stuart's et al. (1987) study, the use of additional trials did not produce conditioning for subjects in the random control group. For this group, the CS, the toothpaste, did not predict the attractive pictures: Sometimes the CS preceded the US, but often the US occurred without being preceded by the US and the CS occurred without being followed by the US. The number of trials improves conditioning, but only when there is a predictive relationship between the CS and the US.

Intensity-Vividness of the CS

In general, the more intense or vivid the CS is, the more effective it will be in eliciting a CR. Mattson and Moore (1964) demonstrated this principle in a study of eyelid conditioning. For one group of subjects, a soft tone served as a CS that predicted a puff of air to the eye, the US, which in turn produced a UR, an eye blink. For a second group of subjects, a loud tone served as the CS. Conditioning was more effective using the loud tone than the soft tone.

The intensity-vividness of the CS may be important in Pavlovian conditioning therapies relying on imagery. People differ greatly in their ability to imagine stimuli (Howard, 1983), suggesting that imagery-based conditioning procedures will be more effective for people who can visualize more vivid images. Dyckman and Cowan (1978) and Glenn and Hughes (1978) found this to be the case. Subjects with better imaginal abilities were more likely to benefit from systematic desensitization for snake phobia than subjects who had poorer imaginal skills. The possible relationship between vividness of imagery and the effectiveness of imaginal conditioning procedures suggests that anything that can be done to improve imaginal abilities also will improve conditioning effectiveness. Some observers (Levin & Gross, 1985; Weir & Marshall, 1980) believe that one effect of relaxation, as used in systematic desensitization, is to improve the vividness of imagined stimuli.

Garcia Effects

Certain CS-US combinations produce stronger Pavlovian conditioning than others. The special abilities some CS-US combinations have in producing conditioning are called *Garcia effects*. In an influential experiment, Garcia and Koelling (1966) conditioned taste aversions in rats. They found that an aversion to a distinctive taste, a CS, could be conditioned much more effectively using a sickness-inducing agent as a US than electric shock. Essentially, the CS-US combination of taste and sickness-inducer worked better to condition an aversion than the combination of taste and electric shock.

Cannon and Baker (1981) found this result in work with alcoholic men. Taste aversions to alcohol could be successfully conditioned to alcohol as the CS with the US of a nausea-inducing drug. However, the taste of alcohol did not become an aversive CS when it predicted shock. One explanation for these findings is evolutionary. Animals that have quickly developed taste aversions to foods that make them sick are more likely to survive, reproduce, and pass on their characteristics to their offspring. Conversely, animals that quickly develop taste aversions to foods associated with externally inflicted pain are more likely to cease looking for food under adverse conditions and fail to survive.

Seligman (1971) made several intriguing proposals about the ability to condition human fear responses with certain CS-US combinations. For example, snake phobias are more common than car or electrical-outlet phobias, even though snakes are far less dangerous to us than cars or electrical hazards. This has led some to speculate that snake stimuli are CSs that are very easily established (or more resistant to extinction) as conditioned aversive stimuli as a result of the history of the human race. In the past, snakes and other reptiles were a greater threat to human survival than they are today. In addition, other research suggests that human facial expressions of fear and anger predispose people to acquire conditioned fears (e.g., Lanzetta & Orr, 1986). Currently, the study of predispositions to fears and fear conditioning is an active area of research. (See McNally [1987] for a review.)

The major practical implication of the Garcia effect is that behavior analysts sometimes have to be selective in finding CS-US combinations that are maximally effective in producing Pavlovian conditioning. If a particular US does not provide good results, it is prudent to look for another, more effective stimulus.

CS Preexposure

In general, exposure to a potential CS before training reduces its effectiveness during the conditioning procedure. (e.g., Björkstrand, 1990; Siddle & Remington, 1987; Stuart et al., 1987). Stuart's et al. (1987) work in conditioning positive emotions toward Brand L Toothpaste, described earlier, included an experiment that examined the effects of CS preexposure. The researchers gave a CS preexposure group 20 5-second presentations of the Brand L Toothpaste slide before 10 conditioning trials in which the toothpaste slide predicted attractive pictures. During the 20 preexposures, the toothpaste slide was presented interspersed among other product slides. A conditioning group received only the 10 conditioning trials. Although the preexposures did not prevent the conditioning of positive emotions and attitudes toward the toothpaste, conditioning was not as effective.

In another study, Shimp, Stuart, and Engle (1991) conditioned positive emotional responses to different colas. The colas included well-known brands (Coke and Pepsi), moderately known brands (RC and Shasta), and obscure brands (Cragmont, Elf, My-Te-Fine, and Target). As in Stuart et al. (1987), they used attractive pictures as the USs. They found that conditioning was more effective with the unknown and moderately known brands than with the well-known brands. One explanation for this result is ceiling effects: Because people have been so extensively conditioned to Coke and Pepsi through advertising, it is difficult in a brief experiment to improve those conditioning effects any further. Another explanation is the CS preexposure effect. It may be more difficult to condition positive responses to well-known brands because people have received extensive preexposure to them (McSweeney & Bierley, 1984).

Animal research has shown that there is also a US preexposure effect (Randich & Lolordo, 1979). Preexposure to the US lessens the effectiveness of conditioning. However, this effect has not been studied extensively with people (though see Blair and Shimp [1992]).

Overshadowing and Blocking Effects

Overshadowing and blocking refer to failures of an NS to become a CS even though it predicts a US. In overshadowing, two NSs predict a US, but only one becomes an effective CS. Often the NS that is more intense, vivid, or prominent will become a CS, but not the other NS. We say that the NS that acquires CS properties overshadows the one that does not. McSweeney and Bierley (1984) have related the overshadowing effect to advertising. For example, suppose on a television commercial for soda pop both the brand name and an attractive close-up of the iced, fizzing liquid predict attractive scenery and music. Both the picture of the fizzing liquid and the brand name predict the USs, but the fizzing liquid might be conditioned as a CS rather than the brand name because it is more prominent. This wouldn't help the soda pop makers because they would be conditioning positive responses toward all soda pops that fizz, not just their brand. It would be better to try to emphasize something distinctive about the brand such as the label, the shape of the bottle, or the color of the can. This overshadowing can be diagrammed as follows:

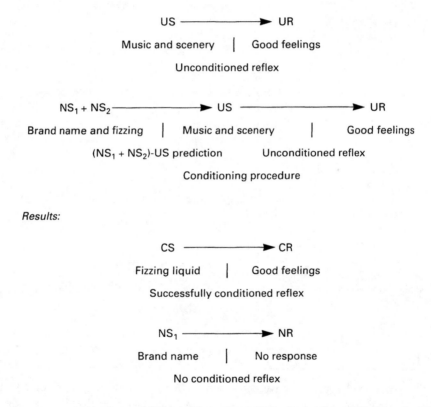

In blocking, a preestablished CS and an NS both predict a US, but the NS fails to become a CS. We say that the NS has not become a CS because it has been blocked by the preexisting CS. For example, suppose that a celebrity has established herself as a CS for a pleasant tune in the same way that Bob Hope and Johnny Carson are associated with characteristic melodies. Our celebrity, now a CS for the CR of the positive emotional responses produced by the tune, is in a car commercial in which both the celebrity and the car now predict the pleasant tune. Here, a blocking effect might occur: The car, the NS, might not be established as a CS (or established as only a weak CS) for the positive emotional responses because of the presence of the preexisting CS, the celebrity, in the ad. We can diagram blocking in the following way:

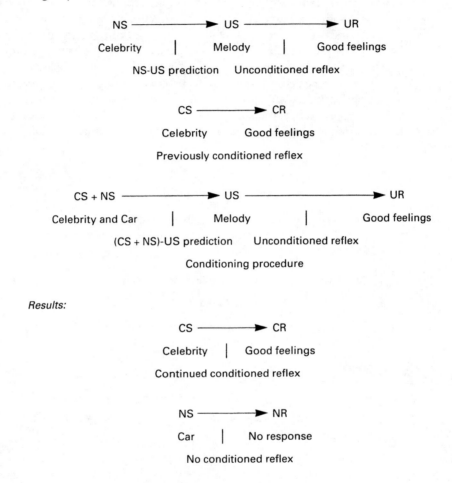

Summary

In this chapter we have examined Pavlovian conditioning, originally studied by the Russian physiologist Ivan Pavlov. Pavlovian conditioning is based on our unconditioned reflexes, unlearned responses we have that are elicited by particular stimuli. The unlearned responses are unconditioned responses (URs), and the stimuli that elicit those responses are unconditioned stimuli (USs). In Pavlovian conditioning, a neutral stimulus (NS) predicts a US. If conditioning is successful, the NS becomes a conditioned stimulus (CS) that can elicit the response, called a conditioned response (CR).

Pavlovian conditioning differs from operant conditioning, changing behavior by using response-dependent consequences. First, in Pavlovian conditioning, conditioning occurs because one stimulus, an NS, predicts another stimulus, a US. The US is therefore presented on a stimulus-dependent basis. In operant conditioning, a consequence for a response occurs dependent on the occurrence or nonoccurrence of a response. As such, in operant conditioning, the consequence occurs on a response-dependent basis. Second, Pavlovian conditioning most readily influences the responding of the autonomic nervous system, which controls responses we normally think of as involuntary. In contrast, operant conditioning most readily affects the skeletal muscles, muscles used to perform actions such as walking and talking, actions we normally think of as voluntary. Third, the language used to describe operant and Pavlovian conditioning differs. Operant behavior is said to be emitted or engaged in, while behavior learned through Pavlovian conditioning is said to be elicited by a prior stimulus.

Pavlovian conditioning occurs when a CS gains the power to elicit a response because it has predicted a US. Pseudoconditioning occurs when a CS gains some ability to elicit a response, but this is due simply to presenting the US, not to a predictive NS-US relationship.

Extinction of Pavlovian conditioning occurs when a CS for a CR is repeatedly presented without predicting a US. This results in the CS losing its ability to elicit a CR. Sometimes it requires many extended presentations of a CS for extinction to take place.

We examined several different therapies based on Pavlovian conditioning, including counterconditioning, systematic and *in vivo* desensitization, aversion therapies, and flooding and exposure therapy. Counterconditioning is used when there is an undesirable CS-CR relationship due to prior conditioning. This undesired relationship is weakened or eliminated by conditioning a new CR to the CS that is the opposite to the old one. Like many other Pavlovian conditioning therapies, the stimuli can either be *in vivo*, actual real-life stimuli, or imagined stimuli.

One specific form of therapy generally based on the idea of counterconditioning is systematic desensitization. In systematic desensitization, relaxation is most often used to countercondition fear responding. The goal of therapy is for the individual to remain relaxed even when she is imagining, and later directly encountering, the most fear-provoking stimuli. *In vivo* desensitization follows this general pattern, except that the person in therapy confronts real rather than imagined stimuli.

Aversion therapy is a method used to develop conditioned aversions to inappropriate stimuli. Clinicians have used aversion therapies to treat many problems including alcoholism, sexual arousal to inappropriate stimuli, and smoking. In one variant of aversion therapy called covert sensitization, the aversive stimulus occurs in imaginal form.

Flooding is a therapy based on the concept of Pavlovian extinction. In flooding, the therapist presents the fear-provoking stimuli in maximum form to the fearful person. By presenting the feared CS stimuli to the individual without them predicting a US, the therapist tries to extinguish the person's fears. Flooding can be conducted *in vivo*, using real stimuli, or though the use of imaginal stimuli. A related treatment is exposure therapy, which generally refers to the method of bringing the fearful person into direct *in vivo* contact with the feared stimuli. Flooding causes considerable discomfort for the patient, a disadvantage of the technique. Other procedures that make use of Pavlovian extinction are graduated extinction and graduated exposure. These methods differ from flooding because the feared stimulus is presented in steps from least to most fearful, while in flooding the most feared stimulus is presented at the beginning of treatment.

Several phenomena are based on classical conditioning, including conditioned aversions and attractions, second-order conditioning, and conditioned suppression.

Studies have shown that through Pavlovian conditioning experiences, people learn fear and other unpleasant responses to certain stimuli. Food aversions, for example, are learned when someone becomes ill after eating a certain food, even though the food itself did not cause the sickness. We briefly saw how food aversions are acquired during chemotherapy. Although most phobias are acquired through direct conditioning, phobias can also be learned through modeling and through rule-governed control.

We examined conditioned attractions, the opposite of conditioned aversions. Through NS-US predictions, people learn to respond with pleasurable emotional or sexual responses to a variety of stimuli. One example of this is a fetish, a sexual attraction to an object. Conditioned attractions, however, are also involved in more conventional attractions people have for one another. Conditioned attractions can be used in advertising to induce people to respond favorably toward commercial products.

Second-order conditioning is another Pavlovian conditioning phenomenon. In this kind of conditioning, an NS predicts a previously established CS for a CR, which changes the NS into a CS capable of eliciting the CR. Many instances of second-order conditioning have used words as previously established CSs. Second order conditioning has shown considerable value as a behavior-change technique useful in altering people's evaluative responses.

We also discussed the way in which Pavlovian and operant conditioning interact with each other. One example of this is conditioning suppression, in which a CS for a fear CR is conditioned. Once the CS is established, presenting it weakens ongoing operant behavior, presumably because the fear responding elicited by the CS interferes with operant performances.

We also examined several factors that contribute to making Pavlovian conditioning effective: the effectiveness of the US, the NS-US timing, the number of conditioning trials, the intensity/vividness of the CS, Garcia effects, CS and US preexposures, and overshadowing and blocking effects. In general, the conditioning is better when a powerful US is used, when the NS precedes the US by a very short period of time, when there are many conditioning trials, when the CS is vivid and intense, when the right NS-US combination is used, and when there is no previous experience with either the CS or the US. It is also useful to have only a single NS predict a US and to avoid coupling an NS with a previously conditioned CS.

Conceptual Exercise   *Pavlovian Conditioning*

For each of the following items, decide if the item is an example of Pavlovian conditioning. For each item, the response in question is highlighted. If the item is an example of Pavlovian conditioning, then identify the US, UR, NS, CS, and CR. If the item is not an example of Pavlovian conditioning, then identify it as an example of operant conditioning, if applicable. Check, your decisions with the analyses in the back of the book.

Note 1: If there is not a predictive relationship between a US and a CS, and there is an apparent CR, the item is not an example of Pavlovian conditioning.

Note 2: If there is an increase in the level of a response due to a reward or a decrease in the level of a response due to punishment, this is an example of operant conditioning.

1. Liz was a 37-year-old woman who had bronchial asthma. She was participating in a medical experiment, during which she sat in front of a box that had several rubber tubes attached. The tubes were connected to a mouthpiece from which Liz was administered various substances. Because there were several tubes, different substances could be given to Liz without her knowing which substances were which. Initial testing showed that when the experimenters gave her an extract of grass and tree pollen, Liz had an asthmatic attack. In contrast, when they gave her a neutral solvent, it had no effect. However, after several days of testing, Liz began to have asthmatic attacks that the neutral solvent alone induced. Eventually, just being fitted with the mouthpiece of the apparatus triggered **asthmatic attacks** in Liz.

2. Lillian was a singer who had epilepsy. It had been discovered that her seizures could be arrested early in their course if she smelled particular odors. Therefore, when she felt a seizure about to occur, she would smell a concentrated odor of jasmine from a vial and this would stop the **seizure**.

3. Madeline and Michelle, aged 34 and 36, suffered from severe constipation. They were unable to defecate without the use of laxatives. Dr. Quarti and Dr. Renaud treated them with a device they had invented. The device was a small transistorized unit, attached by a belt around the patients' waists, that delivered a painless electrical current to the patient. At first, this electric current had no effect on Madeline's and Michelle's bowel movements. The doctors then began inducing bowel movements with laxatives and, just before the patients defecated, the device delivered an electric current. In addition, the patients were told to turn on the current whenever they felt they were about to have a bowel movement and to turn it off once they were finished. Because of this treatment, both Madeline and Michelle could induce a **bowel movement** by turning on the device even when they did not feel a bowel movement about to occur. They no longer required laxatives.

4. Ivan, who was only 32 days old, was fed milk 10 times from a bottle each day for 10 to 15 seconds. Each time a 2-second tone from an organ pipe preceded these feedings and there was a 2-to 3-second interval between tone and bottle. Before the procedure, which continued for 4 months, Ivan would engage in vigorous sucking movements when the nipple of the bottle touched his lips. He didn't react at all to the tone. As a result of this procedure, after 6 days of experimental trials consisting of 29 tone-bottle pairings, the tone came to elicit Ivan's **sucking movements**.

5. Marvin, an undergraduate in college, was participating in a psychology experiment for the first time. He sat in a semireclining chair with several wires attached to his

body. Some of these wires helped to measure his Galvanic Skin Response (GSR), a measure of the electrical conductivity of the skin. (Electric shock produces a strong change in skin conductivity, a reaction often called a GSR.) Wires attached to the middle finger of Marvin's right hand gave him electric shocks. Initially, a faint .25-second light flash from a small bulb had no effect on Marvin's GSR. During the experiment, Marvin was shocked 31 times. As a result of this procedure, the light flash alone produced Marvin's **GSR**.

6. Dr. Hayduk lived in a remote part of Canada where the hearty and robust people have warm hearts, but cold hands. To train hand warming, he had his subjects enter a cold room and put on rubber globes. He instructed them to think of an image of a unique and personally meaningful scene. When the image was clear, they pressed a button and said the nonsense syllable "Wek," immediately after which warm water was injected into a loose-fitting rubber glove. Warmth, as provided by the warm water in this case, naturally elicits a vasodilation response, an increase in blood circulation that produces additional warmth. As a result of 30 trials of this technique, all six subjects were able to **increase their hand warmth** .5 degree Celsius merely by thinking of the thermal image and by saying "Wek." Initially, thinking of the image and saying "Wek" had had no effect on hand warming.

7. Little Albert was a generally happy and healthy nine-month old boy. No one had ever seen him become angry or fearful. However, in preliminary tests, John and Rosalie, the experimenters, found that Albert cried and responded fearfully after a loud noise was made behind his head. After this discovery, in several sessions they put a white rat in front of Albert. While Albert was looking at the rat, John and Rosalie sounded the loud noise, which elicited Albert's crying and other fear responses. As a result of this procedure, when they placed the rat in front of Albert without the loud noise, he began **crying**.

8. Mike was in the experimental group of a psychology research project that consisted of three stages. First, Mike was shown a series of slides of simple mental arithmetic tasks. Mike's task was to use the answer from the last arithmetic problem and add it to, subtract it from, or multiply it by the next number. For example, if the answer to the last problem was 14 and the slide Mike was viewing read +2, then Mike would calculate "14 + 2 = 16" to himself and then use 16 in solving the next problem. The experimenter had arranged these problems such that the number 16 would often be the answer. Second, Mike was presented with slides containing the number 16. After he viewed these for 10 seconds, he was given an electric shock. Third, Mike returned to the first task of solving arithmetic problems, again with the number 16 often being a correct answer to the problem. During this third stage of the experiment, when Mike calculated the answer to be 16, this caused a **GSR response**.

9. Ms. T. was a 46-year-old single woman who made dresses for a living. She had great fear of social situations, especially ones in which she had to interact with men or in which men were arguing or fighting. She had become so fearful that whenever there was even a small emotional disturbance in a social situation, she would run away. She sought help for her problem from Dr. W., who took Ms. T. to social situations and rewarded her with praise if she remained in the situation a progressively longer period of time. This procedure continued until Miss T. was able to **interact in all**

kinds of social situations without escaping. At work she no longer avoided social situations, even when two men fought outside her workroom for an hour.

10. Sweeney, a medical student, had agreed to be a subject in a psychiatric experiment. He and ten other medical students were outfitted with a device that measured the volume of their penises. They watched a series of 10 filmed segments, each lasting about one minute. Half of these segments were films of nude women, and half were films of nude men. The female and male films were alternated. Before each female film, a still photo of a red circle was presented, while before each male film, a green triangle was presented. At first, Sweeney's penile volume increased only when he looked at nude women, and decreased only when he looked at nude men. As a result of this training, Sweeney's **penile volume** increased when he saw the red circle and decreased when he saw the green triangle. Initially these stimuli had had no effect on Sweeney's penile volume.

11. Tarja needed some money so she volunteered to be in a research project in which she would be paid $120 to be given a drug that would make her nauseous. The day the research took place she hadn't eaten anything for the previous 8 hours; when she arrived, she drank a glass of cranberry juice and a then a glass of water. The researcher then injected her with a drug called apomorphine hydrochloride. Within 6 minutes she became nauseated. Two minutes later she vomited. Forty minutes after vomiting, she fell asleep. In two test sessions held 4 days and 1 month after the initial session, Tarja was given cranberry juice to drink. She and the other subjects in her group drank much less than control subjects who had not been made ill. In addition, Tarja felt a twinge of **nausea** during the tests when she sampled the cranberry juice.

12. Chauncey, a student in an introductory psychology course, had volunteered to be in an experiment. During the initial sessions, he received some training in hypnosis and then drank a glass of V-8 juice. At subsequent sessions, the experimenter told him to imagine himself tasting the V-8 juice and then feeling nauseated. After several such imagined sequences, the experimenter had him drink some V-8 and rate how good it tasted. Compared to students who imagined a positive event after they had imagined V-8 consumption, Chauncey and the other students in his group drank much less V-8 at the end of the sessions, rated the V-8 as less palatable, and felt more **nausea** when they drank (or imagined drinking) the V-8 at the end of the sessions.

13. Ross, a 40-year-old man who had been hospitalized due to alcoholism, volunteered to participate in a study designed to help him with his problem. In the study, Ross entered an environment that was designed to look like a bar. There the experimenter invited him to drink what he liked from a selection of available beverages. Immediately after Ross took a drink, he would receive an electric shock. Ross and the others in his treatment group drank the same amount of alcohol as a group of untreated alcoholics. Ross **felt normal** when he drank at the posttest.

14. Alexandra was a subject in a psychology experiment. During one session she viewed red, blue, and yellow slides of geometric figures. After each red slide was shown 10 seconds of music from the film Star Wars was played over headphones

she was wearing. The music was played after half of the blue slides, but after the other half, no music was played. After the yellow slides, no music was played. Before the session, the music produced good feelings in Alexandra, but the colors did not. Due to the training, however, the **good feelings** of Alexandra and the other subjects had changed such that she rated red as her most preferred color, blue as her next most preferred color, and yellow as her least preferred color.

15. Dieter, a German university student, was participating in a psychology experiment. When a blue floodlight was on, Dieter was shown photos of male faces. After each face was presented, a loud 8-second human scream blasted over a speaker. Screams of this sort naturally elicit reactions such as GSR's (i.e., Galvanic Skin Responses, a change in the skin's ability to conduct electricity). When a yellow floodlight was on, Dieter was also shown the faces, but the faces did not predict the screams. During testing, the screaming no longer occurred, but the faces were presented with the blue and yellow lights. The results indicated that Dieter showed more **GSR activity** to the faces when the blue light was on than when the yellow light was on.

16. Pete was a young insurance agent, whose problem was that he was extremely jealous of his fiance, Celia. If Celia even said anything good about another man, Pete would become upset for several days, during which he would be critical of Celia. Initially the therapist had Celia say nice things about other men. If Pete remained cordial to Celia, the therapist praised him. The therapist then had Pete engage in situations in which Celia had something to do with other men. These situations ranged from talking to another man to a situation in which Celia would embrace a male acquaintance in a friendly way or go to a movie with a male friend while Pete was at work. If Pete **remained cordial** and pleasant to Celia in these situations, the therapist praised him for his improvement. After extensive training of this type Pete no longer was unfriendly to Celia even after she had been alone with good-looking men.

17. Frances was in a psychology experiment concerned with fear of snakes. On 12 of 24 trials she viewed a picture of a snake, and on 12 trials she viewed a picture of a flower. After the snake and flower pictures were shown, she was sometimes given a .5 second shock to her right hand. Sometimes she was shocked without any picture present. The experiments measured the subject's **GSR,** and found that neither the snake nor the flower picture had any effect on GSR.

18. Simon had volunteered for an experiment in which his salivation was measured. Over a number of trials, he was shown slides of words, each word for 30 seconds. This procedure continued using different slides; each trial was separated by a 1 to 5 minute interval. The trials continued until Simon **salivated** upon seeing the words on five consecutive trials. This response occurred after 36 trials. Initially, the words had not affected Simon's salivation.

19. Howard was participating in a psychology experiment in which he had been deprived of food for some time. During training sessions, he viewed 2-second slides saying "Support Free Speech," after which the experimenter allowed him to have a snack from a tray of delicious finger sandwiches. He also viewed slides saying "Support Free Trade" for two seconds, but no finger sandwiches were presented

afterward. In a posttest, cotton balls were put into Howard's mouth. The experimenter later weighed the cotton balls to measure how much Howard had salivated. The experimenters found that after training, Howard and the rest of the subjects **salivated to the Free Speech message** but not to the Free Trade message. Before training, there had been no difference in the amount of salivation to the two messages.

20. Sally, a sophomore in an introductory psychology class, was participating in an experiment conducted by Dr. Ellson. She sat in a comfortable chair, on the left arm of which was a small light bulb. For 60 trials, Dr. Ellson would turn on the light and a tone simultaneously. The light was bright enough to see immediately. The tone was initially too quiet to be heard, but it gradually increased in volume so that Sally heard it after about 3 to 4 seconds. As soon as she heard the tone, she pressed a button, as the experimenter had instructed her to do. After these trials were some other test trials on which the light was presented without the tone. Again, Sally was told to press the button if she heard the tone. As a result of the training procedure, Sally also **pressed the button** on these trials several times because she **thought she heard the tone.**

Conceptual Exercise *Pavlovian Conditioning Therapies and Processes*

For each of the following items, decide if the item is an example of counterconditioning, systematic desensitization, *in vivo* desensitization, aversion therapy, covert sensitization, flooding, second-order conditioning, or conditioned suppression. Give a reason for your choice. The items may be an example of more than one process and some items fail to illustrate any of the processes. Check your decisions with the analyses in the back of the book.

Note: In many of the original studies on which the items in this exercise are based, the experimenters made use of the subjects' evaluations as a measure of conditioning. Emotional responses were not directly measured. In these items, we have inferred that the subjects responded emotionally in a way consistent with their evaluative and other responding.

1. Three experimenters were working with cigarette smokers who wanted to quit smoking. Normally, smokers enjoy smoking cigarettes, but the noxious substances in cigarette smoke, when inhaled in large amounts, are a US for the UR of nausea and ill feelings. The experimenters sounded a tone every 6 seconds, and instructed the smokers to inhale their cigarette deeply when the tone came on. This process continued until the individual had smoked three cigarettes, or was unable to continue due to feeling ill. The smokers did this three times per session for six sessions over a 2-week period. This method caused many of the smokers to become nauseated when they saw or smoked a cigarette, which helped many of them to quit.

2. Sixty-four people had volunteered for a study to treat them for fear of flying in an airplane. For each of these subjects, airplane stimuli were CSs for the CR of intense fear

responding. For one group of these people, the therapist had them imagine seven scenes in which there were terrible airplane disasters. The therapist exposed the people to the catastrophic scenes for 350 minutes over seven sessions. This treatment greatly reduced the people's fear responding to airplane stimuli.

3. University students had volunteered for an experiment. For one group of students, a high-pitched tone predicted the appearance of a projected slide showing unpleasant lung surgery procedures, USs for unpleasant emotional responding. As a result of this procedure, the high-pitched tone became a CS for unpleasant emotional responding. Later in the experiment the students did a difficult Stroop task, consisting of reading color names printed in a color other than the color to which the name referred. While engaged in the Stroop task, the high-pitched tone came on, causing unpleasant emotional responding and a decrease in the rate of performance on the Stroop task.

4. Dr. Johnson was treating two patients, Howard and Martha, for fear of dogs. Dr. Johnson trained Howard and Martha in deep muscle relaxation, and gave them daily homework exercises in which they practiced the relaxation techniques they had learned. As a result of this method, Howard's and Martha's fear of dogs diminished considerably. Both could go for walks in their neighborhoods, something that had previously been impossible.

5. Sixty-five female students in the first through fifth grades participated in an experiment. The purpose of the experiment was to see if the girls could unlearn the negative view they had of females due to their cultural conditioning. Students in an experimental group saw pictures of females on a screen for 5 seconds. Each picture predicted a 5-second presentation of a positive word. Through previous conditioning, the positive words had become CSs for the CR of good, positive emotional responses. As a result of this method, the students' positive emotional responses toward other girls increased.

6. Jay was a 24-year-old man whom the police had arrested three times in 5 years for making obscene phone calls. As a treatment for this problem, Jay's therapist had him listen to tapes describing the stimuli Jay imagined associated with his preparation to make an obscene phone call, including dialing the telephone. Jay further imagined scenes in which he associated the telephone and call stimuli with a variety of unpleasant events including snakes, Jay vomiting, choking, having a heart attack, scaring a little girl, and being caught making an obscene call by a priest, his mother, or his grandmother. Jay listened to the 44 the tapes over a 23-day period. This method decreased Jay's sexual arousal to the stimuli involved in making an obscene phone call.

7. Tom, 19, had been committed to a mental hospital because he had assaulted a woman. In doing so, he was carrying out his sadistic fantasy in which he harmed women. Before the assault, many people considered him a model teenager. As a part of Tom's treatment, Tom imagined the sadistic sexual fantasy he normally had. When the image was clear, the therapist delivered a painful shock to Tom's finger. This procedure continued for 14 weeks. As a result of this method, when Tom imagined the sadistic fantasy without being shocked, he had the same unpleasant feel-

ings that previously the shocks had elicited. As a result, Tom ceased having sadistic fantasies. This treatment eventually led to his discharge from the hospital.

8. David was a 38-year-old reservist in the Israeli Army. Due to battlefield experiences, he responded with intense anxiety whenever he heard a loud sudden noise. David's treatment consisted of training to relax and remain relaxed while the therapist presented low-volume noises. This treatment continued, with the therapist presenting increasingly higher volume noises after David could remain relaxed while hearing lower volume noises. The therapist repeated this procedure until David could experience loud noises without anxiety.

9. Roger, 30, had an intense fear of crossing bridges and of heights. His trouble had begun, when in the midst of a marriage crisis, he looked over the side of a bridge and responded with intense fear. Roger's fears caused troubles for him, such as when he became sick when forced to dine with his boss at a restaurant on top of a 52-story building. As treatment, Roger's therapist had him imagine 20 different scenes involving bridges and heights, and then to imagine a pleasant image, such as having a pleasant dinner with friends. The purpose of this method was to help Roger unlearn his fear by learning to respond to bridges and heights with pleasant emotions, the opposite of fear. This method permitted Roger to lose his intense fear of bridges and heights. In a 2-year follow-up observation, Roger continued to have little fear of heights and bridges.

10. An experimenter had alcoholics vividly imagine a scene in which they were drinking beer. The experimenter's descriptions highlighted the appearance, taste, and other sensations associated with beer. Then, the experimenter had the subjects vividly imagine a very unpleasant scene in which nauseous feelings led to intense vomiting. After six sessions, some of the subjects experienced conditioned nausea when imagining drinking without the unpleasant imagery. Conditioned nausea had physical effects including watering eyes, muscular tremors, facial grimacing, and physiological changes.

11. Henry, 22, was a married man who obtained pleasurable feelings when he dressed up in women's clothes. He had sought psychological help because he was afraid that someone might find out that he was a transvestite. His wife had also encouraged him to change his behavior. Before treatment the therapists took photographs of Henry dressed as a woman. During treatment, the therapists gave him injections of apomorphine, a substance that causes nausea and vomiting. While the injection took effect, Henry viewed slides of himself in women's clothing in a darkened room. He continued watching the slides until he vomited or became extremely nauseous. This procedure occurred every 2 hours for 6 days and nights. During this time, Henry received 53 injections of apomorphine and several other doses of other nausea-inducing substances. As a result of this method, when Henry saw slides of himself dressed in women's clothes, he felt sick and unpleasant. Six months after treatment, Henry was no longer dressing in women's clothes. Both he and his wife were very grateful to the therapists for solving the problem.

12. Gidget was a 26-year-old graduate student whose social life revolved around the beach. This situation posed a problem for her because she had an intense fear of

sharks that made being near the beach very uncomfortable for her. At one point, she lost control and ran fearfully from the beach. As a result, she turned down invitations to beach parties. Gidget's treatment consisted of training her in deep muscle-relaxation techniques. In addition, she listed beach and water stimuli that she feared in order from least (walking on the beach on a nice day) to most fearful (swimming in the ocean in water 10 feet deep). Carrying out her therapy at her home, she induced a state of relaxation, then imagined the least feared item on her list. When she could imagine that item without fear, she moved on the next most fearful item, imagining it while remaining relaxed. This process continued until Gidget could relax even when she imagined the most feared item on her list. These techniques caused Gidget to lose her fear of the beach and water. She enjoyed swimming in the ocean, even after viewing the film *Jaws.*

13. Thirty female university students had volunteered for an experiment in which they would receive assistance in overcoming their fear of snakes. The experimenter had one group of students vividly imagine the following scenes: (a) a snake had wrapped itself around the neck of the student, (b) a vicious, biting snake was in the student's stomach, (c) and a huge snake, the size of a person, was attacking the student. This method reduced the students' fear of snakes and 70% of the them were able to pick up a real snake.

14. Alice, 22, had been a victim of incest her father committed when she was 12 to 15 years old. She drank heavily, and originally sought psychological help to assist her with her drinking problem. She also had difficulty sleeping and was troubled by intrusive thoughts and unpleasant emotional responses about her traumatic experience. Alice's therapists treated her by having her vividly imagine the incest scenes. In addition, the scenes were made more terrible by adding fictional details, including (a) the shock of Alice's family, foster family, her fiance, and others upon learning of the incidents and their subsequent rejection of Alice; and (b) Alice verbally and physically attacking her mother for allowing the incidents to occur. The therapists gave Alice five 80-90 minute treatments on 5 consecutive days. After providing these treatments, the therapists told Alice to continue to practice imagining the scenes on her own. As a result of this method, Alice's intrusive thoughts and unpleasant emotional responses about the incest scene were eliminated. A year after treatment, she was no longer troubled by the intrusive thoughts.

15. Two researchers were working with people who had fears of cockroaches, lizards, and spiders. One method that was useful in reducing fear responses was to have the subjects listen to a recording in which a phobic word (e.g., *spider*) was said just before a calming word (e.g., *tame, sedative, drift*). As such, the phobic words predicted the calm words. The calm words were previously established CSs for pleasant emotional responding. This method reduced the subjects fears of the phobic words (e.g., *spider*) and also to the things the phobic words (e.g., *spiders*) represented.

16. Two researchers were working with a group of women who had negative emotional responses toward normal sexual activities. These activities included flirting, public kissing, sexual initiative, sexual intercourse, and looking at a naked man. For these women, these sexual activities were CSs for the CR of negative emotional responses. To try to undo this previous learning, the researchers had the women read

descriptions of the activities, followed by the experimenter reading words that were CSs for positive emotional responses. This procedure reduced the women's negative emotional responses toward the sexual activities.

17. Mark had a fear of public speaking. This fear caused him problems at work because he had to speak in staff meetings, which he had begun to avoid. Mark contacted a therapist for help. As part of Mark's treatment, he was given audiotapes that trained him in deep muscle relaxation. The tapes also provided Mark with instructions. He was to become relaxed and listen to a description of public speaking scenes that he imagined. The scenes were ranked from least to most fearful. One of the first scenes was one in which Mark imagined that he was sitting alone in a conference room. In one of the later scenes, other people at the conference ridiculed Mark for what he was saying. Mark listened to each scene while remaining relaxed. If he began responding fearfully, he stopped the tape recorder, rewound it to the relaxation instructions, and listened to the scene that gave him a problem. As Mark remained relaxed to less fearful scenes, he moved on to more difficult ones. This process continued until Mark could remain relaxed while listening to and imagining the most fearful scenes. A week after finishing the treatment, Mark was able to make a speech at a staff meeting in which he disagreed with previous speakers. In an 8-month follow-up observation, Mark continued to speak in public without fear or anxiety.

18. Edna, 36, was in therapy, being treated for fear of flying in airplanes. As part of her therapy, Dr. Chalmers had Edna engage in deep muscle-relaxation exercises every day. Edna relaxed by listening to a tape of Dr. Chalmers's relaxation instructions. This method diminished Edna's fear and anxiety responses, including those associated with airplanes, enabling her to fly on airplanes.

19. University students had volunteered to be in an experiment. For one group of the students, the experimenter sounded a tone before he gave them a painful electric shock. Later, the students engaged in a button-pushing task in which every 15th button press produced a 4-second view of a slide projected on a screen. When the tone came on as students were viewing the slides, it caused the students to respond emotionally and in turn press the button less frequently.

20. Mr. M., a 22-year-old man, had an extreme fear of both snakes and cemeteries. As a 4-year-old child, Mr. M. had been riding in a car when his cousins put a rubber snake on him. This prank frightened him so much that M.'s parents had to stop the car at a cemetery. This incident established a cemetery phobia in Mr. M. His therapist, Dr. Brown, told Mr. M. to arouse himself sexually by imagining sexual scenes while he was driving. Mr. M did so by thinking of sexual encounters with his wife. Mr. M. was to time his arousal so that it would be maximal when he was driving past a cemetery. If he could not attain a state of sexual arousal, Mr. M. was not to drive past a cemetery. Mr. M. used this method a few times and it caused him to lose his fear of cemeteries.

21. Mrs. J., 27, was a teacher who had an intense fear of hypodermic needles. She had acquired this fear when at 2-years-old, she had received daily injections for an intestinal problem for 4 months. Since then, she had violently resisted all attempts to give her an injection. In one incident in which she needed an injection to treat a

blood clot, she resisted so violently that she broke two hypodermic needles off in her ankle despite the efforts of two orderlies and her husband to restrain her. Due to this incident, she decided to get psychological help. Mrs. J.'s treatment consisted of relaxation training. While Mrs. J. remained relaxed, the therapists showed her gradually larger hypodermic syringes for gradually longer periods of time. In addition, the therapists held the syringes progressively closer to her until Mrs. J. could remain relaxed even when a blood sample was withdrawn from her with a hypodermic syringe. At 6- and 10-month follow-up observations, Mrs. J.'s treatment gains remained.

22. James, a teenager, was a car thief. He had been referred to a medical center for therapy where James told the therapist what brands of cars he liked to steal and under what conditions he normally stole cars. Using this information, the therapist had James imagine that he saw a good-looking sports car and wanted to steal it. Then the therapist had James imagine that (a) he began to feel ill as he approached the car; (b) he vomited on himself and the interior of the car, and the smell of the vomit made him continue vomiting; and (c) he ran from the car and began to feel better. These procedures caused James to feel ill when he approached a car and thought of stealing it.

23. Mel was a 26-year-old retarded man. Three stimulus categories made Mel angry: jokes, criticisms of Mel, and discussions that included sexual content including dating, marriage, and childbirth. Mel's therapist listed the anger-provoking items in each of the three categories and ranked them from least to most anger provoking. The therapist also trained Mel to relax. While Mel remained relaxed, the therapist had him imagine the least anger-provoking item in the joke category. As Mel learned to relax while imagining the less anger-provoking items, the therapist moved on to more anger-provoking items. In this way Mel progressed through the list and learned to remain relaxed while imagining the most anger-provoking item. The therapist also used this method to teach Mel to remain relaxed while imagining the criticisms and sexual content categories. By the end of treatment, Mel's angry responses to jokes, criticism, and discussions with sexual content had been reduced substantially.

Conceptual Exercise   *Making Pavlovian Conditioning Effective*

For each of the following items, a principle that makes Pavlovian conditioning effective has been violated. The principles that make Pavlovian conditioning effective are the effectiveness of the US, the timing of the NS and US, the number of conditioning trials, the intensity-vividness of the CS, Garcia effects, CS preexposure, overshadowing effects, and blocking effects. Identify the principle that has been violated, and provide a brief explanation for your answers. Check your decisions with the analyses at the back of the book.

Note: In this exercise and in the associated quiz items in this unit, when a stimulus that is feared or that otherwise produces undesirable emotional reactions is used as a CS in therapy, it is considered incorrect to say that the problem with the item is the CS preexposure effect. In items of this sort, there is another problem that should be identified.

1. Raymond had a drinking problem and was getting therapy from a behavior analyst. The therapist put shots of vodka, Raymond's favorite alcoholic beverage, in front of him. When Raymond reached for a drink, a very mild electric shock was given to his arm. The shock followed Raymond's reaching for the drink very quickly and many conditioning trials were given. Raymond had not had any kind of electroshock therapy before and the sight of the drinks was a powerful stimulus for Raymond reaching for the drink. This procedure was not as effective as the therapist had hoped.

2. Dr. Lindeman was conducting a demonstration of Pavlovian conditioning. She presented slides of a large triangle and a small square, both neutral stimuli, on a screen. The slides predicted attractive pictures of members of the opposite sex of the subjects. Afterward, she presented the large triangle and the small square individually and had the subjects rate how much the liked each stimulus. The subjects had good feelings toward the large triangle, but neutral feelings toward the small square, as indicated by their evaluative responses.

3. Dr. Brown decided to demonstrate Pavlovian conditioning in her class. Every time she spoke the word "Pavlov," she cracked her ruler across her desk within 1 second of uttering the word. The sound of the ruler made everyone jump. When she said "Pavlov," she said it very loudly and she used a sufficient number of conditioning trials. She had been lecturing on Pavlov and his work for several weeks and so the students were quite familiar with the name.

4. Dr. Cass was working with a man, Lewis, who was troubled by fear of being enclosed in small spaces. As a part of therapy, Dr. Cass trained Lewis to relax. He then described scenes to Lewis depicting situations in which Lewis was in a small room, an enclosed space, and so forth. However, Dr. Cass was not very good at vividly describing scenes, so Lewis had difficulty imagining the enclosed-space scenes. This problem reduced the effectiveness of the therapy. Dr. Cass later took creative writing classes to improve his abilities as a narrator, and this improved the effectiveness of his therapy.

5. Tim was doing a conditioning experiment for his psychology class. He used his little sister as his subject. He would blow a strong puff of air at her right eye and then within one second he would sound a tuning fork very loudly. The goal of this was to get Susie to blink, the CR, when she heard the tuning fork, the CS. Susie, Tim's sister, had not heard tuning forks before. Tim used many conditioning trials and was disappointed when he did not get the conditioning he had expected.

6. In an experiment, a group of subjects were conditioned to respond to a CS, a green cross, by having it predict food. After repeated trials, the green cross came to elicit salivation when it was presented alone. Later, the green cross and a blue triangle were presented together, and they both reliably predicted food. However, despite repeated trials, the blue triangle was not able to elicit salivation when it was presented alone. However, the green cross continued to elicit salivation when it was presented by itself.

7. Robert was very fearful of water. His mother decided to work with him on this problem. She took Robert down to the lake, turned on some taped music, and then imme-

diately took Robert by the hand down to the water. She did this many times. Robert liked the music and hadn't heard it often before, but the music didn't seem to soothe him very much and his fear of the water did not subside. However, when she increased the volume of the music, she found that the procedure was more effective.

8. Louise was receiving help for her fear of reptiles. She was put in a comfortable room where pleasant music could be played. Louise found the music and the room extremely soothing and had no difficulty relaxing. She had not been exposed earlier to this music or the room. The therapist would play a few bars of the music while Louise relaxed and then Louise would be shown a picture of a reptile. After three conditioning trials, Louise returned home. Unfortunately, her fear of reptiles remained strong.

9. Arnie had a fear of both spiders and snakes. He received therapy in which he learned to relax, and then slides of spiders predicted relaxation stimuli, the therapist's relaxation instructions. This procedure established spiders as a CS for the CR of relaxation. After this, slides of both spiders and snakes were presented side by side on the screen and predicted the relaxation stimuli. Despite this procedure, when the snake slides were presented alone, Arnie continued to have intense fear responses; when the spider slides were presented alone, Arnie relaxed.

10. An advertising firm was testing a new advertisement for an automobile. Several volunteers would be shown pictures of the new model. These pictures displayed bright shiny red cars of the new design the manufacturer was promoting. After each picture was presented an exciting music video was immediately shown, making everyone feel very good. Many picture-video trials were given. The people then rated how they felt about the manufacturer's new model and other cars as well. The team was dismayed to find that the people did have good feelings but about all red cars, not specifically the model being promoted.

11. Nina was trying to eat less food. In order to help with this process, she visualized her favorite food, chocolate donuts with chocolate topping and imagined she was eating them. She then imagined that she became very sick and vomited. She did this once one afternoon. In this case, Nina's skills at imagining both the donuts and the vomiting were very good. There were no other stimuli to compete with the donuts. Despite this, Nina still liked chocolate donuts very much and she continued to eat a lot of them every day.

12. Dr. Luz was conducting a classroom demonstration of conditioning. During one session, he set up a predictive relationship between a dim flash of light and a mild electric shock, a stimulus that elicited a skin conductance response. The goal of this demonstration was to see if the light flash could elicit a skin conductance response when presented alone. At first, Dr. Luz was not successful in getting the light flash to elicit the response. However, when he increased the brightness of the flash of light, he was successful in getting conditioning.

13. In a demonstration of conditioning processes in Iowa, Mr. Roberts, a psychology teacher, presented a large American flag to a subject and then gave the subject a mild electric shock, which elicited a skin conductance response. The shock was suffi-

ciently intense to obtain conditioning, he used a sufficient number of trials, and the flag was presented without any competing stimuli. Despite these measures, Mr. Roberts failed to obtain conditioning of the skin conductance response to the flag.

14. In a commercial promoting a laundry detergent, the box of detergent was shown for 10 seconds. After this, there followed 30 seconds of people putting clothes in a washing machine at a Laundromat. After this, music and attractive dancers were shown for 20 seconds. This commercial was not successful in selling the product. In this case, the music and dancers were good at evoking good feelings in the audience. The laundry detergent was not well-known and when the detergent box was presented, it was prominent on the screen and had no competing stimuli. The commercial was also shown many times.

Stimulus and Response Classes: Conceptual Behavior, Generalized Response Classes, and Equivalence Classes

Although he was only a graduate student, Jack Keenan was a more experienced teacher than many of his professors. As an undergraduate, he had worked for several years as a teaching assistant at the University of Massachusetts. As a graduate student at West Virginia University, he continued to teach. During the course of his teaching experience, Jack had become an expert in using methods of behavioral instruction, the use of behavior analysis principles in education. (See Johnson and Ruskin [1977] for an overview of behavioral instruction in university teaching.)

Although Jack felt that behavioral instruction had gone a long way in helping students to learn better, he was not completely satisfied with university teaching. Some students who probably would have failed their first year at university succeeded as a result of the use of behavioral principles. However, Jack felt that these success stories represented only part of the answer. Jack saw that despite the many advantages of behavioral instruction, students still learned pretty much the same old way: They read a textbook or listened to a lecture, and then were tested largely on their ability simply to repeat the words they had read and heard. Jack felt that there was more to truly understanding a subject matter than simply repeating definitions and facts.

Looking for a solution to this problem, Jack turned to educators who had had considerable success in teaching conceptual behavior. These people included Siegfried Engelmann and Wesley Becker, who had worked with younger children, and Keith Miller and Hal Weaver, who had adapted concept learning methods to university teaching. In concept learning, a class of stimuli, rather than a specific stimulus, becomes a set of discriminative stimuli for responding. The stimulus class is defined by a concept feature or set of features. For example, one concept that Jack taught his students was positive reinforcement. The class of positive reinforcement stimuli contains all the examples of positive reinforcement in the world. The class has a set of defining or critical features: a consequence is presented dependent on a behavior and strengthens some measure of that behavior. To be able to say that a student has learned the concept of positive reinforcement, the conceptual class of stimuli must be discriminative stimuli for the student's behavior.

For Jack, the appeal of teaching conceptual behavior was its ability to have an impact beyond the classroom. Jack had seen students who could define a term such as positive reinforcement on a quiz, but who had no real understanding of the meaning of the term. They could not recognize new examples of positive reinforcement, even of their own behavior, and could not apply the concept to change behavior. Jack wanted his students to be able to identify an infinite number of examples of positive reinforcement in the course of their future lives, and apply the concept to their advantage.

Jack set up a special section of an introductory psychology course to do concept-learning research. He recruited nine students from the standard sections of the course, in part by promising them no homework; all studying would be done in class during daily 2-hour sessions. By having the students study in class, Jack could measure their performance and ensure that the students were following his experimental procedures. He provided coffee and tea for the students, making a more relaxed and comfortable study atmosphere.

Jack taught 13 units of material based on chapters in a standard introductory psychology textbook. From each of these chapters, Jack selected 8 concepts to teach. The concepts were typical of those taught in an introductory psychology course. They included several behavior-analysis principles, sensory thresholds, short- and long-term memory, retroactive and proactive inhibition, and some Freudian concepts. For each concept, Jack prepared a set of conceptual-discrimination training materials. He prepared eight illustrations, four of which were examples of the concept and four of which were nonexamples that were missing at least one of the critical features of the concept. For instance, a nonexample of positive reinforcement would be one that included all but one of the critical features of positive reinforcement. The item might fail to indicate an increase in the level of the target behavior. The examples of positive reinforcement were diverse, including different types of people, different situations, and different behaviors.

For each unit of material, Jack had to write 64 training items and 16 test items. With 13 units in the course, Jack wrote 832 training items, 208 quiz items, and 64 final exam items. Because of the other rigorous demands of his graduate program, Jack had to work long hours to get the materials ready for the students. He often worked all night, rapping out examples and nonexamples on an electric typewriter, keeping himself awake by drinking large tumblers of iced coffee. There were some mornings when Jack arrived at class just one step ahead of his students. He never missed a deadline, though, and by the end of the semester, Jack had prepared a book-length set of materials to teach 104 psychology concepts.

As Jack was developing his materials, he was also testing them to see if they really did teach more effectively than conventional textbook materials. In one experimental condition called the *read* condition, the students received only the textbook material to help them learn the concept. In a *define and describe condition*, the students read the textbook material and Jack had them write definitions of the concepts. In an *illustrations* condition, the students read a set of eight examples and nonexamples of the concept, but were not given feedback about which were examples and nonexamples and why. In an *illustrations plus definitions* condition, the students also received the textbook definition of the concept along with the examples and nonexamples. Finally, in an *illustrations plus definitions and feedback* condition, the students received the textbook concept definition, the examples and nonexamples, and feedback that identified the illustrations as examples or nonexamples and explained why.

Figure 14.1 shows some of the results of Jack's study. The data in the figure show how well the students did on unit quizzes due to each of the different teaching techniques Jack used. As you can see, the examples and nonexamples, the definitions, and the feedback all contributed to concept learning. The textbook by itself, without the concept-teaching materials Jack had developed, was relatively poor at teaching the concepts.

After the students learned concepts through his complete training package of examples and nonexamples, definitions, and feedback, Jack found that his students could also write original examples of the concepts. For instance, in the case of positive reinforcement, the students could write examples of positive reinforcement that were different from the ones in the textbook and from Jack's examples. The students' ability to write these original examples showed that they had learned a *generalized response class*. A generalized response class is acquired when learners acquire a class of responses defined by a set of response features rather than by a specific response. Jack's students could write original examples of concepts proving that they had not simply memorized the details of specific examples. Instead, the students had acquired a response class of generating examples that had the critical features of the concept and were original, not like the examples used during training.

What did the students think of Jack's approach to teaching concepts? They liked it a lot. The students enjoyed the approach because the use of many concrete examples was a refreshing change from the dry, completely abstract presentations typical of many textbooks and lectures. In follow-up work, we have collected a variety of student comments about this general approach. Here are a few samples:

1. "The conceptual exercises often clarified confusing points through examples."
2. "The conceptual exercises helped with a practical explanation of the concepts."

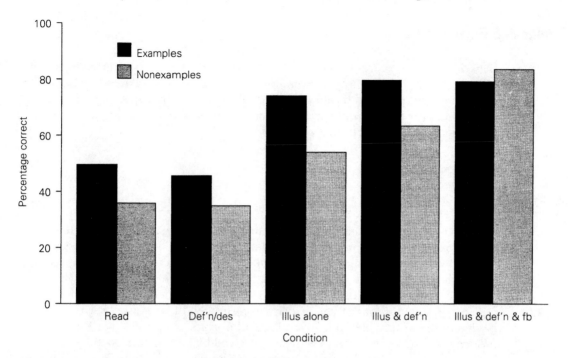

Figure 14.1 *The Effects of Concept Teaching Procedures on the Effectiveness of Concept Teaching*

Student performance in a university course improved when concept teaching techniques were used. Illustrations (examples and nonexamples), concept definitions, and feedback all improved student performance on course quizzes. Figure adapted from Keenan and Grant (1979).

3. "I wish more courses had conceptual exercises."
4. "I found conceptual exercises especially helpful in clarifying and consolidating course content."
5. "Conceptual exercises were very interesting, stimulating, and explanatory."
6. "Conceptual exercises pulled the material together in a practical, understandable manner."
7. "The conceptual exercises helped to define any areas where you may have had incorrect conclusions."

You, yourself, are in an excellent position to judge the merits of Jack's concept-teaching approach. This textbook has been designed along the same concept teaching principles Jack applied. In this sense, you are the main character in this story.*

* Based on Keenan and Grant (1979).

Stimulus and Response Classes

Behavior based on stimulus and response classes is important for many reasons. One of these is that the learning of stimulus and response classes allows the learner to engage in new forms of behavior not specifically trained. Three specific topics we will examine are *conceptual learning,* the learning of *generalized response classes,* and the phenomenon known as *stimulus equivalence.*

Conceptual Discrimination

As we have seen, conceptual behavior occurs when a class of stimuli that share stimulus features act as discriminative stimuli for responding. For example, consider the concept of *inside.* One child might be trained to say that a marble is inside a bottle, but might fail to say that a cat is inside a house. This would not be an example of conceptual behavior because the stimulus feature, insideness, would not be a discriminative stimulus for the child's behavior. This child's response, "inside," would be due to the specific discriminative stimuli of marbles and bottles, not the stimulus property of insideness. In contrast, consider a child who can correctly identify marbles as being inside bottles, cats as being inside houses, planes as being inside hangers, people as being inside countries, and so forth. This would be an example of conceptual behavior because the stimulus feature of insideness would be a discriminative stimulus for the child's behavior. This child can identify insideness even when it occurs in diverse and novel situations.

Another example of a concept is *democracy,* which we might define as a form of government in which the people run the government, by directly casting votes on key policies or by electing representatives who do so. The conceptual stimulus class of democracy is composed of all the instances of democratic governments. We call the members of the stimulus class *concept instances* or *examples.* To be a member of this class, government must have the *critical features* (also called relevant features, defining features, and distinctive features) of democracy: The people make key policy decisions through voting. The stimuli in the conceptual-stimulus class also possess a large range of *variable features,* features of the stimuli in the class that do not define democracy and vary from one stimulus instance to the next. For example, democracies can operate either by the people voting directly on policies, as in some small-town governments, or by the people electing representatives who vote on key policy decisions. This difference is not a defining feature of democracy, but a variable feature. Other variable features of democracy might include the frequency of elections, the number of elected representatives, the size of the government, and so forth. In order for successful concept learning to occur, the learner must discriminate the critical and variable features from each other (Becker, 1986).

The power of concept learning, as we saw in the case of Jack Keenan's students, is in the generality of what is learned. Because the learner acquires responses to classes of stimuli defined by stimulus features, the learner can respond correctly to new stimulus-class members she encounters. The student who has learned the concept of inside, democracy, or positive reinforcement has learned to respond correctly to stimulus features that will occur throughout her life in all sorts of new situations. Without conceptual behavior, our ability to respond to stimuli would be extremely limited. Each new stimulus we encounter would require complete relearning.

Conceptual responding involves both discrimination and generalization processes (Keller & Schoenfeld, 1950). For example, a student who has learned the concept of democracy shows within-class generalization by responding to all the members of the stimulus class of *democracy* in the same way. The student might do this by correctly labeling stimulus instances as "democracy." The student must also show between-class discrimination. She must label members of the democracy stimulus class as such, and not so label other stimulus classes of governments such as monarchies, dictatorships, oligarchies, and sham democracies in which there is no voting on key policies.

Two types of errors in concept learning are called *undergeneralization* and *overgeneralization*, also known as *underextension* and *overextension*. For example, consider a student who has learned to identify one specific instance of democracy. When presented with other types of democracies, the student fails to identify them appropriately. This error pattern is called undergeneralization, in which the learner fails to identify correctly all members of a conceptual-stimulus class as concept instances. Imagine another student who identifies instances of democracies correctly but who also incorrectly identifies sham democracies in which, for example, elected representatives have no power to make policy. This error pattern is called overgeneralization, in which the learner incorrectly identifies concept noninstances outside the conceptual-stimulus class as concept instances.

In order to demonstrate conceptual behavior, it is necessary to show that the critical features of the concept are discriminative stimuli for the learner's response. In order to do this, it is necessary to use novel test items, ones the learner has not encountered before. For example, suppose students learn about democracy through discrimination training in which we use 4 examples of democracies and 8 examples of other types of governments. We have the learner identify each government, and provide differential feedback for correct and incorrect responses. After training, in order to show the stimulus-feature stimulus control of conceptual behavior, it is necessary to use novel examples of governments, ones the learner has not seen before. If the training democracies are used in testing, the learner may have acquired specific labels for each of the specific governments, allowing her to respond correctly on this basis. In contrast, when novel governments are used, the learner can respond correctly to the "test" governments only if she is responding to the critical features of the governmental structure and functions. In the story that introduced this chapter, we also saw how Jack Keenan used novel test items to ensure that his students were responding to the critical features of the concepts he taught.

The World of Concepts and Words

Many concepts have labels, words that refer to the critical feature of the stimulus class. For example, *positive reinforcement, democracy, red, triangle, evil, zebras, cost-*

push inflation, and *acceleration* all refer to stimulus classes, the members of which share a set of critical stimulus features.

As Carroll (1964) discusses, the different parts of speech are themselves organized in terms of types of stimulus features. In the English language, nouns stand for the critical stimulus features that define persons, places, things, and animals. Adjectives stand for the variable features of the stimiuli to which nouns refer. Verbs stand for the critical stimulus (and response) features that define different types of existence, activity, and behavior. Adverbs stand for the variable features of the stimuli to which verbs refer. Many prepositions (e.g., *above, in, beside*) stand for stimulus features involved in relative spatial position. Conjunctions such as *and* and *or* stand for stimulus features involving the logical relations among other stimuli and stimulus features.

Using words to refer to conceptual stimulus classes is one of the major benefits of verbal behavior. This allows us to talk, read, and write about huge classes of stimuli that are too numerous to encounter directly. Through words, children can refer to all zebras, all other children, and good and evil. Through the use of words, we can discuss abstract relations such as the impact of inflation on governmental stability or the relation between the use of behavioral principles and cultural progress. Words that refer to concept features free our thinking from the constraints of specific stimuli by allowing us to refer to stimulus features in isolation and in relation to other stimulus features. In this sense, words put the world at our command.

Differences in the meaning that different people attach to the same words are often due to differences in the conceptual stimulus features that have been established as discriminative stimuli. As such, people's individual concepts of *freedom, democracy,* or *appropriate behavior* show considerable variation due to discriminative stimulus control by different stimulus features. Many times arguments that people have are based on different stimulus features being discriminative stimuli for the same words.

Making Conceptual Discrimination Effective

Conceptual discrimination is a type of stimulus discrimination, so the principles that make stimulus discrimination effective generally apply to conceptual discrimination as well. As such, factors such as active responding, pretraining procedures, the similarity of the stimuli, the relationship between the training and goal stimuli, the similarity of required responses, the rate of stimulus presentation, and the order of stimulus presentation all contribute to the effectiveness of conceptual discrimination. Further, because prompting and fading methods are useful in teaching conceptual discriminations (e.g., Miller & Weaver, 1976), the principles of prompting and fading are also useful in teaching conceptual discriminations.

Concept learning also involves stimulus generalization across members of the conceptual stimulus class. As such, the principles that make stimulus generalization effective, especially the use of multiple training exemplars, also contribute to conceptual discrimination. In this section, we will focus on a few conditions of special importance to conceptual discrimination. These include defining the goal conceptual discrimination through concept analysis, using concept definitions, and discrimination training with examples and nonexamples. (For treatments of conceptual discrimination, see Engelmann and Carnine [1982], Grant [1986], and Tennyson and Cocchiarella [1986].)

Defining the Goal Conceptual Discrimination Through Concept Analysis.   An important consideration in concept teaching is to define the goals of concept teaching in terms of the stimulus classes to which the learner is to respond. We previously discussed this general principle in Chapter 7 in considering stimulus discrimination (Williams, 1969). For example, in teaching a child the concepts of several different animals, a goal might be for the child to discriminate among lions, elephants, and zebras. If this is our goal, we can plan the child's instruction using examples of these animals. However, if our goal is to teach a child the concepts of lions, tigers, panthers, cheetahs, and leopards, this more difficult discrimination would require us to use a very different set of instructional materials and, possibly, discrimination training procedures. The goals of concept teaching must be defined before we can go further.

A specific means of defining the goal of conceptual discrimination is through concept analysis. In concept analysis, a concept is broken down into its critical and variable features (Engelmann, 1969; Markle & Tiemann, 1970; Roid & Haladyna, 1982). This breakdown allows a teacher to construct concept examples and nonexamples for teaching purposes. For example, in a concept analysis of positive reinforcement (Grant, 1986), a teacher would identify three critical features of the concept: (a) response-dependent stimulus presentation; (b) response-rate increase; and (c) response-rate increase due to the response-dependent stimulus presentation. The teacher would also identify variable features of positive reinforcement, concentrating on those features likely to be mistaken for critical features. For example, many beginning students of behavior analysis come to identify positive reinforcers as things that elicit good feelings and do not cause pain. This type of error can be prevented by doing a concept analysis in which this variable feature is identified as important. Later the teacher can construct teaching examples of positive reinforcement in which the reinforcers do not elicit good feelings and are painful. In this way, concept analysis allows the teacher to define the concept explicitly and to anticipate and prevent likely student errors.

An additional benefit of concept analysis is its effect on teachers. Concept analysis demands that teachers identify the components of the concepts their students are learning. This in turn provides teachers with a fresh and precise understanding of concepts they may have taught before, but not thoroughly analyzed (Grant & Spencer, 1983).

Concept Definitions.   A concept definition is a rule that specifies the features of a concept that make it a member of the conceptual stimulus class. For example, the definition of a positive reinforcer, "a response-dependent stimulus presentation that strengthens the response," is a rule for distinguishing between examples and nonexamples of positive reinforcers. A student who learns this definition and then is able to apply it to discriminate between examples and nonexamples of positive reinforcers is demonstrating rule-governed behavior. In many cases, older learners with adequate verbal skills can learn concepts quickly through definitions (e.g., Anderson & Kulhavy, 1972; Johnson & Stratton, 1966).

Concept definitions are often effective because students have previously learned the words in the concept definition. These words then can serve as discriminative stimuli for identifying concept examples and nonexamples. As such, definitions, like other useful rules, are helpful because they take advantage of the student's previous learning of the words in the rule. The words used in a definition must of course be consistent with the student's skill level. For example, Feldman and Klausmeier (1974) found that for fourth graders, a common-language definition of a concept was more effective than a technically stated definition, but for eighth graders, the technical definition was more effective.

Examples and Nonexamples.   Samuel Butler once wrote that "A definition is the enclosing a wilderness of idea within a wall of words." As this suggests, one problem with teaching concepts (i.e., ideas) through definitions alone is that the student does not have the opportunity to discover the range and richness of variation in the examples that make up the conceptual stimulus class. The definition of positive reinforcement, for example, hides actual instances of people's behavior from us. Complete concept learning often also requires that learners encounter concept examples and nonexamples. Important aspects of examples and nonexamples include use of focal examples, use of a broad range of examples that include many different variable features, and use of nonexamples that lack a single critical feature to teach the learners the boundaries of the conceptual stimulus class.

Focal Examples.   In teaching a concept, it is helpful to stress one focal (or prototypical) example that illustrates the concept. This strategy promotes long-term retention of the conceptual discrimination. For example, Park (1984) taught one group of students a concrete focal example of several behavior analysis concepts, including positive reinforcement. He taught another group of students the critical features of the concepts without emphasizing a focal example. During learning, the students who learned the critical features were better at classifying novel concept examples and nonexamples. However, on a test given a week later, the focal example group was better at discriminating novel examples of the concepts.

The focal-example effect is familiar to many university teachers. One such teacher says that when former students visit her, she is honored by the praise they give her courses. However, when she asks them what they recall of the course, they often mention several jokes she told at lectures that had little to do with the instructional content. The jokes, however, were concrete stories that students remember better than the abstract information presented in many courses. Use of the focal example method of teaching allows instructors to promote retention of conceptual discriminations by giving abstract material a concrete representation.

Using a Broad Range of Examples.   Concept learning is improved if a broad range of examples is used to show how concept examples can vary and still qualify as examples (Carnine, 1980; Markle & Tiemann, 1974; Tennyson, Woolley, & Merrill, 1972). Using a broad range of very different examples to illustrate the same concept has been called the *sameness principle* because this allows students to see how all the concept examples are alike.

For example, in teaching the concept of transportation, it would not be appropriate to restrict the range of examples to wheeled vehicles. Doing this would not help learners to generalize to novel examples of transportation that do not make use of wheeled vehicles, which is a variable feature of transportation. Use of a broad range of examples of transportation would include such forms as walking, crawling, horseback riding, spaceflight, sailing, and so forth.

Using Minimally Different Nonexamples.   Concept learning is assisted if the learner is provided with nonexamples of the concept that are minimally different from concept examples (Tennyson et al., 1972). This is called the *minimum difference principle* (Becker, 1986; Engelmann & Carnine, 1982). Minimally different examples and nonexamples differ in that the example possesses all the critical features of the concept, while the nonexample is missing a single critical feature.

Carnine (1980) demonstrated the minimum difference principle in a study in which preschool children learned the concept of *on*. The children studied work sheets with drawings, as illustrated in Figure 14.2. For Group A children, as illustrated in Figure 14.2a, the example and nonexample of *on* were minimally different (they were alike except that the nonexample was not *on*.) For Group B children, the nonexample was far above the example and the hand was removed from the example, making the example and nonexample more different. For Group C children, another difference was introduced because the block was rotated on its side. For Group D children, still another difference was introduced by using a football as part of the nonexample. Finally for Group E children, only examples were used during training, not nonexamples.

The children were tested using 12 novel illustrations of objects that were on or not on. As illustrated in Figure 14.2b, the children in group A performed better than the other groups. In addition, groups B and C did better than groups D and E, showing that the greater the differences between examples and nonexamples, the poorer the students' performance.

When the differences between teaching examples and nonexamples is more than minimal, errors of misconception are likely to occur in which variable features of the concept are responded to as critical features. For example, Carnine's group D children may have mistaken the horizontal feature of the block as a critical feature of *on*. Errors of misconception are also called misrules, especially when the learner

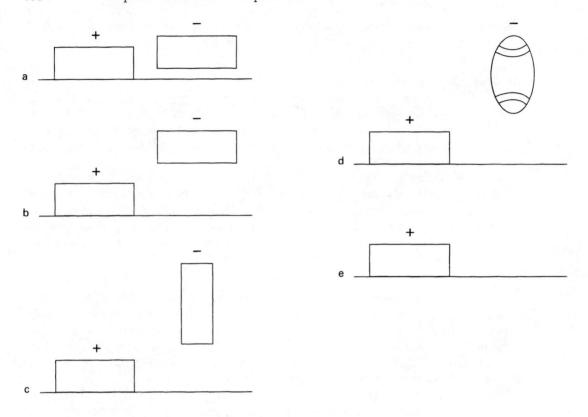

Figure 14.2a *Experimental Groups in Carnine's (1980) Study*

For Group a the nonexamples were minimally different from the examples, For Groups b, c, and d, the difference between the nonexamples and examples became progressively greater. For Group e, nonexamples were omitted. Figure adapted from Carnine (1980).

comes to state the inappropriate rule in verbal form (e.g., "If the block is vertical, it is not *on*").

Generalized Response Classes

In conceptual behavior, *stimulus* features act as discriminative stimuli for a response, allowing the learner to respond correctly to novel-concept examples and nonexamples. Something akin to conceptual behavior occurs on the response side. When a learner is trained to engage in a *response* that has a set of specified *features,* and this training allows the learner to engage in new responses that have those features, we say that the learner has acquired a generalized response class (Becker, 1974; Becker

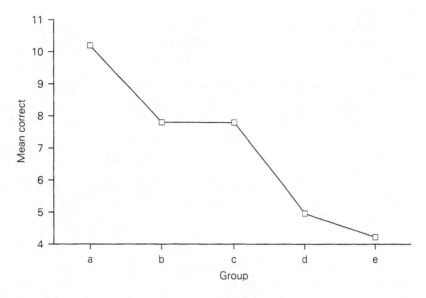

Figure 14.2b *The Effect of Minimally Different Nonexamples*

The mean number of correct responses was highest for group a, which used minimally different nonexamples. Performance became progressively poorer as the differences between the examples and nonexamples increased, as seen in the deteriorating performance of groups b, c, and d. Performance was poorest for group e, which did not use any nonexamples. Figure drawn from Carnine's (1980) data.

& Engelmann, 1978; Peterson, 1968; cf., Skinner, 1935). Generalized response classes are also called operations, and the training that produces a generalized response class is sometimes called operations training (Walls, Sienicki, & Crist, 1981). The word *operant* is also often used to refer to a generalized response class (Skinner, 1969).

In previous chapters, we have already examined several examples of generalized response classes. An example is generalized imitation (Gewirtz, 1971; Gewirtz & Stingle, 1968). In generalized imitation training, the learner's imitations of specific modeled behaviors are prompted and reinforced. This training enables the learner to show generalized imitation, to imitate any new modeled response. This is an example of a generalized response class because in generalized imitation (a) the response has a specified feature: It matches the model's response; and (b) the learner is able to imitate new modeled responses without further training.

There are many examples of generalized response classes other than generalized imitation. For example, Goetz and Baer (1973) trained preschool children to perform novel forms of blockbuilding by reinforcing the building of new forms. This training caused the children to build new forms at a higher rate. This is an example of a generalized response class because (a) the trained response had a specified feature: It had to be different from what the child had done before; and (b) the training resulted in the children being able to perform new responses that had the specified property, novelty. Note that in his work described at the outset of this chapter, Jack Keenan also taught his students generalized response classes based on the behavior feature of response novelty: He required students to write original examples of the concepts he taught. He also showed how this generalized response class could be established through his concept-teaching procedures. This was a generalized response class because the behaviors of writing original examples of a concept all shared common features including those features specified by the concept and response novelty.

Many basic skills that children learn in school consist of generalized response classes. For example, a child who has learned to multiply can multiply using an infinite range of numbers. Although each multiplication response will be different from other multiplication responses because different numbers are multiplied, multiplication is a generalized response class because the response feature, multiplication, remains the same from one behavior to the next. A similar analysis applies to many other mathematical skills in which different types of math problems require the same response features to arrive at a solution (e.g., Engelmann, Carnine, & Steely, 1991).

Personality characteristics and traits can also reflect generalized response classes. For example, suppose different types of a person's honest behaviors have been reinforced. This training might produce a generalized response class of honest behavior, in which the behavioral features of honesty appear in novel honest acts not directly trained. Casey and Burton (1982) established such a generalized response class in children through self-instructional training procedures. Similarly, people who are good listeners have a generalized response class defined by the behavior feature of attending to speech. Research has shown that a generalized response class of listening skills can be established through training (e.g., Cosgrove & Patterson, 1978).

Conceptual behavior and generalized response classes are similar in several respects. First, both are defined in terms of features. In conceptual behavior, stimulus features rather than specific stimuli act as discriminative stimuli for a response. In a generalized response class, the learner is able to engage in a variety of responses that have certain response features in common rather than one specific trained response.

Second, in both conceptual behavior and generalized responses classes, the stimulus and response class members differ from each other in certain respects. In conceptual behavior, different conceptual class members differ because they have different variable features. Likewise, in a generalized response class, responses can differ from each other, as long as they contain the critical response features that define the generalized response class.

Third, the tests for conceptual behavior and generalized response classes are similar because they both require that the learner do something new. To show conceptual behavior, the learner must respond correctly to new stimuli that have the critical concept features. Only in this way can we determine if the learner is responding to the concept features rather than to specific isolated stimuli. To show a generalized response class, the learner must engage in new behaviors that have the critical features of the response class. Only in this way can we determine if the learner has acquired behavior with certain critical response features rather than specific isolated responses. This is typically accomplished through *transfer* or *response-generalization* tests that require the learner to engage in a new response variant of the generalized response class.

One characteristic of generalized response classes is that new response class members can occur without explicit training or without reinforcement of each new response. This aspect of generalized response classes has sometimes been controversial. For example, some observers cite *observational learning* as an example of the acquisition of new behavior without reinforcement or training. These observers have sometimes considered observational learning as proof that reinforcement is not very important in acquiring new behavior. However, as Gewirtz and Stingle (1968) observed, observational learning can be considered as an example of generalized imitation, in which a class of imitative responses is acquired, defined by the response property of matching a model's behavior. Although individual instances of generalized imitation do not require reinforcement, the response class is maintained by intermittent reinforcement of members of the class. The same analysis applies to generalized response classes other than generalized imitation.

Combining Conceptual Behavior With Generalized Response Classes

In many practical teaching situations both conceptual behavior and generalized response classes are taught at the same time. For example, solving a mathematics story problem requires that the learner make conceptual discriminations based on features of the problem, and engage in a generalized response class. She may have to set up an equation and perform mathematical operations.

One teaching method that is explicitly designed to teach both conceptual and generalized response classes at the same time is called *general-case instruction* (Horner & Albin, 1988). General-case instruction is also called *general-case training* and *general-case programming*. It has been used mainly with learners who have severe disabilities, although the basic approach is applicable all learners. Sprague and Horner (1984) used general case instruction to teach six retarded high school students to use novel vending machines, ones they had not been specifically trained to use. This task requires conceptual behavior because the trainees had to respond to general features of vending machines including the coin slots, the prices, the buttons, and the dispenser. This task also required a generalized response class because the trainees were required to engage in behaviors with the same general features, but which also differed from machine to machine.

The basic strategy of general-case instruction is to give the learner a range of teaching tasks in which the same basic stimulus and response features are present, but the specific stimuli and responses in each task vary. Sprague and Horner provided for a range of teaching tasks in their general-case training condition by selecting three vending machines that sampled a wide range of different stimuli and responses.

They compared this general-case training with two other types of training. These included single-instance training, in which the trainees learned only to use a single vending machine, and multiple-instance training, in which the trainees learned to use three vending machines that were similar in stimuli and required responses. Figure 14.3 shows data from the experiment.

The data represent the trainees' performance on novel vending machines not used during training. As shown, when training took place with either a single

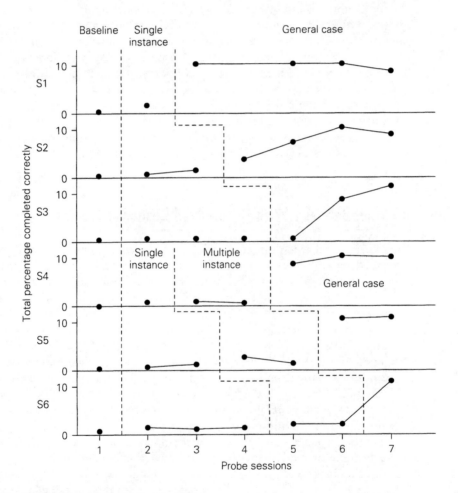

Figure 14.3   *The Effects of General-Case Instruction*

The number of nontrained probe machines completed correctly by students across phases and probe sessions. Students did poorly on novel machines under conditions of single-machine training and multiple-machine training, but performance improved to high levels when the principles of general-case instruction were used in training. Figure adapted from Sprague and Horner (1984).

machine or with three similar machines, performance on the novel machines was poor. However, when the experimenters used general-case instruction, the trainees performed well on the novel machines. Presumably, the general-case training had enabled the trainees to learn basic vending machine stimulus features (i.e., vending machine concepts), and at the same time had established general response features that were successful in operating the novel machines.

Other Combinations of Conceptual Behavior With Generalized Response Classes

General-case instruction provides us with the basic pattern for much complex behavior that involves both conceptual discrimination and generalized response classes. These complex behaviors include such things as applying concepts and principles, rule-learning, applying schemas, using learning strategies, and problem-solving. For example, consider the work of Koegel et al. (1978), which we discussed in the introduction to Chapter 9. In this work, parents learned how to teach their autistic children different skills, and this training generalized to new skills they were asked to teach. The parents acquired conceptual behavior because they were required to respond to features of their children's behavior and the instructional situation. They also acquired a generalized response class because the teaching skills they learned had common response features. Because the parents learned a set of stimulus and response features, rather than specific stimuli and responses, they were eventually able to teach their children new skills without additional training.

Another example of combining conceptual responding and generalized response classes is seen in the problem-solving strategies we discussed in Chapter 11. Problem-solvers use rules that aid in forming concepts. For example, in following the rule "Define the problem," problem-solvers are led to discriminate the critical features of the problem situation, the aspects of the situation that make it a problem. In discriminating these features, problem-solvers learn the concept of what the problem is. Also, in following the problem-solving rule, "Generate alternative solutions," the problem-solver is led to engage in responses that are part of a generalized response class, generating solutions to problems. In turn, when the problem-solvers come to the decision-making stage, they must (a) engage in conceptual behavior by discriminating the critical features of the alternative solutions that are the best solution; and (b) engage in the generalized response class of describing the likely consequences of implementing each of the alternative solutions. As you can see, much complex behavior involves a constant interplay between conceptual responding and generalized response classes.

Chase and Wylie (1985) have described the education of students of behavior analysis in terms of the learning of conceptual behaviors and generalized response classes. This provides us with a good example of how complex behavior involves both conceptual responding and generalized response classes. Table 14.1 lists conceptual behaviors and generalized response classes in the area of applied skills that

---

Table 14.1   *A Task Analysis of General Conceptual and Applied Skills. Table from Chase and Wylie (1985)*

Task Analysis of General Conceptual Skills

A. Identifies ethical issues, designs programs/research consistent with ethical standards, and responds to critiques by review boards.

B. Discusses conceptual issues logically and with relevant citations from the literature.

C. Relates current discussions of issues to historical and philosophical roots.

D. Compares philosophy and science.

E. Compares psychology with other sciences.

F. Compares behavioral psychology with other models of psychology.

G. Describes methods for analyzing psychological events that are difficult to analyze from a behavioral perspective.

H. Pinpoints relations among seemingly disparate events.

I. Pinpoints critical factors within complex and variable situations.

Task Analysis of General Applied Skills

A. Specifies goals, objectives, and task analyses for an applied problem.

B. Assesses relevant entering skills of clients.

C. Designs programs to bring clients from entering level of skills to skills specified in goals and objectives.

D. Designs experimental evaluation system to determine whether the program is working.

E. Implements program and evaluation system.

F. Analyzes data to determine changes that should be made in program.

G. Changes programs based on data/evaluation outcomes.

H. Conducts experimental analyses of unknown relations revealed by program changes.

---

behavior analysts should have. Chase and Wylie stress that by teaching students of behavior analysis conceptual behaviors and general skills (i.e., generalized response classes), the students become capable of successfully applying behavior analysis principles to new behavior problems.

As Chase and Wylie's example illustrates, combining conceptual behavior with generalized response classes is the basis of much of the complex responses involved in intelligent behavior (Becker, 1974; Carnine, 1991).

Making Concept and Generalized Response Class Teaching Effective

When concepts and generalized response classes are taught at the same time, the principles that make teaching effective are similar to those used to teach concepts. However, these principles apply to the response class as well as to the stimulus class. Important considerations include defining the goal tasks, analyzing the critical stimulus and response features, providing rules that identify the critical stimulus and response features for the learner, training using a variety of tasks, and testing for stimulus and response class formation by requiring performance on novel tasks. [See Horner and Albin (1988) for a discussion of the factors that make general case instruction effective and Engelmann and Carnine (1982) for a detailed treatment of teaching various types of skills that require conceptual behavior and the learning of generalized response classes.]

Defining the Goal Tasks.   In teaching any behavior using behavior analysis methods, the first step is to define the target skills the learner is to acquire. When the task is composed of both conceptual behavior and generalized responses classes, this principle also applies. For example, computer programming involves learning conceptual behavior (e.g., responding to stimulus features of a problem or task and the features of the computer language itself) and generalized response classes (e.g., implementing various types of loops and subroutines as needed). Although there are common stimulus and response features of different computer languages, in teaching computer programming, goals for proficiency in specific languages should be set because there are important differences among computer languages.

Analyzing the Stimulus and Response Classes.   In considering conceptual behavior, we saw that it is important to identify the critical and variable features of a concept in order to derive concept illustrations for teaching and testing purposes. The same thing must be done in teaching generalized response classes. A generalized response class will have critical response features that define response class membership and also variable features that will differ from member to member. For example, in teaching a student to divide by fractions (e.g., $1/4 \div 2/3$), the task requires conceptual behavior because features of the problem, like the division symbols and the placement of the fractions, must be S+s for the student's response. The task requires a generalized response class because the student's behavior in solving the problem must show critical response features that are described by the rule "Invert the divisor and multiply." Variable response features of this generalized response class include the specific numbers inverted and multiplied, whether the student inverts and multiplies on paper or as a covert response, whether the student provides the answer on paper or in spoken form, and so forth.

Analyzing the stimuli and responses in teaching complex skills has been described as identifying *samenesses* that exist in a class of tasks (Carnine, 1991; Engelmann, Carnine, & Steely, 1991). *Sameness analysis* means identifying common stimulus and response features that are present in tasks, and making this the basis for instruction. For example, Darch, Carnine, and Gersten (1984) taught fourth-grade students to solve a particular class of mathematics story problems. The problems all demanded that students set up an equation with three terms (i.e., two numbers and a missing number) and to solve for the missing number using either the generalized response class of multiplication or division. Following is an example of one problem:

The following is an example of the type of problem Darch and his colleagues studied:

> Kelly loved to color pages in her coloring book with crayons, so every day Kelly colored 4 pages. Kelly colored 28 pages in all. How many days did Kelly color with crayons?

In this problem, the students would set up the following equation:

4 * X = 28

And solve it by dividing:

(4 * X)/4 = 28/4

X = 7 days

In this problem, the "big number," 28, was given along with one of the smaller numbers. The feature of the story problem of "giving the big number" is a sameness or critical feature that students must learn to set up the equation properly. Conversely, problems in which the big number is not given but two small numbers are is another type of sameness. Once students learn the critical features of this latter type of problem, they can solve them by multiplying:

> Every day Kelly colored 4 pages in her coloring book. She colored for 7 days. How many pages did Kelly color in all?

X = 4 * 7

X = 28 pages

By analyzing critical stimulus and response features, tasks can be divided into classes, and instruction can focus on teaching the samenesses, the essential stimulus and response features that make different tasks alike. However, a common problem is that teachers do not analyze stimuli and responses involved in tasks in this way and therefore cannot teach students the samenesses that exist in tasks such as the mathematics story problems we have briefly considered. As a result, students are left to discover the samenesses for themselves and often fail to do so (Engelmann et al., 1991).

Providing Rules.   In concept learning, we discussed how definitions are a type of rule that help students engage in conceptual behavior by discriminating among the critical features of a class of stimuli. The same general analysis applies to response features: Rules that inform the learner of what critical response features (i.e., samenesses) are required in a task will help the learner be able to acquire the generalized response class. For example, in the work of Darch et al. (1984) in teaching students to solve mathematics story problems, students were taught the rule "Look for the big number to see if it is given." This in turn allowed them to engage in the generalized response class of setting up a proper equation that would lead to a solution.

Rules are generally helpful in teaching learners about stimulus and response features because words in rules can identify critical stimulus and response features. The rule "Invert and multiply" refers not to any specific response, but to response features essential in correctly dividing by fractions. As with the role of rules in concept learning, rules useful in acquiring generalized response classes must make use of words the learner has previously acquired.

Training With Variety.   In teaching skills that incorporate both conceptual behavior and generalized response classes, it is important that the learner receive training in a variety of tasks that sample the stimulus and response variation that exists in the stimulus and response classes to be learned (Horner & Albin, 1988). We saw an example of the importance of variety in stimuli and responses in Sprague and Horner's (1984) work in training people how to use vending machines. Training on three similar machines was found to be more effective than training on a single machine. Training on three machines with different characteristics was in turn found to be superior to training using three similar machines. This benefit of variety in training has been shown with other tasks that require learning stimulus features and acquiring response classes (Day & Horner, 1986, 1989; Horner & McDonald, 1982; Neef et al., 1990).

Testing for Stimulus and Response Class Formation.   In concept learning we saw that it is essential to test with novel stimuli. When teaching concepts and generalized response classes together, it is important to test the learner on tasks that require both responding to novel stimuli and novel responses. Only in this way can we determine if a class of stimuli and responses have been learned rather than specific responses to specific stimuli.

Stimulus Equivalence

With both conceptual behavior and generalized response classes, learners are able to engage in behaviors they were not trained to perform. Untrained skills of this sort are sometimes called *emergent* or *derived*. Another example of emergent skills occurs in *stimulus equivalence* (Sidman & Cresson, 1973; Sidman & Tailby, 1982). In stimulus equivalence, two or more stimuli come to have the same functions and become interchangeable for certain purposes. In ordinary language, people say that stimuli with interchangeable functions "mean" the same thing——for example, a picture of a bear and the word *bear* are said to mean the same thing. The study of stimulus equivalence has implications for several areas of human behavior, including complex language and symbolic processes.

In order for stimulus equivalence to be said to occur, three relationships among stimuli must be demonstrated. Specifically, we must show relations called *reflexivity*, *symmetry*, and *transitivity*.

Reflexivity

Reflexivity is the simplest of these relations and is illustrated in a matching-to-sample discrimination. For example, as shown in Figure 14.4, if the learner is shown the Roman numeral IV as a sample stimulus, and is able to select the IV stimulus from among comparison stimuli that might include III, VI, and IX, we would say that reflexivity has been shown. Reflexivity is demonstrated in correct identity matching in which the learner is able to select a comparison stimulus that matches the sample. Reflexivity can be symbolically represented by $A = A$, indicating that the learner responds to the identicality of stimuli.

Symmetry

In a symmetrical stimulus-response relationship, a stimulus is established as a discriminative stimulus for a response, and this training also results in learning the reverse relation, in which the *response stimulus* assumes the role of discriminative stimulus, and the original discriminative stimulus assumes the role of response. For example, suppose we give a child discrimination training in which IV is the sample stimulus and 2, 4, and 9 are the comparison stimuli. The child learns this discrimination and correctly selects 4 whenever IV is the sample stimulus. This discrimination training very often has another effect: The learner is able to select IV from among comparison stimuli when 4 is shown as the sample stimulus. Because the stimulus-response relationship between 4 and IV has not been directly trained, it is said to be an *emergent* or *derived* relation. At this point, IV and 4 are said to have a symmetrical relation to one another because their roles as stimuli and responses have been reversed or interchanged. Symmetry is illustrated in Figure 14.5. [The same process is seen in the receptive-expressive and expressive-receptive forms of generalization we discussed in Chapter 9.] Symmetry can be symbolically expressed by A = B and B = A, representing the reversibility of stimuli and responses.

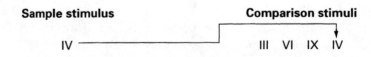

Figure 14.4   *Reflexivity*

Reflexivity is shown when a learner views a sample stimulus (IV) and is able to select the identical stimulus from among comparison stimuli.

Derived Relation

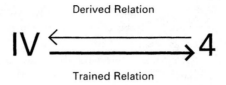

Trained Relation

Figure 14.5 *Symmetrical Relations*

A discriminative stimulus (IV) is established for selecting a response (4). This procedure also sometimes produces a symmetrical relation in which the former response (4) becomes a discriminative stimulus for the response of selecting the former discriminative stimulus (IV).

Transitivity

A third type of relation is transitivity, which is a more complex and complete type of interchangeability of stimuli and responses. Suppose we have established a symmetrical relation between IV and 4. At this point, we continue with stimulus discrimination training, this time using 4 as the S+ sample stimulus and several cards with different numbers of dots on them as the comparison stimuli. We train the learner to select the four-dot card when 4 is shown using differential consequences. Once 4 is an effective S+ for selecting the four-dot card, we can test for transitivity by presenting the stimulus IV and allowing the learner to respond by selecting from among our various dot cards. If the learner selects the card with four dots as a response to IV, this would be an example of a transitive relationship. Transitivity can be symbolically illustrated by the expression: if A = B and B = C, then A = C. Transitivity is illustrated in Figure 14.6.

Stimulus equivalence is said to occur when the combinations of reflexive, symmetric, and transitive relationships are all present. For example, if a transitive relation

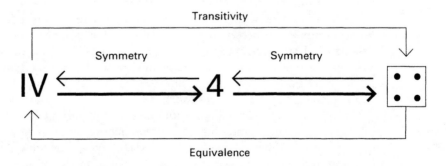

Figure 14.6 *Transitivity and Stimulus Equivalence*

See text for an explanation.

is present without underlying reflexive and symmetric relationships, we do not have stimulus equivalence. However, if all three relations are shown, stimulus equivalence is said to occur, as illustrated in Figure 14.6. In Figure 14.6, the relation in which the dot card is the S+ and selecting IV is the response is labeled equivalence because this derived relation could not exist unless the all the necessary tests of reflexivity, symmetry, and transitivity have been met (Sidman, 1992).

When stimulus equivalence occurs, the stimuli concerned are said to be inter-changeable as stimuli and response and are all members of an *equivalence class.* In ordinary language, we would say that the stimuli in an equivalence class all "mean" the same thing. However, members of an equivalence class can still be discriminated from each other in certain stimulus contexts. For example, in the case of a learner for whom "IV," "4," and a four-dot card are all equivalent, the learner does not go forth and mix the terms indiscriminately (e.g., 3 + 1 = IV). The equivalence class members are equivalent in certain contexts, but the learner can still discriminate dif-ferences between the members when required.

The Importance of Stimulus Equivalence

One reason why stimulus equivalence is so important is that it shows how learners can acquire more discriminative responses than those directly trained. In our exam-ple, IV, 4, and the four-dot card would all be interchangeable as stimuli and responses, even though only two of these relations had been directly trained. Stimulus equivalence permits children to learn to respond to different symbols as if they were the same, at least the same for certain purposes. Through additional train-ing, spoken word stimuli could be added to the equivalence class (e.g., the spoken word *four*), making it too equivalent with the rest of the members of the class. In current behavior analysis research, very large and complex equivalence classes are being studied. In addition, very different kinds of stimuli can participate in stimulus equivalence relationships. Hayes, Tilley, and Hayes (1988), for example, showed that gustatory (taste) stimuli can function much like the verbal stimuli we have examined in stimulus equivalence relationships.

A second reason why stimulus equivalence is important is that it illustrates how dissimilar stimuli can become members of the same stimulus and response classes. With conceptual discrimination and generalized response classes, stimuli and responses must share critical properties and are similar in this respect. However, in stimulus equivalence, completely dissimilar stimuli, such as words and their referents, become members of the same equivalence classes.

Another reason why stimulus equivalence is important is that it is thought to be involved in language meaning and comprehension. For example, we have already suggested that members of an equivalence class "mean" the same thing. In addition, when appropriate equivalence classes have been formed, the learner is not said to have "learned" just specific responses to specific stimuli, but rather is said to "com-prehend" the stimuli, as in reading comprehension in which stimulus pictures, spo-ken words, and written words are all members of an equivalence class (de Rose, de Souza, Rossito, & de Rose 1991; Sidman & Cresson, 1973). Stimulus equivalence offers promise in understanding complex behaviors and it is currently a forefront of behavior analysis research.

Summary

In conceptual behavior a critical feature or set of features acts as discriminative stimuli for behavior. Stimuli that possess the critical features are members of the conceptual stimulus class, and are called concept instances or examples. Each member of a conceptual stimulus class differs in certain respects called variable features. Variable features are characteristics of stimuli that are not important in determining their membership in a conceptual stimulus class.

The power of concept learning is that the learner acquires correct responses to a class of stimuli that have a common set of stimulus features. This allows learners to respond correctly to new stimulus class members when they encounter them.

Conceptual behavior involves both discrimination and generalization processes. Learners must discriminate between examples and nonexamples of the stimulus class by noting the presence or absence of the critical features. And learners must generalize their responses to all examples of the stimulus class.

In testing for conceptual behavior, it is necessary to determine if the critical features of the concept are acting as discriminative stimuli by testing the learner's performance with novel concept examples and nonexamples.

Concepts and words are closely related. We use words to "refer" to conceptual features, a process that makes it possible for us to speak and think about abstract relations. Using concept words is one way we are able to imagine alternative realities, combinations of stimulus features that do not currently exist.

Factors that make conceptual discrimination effective include the factors that make other types of stimulus discrimination effective. Factors of particular importance for conceptual discrimination include defining the goal conceptual discrimination, concept analysis, using concept definitions, and discrimination training with examples and nonexamples.

A generalized response class is a class of responses that have a set of response features in common. Examples of generalized response classes include generalized imitation, creative blockbuilding, writing original examples of concepts, mathematical operations like multiplication, traits like honesty, and listening skills. Generalized response classes are similar to concepts. While concepts are defined by stimulus features, generalized response classes are defined by response features. The test of conceptual behavior is responding correctly to new conceptual class members, while the test of a generalized response class is correctly engaging in new response instances that are members of the generalized response class.

Because many skills involve a combination of conceptual behavior and generalized response classes, they are often taught at the same time. We examined a method for doing this called general-case instruction. We also examined several other instances of skills in which conceptual discriminations and generalized response classes are learned at the same time. These skills included problem-solving and those taught in a behavior-analysis graduate program. The effectiveness of concept and generalized response class teaching is influenced by principles similar to those that make concept teaching effective. The goal task must be defined, the critical stimulus and response features must be analyzed, training must incorporate a variety of tasks, and testing must include novel tasks.

Stimulus equivalence exists when two or more stimuli become interchangeable or "mean the same thing." This is important in reading, for example, because words must come to be interchangeable with the things the words represent. Stimulus equivalence is said to occur when three relations among stimuli are shown: reflexivity, symmetry, and transitivity. Stimulus equivalence has provided insight into processes such as meaning and comprehension.

Conceptual Exercise   *Conceptual Discrimination*

For each of the following items, decide if the item is an example of conceptual discrimination. In each item, the target behavior is highlighted. If the item is an example of conceptual discrimination, identify at least one critical feature of the concept and one variable feature. If the item is an example of faulty conceptual discrimination, specify whether the problem is one of overgeneralization or undergeneralization. Provide brief reasons for your answers. Check your decision with the analyses in the back of the book.

1. Two researchers taught a group of university students about the morpheme, the smallest unit of language that carries meaning, contributes to the meaning of words in which it appears, and cannot be subdivided into smaller units that have meaning. Examples of morphemes include the *s* ending in plural words, words such as *pin, child, load,* and *pray*, the *er* in the word *unloader* and the *hood* in *childhood*. The students did a discrimination training exercise that included a clear definition of the morpheme and responding to examples and nonexamples. As a result of this training, **the students could identify examples and nonexamples of morphemes on a posttest that were not included in the training examples and nonexamples.**

2. A group of high school students was learning about different types of minerals. As part of their instruction, the teacher had each student examine a kit that contained 20 different mineral specimens. The students' task was to learn to identify each specimen by examining it, and then turning over a card placed in front of the specimen to see the name of the mineral. On a midsemester exam, the students were tested on their knowledge of the minerals. The same specimens they had studied earlier were numbered and placed on a table. The students' task was to write down the name of each mineral on their answer sheet. **Dana, one of the students in the class, correctly identified each of the specimens.**

3. University students were learning the poetry concept of trochaic meter. In poetry with trochaic meter, one long or stressed syllable is followed by one short or unstressed

syllable. The students studied a definition of trochaic meter, and then did a discrimination training exercise in which they studied examples and nonexamples of trochaic meter. Byron wrote one of the examples:

> Maid of Athens, ere we part,
> Give, oh give me back my heart!

And Housman wrote one of the nonexamples in which one stressed syllable follows one unstressed syllable:

> When I was one-and-twenty
> I heard a wise man say,
> "Give crowns and pounds of guineas,
> But not your heart away."

As a result of these training methods, **on a posttest the students were able to distinguish between examples and nonexamples of trochaic meter they had not seen before.**

4. Children in a preschool were learning what "on top" means. The teacher showed them several examples of on top, including a ball being on top of a toy truck, a doll being on top of a small wooden block, and a picture book being on top of a mat. Later, the children were tested using novel stimuli that were either on top or not on top of each other. **They were able to correctly identify examples of on top when small items were used. However, when large items on top of one another were shown to the children, they said that the items were not on top of one another. For example, the children failed to identify a roof being on top of a house as being an example of on top.**

5. University students were learning Goldiamond's concept of a constructional approach to behavior change, which emphasizes teaching new forms of useful behavior rather than simply eliminating undesirable responses [See Chapter 3 of this text]. Students were trained to identify examples and nonexamples of this approach in a training program. As a test of learning, the experimenters gave the students new examples of behavior change projects using the constructional approach and new nonexamples in which behavior change occurred without following the constructional approach. **As a result of the training, the students were able to classify correctly the examples and nonexamples of the constructional approach.**

6. A group of preschool school children learning several geometric shapes were trained to identify squares and to distinguish these from nonsquares. After training, the children were tested. Trainers showed the children squares they had not seen before along with other geometric shapes that were not squares. **The students correctly identified the squares as squares, but also identified several other types of closed geometric forms as squares.**

7. Two teachers did an experiment in which they taught the concept of *chide* to university students. They used the definition of chide to mean talking to someone in order to get them to correct their mistakes. The teachers taught chide using various methods, including giving examples of the word in sentence contexts, giving examples of instances of chiding, and giving synonyms of the word. A posttest included exam-

ples of chide that the students had not read during training. Data from the study showed that **all of the training methods were helpful in getting the students to respond correctly to the posttest items.**

8. Several researchers taught a group of 40 preschool children the idea of diagonal. They defined diagonal as a tilted line. During teaching, the researchers showed the children six examples of diagonal that included 4 " lines at angles of 45°, 72.5°, 135°, and 142.5°. The researchers also showed the children two nonexamples of diagonal, 4" black lines at angles of 0 degrees and 90 degrees. Teaching methods included the teacher identifying examples and nonexamples of diagonal. The teacher also required the students to identify examples and nonexamples and praised them for correct responding. On a posttest, the children received examples and nonexamples of diagonal and were required to identify them as examples or nonexamples. The posttest items were different from the training items because the posttest lines were 3 rather than 4 " long, were wavy rather than straight, red rather than black. **Because of the training, the students did well on the posttest.**

9. Else was concerned because many literary concepts are poorly defined and misunderstood. She developed a set of materials to teach students about irony. She defined irony as having three components: (a) dissembling, or hiding under a false appearance; (b) subtlety; and (c) surprise. To teach the concept, she developed a training program that included examples of irony along with nonexamples that were missing one of the critical features of irony. Among the examples and nonexamples, she included ones that were humorous and ones that were tragic. As a result of doing her training program, **on a posttest Else's students were able to identify correctly examples and nonexamples of irony that they had not encountered before.**

10. In a high school course, students were learning the notion of inflation. The textbook presented a definition of inflation and gave an example of inflation that occurred in Germany after World War I. Later, on an exam, the students read several other items describing historical instances of inflation, along with several items describing instances when there had been no inflation. The students had not been previously exposed to the items on the exam. **On the exam, the students tended to say that all the items were examples of inflation.**

11. Preschool children enrolled in a Head-Start program participated in an experiment. During part of their instruction, the teacher showed the children three objects of different sizes. The children's task was to say if the object the teacher indicated was medium-sized. The teacher used several different sets of objects positioned in different places. As a result of this training, **when the teacher showed novel sets of objects to the students, the children were able to identify the medium-sized objects.**

12. Experimenters were working with a group of fourth-, fifth-, and sixth-grade students. The students read 14 brief stories, and the students' task was to identify the motives of characters in the story, particularly to distinguish between apparent motives and actual motives. Training methods included prompting student responding with questions, praise for correct responding, error correction by redirecting the student

to pertinent parts of the story, and correct-answer feedback. As a result of this training, **the students were able to read new stories and correctly identify character motives**.

13. A group of researchers were working with a sixth-grade teacher to improve the reading skills of sixth-grade students enrolled in a remedial program. Part of the training included teaching students to identify the main idea in short reading passages. The students read the passage, underlined the sentence or phrase that contained the main idea, and received feedback by checking the correct answer in the back of the paper on which the passage was written. The students were sometimes tested on their ability to identify the main idea. This was done by giving students reading passages that they has previously read and asking them to identify the main idea by underlining a key sentence or phrase. **These tests showed that the students had learned to identify the main ideas**.

14. In a high school art appreciation class, students were learning about cubism, a style of painting that depicts objects and people in terms of two-dimensional geometric shapes and without realistic detail. Much of Picasso's work exemplifies cubism. After training, to see how much the students had learned the teachers showed them slides of various cubist and noncubist works that the students had not viewed before. **The students correctly classified the noncubist paintings, but they incorrectly classified many of the cubist paintings as noncubist**.

Conceptual Exercise   *Conceptual Behavior and Generalized Response Classes*

For each of the following items, decide if the item is an example of conceptual behavior, a generalized response class, neither, or both. In each item, the target behaviors are italicized. Provide brief reasons for your answers. Check your decision with the analyses in the back of the book.

1. A group of researchers trained retarded adults to use washing machines and dryers. They did this by teaching the trainees to use different types of washers and dryers in which the stimuli (e.g., placement of the controls) and required responses (e.g., the topography of the turn-on response) differed from machine to machine. As a test of teaching effectiveness, the experimenters had the trainees operate new machines that they had not been trained to use. In the new machines, the specific stimulus and response characteristics were different, but the stimulus and response features were of course the same as on almost all washers and dryers. **Because of the teaching methods, the trainees were able to use the new machines correctly**.

2. Roy was a meteorologist, a person who studies and predicts the weather. Roy did his job by studying weather maps and computer printouts of weather data. Part of his skills were made up of being able to look for key aspects of the data, such as a particular pattern of high and low pressure areas. Another part of his skills were made up

of analyzing the data he collected—for example in weighting the various aspects of the data according to their relative importance. **Roy's skills allowed him to accurately predict the weather even under very unusual combinations of conditions he had not encountered before.**

3. Violet was a young girl who hid from dogs whenever she saw one. She hid from all types of dogs including big dogs, little dogs, frisky dogs, tired old dogs, and so on. She did not hide from other animals. When Violet hid, she did so in a wide variety of ways including behind bushes, in her house, in her garage, and behind a fence. All the hiding actions put her out of sight of the dog. **Often she encountered novel dogs in circumstances that required her to hide in new ways, and she did so successfully.**

4. Anders was learning to calculate the length of the hypotenuse (the longest side) of a right triangle when he was given the length of the other two sides. This task demanded that he discriminate several important features of a triangle and apply a formula (i.e., the square of the hypotenuse is equal to the sum of the squares of the other two sides). He practiced with one type of right triangle in which the sides were 3, 4, and 5 units long. Later, he was given problems with other types of right triangles and could not solve them. **The problem was that although he could discriminate the features of right triangles and tell the difference among novel right triangles and other types of novel triangles, he could apply the formula only to the right triangle with sides of 3, 4, and 5 units in length.**

5. Six retarded males ranging in age from 8 to 23 were learning certain dressing skills, how to put on different kinds of pullover shirts. Pullover shirts all have certain stimulus features in common (e.g., big opening at the bottom, smaller openings for neck and arms at the top) and certain response features in common (e.g., positioning the shirt over one's head, putting arms through armholes, pulling the shirt down). However, different types of pullover shirts differ in both the stimulus features the shirts have (e.g., fabric, sleeve length, type of collar, and fit) and the responses features necessary to put on the shirts (e.g., pulling the arms through a long, rather than a short sleeve). The trainees learned how to put on the shirts through training with several different types of pullover shirts. **Because of this training, the subjects were able to put on novel pullover shirts they had not been specifically trained to put on.**

6. Kevin was taking an introductory anthropology course that included instruction in the notions of matriarchal and patriarchal societies. Because his anthropology instructor was enlightened, she used concept teaching principles and taught students these concepts using examples and nonexamples of each type of society. On the final exam for the course, **Kevin was given novel examples of patriarchal and matriarchal societies and was able to classify these examples correctly. However, on the exam he was also directed to provide original examples of the two types of societies. Kevin was unable to write original examples.**

7. Experimenters were working with three teenagers with several disabilities. The goal of training was to open beverage containers. Opening beverage containers requires that the trainee (a) respond to certain essential aspects of the container, such as the type of lid, materials of construction, and placement of the opening; and (b) perform

those actions that share the critical feature of producing an opened container. Of course, types of containers differ in both their stimulus features and the responses needed to open them. The trainees received instruction in opening several different types of containers. **As a result of this training, the trainees were able to discriminate the opening-related features of novel containers and open them.**

8. Donna, 40, Mary, 21, and Jeff, 27 were all legally blind and retarded. They were in a program to train them to clean rooms. Training took place in a model apartment where the researchers taught the trainees a variety of cleaning responses to a variety of stimuli. Although a variety of stimuli and responses were involved, the trainees were taught certain generic cleaning tasks (cleaning a floor) in response to certain generic stimuli (e.g., type and size of the floor). During training, Donna, Mary, and Jeff learned to respond to stimulus features of things in the model apartment and learned to engage in cleaning tasks defined by response features. Later, the trainees were tested in three different novel situations, an office, an infirmary, and a conference room. **Because of the nature of the training, the trainees were able to clean the three rooms at a relatively high level of correct responding.**

9. Agnes, a four-year-old, had learned to imitate 10 different behaviors that her trainer, Jackie, had taught her. Agnes had reached the point at which whenever Jackie demonstrated one of the 10 behaviors and clapped her hands, the signal to imitate, Agnes could imitate the response immediately. However, **when Jackie demonstrated a new behavior and clapped her hands, Agnes simply looked puzzled and could not imitate the response.**

10. June was an art teacher. In her work, **she often examined student's projects and noted whether they showed the characteristics of good art, including such things as balance of elements, composition, originality of style, color coordination, etc. She was also able to tell students how to rearrange the elements in their work in order to improve it. She was able to do both of these things even though every student project was different.**

Conceptual Exercise *Stimulus Equivalence*

For each of the following items, decide if the item is an example of a reflexive relation, a symmetric relation, a transitive relation, or a stimulus equivalence relation. Many of the items will be examples of more than one type of relation. If there are any derived relations, identify each. In each case, concern yourself with the highlighted relations. Check your decisions with the analyses in the back of the book.

Note: In doing this exercise, you may find it helpful to diagram the relations between the stimuli and responses, using the sample diagrams we provided in the text.

Note to advanced students: In our examples, have focused on only one type of stimulus equivalence, that demonstrated by training A-B and B-C relations and testing for A-C relations. For the sake of simplicity in this introductory treatment, we have not included stimulus equivalence trained through A-B and A-C relations and tested through B-C relations. For the same reason, we have also not included more than three elements in our examples.

1. Adam was learning about different colors. His dad showed him a red block, and Adam was required to pick up an identical red block from among three blocks in front of him, only one of which was red. Similarly, when shown a green or blue block, Adam was to select the matching color block. Adam's dad reinforced correct responses with hugs and praise. After some training, **Adam was able to select the block that corresponded to the color of the block his father showed him.**

2. Penny was learning some verbal relationships. When her mother pointed to a picture of a car in an array of several pictures that included only one car, Penny's task was to point to a corresponding card with the word *car* on it in another array of cards with words on them. Penny's mother reinforced correct responses with praise and corrected errors by pointing to the response. Other picture-word relationships she taught at the same time included *toaster, book, stereo,* and *newspaper.* In this way **Penny learned to point to the correct word after her mother pointed to the corresponding picture. Later Penny was tested to see if she could point to the correct picture when her mother pointed to the corresponding word. Even though her mother had not trained her on this task, Penny performed the task without making an error.**

3. Penny continued working with her mother. She had already learned to select correct words when shown pictures, and this training also allowed her to select pictures when shown words. At this point, Penny's mother pointed to words she had used previously (e.g., *car*) and Penny's task was to select another card that had a synonymous word (e.g., *auto*) from another array of cards. Correct responses were reinforced as before. As a result of this training, **Penny was able (a) to select the correct written synonym when her mother pointed to a particular written word; (b) to select the correct written word when her mother pointed to the synonym; (c) to select the synonym when shown the corresponding picture; and (d) to select the correct picture when shown the corresponding synonym. Assume that Penny could do identity matching with all the stimuli used in training (e.g., select the same written word when shown that written word).**

4. Roger was learning about animals by working at a panel of an apparatus. A picture of an animal was shown to him, followed by three animals sounds (e.g., the roar of a lion, the bleating of a sheep, and the meow of a cat). Roger's task was to push a button in a row of three buttons that indicated his sound selection. For example, if a lion picture was shown and the lion roar was the second sound, the correct response was to push the second button. Pieces of delicious candy came down a chute when Roger made a correct response. Incorrect responses stopped the experiment for one minute. As a result of this training, **Roger was able to select the correct animal sound when shown the corresponding animal picture. Roger was also able to select the correct animal picture after he heard the corresponding animal sound.**

5. Mavis was in a psychology experiment. During initial training, American Sign Language (ASL) signs for words were shown to her, and her task was to select the

correct English word, written in all capital letters (e.g., DOVE), that corresponded to the sign from an array of different English words. Mavis received a penny if she pointed to the correct English all-caps word. Then, during the next stage of training, Mavis was shown all-caps words, and her task was to select the corresponding lower-case word from an array of such words (e.g., dove). After Mavis learned how to do this, she was tested. After learning the trained relations, Mavis was tested on other relations. **It was found that she could (a) give the sign when shown the corresponding all-caps word; (b) select the all-caps word when given the corresponding lower-case word. However, Mavis was not able to either (a) give the correct sign when shown the corresponding lower-case word or (b) select the correct lower-case word when shown the corresponding sign. Assume Mavis could do identity matching with all the stimuli used in the experiment.**

6. Pete was learning the names of several types of leaves, such as oak, maple, and birch. At first, the experimenter held up a leaf for Pete to see, and Pete's task was to select the identical leaf from a selection of several leaves. **He did this very well.** In addition, when the experimenter held up a card with the name of the leaf, **Pete was able to select the identical card from several cards with leaf names on them.** Later, the experimenter held up a leaf and Pete's task was to select the card with the corresponding name. **He learned to do this correctly with all the leaf-name pairs.** The experimenter then tested Pete by holding up the leaf-name cards and seeing if Pete could select the correct leaves. **Pete was unable to do this correctly, however.**

Conceptual Exercise *Making Conceptual Discrimination Effective*

For each of the following items one of the factors that make conceptual discrimination effective has been violated. Identify the problem. Confirm your decision with the analyses in the back of the book. Choose from the following factors of special importance to conceptual discrimination: (a) defining the goal conceptual discrimination through concept analysis, (b) using concept definitions, (c) using examples and nonexamples, (d) using focal examples, (e) using a broad range of examples, and (e) using minimally different nonexamples.

Note: Failure to do a proper concept analysis can lead to other problems in teaching, such as failure to use appropriate examples and nonexamples. In the following exercise, when the problem is a failure to do a concept analysis, consider the correct answer only to be this failure and not other problems that follow from this root problem.

1. A new teacher at an elementary school decided to use the behavior analysis skills she had acquired during her teacher training. She was trying to teach her students the conceptual discrimination of *places within which people live.* She carefully analyzed the critical and variable features of dwellings in North America including the variable features of size and construction materials, and the critical features of an enclosure, and so on. She used a small bungalow as a focal example. She properly defined for her students the critical features that make dwellings dwellings. She used pictures of various kinds of dwellings and pictures of other objects, such as vehicles and ani-

mals. The children learned to discriminate among various houses, vehicles, and animals but they did not learn to identify trailers, teepees, and igloos as places within which people live.

2. Ms. B was teaching her first-grade students the concept of triangularity. Prior to teaching, she did an analysis of triangularity in which she identified the critical features of triangles and also variable features of triangles. She presented the students with an equilateral triangle as a focal example and she explained to her students that triangles are geometric shapes having three straight sides all joined. The variable features include color, size, and the length of each side. She used triangles varying in color size and side length to demonstrate the concept of triangularity.

3. Timmy's father was teaching him the concept of *feline.* As a focal example, he used a domestic shorthair cat. He presented pictures of domestic cats of many different breeds so that they varied in color, markings and so on. His nonexamples included other furry small creatures. He pointed out that cats have whiskers and long tails. Although Timmy did very well most of the time, he was unable to identify a cheetah or any other large zoo feline as an example.

4. Peter was training Elizabeth to identify instances of the concept of square. Initially, Peter did a concept analysis of squareness in which he identified the critical and variable features of squareness. During training, Peter used a simple drawing of a square as a focal example in teaching. In addition he defined the concept of square as four straight lines of equal length connected at right angles, and explained this to Elizabeth in terms she could understand. He presented his example of a square with three nonexamples, a circle, a rectangle, a triangle.

5. After using a teaching procedure, Dr. Jones discovered that his student, Nicholas, had failed to learn the concept of *family unit.* Dr. Jones had done a proper concept analysis of a traditional family unit. He had carefully explained to Nicholas that traditionally, a family was a group of people including either one male and one female or at least one adult and at least one youngster who live together. As examples of family units, Dr. Jones used line drawings depicting a wide range of family units. Dr. Jones also used an appropriate range of minimally different nonexamples of a family unit. Nicholas learned the concept of a family unit quite well, but after a few weeks did poorly on a test in which he was required to identify examples and nonexamples of family units.

6. Dr. Bergman was trying to teach her students the behavior analysis concept of shaping. She did an appropriate concept analysis of shaping and used a proper focal example in teaching. She used an appropriate set of examples and nonexamples in teaching. She presented the examples and nonexamples in segments on a videotape. After each segment, the students were required to say whether they had seen an example of shaping. Despite these procedures, the students were still confused about what shaping was after viewing the videotape.

7. Children in a preschool class were learning about the concept of a sphere. The teacher did a concept analysis of spherical, defined the concept in words the children could understand, and used an appropriate focal example of a sphere. The teacher

also used a wide range of different types of examples of spheres. Along with the examples of three-dimensional spheres, the teacher also used a wide range of two-dimensional objects, such as circles, squares, triangles, and rectangles, as nonexamples. The teaching procedure did not work as well as hoped.

Conceptual Exercise   *Making Concept and Generalized Response Class Teaching Effective*

For each of the following, an important factor that makes concept and generalized response class training effective has been violated. Identify the problem and confirm your decision with the analyses in the back of the book. Choose from the following: defining the goal task, analyzing the critical stimulus and response features, training with a variety of tasks, and using novel tasks to test for stimulus and response class formation.

1. Lynn, a retarded woman, was learning various skills in preparation for a new job as the receptionist in a sheltered workshop. A behaviorally trained therapist was working with her. The therapist made a list of the critical and variable features of both the concepts and the responses involved in answering telephone queries. She also explained to Lynn several rules for dealing with telephone queries. For example, Lynn was told that a caller who wanted information about employees at the workshop, should be referred to Mr. Brown. Lynn was then trained with a real telephone. Several calls were made to Lynn asking her different questions about the employees at the workshop. Lynn referred each caller to Mr. Brown. Lynn followed the other rules for other kinds of calls as well. When Lynn began her new job as a receptionist at the sheltered workshop, she did a fine job on the telephone but when she was approached by live people who had queries, she was confused.

2. David was learning his 9 times tables with the help of his mother. She considered all the important features of the goal task as she prepared her examples. She presented problems both on paper and verbally and David sometimes responded verbally and sometimes in written form. When she gave him new problems to solve he did not do very well. David continued to have a lot of trouble with his 9 times tables until his friend Matti showed him the following trick:

   > Subtract 1 from the smaller number in the problem. That is the first digit. The second digit is the number that when added to the first makes 9.

   > For example: 9×3 $3 - 1 = 2$ $2 + 7 = 9$. The answer is 27.

3. Sally was taking a workshop designed to teach her how to use Macintosh computers. Several goal tasks were involved and an analysis of critical features and variables features of different computers was used in teaching Sally the rules for word processing on Macintoshes. In the workshop, the machine that Sally trained on was the Macintosh SE/30. When her training was completed, Sally was tested on a Macintosh IIci. Sally had a lot of problems because this computer was unfamiliar to her.

4. Geoff was being trained to stack and store things at a recycling depot. The job demanded that he be able to stack any glass, paper, or plastic item that was delivered to the depot, and this was the goal of training. The training team analyzed the stimuli and responses involved in the stacking task. Geoff was given general rules for stacking, and he was trained using 12-ounce soda and beer cans, pint-sized liquor bottles, and plastic milk containers. Previous work had shown these items to be of sufficient variety. After a week of training, Geoff was tested using these containers and he accomplished the task without a single major error.

5. Ruth was learning the various concepts involved in positive reinforcement. Her teacher provided many of the rules involved in making positive reinforcement effective. The teacher's goal was to teach general behavioral principles. A variety of positive reinforcement test items requiring a variety of types of responses was used. Ruth was then tested with new items having to do with the procedure called punishment. Although many of the critical features that make reinforcement effective are similar to those that make punishment effective, Ruth was not aware of this.

6. Roy was taking a crash course of exam-writing skills. The goal was to be able to deal with a variety of kinds of questions and to write a variety of kinds of answers. Roy would be given a questions about history in multiple-choice format, or fill-in-the-blank, or short-answer format. Sometimes he would write down his answers, sometimes he would say his answers orally. After training was finished, Roy was tested with items about history he had not seen before. He did well but he did not do well on his first multiple-choice quiz in algebra.

Conceptual Exercise Analyses

Chapter 1 *Describing Behavior*

1. Item (a) is a **summary label** because it refers to a number of different behaviors that have certain features (i.e., creative features) in common. Item (b) is an example of **behavior** because it refers to a specific activity.

2. Items (a) and (b) are examples of **summary labels** because they are terms that refer to a number of different behaviors, those sampled on the test, that have something in common. Item (c) is a **labeling effect** because the labels *introvert* and *extrovert* caused Ms. Adams to respond to the students in terms of the labels. Item (d) is also a **labeling effect** because the students came to respond in label-appropriate ways as a result of their treatment by Ms. Adams. *Source: Snyder and Swann (1978)*

3. Item (a) is an example of a **summary label** because it describes those behaviors involved in doing well at school. Item (b) is an example of an **explanatory fiction**. Mr. Jacobs used the summary label *intelligent* to explain the cause of Arnie's good grades.

4. Items (a) and (b) are both examples of **behavior** because they are descriptions of specific activities that Wilbur engaged in. In item (a), smelling (olfactory behavior) may be considered a form of sensory behavior. Item (b) is also an example of **behavior** because "wishful" sensory behavior can occur in the absence of the stimulus to which it customarily occurs, particularly under conditions of deprivation (i.e., food deprivation in this case).

5. Items (a) and (b) are **summary labels** because they do not refer to specific activities but to a number of different behaviors having certain common features. Items (c) and (d) are **behaviors**. Carol engaged in the specific behaviors of staring at Todd's picture and recalling specific images of their past. Note that Carol's recall of the past was covert behavior, but specific behavior nonetheless.

6. Item (a) is an example of a **summary label** because it describes a feature of a number of different behaviors Betty engages in. Item (b) is an example of an **explanatory fiction** because enthusiasm, a summary label, is identified as a cause of behavior. *Source: Skinner (1953)*

7. Items (a) through (g) are all examples of **behavior** because each refers to a specific activity that Selden engaged in. Items (a) through (c) are examples of observable behaviors. Items (d) through (g) are examples of covert behaviors involved in dreaming. They are nonetheless examples of behavior because they are specific activities.

8. Item (a) is an example of a **summary label** because it refers to a number of different behaviors that have certain common features. Item (b) is an example of an **explanatory fiction**. Duane used the notion of *lazy,* a summary label, to explain why he didn't engage in a work behavior.

9. Items (a), (b), and (c) are examples of **behavior**. In each case, Ansley engaged in a specific activity. Note that sensory activities, such as the visual responses involved in looking and seeing, fall within the behavior analysis definition of behavior. As illustrated in item (b), visual responses can occur in the absence of the specific stimuli that normally produce them. In other words, seeing an object can occur in the absence of that object under certain conditions and the "mistaken" behaviors that are involved here are instances of behavior.

10. Item (a) is an example of a **summary label** because it describes a number of different behaviors that Diane exhibited. Item (b) is an **explanatory fiction** because a summary label is used to explain a cause for a behavior. *Source: Skinner (1953)*

11. Both items (a) and (b) are examples of **behavior**. Hearing, like seeing and smelling, is a form of sensory behavior. In item (b), Sandra's hearing occurs in the absence of music, and she is recalling the music to herself. This covert or private sensory experience qualifies as behavior.

12. Item (a) is an example of a **summary label** because *mildly retarded* is a label for various behaviors that share certain common features. Item (b) is an example of a **labeling effect**. As a result of labeling Dominick as mildly retarded, the teachers responded to him in terms of the label even when the source of his difficulty at school (his poor vision) was removed.

13. Both items (a) and (b) are examples of **behavior**. Tactile responding may be considered a form of sensory behavior. As is suggested in item (b), under certain conditions, tactile responses can occur in the absence of the stimuli that normally produce them.

14. Items (a) and (b) are examples of **behavior** because they are descriptions of specific activities. Note that in item (b), the behavior is defined by its nonoccurrence. That is, the children got extra story time for the nonoccurrence of speaking without raising their hands. Behavior analysts sometimes define behavior in terms of a specific property of behavior (i.e., the absence of that behavior) rather than directly in terms of a concrete action.

15. Item (a) is a **summary label** because it refers to a number of different behaviors that Sergeant Reynolds emitted. Item (b) is an example of an **explanatory fiction** because *authoritarian personality* is a summary label that is used to explain behavior.

16. Item (a) is a description of **behavior** because it identifies a specific activity that Tom engaged in. Item (b) is a **summary label** because it refers to a number of different behaviors that have certain common features.

17. Item (a) is an example of a **summary label**. Senator Morley uses *wimp* as a label for different behaviors his opponent exhibited. In item (b), Senator Morley uses the **summary label** wimp as a cause for Howard's advocacy of a commission to investigate the state police. This illustration represents the use of a summary label as a cause and is therefore an explanatory fiction.

18. Both items (a) and (b) are examples of **behavior**. Item (a) is an example of what is generally considered to be an unlearned behavior. We do not learn to constrict our pupils in response to light. Item (b) is an example of what is generally considered to be a learned behavior. People learn to shield their eyes from the sun with their hand.

19. Item (a) is an example of a **summary label** because it describes smoking behaviors. Item (b) is an **explanatory fiction** because it is the use of a summary label (a tobacco habit) as a cause of smoking. *Source: Skinner (1953)*

20. Both items (a) and (b) are examples of **behavior** because sneezing is a specific activity. Sneezing is generally considered to be an unlearned reaction but as suggested in item (b), sneezing can sometimes be a learned response.

21. Item (a) is an example of a **summary label** because it describes a number of different behaviors that have certain common features. Item (b) is an example of a **labeling effect** because labeling Mr. Marco as *cold* caused the students to respond to him in ways appropriate to the label. *Source: Kelley (1950)*

22. Both items (a) and (b) are examples of **behavior** because each item represents a specific activity the students engaged in. In item (a), the behavior is covert and observable only to Allison, while in item (b), the behavior is overt and observable by other people. Observability by more than one person is not a defining feature of behavior.

23. Item (a) is an example of a **summary label** because it describes a number of different behaviors that have certain features in common. Item (b) is an example of a **labeling effect** because the students responded to George in terms of the label. Item (c) is also a **labeling effect** because the label influenced the students' reactions toward George, causing him to respond in ways appropriate to the label. *Source: Farina, Allen, and Saul (1966)*

24. Both items (a) and (b) are examples of **behavior** because each item represents a specific activity that Basil engaged in. In item (a), the behavior is mainly covert and observable only to Basil, while in item (b), the behavior is overt and observable by other people.

25. Item (a) is an example of a **summary label** because it describes a number of different behaviors that Ben failed to engage in. Item (b) is an example of an **explanatory fiction** because a summary label, memory, is invoked as a cause for the failure of a behavior to occur.

26. Item (a) is an example of a **summary label** because *love* describes a number of different behaviors having certain common features. Item (b) is an **explanatory fiction** because love, a summary label, is used as a cause for one of the behaviors it describes.

Chapter 1   *Selecting Target Behaviors*

1. This item is an example of the **social-comparison method** because behaviors of the good and ordinary poets were compared. This is the data collection phase because there was no effort to improve the fluency of the poorer poets. This finding suggests that, in training poets, fluency in this type of task be used as a target behavior. See Perkins (1981) for some additional considerations. *Source: Perkins (1981)*

2. This item is an example of the **social-comparison method** because the good and ordinary artists were compared to see how their behaviors differed. This item represents the data collection phase because there was no attempt to train the ordinary group in artistic problem-finding activities. This study suggests that art students should be trained in problem-finding activities as well as in pure technical skills. *Source: Getzels and Csikszentmihalyi (1976)*

3. This item is an example of the **subjective-evaluation method** because the judges evaluated the children's general fire-skill competence. It illustrates the intervention phase because the expert evaluations were conducted before and after the children's target behaviors were changed. The **subjective-evaluation method** used here suggests that the researchers selected worthwhile target behaviors. *Source: Jones, Kazdin, and Haney (1981)*

4. This item is an example of the **subjective-evaluation technique** because the teachers rated the value of the students' behaviors. It illustrates the intervention phase because the teachers rated the value of the students' behaviors after a behavior change had taken place. *Source: Stevenson and Fantuzzo (1986)*

5. This item is an example of the **social-comparison method** because two groups of teenagers were used, one group with conduct disorders and a general group. Behavior comparisons of these two groups indicated that the normal teenagers had better problem-solving skills than the conduct-disordered teenagers. It is an example of the intervention phase because the conduct-disordered teenagers were trained in the target behaviors to a level that exceeded that of the normal teenagers. *Source: Tisdelle and St. Lawrence (1988)*

6. This item is an example of the **criterion-validation method** (a) because an experiment established a cause-effect relationship between a reduction in the target behavior (speeding) and reduction in injury accidents; and (b) because reduction in injury accidents is a well-accepted criterion of accomplishment in the field of traffic safety. *Source: Van Houten, Rolider, Nau, Friedman, Becker, Chalodovsky, and Scherer (1985)*

7. This item is an example of.the **criterion-validation method** because (a) an experiment established a cause-effect relationship between the parents' skills and the children's weight loss; and (b) because weight loss in overweight people is a well-accepted standard of accomplishment. *Source: Israel, Stolmaker, and Andrian (1985)*

8. This item is an example of the **subjective-evaluation method** because the 16 expert women rated the worth or usefulness of the four kinds of criticism-handling behaviors. It illustrates the data collection phase because there was no effort to teach anyone to use the highly evaluated assertive behaviors. This research suggests assertive behaviors are more valuable than either passive responding or aggressive behavior when dealing with criticism. *Source: Frisch and Froberg (1987)*

9. This item is an example of the **criterion-validation method** (a) because a cause-effect relationship was established between the treatment procedures and reduction in school vandalism; and (b) because reductions in school vandalism are generally recognized as a significant standard of accomplishment. *Source: Mayer, Butterworth, Nafpaktitis, and Sulzer-Azaroff (1983)*

10. This item is an example of the **social-comparison method** because the behaviors of happy and unhappy couples were compared. It illustrates the data collection phase because there was no effort to teach the unhappy couples the behaviors performed by the happy couples. This research suggests that the use of rewards and punishments is an ingredient to success in marriage. *Source: Williams (1979)*

11. This item is an example of the **subjective-evaluation method** because the judges rated the competence or effectiveness of the behavior. It is the intervention phase because the behavior was evaluated both before and after the behaviors were changed. The evaluations suggest that the target behaviors selected were competent social skills. *Source: Bornstein, Bach, McFall, Friman, and Lyons (1980)*

12. This item is an example of the **social-comparison method** because two groups of successful and unsuccessful performers were compared in terms of their behaviors. It is the data collection phase because differences in the two groups were merely observed. There was no effort to train the problem couples to increase their social contacts. This study suggests that a variety of social interactions is important to success in marriage. *Source: Beach, Arias, and O'Leary (1986)*

13. This item is an example of the **criterion-validation method** (a) because an experiment was conducted that demonstrated a cause-effect relationship between the package of techniques and

electricity conservation; and (b) because electricity conservation is a standard of accomplishment that environmental experts recognize. *Source: Winett, Leckliter, Chinn, Stahl, and Love (1985)*

14. This item is an example of the **subjective-evaluation method** because the raters identified the value of conversational behaviors. It is an example of the data collection phase because there was no effort to change the behaviors of the conversationalists. *Source: Spitzberg and Cupach (1985)*

15. This item is an example of the **criterion-validation method** (a) because an experiment was conducted that showed a cause-effect relationship between the treatment procedure and a reduction in incontinence; and (b) because reduction in incontinence among the elderly is generally recognized as a significant accomplishment in the field of geriatric care. *Source: Schnelle et al. (1983)*

16. This item is an example of the **subjective-evaluation method** because the audiences at the speeches rated the effectiveness of the public speaking behaviors. It illustrates the intervention phase because the evaluations took place both before and after the behavior was changed. This research suggests that the target behaviors selected were important components of good public speaking. *Source: Fawcett and Miller (1975)*

17. This item is an example of the **criterion-validation method** (a) because an experiment was conducted that found a cause-effect relationship between the SQ3R study method and academic achievement and (b) because academic achievement is a generally accepted standard of student accomplishment. *Source: Grant, Keenan, and Hursh (1980)*

18. This item is an example of the **social-comparison method** because two groups were identified, the general women at the shopping mall and the retarded women. When clothing color selections of these groups were compared, it was found that at first the retarded women differed from the general women in their choice of color combinations. It illustrates the intervention phase because the popular color combinations of the general women were used as performance standards for training the retarded women. *Source: Nutter and Reid (1978)*

19. This item is an example of the **criterion-validation method** (a) because the program experimentally demonstrated to cause a reduction in Steve's thefts; and (b) because theft reduction is a well-accepted standard of desirability in our society. *Source: Rosen and Rosen (1983)*

20. This item is an example of the **social-comparison method** because two groups of eaters were identified and compared, the retarded trainees and the restaurant diners. This illustrates the intervention phase because the eating-error levels of the restaurant diners were used as performance standards for retarded trainees to achieve. *Source: O'Brien and Azrin (1972)*

21. This item illustrates the **subjective-evaluation method** because the judges evaluated the creativity of the students' compositional behavior. It illustrates the intervention phase because the judges evaluated the creativity of the stories both before and after writing behaviors had been modified. *Source: Maloney and Hopkins (1973)*

22. This item is an example of the **criterion-validation method** (a) because the program was effective in reducing excessive caffeine consumption and (b) because excessive caffeine consumption is generally recognized as a health risk. *Source: James, Stirling, and Hampton (1985)*

23. This item is an example of the **social-comparison method**, because the behaviors of two groups of veterans with high and low PTSD problems were compared. It is the data collection phase because there was no effort to increase the positive social interactions of the veterans to see if this would reduce the level of PTSD problems. *Source: Barrett and Mizes (1988)*

24. This item is the **social-comparison method** because the behaviors of rapist and nonrapist men were compared. It is the data collection phase because there was no effort to change the behavior of the rapists to meet the standards of the nonrapists. *Source: Quinsey and Chaplin (1984)*

25. This item is the **subjective-evaluation method** because the children rated the value of the different behaviors they were shown. It is the data collection phase because there was no attempt to train any of the desirable behaviors. *Source: DiLorenzo and Foster (1984)*

Chapter 2   *Positive Reinforcement*

1. This item is an example of **positive reinforcement** because arriving on time produced a dependent consequence (receiving the token), resulting in an increase in the level of attendance. *Source: Paschalis (1987)*

2. This item is an example of **positive reinforcement** because responding that resulted in low noise levels produced a dependent consequence (the radio music) and this procedure increased the amount or duration of low noise levels. *Source: Wilson and Hopkins (1973)*

3. This item is an example of **positive reinforcement** because the novel form constructions (the response) produced a dependent consequence (teacher praise and approval) and this procedure resulted in an increase in the number of novel forms. *Source: Goetz and Baer (1973)*

4. This item is an example of **positive reinforcement** because game playing and other special activities were dependent upon doing CPT, and Carol Ann began doing her CPT more frequently. *Source: Stark, Miller, Plienes, and Drabman (1987)*

5. This item is **not an example of positive reinforcement**. In positive reinforcement, a stimulus is presented dependent on a target behavior and this dependency causes that behavior to increase in frequency. In this item, no stimulus is presented dependent on the target behavior, handing in the assignments. Instead, the stimulus was presented dependent on not handing in assignments.

6. This item is an example of **positive reinforcement** because the slap was a consequence dependent on teasing, and caused teasing to become more frequent.

7. This item is **not an example of positive reinforcement**. Although the boy smiled more while Dr. Arnold was talking to him, talking was not dependent on the smiling response.

8. This item is **not an example of positive reinforcement** because the computer voice presentation was not dependent on buckling the seat belt, the target behavior. It is an example of the use of a rule/instruction to engage in a behavior.

9. This item is an example of **positive reinforcement** because the pay bonus was dependent on the target behavior and the procedure increased the level of the target behavior. *Source: Hermann, de Montes, Dominguez, Montes, and Hopkins (1973)*

10. This item is an example of **positive reinforcement** because the target behavior had a dependent consequence and the procedure caused an increase in the target behaviors. The procedure in this study is called a group contingency, wherein consequences are dependent on the total or average performance of the group as a whole rather than on the behavior of any one person. *Source: Slavin, Wodarski, and Blackburn (1981)*

11. This item is **not an example of positive reinforcement** because there was no response-dependent consequence for the target behavior. The increase in the target behavior was due to rules/instructions to engage in the target behavior, not to a response-dependent consequence. *Source: Jacobs, Bailey, and Crews (1984)*

12. This item is an example of **positive reinforcement** because the tokens were a response-dependent consequence that caused correct responding to increase in frequency. The response-dependent tokens produced more correct responding than response-independent tokens, showing that the response-dependent feature of positive reinforcement was important. *Source: Brigham, Finfrock, Breunig, and Bushell (1972)*

13. This item is **not an example of positive reinforcement**. Although the praise and comments were dependent consequences for the target behavior, there is no mention of an increase in the level of the target behavior.

14. This item is an example of **positive reinforcement** because the tokens were response-dependent consequences of the target behavior, and the procedure caused an increase in the target behavior. *Source: Fjellstedt and Sulzer-Azaroff (1973)*

15. This item is an example of **positive reinforcement** because a consequence was presented dependent on the target behavior, and resulted in an increased level of the behavior.

16. This item is an example of **positive reinforcement** because the paid time off and chance for a trip were dependent on the target behaviors, and caused the level of the target behaviors to increase. *Source: Luthans, Paul, and Taylor (1986)*

17. This item is an example of **positive reinforcement** because the presentation of the children's photographs on the bulletin boards was dependent on the target behavior, and caused the level of the target behavior to increase. *Source: Blount and Stokes (1984)*

18. This item is an example of **positive reinforcement** because the consequences, thank-you letters, were response dependent and caused the target behavior, client visits, to increase in frequency. *Source: Clark, Northrop, and Barkshire (1988)*

19. This item is **not an example of positive reinforcement**. The consequences, praise and admiration, were not dependent on the target behavior.

20. This item is **not an example of positive reinforcement** because there was no stimulus presentation dependent on being on-feet, the target behavior. Instead the stimulus change was dependent on being off-feet, behavior other than the target behavior. In order to say that positive reinforcement has occurred, a stimulus must be presented dependent on the target behavior, not other behavior. *Source: Harris, Johnston, Kelley, and Wolf (1964)*

21. This item is an example of **positive reinforcement** because the disruptive behaviors had a response-dependent consequence, teacher disapproval, and this resulted in their increase. Stimuli and events that seem negative, undesirable, or even painful can sometimes act as positive reinforcers.

22. This item is **not an example of reinforcement**. The increase in the target behavior is due to a rule or instruction to engage in a behavior, not to positive reinforcement. Giving a rule or an instruction to engage in a behavior can sometimes strengthen a behavior, but this strengthening is not due to a response-dependent consequence. Indeed, Ohno's lecture/rules improved the student's performance even when they were presented before the target behavior had occurred. In general, do not classify items in which rules or instructions to engage in the behavior are used as examples of positive reinforcement.

23. This is an example of **positive reinforcement**. Being made to stay after school and wash the blackboards was dependent on the target behavior and caused the level of the target behavior to increase. *Source: Mumford (1982)*

24. This is an example of **positive reinforcement**. The tokens awarded for appropriate nighttime behavior served to increase the rate of those behaviors in five of the six children. *Source: Friedman and Ollendick (1989)*

Chapter 2   *Describing Reinforcers*

---

1. This item is an **unconditioned reinforcer** because food is reinforcing without association with other reinforcers. It is an **extrinsic reinforcer** because good behavior does not automatically produce candy bars. It is a **contrived reinforcer** because candy bars are not typical recurring consequences of good behavior in the natural environment for competent performers, and because they have been added specifically to strengthen weak behavior.

2. This item is a **conditioned reinforcer** because people must learn to be reinforced by well-performed ballet. It is a **social reinforcer** because the reinforcer consists of the behavior of people in staging the performance. It is an **intrinsic reinforcer** because the ballet is automatically "produced" by watching it. It is a **natural reinforcer** because all intrinsic reinforcers are natural reinforcers (i.e., because seeing good ballet is a typical recurring outcome of watching good ballet in the natural environment by competent ballet appreciators).

3. This item is a **conditioned reinforcer** because people must learn to be reinforced by engaging in sports. It is a **social reinforcer** because the reinforcer involves other people. It is an **extrinsic reinforcer** because the opportunity to play hockey is not an automatic consequence of doing homework. It is a **contrived reinforcer** because it is intended to strengthen weak studying behavior. It is an **activity reinforcer** because it involves the opportunity to engage in an activity.

4. This item is an **unconditioned reinforcer** because, for most of us, a kiss does not require association with other reinforcers to be effective as a reinforcer. It is a **social reinforcer** because the reinforcer consists of the behavior of another person. It is an **activity reinforcer** because the reinforcer consists of the opportunity to engage in an activity. It is an **extrinsic reinforcer** because kissing is not an automatic result of making dollar payments. It is a **contrived reinforcer** because the opportunity to kiss and be kissed is not typically dependent on paying for skilled performers (i.e., they typically don't have to pay) and because the opportunity for kissing has been specifically added by the fair organizers to strengthen weak behavior (i.e., paying money).

5. This item is an **unconditioned reinforcer**; kissing does not require association with other reinforcers to be effective as a reinforcer. It is a **social reinforcer**; the reinforcer consists of the behavior of another person. It is an **activity reinforcer**; the reinforcer consists of the opportunity to engage in an activity. It is an **extrinsic reinforcer**; kissing is not an automatic result of being kind to someone. It is a **natural reinforcer**; the opportunity to kiss someone or to be kissed by someone is a recurring consequence typically dependent on a competent performer's kind behavior.

6. This item is a **conditioned reinforcer** because music is a learned reinforcer, an acquired taste. It is a **social reinforcer** because a musical performance consists of the behavior of people. It is an **activity reinforcer** because the reinforcer consists of the opportunity to engage in an activity, listening to music. It is an **extrinsic reinforcer** because the performance of a musical score is not an automatic result of composing the score. (*Note:* if the reinforcer, were defined as the musical score as it exists on paper, this would be an intrinsic reinforcer, because the score would be an automatically produced consequence of composing). It is a **natural reinforcer** because musical performances are typical recurring consequences of the behavior of skilled composers.

7. This item is a **conditioned reinforcer** because people must learn to be reinforced by points. It is a **token reinforcer** because its effectiveness is through its association with other reinforcers. It is an **extrinsic reinforcer** because points are not an automatic result of dishwashing. It is a **contrived** reinforcer because it is intended to strengthen weak behavior.

8. This item is a **conditioned reinforcer** because arrival at a particular destination is a learned reinforcer, influenced by association with other reinforcers available at the destination. It is an **extrinsic reinforcer** because arrival at a given destination is not an automatic consequence of driving. It is a **natural reinforcer** because arrival at an intended destination is a typical recurring consequence of the behavior of competent drivers.

9. This item is a **conditioned reinforcer** because one learns to be reinforced by invitations to coffee. It is a **social reinforcer** because the reinforcer consists of the behavior of another person. It is an **extrinsic reinforcer** because being invited for coffee is not an automatic consequence of smiling. It is a **natural reinforcer** because invitations to do things are a typical recurring consequence for skilled smilers. It is an **activity reinforcer** because it involves engaging in an activity.

10. This item is a **conditioned reinforcer** because a university degree obtains its reinforcing effectiveness through association with other reinforcers. It is a **social reinforcer** because the awarding of a degree consists of the behavior of other people. It is an **extrinsic reinforcer** because the awarding of a degree is not an automatic consequence of engaging in educational activities. It is a **contrived reinforcer** because receiving a degree is a nonrecurring consequence that is not typically dependent on the behavior of competent performers (they already either have degrees or don't need them), and because it is a consequence added specifically in order to strengthen the weak behaviors of those in training.

11. This item is a **conditioned reinforcer** because people must learn the virtues of measuring cups. It is an **extrinsic reinforcer** because successful inventions are not automatic results of engaging in inventive activities. It is a **natural reinforcer** because successful inventions are typical and recurring consequences of the behavior of skilled inventors.

12. This item is an **unconditioned reinforcer** because food does not require association with other reinforcers to be effective as a reinforcer. It is an **extrinsic reinforcer** because food is not an automatic consequence of putting weight on one's legs (though the reverse is true). It is a **contrived reinforcer** because food is not a typical recurring consequence of physical-therapy activities, and because the food is a consequence specifically added to strengthen a learner's weak behavior.

13. This item is a **conditioned reinforcer** because books acquire their reinforcing function through association with other reinforcers. It is an **extrinsic reinforcer** because obtaining a book is not an automatic result of asking librarians for help. It is a **natural reinforcer** because obtaining desired books is a typical and recurring consequence of competent help-seekers, not a consequence specifically added to strengthen weak behavior.

14. This item is a **conditioned reinforcer** because people must learn about the reinforcing value of money. It is a **token reinforcer** because money gains its reinforcing effectiveness through exchange for other reinforcers, the things money can buy. It is an extrinsic reinforcer because money is not an automatic result of cleaning. It is a **contrived reinforcer** because money is not a typical recurring consequence of cleaning one's living space on the part of competent and mature individuals and because money is a consequence specifically added to strengthen weak behavior.

15. This item is a **conditioned reinforcer** because people must learn the reinforcing value of clean living spaces. It is an **intrinsic reinforcer** because cleanliness is an automatic consequence of cleaning. It is a **natural reinforcer** because cleanliness is a typical and recurring consequence for cleaning by competent cleaners.

16. This item is a **conditioned reinforcer** because good grades must be associated with other reinforcers in order to gain reinforcing effectiveness. It is an **extrinsic reinforcer** because good grades are not automatic consequences of reading novels. It is a **contrived reinforcer** because good grades are nonrecurring consequences not typically received by competent appreciators of novels, and because good grades are consequences added specifically in order to strengthen weak behavior.

17. This analysis is the same as for item 16, except that this is a **natural reinforcer** because the content of novels is a typical recurring consequence that reinforces the behavior of reading novels on the part of competent appreciators of novels. It is an **extrinsic reinforcer** because reading novels does not always automatically produce reinforcing content, as in the case of poorly written, trashy novels.

Chapter 2 *Making Positive Reinforcement Effective*

1. A problem in this item is that Mr. Kersey's **failure to use instructions** specifying the relationship between the desired behavior and its consequences probably decreased the effectiveness of the honor roll reinforcer. Also, the 1-day **delay of reinforcement** may have decreased the effectiveness of reinforcer, especially because no stimuli were used to bridge the delay between the question-answering and the appearance of the names on the honor roll. If Mr. Kersey had kept his tally on a board all the students could see, it would have bridged the delay. Finally, the students' names merely appeared on the honor roll. Mr. Kersey did not back up this visibility with extra attention and praise for the honored children, and thereby decreased the effectiveness of the honor roll as a reinforcer.

2. A problem with this item is that the effectiveness of the reinforcement involved in the sales staff consultation was diminished by an increase in the **energy required to execute the response**. This situation could be altered by moving Mr. Durer to the same floor as the sales staff.

3. This item is an example of a reinforcer contrast effect, specifically a **negative contrast effect**. In a negative contrast effect, a decrease in the quality or quantity of a reinforcer decreases the effectiveness of the reinforcer compared to what that effectiveness would have been had there been no reduction in the quality or quantity of the reinforcer. Because Adele and Fred were superior entertainers, the reinforcing effectiveness of the entertainment that followed them was lessened because there was a decrease in the quality of the reinforcer of their entertainment relative to the entertainment that followed. A solution to this problem would be for Adele and Fred to close the show, to be the last act presented, which was done. *Source: Satchell (1987).*

4. A problem in this illustration is that Bob and Eileen gave extra attention to June before she was to meet someone, possibly **satiating June on attention as a reinforcer**. Bob and June instead might have tried using mild social deprivation. For example, on the morning when June was scheduled to meet someone, Bob and Eileen might have mildly deprived June of the attention they normally gave her, so as to make attention a more effective reinforcer.

5. A problem in this item is an **insufficient variety of reinforcers**. Inclusion of a number of different types of toys and materials in the play area would have increased its reinforcing effectiveness.

6. The problem with this item is the **low amount of the reinforcer** Jim's parents used. The effectiveness of his parents' reinforcer was much less than that of Tamara's parents' reinforcer, because of the difference in the amount of the reinforcer.

7. This item is an example of the effectiveness of reinforcement being impaired by a source of **extraneous reinforcement**. The parents' social reinforcers for Lionel's grammar had to compete with the peer reinforcers for incorrect language. This competing source of social reinforcement diminished the effectiveness of the parents' positive reinforcement procedure. It is difficult to suggest how the parents could alter the reinforcement practices of Lionel's peer group, except for them to encourage him to interact with peers who would reinforce correct speech, and to support educational programs designed to teach children to use language correctly.

8. A problem in this item is a **failure to make use of predictive conditioned reinforcers**. In this item, nothing is mentioned about what the points could be exchanged for. If the points were exchangeable for desired items (e.g., cigarettes, food snacks, or toiletries) or privileges (e.g., opportunities to view films, opportunities for early parole hearings), then the points would have predicted other reinforcers and would have been more effective.

9. The problem in this item is a reinforcement contrast effect in the form of a **negative contrast effect**. Scheduling the fascinating novel first decreased the reinforcing effectiveness of the moderately interesting play and that of the boring literary criticism. This illustration should be altered by scheduling the criticism first, the play second, and the novel last. This sequence would make it more likely for positive contrast effects to occur.

Chapter 2 *Usage of Terms*

1. This item is **correct**. It means that a procedure of attendance-dependent stimulus presentation caused Barb's attendance to increase.

2. This item is **correct**. Positive reinforcement can refer to a stimulus that, when presented dependent on a response, causes an increase in the level of the response. It would also be correct to say that the positive reinforcers for Barb's attendance at work were presentations of comments of praise.

3. This item is **correct**. It means that presentations of cereal to Randall were dependent on his vocalizations and this caused the level of his vocalizations to increase.

4. This item is **correct**. It means that cereal was made dependent on Randall's vocalizations, causing an increase in the level of those vocalizations.

5. This item is **incorrect** because to reinforce, the verb must apply to a behavior, not to a person. For example, if we say that Belgian chocolates are reinforcers for Alex, does this mean they will strengthen any behavior, that he will lie, steal, and murder for response-dependent Belgian chocolates? These doubts about Alex's moral behavior are politely avoided if we speak of reinforced behaviors rather than a reinforced Alex.

6. This item is **correct**. A positive reinforcement procedure is response-dependent presentation of a suspected reinforcer, which occurred in this item.

7. This item is **correct**. It means that cartoon presentation was dependent on the children's correct identification of colors and this caused a strengthening of these correct identifications.

8. This item is so nice to hear that it is a shame to identify it as **incorrect**. However, it is incorrect, because it does not specify a reinforced behavior. Another problem is that it is not specific about what part of *you* is reinforcing. Is everything about the person referred to reinforcing? Probably not. It would be better to specify what aspects of the person are reinforcing or, when

things have developed this far, to abandon precise behavioral language in favor of ambiguous romantic forms of expression.

Chapter 3 *DRO, DRI, and Extinction*

---

1. This item is an example of **extinction** because the victim's ignoring of Gail's attacks functioned to withhold reinforcement for previously reinforced attacks, and caused the target behavior to occur less often. *Source: Martin and Foxx (1973)*

2. This item is an example of **extinction** because a stimulus change (no nipple to a nipple) that had formerly been dependent on head turns was no longer dependent on head turns, and this caused the frequency of head turns to decrease. *Source: Siqueland (1968)*

3. This item is an example of **DRO** because the praise and stars were dependent on the nonoccurrence of the target behavior and this caused a reduction in the level of the target behavior. *Source: Allen and Harris (1966)*

4. This item is an example of **forgetting**. The weakening of the response is due to the passage of time during which there was no opportunity for the response to occur.

5. This item is an example of **DRI**. A stimulus change was dependent on a response (i.e., sitting), causing a decrease in the level of the target behavior (squirming on the floor). *Source: Twardosz and Sajwaj (1972)*

6. This item is an example of a **DRI** procedure because a stimulus change was dependent on a response (arms down) that was incompatible with the target behavior, and this procedure caused the level of the target behavior to diminish. *Source: Zlutnick, Mayville, and Moffat (1975)*

7. This item is an example of **extinction** because a response-dependent consequence of vomiting (being sent to the dorm) was withheld for the response, and this caused the response to decline in frequency to zero. In the real life case, this item based on extinction was actually combined with positive reinforcement: Praise and M&M candies were dependent on not vomiting. *Source: Wolf, Birnbrauer, Williams, and Lawler (1965)*

8. This item is **not an example of DRO, DRI, or extinction**. It is not DRO or DRI because there was no reinforcement of the absence of the target behavior or behavior incompatible with the target behavior. It is not extinction because there is no indication of a decline in the level of the target behavior.

9. This item is **not an example of DRO, DRI, or extinction**. In DRO, DRI, and extinction there must be a decline in the level of the target behavior. In this example, the level of the target behavior was unchanged. Had head-to-table hitting been the target behavior in this item, it would be an example of DRI. *Source: Young and Wincze (1974)*

10. This item is an example of **DRO** because the praise and hugs were dependent on the absence of the target behavior, and caused the elimination of self-exposures. *Source: Lutzker (1974)*

11. This item is an example of **forgetting** because the weakening of the response is due to the passage of time during which the response did not occur.

12. This item is an example of **extinction** because the stimulus change (i.e., door closed to door

open) that had previously been dependent on the target behavior was withheld, thus causing a decline in the level of the target behavior.

13. This item is **not an example of DRO, DRI, or extinction**. It is not DRO or DRI because there was no reinforcement dependent on the absence of the target behavior or upon behaviors incompatible with the target behavior. It is not extinction because a stimulus changes from television and radio to no television and radio were dependent on the target behavior. In extinction, no stimulus change is dependent on the response on extinction. This is an example of punishment.

14. This item is an example of **DRI** because praise was dependent on a response incompatible with the target behavior, and the procedure caused a reduction in the level of the target behavior. *Source: Lovaas, Freitag, Gold, and Kassorla (1965)*

15. This item is **not an example of DRO, DRI, or extinction**. It is not DRO or DRI because there was no reinforcement dependent on the absence of the target response or upon behavior incompatible with the target response. This is not extinction because the target behavior produced a stimulus change, being sent to the principal. This is an example of punishment.

16. These items are examples of **DRO** because in each case a stimulus change was dependent on the absence of the target behavior, causing the level of the target behavior to decline. *Source: Repp, Deitz, and Speir (1974)*

17. This item is an example of **forgetting** because the weakening of the response occurred due to the passage of time during which there was no opportunity for the response to occur.

18. This item is an example of **extinction** because the stimulus change (a change from a high-demand to a low-demand situation) that had been dependent on the target behavior in the past was withheld, and this caused the level of the target behavior to diminish. Note that being placed in the seat belt was not dependent on Bob's aggression. *Source: Carr, Newsom, and Binkoff (1980)*

19. This item is an example of **extinction** because the attention and medication reinforcers for the asthma attacks were withdrawn, resulting in a decrease in the duration of the attacks. *Source: Neisworth and Moore (1972)*

20. This item is an example of **DRO** because a stimulus change, no food to food, was dependent on the absence of the pica behavior, thus eliminating the pica behavior. *Source: Finney, Russo, and Cataldo (1982)*

21. This item is **not an example of DRO, DRI, or extinction** because there is no mention of a decline in the level of the target behavior.

22. This item is an example of **DRO** because a stimulus change was dependent on the absence of toe walking and this reduced the level of toe walking. *Source: Hobbs, Altman, and Halldin (1980)*

23. This item is **not an example of DRO, DRI, or extinction**. It is not DRO or DRI because there was no reinforcement of the absence of the target behavior or of incompatible behavior. It is not extinction because the vomiting response produced a stimulus change from no required cleaning to required cleaning. In extinction the target behavior produces no stimulus change. This is an example of punishment.

24. This item is an example of **DRO** because a stimulus change was dependent on the absence of stealing food and this caused the level of food stealing to decline. *Source: Page, Stanley, Richman, Deal, and Iwata (1983)*

25. This item is an example of **DRO** because a stimulus change was dependent on the absence of rumination and this caused the level of rumination to decline. *Source: Conrin, Pennypacker, Johnston, and Rast (1982)*

26. This item is an example of **DRO** because a stimulus change (from no opportunity for a walk to an opportunity) was dependent on the absence of seizures and this decreased the level of the seizures. *Source: Burgio, Tice, and Brown (1985)*

27. This item is an example of **extinction** because a consequence (teacher attention) that had previously been dependent on the target behavior was withheld and resulted in a decline in the frequency of the behavior. *Source: Hart, Allen, Buell, Harris, and Wolf (1964)*

28. This item is an example of **DRI** because a stimulus change from no praise and no tokens to praise and tokens was dependent on behavior incompatible with the target behaviors, and caused a reduction in the level of the target behaviors. While clearly not a useful behavior change procedure, it is still an example of DRI. *Source: Kelly and Bushell (1987)*

29. This item is an example of **DRI** because the stimulus change from no light and no praise to light and praise was dependent on mouth-closed behavior incompatible with the target behavior, and because the level of the target behavior was reduced. *Source: Parker et al. (1984)*

30. This item is an example of **DRO** because the stimulus change from no extra-minute-earned to an extra-minute-earned was dependent on the absence of the disruptive behaviors and it reduced the level of these behaviors. *Source: Allen, Gottselig, and Boylan (1982)*

31. This item is an example of **extinction**. Wearing the tubes acted to withhold the stimuli that Rob's bites had previously produced, causing the target behavior to decline. It is an example of sensory extinction because the sensory consequences of the response were removed. *Source: Luiselli (1988)*

32. This item is **not an example of DRO, DRI, or extinction**. It is not DRO or DRI because there is no reinforcement of the absence of the target behavior or of incompatible behavior. It is not extinction because the target behavior produced a dependent stimulus change. In extinction, the target behavior produces no stimulus change. This is an example of punishment.

Chapter 3 *Making Extinction, DRO, and DRI Effective*

1. The problem here is a **failure to use deprivation**. Mild food deprivation, achieved through skipping lunch, would increase the reinforcing effectiveness of the edible treats.

2. A problem here is the **long delay of reinforcement** due to setting the required time interval for reinforcement at such a high value, 10 years. Starting out with a relatively small time interval and gradually increasing the interval size would make the DRO procedure more effective.

3. A problem here is with the **nature of the reinforced behavior when using DRO**. Although Hamlet's talk of his plans to murder his uncle is not the undesired target behavior, it is clearly worse than the target behavior, mere talk of ghosts. Ophelia would be well-advised instead to use a DRI procedure in which she reinforces specific desirable behaviors incompatible with talk of both ghosts and murder.

4. A problem with this example is that the **amount of reinforcement is excessive**. Reinforcers, whether praise, edibles, or tokens, should be provided in sufficient amounts to reinforce the response properly, but in amounts small enough to prevent satiation. A half hour of praise

would be too great an amount of reinforcement because it would likely reduce the effectiveness of Peter's praise due to satiation.

5. A problem with this use of DRI is a **failure to use instructions** to specify the desired behavior. If Rachel had been diplomatic and polite in explaining what Dave stood to gain through appropriate dress, the desired response would be more likely achieved.

6. A problem with this item concerns the **predictiveness of the conditioned reinforcers,** the stars. Because the stars were not exchangeable for anything, they did not predict other reinforcers. This procedure could be improved by making the stars exchangeable for material reinforcers or privileges. The stars might also be made more effective by associating them with teacher attention, such as if Sandy announced daily those students who had earned the most stars and gave those students extra attention.

7. In this item, there is a problem with **variety of reinforcers.** Even if the baked beans were a powerful reinforcer for Roger's behavior, adding other types of edible reinforcers would be likely to increase the overall effectiveness of the DRO procedure.

8. A problem here is the **response energy.** By assigning a large quantity of work, Ted has made it less likely for the DRI procedure to be effective. If he reduced the initial size of the essays, more students would be likely to complete them and benefit from the DRI procedure.

9. A problem with this item is that a **momentary DRO procedure is being used instead of a whole-interval DRO procedure.** The momentary DRO procedure is not as effective in reducing the level of behavior as is the whole-interval DRO method.

10. A problem with this illustration is that Sally **did not combine extinction with positive reinforcement for a desirable alternative response**. It is mentioned that Marvin rarely made complimentary remarks about Sally, indicating that he did sometimes engage in a desirable alternative response that could be reinforced, making the extinction procedure more effective.

11. A problem with this item is that the cheers from Lionel's classmates served as a source of **extraneous reinforcement** for the response, making the extinction procedure unlikely to work. If extinction were to be used successfully in this case, the classmates would have to be enlisted to cooperate in putting Lionel's airplane throwing on extinction.

12. A problem with this illustration is that Kathryn **did not provide instructions** specifying to Benny that she would no longer pay attention to his screaming after his minor injuries. This step would make extinction more rapid.

Chapter 4 *Punishment*

1. This item is an example of **punishment** because a stimulus change from no required activity to required activity was dependent on the target behavior, and caused the level of that behavior to decline. It is an example of a **habit-reversal** activity punisher because the required activity was a response opposite to the undesired response. *Source: Miltenberger, Fuqua, and McKinley (1985)*

2. This item is an example of **punishment** because a stimulus change (being sent to his room), was dependent upon Peter's objectionable behaviors and reduced their frequency. It is an example of **exclusionary timeout** because Peter was temporarily excluded from the situation in which the objectionable behaviors occurred. *Source: Hawkins, Peterson, Schweid, and Bijou (1966)*

3. This item is **not an example of punishment** because no stimulus change was dependent upon the target behaviors. The reduction in behavior was due to instructions, not to punishment.

4. This item is an example of **punishment** because a stimulus change (token loss) was dependent upon rule breaking and reduced the frequency of rule breaking. This item is an example of **response cost** because it consisted of the removal of previously earned reinforcers (the tokens). *Source: Upper (1973)*

5. This item is an example of **punishment**; a stimulus change from no required activity to required face cleansing was dependent on the target behavior and caused its level to be reduced. This item is an example of **restitutional overcorrection** because the activity punisher served to produce facial cleanliness, an outcome opposite to that produced by the target behavior. *Source: Jenner (1984)*

6. This item is **not an example of punishment**; the stimulus change (token loss) was not dependent on the target behaviors or any other behaviors. The token fines were response-independent. The method in this item would not be effective and is included here only to highlight the critical features of punishment.

7. This item is an example of **punishment**; a stimulus change from no scolding to scolding was dependent on Cecil's hitting the door, and this procedure caused hitting to be eliminated. This item is an example of a reprimand.

8. This item is **not an example of punishment** because no stimulus change was dependent on hitting the door. Even though the target behavior was eliminated, this result was not due to a response-dependent stimulus change. Instead, the elimination of the response was due to extinction, in which the reinforcement (buzz elimination) was no longer dependent upon the target behavior. In punishment, response weakening is due to a response-dependent stimulus change. In extinction, response weakening is due to the absence of a response-dependent stimulus change.

9. This item is an example of **punishment**; a stimulus change from no required activity to required jaw exercise was dependent on the target behavior and caused the behavior to be eliminated. This item is an example of a **habit reversal** punisher because the activity punisher was engaging in a response opposite to the undesirable response. *Source: Rosenbaum and Ayllon (1981)*

10. This item is **not an example of punishment**; no mention is made of a decrease in the level of the target behavior. However, in the actual study, the number of directory assistance calls made declined, making this an example of response-cost punishment. *Source: McSweeny (1978)*

11. This item is an example of **punishment** because the elderly lady's waves were dependent upon Dave's waves and caused them to occur less often. Even apparently polite and friendly gestures can function as punishers, but this example is notable for its atypicality: Waves usually act as reinforcers rather than punishers.

12. This item is an example of **punishment**; a stimulus change (no required activity to required hand movements) was dependent on the target behavior and this produced a decrease in the level of the target behavior. This item is an example of **positive-practice overcorrection** because the activity punisher was engaging in a desirable alternative to the target behavior. *Source: Foxx and Azrin (1973)*

13. This item is an example of **punishment**; a stimulus change (no ammonia smell to an ammonia smell) was dependent on the target behavior and eliminated the target behavior. This item is an example of **physical punishment** because the smell of ammonia is an unconditioned punisher that does not need to be paired with other punishers to act as a punisher. *Source: Singh (1979)*

14. This item is an example of **punishment**; a stimulus change (point loss), was dependent upon speech disfluencies and caused speech disfluencies to decline in frequency. This item is a **response-cost** procedure because it consisted of the permanent removal of previously awarded reinforcers (the points). *Source: Siegel, Lenske, and Broen (1969)*

15. This item is **not an example of punishment**. Although the target behavior declined, a response-dependent stimulus change did not cause the decline. Instead, the decline in thumb sucking was due to instructions specifying that Maybelline must not suck her thumb.

16. This item is an example of **punishment** because a stimulus change (no required exercise to required exercise) was dependent upon the target behaviors and reduced their frequency. This procedure, called contingent exercise, is an example of the use of an **arbitrary activity punisher** because the required activity did not produce an outcome that was functionally opposite to the target behavior; there was no logical connection between the target behavior and the required activity. *Source: Luce, Delquadri, and Hall (1980)*

17. This item is **not an example of punishment** because no stimulus change was dependent on the response. The decline in Glenda's letter writing was due to extinction, in which response reduction is due to the absence of a response-dependent stimulus change.

18. This item is an example of **punishment** because a stimulus change from no required activity to required relaxation was dependent on the target behaviors, and reduced their frequency. This item is a **restitutional overcorrection procedure** because the target behavior and the activity punisher were functionally opposite: The outcome of the required activity was opposite to that of the undesirable behaviors. *Source: Webster and Azrin (1973)*

19. This item is an example of **punishment**; a stimulus change (the token fine), was dependent upon crying, and reduced the frequency of crying. This is a **response-cost** procedure, because the punisher was the permanent removal of previously earned reinforcers (the tokens). This procedure was also combined with token and social reinforcement for smiling. *Source: Reisinger (1972)*

20. This item is **not an example of punishment**. In punishment, a stimulus change is dependent on a behavior. In this illustration, there was no stimulus change dependent on the target behavior. Instead, a stimulus change was dependent on the absence of the target behavior. This item is an example of a DRO procedure.

21. This item is an example of **punishment**; a stimulus change from no required activity to required fist clenching was dependent on the target behavior and caused the target behavior to be eliminated. This item is an example of a **habit reversal** punisher because the activity punisher was the opposite of the target behavior. *Source: Tarnowski, Rosen, McGrath, and Drabman (1987)*

22. This item is an example of **punishment**; a stimulus change from food to no food was dependent on the target behaviors and caused a decrease in the frequency of the target behaviors. This item is an example of **nonexclusionary timeout** because the punisher was the withdrawal of food reinforcement for a specified period of time. *Source: Barton, Guess, Garcia, and Baer (1970)*

23. This item is an example of **punishment**; stimulus changes (a warning reprimand and being sent behind a room divider) were dependent on the target behaviors and caused a reduction in them. This item is an example of **exclusionary timeout** because Celia was briefly removed from the situation in which the target behaviors had occurred. It is also an example of the use of **reprimands** because the warnings were verbal response-dependent punishers. *Source: Barton, Brulle, and Repp (1987)*

24. This item is an example of **punishment** because a stimulus change from no required activity to required practice was dependent on the target behavior and reduced that behavior. This item is

an example of **positive-practice overcorrection** because the required activity punisher was to engage in an appropriate alternative to the punished response. *Source: Strauss, Rubinoff, and Atkeson (1983)*

25. This item is an example of **punishment**; a stimulus change from ribbon to no ribbon was dependent on the target behaviors and caused the target behaviors to be reduced. This item is an example of **nonexclusionary timeout** because the punisher was the temporary withdrawal of opportunities for reinforcement for a specified period of time. *Source: Foxx and Shapiro (1978)*

26. This item is **not an example of punishment** because no mention was made of a decrease in some measure of the target behavior.

27. This item is an example of **punishment**; a stimulus change from no mouth washing to mouth washing was dependent on the target behavior and caused it to be reduced. This item is an example of **restitutional overcorrection** because the punisher was an activity (brushing of the teeth and gums with mouthwash), that produced a clean mouth, an outcome functionally opposite to the outcome the undesirable behavior produced. *Source: Foxx and Azrin (1973)*

28. This item is an example of **punishment**; a stimulus change (no required activity to required ball play) was dependent on the target behavior and decreased it. This item is an example of an **arbitrary activity punisher** because the activity punisher was not logically related to the target behavior. *Source: Krivacek and Powell (1978)*

29. This item is an example of **punishment**; a stimulus change (making the curfew earlier) was dependent upon late arrivals and caused a reduction in late arrivals. This item is an example of **nonexclusionary timeout** because the punisher was the temporary withdrawal of the opportunity for reinforcers for a specified period of time. This type of response-consequence relationship is called a group contingency because consequences to the entire group are dependent on the responses of individual group members. *Source: Alexander, Corbett, and Smigel (1976)*

30. This item is an example of **punishment**; a stimulus change (removal to an empty room) was dependent on the target behaviors, and caused the target behaviors to be reduced. This item is an example of **exclusionary timeout** because the punisher was removal of William to a less reinforcing situation. *Source: Vaccaro (1988)*

31. This item is **not an example of punishment**. The drug was administered in the morning whether or not Martin had been aggressive. Even if the drug had been administered dependent upon Martin's aggression, the behavior-drug dependency would not be the cause of the reduction in aggression, since the drug would diminish the aggression whether it had been administered dependent on or independent of the aggression.

32. This item is an example of **punishment** because a stimulus change from no ice to ice was dependent on the target behavior. This item is an example of a **physical punisher** because the punishing effects of cold ice are unconditioned. *Source: Blount, Drabman, Wilson, and Stewart (1982)*

33. This item is an example of **punishment**; a stimulus change from no required activity to required word repetition was dependent on the target behavior and caused it to decline. This item is an example of **positive-practice overcorrection** because the activity punisher was an appropriate alternative to the undesirable punished response. *Source: Singh, Singh, and Winton (1984)*

34. This item is an example of **punishment**; a stimulus change from no required activity to required work was dependent on the target behavior and reduced the target behavior. This item is an example of an **arbitrary-activity punisher** because there was no logical relationship between the undesired-behavior activity punisher. *Source: Carstens (1982)*

Chapter 4   *Making Punishment Effective*

1. In this example, Bruce's father **did not reinforce an alternative response**. It might have been more effective if Bruce's father had given Bruce a toy he could play with every time he touched the unicorn, and then reinforced toy play.

2. This example demonstrates a **lack of consistency**. Punishment, like reinforcement, is most effective if it consistently follows the undesirable response.

3. This example demonstrates how **instructions** can be helpful. Had the day-care workers told the children what was in the storeroom and why they were not allowed to play there, the procedure may have been more effective.

4. This example demonstrates the **reinforcing effects of attention**. Because Julie received little attention at home, any attention at school, even negative, served to reinforce her undesirable behavior. A timeout procedure may have been more effective with Julie.

5. John's **long history of nonpunishment** is a problem in this example. Had John's inappropriate behaviors in the past not gone unpunished, he may have responded more quickly to the punishers at his new school.

6. In this example, the **punisher lacks variety**. Withdrawal of exercise time was the only punisher used.

7. In this example, the problem is the **delay** between the occurrence of the behavior and the delivery of the punisher. Two-year-old children are too young for such a delay to be an effective procedure.

8. In this example, the **punisher is too weak**. Had Jillian been grounded for the whole week rather than for just one night, the procedure might have been more effective.

9. In this example, Tommy's parents failed to carry through with their threats. The loud talk and explanation did **not predict other punishers**.

10. This example demonstrates a **contrast effect**. The mild punishers used in Joy's new school would have had more effect on her behavior if she had not had previous experience with more severe punishers.

Chapter 5   *Escape and Avoidance*

1. This item is an example of **avoidance**; a stimulus change from no grooming requirement to a grooming requirement was dependent on the failure of the target behavior to occur and this dependency strengthened the target behavior. *Source: Foxx (1976)*

2. This item is **not an example of escape or avoidance conditioning**. It is not avoidance because the stimulus change from no permitted grooming to permitted grooming was dependent on the target behavior, not the failure of the target behavior to occur. In avoidance conditioning, the stimulus change is dependent on the absence of the target behavior, not on the target behavior. It is not escape because stimulus presentation rather than stimulus removal was dependent on the target behavior. This illustration is an example of positive reinforcement.

3. This item is an example of **escape conditioning**; removal of the buzz stimulus was dependent on the target behavior of assuming an upright posture and this procedure increased the level of the target behavior. This item is not an example of avoidance, because there is no mention of an increase in the level of the target behavior in the absence of the buzz. *Source: Azrin, Rubin, O'Brien, Ayllon, and Roll (1968)*

4. This item is **not an example of escape conditioning or avoidance conditioning**. In this item, *presentation* of the music stimulus was dependent on the target behavior and this method increased the level of the target behavior. In escape conditioning, *removal* of a stimulus is dependent on the target behavior, while in avoidance conditioning, a stimulus change is dependent on the failure of the target behavior to occur. If assuming an upright posture terminated the music and this increased the duration of time that an upright posture was maintained, this illustration would have been an example of escape conditioning.

5. This item is an example of **avoidance**; a stimulus change from no monster visit to a monster visit was dependent on the absence of the target behavior and caused strengthening of the target behavior.

6. This item is **not an example of avoidance or escape** because there was no stimulus change dependent on the target behavior. The strengthening of the target behavior was due to instructions, rather than to a response-consequence dependency.

7. This item is an example of **avoidance**; a stimulus change from normal prices to doubled prices was dependent on the failure of the target behavior to occur and this procedure strengthened the target behavior. *Source: Winkler (1971)*

8. This item is an example of **avoidance**; a stimulus change from no manual guidance to manual guidance was dependent on the failure of the target behavior to occur and this procedure strengthened the target behavior. *Source: Foxx (1977)*

9. This item is **an example of neither escape nor avoidance**. The stimulus change from no yelling to yelling was not dependent on the target behavior, because the yelling occurred no matter what Cinder did. Although Cinder's behavior did increase in strength, this increase was not due to a response-dependent stimulus change, and therefore, is not an example of escape or avoidance.

10. This item is an example of **avoidance** conditioning; a stimulus change from no nagging to nagging was dependent on the failure of the target behavior to occur and this procedure strengthened the target behavior. This item also involved escape conditioning, because once Joe was being nagged, he could have terminated nagging by engaging in the target behaviors. However, the increase in Joe's target behaviors was measured before any nagging took place, so this item is best interpreted as an example of avoidance. *Source: Fichter, Wallace, Liberman, and Davis (1976)*

11. This item is an example of **neither avoidance** nor escape because there is a decrease in the level of the target behavior. Escape and avoidance both are response-strengthening procedures, not response-weakening procedures. This illustration is an example of punishment. *Source: Le Boeuf (1979)*

12. This item is an example of **avoidance**; a stimulus change from warm to cold feet was dependent on the absence of the target behavior and this procedure increased the level of the target behavior.

13. This item is an example of **escape**; removal of the shock was dependent upon the target behavior and strengthened the target behavior. *Source: Ince (1969)*

14. This item is an example of **avoidance**; a stimulus change from no late-night call to a late-night call was dependent on the absence of the target behavior and strengthened the target behavior of locking the door. *Source: Hughey (1982)*

15. This item is **not an example of avoidance or escape** because there is a decrease in the level of the target behavior. Escape and avoidance cause increases in some measure of the target behavior, not decreases. This is an example of punishment. *Source: Barrett, Staub, and Sisson (1983)*

16. This item is an example of **avoidance**; the consequence, a large electricity bill, was dependent on the failure of the target behavior to occur and this procedure increased the frequency of the target behavior.

17. This item is **neither an example of avoidance nor escape**. The increase in the level of the target behavior in this item was due to instructions, rather than to response-dependent stimulus changes.

18. This item is an example of **avoidance** because the stimulus change from no-louder tone to a louder tone was dependent on the absence of the target behavior (getting up to flip the switch), and because this procedure increased the level of the target behavior. This item is not an example of escape conditioning. Although flipping the switch terminated the first tone, this dependency was insufficient to strengthen the target behavior. Allan's switch flipping was not due to escape from the moderately loud tone, but to avoidance of the very loud tone. *Source: Hansen (1979)*

19. This item is an example of **escape**; termination of the sit-in was dependent on the target behavior and the procedure increased the level of the target behavior.

20. This item is an example of **escape**; removal of the tone was dependent on the target behavior and this procedure strengthened the target behavior when the tone came on. This item has an element of avoidance, because a stimulus change from no tone to a tone was dependent upon the absence of the target behavior. However, it is not indicated whether the level of the target behavior increased when the tone was not present. *Source: Stalonas and Johnson (1979)*

21. This item is an example of **escape** conditioning; removal of the tone was dependent on the target behavior and this procedure increased the level of the target behavior. *Source: Azrin and Powell (1969)*

22. This item is an example of **avoidance**; a stimulus change from no point loss to point loss was dependent on the absence of the target behavior and this procedure strengthened the target behavior. *Source: Semb, Conyers, Spencer, and Sanchez Sosa (1975)*

23. This item is an example of **escape**; removal of the aversive activity (sitting on the toilet), was dependent on the target behavior and the method strengthened the target behavior. This item is also an example of **avoidance**, because a stimulus change from no required toilet sitting to required sitting was dependent on the failure of the target behavior to occur and this procedure strengthened the target behavior. *Source: Rolider and Van Houten (1985b)*

Chapter 5   *Making Escape and Avoidance Conditioning Effective*

1. In this example, the children at the Not-on-the-Ball Day-Care Center were not informed about what would happen following quiet behavior. **Instructions** can help to increase the effectiveness of timeout procedures.

2. In this example, Matilda's mother was **inconsistent** with her use of reprimands. Consistency of the aversive consequences can help to make avoidance training more effective.

3. In this example, Jill learned that she could avoid doing her homework by complaining of illness. Her parents should have **reinforced alternative behavior** on Jill's part.

4. In this example, Biff was being punished for engaging in the desirable avoidance response, being polite. Avoidance training is more effective when **avoidance responses are not punished.**

5. In this example, the problem is the difference in **time interval** between the two classes. In one class, the response postponed the aversive event, being called on, for the entire class period. In the other class, the response postponed the aversive event for only 10 minutes.

6. In this example, Ms. Farrara's students had a **history of response-independent aversive stimulation.** This item is an example of learned helplessness.

Chapter 6   *Shaping*

1. This item is an example of **shaping** because reinforcement was dependent on behaviors that were increasingly like the goal response of playing with the other children. The shaping dimension was the degree of involvement that Ann had with the normal children. *Source: Allen, Hart, Buell, Harris, and Wolf (1964)*

2. This item is **not an example of shaping.** Rather, a single response was reinforced. There was no reinforcement of responses that were increasingly like a goal response.

3. This item is an example of **shaping** because reinforcement was dependent on behavior that was increasing like the goal response, a normal heart rate. The shaping dimension was heart rate. *Source: Scott, Peters, Gillespie, Blanchard, Edmunson, and Young (1973)*

4. This item is an example of **shaping** because reinforcement was dependent on behavior that was increasingly like the goal response, verbal behaviors. The shaping dimension was the topography of the speech responses. *Source: Isaacs, Thomas, and Goldiamond (1960)*

5. This item is **not an example of shaping.** In shaping, reinforcement is dependent on behaviors that are increasingly like a goal behavior. In this example, reinforcement, in increasing amounts, was dependent on an unchanging target behavior, 5 minutes of paying attention. Shaping involves a gradual change in a response, not in the reinforcer for a response.

6. This item is an example of **shaping** because reinforcement was dependent on behavior that was increasingly like the goal response, clear speech. The shaping dimension was speech clarity (topography). *Source: Drudge and Philips (1976)*

7. This item is an example of **shaping** because reinforcement was dependent on behavior that was increasingly like the goal behavior, normal fluid consumption. The shaping dimension was the rate or amount of fluid consumption. *Source: Friedin, Borakove, and Fox (1982)*

8. This item is **not an example of shaping.** In shaping, reinforcement is dependent on responses that are increasingly like a goal response. In this example, reinforcement is always dependent on the same response, correctly naming a pictured object. There is a gradual change in the reinforcer for the response, but in shaping there must be a gradual change in the response itself.

9. This item is an example of **shaping** because reinforcement was dependent on behavior that was increasingly like the goal response, biting through the graham cracker. The shaping dimension was the force or intensity of the biting response. *Source: Butterfield and Parson (1973)*

10. This item is an example of **shaping** because reinforcement was dependent on behavior that was increasingly like the goal response, rolling the ball the full required distance. The shaping dimension was the force or energy the children applied in releasing the ball. *Source: Morris and Dolker (1974)*

11. This item is an example of **shaping** because reinforcement was dependent on behavior that was increasingly like the goal response, speech of normal loudness. The shaping dimension was speech volume or loudness. *Source: Patterson, Teigen, Liberman, and Austin (1975)*

12. This item is an example of **shaping** because reinforcement was dependent on behavior that was increasingly like the goal behavior, a normal urination frequency. The shaping dimension was the rate of urination. Note that this is a DRL schedule in which the time requirement between responses was progressively lengthened. *Source: Masur (1976)*

13. This item is an example of **shaping** because reinforcement was dependent on behaviors that were increasingly like the goal behavior, being able to move normally. The shaping dimension was the topography of normal movements. *Source: Mizes (1985)*

14. This item is an example of **shaping** because reinforcement was made dependent on swallowing responses that were increasingly like the goal response, swallowing the big pills. The shaping dimension was the degree of throat opening necessary to swallow pills. *Source: Dahlquist and Blount (1984)*

15. This item is **not an example of shaping**. In shaping, reinforcement is made dependent on responses more and more like the goal response. In this example, training reinforced the same response, pointing to the correctly spelled name, so there was no change in the behavior that was reinforced. However, there was a change in the stimulus in the presence of which the response was reinforced. This procedure is called fading.

16. This item is an example of **shaping** because reinforcement was dependent on moving increasingly closer to the snake. The shaping dimension was proximity (i.e., closeness) to the snake. *Source: Barlow, Agras, Leitenberg, and Wincze (1970)*

17. This item is an example of **shaping** because reinforcement was dependent on behavior that was increasingly like the target behavior. The shaping dimension was the duration of eye contact. *Source: Lowenstein (1982)*

18. This item is an example of **shaping** because reinforcement was dependent on behaviors that were increasingly like the goal behavior, no binges. This use of shaping involved the use of DRL schedules in which gradually lower rates of binges were required until eventually a state of no binges was required for reinforcement. The shaping dimension was the rate of binges. *Source: Williamson, Lawson, Bennett, and Hinz (1989)*

Chapter 6 *Making Shaping Effective*

1. The problem with this example is that the **goal is not specific enough**. In order to shape successive approximations to a targeted goal, the goal itself must be specified in behavioral terms. The university officials should have delineated exactly what kinds of behaviors made good citizens.

2. The problem is that the **initial step is too large**. It was unrealistic as a first step to expect a student to talk fluently for 10 minutes when that student could not complete a single sentence fluently.

3. The problem is with **too large a second step**. The step from the low hoop to the high hoop was too large.

4. The problem is with the **shaping dimension**. The coach shaped speed, but his goal behavior was the arm movement itself, not swimming speed.

5. The problem is that for Lulu the **steps toward the goal were too small** and she became bored with the entire exercise.

6. The problem is that the **steps were too small**; Anna did not need the training.

7. The problem was that the **final step was too large** and the previous behavior was disrupted.

8. The problem is with the **immediacy of the reinforcer**. In shaping, it is crucial that the reinforcer be delivered as soon as the desired behavior has occurred. Otherwise an inappropriate behavior may be reinforced, which interferes with the shaping process.

Chapter 6   *Reinforcement Schedules*

1. This item is an example of a **fixed-duration schedule,** because reinforcement for the target behavior was dependent on the occurrence of the target behavior for a specific interval of time (90 minutes) that remained fixed from reinforcement to reinforcement.

    If Sam's teacher had made reinforcement dependent on a *certain number of correct problems* that remained constant or fixed from day to day, it would have been an example of a fixed-ratio schedule. If Sam's teacher had made reinforcement dependent on the occurrence of the target behavior for an interval of time that varied from day to day (30 minutes one day, 100 minutes one day, and 15 minutes one day), it would be an example of a variable-duration schedule. Finally, if going to gym period had been made dependent on a number of correct math problems that varied from day to day (40 problems one day, 100 problems one day, and 75 problems one day), it would be an example of a variable-ratio schedule of reinforcement.

2. This item is an example of a **DRL schedule** because reinforcement was dependent on a rate of the target behavior that was below a specified response rate. Further, it is an example of full-session DRL; reinforcement was dependent on driving fewer than a given number of miles per week and per month. *Source: Hake and Foxx (1978)*

3. The target behavior was reinforced according to a **fixed-ratio schedule** of reinforcement, because it was reinforced only when it had occurred a specific and fixed number of times (10) that remained constant.

4. This item is an example of a **variable-ratio schedule** of reinforcement. It is a ratio schedule of reinforcement because the credits were dependent on the number of target behaviors that occurred: The more target behaviors (and the more rolls of the die), the more likely it was for credits to be earned. It is a variable-ratio schedule because the number of target behaviors required for reinforcement varied from reinforcement to reinforcement. Sometimes, the roll of the die would allow several target behaviors to be reinforced in a row. At other times, several rolls of the die would not earn any credits. *Source: Hall, Cooper, Burmaster, and Polk (1977)*

5. This item is a **fixed-interval schedule** of reinforcement. It is an interval schedule of reinforcement because the response of asking is reinforced only after the passage of time. It is a fixed schedule because the length of time that must pass is fixed at 6 ½ to 7 minutes. (If you said it's a variable-interval schedule because the length of time varied between 6 ½ to 7 minutes, consider yourself correct.)

6. This item is an example of a **variable-ratio schedule** of reinforcement. It is a ratio schedule because the reinforcement is produced by the number of times the television set is hit. It is a variable schedule because the number of times the television had to be hit varied from reinforcement to reinforcement.

7. This item is an example of a **DRH schedule** of reinforcement because reinforcement was dependent on a response rate that was above a specified response rate.

8. This item is an example of a **variable-interval schedule** of reinforcement. It is an interval schedule because the response of checking the post office box was reinforced only after it occurred following the passage of intervals of time. It is a variable schedule because the intervals of time that had to pass varied. Note that there was no limited-hold dependency, because once a letter had arrived, it was available indefinitely.

9. This item is an example of a **DRH schedule**; reinforcement was dependent on a response rate that was above a specified response rate. Reinforcement was dependent on a minimum of 61 correct responses during the hour-long math period. *Source: Lovitt and Esveldt (1970)*

10. This item is an example of a **variable-duration schedule** of reinforcement. It is a duration schedule; reinforcement (becoming clean) was dependent on engaging in the target behavior for a certain length of time. It is a variable schedule because the reinforcement was dependent on engaging in the target behavior for lengths of time that varied from day to day.

11. This item illustrates a **fixed-ratio schedule** of reinforcement (FR 100). It is a ratio schedule because reinforcement is dependent on the number of times the response occurs (the number of times the pump is pumped). It is a fixed schedule because the number of times the response had to occur remained constant at 100.

12. This item is an example of **DRL schedule** because the target behavior was reinforced only when its rate of occurrence was sufficiently low (i.e., below the maximum value of three jokes per day).

13. This item is an example of a **variable-interval schedule** of reinforcement. It is an interval schedule because the target behavior is reinforced only after the passage of time, as the timer setting determined. It is a variable schedule because the time that passed before a response would be reinforced varied from reinforcement to reinforcement. *Source: Wolf, Hanley, King, Lachowicz, and Giles (1970)*

14. This item is an example of a **fixed-interval schedule** of reinforcement **with a limited hold**. It is an interval schedule of reinforcement; the target response of observing the groundhog is reinforced only after the passage of 1 year between groundhog days. It is a fixed schedule; the time between groundhog days is fixed at 1 year. There is a limited-hold dependency as well, because the reinforcer is available to the target behavior only when it occurs on groundhog day, not before and not after.

15. This item is an example of a **DRP schedule**; reinforcement is dependent on a response rate that is both above a specified minimum rate and below a specified maximum rate.

16. This item is an illustration of a **variable-interval schedule** of reinforcement **with a limited hold**. It is an interval schedule of reinforcement because the response would be reinforced only after the passage of time, when the night skies were clouded. It is a variable schedule because the length of time that had to pass varied. There was also a limited-hold dependency here, because the reinforcement in the form of a clear sky was available only for a limited period of time. Sooner or later, the sky would cloud over again.

17. This item is an example of a **fixed-interval schedule** of reinforcement. It is an interval schedule of reinforcement because the target behavior is reinforced only after an interval of time has

elapsed. It is a fixed schedule of reinforcement because the amount of time that has to pass before a response is reinforced is fixed at 1 month. If you said that this is a variable-interval schedule because the number of days in a month varies from month to month, consider yourself correct.

18. This item is an example of a **variable-interval** schedule of reinforcement **with a limited hold**. It is an interval schedule because the target behavior was reinforced only after the passage of time (the time between thunderstorms). It is a variable schedule because the amount of time that passed between thunderstorms varied from storm to storm. There was also a limited-hold dependency, because once a thunderstorm had begun, the target behavior would be reinforced only during a limited period of time while the thunderstorm was occurring.

19. This item is an example of a **variable-ratio schedule** of reinforcement. It is a ratio schedule because reinforcers were dependent on the number of times the target behavior occurred: The more times the target behavior occurred, the more reinforcers the riders received. It is a variable schedule; the target behavior was reinforced after it occurred a number of times that varied from reinforcement to reinforcement. *Source: Deslauriers and Everett (1977)*

20. This item is a **DRL schedule** because the reinforcement is dependent on the occurrence of the target behavior at a low rate.

21. This item is a **variable-duration schedule**. It is a duration schedule because reinforcement of the target behavior is dependent on engaging in the behavior for a length of time (the length of time it takes the bus to make the trip). It is a variable schedule because the length of time necessary for the target behavior to be engaged in varies from trip to trip.

22. This item is a **fixed-duration schedule**. It is a duration schedule because reinforcement is dependent on the amount of time the target behavior is engaged in. It is a fixed schedule because reinforcement is dependent on engaging in the target behavior for a fixed amount of time, 6 hours.

23. This item is a **DRP schedule** because reinforcement was dependent on a response rate that was both above a specified minimum rate and below a specified maximum rate.

24. This item is an example of a **fixed-interval schedule** of reinforcement **with a limited hold**. It is an interval schedule because the response could be reinforced only after it occurred following the passage of an interval of time. It is a fixed schedule because the amount of time that had to pass in order for a response to be reinforced was fixed at 55 minutes. Finally, there was a limited-hold dependency because once reinforcement for a response became available (i.e., once the news came on), it was then available for only a limited period of time.

25. This item is an example of a **fixed-ratio schedule** of reinforcement. It is a ratio schedule because reinforcement was dependent on the number of responses made. It is a fixed schedule because the number of required responses was the same from reinforcement to reinforcement.

Chapter 7   *Stimulus Discrimination Training*

1. This item is an example of **stimulus discrimination training** because the students were trained to respond selectively to the stimuli (the faces) and because differential consequences were dependent on correct and incorrect responding. The S+s and S–s were the faces: Each face was an S+ for one number response and an S– for other numbers. This example is **successive discrimination** because one face was presented at a time. It is an example of **social discrimination** because other people came to act as S+s for the responses. It is also an example of **multiple-stimulus multiple-response discrimination** because there 30 stimuli were used during training

with a different correct response for each of those stimuli. *Source: Elliott, Wills, and Goldstein (1973)*

2. This item is **not an example of stimulus discrimination training**. There was no training to respond selectively to two or more stimuli through the use of differential consequences. In this item, the students' self-disclosures were reinforced whenever they occurred. Had there been an effort to encourage self-disclosures in one stimulus situation but not in another, it would have been an example of stimulus discrimination training.

3. This item is an example of **stimulus discrimination training**. The pigeons were trained to respond selectively to the two stimuli, the two types of music by providing differential consequences for responding. The S+ was the Bach music and the S– was the Hindemith music. It was a successive discrimination because one type of music was played at a time. *Source: Porter and Neuringer (1984)*

4. This item is **not an example of stimulus discrimination training**. In this item, the children were trained to respond the same way to different stimuli. In stimulus discrimination training, the learners are trained to respond selectively to stimuli (to respond differently to different stimuli).

5. This item is an example of **stimulus discrimination training** because the infants were trained to respond selectively to the two stimuli (the two colors), through the use of differential consequences for responding. The S+ was the green panel and the S– was the purple panel. This item was a **simultaneous discrimination** because the S+ and the S– were presented at the same time. It was a **multiple-stimulus multiple-response discrimination** because there were two stimuli (the two panels), and two responses (touching the green panel and touching the purple panel). *Source: Simmons (1964)*

6. This item is **not an example of stimulus discrimination** training because there was no use of different consequences for correct and incorrect responding. The students may have learned something from the lecture, but it was not a discrimination training procedure.

7. This item is an example of **stimulus discrimination training** because the infants were trained to respond selectively to the three stimuli through the use of differential consequences. There were two S+s in the study: The stripes were an S+ for head turns to the left while the checkerboard was an S+ for head turns to the right. The stripes were an S– for head turns to the right and the checkerboard was an S– for head turns to the left. The black circle was an S– for head turns both to the right and the left. This was a **successive discrimination** because the three stimuli were presented at different times. It was a **multiple-stimulus multiple-response discrimination** because three stimuli and two responses were involved. *Source: McKenzie and Day (1974)*

8. This item is an example of **stimulus discrimination training** because the children were trained to respond selectively to the stimuli through the use of differential consequences. The S+ was the one of the four letterlike figures that matched the figure in the top window. The S–s were the three letterlike figures that were different from the figure in the top window. It was a **simultaneous discrimination** because the S+ and the S– were presented at the same time. This was a **matching-to-sample discrimination** because reinforcers were dependent on selecting the comparison stimulus that matched the sample stimulus. *Source: Tawney (1972)*

9. This item is an example of **stimulus discrimination training** because the students were trained to respond selectively to the stimuli through the use of differential consequences. It was a **successive discrimination** task because the signals were presented one at a time. The S+s and S–s were the Morse code signals: Each signal was an S+ for writing the correct letter or number and an S– for writing the other letters or numbers. It was a **verbal discrimination** because the stimuli were Morse code signals, verbal stimuli. It was a **multiple-stimulus multiple-response discrimination** because the task required that the students learn several different responses to several different stimuli. *Source: Keller (1943, 1982)*

10. This item is **not an example of stimulus discrimination training** because there was no training in selectively responding to stimuli. In this item, the absence of aggression was reinforced and aggression was punished, with no effort to diminish aggression in some situations and not in others; aggression was discouraged in all situations through the use of DRO and timeout.

11. This item is an example of **stimulus discrimination training** because the children were trained to respond selectively to the pictures through the use of differential consequences. The S+s and S–s were the pictures: Each picture was an S+ for saying the name of that picture and an S– for saying the wrong name. It was a **successive discrimination** task because the cards were presented one at a time. It was a **multiple-stimulus multiple-response discrimination** because the task required that the children learn different responses to several different stimuli. *Source: Kircher, Pear, and Martin (1971)*

12. This item is an example of **stimulus discrimination training** because the students were trained to respond selectively to the pictures through the use of differential consequences. The S+s were the pictures less preferred by experienced artists and the S–s were the pictures more preferred by the artists. It was an example of **simultaneous discrimination** because the S+ and S– pictures were presented at the same time. *Source: Stalling and Tiller (1975)*

13. This item is **not an example of stimulus discrimination training**. In this item there was no use of differential consequences for correct and incorrect performance. The students may have learned from this method, but it was not a stimulus discrimination procedure.

14. This item is an example of **stimulus discrimination training** because the students were trained to respond selectively to the vocabulary word cards through the use of differential consequences. The S+s and S–s were the cards: Each card was an S+ for one response and an S– for all other responses. It is an example of **successive discrimination** because the words were presented one at a time. It is also an example of **verbal discrimination** because the S+s were written words, verbal stimuli. It is an example of **multiple-stimulus multiple-response discrimination** because more than one stimulus and more than one response was used. *Source: Lahey and Drabman (1974)*

15. This item is an example of **stimulus discrimination training** because the students were trained to respond selectively to the instructions through the use of differential consequences. The S+s were instructions: Each instruction for a specific exercise was an S+ for that exercise and an S– for the other exercises and other types of incorrect responses. It is an example of **successive discrimination** because the instructions were presented one at a time. It is an example of **verbal discrimination** because the S+s were the spoken words, verbal stimuli. This is an example of **multiple-stimulus multiple-response discrimination** because more than one stimulus and more than one response were learned. *Source: Fitterling and Ayllon (1983)*

16. This item is an example of **stimulus discrimination training** because the children were trained to respond selectively to the word cards and the sentence cards through the use of differential consequences. The S+ was the matching word in the sentence and the S–s were words that did not match. It was a **simultaneous discrimination** because the S+ and S–were presented at the same time. It was a **verbal discrimination** because the stimuli were words, verbal stimuli. It was an example of a **matching-to-sample discrimination** because the task required that the children match a sample stimulus, the word card, with comparison stimuli, the words in the sentence card. *Source: Littlejohn and Goetz (1989)*

17. This item is **not an example of stimulus discrimination training**. In this item, the students were trained to respond the same way to different stimuli. In stimulus discrimination training, the learners are trained to respond in different ways to different stimuli.

18. This item is an example of **stimulus discrimination training** because the children were trained to respond selectively to the word cards and the sentence cards through the use of differential

consequences, winning the game versus not winning. The S+s were the written words that matched the words the teacher said. The S–s were the written words that did not match the words the teacher pronounced. It was a **simultaneous discrimination** because the S+ and S– were presented at the same time. It was a **verbal discrimination** because the stimuli were words, verbal stimuli. It was a **matching-to-sample discrimination** because children were required to match the written words with the spoken words. It was a symbolic **matching-to-sample** task because the matching relationship between spoken and written words was symbolic. *Source: Kirby, Holborn, and Bushby (1981)*

Chapter 7   *Making Stimulus Discrimination Effective*

1. The teacher **failed to make use of instructions.** Had she explained the distinguishing characteristic between serif and sans serif typefaces, her students would not have attended to an irrelevant dimension such as style.

2. This example **failed to make use of the principle of active responding.** The only student required to respond during the learning phase was Barry and, as a result, he was the only one who did well on the test phase.

3. This item is an example where **pretraining could have helped.** The girl did not have the prerequisite skill of color identification.

4. This item is an example where the **S–s were too similar to the S+s.** Although the S–s were more concrete than the S+s, the similarity was a problem. A progressive technique beginning with more dissimilar examples might have been better.

5. In this example, **the training stimuli were not similar enough to the testing stimuli.** During training, the S–s were either women or children, but in the real world Corey would be expected to tell the difference between his father and other male adults.

6. Davis's mom should have used a **progressive sequence.** She could have started with the first name, then added the middle name, and finally the surname.

7. This item is an example where **rate was too fast** for Cindy. Her impulsive responding suggests that an enforced delay before she was allowed to respond might help her pay more attention to the stimuli.

8. Ms. Farlane failed to remember that a **specific reinforcer** for a particular response works better than a nonspecific reinforcer.

Chapter 8   *Prompting*

1. This item is an example of **prompting**; presenting the brochures was a discriminative stimulus intended to strengthen recycling, and it did indeed increase recycling activities. The **prompt was verbal** because the brochures contained words, verbal stimuli. *Source: Jacobs, Bailey, and Crews (1984)*

2. This item is **not an example of prompting.** Although the sore muscles may have acted as discriminative stimuli that strengthened staying in bed, they were not presented by someone for the purpose of strengthening Janice's bed rest. If someone saw that Janice was having difficulty moving and advised her to stay in bed, it would have been an example of a prompt because the advice would be a discriminative stimulus that someone presented in order to strengthen bed rest.

3. This item is an example of **prompting** because the hat was a discriminative stimulus intended to strengthen waste disposal, and it did so. *Source: O'Neill, Blanck, and Joyner (1980)*

4. This item is an example of **prompting**; the sign was a discriminative stimulus intended to strengthen the use of arm signals by the pedestrians and it did so. The **prompt was verbal** because the sign contained words, verbal stimuli. *Source: Van Houten, Malenfant, and Rolider (1985)*

5. This item is **not an example of prompting**. Although the accident may have served as a discriminative stimulus for safety-related behaviors, the accident was not staged with that intent. A prompt is a discriminative stimulus presented with the intention of strengthening a response. If the men had watched films depicting accidents that unsafe behaviors caused, it would have been a prompt because the film would have been presented for the purpose of strengthening safe behaviors.

6. This item is an example of **prompting**; because the sign was a discriminative stimulus intended to strengthen low-fat food selection and did so. **The prompt was verbal** because it consisted of words, verbal stimuli. *Source: Mayer, Heins, Vogel, Morrison, Lakester, and Jacobs (1986)*

7. This item is an example of **prompting**; the sign was a discriminative stimulus intended to strengthen seat-belt use, and it did so. **The prompt was verbal** because the sign consisted of words, verbal stimuli. *Source: Williams, Thyer, Bailey, and Harrison (1989)*

8. This item is an example of **prompting**; the mailed messages were discriminative stimuli intended to strengthen breast self-exams and they did so. **The prompt was verbal** because it consisted of written words, verbal stimuli. *Source: Craun and Deffenbacher (1987)*

9. This item is **not an example of prompting**. Although the stench from the pulp mill may well have acted as a discriminative stimulus, it was not presented for that purpose. Prompts are discriminative stimuli that are presented by someone specifically for the purpose of strengthening a particular behavior. In this case, the purpose of the smell was not to strengthen use of a particular road.

10. This item is an example of **prompting**; the nurse and computer reminders were discriminative stimuli intended to strengthen use of the preventative procedures and they did so. The **prompts were verbal** because they consisted of words, verbal stimuli. *Source: Harris, O'Malley, Fletcher, and Knight (1990)*

11. This item is an example of **prompting**; the advertising messages and video pictures were discriminative stimuli intended to strengthen reading medication labels and they did so. **The message prompt was verbal** because it consisted of words, verbal stimuli. The video pictures of people reading labels can be interpreted either as **picture prompts** or **modeling prompts** because they demonstrated the target behaviors. *Source: Wright (1979)*

12. This item is an example of **prompting**; the experimenter's suggestions were discriminative stimuli intended to strengthen donations and they did so. The suggestions were **verbal prompts** because they consisted of words, verbal stimuli. *Source: Gelfand, Hartmann, Cromer, Smith, and Page (1975)*

13. This item is an example of **prompting**; the signs and the red circles were discriminative stimuli intended to weaken shoplifting and they did so. The signs were **verbal prompts** because they consisted of words, verbal stimuli. *Source: Carter, Hansson, Holmberg, and Melin (1979)*

14. This item is an example of **prompting** because **gestural** (pointing), **verbal** (command), and **physical** (guiding) **prompts** were used. It is an example of the increasing assistance prompting

method because the weakest prompt (gestural prompt) was used first and increasingly stronger prompts (direct verbal prompts and physical prompts) were used only if necessary.

15. This item is an example of **prompting** because the buzzer, question, and list were intended to strengthen service-requesting behavior and they did so. It is an example of the increasing assistance method because the weaker buzzer prompt was followed by a stronger verbal prompt and an even stronger verbal prompt only if the weaker prompts had failed.

Chapter 8   *Fading and Delayed Prompting*

1. This item is an example of **fading**; the discriminative stimuli for the response were gradually changed so that they became increasingly like the goal discriminative stimuli, distinct circles and ellipses. The fading dimension was the darkness-distinctness of the ellipses because this was the feature of the discriminative stimuli that was gradually changed. This practice of fading made use of **within-stimulus prompts** because the distinctness of the ellipses was a part of the ellipses and therefore was contained in the goal discriminative stimuli. *Source: Sidman and Stoddard (1967)*

2. This item is **neither an example of fading** (there was no gradual change in the discriminative stimuli for the response) nor of delayed prompting (no delayed prompts were used). It is an example of shaping, in which the *response* becomes increasingly similar to a *goal response*. In fading, the *discriminative stimuli* for the response become increasingly similar to the goal *discriminative stimuli*.

3. This item is an example of **fading**; the discriminative stimuli for the response were gradually changed so that they became increasingly like the goal discriminative stimuli , red and red-orange lights. The fading dimension was the color (the wavelength) of the light, because this feature of the discriminative stimuli gradually changed from yellow to pink to red-orange. This is an example of **within-stimulus prompting** because the prompts were the color of the lights and the color of the lights were part of the lights, the goal-discriminative stimuli. *Source: Powers, Cheney, and Agostino (1970)*

4. This item is an example of **delayed prompting**. At first, the color-card prompts were presented before there was an opportunity to respond to the signs. Later, the signs were presented before the color-card prompt, providing an opportunity to respond in the absence of the prompt. The prompts used were **extra-stimulus prompts** because the color-card prompts were not a part of the goal discriminative stimuli, the color signs. *Source: Smeets and Streifel (1976)*

5. This item is an example of **fading** because the discriminative stimuli for the response were gradually changed, becoming increasingly like the goal discriminative stimuli (the printed words presented alone). The fading dimension was the distinctness (or faintness) of the pictures because this feature of the discriminative stimuli gradually changed from very distinct to indistinct. It is an example of **extra-stimulus prompting** because the picture prompts were not a part of the words (the goal discriminative stimuli). *Source: Dorry and Zeaman (1973)*

6. This item is **neither an example of fading** (no discriminative stimuli for the response were gradually changed so that they became more like goal discriminative stimuli) **nor of delayed prompting** (no use of delayed prompts induced the learner to respond to a stimulus in the absence of prompts). In this example, there was a gradual change in the frequency of reinforcement for the response. It is an example of thinning a reinforcement schedule.

7. This item is **neither an example of fading** (the discriminative stimuli for the response did not become more like goal discriminative stimuli) **nor of delayed prompting** (no delayed prompts

were used). In this item, the handwriting responses gradually changed, not the discriminative stimuli for those responses. This item is an example of shaping.

8. This item is an example of **fading** because the discriminative stimuli for the response were gradually changed, becoming increasingly like the goal discriminative stimuli, the braille patterns presented alone. The fading dimension was the degree of focus of the letters. It is an example of **extra-stimulus prompting** because the prompts (the letters were not a part of the braille patterns (the goal discriminative stimuli). *Source: Fields (1980)*

9. This item is an example of **delayed prompting** because at first, responding to the discriminative stimuli was prompted and over time, the prompts were presented only after a delay. At first, job pictures and the job-name prompts were presented at the same time. Later, there was a progressively longer delay between the job-picture presentation and the job-name-prompt presentation. This item is an example of **extra-stimulus prompting** because the job-name prompts were not part of the job pictures, the goal discriminative stimuli. *Source: Wolery, Gast, Kirk, and Schuster (1988)*

10. This item is an example of **delayed prompting** because at first, responding to the discriminative stimuli was prompted and over time, the prompts were presented only after a delay. At first, the words and picture prompts were presented together. Over time, there was a progressively longer delay between the presentation of the words and the picture prompts. It is an example of **extra-stimulus prompting** because the pictures were not a part of the words, the goal discriminative stimuli. *Source: McGee and McCoy (1981)*

11. This item is **not an example of fading**; there was no gradual change in the discriminative stimuli for responding in the direction of goal discriminative stimuli. In this item, there was a gradual reduction in the frequency of reinforcement, not a gradual change in any discriminative stimuli. This is an example of the thinning of a variable-interval reinforcement schedule.

12. This item is an example of **fading**; the discriminative stimuli for the response were gradually changed, becoming increasingly like the goal discriminative stimulus, the tape recorder. At first, modeling, verbal, and physical prompts were used to get the response to occur. These prompts were gradually faded. The fading dimension was the degree to which the modeling, verbal, and physical prompts were used because this feature of the discriminative stimuli was gradually changed. It is an example of **extra-stimulus prompting** because the modeling, verbal, and physical prompts were not a part of the tape recorder, the goal discriminative stimulus. *Source: Walls, Crist, Sienicki, and Grant (1981)*

13. This item is an example of **fading**; the discriminative stimuli for the response were gradually changed so that they became increasingly like the goal discriminative stimuli, the letters presented for copying without dots. The fading dimension was the degree to which the dots were used as discriminative stimuli for copying the letters, because this feature was altered. It is an example of **within-stimulus prompting** because during training the dots were part of the letters, the goal discriminative stimuli. *Source: Hartley and Salzwedel (1980)*

14. This item is an example of **fading**; there was a gradual change in the discriminative stimuli for the happy behavior toward a goal discriminative stimuli, the preschool without Maria's mother. The fading dimension was the length of time Maria's mother was gone. It is an example of **extra-stimulus prompting** because Maria's mother was not a part of the preschool environment, the goal discriminative stimuli. *Source: Neisworth, Madle, and Goeke (1975)*

15. This item is an example of **fading**; there was a gradual change in the discriminative stimuli for the response toward goal discriminative stimuli, letters presented at a distance from the subjects. The fading dimension was the distance between the subjects and the letters because it was this feature of the discriminative stimuli that was altered. It is an example of **within-stimulus prompting** because the distance between the subject and the letters was an essential part

of the stimuli that were involved in the goal discrimination. This use of fading may eventually be useful for teaching people with myopia to see without corrective lenses. However, at present, research has not clearly established that the improvements in visual acuity that subjects make during training will persist outside the training situation. *Source: Ricci and Collins (1988)*

Chapter 8　*Stimulus-Response Chaining*

1. This item is an example of a **stimulus-response chaining** procedure because the method was designed to build a sequence of different behaviors. It is an example of the **whole-task method** of teaching stimulus-response chains because the trainees learned the whole task at once: The experimenters did not require the learners to master one step of the assembly skill before adding additional steps. *Source: Spooner, Weber, and Spooner (1983)*

2. This item is an example of a **stimulus-response chaining** procedure because it was a method designed to build a sequence of different behaviors. It is an example of **backward chaining** because (a) the task was broken down into a series of steps; (b) the students learned the last step first; (c) as each new step was learned, the experimenters added the preceding step to the training; and (d) this process continued until all the steps had been added in the order from last to first. *Source: Wightman and Sistrunk (1987)*

3. This item is **not an example of a stimulus-response chaining** procedure because there was no mention of building a sequence of behavior by adding new behaviors. It is an example of shaping, in which behavior that was more and more like a goal response (dark printing) was reinforced. In this case, the shaping dimension was how hard Lois pressed her pencil against the paper when writing.

4. This item is an example of a **stimulus-response chaining** procedure because it was a method designed to build a sequence of different behaviors. It is an example of the **whole-task method** of teaching stimulus-response chains because the students learned the whole task at once: The experimenters did not require the learners to master one step of the assembly skill before adding additional steps. *Source: McGregor and Axelrod (1988)*

5. This item is an example of a **stimulus-response chaining** procedure because it was a method designed to build a sequence of different behaviors. It is an example of **backward chaining** because (a) the task was broken down into a series of steps; (b) the trainees learned the last step first; (c) as each new step was learned, the experimenters added the preceding step to the training; and (d) this process continued until all the steps had been added in the order from last to first. *Source: McDonnell and Laughlin (1989)*

6. This item is **not an example of a procedure to teach a stimulus-response chain** because there is no mention of building a sequence of behavior by adding new behaviors. It is an example of fading, in which the discriminative stimulus for a response is gradually altered.

7. This item is an example of a **stimulus-response chaining** procedure because it was a method designed to build a sequence of different behaviors. It is an example of **forward chaining** because (a) the task was broken down into a series of steps; (b) the trainees learned the first step first; (c) as each new step was learned, the experimenters added the following step to the training; and (d) this process continued until all the steps had been added in the order from first to last. *Source: LaCampagne and Cipani (1987)*

8. This item is an example of a **stimulus-response chaining** procedure because it was a method designed to build a sequence of different behaviors. It is an example of **forward chaining**

because (a) the task was broken down into a series of steps; (b) the trainees learned the first step first; (c) as each new step was learned, the experimenters added the following step to the training; and (d) this process continued until all the steps had been added in the order from first to last. *Source: Ash and Holding (1990)*

9. This item is an example of a **stimulus-response chaining** procedure because it was a method designed to build a sequence of different behaviors. It is an example of **backward chaining** because (a) the task was broken down into a series of steps; (b) the trainees learned the last step first; (c) as each new step was learned, the experimenters added the preceding step to the training; and (d) this process continued until all the steps had been added in the order from last to first. *Source: Wilcox (1974)*

10. This item is **not an example of a stimulus-response chaining** procedure because there is no mention of building a sequence of different behaviors. It is an example of shaping in which the duration of upright behavior was shaped toward longer durations. In chaining, different behaviors are added to a sequence of behavior; the duration of behavior is not simply increased.

11. This item is an example of a **stimulus-response chaining** procedure because it was a method designed to build a sequence of different behaviors. It is an example of **forward chaining** because (a) the task was broken down into a series of steps; (b) Ted learned the first step first; (c) as each new step was learned, the trainer added the following step to the training; and (d) this process continued until all the steps had been added in the order from first to last. *Source: Cohen (1984)*

12. This item is an example of a **stimulus-response chaining** procedure because it was a method designed to build a sequence of different behaviors. It is an example of the **whole-task method** of teaching stimulus-response chains because the students learned the whole task at once: The experimenters did not require the learners to practice the entire task from start to finish, rather than breaking the task up into steps. *Source: Walls, Dowler, Haught, and Zawlocki (1984)*

Chapter 8   *Making Prompting and Fading Effective*

1. A problem here is the **impersonal nature of the verbal prompt**. Had the director sent personalized requests to the alumni, or even better, had she met with each of them, she may have had better luck.

2. A problem here is **step size**. Lulu's mother would have been wiser to continue her procedure with small steps.

3. The problem here is the **lack of distinctiveness of the fading dimension**. Laurie learned to attend to leash wearing that, although a discriminative feature of many dogs, isn't a feature restricted to dogs.

4. A problem here is that with retarded children in particular, it is confusing to use **extra-stimulus prompts**. The trainers might instead have incorporated their picture prompts into the stimulus.

5. The problem here is the **lengthy delay** at the beginning of the procedure. His mother should have given David the prompt sooner.

6. The problem here is that the fading dimension was along the S– (a talking cat). It might have been better to **fade along the S+** (a talking dog).

7. The **step size** is a problem. Charlie's father would have been wiser to continue with his gradual procedure.

8. The problem here is that the **fading dimension is not distinctive**. The teacher might have been wiser to fade the "e" letter, rather than the nondistinctive "a."

9. The problem here is that the teacher used **extra-stimulus prompts**. With autistic children, in particular, extra-stimulus prompts are distracting and make the task more difficult. The teacher might have been wiser to use the red apple itself as the S+, and then fade out the picture to the color patch.

Chapter 9   *Types of Generalization*

1. This item is an example of **response generalization**; strengthening correct responses of one component of a stroke also strengthened correct responses of other components of that same stroke. *Source: Koop and Martin (1983)*

2. This item is an example of **stimulus generalization** in the specific form of **setting generalization**. The training in the learning resource room strengthened the students' question-asking behaviors and the effects of this training generalized to another setting, regular math class. *Source: Knapczyk (1989)*

3. This item is an example of **subject generalization** because the behavior change procedures that were applied to three target subjects, Dan, Hank, and Ricky, also improved the behavior of non-target subjects to whom the procedures were not directly applied. *Source: Strain, Shores, & Kerr (1976)*

4. This item is an example of **behavior maintenance** because the increase in the target behaviors was continued after training ended. *Source: Briscoe, Hoffman, and Bailey (1975)*

5. This item is an example of **expressive-receptive generalization** because Leonard's training in an expressive task generalized to his performance in a receptive task. At first, Leonard engaged in a receptive task: He was shown an object and required to say the French word for the object. Later, Leonard was tested at a receptive task: He was presented with a French word and required to select the object represented by the word from among a group of alternatives. As a result of the expressive task training, Leonard's performance on the receptive task was improved.

6. This item is an example of **receptive-expressive generalization**; training the children in a receptive task generalized to the children's performance in an expressive task. At first, the children engaged in a receptive task: They were given the names of objects and required to select the correct object from among alternatives. Then, the children were tested on an expressive task: They were required to say the name of an object when the experimenter pointed to it. As a result of the receptive-task training, the children's performance on the expressive task was improved. *Source: (cf., Mann & Baer, 1971).*

7. This item is **not an example of stimulus generalization** because the training effects were specific to the training situation, the reading lessons, and did not extend to language arts or math lessons. *Source: Horton (1975)*

8. This item is an example of **both stimulus and response generalization**. It is an example of stimulus generalization because the effects of training with one set of stimuli, the practice pitchers, also improved performance with similar stimuli, the 16 test pitchers. It is an example of response generalization because training the pouring response with the practice pictures also improved similar pouring responses with the 16 test pitchers. *Source: Day and Horner (1989)*

9. This item is an example of **receptive-expressive generalization** because training the children in a receptive task generalized to the children's performance in a productive task. At first, the chil-

dren engaged in a receptive task: They were given the Spanish names of objects and required to select the correct object from alternatives. Then, the children were tested on an expressive task: They were required to say the name of an object when the experimenter told them the Spanish name for the object. As a result of the receptive task training, the children's performance on the expressive task was improved. *Source: Ruder, Hermann, and Schiefelbusch (1977)*

10. This item is an example of **stimulus generalization** because the improvement in the trainees' performance in the training situation, the school cafeteria, was also observed in the stores in which training had not occurred. It is also an example of behavior maintenance, because correct responding continued to occur after training ceased. *Source: Haring, Kennedy, Adams, and Pitts-Conway (1987)*

11. This item is an example of **stimulus generalization** because for all four children, the strengthening of correct naming of real objects in the training situation also strengthened correct naming in the test situation. For the fourth child, there was additional stimulus generalization because training in picture and photograph naming in the training situation strengthened real-object naming in the natural environment. *Source: Welch and Pear (1980)*

12. This item is an example of **subject generalization** because the behavior change procedures that were applied to Charlotte, the target subject, also changed the behaviors of the nontarget subjects, Charlotte's classmates. *Source: Drabman and Lahey (1974)*

13. This item is an example of **behavior maintenance**; the improvement in the target behaviors remained, even after training had been discontinued. *Source: Johnson and Cuvo (1981)*

14. This item is an example of **stimulus generalization**; training the children to interact with one another in one stimulus situation, the lunchroom, caused an increase in the children's interactions in another stimulus situation, the free-play environment. This specific type of stimulus generalization is called **setting generalization**. There was no behavior maintenance because the effects of the training did not endure when the training was discontinued. *Source: Hauserman, Walen, and Behling (1973)*

15. This item is an example of **response generalization** because the token reinforcement, which strengthened Jenny's putting away her toys, also strengthened similar room-cleaning behaviors, including putting away clothes and making the bed. *Source: Bucher and Reaume (1979)*

16. This item is an example of **stimulus generalization**; the procedure that strengthened the response in one set of stimuli, those in the library, also strengthened responding in another stimulus situation, the classroom. It is **setting generalization** because the generalization took place across different settings. *Source: Fishbein and Wasik (1981)*

17. This item is an example of **stimulus generalization** because the procedure that strengthened the appropriate public speaking responses to one set of stimuli, the trainees, also strengthened responding in another stimulus situation, the larger audience. It may be considered an example of **setting generalization** because the small and large audiences represented different settings. *Source: Hayes and Marshall (1984)*

18. This item is an example of **stimulus generalization** in the specific form of **setting generalization**; the strengthening of the student's attendance in one setting, English and math classes, also strengthened the students attendance at another setting, science and social studies classes. *Source: Reese and Filipczak (1980)*

19. This item is an example of **stimulus and response generalization**. It is stimulus generalization because training using the miniature street generalized to similar stimuli on a real street. It is response generalization because the training in moving the doll on the miniature street

strengthened correct doll movements and correct pedestrian behaviors on a real street. *Source: Page, Iwata, and Neef (1976)*

20. This item is an example of **subject generalization;** the behavior change procedures that were applied to Allan, the target subject, also changed the behaviors of Allan's brother Bert, the non-target subject. *Source: Peterson, Farmer, and Selby (1988)*

21. This item is an example of **response generalization;** strengthening one response, healthy talk, also improved another response, correct interpretation of proverbs. *Source: Meichenbaum (1969)*

22. This item is an example of **expressive-receptive generalization** because Isabel's training in an expressive task generalized to her performance in a receptive task. At first, Isabel engaged in a receptive task: She was shown a flower and required to say its name. Later, Isabel was tested at a receptive task: She was presented with the name of a flower and required to select the correct drawing of that flower from alternatives. As a result of the expressive task training, Isabel's performance on the receptive task was improved.

Chapter 9 *Making Generalization Effective*

1. The use of **multiple trainers** would have increased the likelihood that generalization would occur.

2. The **training and generalization situations were not similar enough.**

3. Reg might have shown more generalization if **natural reinforcers** had been used along with the tokens.

4. This item is an example where **intermittent reinforcement** should have been used.

5. This item is an example of an **inappropriate target behavior.**

6. The use of **delayed reinforcement** was more effective in inducing generalization.

7. Elsa's behavior might have generalized if a **self-control procedure** had been used for her, as well as for Ruth.

8. The use of **intermittent reinforcement** might have been helpful in this case.

9. The **training and generalization situations were dissimilar.**

Chapter 10 *Modeling and Related Processes*

1. This item is an example of **modeling, vicarious reinforcement,** and **vicarious punishment.** It illustrates modeling because viewing the model's selections caused the observers to imitate those selections. It is an example of vicarious reinforcement because the rewards for the model's selections made the observers more likely to imitate those selections. It is an example of vicarious punishment because the disapproval of the model's selections made the observers less likely to imitate those selections. *Source: Liebert and Fernandez (1970)*

2. This item is an example of **modeling** in the specific form of **vicarious reinforcement.** It is an example of vicarious reinforcement because rewarding consequences followed the model's

(Dan's) attentive behavior, and this made the observer (Phil) more likely to imitate the behavior. *Source: Kazdin (1977c)*

3. This item is an example of **modeling** because the observer children imitated the feature of the filmed model's behavior of choosing an easy or a difficult task. It is an example of **symbolic modeling** because the model's behavior was presented on film rather than live. *Source: Sagotsky and Lepper (1982)*

4. This item is an example of **participant modeling** because the task was broken down into steps from easy-to-imitate to difficult-to-imitate, each step was modeled, the learner was prompted to imitate each modeled response, and, after each step was successfully imitated, the next step was attempted. *Source: Rachman and Lopatka (1988)*

5. This item is **not an example of modeling**. Although the students all behaved alike by quieting down when their teacher entered the classroom, it was due to the stimulus control of the teacher's presence rather than to the students' imitating each other's behavior.

6. This item is an example of **modeling** because the teacher's demonstration of correct reading responses strengthened imitative behavior in the observer children. *Source: D. D. Smith (1979)*

7. This item is an example of **modeling** because the videotaped demonstration of the divulging and question-asking behaviors strengthened imitative responding on the part of the patients. It is **symbolic modeling** because the model's behavior was presented on videotape rather than live. *Source: Anderson, DeVellis, and DeVellis (1987)*

8. This item is an example of **modeling** in the specific form of **self-modeling**; instances of the children's desirable swimming behaviors were videotaped and viewing these tapes caused the children to imitate their own desirable performances. *Source: Dowrick and Dove (1980)*

9. This item is an example of **modeling** because the adult models' demonstration of conversational skills strengthened imitative responding of those skills in the observer children. It is **symbolic modeling** because the modeled conversations were presented on videotapes rather than live. *Source: Charlop and Milstein (1989)*

10. This item is an example of **generalized imitation** because the boys were able to imitate different responses (the Spanish words) that had not been trained and that were not reinforced. *Source: Burgess, Burgess, and Esveldt (1970)*

11. This item is **not an example of modeling**. Although many people engaged in the same behavior of buying a new house, it was due to the drop in housing prices, not to people imitating one another's home purchases.

12. This item is an example of **peer modeling** because the girls imitated the behavior of a peer model. It is an example of **symbolic modeling** because the model was filmed rather than live. *Source: Gilbert et al. (1982)*

13. This item is an example of **modeling** because the model's demonstration of the response strengthened imitative responding in the observers. It is an example of **symbolic modeling** because the model's performance was videotaped rather than live. *Source: Smith and Hailey (1988)*

14. This item is an example of **generalized imitation**. Due to reinforcement of previous imitative responding, Billy was able to imitate many different modeled words the first time he observed them. In addition, it was not necessary for each instance of Billy's imitative responding to be reinforced. *Source: Lovaas, Berberich, Perloff, and Schaeffer (1966)*

15. This item is an example of **covert modeling;** rather than actually observing the modeled response, the students imagined someone modeling the response. *Source: Rosenthal and Reese (1976)*

16. This item is an example of **participant modeling;** the task was broken down into steps, behavior at each step was modeled, the patients were prompted to imitate each behavior, and after one step was completed, they moved on to the next step. *Source: Downs, Rosenthal, and Lichstein (1988)*

17. This item is an example of **peer modeling** because audiotaped peers served as models for imitative responding. It is an example of symbolic modeling because the model's performance was audiotaped rather than live. Note that this is not participant modeling because the students were not required to perform the modeled responses after watching demonstrations. It is an example of a special type of modeling in which the *absence* of a behavior was modeled and imitated. *Source: Horne and Matson (1977)*

18. This item is an example of **vicarious reinforcement** because the rewarding consequences that followed the boy's injury caused Vikka to imitate features of the behavior that produced it. *Source: Fyodorova and Frankel (1979)*

19. This item is an example of both **vicarious punishment** and **vicarious reinforcement.** It is vicarious reinforcement because the rewarding praise that followed the model's aggression strengthened imitation of the aggression. It is vicarious punishment because among the younger children, reprimanding the model's aggression caused these children to be less aggressive. Note that this description of the original study has been altered in order to illustrate more clearly the vicarious reinforcement and punishment effects. In the original study, the control group did not observe a model. Vicarious reinforcement and punishment are best experimentally tested using a control group that observes a model whose behavior is neither rewarded nor penalized. *Source: Rosekrans and Hartup (1967)*

20. This item is an example of **participant modeling;** the task was broken down into steps, each step was modeled, the learners were prompted to imitate each modeled behavior, and more difficult steps were attempted after the learners had succeeded at the easier steps. *Source: Ritter (1969)*

21. This item is **not an example of modeling.** Although the office workers behaved alike by closing the shades of the windows, these behaviors were due to the bright sunlight, not to imitation of each other's behavior.

22. This item is an example of **self-modeling;** Chuck's desirable behaviors were videotaped and shown to him, causing him to imitate his own desirable performances. It is an example of **symbolic modeling** because the modeled behaviors were videotaped, not live. *Source: Creer and Miklich (1970)*

23. This item is an example of **covert modeling** because the students did not observe a real model, but instead imagined a model performing a behavior. Note that this is not participant modeling. Although the task was broken down into steps, the learners did not imitate the model's behavior at each step level. *Source: Thase and Moss (1976)*

24. This item is an example of **self-modeling;** instances of the man's desirable behaviors were taped and shown to him, causing him to imitate features of his own behavior. *Source: Hosford (1981)*

25. This item is an example of **vicarious punishment;** punitive consequences followed the model's behavior, making the observer boys less likely to imitate the modeled response. *Source: Walters and Parke (1964)*

26. This item is an example of **peer modeling** because the confederates, who were peers of the subjects, modeled a certain rate of beer consumption, causing the subjects to imitate that rate. Source: Garlington and Dericco (1977)

Chapter 10   *Making Modeling Effective*

1. In this item the **target behavior was too complex.**

2. The **perceived competence of the model** could have been a problem in this item.

3. In this item the **model may have been too dissimilar** to the learners.

4. This procedure would have been more effective **if at each step learners had been trained to master the criterion** before going on to the next step.

5. The teacher should **use mediating labels** in this example.

6. Modeling would have been more effective if **rehearsal** had been permitted.

7. In this item, the **model may not have been similar enough** to the learners to be an effective model.

8. Lack of **rehearsal** is a problem in this item.

9. Modeling would have been more effective if the **model had been rewarded.**

Chapter 11   *Rule-Governed and Contingency-Shaped Behavior*

1. This item is an example of **rule-governed behavior;** Regulas's behavior of positioning his ship was due to rules that specified where the satellite would come down when influenced by various factors. *Source: Skinner (1969)*

2. This item is an example of **rule-governed behavior;** the poem was a verbal specification of desired behavior that caused Biff to operate the bellows properly. *Source: Skinner (1969)*

3. This item is an example of **contingency-shaped behavior** because shifting gears is due to the past consequences of correct and incorrect shifts. In addition, Carol can carry on other verbal activities while shifting gears, suggesting that self-instructions did not influence her performance.

4. This item is an example of **rule-governed behavior;** Mike's wearing white at night was governed by the verbal stimulus of "Wear white at night."

5. This item is an example of **contingency-shaped behavior** because Chris's movement of pulling down her hat brim was due to the past consequences of the response, not to a rule.

6. This item is an example of **rule-governed behavior** because Martha's spelling response was governed by the rule "i before e except after c."

7. This item is an example of **contingency-shaped behavior;** Bob's behavior of judging the trajectory of the balls and positioning himself properly was due to previous reinforcers and punishers associated with catching or not catching fly balls. *Source: Skinner (1969)*

8. This item is an example of **contingency-shaped behavior** because the turning movements were due to the past consequences of turning, not to rules.

9. This item is an example of **rule-governed behavior** because the rule in the book governed the response of calling people by name.

10. This item is an example of **contingency-shaped behavior** because shaving was due to the consequences of the response rather than to a rule.

Chapter 11   *Rule-Governed Behavior Change Procedures*

1. This item is an example of the use of **self-instructions** because the children learned to say and recall rules that influenced their behavior. It is not an example of a self-instructional package because the sequence of instructions used in Meichanbaum and Goodman's system was not employed. *Source: Kanfer, Karoly, and Newman (1975)*

2. This item is an example of **Meichanbaum and Goodman's self-instructional package** because the children learned a sequence of self rules: (a) defining the goal; (b) making and following a plan to meet the goal; (c) using task-specific self-instructions to carry out the plan; and (d) providing self-rewards for good performance and correcting errors. Although these researchers found self-instructions effective, training the children to say the self-instructions was so time-consuming that they did not recommend use of the procedure to improve kindergartners' letter writing. *Source: Robin, Armel, and O'Leary (1975)*

3. This item is **not an example of rule-governed behavior** because there is no mention of a rule, instruction, or other verbal stimulus for the acting responses. It is an example of modeling.

4. This item is an example of **problem solving** because the treatment consisted of recognizing and defining the problem, generating alternative solutions to the problem, selecting a solution, and evaluating the results. *Source: Kleiner, Marshall, and Spevak (1987)*

5. This item is an example of **cognitive therapy** because the procedure consisted of replacing maladaptive self-rules about the women's bodies with more positive self-rules. *Source: Rosen, Saltzberg, and Srebnik (1989)*

6. This item is an example of **cognitive therapy** because the procedure consisted of replacing maladaptive self-rules with helpful self-rules. Note that although this method has certain elements in common with problem solving, there was no training in defining problems, a key element of problem-solving treatments. *Source: Jarrett and Nelson (1987)*

7. This item is an example of **problem solving** because the treatment consisted of training in problem definition, generating alternative solutions, implementing the solutions, and evaluating the outcomes. Note that in this item, problems are called difficulties, but all the essential features of the problem-solving method are present. *Source: Lerner and Clum (1990)*

8. This item is an example of **cognitive therapy** because the procedure consisted of replacing maladaptive self-rules, the delusional beliefs, with more helpful self-rules. *Source: Lowe and Chadwick (1990)*

9. This item is **not an example of rule-governed behavior** because there is no mention of a rule, instruction, or other type of verbal stimulus governing the response. It is an example of reinforcement and extinction, rather than rule-governed behavior.

10. This item is an example of **Meichanbaum and Goodman's self-instructional package** because Terry learned a sequence of self-rules: (a) defining the task; (b) devising and following a plan to

meet the goal; (c) using task-specific self-instructions to carry out the plan; and (d) providing self-rewards for good performance and correcting mistakes. *Source: Gumaer and Headspeth (1985)*

11. This item is an example of the use of **self-instructions**. Two types of self-instructions were found to be effective, ones specifying a reduction in negative thoughts and ones specifying that the subjects try to pay attention to things other than the pain. It is not an example of a self-instructional package because there is no mention of use of the four-step sequence of self-instructions that Meichanbaum and Goodman use. *Source: Heyneman, Fremouw, Gano, Kirkland, and Heiden (1990)*

12. This item is an example of the use of **self-instructions** because the children learned self-rules specifying that they engage in honest behavior. It is not an example of a self-instructional package because the self-rules were simple and did not make use of the four-step sequence of self-instructions that Meichanbaum and Goodman suggested. *Source: Casey and Burton (1982)*

13. This item is an example of **problem solving** because the treatment consisted of training in defining problems, generating alternative solutions, and carrying out the solution thought to be the best one. *Source: Robin, Kent, O'Leary, Foster, and Prinz (1977)*

14. This item is an example of **cognitive therapy** because the procedure consisted of replacing maladaptive self-rules, the negative thoughts and self-instructions, with more helpful self-rules. *Source: Kendrick, Craig, Lawson, and Davidson (1982)*

15. This item is an example of **Meichanbaum and Goodman's self-instructional package** because the children learned a sequence of self-rules: (a) defining the task goals; (b) making and following a plan to meet the goal; (c) using task-specific self-instructions to carry out the plan; and (d) providing self-rewards for good performance and correcting errors. *Source: Mahn and Greenwood (1990)*

16. This item is an example of **problem solving** because the treatment consisted of training in problem definition, generating alternative solutions, implementing the solutions, and evaluating the outcomes. *Source: Camp, Blom, Herbert, and van Doorninck (1977)*

Chapter 11   *Making Rules Effective*

1. In this item there were **no differential consequences** for following or not following the rule.

2. In this item there were **no differential consequences** for following or not following the rule.

3. In this item the **rule was not specific enough**. Although general rules may have advantages in producing generalized changes in behavior, often they must be supplemented with more specific rules.

4. Matti might have been more likely to follow the rule if **the reason given included information about the natural consequences** of picking up sharp axes.

Chapter 11   *Making Self-Instructions Effective*

1. This item might have been more effective if Marissa has **stated her self-rule aloud**.

2. Lance might have been more successful if he had made a **public commitment** about his intention to quit smoking.

3. Merrilyn might have been more successful if she had **rewarded herself** for working out.

4. Luis should have been told to **say his rule aloud.**

5. Bernice might have **rewarded herself for following her rule.**

Chapter 11 *Making Problem-Solving Effective*

1. Marissa might have done better if she had **generated more alternatives** rather than just one to find the best solution for her problem.

2. This group might have done better had they **received feedback** about their performance.

3. Group B would have done better if they had had the opportunity to **practice their skills,** as Group A did.

Chapter 12 *Types of Feedback*

1. This item is an example of **publicly posted feedback**. It is feedback because the graphs were consequences of the students' cleaning behaviors. It is an example of public posting because the researchers placed the graphs in an area where everyone could see them. Although in this study, each student employee was identified by number rather than name, it is still an example of public posting. *Source: Anderson, Crowell, Hantula, and Siroky (1988)*

2. This item is an example of **spoken feedback**. The clinical director provided performance consequences by evaluating the treatment activities and discussing them with the unit coordinators. In this case, the feedback was effective in improving performance. *Source: Prue, Krapfl, Noah, Cannon, and Maley (1980)*

3. This item is an example of **correct-response feedback** and **written feedback**. It is an example of feedback because the students received a consequence for underlining: They saw the words under the sticky-backed paper that they peeled from the page. It is an example of correct-response feedback because the consequences for the students' responses were the correct responses, the real main ideas of the material the students had read. It is written feedback because the feedback was in written form. *Source: Glover, Zimmer, Filbeck, and Plake (1980)*

4. This item is an example of **labeled praise**. The children received praise for doing well, coupled with messages specifically labeling what they had done well. *Source: Fueyo, Saudargas, and Bushell (1975)*

5. This item is **not an example of feedback**. The videotaped information was provided to the employees before they had done any inspections rather than being dependent on any behaviors. Feedback consists of response-dependent consequences for behavior, not instructions that are presented before the behavior has occurred.

6. This item is an example of **biofeedback** and **automated feedback**. It is feedback because the increased neural activity was a consequence of the patients' attempts to increase it. It is biofeedback because the neural activity is a physiological response. It is automated feedback because the feedback was presented automatically by a device. *Source: Finley (1983)*

7. This item is an example of **written feedback, correct-response feedback,** and **why feedback**. It is written feedback because the students received the consequences in written form. It is correct response-feedback because the students received the correct response to each picture after

they had responded to it. It is why-feedback because they received reasons why each picture was or was not an example of the RX$_2$ structure. *Source: Tennyson, Steve, and Boutwell (1975)*

8. This item is an example of **self-monitoring** because the people recorded their own behavior, electricity use, and kept the results in the form of a chart or graph. It can also be considered automated feedback because a machine was used to provide the feedback. *Source: Winett, Neale, and Grier (1979)*

9. This item is an example of **corrective feedback, spoken feedback,** and **correct-response feedback.** It is corrective feedback because the sequence of prompts the instructor used were dependent only on incorrect responses and they prompted the correct response. It is spoken feedback because the teacher gave the feedback through spoken words. It is an example of correct-response feedback because the last prompt used in the sequence was the correct response. *Source: Pany and McCoy (1988)*

10. This item is an example of **publicly posted feedback.** It is feedback because the diagrams were consequences of the employees' thefts from the store. It is an example of public posting because the graphs were placed in an area where everyone could view them. *Source: Carter, Holström, Simpanen, and Melin (1988)*

11. This item is an example of **automated feedback,** specifically videotaped feedback. It is a feedback procedure because the videotapes were consequences of the boys' behavior. It is an automated feedback procedure because the feedback came from a machine, the videotape recorder-player. *Source: Esveldt, Dawson, and Forness (1974)*

12. This item is an example of **written feedback.** It is feedback because the hazard information messages were consequences of the performance of the supervisors and the workers at the factory. It is written feedback because the feedback messages were presented in written form. Spoken feedback was also used because the vice president sometimes presented the feedback in this form. *Source: Sulzer-Azaroff and de Santamaria (1980)*

13. This item is an example of **correct-response feedback, why feedback,** and **automated feedback.** It is correct-response feedback because the learners received the correct response as a consequence of their responding. It is why feedback because the learners got an explanation of why the correct responses were correct. It is automated feedback because a machine, a computer, was used to provide the feedback automatically. *Source: Kim and Phillips (1991)*

14. This item is an example of **labeled praise** because the teacher gave the students positive verbal feedback for complex questions and told the students what behaviors had merited the praise. *Source: Glover and Zimmer (1982)*

15. This item is **not an example of feedback.** The aide gave the new children the rules and information about why the rules should be followed before the children entered the classroom. Feedback consists of consequences for behavior and in this case the stimuli were provided before the child had an opportunity to behave.

16. This item is an example of **biofeedback** and **automated feedback.** It is an example of feedback because the video-display feedback was a consequence of the patients' responding. It is biofeedback because the feedback consisted of data about a physiological response, blood flow to the brain. It is automated feedback because the feedback came automatically from a machine. In this study, some patients learned to increase blood flow and some learned to decrease it. Depending on the stage of a migraine headache, it may be desirable either to increase or decrease blood flow. See the source article for details about the theory of the causes of migraine headaches. *Source: Lisspers and Öst (1990)*

17. This item is an example of **written feedback** and **corrective feedback**. It is feedback because these notes were dependent on the behavior of dropping and tilting the blinds. It is individual feedback because the staff received individual notes on their desks. It is corrective feedback because the notes were dependent only on incorrect responses. It may also be considered correct-response corrective feedback because the notes illustrated the proper way the blinds should be adjusted. *Source: Luyben (1984)*

18. This item is an example of **publicly posted feedback**. It is feedback because the performance graphs were consequences of the players' bodychecking behaviors. It is publicly posted feedback because the feedback graphs were posted where everyone could see them.
In addition, this use of feedback combined with goal setting helped the team to its first winning season in five years and a 23–15–2 record. *Source: Anderson, Crowell, Doman, & Howard (1988)*

19. This item is an example of **self-monitoring** because the man recorded aspects of his own behavior, arrival time at work and on-task time, and kept these in the form of a chart. *Source: Lamal and Benfield (1978)*

20. This item is an example of **written feedback** and **why feedback**. It is an example of feedback because the messages from the students were consequences of the professors' teaching behaviors. It is an example of individual-written feedback because the professors received the feedback privately. It is an example of why feedback because the feedback messages included the students' reasons why they rated the professor as they did. *Source: Sherman (1978)*

21. This item is an example of both **written** and **spoken feedback**. It is feedback because the graph and the discussions were consequences of the salespersons' performances. It was individual written and spoken feedback because the feedback took the form of both written materials (the graphs) and a spoken message (the discussion of performance). *Source: Brown, Malott, Dillon, and Keeps (1980)*

22. This item is an example of s**poken feedback, corrective feedback,** and **correct-response feedback**. It is spoken feedback because the feedback was presented in spoken form. It is corrective feedback because special consequences were dependent only on incorrect responses. It is correct-response feedback because the feedback included the correct response used as a modeling prompt. *Source: Goldstein (1984)*

23. This item is **not an example of feedback**. The coach's demonstration and explanation of the fade-away jump shot were not consequences of behavior because they occurred before the players had tried the shot. Feedback consists of consequences for behavior and feedback does not include information presented before a behavior has occurred.

24. This item is an example of **written corrective feedback** because the teacher provided checklists dependent on the students' errors and because the checklists acted as prompts for correct responding. It may also be considered an example of **self-monitoring** because in checking off the items, the students recorded their own behaviors. *Source: Dunlap and Dunlap (1989)*

25. This item is an example of **biofeedback** and **automated feedback**. It is feedback because the movements of the polygraph pen were consequences of what the patients did to control their sphincter muscles. It is biofeedback because the feedback information was reported on a physiological response. It is automated feedback because a machine provided the feedback. *Source: Engel, Nikoomanesh, and Schuster (1974)*

26. This item is an example of **labeled praise** because Mark's mother praised Mark and specifically described the praised behaviors. It is also spoken feedback because the labeled praise was presented orally. *Source: Dachman, Halasz, Bickett, and Lutzker (1984)*

Chapter 12   *Making Feedback Effective*

1. Johnny might have done better had the teacher given **immediate feedback** rather than waiting until five problems had been given.

2. The problem is that the **feedback should have been combined with goal setting**.

3. Peter might have benefited more had his teacher given more **specific feedback** than simply saying his pronunciation was right or wrong.

4. The teacher should have **required a response before providing feedback.**

5. The company should have provided more of an incentive, a **contrived money reinforcer,** for employees who submitted excellent suggestions.

6. The policeman was a very credible source of feedback for David. But David was a **less credible** source for his friend Aaron.

7. The problem is that the students were not given **drill and practice** in the skills with which they had difficulties.

8. The inspectors would have been wiser to give feedback on a **less predictable schedule.**

9. The feedback from the auditors should have been **more frequent** than once every 5 years.

Chapter 13   *Pavlovian Conditioning*

1. This item is an example of **Pavlovian conditioning.** The USs for asthma were the pollen extracts and the UR was the asthmatic attack. The neutral solvent and exposure to the mouthpiece were initially neutral stimuli. They predicted the US during the study, thus establishing the neutral solvent and the mouthpiece as CSs for the CR of a conditioned asthmatic attack. *Source: Dekker, Pelser, and Groen (1964)*

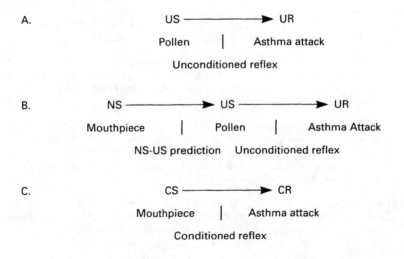

2. This item is **not an example of Pavlovian conditioning**. The smell of jasmine can be considered as a US for the UR of arresting a seizure. However, no CS predicted the US, so no conditioning took place. *Source: cf., Efron (1964)*

3. This item is an example of **Pavlovian conditioning**. Here the USs were the internal stimuli that normally precede a bowel movement and the UR was the bowel movement itself. The CS was the electrical current from the device, which predicted the US, the internal stimuli associated with an incipient bowel movement. The CR was the bowel movement that the electrical stimulation induced. *Source: Quarti and Renaud (1964)*

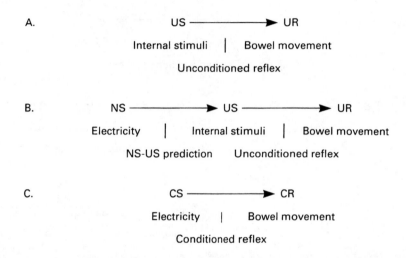

4. This item is an example of **Pavlovian conditioning**. The US is the bottle touching Ivan's lips and the UR is the sucking response. The CS (the organ tone) predicted the US, and this eventually gave the CS the ability to evoke the CR (the sucking movements). *Source: Kasatkin and Levikova (1935)*

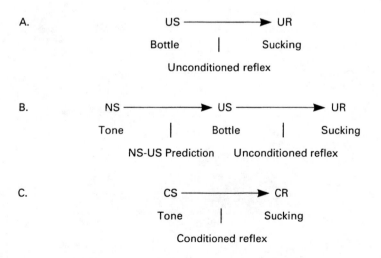

5. This item is **not an example of Pavlovian conditioning**. A US is the electric shock and the associated UR is the GSR. The light, an initially neutral stimulus, did not predict electric shock. Although the light elicited a GSR, it did so for reasons other than predicting the US and, therefore, it is not an example of Pavlovian conditioning.

6. This item is an example of **Pavlovian conditioning**. The US was the warm water and the UR was the vasodilation response. The thermal image and saying "Wek," initially neutral stimuli, became CSs by predicting the warm water flush. As a result, the thermal image and "Wek" acquired the ability to elicit hand warming, the CR. *Source: Hayduk (1980)*

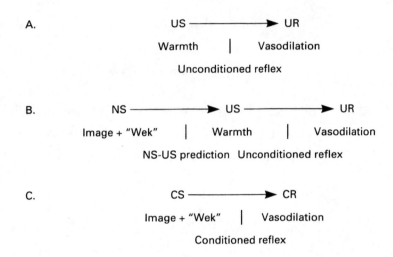

7. This item is an example of **Pavlovian conditioning**. The loud noise was the US and the crying and other fear responses were the UR. The white rat, initially a neutral stimulus in that it did not elicit Albert's fear responding, predicted the loud noise. In this way, it became a CS for the fear responses. *Source: Watson and Rayner (1920)*

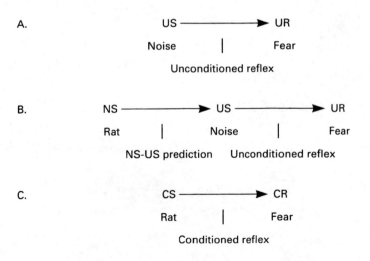

8. This item is an example of **Pavlovian conditioning**. The US is electric shock and the UR is the GSR response. The number 16, a formerly neutral stimulus, became a CS when it predicted the onset of shock. The number thus acquired the ability to elicit GSRs, the CR. This experiment shows that our thinking behavior, as exemplified by thoughts of the number 16 when derived as an answer to an arithmetic problem, can function as a CS. *Source: Doerr (1981)*

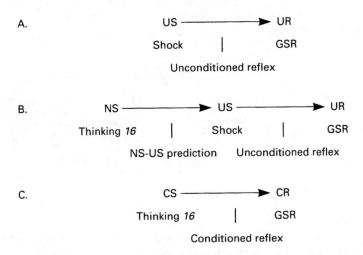

A.
$$US \longrightarrow UR$$
Shock | GSR
Unconditioned reflex

B.
$$NS \longrightarrow US \longrightarrow UR$$
Thinking *16* | Shock | GSR
NS-US prediction   Unconditioned reflex

C.
$$CS \longrightarrow CR$$
Thinking *16* | GSR
Conditioned reflex

9. This item is **not an example of Pavlovian conditioning**. In this example remaining in a social situation for progressively longer periods of time was rewarded. As such, response-dependent consequences were provided for engaging in social situations. In Pavlovian conditioning, response-dependent consequences are not used. This item is an example of shaping, an operant conditioning procedure.

10. This item is an example of **Pavlovian conditioning**. The USs were the films of nude men and women, and the URs were the changes in the size of Sweeney's penis. The CSs, the red circle and the green triangle, predicted the appearance of the USs and came to elicit the CRs, increases and decreases in penile volume. *Source: McConaghy (1970)*

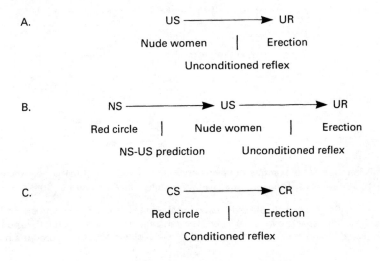

A.
$$US \longrightarrow UR$$
Nude women | Erection
Unconditioned reflex

B.
$$NS \longrightarrow US \longrightarrow UR$$
Red circle | Nude women | Erection
NS-US prediction   Unconditioned reflex

C.
$$CS \longrightarrow CR$$
Red circle | Erection
Conditioned reflex

11. This item is an example of **Pavlovian conditioning**. The US was the nausea-inducing drug and the UR was the nausea. Because the cranberry juice predicted the drug, the juice became a CS for nausea, the CR. *Source: Cannon, Best, Batson, and Feldman (1983)*

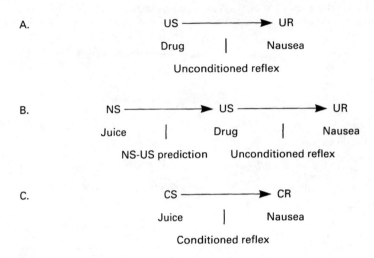

12. This item is an example of **Pavlovian conditioning**. The US was the instruction to imagine nausea and the UR was the nausea that the instructions elicited. The imagined drinking of V-8 juice predicted the nausea instructions, which established the V-8 as a CS for the unpleasant nausea feelings, the CR. The CS, the imagined drinking of V-8, appeared to generalize to actual V-8. *Source: Clarke and Hayes (1984)*

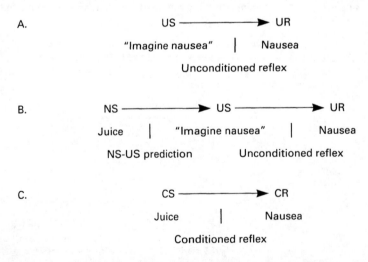

13. This item is **not an example of Pavlovian conditioning**. The shock consequence was dependent upon the drinking. The shock also had no effect on any measure of Ross's behavior.

14. This item is an example of **Pavlovian conditioning**. The US was the music and the UR was the good feelings that the music elicited. The red slides always predicted the music, the blue slides predicted the music half the time, and the yellow slides never predicted the music. This pattern

resulted in red acquiring the ability to function as a CS for the good feelings, the CR. *Source: Bierley, McSweeney, and Vannieuwkerk (1985)*

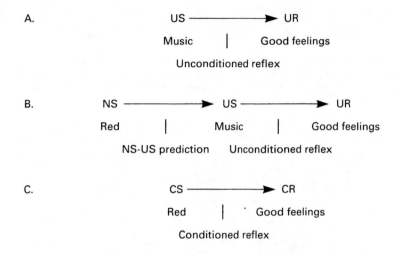

A.

US ─────────► UR

Music | Good feelings

Unconditioned reflex

B.

NS ─────────► US ─────────► UR

Red | Music | Good feelings

NS-US prediction Unconditioned reflex

C.

CS ─────────► CR

Red | Good feelings

Conditioned reflex

15. This item is an example of **Pavlovian conditioning**. The US was the scream and the UR was the GSR. The CS, the blue light plus the faces, predicted the US, which eventually gave the CS the ability to evoke the CR, the GSR. *Source: Vaitl, Gruppe, and Kimmel (1983)*

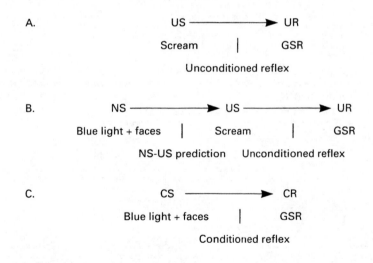

A.

US ─────────► UR

Scream | GSR

Unconditioned reflex

B.

NS ─────────► US ─────────► UR

Blue light + faces | Scream | GSR

NS-US prediction Unconditioned reflex

C.

CS ─────────► CR

Blue light + faces | GSR

Conditioned reflex

16. This item is **not an example of Pavlovian conditioning**. In this example, Pete's cordial responses toward Celia were rewarded. As such, response-dependent consequences were provided for engaging in pleasant behavior. In Pavlovian conditioning, response-dependent consequences are not used. This item is an example of **operant conditioning**.

17. This item is **not an example of Pavlovian conditioning**. In this example, a US was the shock and a UR was the GSR. However, no CS predicted the US and neither of the pictures came to evoke the GSR.

18. This item is **not an example of Pavlovian conditioning.** In this item, the stimuli, the word slides, were repeatedly presented, which somehow caused them to evoke salivation responses. The word pictures did not predict any US for the UR of salivation. Because the NS, the word pictures, came to evoke salivation for reasons other than a predictive relationship between the NS and a US, this item is not an example of Pavlovian conditioning.

19. This item is an example of **Pavlovian conditioning.** The USs were the finger sandwiches and the UR was salivation. The CS was the "Support Free Speech" message because it predicted the US, the sandwiches, and because it came to evoke the CR, salivation. *Source: cf., Razran (1949)*

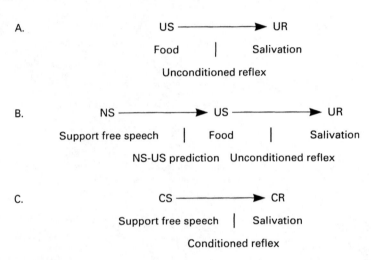

20. This item is an example of **Pavlovian conditioning.** The US was the tone and the UR was hearing the tone (or pressing the button). The CS was the light, which predicted the tone. The CR was hearing the tone in the absence of the tone (or pressing the button to show that the tone had been heard). As this example illustrates, Pavlovian conditioning can work to produce subtle types of hallucinations like this one. *Source: Ellson (1941)*

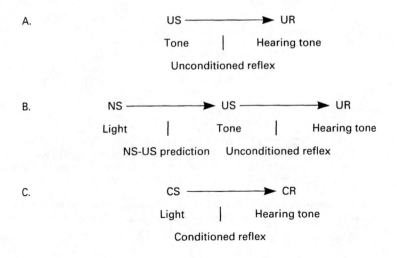

Chapter 13   *Pavlovian Conditioning Therapies and Processes*

---

1. This item is an example of **aversion therapy** because Pavlovian conditioning established a conditioned aversion to cigarettes, inappropriate stimuli that previously elicited good feelings and act as positive reinforcers. Conditioning occurred by setting up a predictive relationship between the cigarettes and the large amounts of noxious smoke that was a US for the UR of nausea. It is also an example of **counterconditioning** because the procedure established a CR, nausea, that was opposite to the response normally elicited by the cigarettes, good feelings. In the study this example is based on, the experimenters also found it useful to provide counseling to the smokers to help them quit. *Source: Tiffany, Martin, and Baker (1986)*

2. This item is an example of **flooding** because the therapists presented the CSs for fear responding (scenes of an airplane disaster) in intensive, maximum form without predicting a US for fear responding. It is not an example of aversion therapy because the purpose of the procedure was not to establish a conditioned aversion to a pleasurable stimulus. It is not counterconditioning because there was no attempt to condition a response that was opposite to the problem CR, fear responding. It is not systematic desensitization because there was no relaxation training. *Source: Howard, Murphy, and Clark (1983)*

3. This item is an example of **conditioned suppression** because presentation of the CS that had predicted the unpleasant slides caused a reduction in the frequency of performance on the Stroop task. *Source: Desbien and Yelen (1980)*

4. This item is **not an example** of any of the therapies or processes. This item has some similarity to systematic and *in vivo* desensitization because it makes use of relaxation training. However, in this item, relaxation training was the only method used. In the desensitization therapies, the therapist gradually introduces the feared stimuli (dogs, in this case) while the patient remains relaxed. It is not an example of counterconditioning because in counterconditioning, there is an attempt to condition a new CR to a CS that is opposite to the original CS. In this item, there was no attempt to condition relaxation to dog CSs, just an attempt to teach the patients to relax.

5. This item is an example of **second-order conditioning** because there was a predictive relationship between the pictures of females and previously established conditioned stimuli, the positive words. It may also be considered an example of **counterconditioning** because the purpose of the procedure was to establish CRs, positive emotional responses, that were opposite to the negative emotional responses previously elicited by females.*Source: Parish, Bryant, and Prawat (1977)*

6. This item is an example of **covert sensitization.** It is covert sensitization because the aversive stimuli used to establish the telephone stimuli as conditioned aversive stimuli were imaginal. It is also an example of a **counterconditioning** procedure because the purpose of the method was to establish CRs, unpleasant emotional responses, that were opposite to the pleasant emotional responses that obscene phone calls previously elicited. *Source: Moergen, Merkel, & Brown (1990)*

7. This item is an example of **aversion therapy** because Pavlovian conditioning established a conditioned aversion to the sadistic fantasy, an inappropriate stimulus that previously elicited good feelings. Conditioning occurred by setting up a predictive relationship between the sadistic fantasy stimuli and the shock, a US for the UR of unpleasant feelings. It is also an example of **counterconditioning** because the procedure established CRs, unpleasant feelings, that were opposite to the response normally elicited by the fantasy, pleasurable feelings. In this study, the man's nonsadistic fantasies were also encouraged to replace the sadistic fantasies. *Source: Mees (1966)*

8. This item is an example of *in vivo* **desensitization.** It is desensitization because relaxation training was used, the fear-provoking items were presented in a hierarchy from least to most fearful, and more fearful stimuli were introduced only when the man could relax when fewer fearful stimuli were presented. It is *in vivo* desensitization because actual noises were used rather
   than imagined noises. It is also an example of **counterconditioning** because the purpose of the
   procedure was to establish relaxation responding to the CS stimuli, and relaxation is opposite
   to fear and anxiety. *Source: Kipper (1977)*

9. This item is an example of **counterconditioning** because the purpose of the procedure was to
   establish pleasant emotional responding to the CS stimuli, and pleasant responding is opposite
   to intense fear. It is not an example of systematic desensitization; systematic desensitization
   makes use of relaxation training and an anxiety hierarchy, which the therapists did not use in
   this study. *Source: Hurley (1976)*

10. This item is an example of **covert sensitization** because the aversive stimuli used to establish
    beer as a conditioned aversive stimulus were imaginal. It is also an example of a **countercondi-
    tioning** procedure because the purpose of the method was to establish CRs, unpleasant nausea
    responses, that were opposite to the pleasant emotional responses that alcoholic drinks previ-
    ously elicited. In the actual study this example is based on, the experimenter got the condi-
    tioned nausea effect with 24 of 52 subjects. *Source: Elkins (1980)*

11. This item is an example of **aversion therapy** because Pavlovian conditioning established a con-
    ditioned aversion to Henry dressed in women's clothes, a stimulus that previously elicited
    good feelings. Conditioning occurred by setting up a predictive relationship between Henry's
    cross dressing and the apomorphine injections, a US for the UR of nausea and vomiting. It is
    also an example of **counterconditioning** because the procedure established CRs, unpleasant
    feelings, that were opposite to the responses of pleasurable feelings previously elicited by
    dressing in women's clothes. *Source: Lavin, Thorpe, Barker, Blakemore, and Conway (1961)*

12. This item is an example of **systematic desensitization.** It is desensitization because the thera-
    pist used relaxation training, presented the fear-provoking items in a hierarchy from least to
    most fearful, and introduced more fearful stimuli only when Gidget could relax in the presence
    of less fearful stimuli. It is systematic desensitization because the therapists had Gidget imag-
    ine the beach and water stimuli during therapy. It is also an example of **counterconditioning**
    because the purpose of the procedure was to establish relaxation responding to the CS stimuli,
    and relaxation is opposite to fear and anxiety. *Source: Krop and Krause (1976)*

13. This item is an example of **flooding** because the therapist presented the CSs for fear respond-
    ing, scenes of snakes, in intensive, maximum form without predicting a US for fear responding.
    It is not an example of aversion therapy because the purpose of the procedure was not to
    establish a conditioned aversion to a pleasurable stimulus. It is not counterconditioning
    because there was no attempt to condition a response that was opposite to the problem CR,
    fear responding. This is not systematic desensitization because there was no relaxation train-
    ing. *Source: Hogan and Kirchner (1968)*

14. This item is an example of **flooding** because the therapists presented the incest scenes, the CSs
    for undesired emotional responding, in intensive, maximum form without predicting a US for
    fear responding. It is not an example of aversion therapy because the purpose of the procedure
    was not to establish a conditioned aversion to a pleasurable stimulus. It is not systematic
    desensitization because there was no relaxation training and no gradual introduction of the CS.
       In the actual experiment this item is based on, relaxation training was used, so the proce-
    dure was a counterconditioning technique. We have omitted this detail to show it as an unam-
    biguous example of flooding. This experiment also provoked some controversy about the
    appropriateness of applying flooding to the problem of sexual assault. [See Kilpatrick and Best
    (1984) and Rychtarik, Silverman, Van Landingham, and Prue (1984b)]. *Source: Rychtarik,
    Silverman, Van Landingham, and Prue (1984a)*

15. This item is an example of **second-order conditioning**. It is second-order conditioning because there was a predictive relationship between the phobic words and previously established conditioned stimuli, the calm words. It is also an example of **counterconditioning** because the purpose of the procedure was to establish CRs, calm pleasant feelings, that were opposite to the unpleasant fear responses that the phobic stimuli previously elicited. *Source: Weiss and Evans (1978)*

16. This item is an example of **second-order conditioning**. It is second-order conditioning because there was a predictive relationship between the sexual activity words and previously established conditioned stimuli, the words that elicited positive emotional responses. It is also an example of **counterconditioning** because the purpose of the procedure was to establish CRs, more positive emotional responses, that were opposite to the negative emotional responses that the sexual activities had previously elicited. *Source: Tryon and Briones (1985)*

17. This item is an example of **systematic desensitization**. It is desensitization because the therapist used relaxation training, presented the fear-provoking items in a hierarchy from least to most fearful, and introduced more fearful stimuli only when Mark could relax in the presence of the less fearful stimuli. It is systematic desensitization because the public-speaking stimuli occurred in imaginal form during therapy. It is also an example of **counterconditioning** because the purpose of the procedure was to establish relaxation responding to the CS stimuli, and relaxation is opposite to fear and anxiety. *Source: Migler and Wolpe (1967)*

18. This item is **not an example** of any of the therapies or processes. In this item, the therapist simply trained the patient to relax. Because the feared stimuli were not introduced in imaginal or *in vivo* form during therapy, it is not an example of the desensitization therapies, counterconditioning, or flooding. All these therapies make use of presentation of the feared stimuli.

19. This item is an example of **conditioned suppression** because presentation of the CS that had predicted shock caused a reduction in the frequency of operant button pushing. *Source: Di Giusto and Bond (1978)*

20. This item is an example of **counterconditioning** because the purpose of the procedure was to establish sexual responding to the CS stimuli, and sexual responding is opposite to fear. It is not an example of systematic desensitization because systematic desensitization makes use of relaxation training. *Source: Brown (1978)*

21. This item is an example of *in vivo* **desensitization**. It is desensitization because the therapists used relaxation training, presented the fear-provoking items in a hierarchy from least to most fearful, and introduced more fearful stimuli only when the man could relax in the presence of less fearful stimuli. It is *in vivo* desensitization because the therapists used real hypodermic syringes rather than imagined syringes. It is also an example of **counterconditioning** because the purpose of the procedure was to establish relaxation responding to the CS stimuli, and relaxation is opposite to fear and anxiety. *Source: Turnage and Logan (1974)*

22. This item is an example of **covert sensitization**. It is covert sensitization because imaginal rather than real aversive stimuli used to establish the to-be-stolen car as a conditioned aversive stimulus. It is also an example of a counterconditioning procedure because the purpose of the method was to establish CRs, unpleasant sickness responses, that were opposite to the pleasant emotional responses previously elicited by a car to be stolen. In the actual study this example is based on, the therapist did not report the outcome of this case. *Source: Cautela (1967)*

23. This item is an example of **systematic desensitization**. It is desensitization because the therapist used relaxation training, presented the anger-inducing items in a hierarchy from least to most provocative, and introduced more anger-provoking stimuli only when Mel could relax in the presence of less provocative stimuli. It is systematic desensitization because the anger-provoking stimuli were imaginal in form during therapy. It is also an example of **countercondition-

ing because the purpose of the procedure was to establish relaxation responding to the CS stimuli, and relaxation is opposite to anger. *Source: Schloss, Smith, Santora, and Bryant (1989)*

Chapter 13   *Making Pavlovian Conditioning Effective*

1. This procedure might have been more effective if the **US (the shock) had been more intense.** Also, Garcia effects work against the use of shock as a US in this kind of application.

2. The problem is **overshadowing**. The large triangle was a more prominent stimulus than the small square. When two neutral stimuli are presented together and both predict the US, overshadowing often will occur: The more prominent, intense, or vivid stimulus will become a CS, not the less prominent one.

3. The problem here is **CS preexposure**: The students had been exposed frequently to the word prior to the procedure. Dr. Brown might have had more effective startle conditioning had she used a word the students were not so familiar with.

4. Because Dr. Cass could not describe the scene vividly enough for Lewis to imagine the scene, the **CS was insufficiently intense and vivid.**

5. The problem here is with the **timing of the NS and the US.** Tim used backward conditioning, which is not as effective as forward conditioning. He would have been more successful if the NS (sound) had preceded the US (air puff).

6. The problem here is **blocking**. The green cross, a preestablished CS, was presented with the blue triangle, a neutral stimulus. Under these conditions, the blue triangle will often not become a CS.

7. The problem here is that the **US, the music, was initially not sufficiently intense** and counter-conditioning was not successful.

8. The problem here is with the **number of conditioning trials.** Three trials probably were not enough to produce effective conditioning.

9. The problem is **blocking**. The spider slides, a preestablished CS, were presented with the snake slides, stimuli that did not elicit relaxation. The snake slides should have been presented alone in this procedure, not alongside the spider slides.

10. The problem here is that the model-type CS was **overshadowed** by the color CS. The advertisers should have made sure that the particular model was the most vivid CS.

11. In this item, the covert sensitization procedure took place only in a single trial. Use of a **greater number of conditioning trials** is needed.

12. The problem is **CS intensity**. At first the CS, the flash of light, was insufficiently intense to obtain conditioning.

13. The problem is **CS preexposure**. The American flag is a stimulus to which people in Iowa would have received extensive preexposure.

14. The problem is the **timing of the NS,** the laundry detergent box, **and the US,** the music and dancing. The interval of time elapsing between the NS and US was too long.

Chapter 14   *Conceptual Discrimination*

1. This item is an example of **conceptual discrimination** because on the posttest the students could discriminate the critical features of morphemes, as their ability to discriminate novel examples and nonexamples of the morpheme shows. Critical features of the morpheme included a unit of languages (a) that carry meaning; (b) that contribute to the meaning of words in which they appear; and (c) cannot be subdivided into smaller units that have meaning. Variable features of the morpheme include whether the unit is a word or part of a word, the length of the unit, the spelling of the unit, and so forth. *Source: Markle and Tiemann (1974)*

2. This item is **not an example of conceptual discrimination**. On the exam, the students were tested using the same mineral specimens they had used during training. Because of this, the students' correct exam responding could be due to learning names for the specific specimens used in training rather than learning the names of the critical features of each mineral. In order to test for conceptual behavior, the exam would have had to use novel mineral specimens the students had not examined before. This would have provided a test of the discriminative control of stimulus features, rather than specific stimuli, that defines conceptual behavior.

3. This item is an example of **conceptual discrimination** because on the posttest the students could discriminate the critical features of trochaic meter, as shown by their ability to discriminate novel examples and nonexamples of this concept. The critical feature of trochaic meter is that it is a stress pattern of poetry in which one stressed syllable is followed by one unstressed syllable. Variable features of trochaic meter include the content of the poem, stylistic features of the poem, the quality of the poem, and so forth. *Source: Tennyson, Woolley, and Merrill (1972)*

4. This item is an example of a **faulty conceptual discrimination**. It has elements of a conceptual discrimination because the students could identify the critical features of *on top* with small objects. However, the critical features of *on top* did not control the students' responding with large objects. It is an example of **undergeneralization** because the students identified some concept examples as nonexamples.

5. This item is an example of **conceptual discrimination** because on the posttest the students could discriminate the critical features of the constructional approach, as shown by their ability to discriminate novel examples and nonexamples of this concept. The critical feature of the constructional approach is that new useful behavior is trained. Variable features of the constructional approach include the specific type of behavior taught, the subject population, and the methods used to teach the new behavior. *Source: Chase, Johnson, and Sulzer-Azaroff (1985) and Johnson and Chase (1981)*

6. This item is an example of a **faulty conceptual discrimination**. The testing procedure was appropriate for testing conceptual discrimination, because it used novel examples and nonexamples. However, the critical features of squareness did not control the children's responding on the test, as their identification of nonsquare forms as squares shows. It is an example of **overgeneralization** because the children identified some concept nonexamples as examples.

7. This item is an example of **conceptual discrimination** because on the posttest the students could discriminate the critical features of chide, as their ability to discriminate novel examples and nonexamples of this concept shows. The critical feature of chide is that there is criticism of one person's performance by another person or other people. Variable features of chide include the nature of the criticism, the form (e.g., written, spoken) of the criticism, and its length and intensity. Note that in this item, conceptual behavior was taught using various methods. The method used to teach conceptual behavior is not a critical feature of conceptual behavior. *Source: Johnson and Stratton (1966)*

8. This item is an example of **conceptual discrimination** because on the posttest the students could discriminate the critical features of diagonal, as shown by their ability to discriminate novel examples and nonexamples of this concept. The critical feature of diagonal is that the line angle be discernibly different from either 0 or 90°. Variable features of diagonal include the length, color, thickness, and specific angle of the lines within the acceptable range of variation. Note that on the posttest, the same angles were used as the ones used in training, but the stimuli were made novel by altering the variable features of the lines. *Source: Gersten, White, Falco, and Carnine (1982)*

9. This item is an example of **conceptual discrimination** because on the posttest the students could discriminate the critical features of irony, as shown by their ability to discriminate novel examples and nonexamples of this concept. Critical features of irony include the dissembling feature, subtlety, and surprise. Variable features include humorous or tragic content. *Source: Kennedy (1990)*

10. This item is an example of a **faulty conceptual discrimination**. For these students, the critical features of inflation were not discriminative stimuli for their behavior, because they could not correctly identify nonexamples of inflation. It is an example of overgeneralization because the students identified nonexamples of inflation as examples.

11. This item is an example of **conceptual discrimination** because on the posttest the students could discriminate the critical features of *medium-sized,* as their ability to discriminate novel examples and nonexamples of this concept shows. The critical feature of *medium-sized* is that an object be intermediate in size relative to two comparison objects. Variable features of *medium-sized* include the type of the objects, the shapes of the objects, the color of the objects, and the weight of the objects. *Source: Seifert and Schwarz (1991)*

12. This item is an example of **conceptual discrimination** because after training, the students could discriminate the critical feature of character motives, as their ability to discriminate novel examples and nonexamples of this concept shows. The critical feature of a character's motive is the reason why the character acts as she does in a story. Variable features of a character's motive include the apparent reason for the character's actions, the age of the character, and whether the character's motives are good or bad. *Source: Carnine, Stevens, Clements, and Kameenui (1982)*

13. This item is **not an example of conceptual discrimination**. The students were tested using the same reading passages that they had used during training. Because of this, the students' correct responding on the tests could be due to learning the specific main ideas of each passage rather than learning the critical features of the main idea. In order to test for conceptual behavior, the tests would have had to use novel reading passages, ones the students had not read before. This would have provided a test of whether the critical features of the concept were discriminative stimuli for the students' responding. *Source: Glover, Zimmer, Filbeck & Plake (1980)*

14. This item is an example of a **faulty conceptual discrimination**. It has elements of a conceptual discrimination; the students could identify the critical features represented in some of the cubist paintings. However, the critical features of cubism did not properly control the students' responding to all the cubist paintings because some examples of cubism were classified as nonexamples. It is an example of **undergeneralization** because the students identified some concept examples as nonexamples.

| **Chapter 14** | *Conceptual Behavior and Generalized Response Classes* |

1. This item is an example of **both conceptual behavior and a generalized response class.** It is conceptual behavior because the trainees responded correctly to the stimulus features of the washers and dryers, as shown by their performance on novel machines. It is a generalized response class because the trainees learned response features on the training machines, and these response features allowed for correct responding on the new machines, which required novel responses. It is an example of general-case instruction. *Source: Neef, Lensbower, Hockersmith, DePalma, and Gray (1990)*

2. This item is an example of **both conceptual behavior and a generalized response class.** It is conceptual behavior because Roy's behavior was controlled by certain critical features of weather conditions rather than specific signals. This was shown by his ability to respond correctly to those features even when they occurred in novel combinations. It is also a generalized response class because Roy's analyses and predictions involved different weather conditions, but shared certain general features, such as giving conditions the appropriate weightings. Roy's generalized response class was highlighted by his accuracy in making novel predictions under unusual conditions.

3. This item is an example of **both conceptual behavior and of a generalized response class.** It is conceptual behavior because Violet's responses were controlled by the critical features of a dog (i.e., *dogness*) rather than by a specific dog. This was shown by her discriminative responding to novel dogs. This is also a generalized response class because Violet's hiding behaviors were all different, but shared the response feature of putting her out of sight of dogs. Violet's learning of a generalized response class was demonstrated by her responding in new situations that required novel hiding behaviors. *Source: Skinner (1935)*

4. This item is an **example of conceptual behavior** because Anders could discriminate right triangles from other types of triangles. However, this is not a generalized response class because Anders could not apply the formula to solve a range of problems involving the calculation of the sides of right triangles.

5. This item is an example of **both conceptual behavior and a generalized response class.** It is conceptual behavior because the trainees responded correctly to the stimulus features of the pullover shirts, as shown by their performance with novel shirts. It is a generalized response class because the trainees learned response features on the training shirts. These response features allowed for correct responding on the untrained test shirts, which required slightly different responses, but having the same response features as those that were trained. It is an example of general-case instruction. *Source: Day and Horner (1986)*

6. This item is an **example of conceptual behavior** because Kevin could respond to the critical features of matriarchal and patriarchal societies, as shown by his ability to classify novel examples of these societies. It is **not an example of a generalized response class** because Kevin could not engage in responses, writing novel examples of matriarchal and patriarchal societies, that were defined by a set of response features (i.e., the features of matriarchal and patriarchal societies).

7. This item is an example of **both conceptual behavior and a generalized response class.** It is conceptual behavior because the trainees responded correctly to the stimulus features of the containers, as shown by their performance with novel containers. It is a generalized response class because the trainees learned response features on the training containers. These response features allowed for correct responding on the untrained test containers, which required slightly different responses, but responses having the same essential response features as those that

were trained. It is an example of general-case instruction. *Source: Steere, Strauch, Powell, & Butterworth (1990)*

8. This item is an example of **both conceptual behavior and of a generalized response class**. It is conceptual behavior because the trainees responded correctly to the stimulus features of the things in the model apartment, as shown by their performance in the novel rooms to be cleaned. It is a generalized response class because the trainees learned response features in the model apartment, and these response features allowed for correct responding on the untrained test rooms. It is an example of general-case instruction. *Source: Lengyel, Domaracki, and Lyon (1990)*

9. This item is **not an example of either conceptual behavior or a generalized response class**. It is not conceptual behavior because Agnes was not responding to stimulus features, but instead to 10 different stimuli, the modeled responses. It is not a generalized response class because Agnes could not engage in novel responses that shared a response feature such as imitativeness.

10. This item is an **example of conceptual behavior** because June's behavior was under the control of stimulus features, the artistic features of the students' projects. This stimulus-feature control is shown by June's ability to identify the critical stimulus features in novel projects. It is also an **example of a generalized response class** because June could correctly explain how to rearrange the elements of the students' projects, which were all novel to her.

Chapter 14   *Stimulus Equivalence*

1. This item is an example of a **reflexive relation** because Adam could correctly perform this identity matching task. There are no derived relations learned in this item.

2. This item is an example of a **symmetric relation** because the pictures were S+s for selecting the corresponding written word and the reverse was also true: The words were S+s for selecting the correct pictures. A derived relation was the one in which the written words were S+s for selecting the corresponding pictures. This relation was derived because it was not directly established through stimulus discrimination training.

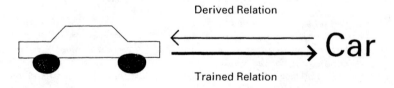

3. This item is an example of **reflexive, symmetric, transitive**, and **equivalence relations**. It is stated that Penny could do identity matching with all the stimuli, so this illustrates reflexivity. Similarly, for each S+ ⟶ Response relation Penny learned, the reverse relation was also learned, illustrating symmetrical relations. Penny was also able to select the synonyms when shown the corresponding pictures, illustrating transitivity. Finally, Penny was able to select the correct pictures when shown the corresponding synonyms, illustrating equivalence. One equiv-

alence class contained three members, the picture of a car, the word *car,* and the word *auto.*
There are four derived relations in this item. They are, with the S+ listed first: (a) *Car* ———▶ Car
picture; (b) *Auto* ———▶ *Car;* (c) Picture of car ———▶ *Auto;* (d) *Auto* ———▶ Picture of car.

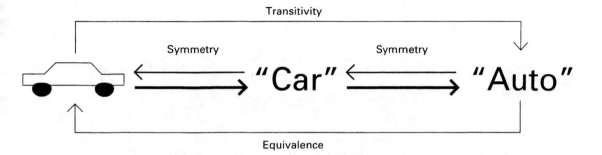

4. This item is an example of a **symmetric relation** because the animal pictures were S+s for
   selecting the corresponding animal sounds and the reverse was also true: The animal sounds
   were S+s for selecting the correct animal pictures. A derived relation was the one in which the
   animal sounds were S+s for selecting the animal pictures because this relation was not directly
   established through stimulus discrimination training.

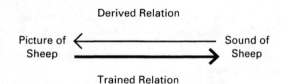

5. This item is an example of **reflexive relations** because Mavis could do identity matching with all
   the stimuli in the experiment. It is an example of a **symmetric relation** because as a result of
   training the ASL-sign ———▶ all-caps-word relation, the reverse relation (all-caps word ———▶
   ASL sign) was also established. Another symmetric relation was seen in Mavis's ability to select
   the correct all-caps word when given the corresponding lower-case word. However, this is not
   an example of transitivity or stimulus equivalence because Mavis could not select the correct
   lower-case word when given the corresponding ASL sign or do the correct sign when shown
   the corresponding ASL word. The derived relations were the two symmetric relations.

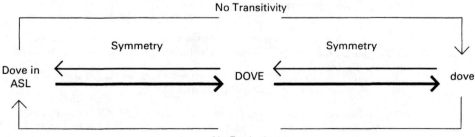

6. This item is an example of **reflexivity** because Pete could do identity matching with both the leaves and the leaf-name cards. It is not an example of symmetry because after training the leaf ——► leaf-name relation, the reverse relation was not established. There are no derived relations in this item.

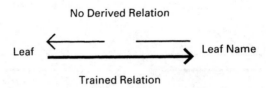

No Derived Relation

Leaf   Leaf Name

Trained Relation

Chapter 14   *Making Conceptual Discrimination Effective*

1. The problem here is **failure to use a sufficiently broad range of examples** teaching. Although a proper concept analysis was done that specified the critical and variable features of dwellings, an insufficiently broad range of dwellings was included in the teaching examples.

2. The problem here is that Ms. B **failed to present nonexamples.** Her students would have learned the concept triangularity better if they had some exposure to figures that were similar but were not in fact triangles.

3. The problem here is that Timmy's father **failed to do a concept analysis.** This in turn led to failure to include a broad range of examples of felines that varied in the size of the animals.

4. The problem here is that Peter **did not use a wide range of examples and nonexamples** in his training procedure.

5. The problem with this item is that Dr. Jones **did not use a focal example** of a family unit. Use of focal examples promotes longer-term retention of conceptual discriminations.

6. The problem is that Dr. Bergman **did not provide a definition** of shaping.

7. The problem is a **failure to use minimally different nonexamples.** Because only two-dimensional nonexamples were used, the nonexamples were not minimally different from the examples, which were all three-dimensional.

Chapter 14   *Making Concept and Generalized Response Class Teaching Effective*

1. In this item the goal tasks that Lynn needed to learn were not well defined. The therapist should have **defined the goal more broadly** to include queries from visitors, staff, and so on.

2. David's mother would have had more success if **she had taught David the rule** that he could use with any problem involving multiplying by 9.

3. The problem here is that the goal task involved training Sally to use a class of computers, but her **training involved only one type.** The workshop should have had a variety of models for Sally to learn on.

4. The problem is a **failure to test using novel stimuli and novel responses.**

5. The problem here is that if the teacher's goal was to teach general principles, she should have analyzed the task with the intention of training Ruth the similarities or samenesses between the two behavioral procedures.

6. Because the goal was general exam skills, there should have been more variety among the kinds of items used as training items.

References/Author Index

The numbers in brackets at the end of each reference indicate the pages in this text where the reference is cited. The numbers in parentheses after the page numbers indicate conceptual-exercise item numbers.

Abernethy, E. M. (1940). The effect of changed environmental conditions on the results of college examinations. *Journal of Psychology, 10,* 293–301. [180]

Abramowitz, A. J., & O'Leary, S. G. (1990). Effectiveness of delayed punishment in an applied setting. *Behavior Therapy, 21,* 231–239. [116]

Abramowitz, A. J., O'Leary, S. G., & Futtersak, M. W. (1988). The relative impact of long and short reprimands on children's off-task behavior in the classroom. *Behavior Therapy, 19,* 243–247. [113]

Acker, M. M., & O'Leary, S. G. (1988). Effects of consistent and inconsistent feedback on inappropriate child behavior. *Behavior Therapy, 19,* 619–624. [110]

Ackerman, A. M., & Shapiro, E. S. (1984). Self-monitoring and work productivity with mentally retarded adults. *Journal of Applied Behavior Analysis, 17,* 403–407. [354]

Ader, R., & Seibetta, J. (1964). Temporal parameters in the acquisition of a free-operant avoidance response in human subjects. *Psychonomic Science, 1,* 385–386. [148]

Alavosius, M. P., & Sulzer-Azaroff, B. (1990). Acquisition and maintenance of health-care routines as a function of feedback density. *Journal of Applied Behavior Analysis, 23,* 151–162. [363]

Alexander, R. N., & Apfel, C. H. (1976). Altering schedule of reinforcement for improved classroom behavior. *Exceptional Children, 43,* 97–99. [170, 171]

Alexander, R. N., Corbett, T. F., & Smigel, J. (1976). The effects of individual and group consequences on school attendance and curfew violations with predelinquent adolescents. *Journal of Applied Behavior Analysis, 9,* 221–226. [126–127(29), 478]

Allen, K. E., & Harris, F. R. (1966). Elimination of a child's excessive scratching by training the mother in reinforcement procedures. *Behavior Research and Therapy, 2,* 79–84. [84(3), 472]

Allen, K. E., Hart, B. M., Buell, J. S., Harris, F. R., & Wolf, M. M. (1964). Effects of social reinforcement on isolate behavior of a nursery school child. *Child Development, 35,* 511–518. [182(1), 482]

Allen, L. D., Gottselig, M., & Boylan, S. (1982). A practical mechanism for using free time as a reinforcer in classrooms. *Education and Treatment of Children, 5,* 347–353. [88(30), 474]

Alloy, L. B., & Abramson, L. Y. (1979). Judgment of contingency in depressed and nondepressed students: Sadder but wiser? *Journal of Experimental Psychology: General, 108,* 441–485. [334]

Alloy, L. B., & Ahrens, A. H. (1987). Depression and pessimism for the future: Biased use of statistically relevant information in predictions for self versus others. *Journal of Personality and Social Psychology, 52,* 366–378. [334]

Anderson, D. C., Crowell, C. R., Doman, M., & Howard, G. S. (1988). Performance posting, goal setting, and activity-contingent praise as applied to a university hockey team. *Journal of Applied Psychology, 73,* 87–95. [371(18), 505]

Anderson, D. C., Crowell, C. R., Hantula, D. A., & Siroky, L. M. (1988). Task clarification and individual performance posting for improving cleaning in a student-managed university bar. *Journal of Organizational Behavior Management, 9,* 73–90. [368(1), 503]

Anderson, L. A., DeVellis, B. M., & DeVellis, R. F. (1987). Effects of modeling on patient communication, satisfaction, and knowledge. *Medical Care, 25,* 1044–1056. [305(7), 498]

Anderson, R. C., & Kulhavy, R. W. (1972). Learning concepts from definitions. *American Educational Research Journal, 9,* 385–390. [434]

Anderson, R. C., Kulhavy, R. W., & Andre, T. (1972). Conditions under which feedback facilitates learning from programmed lessons. *Journal of Educational Psychology, 63,* 186–188. [362]

Andrewes, D. (1989). Management of disruptive behavior in the brain-damaged patient using selective reinforcement. *Journal of Behavior Therapy and Experimental Psychiatry, 20,* 261–264. [109]

Arnett, M. S., & Ulrich, R. E. (1975). Behavior control in a home setting. *The Psychological Record, 25,* 395–413. [174–175]

Aronfreed, J., & Reber, A. (1965). Internalized behavioral suppression and the timing of social punishment. *Journal of Personality and Social Psychology, 1,* 3–16. [116]

Ash, D. W., & Holding, D. H. (1990). Backward versus forward chaining in the acquisition of a keyboard skill. *Human Factors, 32,* 139–146. [235, 245(8), 494]

Ashem, B. (1963). The treatment of a disaster phobia by systematic desensitization. *Behavior Research and Therapy, 1,* 81–84. [376–378]

Ashford, S. J., & Tsui, A. S. (1991). Self-regulation for managerial effectiveness: The role of active feedback seeking. *Academy of Management Journal, 34,* 251–280. [361]

At Emery Air Freight: Positive reinforcement boosts performance. (1973, 1, Winter). *Organizational Dynamics.* pp. 41–50. [343–345]

Ayllon, T., & Azrin, N. H. (1964). Reinforcement and·instructions with mental patients. *Journal of the Experimental Analysis of Behavior, 7,* 327–331. [41–42, 319]

Ayllon, T., & Azrin, N. H. (1965). The measurement and reinforcement of behavior of psychotics. *Journal of the Experimental Analysis of Behavior, 8,* 357–383. [35, 37]

Ayllon, T., & Azrin, N. H. (1968). *The token economy: A motivational system for therapy and rehabilitation.* New York: Appleton-Century-Crofts. [35, 261]

Ayllon, T., Kuhlman, C., & Warzak, W. J. (1982). Programming resource room generalization using lucky charms. *Child and Family Behavior Therapy, 4,* 61–67. [263]

Ayllon, T., & Michael, J. (1959). The psychiatric nurse as a behavioral engineer. *Journal of the Experimental Analysis of Behavior, 2,* 323–334. [48]

Ayllon, T., & Roberts, M. D. (1974). Eliminating discipline problems by strengthening academic performance. *Journal of Applied Behavior Analysis, 7,* 71–76. [12]

Azrin, N. H., & Holz, W. C. (1966). Punishment. In W. K. Honig (Ed.), *Operant behavior: Areas of research and application* (pp. 380–447). New York: Appleton. [97]

Azrin, N. H., Hutchinson, R. R., & Hake, D. F. (1966). Extinction-induced aggression. *Journal of the Experimental Analysis of Behavior, 9,* 191–204. [65]

Azrin, N. H., & Nunn, R. G. (1973). Habit reversal: A method of eliminating nervous habits and tics. *Behavior Research and Therapy, 11,* 619–628. [103]

Azrin, N. H., & Peterson, A. L. (1988). Habit reversal for the treatment of Tourette Syndrome. *Behavior Research and Therapy, 26,* 347–351. [103–104, 105]

Azrin, N. H., & Powell, J. (1968). Behavioral engineering: The reduction of smoking behavior by a conditioning apparatus and procedure. *Journal of Applied Behavior Analysis, 1,* 193–200. [108]

Azrin, N. H., & Powell, J. (1969). Behavioral engineering: The use of response priming to improve prescribed self-medication. *Journal of Applied Behavior Analysis, 2,* 39–42. [156(21), 481]

Azrin, N. H., & Powers, M. A. (1975). Eliminating classroom disturbances of emotionally disturbed children by positive practice procedures. *Behavior Therapy, 6,* 525–534. [102,103]

Azrin, N. H., Rubin, H., O'Brien, F., Ayllon, T., & Roll, D. (1968). Behavioral engineering: Postural control by a portable operant apparatus. *Journal of Applied Behavior Analysis, 1,* 99–108. [156(3), 480]

Azrin, N. H., & Wesolowski, M. D. (1974). Theft reversal: An overcorrection procedure for eliminating stealing by retarded persons. *Journal of Applied Behavior Analysis, 7,* 577–581. [103]

Azrin, R. D., & Hayes, S. C. (1984). The discrimination of interest within a heterosexual interaction: Training, generalization, and effects on social skills. *Behavior Therapy, 15,* 173–184. [199]

Babbitt, R., Hoch, T., Krell, D., & Williams, K. (1992). *Respondent and operant treatment of nonmotivational swallowing skill deficit.* Paper presented at the 18th annual convention of the Association for Behavior Analysis. [378]

Babcock, R. A., Sulzer-Azaroff, B., & Sanderson, M. (1992). Increasing nurses' use of feedback to promote infection-control practices in a head-injury treatment center. *Journal of Applied Behavior Analysis, 25,* 621–627. [350, 351]

Baer, D. M., Peterson, R. F., & Sherman, J. A. (1967). The development of imitation by reinforcing behavioral similarity to a model. *Journal of the Experimental Analysis of Behavior, 10,* 405–416. [292–293]

Baer, D. M., Wolf, M. M., & Risley, T. R. (1968). Some current dimensions of applied behavior analysis. *Journal of Applied Behavior Analysis, 1,* 91–97. [7, 8, 9]

Baer, D. M., Wolf, M. M., & Risley, T. R. (1987). Some still-current dimensions of applied behavior analysis. *Journal of Applied Behavior Analysis, 20,* 313–327. [7, 8]

Baeyens, F., Eelen, P., Crombez, G., & Van den Bergh, O. (1992). Human evaluative conditioning: Acquisition trials, presentation schedule, evaluative style, and contingency awareness. *Behavior Research and Therapy, 30,* 133–142. [405, 406]

Bailey, J. S., Wolf, M. M., & Phillips, E. L. (1970). Home-based reinforcement and the modification of pre-delinquents' classroom behavior. *Journal of Applied Behavior Analysis, 3,* 223–233. [114–115]

Balcazar, F., Hopkins, B. L., & Suarez, Y. (1986). A critical, objective review of performance feedback. *Journal of Organizational Behavior Management, 7,* 65–89. [351, 364]

Balzer, W. K., Doherty, M. E., & O'Conner, R., Jr. (1989). Effects of cognitive feedback on performance. *Psychological Bulletin, 106,* 410–433. [358–359]

Bandura, A. (1965). Influence of models' reinforcement contingencies on the acquisition of imitative responses. *Journal of Personality and Social Psychology, 1,* 589–595. [289–290]

Bandura, A. (1969). *Principles of behavior modification.* New York: Holt, Rinehart, & Winston. [282, 297, 298, 389, 392]

Bandura, A., & Jeffery, R. W. (1973). Role of symbolic coding and rehearsal processes in observational learning. *Journal of Personality and Social Psychology, 26,* 122–130. [302]

Bandura, A., & Menlove, F. L. (1968). Factors determining vicarious extinction of avoidance behavior through symbolic modeling. *Journal of Personality and Social Psychology, 8,* 99–108. [301]

Bangert-Drowns, R. L., Kulik, C-L. C., Kulik, J. A., & Morgan, M. (1991). The instructional effect of feedback in test-like events. *Review of Educational Research, 61,* 213–238. [362, 363]

Banks, R. K., & Vogel-Sprott, M. D. (1965). The effect of delayed punishment on an immediately rewarded response in humans. *Journal of Experimental Psychology, 70,* 357–359. [114]

Barbetta, P. M., Heward, W. L., Bradley, D., & Miller, A. D. (1992). *Relative effects of immediate and delayed error correction on the acquisition and maintenance of sight words by students with developmental handicaps.* Paper presented at the 18th annual convention of the Association for Behavior Analysis. [362]

Barlow, D. H., Agras, W. S., Leitenberg, H., & Wincze, J. P. (1970). An experimental analysis of the effectiveness of "shaping" in reducing maladaptive avoidance behavior: An analogue study. *Behavior Research and Therapy, 8,* 165–173. [185(17), 483]

Barlow, D. H., & Wolfe, B. E. (1981). Behavioral approaches to anxiety disorders: A report on the NIMH-SUNY, Albany, research conference. *Journal of Consulting and Clinical Psychology, 49,* 448–454. [391]

Baron, A. (1973). Postdiscrimination gradients of human subjects on a tone continuum. *Journal of Experimental Psychology, 101,* 337–342. [251–252, 261]

Baron, R. A. (1970). Attraction toward the model and model's competence as determinants of adult imitative behavior. *Journal of Personality and Social Psychology, 14,* 345–351. [300, 301]

Barrett, R. P., Staub, R. W., & Sisson, L. A. (1983). Treatment of compulsive rituals with visual screening: A case study with long-term follow-up. *Journal of Behavior Therapy and Experimental Psychiatry, 14,* 55–59. [155(15), 481]

Barrett, T. W., & Mizes, J. S. (1988). Combat level and social support in the development of posttraumatic stress disorder in Vietnam veterans, *Behavior Modification*, **12**, 100–115. [27(23), 465]

Barry, N. J., & Overmann, P. B. (1977). Comparison of the effectiveness of adult and peer models with EMR children. *American Journal of Mental Deficiency*, **82**, 33–36. [294]

Barton, E. S., Guess, D., Garcia, E., & Baer, D. M. (1970). Improvement of retardates' mealtime behaviors by timeout procedures using multiple-baseline techniques. *Journal of Applied Behavior Analysis*, **3**, 77–84. [125(22), 477]

Barton, L. E., Brulle, A. R., & Repp, A. C. (1986). Maintenance of therapeutic change by momentary DRO. *Journal of Applied Behavior Analysis*, **19**, 277–282. [79]

Barton, L. E., Brulle, A. R., & Repp, A. C. (1987). Effects of differential scheduling of timeout to reduce maladaptive responding. *Exceptional Children*, **53**, 351–356. [120, 126(23), 477]

Bayes, R., Masvidal, A. E., & Moros, J. (1982). Efectos del auto-registro en un caso de insomnio cronico. [Effects of self-monitoring in a case of chronic insomnia]. *Analisis y Modificacion de Conducta*, **8**, 349–358. [354]

Beach, S. R. H., Arias, I., & O'Leary, K. D. (1986). The relationship of marital satisfaction and social support to depressive symptomatology. *Journal of Psychopathology and Behavioral Assessment*, **8**, 305–316. [25(12), 464]

Beck, A. T. (1976). *Cognitive therapy and the emotional disorders*. Madison, CT: International Universities Press. [325]

Beck, A. T., Rush, A. J., Shaw, B. F., & Emery, G. (1979). *Cognitive therapy of depression*. New York: Guilford Press. [320, 325]

Becker, J. V., Turner, S. M., & Sajwaj, T. E. (1978). Multiple behavioral effects of the use of lemon juice with a ruminating toddler-age child. *Behavior Modification*, **2**, 267–278. [121]

Becker, W. C. (1974). Teaching concepts and operations, or how to make kids smart. In R. Ulrich, T. Stachnik, & J. Mabry (Eds.), *Control of human behavior: Vol. 3. Behavior modification in education* (pp. 299–312). Glenview, IL: Scott, Foresman. [437, 442]

Becker, W. C. (1986). *Applied psychology for teachers: A behavioral cognitive approach*. Palo Alto, CA: SRA. [430, 436]

Becker, W. C., & Engelmann, S. (1978). Systems for basic instruction: Theory and applications. In T. A. Brigham & A. C. Catania (Eds.), *Handbook of applied behavior analysis: Social and instructional processes* (pp. 325–377). New York: Irvington. [437]

Bentall, R. P., & Lowe, C. F. (1987). The role of verbal behavior in human learning: III. Instructional effects in children. *Journal of the Experimental Analysis of Behavior*, **47**, 177–190. [320]

Bentall, R. P., Lowe, C. F., & Beasty, A. (1985). The role of verbal behavior in human learning: II. Developmental differences. *Journal of the Experimental Analysis of Behavior*, **43**, 165–181. [320]

Bernhardt, A. J., & Forehand, R. (1975). The effects of labeled and unlabeled praise upon lower and middle class children. *Journal of Experimental Child Psychology*, **19**, 536–543. [355]

Bernhardt, A. J., Fredericks, S., & Forbach, G. B. (1978). Comparison of effects of labeled and unlabeled praise and time-out upon children's discrimination learning. *Psychological Reports*, **42**, 771–776. [355]

Bernstein, I. L., & Webster, M. M. (1980). Learned taste aversions in humans. *Physiology and Behavior*, **25**, 363–366. [394]

Bierley, C., McSweeney, F. K., & Vannieuwkerk, R. (1985). Classical conditioning of preferences for stimuli. *Journal of Consumer Research*, **12**, 316–323. [395, 398, 416(14), 511]

Biglan, A., Hops, H., Sherman, L., Friedman, L. S., Arthur, J., & Osteen, V. (1985). Problem-solving interactions of depressed women and their husbands. *Behavior Therapy*, **16**, 431–451. [15, 143]

Bijou, S. W. (1961). Discrimination performance as a baseline for individual analysis of young children. *Child Development*, **32**, 163–170. [198]

Birch, L. L. (1980). Effects of peer models' food choices and eating behaviors on preschoolers' food preferences. *Child Development*, **51**, 489–496. [294]

Björkstrand, P-Å. (1990). Effects of conditioned stimulus pre-exposure on human electrodermal conditioning to fear-relevant and fear-irrelevant stimuli. *Biological Psychology*, **30**, 35–50. [408]

Blair, M. E., & Shimp, T. A. (1992). Consequences of an unpleasant experience with music: A second-order negative conditioning perspective. *Journal of Advertising, 21,* 35–43. [408]

Blanchard, E. B., McCoy, G. C., Musso, A., Gerardi, M. A., Pallmeyer, T. P., Gerardi, R. J., Cotch, P. A., Siracusa, K., & Andrasik, F. (1986). A controlled comparison of thermal biofeedback and relaxation training in the treatment of essential hypertension: I. Short-term and long-term outcome. *Behavior Therapy, 17,* 563–579. [359]

Blount, R. L., Drabman, R. S., Wilson, N., & Stewart, D. (1982). Reducing severe diurnal bruxism in two profoundly retarded females. *Journal of Applied Behavior Analysis, 15,* 565–571. [127(32), 478]

Blount, R. L., & Stokes, T. F. (1984). Contingent public posting of photographs to reinforce dental hygiene. *Behavior Modification, 8,* 79–92. [54(17), 467]

Boersma, F. J. (1966). Effects of delay of information feedback and length of postfeedback interval on linear programed learning. *Journal of Educational Psychology, 57,* 140–145. [362]

Bohannon, J. N., III., & Stanowicz, L. (1988). The issue of negative evidence: Adult responses to children's language errors. *Developmental Psychology, 24,* 684–689. [350–351]

Bohannon, J. N., III., MacWhinney, B., & Snow, C. (1990). No negative evidence revisited: Beyond learnability or who has to prove what to whom. *Developmental Psychology, 26,* 221–226. [351]

Boland, F. J., Mellor, C. S., & Revusky, S. (1978). Chemical aversion treatment of alcoholism: Lithium as the aversive agent. *Behavior Research and Therapy, 16,* 401–409. [389–390]

Booth, R., & Rachman, S. (1992). The reduction of claustrophobia—I. *Behavior Research and Therapy, 30,* 207–221. [391]

Boren J. J., & Colman, A. D. (1970). Some experiments on reinforcement principles within a psychiatric ward for delinquent soldiers. *Journal of Applied Behavior Analysis, 3,* 29–37. [108]

Borgen, W. A., & Calder, P. (1980). Relative effects of a segmented model versus a combined model in teaching appropriate group discussion skills to children. *Canadian Counsellor, 14,* 163–166. [299]

Bornstein, P. H. (1985). Self-instructional training: A commentary and state-of-the-art. *Journal of Applied Behavior Analysis, 18,* 69–72. [321]

Bornstein, P. H., & Quevillon, R. P. (1976). The effects of a self-instructional package on overactive preschool boys. *Journal of Applied Behavior Analysis, 9,* 179–188. [321]

Bornstein, P. H., Bach, P. J., McFall, M. E., Friman, P. C., & Lyons, P. D. (1980). Application of a social skills training program in the modification of interpersonal deficits among retarded adults: A clinical replication. *Journal of Applied Behavior Analysis, 13,* 171–176. [25(11), 464]

Boulougouris, J. C., Marks, I. M., & Marset, P. (1971). Superiority of flooding (implosion) to desensitisation for reducing pathological fear. *Behavior Research and Therapy, 9,* 7–16. [391]

Boyd, T. L., & Levis, D. J. (1980). Depression. In R. J. Daitzman (Ed.), *Clinical behavior therapy and behavior modification* (Vol. 1). New York: Garland STPM Press. [143]

Brackbill, Y., & Kappy, M. S. (1962). Delay of reinforcement and retention. *Journal of Comparative and Physiological Psychology, 55,* 14–18. [50]

Brantner, J. P., & Doherty, M. A. (1983). A review of timeout: A conceptual and methodological analysis. In S. Axelrod & J. Apsche (Eds.), *The effects of punishment on human behavior* (pp. 87–132). New York: Academic Press. [104]

Brasted, W. S., & Callahan, E. J. (1984). A behavioral analysis of the grief process. *Behavior Therapy, 15,* 529–543. [401]

Brigham, T. A., & Sherman, J. A. (1973). Effects of choice and immediacy of reinforcement on single response and switching behavior of children. *Journal of the Experimental Analysis of Behavior, 19,* 425–435. [50]

Brigham, T. A., Finfrock, S. R., Breunig, M. K., & Bushell, D. (1972). The use of programmed materials in the analysis of academic contingencies. *Journal of Applied Behavior Analysis, 5,* 177–182. [48–49, 53–54(12), 467]

Briscoe, R. V., Hoffman, D. B., & Bailey, J. S. (1975). Behavioral community psychology: Training a community board to problem solve. *Journal of Applied Behavior Analysis, 8,* 157–168. [272(4), 495]

Broden, M., Bruce, C., Mitchell, M. A., Carter, V., & Hall, R. V. (1970). Effects of teacher attention on attending behavior of two boys at adjacent desks. *Journal of Applied Behavior Analysis,* **3,** 199–203. [257]

Brody, G. H., & Stoneman, Z. (1981). Selective imitation of same-age, older, and younger peer models. *Child Development,* **52,** 717–720. [300]

Bromfield, R., Bromfield, D., & Weiss, B. (1988). Influence of the sexually abused label on perceptions of a child's failure. *Journal of Educational Research,* **82,** 96–98. [5]

Bromfield, R., Weisz, J. R., & Messer, T. (1986). Children's judgments and attributions in response to the "mentally retarded" label: A developmental approach. *Journal of Abnormal Psychology,* **95,** 81–87. [5]

Brown, G. E. (1978). Self-administered desensitization of a cemetery phobia using sexual arousal to inhibit anxiety. *Journal of Behavior Therapy and Experimental Psychiatry,* **9,** 73–74. [422(20), 515]

Brown, I., Jr., & Inouye, D. K. (1978). Learned helplessness through modeling: The role of perceived similarity in competence. *Journal of Personality and Social Psychology,* **36,** 900–908. [300]

Brown, M. G., Malott, R. W., Dillon, M. J., & Keeps, E. J. (1980). Improving customer service in a large department store through the use of training and feedback. *Journal of Organizational Behavior Management,* **2,** 251–265. [372(21), 505]

Brown, R. E., Copeland, R. E., & Hall, R. V. (1974). School phobia: Effects of behavior modification treatment applied by an elementary school principal. *Child Study Journal,* **4,** 125–133. [164, 165]

Bryant, L. E., & Budd, K. S. (1982). Self-instructional training to increase independent work performance in preschoolers. *Journal of Applied Behavior Analysis,* **15,** 259–271. [321]

Bucher, B., & Reaume, J. (1979). Generalization of reinforcement effects in a token program in the home. *Behavior Modification,* **3,** 63–72. [274(15), 496]

Burchard, J. D., & Barrera, F. (1972). An analysis of timeout and response cost in a programmed environment. *Journal of Applied Behavior Analysis,* **5,** 271–282. [117]

Burgess, R. L., Burgess, J. M., & Esveldt, K. C. (1970). An analysis of generalized imitation. *Journal of Applied Behavior Analysis,* **3,** 39–46. [305–306(10), 498]

Burgio, L. D., Whitman, T. L., & Johnson, M. R. (1980). A self-instructional package for increasing attending behavior in educable mentally retarded children. *Journal of Applied Behavior Analysis,* **13,** 443–459. [321]

Burgio, L., Tice, L., & Brown, K. (1985). The reduction of seizure-like behaviors through contingency management. *Journal of Behavior Therapy and Experimental Psychiatry,* **16,** 71–75. [87–88(26), 474]

Buskist, W. F., & Miller, H. L., Jr. (1986). Interaction between rules and contingencies in the control of human fixed-interval performance. *The Psychological Record,* **36,** 109–116. [318]

Butterfield, W. H., & Parson, R. (1973). Modeling and shaping by parents to develop chewing behavior in their retarded child. *Journal of Behavior Therapy and Experimental Psychiatry,* **4,** 285–287. [183–184(9), 482]

Cairns, R. B. (1967). The information properties of verbal and nonverbal events. *Journal of Personality and Social Psychology,* **5,** 353–357. [44]

Cairns, R. B. (1970). Meaning and attention as determinants of social reinforcer effectiveness. *Child Development,* **41,** 1067–1082. [44]

Cairns, R. B., & Paris, S. G. (1971). Informational determinants of social reinforcement effectiveness among retarded children. *American Journal of Mental Deficiency,* **76,** 362–369. [44]

Calicchia, J. P. (1973). Effects of magnitude and schedule of reward for counterattitudinal advocacy on subsequent attitude change. *The Journal of Social Psychology,* **91,** 239–249. [179]

Calpin, J. P., Edelstein, B., & Redmon, W. K. (1988). Performance feedback and goal setting to improve mental health center staff productivity. *Journal of Organizational Behavior Management,* **9,** 35–58. [354]

Camp, B. W., Blom, G. E., Hebert, F., & van Doorninck, W. J. (1977). "Think aloud": A program for developing self-control in young aggressive boys. *Journal of Abnormal Child Psychology,* **5,** 157–169. [340(16), 502]

Campbell, C. R., & Stremel-Campbell, K. (1982). Programming "loose training" as a strategy to facilitate language generalization. *Journal of Applied Behavior Analysis, 15,* 295–301. [264]

Cannon, D. S., & Baker, T. B. (1981). Emetic and electric shock alcohol aversion therapy: Assessment of conditioning. *Journal of Consulting and Clinical Psychology, 49,* 20–33. [407]

Cannon, D. S., Best, M. R., Batson, J. D., & Feldman, M. (1983). Taste familiarity and apomorphine-induced taste aversions in humans. *Behavior Research and Therapy, 21,* 669–673. [415(11), 510]

Carey, M. P., & Burish, T. G. (1988). Etiology and treatment of the psychological side effects associated with cancer chemotherapy: A critical review and discussion. *Psychological Bulletin, 104,* 307–325. [394]

Carey, R. G., & Bucher, B. (1981). Identifying the educative and suppressive effects of positive practice and restitutional overcorrection. *Journal of Applied Behavior Analysis, 14,* 71–80. [102, 105]

Carlsen, G. R. (1971). *Books and the teen-age reader: A guide for teachers, librarians, and parents.* New York: Bantam Books. [16]

Carlson, C. S., Arnold, C. R., Becker, W. C., & Madsen, C. H. (1968). The elimination of tantrum behavior of a child in an elementary classroom. *Behavior Research and Therapy, 6,* 117–119. [70]

Carnine, D. W. (1976a). Effects of two teacher-presentation rates on off-task behavior, answering correctly, and participation. *Journal of Applied Behavior Analysis, 9,* 199–206. [207]

Carnine, D. W. (1976b). Similar sound separation and cumulative introduction in learning letter-sound correspondences. *Journal of Educational Research, 69,* 368–372. [208]

Carnine, D. (1980). Relationships between stimulus variation and the formation of misconceptions. *Journal of Educational Research, 74,* 106–110. [435, 436–437]

Carnine, D. W. (1991). Curricular interventions for teaching higher order thinking to all students: Introduction to the special series. *Journal of Learning Disabilities, 24,* 261–269. [442, 443]

Carnine, D., Stevens, C., Clements, J., & Kameenui, E. J. (1982). Effects of facilitative questions and practice on intermediate students' understanding of character motives. *Journal of Reading Behavior, 14,* 179–190. [452(12), 518]

Carr, E. G., & Durand, V. M. (1985). Reducing behavior problems through functional communication training. *Journal of Applied Behavior Analysis, 18,* 111–126. [141]

Carr, E. G., Newsom, C. D., & Binkoff, J. A. (1980). Escape as a factor in the aggressive behavior of two retarded children. *Journal of Applied Behavior Analysis, 13,* 101–117. [86(18), 473]

Carroll, J. B. (1964). Words, meanings, and concepts. *Harvard Educational Review, 34,* 178–202. [432]

Carstens, C. (1982). Application of a work penalty threat in the treatment of a case of juvenile fire setting. *Journal of Behavior Therapy and Experimental Psychiatry, 13,* 159–161. [127(34), 478]

Carstensen, L. L., & Erickson, R. J. (1986). Enhancing the social environments of elderly nursing home residents: Are high rates of interaction enough? *Journal of Applied Behavior Analysis, 19,* 349–356. [13]

Carter, N., Hansson, L., Holmberg, B., & Melin L. (1979). Shoplifting reduction through the use of specific signs. *Journal of Organizational Behavior Management, 2,* 73–84. [240(13), 491]

Carter, N., Holström, A., Simpanen, M., & Melin, L. (1988). Theft reduction in a grocery store through product identification and graphing of losses for employees. *Journal of Applied Behavior Analysis, 21,* 385–389. [369–370(10), 504]

Casey, W. M., & Burton, R. V. (1982). Training children to be consistently honest through verbal self-instructions. *Child Development, 53,* 911–919. [321, 328, 339(12), 438, 502]

Catania, A. C. (1984). *Learning* (2nd ed.). New York: Prentice-Hall. [31, 382]

Cautela, J. R. (1967). Covert sensitization. *Psychological Reports, 20,* 459–468. [390, 422(22), 516]

Cautela, J. R., Flannery, R. B., Jr., & Hanley, S. (1974). Covert modeling: An experimental test. *Behavior Therapy, 5,* 494–502. [295]

Cecil, J. S., Weiss, R. F., & Feinberg, R. A. (1978). The reinforcing effects of the recommendation in threatening communication. *The Journal of General Psychology, 98,* 65–77. [141]

Charlop, M. H., Burgio, L. D., Iwata, B. A., & Ivancic, M. T. (1988). Stimulus variation as a means of enhancing punishment effects. *Journal of Applied Behavior Analysis, 21,* 89–95. [113–114]

Charlop, M. H., Kurtz, P. F., & Casey, F. G. (1990). Using aberrant behaviors as reinforcers for autistic children. *Journal of Applied Behavior Analysis, 23,* 163–181. [37]

Charlop, M. H., & Milstein, J. P. (1989). Teaching autistic children conversational speech using video modeling. *Journal of Applied Behavior Analysis, 22,* 275–285. [305(9), 498]

Chase, P. N., & Danforth, J. S. (1991). The role of rules in concept learning. In L. J. Hayes and P. N. Chase (Eds.), *Dialogues on verbal behavior* (pp. 205–225). Reno, NV: Context Press. [334]

Chase, P. N., & Wylie, R. G. (1985). Doctoral training in behavior analysis: Training generalized problem-solving skills. *The Behavior Analyst, 8,* 159–176. [324, 441, 442]

Chase, P. N., Johnson, K. R., & Sulzer-Azaroff, B. (1985). Verbal relations within instruction: Are there subclasses of the intraverbal? *Journal of the Experimental Analysis of Behavior, 43,* 301–313. [451(5), 517]

Cheyne, J. A. (1971). Some parameters of punishment affecting resistance to deviation and generalization of a prohibition. *Child Development, 42,* 1249–1261. [116, 328, 329]

Chhokar, J. S., & Wallin, J. A. (1984). A field study of the effect of feedback frequency on performance. *Journal of Applied Psychology, 69,* 524–530. [363–364]

Cicero, S. D., & Tryon, W. W. (1989). Classical conditioning of meaning—II. A replication and triplet associate extension. *Journal of Behavior Therapy and Experimental Psychiatry, 20,* 197–202. [398]

Clark, H. B., Northrop, J. T., & Barkshire, C. T. (1988). The effects of contingent thank-you notes on case managers' visiting residential clients. *Education and Treatment of Children, 11,* 45–51. [54–55(18), 467]

Clark, H. B., Rowbury, T., Baer, A. M., & Baer, D. M. (1973). Timeout as a punishing stimulus in continuous and intermittent schedules. *Journal of Applied Behavior Analysis, 6,* 443–455. [110–111]

Clarke, J. C., & Hayes, K. (1984). Covert sensitization, stimulus relevance and the equipotentiality premise. *Behavior Research and Therapy, 22,* 451–454. [415–416(12), 510]

Cohen, I. L. (1984). Establishment of independent responding to a fire alarm in a blind, profoundly retarded adult. *Journal of Behavior Therapy and Experimental Psychiatry, 15,* 365–367. [246(11), 494]

Collins, R. L., Parks, G. A., & Marlatt, G. A. (1985). Social determinants of alcohol consumption: The effects of social interaction and model status on self-administration of alcohol. *Journal of Consulting and Clinical Psychology, 53,* 189–200. [301]

Conrin, J., Pennypacker, H. S., Johnston, J., & Rast, J. (1982). Differential reinforcement of other behaviors to treat chronic rumination of mental retardates. *Journal of Behavior Therapy and Experimental Psychiatry, 13,* 325–329. [87(25), 473]

Cook, S. W., & Harris, R. E. (1927). The verbal conditioning of the galvanic skin reflex. *Journal of Experimental Psychology, 21,* 202–210. [394]

Coon, R. C., Lipscomb, T. J., & Copple, C. E. (1982). Effects of listener feedback on the messages of kindergarten children in a referential communication task. *Journal of Applied Developmental Psychology, 3,* 337–346. [363]

Cooper, N. A., & Clum, G. A. (1989). Imaginal flooding as a supplementary treatment for PTSD in combat veterans: A controlled study. *Behavior Therapy, 20,* 381–391. [392]

Cormier, W. H., Otani, A., & Cormier, S. (1986). The effects of problem-solving training on two problem-solving tasks. *Cognitive Therapy and Research, 10,* 95–108. [331]

Corte, H. E., Wolf, M. M., & Locke, B. J. (1971). A comparison of procedures for eliminating self-injurious behavior of retarded adolescents. *Journal of Applied Behavior Analysis, 4,* 201–213. [77]

Cosgrove, J. M., & Patterson, C. J. (1978). Generalization of training for children's listener skills. *Child Development, 49,* 513–516. [438]

Cowdery, G. E., Iwata, B. A., & Pace, G. M. (1990). Effects and side effects of DRO as a treatment for self-injurious behavior. *Journal of Applied Behavior Analysis, 23,* 497–506. [77]

Craun, A. M., & Deffenbacher, J. L. (1987). The effects of information, behavioral rehearsal, and prompting on breast self-exams. *Journal of Behavioral Medicine, 10,* 351–365. [239(8), 490]

Creer, T. L., & Miklich, D. R. (1970). The application of a self-modeling procedure to modify inappropriate behavior: A preliminary report. *Behavior Research and Therapy, 8,* 91–92. [308(22), 500]

Crespi, L. P. (1942). Quantitative variation in incentive and performance in the white rat. *American Journal of Psychology, 55,* 467–517. [46]

Critchfield, T. S. (1989). Self-recording mutually exclusive multiple responses. *Behavior Modification, 13,* 361–375. [354]

Croghan, L., & Musante, G. J. (1975). The elimination of a boy's high-building phobia by in vivo desensitization and game playing. *Journal of Behavior Therapy and Experimental Psychiatry, 6,* 87–88. [385]

Cross, S. M., Dickson, A. L., & Sisemore, D. A. (1978). A comparison of three response-elimination procedures following VR training with institutionalized, moderately retarded individuals. *The Psychological Record, 28,* 589–594. [79]

Cuvo, A. J. (1974). Incentive level influence on overt rehearsal and free recall as a function of age. *Journal of Experimental Child Psychology, 18,* 167–181. [43]

Cuvo, A. J., & Riva, M. T. (1980). Generalization and transfer between comprehension and production: A comparison of retarded and nonretarded persons. *Journal of Applied Behavior Analysis, 13,* 315–331. [259–260]

Dachman, R. S., Halasz, M. M., Bickett, A. D., & Lutzker, J. R. (1984). A home-based ecobehavioral parent-training and generalization package with a neglectful mother. *Education and Treatment of Children, 7,* 183–202. [373(26), 506]

Dahlquist, L. M. (1990). The treatment of persistent vomiting through shaping and contingency management. *Journal of Behavior Therapy and Experimental Psychiatry, 21,* 77–80. [164]

Dahlquist, L. M., & Blount, R. L. (1984). Teaching a six-year-old girl to swallow pills. *Journal of Behavior Therapy and Experimental Psychiatry, 15,* 171–173. [184(14), 483]

Danforth, J. S., Chase, P. N., Dolan, M., & Joyce, J. H. (1990). The establishment of stimulus control by instructions and by differential reinforcement. *Journal of the Experimental Analysis of Behavior, 54,* 97–112. [319]

Darch, C., Carnine, D., & Gersten, R. (1984). Explicit instruction in mathematics problem solving. *Journal of Educational Research, 77,* 351–359. [291]

Davies, G. R., McMahon, R. J., Flessati, E. W., & Tiedemann, G. L. (1984). Verbal rationales and modeling as adjuncts to parenting for child compliance. *Child Development, 55,* 1290–1298. [328]

Day, M. H., & Horner, R. H. (1986). Response variation and the generalization of a dressing skill: Comparison of single instance and general case instruction. *Applied Research in Mental Retardation, 7,* 189–202. [445, 454(5), 519]

Day, M. H., & Horner, R. H. (1989). Building response classes: A comparison of two procedures for teaching generalized pouring to learners with severe disabilities. *Journal of Applied Behavior Analysis, 22,* 223–229. [272–273(8), 445, 496]

Day, W. F., Jr. (1980). The historical antecedents of contemporary behaviorism. In R. W. Rieber & K. Salzinger (Eds.), *Psychology: Theoretical-historical perspectives* (pp. 203–262). New York: Academic Press. [8]

de Rose, J. C., de Souza, D. G., Rossito, A. L., & de Rose, T. M. S. (1992). Stimulus equivalence and generalization in reading after matching to sample by exclusion. In S. C. Hayes and L. J. Hayes (Eds.), *Understanding verbal relations* (pp. 69–82). Reno, NV: Context Press. [448]

Deguchi, H., Fujita, T., & Sato, M. (1988). Reinforcement control of observational learning in young children: A behavioral analysis of modeling. *Journal of Experimental Child Psychology, 46,* 362–371. [291]

Dekker, E., Pelser, H. E., & Groen, J. (1964). Conditioning as a cause of asthmatic attacks; a laboratory study. In C. M. Franks (Ed.), *Conditioning techniques in clinical practice and research* (pp. 116–131). New York: Springer. [413(1), 506]

Delclos, V. R., & Harrington, C. (1991). Effects of strategy monitoring and proactive instruction on children's problem-solving performance. *Journal of Educational Psychology, 83,* 35–42. [354]

Demchak, M. A. (1990). Response prompting and fading methods: A review. *American Journal on Mental Retardation, 94,* 603–615. [225, 233]

DeNike, L. D. (1964). The temporal relationship between awareness and performance in verbal conditioning. *Journal of Experimental Psychology*, **68**, 521–529. [333]

Desbien, D., & Yelen, D. (1980). Task difficulty and conditioned suppression in humans. *Bulletin of the Psychonomic Society*, **16**, 197–198. [418(3), 513]

Deslauriers, B. C., & Everett, P. B. (1977). Effects of intermittent and continuous token reinforcement on bus ridership. *Journal of Applied Psychology*, **62**, 369–375. [191(19), 486]

DeVellis, R. F., DeVellis, B. M., & McCauley, C. (1978). Vicarious acquisition of learned helplessness. *Journal of Personality and Social Psychology*, **36**, 894–899. [291–292]

Di Giusto, E. L., & Bond, N. W. (1978). One-trial conditioned suppression: Effects of instructions on extinction. *American Journal of Psychology*, **91**, 313–319. [421(19), 515]

Dietz, S. M. (1977). An analysis of programming DRL schedules in educational settings. *Behavior Research and Therapy*, **15**, 103–111. [172, 173]

Dietz, S. M., & Repp, A. C. (1973). Decreasing classroom misbehavior through the use of DRL schedules of reinforcement. *Journal of Applied Behavior Analysis*, **6**, 457–463. [173, 174]

DiLorenzo, T. M., & Foster, S. L. (1984). A functional assessment of children's ratings of interaction patterns. *Behavioral Assessment*, **6**, 291–302. [27(25), 466]

Dinsmore, J. A. (1977). Escape, avoidance, punishment: Where do we stand? *Journal of the Experimental Analysis of Behavior*, **28**, 83–95. [120]

Dixon, L. S. (1981). A functional analysis of photo-object matching skills of severely retarded adolescents. *Journal of Applied Behavior Analysis*, **14**, 465–478. [261–262]

Doerr, H. O. (1981). Cognitive derivation of generalization stimuli: Separation of components. *Bulletin of the Psychonomic Society*, **17**, 73–75. [414–415(8, 509)]

Doleys, D. M., Wells, K. C., Hobbs, S. A., Roberts, M. W., & Cartelli, L. M. (1976). The effects of social punishment on noncompliance: A comparison with timeout and positive practice. *Journal of Applied Behavior Analysis*, **9**, 471–482. [98]

Dorry, G. W., & Zeaman, D. (1973). The use of a fading technique in paired-associate teaching of a reading vocabulary with retardates. *Mental Retardation*, **11**, 3–6. [242(5), 492]

Dorsey, M. F., Iwata, B. A., Ong, P., & McSween, T. E. (1980). Treatment of self-injurious behavior using a water mist: Initial response suppression and generalization. *Journal of Applied Behavior Analysis*, **13**, 343–353. [118]

Dorsey, M. F., Iwata, B. A., Reid, D. H., & Davis, P. A. (1982). Protective equipment: Continuous and contingent application in the treatment of self-injurious behavior. *Journal of Applied Behavior Analysis*, **15**, 217–230. [68]

Downs, A. F. D., Rosenthal, T. L., & Lichstein, K. L. (1988). Modeling therapies reduce avoidance of bath-time by the institutionalized elderly. *Behavior Therapy*, **19**, 359–368. [307(16), 499]

Dowrick, P. W., & Dove, C. (1980). The use of self-modeling to improve the swimming performance of spina bifida children. *Journal of Applied Behavior Analysis*, **13**, 51–56. [305(8), 498]

Dowrick, P. W., & Hood, M. (1981). Comparison of self-modeling and small cash incentives in a sheltered workshop. *Journal of Applied Psychology*, **66**, 394–397. [296]

Drabman, R. S., & Lahey, B. B. (1974). Feedback in classroom behavior modification: Effects on the target and her classmates. *Journal of Applied Behavior Analysis*, **7**, 591–598. [273(12), 496]

Drudge, M. K., & Philips, B. J. (1976). Shaping behavior in voice therapy. *Journal of Speech and Hearing Disorders*, **41**, 398–411. [183(6), 482]

Duncan, P. K., & Bruwelheide, L. R. (1986). Feedback: Use and possible behavioral functions. *Journal of Organizational Behavior Management*, **7**, 91–114. [346]

Dunlap, G., Koegel, R. L., Johnson, J., & O'Neill, R. E. (1987). Maintaining performance of autistic clients in community settings with delayed contingencies. *Journal of Applied Behavior Analysis*, **20**, 185–191. [51]

Dunlap, L. K., & Dunlap, G. (1989). A self-monitoring package for teaching subtraction with regrouping to students with learning disabilities. *Journal of Applied Behavior Analysis*, **22**, 309–314. [354, 372(24), 506]

Durand, V. M., & Carr, E. G. (1987). Social influences on "self-stimulatory" behavior: Analysis and treatment applications. *Journal of Applied Behavior Analysis*, **20**, 119–132. [142]

Durand, V. M., & Kishi, G. (1987). Reducing severe behavior problems among persons with dual sensory impairments: An evaluation of a technical assistance model. *Journal of the Association for Persons with Severe Handicaps*, 12, 2–10. [142]

Duus, R. E. (1988). Response class in the organizational setting: The effects of location-specific feedback. *Psychological Record*, 38, 49–65. [348]

Dyckman, J. M., & Cowan, P. A. (1978). Imaging vividness and the outcome of in vivo and imagined scene desensitization. *Journal of Consulting and Clinical Psychology*, 46, 1155–1156. [407]

Dyer, K., Christian, W. P., & Luce, S. C. (1982). The role of response delay in improving the discrimination performance of autistic children. *Journal of Applied Behavior Analysis*, 15, 231–240. [207]

D'Zurilla, T. J., & Goldfried, M. R. (1971). Problem solving and behavior modification. *Journal of Abnormal Psychology*, 78, 107–126. [322–324]

D'Zurilla, T. J., & Nezu, A. (1980). A study of the generation-of-alternatives process in social problem solving. *Cognitive Therapy and Research*, 4, 67–72. [331–332]

Earley, P. C. (1988). Computer-generated performance feedback in the magazine-subscription industry. *Organizational Behavior and Human Decision Processes*, 41, 50–64. [351]

Early, C. J. (1968). Attitude learning in children. *Journal of Educational Psychology*, 59, 176–180. [396–398]

Eckerman, D. A., & Vreeland, R. (1973). Response variability for humans receiving continuous, intermittent, or no positive reinforcement feedback. *Bulletin of the Psychonomic Society*, 2, 297–299. [179]

Eckman, T. A., Wirshing, W. C., Marder, S. R., Liberman, R. P., Johnston-Cronk, K., Zimmermann, K., & Minta, J. (1992). *Technology for training schizophrenics in illness self-management: A controlled trial*. Unpublished manuscript. [63]

Efron, R. (1964). The conditioned inhibition of uncinate fits. In C. M. Franks (Ed.), *Conditioning techniques in clinical practice and research* (pp. 132–143). New York: Springer. [413(2), 507]

Egel, A. L. (1981). Reinforcer variation: Implications for motivating developmentally disabled children. *Journal of Applied Behavior Analysis*, 14, 345–350. [44–45]

Egel, A. L., Richman, G. S., & Koegel, R. L. (1981). Normal peer models and autistic children's learning. *Journal of Applied Behavior Analysis*, 14, 3–12. [294]

Egeland, B. (1975). Effects of errorless training on teaching children to discriminate letters of the alphabet. *Journal of Applied Psychology*, 60, 533–536. [227]

Eifert, G. H. (1984). The effects of language conditioning on various aspects of anxiety. *Behavior Research and Therapy*, 22, 13–21. [385]

Eifert, G. H., Craill, L., Carey, E., & O'Connor, C. (1988). Affect modification through evaluative conditioning with music. *Behavior Research and Therapy*, 26, 321–330. [385]

Eisenberger, R. (1970). Is there a deprivation-satiation function for social approval? *Psychological Bulletin*, 74, 255–275. [40]

Elawar, M. C., & Corno, L. (1985). A factorial experiment in teachers' written feedback on student homework: Changing teacher behavior a little rather than a lot. *Journal of Educational Psychology*, 77, 162–173. [349–350]

Elkins, R. L. (1980). Covert sensitization treatment of alcoholism: Contributions of successful conditioning to subsequent abstinence maintenance. *Addictive Behaviors*, 5, 67–89. [419(10), 514]

Elkins, R. L. (1991a). An appraisal of chemical aversion (emetic therapy) approaches to alcoholism treatment. *Behavior Research and Therapy*, 29, 387–418. [387–389, 390, 405]

Elkins, R. L. (1991b). Chemical aversion (emetic therapy) treatment of alcoholism: Further comments. *Behavior Research and Therapy*, 29, 421–428. [390]

Elliott, E. S., Wills, E. J., & Goldstein, A. G. (1973). The effects of discrimination training on the recognition of white and oriental faces. *Bulletin of the Psychonomic Society*, 2, 71–73. [210(1), 487]

Ellis, A., & Grieger, R. (1977). *Handbook of rational-emotive therapy*. New York: Springer. [325]

Ellson, D. G. (1941). Hallucinations produced by sensory conditioning. *Journal of Experimental Psychology*, 28, 1–20. [417(20), 512]

Emmelkamp, P. M. G., & Wessels, H. (1975). Flooding in imagination vs flooding in vivo: A comparison with agoraphobics. *Behavior Research and Therapy*, 13, 7–15. [391]

Engel, B. T., Nikoomanesh, P., & Schuster, M. M. (1974). Operant conditioning of rectosphincteric responses in the treatment of fecal incontinence. *New England Journal of Medicine,* **290,** 646–649. [372(25), 506]

Engelmann, S. (1969). *Conceptual learning.* San Rafael, CA: Dimensions. [433]

Engelmann, S., & Carnine, D. (1982). *Theory of instruction: Principles and applications.* New York: Irvington. [236, 357, 366, 433, 436, 443]

Engelmann, S., Carnine, D., & Steely, D. G. (1991). Making connections in mathematics. *Journal of Learning Disabilities,* **24,** 292–303. [438, 443, 444]

English, H. B. (1929). Three cases of the "conditioned fear response." *Journal of Abnormal and Social Psychology,* **34,** 221–225. [380]

Epling, W. F., & Pierce, W. D. (1983). Applied behavior analysis: New directions from the laboratory. *The Behavior Analyst,* **6,** 27–37. [80]

Epstein, L. H., Doke, L. A., Sajwaj, T. E., Sorrell, S., & Rimmer, B. (1974). Generality and side effects of overcorrection. *Journal of Applied Behavior Analysis,* 7, 385–390. [68]

Epstein, M. H., Repp, A. C., & Cullinan, D. (1978). Decreasing "obscene" language of behaviorally disordered children through the use of a DRL schedule. *Psychology in the Schools,* **15,** 419–423. [162–163, 173–174]

Erez, M. (1977). Feedback: A necessary condition for the goal setting–performance relationship. *Journal of Applied Psychology,* **62,** 624–627. [365]

Erickson, L. M., Tiffany, S. T., Martin, E. M., & Baker, T. B. (1983). Aversive smoking therapies: A conditioning analysis of therapeutic effectiveness. *Behavior Research and Therapy,* **21,** 595–611. [403]

Erikson, M., & Lipsitt, L. (1960). Effects of delayed reward on simultaneous and successive discrimination learning in children. *Journal of Comparative and Physiological Psychology,* **53,** 256–260. [50]

Esveldt, K. C., Dawson, P. C., & Forness, S. R. (1974). Effect of videotape feedback on children's classroom behavior. *Journal of Educational Research,* **67,** 453–456. [370(11), 504]

Farina, A., Allen, J., & Saul, G. (1966). The role of the stigmatized person in affecting social relationships. *Journal of Personality,* **71,** 421–428. [22(23), 463]

Fawcett, S. B., & Miller, L. K. (1975). Training public-speaking behavior: An experimental analysis and social validation. *Journal of Applied Behavior Analysis,* **8,** 125–135. [19–20(16), 465]

Fehrenbach, P. A., Miller, D. J., & Thelen, M. H. (1979). The importance of consistency of modeling behavior upon imitation: A comparison of single and multiple models. *Journal of Personality and Social Psychology,* **37,** 1412–1417. [301]

Feindler, E. J., Marriott, S. A., & Iwata, M. (1984). Group anger control training for junior high school delinquents. *Cognitive Therapy and Research,* **8,** 299–311. [324]

Feldman, K. V., & Klausmeier, H. J. (1974). The effects of two kinds of definitions on the concept attainment of fourth- and eighth-grade students. *Journal of Educational Research,* **67,** 219–223. [434]

Ferritor, D. E., Buckholdt, D., Hamblin, R. L., & Smith, L. (1972). The noneffects of contingent reinforcement for attending behavior on work accomplished. *Journal of Applied Behavior Analysis,* **5,** 7–18. [12]

Ferster, C. B. (1967). Arbitrary and natural reinforcement. *The Psychological Record,* 17, 341–347. [226]

Fichter, M. M., Wallace, C. J., Liberman, R. P., & Davis, J. R. (1976). Improving social interaction in a chronic psychotic using discriminated avoidance ("nagging"): Experimental analysis and generalization. *Journal of Applied Behavior Analysis,* **9,** 377–386. [136, 154–155(10), 480]

Fields, L. (1980). Enhanced learning of new discriminations after stimulus fading. *Bulletin of the Psychonomic Society,* **15,** 327–330. [242(8), 492]

Fink, W. T., & Carnine, D. W. (1975). Control of arithmetic errors using informational feedback and graphing. *Journal of Applied Behavior Analysis,* **8,** 461. [354]

Finley, W. W. (1983). Operant conditioning of the short-latency cervical somatosensory evoked potential in quadriplegics. *Experimental Neurology,* **81,** 542–558. [369(6), 504]

Finney, J. W., Russo, D. C., & Cataldo, M. F. (1982). Reduction of pica in young children with lead poisoning. *Journal of Pediatric Psychology,* **7,** 197–207. [86(20), 473]

Fischer, J., & Nehs, R. (1978). Use of a commonly available chore to reduce a boy's rate of swearing. *Journal of Behavior Therapy and Experimental Psychiatry, 9*, 81–83. [101]

Fishbein, J. E., & Wasik, B. H. (1981). Effect of the good behavior game on disruptive library behavior. *Journal of Applied Behavior Analysis, 14*, 89–93. [274(16), 497]

Fitterling, J. M., & Ayllon, T. (1983). Behavioral coaching in classical ballet. *Behavior Modification, 7,* 345–368. [212(15), 488]

Fjellstedt, N., & Sulzer-Azaroff, B. (1973). Reducing the latency of a child's responding to instructions by means of a token system. *Journal of Applied Behavior Analysis, 6*, 125–130. [54(14), 467]

Fonagy, P., & Slade, P. (1982). Punishment vs negative reinforcement in the aversive conditioning of auditory hallucinations. *Behavior Research and Therapy, 20*, 483–492. [116]

Fowler, S., & Baer, D. M. (1981). "Do I have to be good all day?" The timing of delayed reinforcement as a factor in generalization. *Journal of Applied Behavior Analysis, 14*, 13–24. [50, 51, 265–266]

Foxx, R. M. (1976). Increasing a mildly retarded woman's attendance at self-help classes by overcorrection and instruction. *Behavior Therapy, 7*, 390–396. [153(1), 479]

Foxx, R. M. (1977). Attention training: The use of overcorrection avoidance to increase the eye contact of autistic and retarded children. *Journal of Applied Behavior Analysis, 10*, 489–499. [154(8), 480]

Foxx, R. M. (1984). The use of a negative reinforcement procedure to increase the performance of autistic and mentally retarded children on discrimination training tasks. *Analysis and Intervention in Developmental Disabilities, 4*, 253–265. [136]

Foxx, R. M., & Azrin, N. H. (1972). Restitution: A method of eliminating aggressive-disruptive behavior of retarded and brain damaged patients. *Behavior Research and Therapy, 10*, 15–27. [102, 105]

Foxx, R. M., & Azrin, N. H. (1973). The elimination of autistic self-stimulatory behavior by overcorrection. *Journal of Applied Behavior Analysis, 6*, 1–14. [124(12), 126(27), 476, 478]

Foxx, R. M., & Bechtel, D. R. (1983). Overcorrection: A review and analysis. In S. Axelrod & J. Apsche (Eds.), *The effects of punishment on human behavior* (pp. 133–220). New York: Academic Press. [102, 103, 104, 105]

Foxx, R. M., & Shapiro, S. T. (1978). The timeout ribbon: A nonexclusionary timeout procedure. *Journal of Applied Behavior Analysis, 11*, 125–136. [188(25), 478]

Fredericksen, L. W., Richter, W. T., Jr., Johnson, R. P., & Solomon, L. J. (1982). Specificity of performance feedback in a professional service delivery setting. *Journal of Organizational Behavior Management, 3*, 41–53. [363]

Freed, L. M., & Freed, W. J. (1977). Effects of schedules of reinforcement on hypothesis-refining behavior. *American Journal of Psychology, 90*, 517–525. [179]

Friedin, B. D., Borakove, L. S., & Fox, K. T. (1982). Treatment of an abnormal avoidance of fluid consumption. *Journal of Behavior Therapy and Experimental Psychiatry, 13*, 85–87. [183(7), 482]

Friedman, A. G., & Ollendick, T. H. (1989). Treatment programs for severe night-time fears: A methodological note. *Journal of Behavior Therapy and Experimental Psychiatry, 20*, 171–178. [55–56(24), 468]

Frisch, M. B., & Froberg, W. (1987). Social validation of assertion strategies for handling aggressive criticism: Evidence for consistency across situations. *Behavior Therapy, 18*, 181–191. [24(8), 464]

Fueyo, V., Saudargas, R. A., & Bushell, D. (1975). Two types of feedback in teaching swimming skills to handicapped children. *Perceptual and Motor Skills, 40*, 963–966. [369(4), 504]

Fyodorova, V., & Frankel, H. (1979). *The Admiral's Daughter*. New York: Dell. [307(18), 499]

Galizio, M. (1979). Contingency-shaped and rule-governed behavior: Instructional control of human loss avoidance. *Journal of the Experimental Analysis of Behavior, 31*, 53–70. [143, 326]

Gallimore, R., Tharp, R. G., & Kemp, B. (1969). Positive reinforcing functions of "negative attention." *Journal of Experimental Child Psychology, 8*, 140–146. [36,113]

Garcia, J., & Koelling, R. A. (1966). Relation of cue to consequence in avoidance learning. *Psychonomic Science, 4*, 123–124. [407]

Garlington, W. K., & Dericco, D. A. (1977). The effect of modelling on drinking rate. *Journal of Applied Behavior Analysis, 10*, 207–211. [308(26), 500]

Gaylord-Ross, R. J., Weeks, M., & Lipner, C. (1980). An analysis of antecedent, response, and conse-quence events in the treatment of self-injurious behavior. *Education and Training of the Mentally Retarded,* **15,** 35–42. [142]

Gear, T. E., Marsh, N. R., & Sergent, P. (1985). Semi-automated feedback and team behavior. *Human Relations,* **38,** 707–721. [352, 353]

Geis, G. L. (1974). Information about instruction: Before, during and after learning. *Improving Human Performance,* **3,** 1–6. [359]

Gelfand, D. M. (1962). The influence of self-esteem on rate of verbal conditioning and social matching behavior. *Journal of Abnormal and Social Psychology,* **65,** 259–265. [300]

Gelfand, D. M., Hartmann, D. P., Cromer, C. C., Smith, C. L., & Page, B. C. (1975). The effects of instructional prompts and praise on children's donation rates. *Child Development,* **46,** 980–983. [240(12), 491]

Gelfand, D. M., Hartmann, D. P., Lamb, A. K., Smith, C. L., Mahan, M. A., & Paul, S. C. (1974). The effects of adult models and described alternatives on children's choice of behavior management techniques. *Child Development,* **45,** 585–593. [106–107]

George, J. T., & Hopkins, B. L. (1989). Multiple effects of performance-contingent pay for waitpersons. *Journal of Applied Behavior Analysis,* **22,** 131–141. [172]

Gerst, M. D. (1971). Symbolic coding processes in observational learning. *Journal of Personality and Social Psychology,* **19,** 7–17. [302]

Gersten, R. M., White, W. A. T., Falco, R., & Carnine, D. (1982). Teaching basic discriminations to handicapped and nonhandicapped individuals through a dynamic presentation of instructional stimuli. *Analysis and Intervention in Developmental Disabilities,* **2,** 305–317. [451–452(8), 518]

Getzels, J., & Csikszentmihalyi, M. (1976). *The creative vision: A longitudinal study of problem finding in art.* New York: Wiley. [23(2), 463]

Gewirtz, J. L. (1971). Conditional responding as a paradigm for observational imitative learning and vic-arious reinforcement. In H. W. Reese (Ed.), *Advances in Child Development and Behavior* (Vol. 6, pp. 273–304). New York: Academic Press. [437]

Gewirtz, J. L., & Baer, D. M. (1958a). Deprivation and satiation of social reinforcers as drive conditions. *Journal of Abnormal and Social Psychology,* **57,** 165–172. [40]

Gewirtz, J. L., & Baer, D. M. (1958b). The effect of brief social deprivation on behaviors of a social rein-forcer. *Journal of Abnormal and Social Psychology,* **56,** 49–56. [40]

Gewirtz, J. L., & Stingle, K. G. (1968). Learning of generalized imitation as the basis for identification. *Psychological Review,* **75,** 374–397. [437, 439]

Gibbs, J. W., & Luyben, P. D. (1985). Treatment of self-injurious behavior: Contingent versus noncon-tingent positive practice overcorrection. *Behavior Modification,* **9,** 3–21. [102, 103]

Gibson, E. J. (1969). *Principles of perceptual learning and development.* New York: Appleton-Century-Crofts. [227]

Gilbert, B. O., Johnson, S. B., Spillar, R., McCallum, M., Silverstein, J. H., & Rosenbloom, A. (1982). The effects of a peer-modeling film on children learning to self-inject insulin. *Behavior Therapy,* **13,** 186–193. [306(12), 499]

Gilbert, T. F. (1978). *Human competence.* New York: McGraw-Hill. [12]

Gilden, J. L., Casia, C., Hendryx, M., & Singh, S. P. (1990). Effects of self-monitoring of blood glucose on quality of life in elderly diabetic patients. *Journal of the American Geriatrics Society,* **38,** 511–515. [354]

Glenn, S. S., & Hughes, H. H. (1978). Imaginal response events in systematic desensitization: A pilot study. *Biological Psychology,* **7,** 303–309. [407]

Glover, J. A., & Zimmer, J. W. (1982). Procedures to influence levels of questions asked by students. *Journal of General Psychology,* **107,** 267–276. [380(14), 505]

Glover, J. A., Zimmer, J. W., Filbeck, R. W., & Plake, B. S. (1980). Effects of training students to identi-fy the semantic base of prose materials. *Journal of Applied Behavior Analysis,* **13,** 655–667. [368(3), 452–453(13), 504, 518]

Goetz, E. M., & Baer, D. M. (1973). Social control of form diversity and the emergence of new forms in children's blockbuilding. *Journal of Applied Behavior Analysis,* **6,** 209–217. [52(3), 81–82, 437, 466]

Goldiamond, I. (1974). Toward a constructional approach to social problems. *Behaviorism,* **2,** 1–84. [63]

Goldstein, H. (1984). Effects of modeling and corrected practice on generative language learning of preschool children. *Journal of Speech and Hearing Disorders,* **49,** 389–398. [372(22), 505]

Goldstein, S. B., & Siegel, A. W. (1971). Observing behavior and children's discrimination learning. *Child Development,* **42,** 1608–1613. [50]

Goldstein, S. B., & Siegel, A. W. (1972). Facilitation of discrimination learning with delayed reinforcement. *Child Development,* **43,** 1004–1011. [50]

Gorn, G. J. (1982). The effects of music in advertising on choice behavior: A classical conditioning approach. *Journal of Marketing,* **46,** 94–101. [395]

Grant, L. (1986). Categorizing and concept learning. In H. W. Reese & L. J. Parrott (Eds.), *Behavior science: Philosophical, methodological, and empirical advances* (pp. 139–162). Hillsdale, NJ: Erlbaum. [433]

Grant, L. (1989). Word diagrams in teaching Pavlovian conditioning. Unpublished manuscript. [379]

Grant, L., & Evans, A. N. (1992). Acceptance of labels for behavioral response-reduction procedures and the users of those procedures. *The Psychological Record,* **42,** 355–368. [96]

Grant, L., & Spencer, R. E. (1983). The psychology of concept learning and teaching. *Alberta Psychology,* **12,** 7–8. [433]

Grant, L., Keenan, J. B., & Hursh, D. E. (1980). The effects of study questions, the SQ3R system of studying, and reading and rereading on academic performance. *Journal of Personalized Instruction,* **4,** 142–147. [26(17), 360, 465]

Grant, L., Keenan, J. B., & Hursh, D. E. (1982). Studying in college: A review of research. In J. G. Sherman, R. S. Ruskin, & G. B Semb (Eds.), *The personalized system of instruction: 48 seminal papers* (pp. 92–128). Lawrence, Kansas: TRI Publications. [360]

Grant, L., McAvoy, R., & Keenan, J. B. (1982). Prompting and feedback variables in concept programming. *Teaching of Psychology,* **9,** 173–177. [357, 358]

Green, G. R., Linsk, N. L., & Pinkston, E. M. (1986). Modification of verbal behavior of the mentally impaired elderly by their spouses. *Journal of Applied Behavior Analysis,* **19,** 329–336. [28–29]

Greer, S. E., & D'Zurilla, T. J. (1975). Behavioral approaches to marital discord and conflict. *Journal of Marriage and Family Counseling,* **1,** 299–315. [324]

Griffiths, R. R., Bigelow, G., & Liebson, I. (1977). Comparison of social time-out and activity time-out procedures in suppressing ethanol self-administration in alcoholics. *Behavior Research and Therapy,* **15,** 329–336. [99–100]

Grings, W. W., & Schandler, S. L. (1977). Interaction of learned relaxation and aversion. *Psychophysiology,* **14,** 275–280. [387, 388]

Gross, D. K., & Gutman, A. (1988). Effects of schedule and length of training on reward-induced stereotypy and negative transfer in humans. *The Psychological Record,* **38,** 567–594. [179]

Gumaer, J., & Headspeth, T. (1985). Self-instructional training with an adolescent schizophrenic. *The School Counselor,* **32,** 371–380. [339(10), 502]

Hake, D. F., & Foxx, R. M. (1978). Promoting gasoline conservation: The effects of reinforcement schedule, a leader, and self-recording. *Behavior Modification,* **2,** 339–370. [188(2), 484]

Hall, J. F. (1984). Backward conditioning in Pavlovian type studies: Reevaluation and present status. *Pavlovian Journal of Biological Science,* **19,** 163–168. [405]

Hall, S. M., Cooper, J. L., Burmaster, S., & Polk, A. (1977). Contingency contracting as a therapeutic tool with methadone maintenance clients: Six single subject studies. *Behavior Research and Therapy,* **15,** 438–441. [188–189(4), 484]

Handen, B. L., & Zane, T. (1987). Delayed prompting: A review of procedural variations and results. *Research in Developmental Disabilities,* **8,** 307–330. [233]

Hansen, D. J., St. Lawrence, J. S., & Christoff, K. A. (1988). Conversational skills of inpatient conduct-disordered youths: Social validation of component behaviors and implications for skills training. *Behavior Modification,* **12,** 424–444. [137]

Hansen, G. D. (1979). Enuresis control through fading, escape, and avoidance training. *Journal of Applied Behavior Analysis,* **12,** 303–307. [156(18), 481]

Haring, T. G., Kennedy, C. H., Adams, M. J., & Pitts-Conway, V. (1987). Teaching generalization of purchasing skills across community settings to autistic youth using videotape modeling. *Journal of Applied Behavior Analysis,* **20,** 89–96. [273(10), 496]

Harris, F. R., Johnston, M. K., Kelley, C. S., & Wolf, M. M. (1964). Effects of positive social reinforcement on regressed crawling of a nursery school child. *Journal of Educational Psychology,* **55,** 35–41. [55(20), 467]

Harris, K. R. (1986a). Self-monitoring of attentional behavior versus self-monitoring of productivity: Effects on on-task behavior and academic response rate among learning disabled children. *Journal of Applied Behavior Analysis,* **19,** 417–423. [12]

Harris, K. R. (1986b). The effects of cognitive-behavior modification of private speech and task performance during problem solving among learning-disabled and normally achieving children. *Journal of Abnormal Child Psychology,* **14,** 63–67. [324]

Harris, M. B., & Evans, R. C. (1974). The effects of modeling and instructions on creative responses. *The Journal of Psychology,* **86,** 123–130. [287–288]

Harris, R. P., O'Malley, M. S., Fletcher, S. W., & Knight, B. P. (1990). Prompting physicians for preventive procedures: A five-year study of manual and computer reminders. *American Journal of Preventive Medicine,* **6,** 145–152. [239(9), 490]

Harris, S. L., & Ersner-Hershfield, R. (1978). Behavioral suppression of severely disruptive behavior in psychotic and retarded patients: A review of punishment and its alternatives. *Psychological Bulletin,* **85,** 1352–1375. [77]

Hart, B. M., Allen, K. E., Buell, J. S., Harris, F. R., & Wolf, M. M. (1964). Effects of social reinforcement on operant crying. *Journal of Experimental Child Psychology,* **1,** 145–153. [88(27), 474]

Hartley, S. T., & Salzwedel, K. D. (1980). Behavioral writing for an autistic-like child. *Academic Therapy,* **16,** 101–110. [243(13), 493]

Harzem, P., & Miles, T. R. (1978). *Conceptual issues in operant psychology.* Chichester, UK: John Wiley [96]

Haught, P., Walls, R. T., & Crist, K. (1984). Placement of prompts, length of task, and level of retardation in learning complex assembly tasks. *American Journal of Mental Deficiency,* **89,** 60–66. [347]

Hauserman, N., Walen, S. R., & Behling, M. (1973). Reinforced racial integration in the first grade: A study in generalization. *Journal of Applied Behavior Analysis,* **6,** 193–200. [274(14), 496]

Hawkins, R. P. (1975). Who decided that was the problem? Two stages of responsibility for applied behavior analysts. In W. S. Wood (Ed.), *Issues in evaluating behavior modification,* (pp. 195–214). Champaign, IL: Research Press. [12]

Hawkins, R. P., Peterson, R. F., Schweid, E., & Bijou, S. S. (1966). Behavior therapy in the home: Amelioration of parent-child relations with parent in a therapeutic role. *Journal of Experimental Child Psychology,* **4,** 99–107. [122(2), 475]

Hay, W. M., Hay, L. R., & Nelson, R. O. (1977). Direct and collateral changes in on-task and academic behavior resulting from on-task versus academic contingencies. *Behavior Therapy,* **8,** 431–441. [12]

Hayduk, A. W. (1978). Peer selected modeling: A rapid treatment for aggressive-disruptive behavior. *Canadian Counsellor,* **12,** 123–127. [278–282, 283, 288, 294, 300]

Hayduk, A. W. (1980). Increasing hand efficiency at cold temperatures by training hand vasodilation with a classical conditioning-biofeedback overlap design. *Biofeedback and Self-Regulation,* **5,** 307–326. [414(6), 508]

Hayes, B. J., & Marshall, W. L. (1984). Generalization of treatment effects in training public speakers. *Behavior Research and Therapy,* **22,** 519–533. [274(17), 376, 497]

Hayes, L. J., Tilley, K. J., & Hayes, S. C. (1988). Extending equivalence class membership to gustatory stimuli. *Psychological Record,* **38,** 473–482. [448]

Hayes, S. C., & Barlow, D. H. (1977). Flooding relief in a case of public transportation phobia. *Behavior Therapy,* **8,** 742–746. [130–132]

Hayes, S. C., Brownstein, A. J., Zettle, R. D., Rosenfarb, I., & Korn, Z. (1986). Rule-governed behavior and sensitivity to changing consequences of responding. *Journal of the Experimental Analysis of Behavior, 45,* 237–256. [319]

Hayes, S. C., & Hayes, L. J. (1989). The verbal action of the listener as a basis for rule governance. In S. C. Hayes (Ed.), *Rule-governed behavior: Cognition, contingencies, and instructional control* (pp. 153–190). New York: Plenum Press. [316]

Hayes, S. C., Kohlenberg, B. S., & Melancon, S. M. (1989). Avoiding and altering rule-control as a strategy of clinical intervention. In S. C. Hayes (Ed.), *Rule-governed behavior: Cognition, contingencies, and instructional control* (pp. 359–385). New York: Plenum Press. [334]

Hayes, S. C., & Wolf, M. R. (1984). Cues, consequences and therapeutic talk: Effects of social context and coping statements on pain. *Behavior Research and Therapy, 22,* 385–392. [329–331]

Heckel, R. V., Wiggins, S. L., & Salzberg, H. C. (1962). Conditioning against silences in group therapy. *Journal of Clinical Psychology, 18,* 216–217. [137]

Hegel, M. T., Ayllon, T., VanderPlate, C., & Spiro-Hawkins, H. (1986). A behavioral procedure for increasing compliance with self-exercise regimens in severely burn-injured patients. *Behavior Research and Therapy, 24,* 521–528. [140]

Hendrickson, L. N., & Muehl, S. (1962). The effect of attention and motor response pretraining on learning to discriminate b and d in kindergarten children. *Journal of Educational Psychology, 53,* 236–241. [205]

Hendrix, E. M., Thompson, L. M., & Rau, B. W. (1978). Behavior treatment of an "hysterically" clenched fist. *Journal of Behavior Therapy and Experimental Psychiatry, 9,* 273–276. [142–143]

Herbert, E. W., & Baer, D. M. (1972). Training parents as behavior modifiers: Self-recording of contingent attention. *Journal of Applied Behavior Analysis, 5,* 139–149. [354]

Herman, R. L., & Azrin, N. H. (1964). Punishment by noise in an alternative response situation. *Journal of the Experimental Analysis of Behavior, 7,* 185–188. [109]

Hermann, J. A., de Montes, A. I., Dominguez, B., Montes, F., & Hopkins, B. L. (1973). Effects of bonuses for punctuality on the tardiness of industrial workers. *Journal of Applied Behavior Analysis, 6,* 563–570. [53(9), 466]

Herren, C. M. (1989). A self-monitoring technique for increasing productivity in multiple media. *Journal of Behavior Therapy and Experimental Psychiatry, 20,* 69–72. [354]

Herrnstein, R. J. (1970). On the law of effect. *Journal of the Experimental Analysis of Behavior, 4,* 267–272. [48]

Heyneman, N. E., Fremouw, W. J., Gano, D., Kirkland, F., Heiden, L. (1990). Individual differences and the effectiveness of different coping strategies for pain. *Cognitive Therapy and Research, 14,* 63–77. [321–322, 339(11), 502]

Higgins, S. T., & Morris, E. K. (1984). Generality of free-operant avoidance conditioning to human behavior. *Psychological Bulletin, 96,* 247–272. [136, 143]

Higgins, S. T. & Morris, E. K. (1985). A comment on contemporary definitions of reinforcement as a behavioral process. *The Psychological Record, 35,* 81–88. [31]

Hineline, P. N., & Wanchisen, B. A. (1989). Correlated hypothesizing and the distinction between contingency-shaped and rule-governed behavior. In S. C. Hayes (Ed.), *Rule-governed behavior: Cognition, contingencies, and instructional control* (pp. 221–268). New York: Plenum Press. [333]

Hiroto, D. S., & Seligman, M. E. P. (1975). Generality of learned helplessness in man. *Journal of Personality and Social Psychology, 31,* 311–327. [148]

Hobbs, S. A., Altman, K., & Halldin, M. A. (1980). Modification of a child's deviant walking pattern: An alternative to surgery. *Journal of Behavior Therapy and Experimental Psychiatry, 11,* 227–229. [87(22), 473]

Hobbs, S. A., & Forehand, R. (1975). Effects of differential release from timeout on children's deviant behavior. *Journal of Behavior Therapy and Experimental Psychiatry, 6,* 256–257. [133]

Hobbs, S. A., Forehand, R., & Murray, R. G. (1978). Effects of various durations of timeout on non-compliant behavior of children. *Behavior Therapy, 9,* 652–656. [138]

Hogan, R. A., & Kirchner, J. H. (1968). Implosive, eclectic verbal and bibliotherapy in the treatment of fears of snakes. *Behavior Research and Therapy,* **6,** 167–171. [420(13), 514]

Holz, W. C., Azrin, N. H., & Ayllon, T. (1963). Elimination of behavior of mental patients by response-produced extinction. *Journal of the Experimental Analysis of Behavior,* **6,** 407–412. [109]

Hom, G. L. (1967). Effects of amount of reinforcement on the concurrent performance of retardates. *Psychological Reports,* **20,** 887–892. [43]

Homer, A. L., & Peterson, L. (1980). Differential reinforcement of other behavior: A preferred response elimination procedure. *Behavior Therapy,* **11,** 449–471. [77]

Homme, L. E., deBaca, P. C., Devine, J. V., Steinhorst, R., & Rickert, E. J. (1963). Use of the Premack principle in controlling the behavior of nursery school children. *Journal of the Experimental Analysis of Behavior,* **6,** 544. [36]

Honig, W. K., Boneau, C. A., Burstein, K. R., & Pennypacker, H. S. (1963). Positive and negative generalization gradients obtained after equivalent training conditions. *Journal of Comparative and Physiological Psychology,* **56,** 111–116. [252]

Horne, A. M., & Matson, J. L. (1977). A comparison of modeling, desensitization, flooding, study skills, and control groups for reducing test anxiety. *Behavior Therapy,* **8,** 1–8. [307(17), 391, 499]

Horner, R. D., & Keilitz, I. (1975). Training mentally retarded adolescents to brush their teeth. *Journal of Applied Behavior Analysis,* **8,** 301–309. [224]

Horner, R. H., & Albin, R. W. (1988). Research on general-case procedures for learners with severe disabilities. *Education and Treatment of Children,* **11,** 375–388. [439, 443, 445]

Horner, R. H., & McDonald, R. S. (1982). Comparison of single instance and general case instruction in teaching a generalized vocational skill. *The Journal of the Association for the Severely Handicapped,* **8,** 7–20. [445]

Horton, G. O. (1975). Generalization of teacher behavior as a function of subject matter specific discrimination training. *Journal of Applied Behavior Analysis,* **8,** 311–319. [272(7), 496]

Hosford, R. E. (1981). Self-as-a-model: A cognitive social learning technique. *The Counseling Psychologist,* **9,** 45–61. [296, 308(24), 500]

Houlihan, D. D., & Jones, R. N. (1989). Treatment of a boy's school phobia with in vivo systematic desensitization. *Professional School Psychology,* **4,** 285–293. [385]

Howard, D. V. (1983). *Cognitive psychology.* New York: Macmillan. [407]

Howard, M. O., & Jenson, J. M. (1990). Chemical aversion treatment of alcohol dependence. I. Validity of current criticisms. *The International Journal of the Addictions,* **25,** 1227–1262. [390]

Howard, W. A., Murphy, S. M., & Clarke, J. C. (1983). The nature and treatment of fear of flying: A controlled investigation. *Behavior Therapy,* **14,** 555–567. [418(2), 513]

Howie, P. M., & Woods, C. L. (1982). Token reinforcement during the instatement and shaping of fluency in the treatment of stuttering. *Journal of Applied Behavior Analysis,* **15,** 55–64. [175–176]

Hughey, A. W. (1982). Use of Sidman avoidance to increase door-locking behavior among college students living in residence halls. *Psychological Reports,* **50,** 1055–1058. [155(14), 481]

Hurley, A. D. (1976). Unsystematic desensitization using pleasurable images to inhibit anxiety. *Journal of Behavior Therapy and Experimental Psychiatry,* **7,** 295. [419(9), 514]

Ince, L. P. (1969). Escape and avoidance conditioning of responses in the plegic arm of stroke patients: A preliminary study. *Psychonomic Science,* **16,** 49–50. [155(13), 480]

Intagliata, J. C. (1978). Increasing the interpersonal problem-solving skills of an alcoholic population. *Journal of Consulting and Clinical Psychology,* **46,** 489–498. [324]

Isaacs, W., Thomas, J., & Goldiamond, I. (1960). Application of operant conditioning to reinstate verbal behavior in psychotics. *Journal of Speech and Hearing Disorders,* **25,** 8–12. [183(4), 482]

Israel, A. C., & O'Leary, K. D. (1973). Developing correspondence between children's words and deeds. *Child Development,* **44,** 575–581. [326–327]

Israel, A. C., Stolmaker, L., & Andrian, C. A. G. (1985). The effects of training parents in general child management skills on a behavioral weight loss program for children. *Behavior Therapy,* **16,** 169–180. [24(7), 464]

Iwata, B. A. (1987). Negative reinforcement in applied behavior analysis: An emerging technology. *Journal of Applied Behavior Analysis,* **20,** 361–378. [143]

Iwata, B. A., & Bailey, J. S. (1974). Reward versus cost token systems: An analysis of the effects on students and teachers. *Journal of Applied Behavior Analysis, 7,* 567–576. [136]

Iwata, B. A., Pace, G. M., Kalsher, M. J., Cowdery, G. E., & Cataldo, M. F. (1990). Experimental analysis and extinction of self-injurious escape behavior. *Journal of Applied Behavior Analysis, 23,* 11–27. [141]

Jaanus, H., Defares, P. B., & Zwaan, E. J. (1990). Verbal classical conditioning of evaluative responses. *Advances in Behavior Research and Therapy, 12,* 123–151. [401]

Jacobs, H. E., Bailey, J. S., & Crews, J. I. (1984). Development and analysis of a community-based resource recovery program. *Journal of Applied Behavior Analysis, 17,* 127–145. [53(11), 222, 238(1), 467, 490]

Jacobson, N. S. (1977). Problem solving and contingency contracting in the treatment of marital discord. *Journal of Consulting and Clinical Psychology, 45,* 92–100. [324]

Jacobson, N. S., & Anderson, E. A. (1980). The effects of behavior rehearsal and feedback on the acquisition of problem-solving skills in distressed and nondistressed couples. *Behavior Research and Therapy, 18,* 25–36. [331–332]

Jacobson, N. S., Follette, V. M., Follette, W. C., Holtzworth-Munroe, A., Katt, J. L., & Schmaling, K. B. (1985). A component analysis of behavioral marital therapy: 1-year follow-up. *Behavior Research and Therapy, 23,* 549–555. [324]

James, J. E., Stirling, K. P., & Hampton, B. A. M. (1985). Caffeine fading: Behavioral treatment of caffeine abuse. *Behavior Therapy, 16,* 15–27. [26–27(22), 465]

Jarrett, R. B., & Nelson, R. O. (1987). Mechanisms of change in cognitive therapy of depression. *Behavior Therapy, 18,* 227–241. [338(6), 502]

Jenkins, J. R., & Larson, K. (1979). Evaluating error-correction procedures for oral reading. *Journal of Special Education, 13,* 145–156. [366]

Jenner, S. (1984). The effectiveness of abbreviated overcorrection-based treatments. *Behavioural Psychotherapy, 12,* 175–187. [123(5), 476]

Johnson, B. F., & Cuvo, A. J. (1981). Teaching mentally retarded adults to cook. *Behavior Modification, 5,* 187–202. [273(13), 496]

Johnson, D. L., McGlynn, F. D., & Topping, J. S. (1973). The relative efficiency of four response-elimination techniques following variable-ratio reinforcement training. *The Psychological Record, 23,* 203–208. [76]

Johnson, D. M., & Stratton, R. P. (1966). Evaluation of five methods of teaching concepts. *Journal of Educational Psychology, 57,* 48–53. [434, 451(7), 518]

Johnson, K. R., & Chase, P. N. (1981). Behavior analysis in instructional design: A functional typology of verbal tasks. *The Behavior Analyst, 4,* 103–121. [451(5), 517]

Johnson, K. R., & Layng, T. V. J. (1991). *Breaking the structuralist barrier: Literacy and numeracy with fluency.* Seattle, WA: Morningside Corporation. [3]

Johnson, K. R., & Ruskin, R. S. (1977). *Behavioral instruction: An evaluative review.* Washington, DC: American Psychological Association. [363, 426]

Johnston, J. M. (1972). Punishment of human behavior. *American Psychologist, 27,* 1033–1054. [104]

Johnston, J. M., & Pennypacker, H. S. (1981). *Strategies and tactics of human behavioral research.* Hillsdale, NJ: Lawrence Erlbaum. [8]

Jones, F. H., Fremouw, W., & Carples, S. (1977). Pyramid training of elementary school teachers to use a classroom management "skill package." *Journal of Applied Behavior Analysis, 10,* 239–253. [258]

Jones, M. C. (1924). The elimination of children's fears. *Journal of Experimental Psychology, 7,* 382–390. [385]

Jones, R. N., Sloane, H. N., & Roberts, M. W. (1992). Limitations of "don't" instructional control. *Behavior Therapy, 23,* 131–140. [113]

Jones, R. T., Kazdin, A. E., & Haney, J. I. (1981). Social validation and training of emergency fire safety skills for potential injury prevention and life saving. *Journal of Applied Behavior Analysis, 14,* 249–260. [23–24(3), 463]

Joyce, J. H., & Chase, P. N. (1990). Effects of response variability on the sensitivity of rule-governed behavior. *Journal of the Experimental Analysis of Behavior, 54,* 251–262. [320]

Kandel, H. J., Ayllon, T., & Rosenbaum, M. S. (1977). Flooding or systematic exposure in the treatment of extreme social withdrawal in children. *Journal of Behavior Therapy and Experimental Psychiatry*, **8**, 75–81. [391]

Kanfer, F. H., Karoly, P., & Newman, H. (1975). Reduction of children's fear of the dark by competence-related and situational threat-related verbal cues. *Journal of Consulting and Clinical Psychology*, **43**, 251–258. [337(1), 501]

Karan, B. S., & Kopelman, R. E. (1986). The effects of objective feedback on vehicular and industrial accidents: A field experiment using outcome feedback. *Journal of Organizational Behavior Management*, **8**, 45–56. [348]

Karsh, E. B., & Williams, J. P. (1964). Punishment and reward in children's instrumental learning. *Psychonomic Science*, **1**, 359–360. [113]

Kasatkin, N. I., & Levikova, A. M. (1935). On the development of early conditioned reflexes and differentiations of auditory stimuli in infants. *Journal of Experimental Psychology*, **18**, 1–19. [414(4), 507]

Kassorla, I. C. (1984). *Go for it! How to win at love, work, and play.* New York: Delacorte. [5, 322, 325]

Kaufman, A., Baron, A., & Kopp, R. E. (1966). Some effects of instructions on human operant behavior. *Psychonomic Monograph Supplements*, **1**, 243–250. [319]

Kazdin, A. E. (1973). The failure of some patients to respond to token programs. *Journal of Behavior Therapy and Experimental Psychiatry*, **4**, 7–14. [136]

Kazdin, A. E. (1974). Covert modeling, model similarity, and reduction in avoidance behavior. *Behavior Therapy*, **5**, 325–340. [300, 301–302]

Kazdin, A. E. (1975). Covert modeling, imagery assessment, and assertive behavior. *Journal of Consulting and Clinical Psychology*, **43**, 716–724. [300, 301–302]

Kazdin, A. E. (1976). Effects of covert modeling, multiple models, and model reinforcement on assertive behavior. *Behavior Therapy*, **7**, 211–222. [300, 301–302]

Kazdin, A. E. (1977a). Assessing the clinical or applied importance of behavior change through social validation. *Behavior Modification*, **1**, 427–452. [16]

Kazdin, A. E. (1977b). *The token economy: A review and evaluation.* New York: Plenum. [35]

Kazdin, A. E. (1977c). Vicarious reinforcement and the direction of behavior change in the classroom. *Behavior Therapy*, **8**, 57–63. [304(2), 498]

Kazdin, A. E. (1979). Effects of covert modeling and coding of modeled stimuli on assertive behavior. *Behavior Research and Therapy*, **17**, 53–61. [302]

Kazdin, A. E. (1980a). Acceptability of alternative treatments for deviant child behavior. *Journal of Applied Behavior Analysis*, **13**, 259–273. [77, 97, 108]

Kazdin, A. E. (1980b). Acceptability of time-out from reinforcement procedures for disruptive child behavior. *Behavior Therapy*, **11**, 329–344. [77, 100, 108, 112]

Kazdin, A. E. (1981). Acceptability of child treatment techniques: The influence of treatment efficacy and adverse side effects. *Behavior Therapy*, **12**, 493–506. [77, 78]

Kazdin, A. E. (1982a). Methodological strategies in behavior-therapy research. In G. T. Wilson & C. M. Franks (Eds.), *Contemporary behavior therapy: Conceptual and empirical foundations* (pp. 403–442). New York: Guilford Press. [15, 16]

Kazdin, A. E. (1982b). Symptom substitution, generalization, and response covariation: Implications for psychotherapy outcome. *Psychological Bulletin*, **91**, 349–365. [70, 80]

Kazdin, A. E. (1982c). The separate and combined effects of covert and overt rehearsal in developing assertive behavior. *Behavior Research and Therapy*, **20**, 17–25. [295]

Kazdin, A. E. (1985). Selection of target behaviors: The relationship of treatment focus to clinical dysfunction. *Behavioral Assessment*, **7**, 33–47. [12, 13]

Kazdin, A. E., & Bootzin, R. R. (1972). The token economy: An evaluative review. *Journal of Applied Behavior Analysis*, **5**, 343–372. [267]

Kazdin, A. E., French, N. H., & Sherick, R. B. (1981). Acceptability of alternative treatments for children: Evaluations by inpatient children, parents, and staff. *Journal of Consulting and Clinical Psychology*, **49**, 900–907. [103, 108]

Kazdin, A. E., & Mascitelli, S. (1982). Covert and overt rehearsal and homework practice in developing assertiveness. *Journal of Consulting and Clinical Psychology, 50,* 250–258. [299]

Kazdin, A. E., & Polster, R. (1973). Intermittent token reinforcement and response maintenance in extinction. *Behavior Therapy, 4,* 386–391. [177, 178, 181]

Keane, T. M., & Kaloupek, D. G. (1982). Imaginal flooding in the treatment of a posttraumatic stress disorder. *Journal of Consulting and Clinical Psychology, 50,* 138–140. [392]

Keane, T. M., Fairbank, J. A., Caddell, J. M., & Zimering, R. T. (1989). Implosive (flooding) therapy reduces symptoms of PTSD in Vietnam combat veterans. *Behavior Therapy, 20,* 245–260. [392]

Keenan, J. B., & Grant, L. (1979). *The effects of definitions, examples and nonexamples, and feedback on student conceptual responding.* Paper presented at the Fifth National Conference on Personalized Instruction, Washington, DC. [426–429]

Keller, F. S. (1943). Studies in international Morse code: I. A new method of teaching code reception. *Journal of Applied Psychology, 27,* 407–415. [211(9), 488]

Keller, F. S. (1968). "Goodbye, teacher. . ." *Journal of Applied Behavior Analysis, 1,* 79–89. [204, 363]

Keller, F. S. (1982). *Pedagogue's progress.* Lawrence, KS: TRI Publications. [211(9), 488]

Keller, F. S., & Schoenfeld, W. N. (1950). *Principles of psychology.* New York: Appleton-Century-Crofts. [32, 255, 431]

Kelley, H. H. (1950). The warm-cold variable in first impressions of persons. *Journal of Personality, 18,* 431–439. [22(21), 463]

Kelly, J. F., & Hake, D. F. (1970). An extinction-induced increase in an aggressive response with humans. *Journal of the Experimental Analysis of Behavior, 14,* 153–164. [65–66]

Kelly, M. B., & Bushell, D., Jr. (1987). Student achievement and differential reinforcement of incompatible behavior: Hand raising. *Psychology in the Schools, 24,* 273–281. [88(28), 474]

Kelly, M. L., Scott, W. O. M., Prue, D. M., & Rychtarik, R. G. (1985). A component analysis of problem-solving skills training. *Cognitive Therapy and Research, 9,* 429–441. [324]

Kelly, W. J., Salzberg, C. L., Levy, S. M., Warrenteltz, R. B., Adams, T. W., Crouse, T. R., & Beegle, G. P. (1983). The effects of role-playing and self-monitoring on the generalization of vocational social skills by behaviorally disordered adolescents. *Behavioral Disorders, 9,* 27–35. [354]

Kendall, P. C. (1992). Healthy thinking. *Behavior Therapy, 23,* 1–11. [322, 334]

Kendall, P. C., & Braswell, L. (1985). *Cognitive-behavioral therapy for impulsive children.* New York: Guilford Press. [321]

Kendall, P. C., & Grove, W. M. (1988). Normative comparisons in therapy outcome. *Behavioral Assessment, 10,* 147–158. [15]

Kendrick, M. J., Craig, K. D., Lawson, D. M., & Davidson, P. O. (1982). Cognitive and behavioral therapy for musical-performance anxiety. *Journal of Consulting and Clinical Psychology, 50,* 353–362. [340(14), 502]

Kennedy, E. M. (1990). *The concept of irony.* Unpublished manuscript. [452(9), 518]

Kilpatrick, D. G., & Best, C. L. (1984). Some cautionary remarks on treating sexual assault victims with implosion. *Behavior Therapy, 15,* 421–423. [515]

Kim, J.-Y. L., & Phillips, T. L. (1991). The effectiveness of two forms of corrective feedback in diabetes education. *Journal of Computer-Based Instruction, 18,* 14–18. [359, 370(13), 505]

Kim, J. S., & Hammer, W. C. (1976). Effect of performance feedback and goal setting on productivity and satisfaction in an organizational setting. *Journal of Applied Psychology, 61,* 48–57. [365]

Kim, Y. C., Marx, M. H., & Broyles, J. W. (1981). The stubborn-error effect in verbal discrimination learning. *Bulletin of the Psychonomic Society, 18,* 5–8. [347]

King, G. R., & Logue, A. W. (1987). Choice in a self-control paradigm with human subjects: Effects of changeover delay duration. *Learning and Motivation, 18,* 421–438. [43]

King, G. R., & Logue, A. W. (1990). Humans' sensitivity to variation in reinforcer amount: Effects of the method of reinforcer delivery. *Journal of the Experimental Analysis of Behavior, 53,* 33–45. [49, 51]

King, N. J., & Gullone, E. (1990). Acceptability of fear reduction procedures with children. *Journal of Behavior Therapy and Experimental Psychiatry, 21,* 1–8. [391–392]

Kipper, D. A. (1977). Behavior therapy for fears brought on by war experiences. *Journal of Consulting and Clinical Psychology*, **45**, 216–221. [419(8), 514]

Kirby, F. D., & Shields, F. (1972). Modification of arithmetic response rate and attending behavior in a seventh-grade student. *Journal of Applied Behavior Analysis*, **5**, 79–84. [12, 168]

Kirby, K. C., Holborn, S. W., & Bushby, H. T. (1981). Word game bingo: A behavioral treatment package for improving textual responding to sight words. *Journal of Applied Behavior Analysis*, **14**, 317–326. [212(18), 489]

Kircher, A. S., Pear, J. J., & Martin, G. L. (1971). Shock as a punishment in a picture-naming task with retarded children. *Journal of Applied Behavior Analysis*, **4**, 227–233. [111, 211(11), 488]

Kirsch, I., Wolpin, M., & Knutson, J. L. (1975). A comparison of *in vivo* methods for rapid reduction of "stage fright" in the college classroom: A field experiment. *Behavior Therapy*, **6**, 165–171. [166]

Klass, E. T. (1979). Relative influence of sincere, insincere, and neutral symbolic models. *Journal of Experimental Child Psychology*, **27**, 48–59. [301]

Kleiner, L., Marshall, W. L., & Spevack, M. (1987). Training in problem-solving and exposure treatment for agoraphobics with panic attacks. *Journal of Anxiety Disorders*, **1**, 219–238. [324, 338(4), 501]

Knapczyk, D. R. (1989). Generalization of student question asking from special class to regular class settings. *Journal of Applied Behavior Analysis*, **22**, 77–83. [271–272(2), 495]

Knapp, T. J., Crosby, H. W., & O'Boyle, M. W. (1978). Using the natural environment in counseling for therapeutic change: A case study. *Psychological Reports*, **42**, 1048–1050. [262]

Knapp, T. J., & Shodahl, S. A. (1974). Ben Franklin as a behavior modifier: A note. *Behavior Therapy*, **5**, 656–660. [353]

Kobre, K. R., & Lipsitt, L. P. (1972). A negative contrast effect in newborns. *Journal of Experimental Child Psychology*, **14**, 81–91. [46–48]

Koegel, R. L., Egel, A. L., & Williams, J. A. (1980). Behavioral contrast and generalization across settings in the treatment of autistic children. *Journal of Experimental Child Psychology*, **30**, 422–437. [269]

Koegel, R. L., Firestone, P. B., Kramme, K. W., & Dunlap, G. (1974). Increasing spontaneous play by suppressing self-stimulation in autistic children. *Journal of Applied Behavior Analysis*, **7**, 521–528. [68]

Koegel, R. L., Glahn, T. J., & Nieminen, G. S. (1978). Generalization of parent-training results. *Journal of Applied Behavior Analysis*, **11**, 95–109. [249–251, 442]

Koegel, R. L., O'Dell, M., & Dunlap, G. (1988). Producing speech use in nonverbal autistic children by reinforcing attempts. *Journal of Autism and Developmental Disorders*, **18**, 525–538. [167]

Koegel, R. L., Schreibman, L., Britten, K., & Laitinen, R. (1979). The effects of schedule of reinforcement on stimulus overselectivity in autistic children. *Journal of Autism and Developmental Disorders*, **9**, 383–397. [177–178, 179]

Komaki, J. L. (1986). Toward effective supervision: An operant analysis and comparison of managers at work. *Journal of Applied Psychology*, **71**, 270–279. [360]

Komaki, J. L., Collins, R. L., & Penn, P. (1982). The role of performance antecedents and consequences in work motivation. *Journal of Applied Psychology*, **67**, 334–340. [348]

Komaki, J. L., Desselles, M. L., & Bowman, E. D. (1989). Definitely not a breeze: Extending the operant model of effective supervision to teams. *Journal of Applied Psychology*, **74**, 522–529. [360]

Komaki, J. L., Waddell, W. M., & Pearce, M. G. (1977). The applied behavior analysis approach and individual employees: Improving performance in two small businesses. *Organizational Behavior and Human Performance*, **19**, 337–352. [348]

Koop, S., & Martin, G. L. (1983). Evaluation of a coaching strategy to reduce swimming stroke errors with beginning age-group swimmers. *Journal of Applied Behavior Analysis*, **16**, 447–460. [271(1), 495]

Kornhaber, R. C., & Schroeder, H. E. (1975). Importance of model similarity on extinction of avoidance behavior in children. *Journal of Consulting and Clinical Psychology*, **43**, 601–607. [300]

Kozma, A. (1969). The effects of anxiety, stimulation, and isolation on social reinforcer effectiveness. *Journal of Experimental Child Psychology*, **8**, 1–8. [40–41]

Krivacek, D., & Powell, J. (1978). Negative preference management: Behavioral suppression using Premack's punishment hypothesis. *Education and Treatment of Children*, **1**, 5–13. [126(28), 478]

Krop, H., & Krause, S. (1976). The elimination of a shark phobia by self-administered systematic desensitization: A case study. *Journal of Behavior Therapy and Experimental Psychiatry, 7,* 293–294. [420(12), 514]

Kulhavy, R. W. (1977). Feedback in written instruction. *Review of Educational Research, 47,* 211–232. [362]

Kulik, J. A., & Kulik, C.-L. C. (1988). Timing of feedback and verbal learning. *Review of Educational Research, 58,* 79–97. [262]

Kymissis, E., & Poulson, C. L. (1990). The history of imitation in learning theory: The language acquisition process. *Journal of the Experimental Analysis of Behavior, 54,* 113–127. [288]

Labrum, W. D. (1976). The 55 mph speed limit and fatality reduction in Utah. *Traffic Engineering, 46,* 13–16. [348]

LaCampagne, J., & Cipani, E. (1987). Training adults with mental retardation to pay bills. *Mental Retardation, 25,* 293–303. [245(7), 494]

Lahey, B. B., & Drabman, R. S. (1974). Facilitation of the acquisition and retention of sight-word vocabulary through token reinforcement. *Journal of Applied Behavior Analysis, 7,* 307–312. [212(14), 488]

Lalli, E. P., & Shapiro, E. S. (1990). The effects of self-monitoring and contingent reward on sight-word acquisition. *Education and Treatment of Children, 13,* 129–141. [354]

Lamal, P. A., & Benfield, A. (1978). The effect of self-monitoring on job tardiness and percentage of time spent working. *Journal of Organizational Behavior Management, 1,* 142–149. [371(19), 505]

Lancioni, G. E., Coninx, F., & Smeets, P. M. (1989). A classical conditioning procedure for the hearing assessment of multiply handicapped persons. *Journal of Speech and Hearing Disorders, 54,* 88–93. [401]

Landers, D. M., & Landers, D. M. (1973). Teacher versus peer models: Effects of model's presence and performance level on motor behavior. *Journal of Motor Behavior, 5,* 129–139. [300]

Lane, I. M., Wesolowski, M. D., & Burke, W. H. (1989). Teaching socially appropriate behavior to eliminate hoarding in a brain-injured adult. *Journal of Behavior Therapy and Experimental Psychiatry, 20,* 79–82. [109–110]

Lane, R. G., & Domrath, R. P. (1970). Behavior therapy: A case history. *Hospital and Community Psychiatry, 21,* 150–153. [61–63]

Lanzetta, J. T., & Orr, S. P. (1986). Excitatory strength of expressive faces: Effects of happy and fear expression and context on the extinction of a conditioned fear response. *Journal of Personality and Social Psychology, 50,* 190–194. [408]

Larson, K., & Ayllon, T. (1990). The effects of contingent music and differential reinforcement on infantile colic. *Behavior Research and Therapy, 28,* 119–125. [109]

Lattal, K. A., & Poling, A. D. (1981). Describing response-event relations: Babel revisited. *The Behavior Analyst, 4,* 143–152. [31]

Lauten, M. H., & Birnbrauer, J. S. (1974). The efficacy of "right" as a function of its relationship with reinforcement. *Journal of Experimental Child Psychology, 18,* 159–166. [44, 267]

Lavin, N. I., Thorpe, J. G., Barker, J. C., Blakemore, C. B., & Conway, C. G. (1961). Behavior therapy in a case of transvestism. *Journal of Nervous and Mental Disease, 133,* 346–353. [419–420(11), 514]

Le Boeuf, A. (1979). A behavioral treatment of chronic sleeptalking. *Journal of Behavior Therapy and Experimental Psychiatry, 10,* 83–84. [155(11), 480]

Leal, L., Crays, N., & Moely, B. E. (1985). Training children to use a self-monitoring study strategy in preparation for recall: Maintenance and generalization effects. *Child Development, 56,* 643–653. [354, 360]

LeFrancois, j. R., Chase, P. N., & Joyce, J. H. (1988). The effects of a variety of instructions on human fixed-interval performance. *Journal of the Experimental Analysis of Behavior, 49,* 383–393. [320]

Lengyel, L. M., Domaracki, J. W., & Lyon, S. R. (1990). General case simulation instruction of generalized housekeeping skills in blind, multihandicapped adults. *Journal of Visual Impairment and Blindness, 84,* 166–170. [454–455(8), 520]

Lennox, D. B., Miltenberger, R. G., & Donnelly, D. R. (1987). Response interruption and DRL for the reduction of rapid eating. *Journal of Applied Behavior Analysis, 20,* 279–284. [172–173]

Lerner, M. S., & Clum, G. A. (1990). Treatment of suicide ideators: A problem-solving approach. *Behavior Therapy, 21,* 403–411. [338(7), 502]

Levin, R., & Gross, A. M. (1985). The role of relaxation in systematic desensitization. *Behavior Research and Therapy, 23,* 187–196. [407]

Levine, G. F. (1977). "Learned helplessness" and the evening news. *Journal of Communication, 27,* 100–105. [292]

Levis, D. J., & Malloy, P. F. (1982). Research in infrahuman and human conditioning. In G. T. Wilson & C. M. Franks (Eds.), *Contemporary behavior therapy: Conceptual and empirical foundations* (pp. 65–118). New York: Guilford Press. [149]

Lewis, D. J., & Duncan, C. P. (1956). Effect of different percentages of money reward on extinction of a lever-pulling response. *Journal of Experimental Psychology, 52,* 23–27. [72, 73]

Lewis, D. J., & Duncan, C. P. (1957). Expectation and resistance to extinction of a lever-pulling response as functions of percentage of reinforcement and amount of reward. *Journal of Experimental Psychology, 54,* 115–120. [72]

Leyens, J.-P., Camino, L., Parke, R. D., & Berkowitz, L. (1975). Effects of movie violence on aggression in a field setting as a function of group dominance and cohesion. *Journal of Personality and Social Psychology, 32,* 346–360. [284, 285]

Liberman, R. P., Teigen, J., Patterson, R., & Baker, V. (1973). Reducing delusional speech in chronic paranoid schizophrenics. *Journal of Applied Behavior Analysis, 6,* 57–64. [254]

Liberman, R. P. (1992). *Behavioral rehabilitation for persons with serious mental disorders: Can coping and competence overcome stress and vulnerability?* Paper presented at the 18th annual convention of the Association for Behavior Analysis. [9, 63]

Liberman, R. P., Corrigan, P. W., & Schade, M. L. (1989). Drug and psychosocial treatment interactions in schizophrenia. *International Review of Psychiatry, 1,* 283–294. [63]

Lichstein, K. L., & Schreibman, L. (1976). Employing electric shock with autistic children: A review of the side effects. *Journal of Autism and Childhood Schizophrenia, 6,* 163–173. [104, 105]

Liebert, R. M., & Fernandez, L. E. (1970). Effects of vicarious consequences on imitative performance. *Child Development, 41,* 921–926. [304(1), 498]

Lindsley, O. R. (1992). Precision teaching: Discoveries and effects. *Journal of Applied Behavior Analysis, 25,* 51–57. [3]

Link, B. G., Cullen, F. T., Frank, J., & Wozniak, J. F. (1987). The social rejection of former mental patients: Understanding why labels matter. *American Journal of Sociology, 92,* 1461–1500. [5]

Lipinski, D., & Nelson, R. (1974). The reactivity and unreliability of self-recording. *Journal of Consulting and Clinical Psychology, 42,* 118–123. [354]

Lisspers, J., & Öst, L.-G. (1990). BVP-biofeedback in the treatment of migraine: The effects of constriction and dilatation during different phases of the migraine attack. *Behavior Modification, 14,* 200–221. [371(16), 505]

Litt, M. D., & Schreibman, L. (1981). Stimulus-specific reinforcement in the acquisition of receptive labels by autistic children. *Analysis and Intervention in Developmental Disabilities, 1,* 171–186. [208]

Little, L. M., & Kelley, M. L. (1989). The efficacy of response cost procedures for reducing children's noncompliance to parental instructions. *Behavior Therapy, 20,* 525–534. [139]

Littlejohn, T. D., & Goetz, E. M. (1989). Beginnings of reading: The effects of the preschool reading center. *Behavior Modification, 13,* 306–321. [212(16), 489]

Loess, H. B., & Duncan, C. P. (1952). Human discrimination learning with simultaneous and successive presentation of stimuli. *Journal of Experimental Psychology, 44,* 215–221. [198]

Logue, A. W., Ophir, I., & Strauss, K. E. (1981). The acquisition of taste aversions in humans. *Behavior Research and Therapy, 19,* 319–333. [393–394]

Logue, A. W., Pena-Correal, T. E., Rodriguez, M. L., & Kabela, E. (1986). Self-control in adult humans: Variation in positive reinforcer amount and delay. *Journal of the Experimental Analysis of Behavior, 46,* 159–173. [43, 49]

Lovaas, O. I., Berberich, J. P., Perloff, B. F., & Schaeffer, B. (1966). Acquisition of imitative speech by schizophrenic children. *Science, 151,* 705–707. [306(14), 499]

Lovaas, O. I., Freitag, G., Gold, V., & Kassorla, I. (1965). Experimental studies in childhood schizophrenia: Analysis of self-destructive behavior. *Journal of Experimental Child Psychology, 2,* 67–84. [85(14), 473]

Lovaas, O. I., Freitag, G., Kinder, M. I., Rubenstein, B. D., Schaeffer, B., & Simmons, J. Q. (1966). Establishment of social reinforcers in two schizophrenic children on the basis of food. *Journal of Experimental Child Psychology, 4,* 109–125. [44]

Lovaas, O. I., Koegel, R., Simmons, J. Q., & Long, J. S. (1973). Some generalization and follow-up measures on autistic children in behavior therapy. *Journal of Applied Behavior Analysis, 6,* 131–166. [258–259]

Lovaas, O. I., & Schreibman, L. (1971). Stimulus overselectivity of autistic children in a two stimulus situation. *Behavior Research and Therapy, 9,* 305–310. [201, 202]

Lovitt, T. C., & Esveldt, K. A. (1970). The relative effects on math performance of single- versus multiple-ratio schedules: A case study. *Journal of Applied Behavior Analysis, 3,* 261–270. [159(9), 485]

Lowe, C. F., & Chadwick, P. D. J. (1990). Verbal control of delusions. *Behavior Therapy, 21,* 461–479. [322, 338–339(8), 502]

Lowenstein, L. F. (1982). The treatment of extreme shyness in maladjusted children by implosive, counselling, and conditioning approaches. *Acta Psychiatrica Scandinavica, 66,* 173–189. [185(16), 483]

Luce, S. C., Delquadri, J., & Hall, R. V. (1980). Contingent exercise: A mild yet powerful procedure for suppressing inappropriate verbal and aggressive behavior. *Journal of Applied Behavior Analysis, 13,* 583–594. [124–125(16), 477]

Luciano, M. C., & Polaino-Lorente, A. (1986). Effects of the acquisition of prerequisite behavior on the learning of nonvocal verbal behavior and vocal imitation in children with severe retardation. *The Psychological Record, 36,* 315–332. [298]

Ludwig, T. D., & Geller, E. S. (1991). Improving the driving practices of pizza deliverers: Response generalization and moderating effects of driving history. *Journal of Applied Behavior Analysis, 24,* 31–44. [256]

Luiselli, J. K. (1988). Comparative analysis of sensory extinction treatments for self-injury. *Education and Treatment of Children, 11,* 149–156. [88(31), 474]

Luthans, F., Paul, R., & Taylor, L. (1986). The impact of contingent reinforcement on retail salespersons' performance behaviors: A replicated field experiment. *Journal of Organizational Behavior Management, 7,* 25–35. [54(16), 467]

Lutzker, J. R. (1974). Social reinforcement control of exhibitionism in a profoundly retarded adult. *Mental Retardation, 12* (Oct.), 46–47. [85(10), 472]

Luyben, P. D. (1984). Drop and tilt: A comparison of two procedures to increase the use of venetian blinds to conserve energy. *Journal of Community Psychology, 12,* 149–154. [371(17), 505]

Luyben, P. D., Funk, D. M., Morgan, J. K., Clark, K. A., & Delulio, D. W. (1986). Team sports for the severely retarded: Training a side-of-the-foot soccer pass using a maximum-to-minimum prompt reduction strategy. *Journal of Applied Behavior Analysis, 19,* 431–436. [221]

Mace, F. C., & Belfiore, P. (1990). Behavioral momentum in the treatment of escape-motivated stereotypy. *Journal of Applied Behavior Analysis, 23,* 507–514. [142, 329]

Mace, F. C., Browder, D. M., & Lin, Y. L. (1987). Analysis of demand conditions associated with stereotypy. *Journal of Behavior Therapy and Experimental Psychiatry, 18,* 25–31. [142]

Macht, J. (1970). Examination and reevaluation of prosthetic lenses employing an operant procedure for measuring subjective visual acuity in a retarded child. *Journal of Experimental Child Psychology, 10,* 139–145. [217]

Madsen, C. H., Jr., Becker, W. C., Thomas, D. R., Koser, L., & Plager, E. (1968). An analysis of the reinforcing function of "sit-down" commands. In R. K. Parker (Ed.), *Readings in educational psychology* (pp. 265–278). Boston: Allyn and Bacon. [36, 113]

Madsen, C. H., Becker, W. C., & Thomas, D. R. (1968). Rules, praise, and ignoring: Elements of elementary classroom control. *Journal of Applied Behavior Analysis, 1,* 139–150. [64, 70]

Mahn, C. S., & Greenwood, G. E. (1990). Cognitive behavior modification: Use of self-instruction strategies by first graders on academic tasks. *Journal of Educational Research, 83,* 158–161. [340(15), 502]

Malloy, P., & Levis, D. J. (1988). A laboratory demonstration of persistent human avoidance. *Behavior Therapy, 19,* 229–241. [136]

Maloney, K. B., & Hopkins, B. L. (1973). The modification of sentence structure and its relationship to subjective judgements of creativity in writing. *Journal of Applied Behavior Analysis, 6,* 425–433. [26(21), 465]

Malott, R. W. (1986). Self-management, rule-governed behavior, and everyday life. In H. W. Reese and L. J. Parrott (Eds.), *Behavior science: Philosophical, methodological, and empirical advances* (pp. 207–228). Hillsdale, NJ: Lawrence Erlbaum. [317]

Malott, R. W. (1989). The achievement of evasive goals: Control by rules describing contingencies that are not direct acting. In S. C. Hayes (Ed.), *Rule-governed behavior: Cognition, contingencies, and instructional control* (pp. 269–322). New York: Plenum Press. [317]

Maltzman, I., Langdon, B., Pendery, M., & Wolff, C. (1977). Galvanic skin response—orienting reflex and semantic conditioning and generalization with different unconditioned stimuli. *Journal of Experimental Psychology: General, 106,* 141–171. [402–403]

Mank, D. M., & Horner, R. H. (1987). Self-recruited feedback: A cost-effective procedure. *Research in Developmental Disabilities, 8,* 91–112. [268]

Mann, R. A., & Baer, D. M. (1971). The effects of receptive language training on articulation. *Journal of Applied Behavior Analysis, 4,* 291–298. [272(6), 496]

Mann, R. B., & Decker, P. J. (1984). The effect of key behavior distinctiveness on generalization and recall in behavior modeling training. *Academy of Management Journal, 27,* 900–910. [299]

Mansdorf, I. J. (1977). Rapid token training of an institution ward using modeling. *Mental Retardation, 15,* 37–39. [291]

Marholin, D., II, & Steinman, W. M. (1977). Stimulus control in the classroom as a function of the behavior reinforced. *Journal of Applied Behavior Analysis, 10,* 465–478. [12]

Markle, S. M., & Tiemann, P. W. (1970). *Really understanding concepts.* Champaign, IL: Stipes. [433]

Markle, S. M., & Tiemann, P. W. (1974). Some principles of instructional design at higher cognitive levels. In R. Ulrich, T. Stachnik, & J. Mabry (Eds.), *Control of human behavior* (Vol. 3, pp. 312–323). Glenview, IL: Scott, Foresman. [435, 450(1), 517]

Marshall, W. L. (1985). Effects of variable exposure in flooding therapy. *Behavior Therapy, 16,* 117–135. [383]

Martella, R. C., Agran, M., & Marchand-Martella, N. E. (1992). Problem solving to prevent work injuries in supported employment. *Journal of Applied Behavior Analysis, 25,* 637–645. [324]

Martin, P. L., & Foxx, R. M. (1973). Victim control of the aggression of an institutionalized retardate. *Journal of Behavior Therapy and Experimental Psychiatry, 4,* 161–165. [83(1), 472]

Mash, E. J. (1985). Some comments on target selection in behavior therapy. *Behavioral Assessment, 7,* 63–78. [12]

Masur, F. T. (1976). Behavior therapy in a case of pollakiuria. *Journal of Behavior Therapy and Experimental Psychiatry, 7,* 175–178. [184(12), 483]

Matson, J. L., & Taras, M. E. (1989). A 20-year review of punishment and alternative methods to treat problem behaviors in developmentally delayed persons. *Research in developmental disabilities, 10,* 85–104. [104, 105]

Matthews, B. A., & Shimoff, E. (1974). Human responding on a temporally defined schedule of point-loss avoidance. *The Psychological Record, 24,* 209–219. [146]

Mattson, M., & Moore, J. W. (1964). Intertrial responding and CS intensity in classical eyelid conditioning. *Journal of Experimental Psychology, 68,* 396–401. [407]

Mausner, B. (1953). Studies in social interaction: III. Effect of variation in one partner's prestige on the interaction of observer pairs. *Journal of Applied Psychology, 37,* 391–393. [300]

Mausner, B. (1954). The effect of one partner's success in a relevant task on the interaction of observer pairs. *Journal of Abnormal and Social Psychology, 49,* 557–560. [300]

Mayer, G. R., Butterworth, T., Nafpaktitis, M., & Sulzer-Azaroff, B. (1983). Preventing school vandalism and improving discipline: A three-year study. *Journal of Applied Behavior Analysis, 16,* 355–369. [24–25(9), 464]

Mayer, J. A., Heins, J. M., Vogel, J. M., Morrison, D. C., Lankester, L. D., & Jacobs, A. L. (1986). Promoting low-fat entree choices in a public cafeteria. *Journal of Applied Behavior Analysis, 19,* 397–402. [239(6), 490]

Mayhew, G. L., & Anderson, J. (1980). Delayed and immediate reinforcement: Retarded adolescents in an educational setting. *Behavior Modification, 4,* 527–545. [266]

Mayo, L. L., & Norton, G. R. (1980). The use of problem solving to reduce examination and interpersonal anxiety. *Journal of Behavior Therapy and Experimental Psychiatry, 11,* 287–289. [324]

McConaghy, N. (1970). Penile response conditioning and its relationship to aversion therapy in homosexuals. *Behavior Therapy, 1,* 213–221. [415(10), 509]

McCullagh, P. (1986). Model status as a determinant of observational learning and performance. *Journal of Sport Psychology, 8,* 319–331. [300]

McCullagh, P. (1987). Model similarity effects on motor performance. *Journal of Sport Psychology, 9,* 249–260. [300]

McDonnell, J., & Ferguson, B. (1989). A comparison of time delay and decreasing prompt hierarchy strategies in teaching banking skills to students with moderate handicaps. *Journal of Applied Behavior Analysis, 22,* 85–91. [224–225]

McDonnell, J., & Laughlin, B. (1989). A comparison of backward and concurrent chaining strategies in teaching community skills. *Education and Training in Mental Retardation, 24,* 230–238. [245(5), 494]

McDowell, J. J. (1982). The importance of Herrnstein's mathematical statement of the law of effect for behavior therapy. *American Psychologist, 37,* 771–779. [80, 121]

McDowell, J. J. (1988). Matching theory in natural human environments. *The Behavior Analyst, 11,* 95–109. [48, 80, 121]

McGee, G. G., & McCoy, J. F. (1981). Training procedures for acquisition and retention of reading in retarded youth. *Applied Research in Mental Retardation, 2,* 263–276. [243(10), 492]

McGovern, L. P., Ditzian, J. L., & Taylor, S. P. (1975). The effect of one positive reinforcement in helping with cost. *Bulletin of the Psychonomic Society, 5,* 421–423. [112]

McGregor, G., & Axelrod, S. (1988). Microcomputers in the classroom: Teaching students with severe handicaps to use a computer. *Education and Treatment of Children, 11,* 230–238. [245(4), 493]

McKenzie, B., & Day, R. H. (1974). Operant learning of visual pattern discrimination in young infants. *Journal of Experimental Child Psychology, 11,* 45–53. [211(7), 487]

McKenzie, T. L., & Rushall, B. S. (1974). Effects of self-recording on attendance and performance in a competitive swimming training environment. *Journal of Applied Behavior Analysis, 7,* 199–206. [354]

McNally, R. J. (1987). Preparedness and phobias: A review. *Psychological Bulletin, 101,* 283–303. [408]

McNally, R. J., & Steketee, G. S. (1985). The etiology and maintenance of severe animal phobias. *Behavior Research and Therapy, 23,* 431–435. [394]

McSweeney, F. K., & Bierley, C. (1984). Recent developments in classical conditioning. *Journal of Consumer Research, 11,* 619–631. [408, 409]

McSweeny, A. J. (1978). Effects of response cost on the behavior of a million persons: Charging for directory assistance in Cincinnati. *Journal of Applied Behavior Analysis, 11,* 47–51. [124(10), 476]

Mees, H. L. (1966). Sadistic fantasies modified by aversive conditioning and substitution: A case study. *Behavior Research and Therapy, 4,* 317–320. [419(7), 514]

Meichenbaum, D. H. (1969). The effects of instructions and reinforcement on thinking and language behavior of schizophrenics. *Behavior Research and Therapy, 7,* 101–114. [275(21), 497]

Meichenbaum, D., & Cameron, R. (1973). Training schizophrenics to talk to themselves: A means of developing attentional controls. *Behavior Therapy, 4,* 515–534. [322, 329]

Meichenbaum, D., & Goodman, J. (1969). The developmental control of operant motor responding by verbal operants. *Journal of Experimental Child Psychology, 7,* 553–565. [329]

Meichenbaum, D. H., & Goodman, J. (1971). Training impulsive children to talk to themselves: A means of developing self-control. *Journal of Abnormal Psychology, 77,* 115–126. [321]

Meltzoff, A. N. (1988). Infant imitation after a 1-week delay: Long-term memory for novel acts and multiple stimuli. *Developmental Psychology, 24,* 470–476. [293]

Mento, A. J., Steel, R. P., & Karren, R. J. (1987). A meta-analytic study of the effects of goal setting on task performance: 1966–1984. *Organizational Behavior and Human Decision-Processes, 39,* 52–83. [365–366]

Merckelbach, H., de Ruiter, C., van den Hout, M. A., & Hoekstra, R. (1989). Conditioning experiences and phobias. *Behavior Research and Therapy, 27,* 657–662. [394]

Michelson, L., Mavissakalian, M., & Marchione, K. (1988). Cognitive, behavioral, and psychophysiological treatments of agoraphobia: A comparative outcome investigation. *Behavior Therapy, 19,* 97–120. [392]

Migler, B., & Wolpe, J. (1967). Automated self-desensitization: A case report. *Behavior Research and Therapy, 5,* 133–135. [421(17), 515]

Millar, W. S., & Watson, J. S. (1979). The effect of delayed feedback on infant learning reexamined. *Child Development, 50,* 747–751. [50]

Millenson, J. R., & Leslie, J. C. (1979). *Principles of behavioral analysis* (2nd ed.). New York: Macmillan. [382]

Miller, F. D., Kalin, R. S., Eckenroth, W. N., & Meyer, P. A. (1970). Acquisition variables in human avoidance behavior. *Psychonomic Science, 21,* 233–235. [136, 143–144, 327]

Miller, F. D., Kalin, R. S., & Meyer, P. A. (1970). The effects of temporal variables on the acquisition of human avoidance behavior. *Psychonomic Science, 21,* 241–243. [136]

Miller, L. K. (1968a). Escape from an effortful situation. *Journal of the Experimental Analysis of Behavior, 11,* 619–627. [141, 146, 168, 169]

Miller, L. K. (1968b). The effects of response force on avoidance rate. *Journal of the Experimental Analysis of Behavior, 11,* 809–812. [146]

Miller, L. K., & Weaver, H. (1976). A behavioral technology for producing concept formation in university students. *Journal of Applied Behavior Analysis, 9,* 289–300. [432]

Miller, P. M. (1972). The use of behavioral contracting in the treatment of alcoholism: A case report. *Behavior Therapy, 3,* 593–596. [100–101]

Miller, W. R., & Seligman, M. E. P. (1975). Depression and learned helplessness in man. *Journal of Abnormal Psychology, 84,* 228–238. [149]

Miltenberger, R. G., & Fuqua, R. W. (1985). A comparison of contingent vs non-contingent competing response practice in the treatment of nervous habits. *Journal of Behavior Therapy and Experimental Psychiatry, 16,* 195–200. [104]

Miltenberger, R. G., Fuqua, R. W., & McKinley, T. (1985). Habit reversal with muscle tics: Replication and component analysis. *Behavior Therapy, 16,* 39–50. [106, 122(1), 475]

Miltenberger, R. G., Lennox, D. B., & Erfanian, N. (1989). Acceptability of alternative treatments for persons with mental retardation: Ratings from institutional and community-based staff. *American Journal on Mental Retardation, 93,* 388–395. [97, 103, 108]

Minkin, N., Braukmann, C. J., Minkin, B. L., Timbers, G. D., Timbers, B. J., Fixsen, D. L., Phillips, E. L., & Wolf, M. M. (1976). The social validation and training of conversational skills. *Journal of Applied Behavior Analysis, 9,* 127–139. [16]

Mischel, W. (1984). Convergences and challenges in the search for consistency. *American Psychologist, 39,* 351–364. [50]

Mischel, W. (1986). *Introduction to personality* (4th ed.). New York: Holt, Rinehart, and Winston. [50]

Mizes, J. S. (1985). The use of contingent reinforcement in the treatment of a conversion disorder: A multiple baseline study. *Journal of Behavior Therapy and Experimental Psychiatry, 16,* 341–345. [143, 184(13), 483]

Moeller, G. (1954). The CS-UCS interval in GSR conditioning. *Journal of Experimental Psychology, 48,* 162–166. [404]

Moergen, S. A., Merkel, W. T., & Brown, S. (1990). The use of covert sensitization and social skills training in the treatment of an obscene telephone caller. *Journal of Behavior Therapy and Experimental Psychiatry, 21*, 269–275. [418–419(6), 513]

Moffat, G. H. (1972). Avoidance conditioning in young children with interruption of a positive stimulus as the aversive event. *Journal of Experimental Child Psychology, 13*, 21–28. [147]

Moffat, G. H., & Miller, F. D. (1971). Effect of pretraining and instructions on avoidance conditioning in preschool children. *Journal of Experimental Child Psychology, 11*, 133–138. [143]

Moore, L. P., Moore, J. W., & Hauck, W. E. (1982). Conditioning children's attitudes toward alcohol, smoking, and drugs. *Journal of Experimental Education, 50*, 154–158. [397]

Moore, S. G., & Olson, F. (1969). The effects of explicitness of instructions on the generalization of a prohibition in young children. *Child Development, 40*, 945–949. [327]

Moran, G. (1981). Second-order classical conditioning of meaning in the Staats format. *Bulletin of the Psychonomic Society, 18*, 299–300. [395]

Morgan, Wesley G. (1974). The shaping game: A teaching technique. *Behavior Therapy, 5*, 271–272. [161]

Morris, E. K. (1992). [Review of L. D. Fernald's *Walking tour of Walden Two: A student's guidebook.*] *The Behavior Analyst, 15*, 77–79. [10]

Morris, E. K., & Redd, W. H. (1975). Children's performance and social preference for positive, negative, and mixed adult-child interactions. *Child Development, 46*, 525–531. [108]

Morris, R. J., & Dolker, M. (1974). Developing cooperative play in socially withdrawn retarded children. *Mental Retardation, 12*, 24–27. [184(10), 483]

Mowrer, O. H. (1947). On the dual nature of learning—A re-interpretation of "conditioning" and "problem-solving." *Harvard Educational Review, 17*, 102–148. [149]

Mulick, J. A. (1990). The ideology and science of punishment in mental retardation. *American Journal on Mental Retardation, 95*, 142–156. [96]

Mumford, L. (1982). *Sketches from life: The autobiography of Lewis Mumford, The early years.* New York: The Dial Press. [55(23), 468]

Munjack, D. J. (1984). The onset of driving phobias. *Journal of Behavior Therapy and Experimental Psychiatry, 15*, 305–308. [394]

Murphy, J., Bates, P., & Anderson, J. (1984). The effect of self-instruction training of counting skills by pre-school handicapped students. *Education and Treatment of Children, 7*, 247–257. [321]

Narayan, J. S., Heward, W. L., Gardner, R., III, Courson, F. H., & Omness, C. K. (1990). Using response cards to increase student participation in an elementary school classroom. *Journal of Applied Behavior Analysis, 23*, 483–490. [204]

Nation, J. R., & Cooney, J. B. (1982). The time course of extinction-induced aggressive behavior in humans: Evidence for a stage model of extinction. *Learning and Motivation, 13*, 95–112. [65]

Nedelman, D., & Sulzbacher, S. I. (1972). Dicky at 13 years of age: A long term-success following early application of operant conditioning procedures (pp. 3–10). In G. Semb (Ed.), *Behavior Analysis & Education*—1972. Lawrence, KS: Department of Human Development, University of Kansas. [159–161]

Neef, N. A., Lensbower, J., Hockersmith, I., DePalma, V., & Gray, K. (1990). In vivo versus simulation training: An interactional analysis of range and type of training exemplars. *Journal of Applied Behavior Analysis, 23*, 447–458. [264, 445, 453(1), 519]

Neef, N. A., Shafer, M. S., Egel, A. L., Cataldo, M. F., & Parrish, J. M. (1983). The class specific effects of compliance training with "do" and "don't" requests: Analogue analysis and classroom application. *Journal of Applied Behavior Analysis, 16*, 81–99. [326, 327]

Neisworth, J. T., Hunt, F. M., Gallop, H. R., & Madle, R. A. (1985). Reinforcer displacement: A preliminary study of the clinical application of the CRF/EXT effect. *Behavior Modification, 9*, 103–115. [72, 73]

Neisworth, J. T., Madle, R. A., & Goeke, K. E. (1975). "Errorless" elimination of separation anxiety: A case study. *Journal of Behavior Therapy and Experimental Psychiatry, 6*, 79–82. [242–243(14), 493]

Neisworth, J. T., & Moore, F. (1972). Operant treatment of asthmatic responding with the parent as therapist. *Behavior Therapy, 3,* 95–99. [86(19), 473]

Nelson, R. O., & Hayes, S. C. (1979). The nature of behavioral assessment: A commentary. *Journal of Applied Behavior Analysis,* 12, 491–500. [11, 16]

Nelson, W. J., & Birkimer, J. C. (1978). Role of self-instruction and self-reinforcement in the modification of impulsivity. *Journal of Consulting and Clinical Psychology,* 46, 183. [331]

Nevo, O., & Shapira, J. (1988). The use of humor by pediatric dentists. *Journal of Children in Contemporary Society,* 20, 171–178. [385]

New tool: 'Reinforcement' for good work. (1971, December 18). *Business Week,* pp. 76–77. [343–345]

Newsom, C. D., & Simón, K. M. (1977). A simultaneous discrimination procedure for the measurement of vision in nonverbal children. *Journal of Applied Behavior Analysis,* 10, 633–644. [216–219, 220, 223, 225–226]

Newsom, C., Favell, J. E., & Rincover, A. (1983). The side effects of punishment. In S. Axelrod and J. Apsche (Eds.), *The effects of punishment on human behavior* (pp. 285–316). New York: Academic Press. [105]

Nezu, A., & D'Zurilla, T. J. (1981). Effects of problem definition and formulation on decision making in the social problem-solving process. *Behavior Therapy,* 12, 100–106. [331]

Nisbett, R. E., Fong, G. T., Lehman, D. R., & Cheng, P. W. (1987). Teaching reasoning. *Science,* 238, 625–631. [317]

Nordstrom, R., Lorenzi, P., & Hall, R. V. (1990). A review of public posting of performance feedback in work settings. *Journal of Organizational Behavior Management,* 11, 101–123. [348]

Nurnberger, J. I., & Zimmerman, J. (1970). Applied analysis of human behavior: An alternative to conventional motivational inferences and unconscious determination in therapeutic programming. *Behavior Therapy,* 1, 59–69. [139–140]

Nutter, D., & Reid, D. H. (1978). Teaching retarded women a clothing selection skill using community norms. *Journal of Applied Behavior Analysis,* 11, 475–487. [26(18), 465]

O'Brien, F., & Azrin, N. H. (1972). Developing proper mealtime behaviors of the institutionalized retarded. *Journal of Applied Behavior Analysis,* 5, 389–399. [26(20), 465]

O'Leary, S. G. (1974). Children's avoidance responses to three probabilities of threatened consequences. *Journal of Experimental Child Psychology,* 17, 507–518. [145]

O'Neill, G. W., Blanck, L. S., & Joyner, M. A. (1980). The use of stimulus control over littering in a natural setting. *Journal of Applied Behavior Analysis,* 13, 379–381. [238(3), 490]

O'Shea, L. J., Munson, S. M., & O'Shea, D. J. (1984). Error correction in oral reading: Evaluating the effectiveness of three procedures. *Education and Treatment of Children,* 7, 203–214. [366]

Oldenquist, A. (1990). How not to make moral arguments. *American Journal on Mental Retardation,* 95, 171–172. [96]

Oliver, S. D., West, R. C., & Sloane, H. N., Jr. (1974). Some effects on human behavior of aversive events. *Behavior Therapy,* 5, 481–493. [106, 149]

Ollendick, T. H., & Shapiro, E. S. (1984). An examination of vicarious reinforcement processes in children. *Journal of Experimental Child Psychology,* 37, 78–91. [291]

Öst, L.-G., & Hugdahl, K. (1985). Acquisition of blood and dental phobia and anxiety response patterns in clinical patients. *Behavior Research and Therapy,* 23, 27–34. [394]

Page, T. J., Iwata, B. A., & Neef, N. A. (1976). Teaching pedestrian skills to retarded persons: Generalization from the classroom to the natural environment. *Journal of Applied Behavior Analysis,* 9, 433–444. [274–275(19), 497]

Page, T. J., Stanley, A. E., Richman, G. S., Deal, R. M., & Iwata, B. A. (1983). Reduction of food theft and long-term maintenance of weight loss in a Prader-Willi adult. *Journal of Behavior Therapy and Experimental Psychiatry,* 14, 261–268. [87(24), 473]

Palace, E. M., & Johnston, C. (1989). Treatment of recurrent nightmares by the dream reorganization approach. *Journal of Behavior Therapy and Experimental Psychiatry,* 20, 219–226. [312–314]

Paniagua, F. A. (1990). A procedural analysis of correspondence training techniques. *The Behavior Analyst,* 13, 107–119. [327]

Pany, D., & McCoy, K. M. (1988). Effects of corrective feedback on word accuracy and reading comprehension of readers with learning disabilities. *Journal of Learning Disabilities, 9,* 546–550. [369(9), 504]

Parish, T. S., Bryant, W. T., & Prawat, R. S. (1977). Reversing effects of sexism in elementary school girls through counterconditioning. *Journal of Instructional Psychology, 4,* 11–16. [418(5), 513]

Parish, T. S., Buntman, A. D., & Buntman, S. R. (1976). Effect of counterconditioning on test anxiety as indicated by digit span performance. *Journal of Educational Psychology, 68,* 297–299. [397]

Parish, T. S., Shirazi, A., & Lambert, F. (1976). Conditioning away prejudicial attitudes in children. Can attitudes be modified through classical conditioning? *Perceptual and Motor Skills, 43,* 907–912. [397]

Park, H.-P., & Gaylord-Ross, R. (1989). A problem-solving approach to social skills training in employment settings with mentally retarded youth. *Journal of Applied Behavior Analysis, 22,* 373–380. [324]

Park, O.-C. (1984). Example comparison strategy versus attribute identification strategy in concept learning. *American Educational Research Journal, 21,* 145–162. [434]

Parke, R. D. (1969). Effectiveness of punishment as an interaction of intensity, timing, agent nurturance, and cognitive structuring. *Child Development, 40,* 213–235. [111–112, 116, 328]

Parker, L. H., Cataldo, M. F., Bourland, G., Emurian, C. S., Corbin, R. J., & Page, J. M. (1984). Operant treatment of orofacial dysfunction in neuromuscular disorders. *Journal of Applied Behavior Analysis, 17,* 413–427. [88(29), 474]

Paschalis, A. P. (1987). Tokens and their economy: The Greeks had a use for them. *Journal of Applied Behavior Analysis, 20,* 427. [52(1), 466]

Patterson, R. L., Teigen, J. R., Liberman, R. P., & Austin, N. K. (1975). Increasing speech intensity of chronic patients ("mumblers") by shaping techniques. *The Journal of Nervous and Mental Disease, 160,* 182–187. [184(11), 483]

Pavlov, I. P. (1960). *Conditioned reflexes: An investigation of the physiological activity of the cerebral cortex* (G. V. Anrep, Trans. and Ed.). New York: Dover. (Original edition published 1927) [379]

Pereira, F., & Pérez, R. (1987). Conducta gobernada por la regla y ejecución en un proceso de discriminación. II. Verbalización de las contingencies y exito en la discriminación. [Behavior governed by rule and execution in a process of discrimination. II. Verbalization of the contingencies and success in the discrimination.] *Revista Latinoamericana de Psicologia, 19,* 63–70. [319]

Perkins, D. N. (1981). *The mind's best work.* Cambridge, MA: Harvard University Press. [23(1), 463]

Perry, D. G., & Parke, R. D. (1975). Punishment and alternative response training as determinants of response inhibition in children. *Genetic Psychology Monographs, 91,* 257–279. [109]

Persinger, M. A. (1985). Death anxiety as a semantic conditioned suppression paradigm. *Perceptual and Motor Skills, 60,* 827–830. [401]

Peterson, C., & Bossio, L. M. (1989). Learned helplessness. In R. C. Curtis (Ed.), *Self-defeating behaviors: Experimental research, clinical impressions, and practical implications.* New York: Plenum Press. [149]

Peterson, L. (1987). Not safe at home: Behavioral treatment of a child's fear of being at home alone. *Journal of Behavior Therapy and Experimental Psychiatry, 18,* 381–385. [321]

Peterson, L., Farmer, J. E., & Selby, V. (1988). Unprompted between subject generalization of home safety skills. *Child and Family Behavior Therapy, 10,* 107–119. [257(20), 497]

Peterson, R. F. (1968). Some experiments on the organization of a class of imitative behaviors. *Journal of Applied Behavior Analysis, 1,* 225–235. [437]

Pfiffner, L. J., & O'Leary, S. G. (1989). Effects of maternal discipline and nurturance on toddler's behavior and affect. *Journal of Abnormal Child Psychology, 17,* 527–540. [113]

Pierce, C. H., & Risley, T. R. (1974). Recreation as a reinforcer: Increasing membership and decreasing disruptions in an urban recreation center. *Journal of Applied Behavior Analysis, 7,* 403–411. [111]

Platt, J. J., & Spivack, G. (1972). Problem-solving thinking of psychiatric patients. *Journal of Consulting and Clinical Psychology, 39,* 148–151. [324]

Platt, J. J., Spivack, G., Altman, N., Altman, D., & Peizer, S. B. (1974). Adolescent problem-solving thinking. *Journal of Consulting and Clinical Psychology, 42,* 787–793. [324]

Plummer, S., Baer, D. M., & LeBlanc, J. M. (1977). Functional considerations in the use of procedural timeout and an effective alternative. *Journal of Applied Behavior Analysis,* 10, 689–705. [100, 142, 147]

Podsakoff, P. M., & Farh, J.-L. (1989). Effects of feedback sign and credibility on goal setting and task performance. *Organizational Behavior an Human Decision Processes,* 44, 45–67. [365]

Porter, D., & Neuringer, A. (1984). Music discrimination by pigeons. *Journal of Experimental Psychology: Animal Behavior Processes,* 10, 138–148. [210(3), 487]

Poulson, C. L., Kymissis, E., Reeve, K. F., Andreatos, M., & Reeve, L. (1991). Generalized vocal imitation in infants. *Journal of Experimental Child Psychology,* 51, 267–279. [293]

Powers, R. B., Cheney, C. D., & Agostino, N. R. (1970). Errorless training of a visual discrimination in preschool children. *The Psychological Record,* 20, 45–50. [241(3), 491]

Premack, D. (1959). Toward empirical behavior laws: I. Positive reinforcement. *Psychological Review,* 66, 219–233. [36]

Pritchard, R. D., Hollenback, J., & DeLeo, P. J. (1980). The effects of continuous and partial schedules of reinforcement on effort, performance, and satisfaction. *Organizational Behavior and Human Performance,* 25, 336–353. [172]

Pritchard, R. D., Jones, S. D., Roth, P. L., Stuebing, K. K., & Ekeberg, S. E. (1988). Effects of group feedback, goal setting, and incentives on organizational productivity. *Journal of Applied Psychology,* 73, 337–358. [365]

Pritchard, R. D., Leonard, D. W., Von Bergen, C. W., & Kirk, R. J. (1976). The effects of varying schedules of reinforcement on human task performance. *Organizational Behavior and Human Performance,* 16, 205–230.

Prue, D. M., & Fairbank, J. A. (1981). Performance feedback in organizational behavior management: A review. *Journal of Organizational Behavior Management,* 3, 1–16. [347, 348, 351]

Prue, D. M., Krapfl, J. E., Noah, J. C., Cannon, S., & Maley, R. F. (1980). Managing the treatment activities of state hospital staff. *Journal of Organizational Behavior Management,* 2, 165–181. [368(2), 503]

Pryor, K. W., Haag, R., & O'Reilly, J. (1969). The creative porpoise: Training for novel behavior. *Journal of the Experimental Analysis of Behavior,* 12, 653–661. [81]

Quarti, C., & Renaud, J. (1964). A new treatment of constipation by conditioning: A preliminary report. In C. M. Franks (Ed.), *Conditioning techniques in clinical practice and research* (pp. 219–227). New York: Springer. [413–414(3), 507]

Quinsey, V. L, & Chaplin, T. C. (1984). Stimulus control of rapists' and non-sex offenders' sexual arousal. *Behavioral Assessment,* 6, 169–176. [27(24), 466]

Quotation on stimulus control. (1977). *Journal of the Experimental Analysis of Behavior,* 27, 432. [196]

Rabin-Bickelman, E., & Marholin, D., II, (1978). Programming generalization of treatment effects: A stimulus control procedure. *Journal of Behavior Therapy and Experimental Psychiatry,* 9, 277–281. [195, 196]

Rachlin, H. (1974). Self-control. *Behaviorism,* 2, 94–107. [51]

Rachman, S., & Hodgson, R. J. (1968). Experimentally-induced "sexual fetishism": Replication and development. *The Psychological Record,* 18, 25–27. [395]

Rachman, S., & Lopatka, C. (1988). Return of fear: Underlearning and overlearning. *Behavior Research and Therapy,* 26, 99–104. [305(4), 498]

Ramey, C. T., & Ourth, L. L. (1971). Delayed reinforcement of vocalization rates in infants. *Child Development,* 42, 291–297. [49–50]

Randich, A., & LoLordo, V. M. (1979). Associative and nonassociative theories of the UCS preexposure phenomenon: Implications for Pavlovian conditioning. *Psychological Bulletin,* 86, 523–548. [408]

Razran, G. (1949). Sentential and propositional generalization of salivary conditioning to verbal stimuli. *Science,* 109, 447–448. [417(19), 512]

Reber, R. A., & Wallin, J. A. (1984). The effects of training, goal setting, and knowledge of results on safe behavior: A component analysis. *Academy of Management Journal,* 27, 544–560. [365]

Redd, W. H., Amen, D. L., Meddock, T. D., & Winston, A. S. (1974). Children's compliance as a function of type of instructions and payoff for noncompliance. *Bulletin of the Psychonomic Society, 4,* 597–599. [111, 328]

Redd, W. H., & Birnbrauer, J. S. (1969). Adults as discriminative stimuli for different reinforcement contingencies with retarded children. *Journal of Experimental Child Psychology, 7,* 440–447. [199]

Redd, W. H., Morris, E. K., & Martin, J. A. (1975). Effects of positive and negative adult-child interactions on children's social preference. *Journal of Experimental Child Psychology, 19,* 153–164. [108]

Reese, E. P. (1986). Learning about teaching from teaching about learning: Presenting behavioral analysis in an introductory survey course. In V. P. Makosky (Ed.) *The G. Stanley Hall lectures* (Vol. 6). Washington, DC: American Psychological Association. [9]

Reese, E. P., Howard, J., & Reese, T. W. (1978). *Human operant behavior* (2nd ed.). Dubuque, IA: W. C. Brown. [106, 134]

Reese, S. C., & Filipczak, J. (1980). Assessment of skill generalization: Measurement across setting, behavior, and time in an educational setting. *Behavior Modification, 4,* 209–224. [274(18), 497]

Reiher, R. H., & Dembo, M. H. (1984). Changing academic task persistence through a self-instructional attribution training program. *Contemporary Educational Psychology, 9,* 84–94. [321, 322]

Reisinger, J. J. (1972). The treatment of "anxiety-depression" via positive reinforcement and response cost. *Journal of Applied Behavior Analysis, 5,* 125–130. [125(19), 477]

Reiter, L. A., & DeVellis, B. M. (1976). Conditioned suppression in humans produced by a human stimulus. *Journal of Personality and Social Psychology, 34,* 223–227. [400]

Reitz, A. L., & Hawkins, R. P. (1982). Increasing the attendance of nursing home residents at group recreation activities. *Behavior Therapy, 13,* 283–290. [222, 329]

Renner, K. E. (1964). Delay of reinforcement: A historical review. *Psychological Bulletin, 61,* 341–361. [50]

Repp, A. C., Barton, L. E., & Brulle, A. R. (1983). A comparison of two procedures for programming the differential reinforcement of other behaviors. *Journal of Applied Behavior Analysis, 16,* 435–445. [79–80]

Repp, A. C., Deitz, S. M., & Speir, N. C. (1974). Reducing stereotypic responding of retarded persons by the differential reinforcement of other behavior. *American Journal of Mental Deficiency, 79,* 279–284. [86(16), 473]

Repp, A., Felce, D., Barton, L. (1988). Basing the treatment of stereotypic and self-injurious behavior on hypotheses of their causes. *Journal of Applied Behavior Analysis, 21,* 281–289. [141]

Repp, A. C., & Slack, D. J. (1977). Reducing responding of retarded persons by DRO schedules following a history of low-rate responding: A comparison of ascending interval sizes. *The Psychological Record, 27,* 581–588. [79]

Ribes, E., & Martinez, H. (1990). Interaction of contingencies and rule instructions in the performance of human subjects in conditional discrimination. *The Psychological Record, 40,* 565–586. [320]

Ricci, J. A., & Collins, F. L., Jr. (1988). Visual acuity improvement following fading and feedback training—III. Effects on acuity for stimuli in the natural environment. *Behavior Research and Therapy, 26,* 475–480. [244(15), 493]

Richards, C. S. (1975). Behavior modification of studying through study skills advice and self-control procedures. *Journal of Counseling Psychology, 22,* 431–436. [14, 354]

Richards, C. S. (1978). When self-control fails: A case study of the maintenance problem in self-control treatment programs. *Cognitive Therapy and Research, 2,* 397–401. [324]

Richards, C. S., McReynolds, W. T., Holt, S., & Sexton, T. (1976). The effects of information feedback and self-administered consequences on self-monitoring study behavior. *Journal of Counseling Psychology, 23,* 316–321. [268]

Richman, G. S., Riordan, M. R., Reiss, M. L., Pyles, D. A. M., & Bailey, J. S. (1988). Effects of self-monitoring and supervisor feedback on staff performance in a residential setting. *Journal of Applied Behavior Analysis, 21,* 401–409. [354]

Rilling, M. (1977). Stimulus control and inhibitory processes. In W. K. Honig & J. E. R. Staddon (Eds.), *Handbook of operant behavior.* Englewood Cliffs, NJ: Prentice-Hall. [252]

Rincover, A. (1978a). Sensory extinction: A procedure for eliminating self-stimulatory behavior in developmentally disabled children. *Journal of Abnormal Child Psychology, 6,* 299–310. [67]

Rincover, A. (1978b). Variables affecting stimulus fading and discriminative responding in psychotic children. *Journal of Abnormal Psychology, 87,* 541–553. [227–228]

Rincover, A., Cook, R., Peoples, A., & Packard, D. (1979). Sensory extinction and sensory reinforcement principles for programming multiple adaptive behavior change. *Journal of Applied Behavior Analysis, 12,* 221–234. [67, 68]

Rincover, A., & Ducharme, J. M. (1987). Variables influencing stimulus overselectivity and "tunnel vision" in developmentally delayed children. *American Journal of Mental Deficiency, 91,* 422–430. [229]

Rincover, A., & Koegel, R. L. (1975). Setting generality and stimulus control in autistic children. *Journal of Applied Behavior Analysis, 8,* 235–246. [262]

Ritter, B. (1969). The use of contact desensitization, demonstration-plus-participation and demonstration-alone in the treatment of acrophobia. *Behavior Research and Therapy, 7,* 157–164. [307(20), 499]

Roberts, M. C., Santogrossi, D. A., & Thelen, M. H. (1977). The effects of model affect on imitation. *Personality and Social Psychology Bulletin, 3,* 75–78. [301]

Roberts, M. W. (1988). Enforcing chair timeouts with room timeouts. *Behavior Modification, 12,* 353–370. [100]

Robin, A. L. (1979). Problem-solving communication training: A behavioral approach to the treatment of parent-adolescent conflict. *American Journal of Family Therapy, 7,* 69–82. [324]

Robin, A. L., Armel, S., & O'Leary, K. D. (1975). The effects of self-instruction on writing deficiencies. *Behavior Therapy, 6,* 178–187. [337(2), 501]

Robin, A. L., Kent, R., O'Leary, K. D., Foster, S., & Prinz, R. (1977). An approach to teaching parents and adolescents problem-solving communication skills: A preliminary report. *Behavior Therapy, 8,* 639–643. [339–340(13), 502]

Rogers, R. W., Rogers, J. S., Bailey, J. S., Runkle, W., & Moore, B. (1988). Promoting safety belt use among state employees: The effects of prompting and a stimulus-control intervention. *Journal of Applied Behavior Analysis, 21,* 263–269. [144–145]

Roid, G. H., & Haladyna, T. M. (1982). *A technology for test-item writing.* New York: Academic Press. [433]

Rolider, A., & Van Houten, R. (1984). The effects of DRO alone and DRO plus reprimands on the undesirable behavior of three children in home settings. *Education and Treatment of Children, 7,* 17–31. [97–98]

Rolider, A., & Van Houten, R. (1985a). Suppressing tantrum behavior in public places through the use of delayed punishment mediated by audio recordings. *Behavior Therapy, 16,* 181–194. [115]

Rolider, A., & Van Houten, R. (1985b). Treatment of constipation-caused encopresis by a negative reinforcement procedure. *Journal of Behavior Therapy and Experimental Psychiatry, 16,* 67–70. [156–157(23), 481]

Rollings, J. P., & Baumeister, A. A. (1981). Stimulus control of stereotypic responding: Effects on target and collateral behavior. *American Journal of Mental Deficiency, 86,* 67–77. [252–253]

Rooney, K. J., & Hallahan, D. P. (1988). The effects of self-monitoring on adult behavior and student independence. *Learning Disabilities Research, 3,* 88–93. [354]

Roper, G., Rachman, S., & Hodgson, R. (1973). An experiment on obsessional checking. *Behavior Research and Therapy, 11,* 271–277. [150]

Rosekrans, M. A., & Hartup, W. W. (1967). Imitative influences of consistent and inconsistent responses consequences of a model on aggressive behavior in children. *Journal of Personality and Social Psychology, 7,* 429–434. [307(19), 499]

Rosen, H. S., & Rosen, L. A. (1983). Eliminating stealing: Use of stimulus control with an elementary student. *Behavior Modification, 7,* 56–63. [26(19), 465]

Rosen, J. C., Saltzberg, E., & Srebnik, D. (1989). Cognitive behavior therapy for negative body image. *Behavior Therapy, 20,* 393–404. [338(5), 501]

Rosenbaum, M. S., & Ayllon, T. (1981). Treating bruxism with the habit-reversal technique. *Behavior Research and Therapy, 19,* 87–96. [123–124(9), 476]

Rosenberg, M. S. (1986). Error-correction during oral reading: A comparison of three techniques. *Learning Disability Quarterly, 9,* 182–192. [366]

Rosenfarb, I., & Hayes, S. C. (1984). Social standard setting: The Achilles heel of informational accounts of therapeutic change. *Behavior Therapy, 15,* 515–528. [329–330]

Rosenfarb, I. S., Hayes, S. C., & Linehan, M. M. (1989). Instructions and experiential feedback in the treatment of social skills deficits in adults. *Psychotherapy, 26,* 242–251. [347]

Rosenthal, T. L., & Reese, S. L. (1976). The effects of covert and overt modeling on assertive behavior. *Behavior Research and Therapy, 14,* 463–469. [306(15), 499]

Rovetto, F. M. (1983). *In vivo* desensitization of a severe driving phobia through radio contact with tele-monitoring of neurophysiological reactions. *Journal of Behavior Therapy and Experimental Psychiatry, 14,* 49–54. [385]

Ruder, K. F., Hermann, P., & Schiefelbusch, R. (1977). Effects of verbal imitation and comprehension training on verbal production. *Journal of Psycholinguistic Research, 6,* 59–72. [273(9), 496]

Rudestam, K. E., & Bedrosian, R. (1977). An investigation of the effectiveness of desensitization and flooding with two types of phobias. *Behavior Research and Therapy, 15,* 23–30. [391]

Rychtarik, R. G., Silverman, W. K., Van Landingham, W. P., & Prue, D. M. (1984a). Treatment of an incest victim with implosive therapy: A case study. *Behavior Therapy, 15,* 410–420. [420–421(14), 515]

Rychtarik, R. G., Silverman, W. K., Van Landingham, W. P., & Prue, D. M. (1984b). Further considerations in treating sexual assault victims with implosion. *Behavior Therapy, 15,* 423–426. [515]

Saari, L. M., & Latham, G. P. (1982). Employee reactions to continuous and variable-ratio reinforcement schedules involving a monetary incentive. *Journal of Applied Psychology, 67,* 506–508. [109]

Sachs, D. H. (1975). Conditioning of affect to a neutral stimulus: Number of trials. *Perceptual and Motor Skills, 40,* 895–901. [405]

Sagotsky, G., & Lepper, M. R. (1982). Generalization of changes in children's preferences for easy or difficult goals induced through peer modeling. *Child Development, 53,* 372–375. [304–305(3), 498]

Sajwaj, T., Libet, J., & Agras, S. (1974). Lemon-juice therapy: The control of life-threatening rumination in a six-month-old infant. *Journal of Applied Behavior Analysis, 7,* 557–563. [92–95]

Sajwaj, T., Twardosz, S., & Burke, M. (1972). Side effects of extinction procedures in a remedial preschool. *Journal of Applied Behavior Analysis, 5,* 163–175. [70]

Salzberg, B. H., Wheeler, A. J., Devar, L. T., & Hopkins, B. L. (1971). The effect of intermittent feedback and intermittent contingent access to play on printing of kindergarten children. *Journal of Applied Behavior Analysis, 4,* 163–171. [367]

Sanders, M. R., & James, J. E. (1982). Enhancing generalization and maintenance effects in systematic parent training: The role of self-management skills. *Australian Psychologist, 17,* 151–164. [354]

Saper, B. (1988). On learning terrorism. *Terrorism, 11,* 13–27. [386]

Satchell, T. (1987). *Astaire: The biography.* London: Hutchinson. [58(3), 470]

Saudargas, R. W., Madsen, C. H., & Scott, J. W. (1977). Differential effects of fixed- and variable-time feedback on production rates of elementary school children. *Journal of Applied Behavior Analysis, 10,* 673–678. [364]

Saul, L, J., Rome, H., & Leuser, E. (1946). Desensitization of combat fatigue patients. *American Journal of Psychiatry, 102,* 476–478. [392–393]

Scarboro, M. E., & Forehand, R. (1975). Effects of two types of response-contingent timeout on compliance and oppositional behavior of children. *Journal of Experimental Child Psychology, 19,* 252–264. [138]

Schloss, C. N., Schloss, P. J., Smith, M. A. (1988). Enhancement of employment interview skills using self-monitoring with communicatively impaired youths. *Education and Treatment of Children, 11,* 19–28. [354]

Schloss, P. J., Smith, M., Santora, C., & Bryant, R. (1989). A respondent conditioning approach to reducing anger responses of a dually diagnosed man with mild mental retardation. *Behavior Therapy, 20,* 459–464. [422(23), 516]

Schloss, P. J., Smith, M. A., & Schloss, C. N. (1988). Analysis of the relative efficacy of self-monitoring and feedback in the development of emotion adjectives with hearing-impaired persons. *Behavior Modification, 12,* 82–99. [354]

Schloss, P. J., & Wood, C. E. (1990). Effect of self-monitoring on maintenance and generalization of conversational skills of persons with mental retardation. *Mental Retardation, 28,* 105–113. [354]

Schmid, T. L. (1986). Reducing inappropriate behavior of retarded children through interpolated reinforcement. *American Journal of Mental Deficiency, 91,* 286–293. [72]

Schnelle, J. F., Traughber, B., Morgan, D. B., Embry, J. E., Binion, A. F., & Coleman, A. (1983). Management of geriatric incontinence in nursing homes. *Journal of Applied Behavior Analysis, 16,* 235–241. [25(15), 465]

Schrader, C., & Levine, M. D. (1989). The great escape: Public broadcasting goes behavioral. *Journal of Applied Behavior Analysis, 22,* 121–122. [139]

Schreibman, L. (1975). Effects of within-stimulus and extra-stimulus prompting on discrimination learning in autistic children. *Journal of Applied Behavior Analysis, 8,* 91–112. [228]

Schreibman, L., & Charlop, M. H. (1981). S+ versus S– fading in prompting procedures with autistic children. *Journal of Experimental Child Psychology, 31,* 508–520. [226]

Schroeder, S. R. (1972). Parametric effects of reinforcement frequency, amount of reinforcement, and required response force on sheltered workshop behavior. *Journal of Applied Behavior Analysis, 5,* 431–441. [45–46]

Schwarz, M. L., & Hawkins, R. P. (1970). Application of delayed reinforcement procedures to the behavior of an elementary school child. *Journal of Applied Behavior Analysis, 3,* 85–96. [51]

Scott, R. W., Peters, R. D., Gillespie, W. J., Blanchard, E. G., Edmunson, E. D., & Young, L. D. (1973). The use of shaping and reinforcement in the operant acceleration and deceleration of heart rate. *Behavior Research and Therapy, 11,* 179–185. [163–164, 182–183(3), 482]

Scotti, J. R., Vittimberga, G., Ridley, J., & Cornell, K. (1992). *The conditioned emotional response paradigm in the analysis of conditioned fear in combat-related post-traumatic stress disorder.* Paper presented at the 18th annual convention of the Association for Behavior Analysis. [400–401]

Seifert, H., & Schwarz, I. (1991). Treatment effectiveness of large group basic concept instruction with Head Start students. *Language, Speech, and Hearing Services in the Schools, 22,* 60–64. [452(11), 518]

Seligman, M. E. P. (1971). Phobias and preparedness. *Behavior Therapy, 2,* 307–320. [395, 407–408]

Semb, G. (1974). The effects of mastery criteria and assignment length on college student test performance. *Journal of Applied Behavior Analysis, 7,* 61–71. [363]

Semb, G., Conyers, D., Spencer, R., & Sanchez Sosa, J. J. (1975). An experimental comparison of four pacing contingencies. In J. M. Johnston (Ed.), *Behavior research and technology in higher education* (pp. 348–368). Springfield, IL: Charles C. Thomas. [156(22), 481]

Semb, G., & Semb, S. (1975). A comparison of fixed-page and fixed-time reading assignments in elementary school children. In E. Ramp and G. Semb (Eds.), *Behavior analysis: Areas of research and application* (pp. 233–243). Englewood Cliffs, NJ: Prentice-Hall. [171]

Setterington, R. G., & Walters, R. H. (1964). Effects of concurrent delays of material rewards and punishments on problem-solving in children. *Child Development, 35,* 275–280. [114]

Seybert, J. A., & Weiss, R. F. (1974). The negative reinforcing functions of nonconformity. *Memory and Cognition, 2,* 791–795. [141]

Seymour, F. W., & Stokes, T. F. (1976). Self-recording in training girls to increase work and evoke staff praise in an institution for offenders. *Journal of Applied Behavior Analysis, 9,* 41–54. [267–268, 361]

Sharenow, E. L., Fuqua, R. W., & Miltenberger, R. G. (1989). The treatment of muscle tics with dissimilar competing response practice. *Journal of Applied Behavior Analysis, 22,* 35–42. [104]

Sherman, T. M. (1978). The effects of student formative evaluation of instruction on teacher behavior. *Journal of Educational Technology Systems, 6,* 209–217. [371–372(20), 505]

Shimoff, E., Catania, A. C., & Matthews, B. A. (1981). Uninstructed human responding: Sensitivity of low-rate performance to schedule contingencies. *Journal of the Experimental Analysis of Behavior, 36,* 207–220. [319]

Shimp, T. A., Stuart, E. W., & Engle, R. W. (1991). A program of classical conditioning experiments testing variations in the conditioned stimulus and context. *Journal of Consumer Research,* **18,** 1–12. [408]

Siddle, D. A. T., & Remington, B. (1987). Latent inhibition and human Pavlovian conditioning: Research and relevance. In G. Davey (Ed.), *Cognitive processes and Pavlovian conditioning in humans* (pp. 115–146). Chichester: John Wiley. [408]

Sidman, M. (1960). *Tactics of scientific research.* New York: Basic Books. [8]

Sidman, M. (1966). Avoidance behavior. In W. K. Honig (Ed.), *Operant behavior: Areas of research and application* (pp. 448–498). New York: Appleton-Century-Crofts. [148]

Sidman, M. (1989). *Coercion and its fallout.* Boston, MA: Authors Cooperative. [39, 361]

Sidman, M. (1992). Equivalence relations: Some basic considerations. In S. C. Hayes and L. J. Hayes (Eds.), *Understanding Verbal Relations* (pp. 15–27). Reno, NV: Context Press. [447]

Sidman, M., & Cresson, O., Jr. (1973). Reading and crossmodal transfer of stimulus equivalences in severe retardation. *American Journal of Mental Deficiency,* 77, 515–523. [445, 448]

Sidman, M., & Stoddard, L. T. (1967). The effectiveness of fading in programming a simultaneous form discrimination for retarded children. *Journal of the Experimental Analysis of Behavior,* 10, 3–15. [223, 241(1), 491]

Sidman, M., & Tailby, W. (1982). Conditional discrimination vs matching to sample: An expansion of the testing paradigm. *Journal of the Experimental Analysis of Behavior,* 37, 5–22. [445]

Siegel, G. M., Lenske, J., & Broen, P. (1969). Suppression of normal speech disfluencies through response cost. *Journal of Applied Behavior Analysis,* 2, 265–276. [124(14), 476]

Siegel, P. S., & Foshee, J. G. (1953). The law of primary reinforcement in children. *Journal of Experimental Psychology,* 45, 12–14. [68–69]

Simmons, M. W. (1964). Operant discrimination learning in human infants. *Child Development,* **35,** 737–748. [198, 210(5), 487]

Simón, A. (1979). Violence in the mass media: A case of modelling. *Perceptual and Motor Skills,* **48,** 1081–1082. [285–286]

Singh, N. N. (1979). Aversive control of breath-holding. *Journal of Behavior Therapy and Experimental Psychiatry,* 10, 147–149. [124(13), 476]

Singh, N. N. (1990). Effects of two error-correction procedures on oral reading errors: Word supply versus sentence repeat. *Behavior Modification,* 14, 188–199. [366]

Singh, N. N., & Katz, R. C. (1985). On the modification of acceptability ratings for alternative child treatments. *Behavior Modification,* **9,** 375–386. [77, 103, 108]

Singh, N. N., Singh, J., & Winton, A. S. W. (1984). Positive practice overcorrection of oral reading errors. *Behavior Modification,* **8,** 23–37. [127(33), 478]

Singh, N. N., Watson, J. E., & Winton, A. S. W. (1987). Parents' acceptability ratings of alternative treatments for use with mentally retarded children. *Behavior Modification,* **11,** 17–26. [77, 108]

Siqueland, E. R. (1968). Reinforcement patterns and extinction in human newborns. *Journal of Experimental Child Psychology,* **6,** 431–442. [84(2), 472]

Skinner, B. F. (1935). The generic nature of the concepts of stimulus and response. *Journal of General Psychology,* 12, 40–65. [437, 453(3), 519]

Skinner, B. F. (1938). *The behavior of organisms.* New York: Appleton-Century-Crofts. [7, 65, 332]

Skinner, B. F. (1948). *Walden two.* New York: Macmillan. [10, 51]

Skinner, B. F. (1953). *Science and human behavior.* New York: Macmillan. [1, 6, 7, 20(6, 10), 21–22(19), 79, 268, 322, 461, 463]

Skinner, B. F. (1956). A case history in the scientific method. *American Psychologist,* **11,** 221–233. [8]

Skinner, B. F. (1957). *Verbal Behavior.* New York: Appleton-Century-Crofts. [8]

Skinner, B. F. (1968). *The technology of teaching.* New York: Appleton-Century-Crofts. [362]

Skinner, B. F. (1969). *Contingencies of reinforcement: A theoretical analysis.* New York: Appleton-Century-Crofts. [9, 315, 316–317, 318, 326, 334, 335(1), 335–336(2), 336(7), 437, 500, 501]

Skinner, B. F. (1971). *Beyond freedom and dignity.* New York: Knopf. [39]

Skinner, B. F. (1980). *Notebooks.* Englewood Cliffs, NJ: Prentice-Hall. [33]

Skinner, B. F. (1983). *A matter of consequences.* New York: Knopf. [69, 107–108, 204]

Skinner, B. F. (1989). The behavior of the listener. In S. C. Hayes (Ed.), *Rule-governed behavior: Cognition, contingencies, and instructional control* (pp. 85–96). New York: Plenum Press. [317]

Skinner, B. F., & Vaughan, M. E. (1983). *Enjoy old age: A program of self-management.* New York: W. W. Norton. [69]

Slavin, R. E., Wodarski, J. S., & Blackburn, B. L. (1981). A group contingency for electricity conservation in master-metered apartments. *Journal of Applied Behavior Analysis, 14,* 357–363. [53(10), 466]

Smeets, P. M., & Striefel, S. (1976). Acquisition of sign reading by transfer of stimulus control in a retarded deaf girl. *Journal of Mental Deficiency Research, 20,* 197–205. [241–242(4), 491]

Smith, D. D. (1979). The improvement of children's oral reading through the use of teacher modeling. *Journal of Learning Disabilities, 12,* 39–42. [305(6), 498]

Smith, J. W. (1982). Treatment of alcoholism in aversion conditioning hospitals. In E. M. Pattison and E. Kaufman (Eds.), *Encyclopedic handbook of alcoholism* (pp. 874–884). New York: Gardener. [389]

Smith, P. C., & Hailey, B. J. (1988). Compliance with instructions for regular breast self-examination. *The Journal of Compliance in Health Care, 3,* 151–161. [306(13), 499]

Smith, R. E. (1973). The use of humor in the counterconditioning of anger responses: A case study. *Behavior Therapy, 4,* 576–580. [383–385]

Smith, S. M. (1979). Remembering in and out of context. *Journal of Experimental Psychology: Human Learning and Memory, 5,* 460–471. [180]

Snyder, J., & Patterson, G. R. (1986). The effects of consequences on patterns of social interaction: A quasi-experimental approach to reinforcement in natural interaction. *Child Development, 57,* 1257–1268. [35]

Snyder, M., & Swann, W. B. (1978). Hypothesis-testing processes in social interaction. *Journal of Personality and Social Psychology, 36,* 1202–1212. [19(2), 461]

Solnick, J. V., Rincover, A., & Peterson, C. R. (1977). Some determinants of the reinforcing and punishing effects of timeout. *Journal of Applied Behavior Analysis, 10,* 415–424. [100]

Speas, C. M. (1979). Job-seeking interview skills training: A comparison of four instructional methods. *Journal of Counseling Psychology, 26,* 405–412. [351–352]

Speltz, M. L., & Bernstein, D. A. (1979). The use of participant modeling for claustrophobia. *Journal of Behavior Therapy and Experimental Psychiatry, 10,* 251–255. [296–297]

Spence, J. T., Armstrong, J., & Conrad, R. (1969). Contribution of instructions to the effects of two types of symbolic reinforcers on the discrimination learning of children. *Psychonomic Science, 17,* 107–108. [203–204, 329]

Spencer, R. E., & Semb, G. (1978). Giving students the opportunity to increase unit size: A performance-based system for personalized instruction. *Journal of Personalized Instruction, 2,* 76–80. [364]

Spetch, M. L., Wilkie, D. M., & Pinel, J. P. J. (1981). Backward conditioning: A reevaluation of the empirical evidence. *Psychological Bulletin, 89,* 163–175. [405]

Spiker, C. C., & Holton, R. B. (1959). Similarity of stimuli and of responses in the successive discrimination problem. *Child Development, 30,* 471–480. [205]

Spitzberg, B. H., & Cupach, W. R. (1985). Conversational skill and the locus of perception. *Journal of Psychopathology and Behavioral Assessment, 7,* 207–220. [25(14), 465]

Spooner, F., Weber, L. H., & Spooner, D. (1983). The effects of backward chaining and total task presentation on the acquisition of complex tasks by severely retarded adolescents and adults. *Education and Treatment of Children, 6,* 401–420. [244(1), 493]

Sprague, J. R., & Horner, R. H. (1984). The effects of single instance, multiple instance, and general case training on generalized vending machine use by moderately and severely handicapped students. *Journal of Applied Behavior Analysis, 17,* 273–278. [439–440, 445]

Spreat, S., Lipinski, D., Dickerson, R., Nass, R., & Dorsey, M. (1989). The acceptability of electric shock programs. *Behavior Modification, 13,* 245–256. [97]

Staats, C. K., & Staats, A. W. (1957). Meaning established by classical conditioning. *Journal of*

Experimental Psychology, 54, 74–80. [395–396, 398]

Stalling, R. B., & Tiller, J. (1975). Modifying a response class of artistic taste with signal-light reinforcers. *The Psychological Record, 25,* 65–69. [211–212(12), 488]

Stalonas, P. M., & Johnson, W. G. (1979). Conversational skills training for obsessive speech using an aversive-cueing procedure. *Journal of Behavior Therapy and Experimental Psychiatry, 10,* 61–63. [156(20), 481]

Stampfl, T. G., & Levis, D. J. (1967). Essentials of implosive therapy: A learning-theory-based psycho-dynamic behavioral therapy. *Journal of Abnormal Psychology, 72,* 157–163. [390]

Stark, K. D., Reynolds, W. M., & Kaslow, N. J. (1987). A comparison of the relative efficacy of self-control therapy and a behavioral problem-solving therapy for depression in children. *Journal of Abnormal Child Psychology, 15,* 91–113. [324]

Stark, L. J., Miller, S. T., Plienes, A. J., & Drabman, R. S. (1987) Behavioral contracting to increase chest physiotherapy. *Behavior Modification, 11,* 75–86. [52–53(4), 466]

Steege, M. W., Wacker, D. P., Berg, W. K., Cigrand, K. K., & Cooper, L. J. (1989). The use of behav-ioral assessment to prescribe and evaluate treatments for severely handicapped children. *Journal of Applied Behavior Analysis, 22,* 23–33. [141–142]

Steege, M. W., Wacker, D. P., Berg, W. K., Novak, C. G., Reimers, T. M., Sasso, G. M., & DeRaad, A. (1990). Use of negative reinforcement in the treatment of self-injurious behavior. *Journal of Applied Behavior Analysis, 23,* 459–467. [142]

Steere, D. E., Strauch, J. D., Powell, T. H., Butterworth, J., Jr. (1990). Promoting generalization from a teaching setting to a community-based setting among persons with severe disabilities: A general case programming approach. *Education and Treatment of Children, 13,* 5–20. [454(7), 520]

Steeves, J. M., Martin, G. L., & Pear, J. J. (1970). Self-imposed time-out by autistic children during an operant training program. *Behavior Therapy, 1,* 371–381. [179–180]

Steinman, W. M. (1968). The strengthening of verbal approval in retardates by discrimination training. *Journal of Experimental Child Psychology, 6,* 100–112. [44]

Stella, M. E., & Etzel, B. C. (1986). Stimulus control of eye orientations: Shaping S+ only versus shaping S– only. *Analysis and Intervention in Developmental Disabilities, 6,* 137–153. [226–227]

Stendhal. (1983). *On Love* (H. B. V., Trans.). New York: Da Capo Press. (Original work published 1822) [33]

Stephens, C. E., Pear, J. J., Wray, L. D., & Jackson, G. C. (1975). Some effects of reinforcement sched-ules in teaching picture names to retarded children. *Journal of Applied Behavior Analysis, 8,* 435–447. [179]

Sterling, R. M., Barbetta, P. M., Heward, W. L., & Heron, T. E. (1992). *A comparison of active student response and on-task instruction on the acquisition and maintenance of health facts by fourth grade special education students.* Paper presented at the 18th annual convention of the Association for Behavior Analysis. [366]

Stevenson, H. C., & Fantuzzo, J. W. (1986). The generality and social validity of a competency-based self-control training intervention for underachieving students. *Journal of Applied Behavior Analysis, 19,* 269–276. [24(4), 464]

Stockwell, R. P., Bowen, J. D., & Silva-Fuenzalida, I. (1985). *Mastering Spanish.* Hauppague, NY: Barron's Educational Series. [298]

Stoddard, L. T., & McIlvane, W. J. (1989). Generalization after intradimensional discrimination training in 2-year-old children. *Journal of Experimental Child Psychology, 47,* 324–334. [206]

Stokes, T. F., & Baer, D. M. (1977). An implicit technology of generalization. *Journal of Applied Behavior Analysis, 10,* 349–367. [51, 250, 261]

Stokes, T. F., Baer, D. M., & Jackson, R. L. (1974). Programming the generalization of a greeting response in four retarded children. *Journal of Applied Behavior Analysis, 7,* 599–610. [263–264]

Stokes, T. F., Fowler, S. A., & Baer, D. M. (1978). Training preschool children to recruit natural com-munities of reinforcement. *Journal of Applied Behavior Analysis, 11,* 285–303. [267]

Stokes, T. F., & Osnes, P. G. (1989). An operant pursuit of generalization. *Behavior Therapy, 20,* 337–355. [261]

Stone, D. L., & Stone, E. F. (1985). The effects of feedback consistency and feedback favorability on self-perceived task competence and perceived feedback accuracy. *Organizational Behavior and Human Decision Processes, 36,* 167–185. [365]

Stotland, E., Zander, A., & Natsoulas, T. (1961). Generalization of interpersonal similarity. *Journal of Abnormal and Social Psychology, 62,* 250–256. [300]

Stouwie, R. J. (1971). Inconsistent verbal instructions and children's resistance-to-temptation behavior. *Child Development, 42,* 1517–1531. [328]

Strain, P. S., Shores, R. E., & Kerr, M. M. (1976). An experimental analysis of "spillover" effects of the social interaction of behaviorally handicapped preschool children. *Journal of Applied Behavior Analysis, 9,* 31–41. [272(3), 495]

Strauss, C. C., Rubinoff, A., & Atkeson, B. M. (1983). Elimination of nocturnal headbanging in a normal seven-year-old girl using overcorrection plus rewards. *Journal of Behavior Therapy and Experimental Psychiatry, 14,* 269–273. [126(24), 477]

Stuart, E. W., Shimp, T. A., & Engle, R. W. (1987). Classical conditioning of consumer attitudes: Four experiments in an advertising context. *Journal of Consumer Research, 14,* 334–349. [395, 405–406, 408]

Sullivan, M. A., & O'Leary, S. G. (1990). Maintenance following reward and cost token programs. *Behavior Therapy, 21,* 139–149. [136]

Sulzer-Azaroff, B., & de Santamaria, C. (1980). Industrial safety hazard reduction through performance feedback. *Journal of Applied Behavior Analysis, 13,* 287–295. [370(12), 504]

Taffel, S. J., & O'Leary, K. D. (1976). Reinforcing math with more math: Choosing special academic activities as a reward for academic performance. *Journal of Educational Psychology, 68,* 579–587. [36–37]

Taffel, S. J., O'Leary, K. D., & Armel, S. (1974). Reasoning and praise: Their effects on academic behavior. *Journal of Educational Psychology, 66,* 291–295. [50]

Tarnowski, K. J., Mulick, J. A., & Rasnake, L. K. (1990). Acceptability of behavior interventions for self-injurious behavior: Replication and interinstitutional comparison. *American Journal on Mental Retardation, 95,* 182–187. [97, 108]

Tarnowski, K. J., Rasnake, L. K., Mulick, J. A., & Kelly, P. A. (1989). Acceptability of behavioral interventions for self-injurious behavior. *American Journal on Mental Retardation, 93,* 575–580. [97, 108]

Tarnowski, K. J., Rosén, L. A., McGrath, M. L., & Drabman, R. S. (1987). A modified habit reversal procedure in a recalcitrant case of trichotillomania. *Journal of Behavior Therapy and Experimental Psychiatry, 18,* 157–163. [125(21), 477]

Tawney, J. W. (1972). Training letter discrimination in four-year-old children. *Journal of Applied Behavior Analysis, 5,* 455–465. [211(8), 487]

Taylor, G. E., & Rickard, H. C. (1974). Generalization of stimulus control in a summer camp. *Psychological Reports, 34,* 419–423. [196]

Taylor, S. E., & Brown, J. D. (1988). Illusion and well-being: A social psychological perspective on mental health. *Psychological Bulletin, 96,* 465–490. [334]

Tennyson, R. D., & Cocchiarella, M. J. (1986). An empirically based instructional design theory for teaching concepts. *Review of Educational Research, 56,* 40–71. [433]

Tennyson, R. D., Steve, M. W., & Boutwell, R. C. (1975). Instance sequence and analysis of instance attribute representation in concept acquisition. *Journal of Educational Psychology, 67,* 821–827. [369(7), 504]

Tennyson, R. D., Woolley, F. R., & Merrill, M. D. (1972). Exemplar and nonexemplar variables which produce correct concept classification behavior and specified classification errors. *Journal of Educational Psychology, 63,* 144–152. [450–451(3), 517]

Terrace, H. S. (1963). Discriminative learning with and without errors. *Journal of the Experimental Analysis of Behavior, 6,* 1–27. [223]

Terrell, D. J., & Johnston, J. M. (1989). Logic, reasoning, and verbal behavior. *The Behavior Analyst, 12,* 35–44. [317, 319]

Terrell, G. (1965). Delayed reinforcement effects. In L. P. Lipsitt & C. C. Spiker (Eds.), *Advances in child development and behavior* (pp. 127–158). New York: Academic Press. [50]

Terrell, G., & Ware, R. (1963). Emotionality as a function of delay of reward. *Child Development,* **34,** 495–501. [49]

Thase, M. E., & Moss, M. K. (1976). The relative efficacy of covert modeling procedures and guided participant modeling on the reduction of avoidance behavior. *Journal of Behavior Therapy and Experimental Psychiatry,* 7, 7–12. [308(23), 500]

Thelen, M. H., & Kirkland, K. D. (1976). On status and being imitated: Effects on reciprocal imitation and attraction. *Journal of Personality and Social Psychology,* **33,** 691–697. [300]

Thompson, T., Heistad, G. T., & Palermo, D. S. (1963). Effect of amount of training on rate and duration of responding during extinction. *Journal of the Experimental Analysis of Behavior,* **6,** 155–161. [69]

Thomson, W. J. (1983). Effects of control on choice of reward or punishment. *Bulletin of the Psychonomic Society,* **21,** 462–464. [112]

Thyer, B. A., Baum, M., & Reid, L. D. (1988). Exposure techniques in the reduction of fear: A comparative review of the procedure in animals and humans. *Advances in Behavior Research and Therapy,* **10,** 105–127. [391]

Tiffany, S. T., Martin, E. M., & Baker, T. B. (1986). Treatments for cigarette smoking: An evaluation of the contributions of aversion and counseling procedures. *Behavior Research and Therapy,* **24,** 437–452. [418(1), 513]

Till, J. A., & Toye, A. R. (1988). Acoustic phonetic effects of two types of verbal feedback in dysarthric subjects. *Journal of Speech and Hearing Disorders,* **53,** 449–458. [363]

Tisdelle, D. A., & St. Lawrence, J. S. (1988). Adolescent interpersonal problem-solving skill training: Social validation and generalization. *Behavior Therapy,* **19,** 171–182. [24(5), 464]

Topping, J. S., Larmi, O. K., & Johnson, D. L. (1972). Omission training: Effects of gradual introduction. *Psychonomic Science,* **28,** 279–280. [79]

Touchette, P. E. (1968). The effects of graduated stimulus change on the acquisition of a simple discrimination in severely retarded boys. *Journal of the Experimental Analysis of Behavior,* **11,** 39–48. [223]

Touchette, P. E. (1971). Transfer of stimulus control: Measuring the moment of transfer. *Journal of the Experimental Analysis of Behavior,* **15,** 347–354. [230]

Touchette, P. E., & Howard, J. S. (1984). Errorless learning: Reinforcement contingencies and stimulus control transfer in delayed prompting. *Journal of Applied Behavior Analysis,* **17,** 175–188. [232, 233]

Tryon, W. W. (1976). Models of behavior disorder: A formal analysis based on Woods's taxonomy of instrumental conditioning. *American Psychologist,* **31,** 509–518. [152]

Tryon, W. W. (1978). An operant explanation of Mowrer's neurotic paradox. *Behaviorism,* **6,** 203–211. [152]

Tryon, W. W., & Briones, R. G. (1985). Higher-order sematic counterconditioning of Filipino women's evaluations of heterosexual behaviors. *Journal of Behavior Therapy and Experimental Psychiatry,* **16,** 125–131. [421(16), 515]

Tryon, W. W., & Cicero, S. D. (1989). Classical conditioning of meaning—I. A replication and higher-order extension. *Journal of Behavior Therapy and Experimental Psychiatry,* **20,** 137–142. [398]

Turkkan, J. S. (1989). Classical conditioning: The new hegemony. *Behavioral and Brain Sciences,* **12,** 121–179. [401]

Turnage, J. R., & Logan, D. L. (1974). Treatment of a hypodermic needle phobia by *in vivo* systematic desensitization. *Journal of Behavior Therapy and Experimental Psychiatry,* **5,** 67–69. [422(21), 515]

Twardosz, S., & Sajwaj, T. (1972). Multiple effects of a procedure to increase sitting in a hyperactive, retarded boy. *Journal of Applied Behavior Analysis,* **5,** 73–78. [84(5), 472]

Tziner, A., & Latham, G. P. (1989). The effects of appraisal instrument, feedback and goal-setting on worker satisfaction and commitment. *Journal of Organizational Behavior,* **10,** 145–153. [363, 365]

Ullmann, L. P., & Krasner, L. (1975). *A psychological approach to abnormal behavior* (2nd ed.). Englewood Cliffs, NJ: Prentice-Hall. [70, 143]

Underwood, B. J., & Hughes, R. H. (1950). Gradients of generalized verbal responses. *American Journal of Psychology,* **63,** 422–430. [255–256]

Upper, D. (1973). A "ticket" system for reducing ward rules violations on a token economy program. *Journal of Behavior Therapy and Experimental Psychiatry,* **4,** 137–140. [123(4), 476]

Vaccaro, F. J. (1988). Successful operant conditioning procedures with an institutionalized aggressive geriatric patient. *International Journal of Aging and Human Development,* **26,** 71–79. [127(30), 478]

Vaitl, D., Gruppe, H., & Kimmel, H. D. (1985). Contextual stimulus control of conditional vasomotor and electrodermal reactions to angry and friendly faces. *The Pavlovian Journal of Biological Science,* **20,** 124–131. [416(15), 511]

Van Houten, R. (1979). Social validation: The evolution of standards of competency for target behaviors. *Journal of Applied Behavior Analysis,* **12,** 581–591. [15]

Van Houten, R., Malenfant, L., & Rolider, A. (1985). Increasing driver yielding and pedestrian signaling with prompting, feedback, and enforcement. *Journal of Applied Behavior Analysis,* **18,** 103–110. [238–239(4), 348, 490]

Van Houten, R., & Nau, P. A. (1981). A comparison of the effects of posted feedback and increased police surveillance on highway speeding. *Journal of Applied Behavior Analysis,* **14,** 261–271. [348]

Van Houten, R., & Nau, P. A. (1983). Feedback interventions and driving speed: A parametric and comparative analysis. *Journal of Applied Behavior Analysis,* **16,** 253–281. [348]

Van Houten, R., Nau, P. A., MacKenzie-Keating, S. E., Sameoto, D., & Colavecchia, B. (1982). An analysis of some variables influencing the effectiveness of reprimands. *Journal of Applied Behavior Analysis,* **15,** 65–83. [118]

Van Houten, R., Nau, P., & Marini, Z. (1980). An analysis of public posting in reducing speeding behavior on an urban highway. *Journal of Applied Behavior Analysis,* **13,** 383–395. [348]

Van Houten, R., & Rolider, A. (1988). Recreating the scene: An effective way to provide delayed punishment for inappropriate motor behavior. *Journal of Applied Behavior Analysis,* **21,** 187–192. [115–116]

Van Houten, R., & Rolider, A. (1989). An analysis of several variables influencing the efficacy of flash card instruction. *Journal of Applied Behavior Analysis,* **22,** 111–118. [208]

Van Houten, R., Rolider, A., Nau, P. A., Friedman, R., Becker, M., Chalodovsky, I., & Scherer, M. (1985). Large-scale reductions in speeding and accidents in Canada and Israel: A behavioral ecological perspective. *Journal of Applied Behavior Analysis,* **18,** 87–93. [24(6), 348, 464]

Van Houten, R., & Van Houten, J. (1977). The performance feedback system in the special education classroom: An analysis of public posting and peer comments. *Behavior Therapy,* **8,** 366–376. [348]

Van Luit, J. E. H., & Van der Aalsvoort, G. M. (1985). Learning subtraction in a special school: A self-instructional training strategy for educable mentally retarded children with arithmetic deficits. *Instructional Science,* **14,** 179–189. [321]

Vance, B. J., & Siegel, A. W. (1971). The relative effectiveness of observing response vs predifferentiation pretraining on children's discrimination learning. *Psychonomic Science,* **24,** 183–185. [205]

Vance, R. J., & Colella, A. (1990). Effects of two types of feedback on goal acceptance and personal goals. *Journal of Applied Psychology,* **75,** 68–76. [327–328]

Vargas, J. S. (1972). *Writing worthwhile behavioral objectives.* New York: Harper and Row. [327]

Vaughan, M. E. (1985). Repeated acquisition in the analysis of rule-governed behavior. *Journal of the Experimental Analysis of Behavior,* **44,** 175–184. [319]

Vaughan, M. E., & Michael, J. (1982). Automatic reinforcement: An important but ignored concept. *Behaviorism,* **10,** 217–227. [37]

Venn, J. R., & Short, J. G. (1973). Vicarious classical conditioning of emotional responses in nursery school children. *Journal of Personality and Social Psychology,* **2,** 249–255. [394]

Verna, G. B. (1977). The effects of four-hour delay of punishment under two conditions of verbal instruction. *Child Development,* **48,** 621–624. [114]

Vogel-Sprott, M. D. (1967). The effect of short delays in punishment on an immediately rewarded response in humans. *Psychonomic Science, 9,* 83–84. [114, 115]

Wahler, R. G. (1969). Oppositional children: A quest for parental reinforcement control. *Journal of Applied Behavior Analysis, 2,* 159–170. [199–200]

Walk, R. D. (1966). Perceptual learning and the discrimination of wines. *Psychonomic Science, 5,* 57–58. [205]

Walk, R. D., & Gibson, E. J. (1961). A comparative and analytical study of visual depth perception. *Psychological Monographs, 75,* No. 15. [97]

Wallace, C. J., Liberman, R. P., MacKain, S. J., Blackwell, G., & Eckman, T. A. (1992). *The effectiveness and replicability of modules to train social and instructional skills in the severely mentally ill.* Unpublished manuscript. [63]

Wallace, I., & Pear, J. J. (1977). Self-control techniques of famous novelists. *Journal of Applied Behavior Analysis, 10,* 515–525. [354]

Walls, R. T., Crist, K., Sienicki, D. A., & Grant, L. (1981). Prompting sequences in teaching independent living skills. *Mental Retardation, 19,* 243–246. [243(12), 492]

Walls, R. T., Dowler, D. L., Haught, P. A., & Zawlocki, R. J. (1984). Progressive delay and unlimited delay of prompts in forward chaining and whole-task training strategies. *Education and Training of the Mentally Retarded, 19,* 276–284. [236, 246(12), 494]

Walls, R. T., Haught, P., & Dowler, D. L. (1982). Moments of transfer of stimulus control in practical assembly tasks by mentally retarded adults. *American Journal of Mental Deficiency, 87,* 309–315. [230–233]

Walls, R. T., Sienicki, D. A., & Crist, K. (1981). Operations training in vocational skills. *American Journal of Mental Deficiency, 85,* 357–367. [437]

Walls, R. T., & Smith, T. S. (1970). Development of preference for delayed reinforcement in disadvantaged children. *Journal of Educational Psychology, 6,* 118–123. [51]

Walls, R. T., Zane, T., & Ellis, W. D. (1981). Forward and backward chaining, and whole task methods. *Behavior Modification, 5,* 61–74. [234–235]

Walters, R. H. (1964). Delay-of-reinforcement gradients in children's learning. *Psychonomic Science, 1,* 307–308. [114]

Walters, R. H., & Parke, R. D. (1964). Influence of response consequences to a social model on resistance to deviation. *Journal of Experimental Child Psychology, 1,* 269–280. [308(25), 500]

Walters, R. H., Parke, R. D., & Cane, V. A. (1965). Timing of punishment and the observation of consequences to others as determinants of response inhibition. *Journal of Experimental Child Psychology, 2,* 10–30. [116]

Waranch, H. R., Iwata, B. A., Wohl, M. K., & Nidiffer, F. D. (1981). Treatment of a retarded adult's mannequin phobia through *in vivo* desensitization and shaping approach responses. *Journal of Behavior Therapy and Experimental Psychiatry, 12,* 359–362. [225]

Ware, R., & Terrell, G. (1961). Effects of delayed reinforcement on associative and incentive factors. *Child Development, 32,* 789–793. [49]

Warren, V. L., & Cairns, R. B. (1972). Social reinforcement satiation: An outcome of frequency or ambiguity? *Journal of Experimental Child Psychology, 13,* 249–260. [44]

Warzak, W. J., Kewman, D. G., Stefans, V., & Johnson, E. (1987). Behavioral rehabilitation of functional alexia. *Journal of Behavior Therapy and Experimental Psychiatry, 18,* 171–177. [137]

Watson, J. B., & Rayner, R. (1920). Conditioned emotional reactions. *Journal of Experimental Psychology, 3,* 1–20. [414(7), 508]

Watson, J. P., Gaind, R., & Marks, I. M. (1971). Prolonged exposure: A rapid treatment for phobias. *British Medical Journal, 1,* 13–15. [391]

Watson, J. P., Mullett, G. E., & Pillay, H. (1973). The effects of prolonged exposure to phobic situations upon agoraphobic patients treated in groups. *Behavior Research and Therapy, 11,* 531–545. [391]

Weber, R. J. (1980). Energy conservation and feedback metering for the automobile: Ideal requirements. *Bulletin of the Psychonomic Society, 16,* 301–302. [352]

Webster, D. R., & Azrin, N. H. (1973). Required relaxation: A method of inhibiting agitative-disruptive behavior of retardates. *Behavior Research and Therapy, 11,* 67–78. [125(18), 477]

Weeks, M., & Gaylord-Ross, R. (1981). Task difficulty and aberrant behavior in severely handicapped students. *Journal of Applied Behavior Analysis, 14,* 449–463. [142]

Weiner, H. (1970). Instructional control of human operant responding during extinction following fixed-ratio conditioning. *Journal of the Experimental Analysis of Behavior, 13,* 391–394. [71–72, 329]

Weinstein, L. (1969). Decreased sensitivity to punishment. *Psychonomic Science, 14,* 264, 266. [114]

Weir, R. O., & Marshall, W. L. (1980). Relaxation and distraction in experimental desensitization. *Journal of Clinical Psychology, 36,* 246–252. [407]

Weiss, A. R., & Evans, I. M. (1978). Process studies in language conditioning—I: Counterconditioning of anxiety by "calm" words. *Journal of Behavior Therapy and Experimental Psychiatry, 9,* 115–119. [421(15), 515]

Weiss, R. F., Boyer, J. L., Lombardo, J. P., & Stich, M. H. (1973). Altruistic drive and altruistic reinforcement. *Journal of Personality and Social Psychology, 25,* 390–400. [140, 145, 147]

Weiss, R. F., Buchanan, W., Altstatt, L., & Lombardo, J. P. (1971). Altruism is rewarding. *Science, 171,* 1262–1263. [141]

Weiss, R. F., Cecil, J. S., & Frank, M. J. (1973). Steep delay of reinforcement gradient in escape conditioning with altruistic reinforcement. *Bulletin of the Psychonomic Society, 2,* 372–374. [140, 146]

Weiss, R. F., Feinberg, R. A., Cramer, R. E., & Schoedel, J. (1976). Delay of the reinforcing opportunity to speak in reply under invariable initial disagreement. *Bulletin of the Psychonomic Society, 8,* 199–200. [140–141]

Weiss, R. F., Lombardo, J. P., Warren, D. R., & Kelley, K. A. (1971). Reinforcing effects of speaking in reply. *Journal of Personality and Social Psychology, 20,* 186–199. [140, 145]

Welch, S. J., & Pear, J. J. (1980). Generalization of naming responses to objects in the natural environment as a function of training stimulus modality with retarded children. *Journal of Applied Behavior Analysis, 13,* 629–643. [273(11), 496]

Whaley, D. L. (1973). *Hope.* Unpublished manuscript. [322]

Whaley, D. L., & Malott, R. W. (1971). *Elementary principles of behavior.* Englewood Cliffs, NJ: Prentice-Hall. [293]

White, G. D., Nielsen, G., & Johnson, S. M. (1972). Timeout duration and the suppression of deviant behavior in children. *Journal of Applied Behavior Analysis, 5,* 111–120. [119–120]

White, G. W., Mathews, R. M., & Fawcett, S. B. (1989). Reducing risk of pressure sores: Effects of watch prompts and alarm avoidance on wheel chair push-ups. *Journal of Applied Behavior Analysis, 22,* 287–295. [138]

Whitney, J. L., & Goldstein, H. (1989). Using self-monitoring to reduce disfluencies in speakers with mild aphasia. *Journal of Speech and Hearing Disorders, 54,* 576–586. [354]

Wiens, A. N., & Menustik, C. E. (1983). Treatment outcome and patient characteristics in an aversion therapy program for alcoholism. *American Psychologist, 38,* 1089–1096. [389]

Wightman, D. C., & Sistrunk, F. (1987). Part-task training strategies in simulated carrier landing final-approach training. *Human Factors, 29,* 245–254. [235, 244(2), 493]

Wigton, R. S., Patil, K. D., & Hoellerich, V. L. (1986). The effects of feedback in learning clinical diagnosis. *Journal of Medical Education, 61,* 816–822. [357–358]

Wilcox, B. (1974). The teaching of serial tasks using chaining strategies. *British Journal of Educational Psychology, 44,* 175–183. [235, 245–246(9), 494]

Williams, A. M. (1979). The quantity and quality of marital interaction related to marital satisfaction: A behavioral analysis. *Journal of Applied Behavior Analysis, 12,* 665–678. [25(10), 63–64, 464]

Williams, C. D. (1959). The elimination of tantrum behavior by extinction procedures. *Journal of Abnormal and Social Psychology, 59,* 269. [65, 72, 74]

Williams, J. P. (1969). Training kindergarten children to discriminate letter-like forms. *American Educational Research Journal, 6,* 501–514. [206, 207, 433]

Williams, M., Thyer, B. A., Bailey, J. S., & Harrison, D. F. (1989). Promoting safety belt use with traffic signs and prompters. *Journal of Applied Behavior Analysis, 22,* 71–76. [222, 239(7), 490]

Williamson, D. A., Lawson, O. D., Bennett, S. M., & Hinz, L. (1989). Behavioral treatment of night bingeing and rumination in an adult case of bulimia nervosa. *Journal of Behavior Therapy and*

Experimental Psychiatry, 20, 73–77. [185(18), 483]

Wilson, C. W., & Hopkins, B. L. (1973). The effects of contingent music on the intensity of noise in junior high home economics classes. *Journal of Applied Behavior Analysis, 6,* 269–275. [52(2), 466]

Wilson, G. T. (1991). Chemical aversion conditioning in the treatment of alcoholism: Further comments. *Behavior Research and Therapy, 29,* 415–419. [390]

Wincze, J. P., Leitenberg, H., & Agras, W. S. (1972). The effects of token reinforcement and feedback on the delusional verbal behavior of chronic paranoid schizophrenics. *Journal of Applied Behavior Analysis, 5,* 247–262. [366–367]

Winett, R. A., Leckliter, I. N., Chinn, D. E., Stahl, B., & Love, S. Q. (1985). Effects of television modeling on residential energy conservation. *Journal of Applied Behavior Analysis, 18,* 33–44. [25(13), 465]

Winett, R. A., Neale, M. S., & Grier, H. C. (1979). Effects of self-monitoring and feedback on residential electricity consumption. *Journal of Applied Behavior Analysis, 12,* 174–184. [354, 369(8), 504]

Winett, R. A., & Roach, A. M. (1973). The effects of reinforcing academic performance on social behavior: A brief report. *Psychological Record, 23,* 391–396. [12]

Winkler, R. C. (1971). Reinforcement schedules for individual patients in a token economy. *Behavior Therapy, 22,* 534–537. [154(7), 480]

Winner, E. (1982). *Invented worlds: The psychology of the arts.* Cambridge, MA: Harvard University Press. [68, 295]

Wirshing, W. C., Eckman, T. A., Liberman, R. P., & Marder, S. R. (1989). *Management of risk of relapse through skills training of chronic schizophrenics.* Unpublished manuscript. [63]

Wispe, L. G., & Drambarean, N. C. (1953). Physiological need, word frequency, and visual duration thresholds. *Journal of Experimental Psychology, 46,* 25–31. [41]

Witt, J. C., & Robbins, J. R. (1985). Acceptability of reductive interventions for the control of inappropriate child behavior. *Journal of Abnormal Child Psychology, 13,* 59–67. [97, 108]

Wolery, M., Gast, D. L., Kirk, K., & Schuster, J. (1988). Fading extra-stimulus prompts with autistic children using time delay. *Education and Treatment of Children, 11,* 29–44. [242–243(9), 492]

Wolf, M. M. (1978). Social validity: The case for subjective measurement or how applied behavior analysis is finding its heart. *Journal of Applied Behavior Analysis, 11,* 203–214. [16]

Wolf, M. M., Birnbrauer, J. S., Williams, T., & Lawler, J. (1965). A note on apparent extinction of the vomiting behavior of a retarded child. In L. P. Ullmann & L. Krasner (Eds.), *Case studies in behavior modification* (pp. 364–366). New York: Holt, Rinehart, and Winston. [84(7), 472]

Wolf, M. M., Giles, D. K., & Hall, R. V. (1968). Experiments with token reinforcement in a remedial classroom. *Behavior Research and Therapy, 6,* 51–54. [43]

Wolf, M. M., Hanley, E. L., King, L. A., Lachowicz, J., & Giles, D. K. (1970). The timer-game: A variable interval contingency for the management of out-of-seat behavior. *Exceptional Children, 37,* 113–117. [190(13), 485]

Wolf, M. M., Risley, T., & Mees, H. (1964). Application of operant conditioning procedures to the behavior problems of an autistic child. *Behavior Research and Therapy, 1,* 305–312. [159–161, 167]

Wolfe, V. F., & Cuvo, A. J. (1978). Effects of within-stimulus and extra-stimulus prompting on letter discrimination by mentally retarded persons. *American Journal of Mental Deficiency, 83,* 297–303. [228]

Wolner, M., & Pyle, W. H. (1933). An experiment in individual training of pitch-deficient children. *Journal of Educational Psychology, 24,* 602–608. [193–194]

Woods, P. J. (1974). A taxonomy of instrumental conditioning. *American Psychologist, 29,* 584–597. [152]

Woods, T. S. (1983). DRO and DRI: A false dichotomy? *The Psychological Record, 33,* 59–66. [80, 82]

Wright, P. (1979). Concrete action plans in TV messages to increase reading of drug warnings. *Journal of Consumer Research, 6,* 256–269. [239–240(11), 491]

Wulbert, M., Nyman, B. A., Snow, D., & Owen, Y. (1973). The efficacy of stimulus fading and contin-